THE

Nature

AND

Conditions

OF

Learning

PRENTICE-HALL PSYCHOLOGY SERIES

HOWARD L. KINGSLEY

Revised by **RALPH GARRY**

School of Education
Boston University

THE

Nature

AND

Conditions

OF

Learning

SECOND EDITION

Englewood Cliffs, N. J.
PRENTICE-HALL, INC.

LIBRARY OF CONGRESS
CATALOG CARD NO.: 57-5937

First printing .... *January, 1957*
Second printing .... *July, 1957*
Third printing .... *August, 1958*
Fourth printing .... *July, 1959*

PRINTED IN THE UNITED STATES OF AMERICA
61062

Preface

However factually written, a book cannot avoid reflecting the biases of its authors. *The Nature and Conditions of Learning,* in both the original edition and the present revision, is no exception. The intent of the authors has been to present experimental and empirical evidence and data about learning and to provide a broad factual base for the concepts and principles involved.

Considerable latitude is possible in the sequence in which the topics may be studied. Aside from the introductory chapter, all the chapters in Part 1 may be shifted to follow Chapter 17, in keeping with individual preferences. The chapter, "Theories of Learning," may be omitted if desired.

Attempting to bridge the fields of psychology and education presents problems, for there is only limited experimental evidence in several areas of learning with which the readers are vitally concerned. Part 2 presents the psychological data available regarding the variables affecting learning; Part 3 attempts to relate this evidence to various aspects of learning traditionally associated with formal instruction. In this latter connection, more empirical observational information is introduced, particularly where experiment may be missing.

The authors wish to acknowledge indebtedness to all the psychologists whose names appear in the chapter references and bibliography and to the publishers who generously gave permission to quote or use materials from their publications. Friends and relatives have contributed helpful suggestions, criticisms, and various forms of assistance in preparing and correcting the manuscript. To all of them go our appreciation and thanks.

R. G.

Contents

Part 2

Variables Influencing Learning

Part 3

Learning in Behavioral Areas

Part 1

The Study of Learning

Chapter One

The Nature of Learning

*Learning is a fundamental process of
life. Every individual learns, and through
learning he develops the modes
of behavior by which he lives. All
human activities and achievements manifest
the results of learning. Whether we regard life
in terms of the race, of the community,
or of the individual, we are confronted on
every side by the pervasive effects of learning.
Through the centuries, each generation
has been able to profit by learning
from the experiences and discoveries of the
generations that have preceded it, and, in turn, has
added its contribution to the ever-growing fund
of human knowledge and skills. Customs,
laws, religions, languages, and social*

institutions have been developed and maintained as a result of man's ability to learn.

We see the products of learning in the skilled performances of the builder, the engineer, the craftsman, the surgeon, and the artist. They are evident in the spectacular discoveries and inventions of modern science, in the thought of the philosopher, and in the decisions of the statesman. The everyday behavior of common people, their beliefs, their fears, and their adherence to tradition are determined largely by tendencies and predispositions acquired through learning.

As soon as a child is born, or possibly before, he begins to learn, and he continues to do so throughout his whole life. Within a few days he learns to call his mother by his cries. By the end of his first year he has become acquainted with many of the objects that make up his new world, has acquired a measure of control over his hands and feet, and has made a respectable beginning on the process of developing a spoken language. At the age of five or six he goes to school, where through directed learning he adds the habits, skills, information, understandings, and attitudes that society deems essential to good citizenship.

When we consider all the skills, interests, attitudes, and information acquired both outside and inside the school, and the relation of these to conduct, personality, and manner of living, we find learning to be a momentous and continuous feature of life. Through it man improves his performance of manual tasks, profits by his mistakes, and acquires knowledge of nature and an understanding of his fellows. It enables him to adjust adequately to his social and physical environment. We "live and learn." By learning we may live better or we may live worse, but we are sure to live according to what we learn.

It is evident that learning is a process and an activity which engages a major portion of every individual's life. It is a process so important to the successful survival of human beings that the institution of education and the school has been devised as a procedure for making learning more efficient. The tasks to be learned are so complex and so important that they cannot be left to chance. Nor can it be said that the tasks which human beings are called upon to learn are "normal" to human development and growth, for adding, multiplying, reading, using tooth brushes, lacing shoes, operating typewriters, and a host of other skills to be acquired are not activities that normally would be learned. In fact, many of the routines to be learned by children and adults are those which do not come naturally.

Experience long has been called the best teacher. Yet the phrase is meaningless, for experience may be said to be the only teacher; it is seeing, smelling, tasting, feeling, hearing, — in short, receiving and interpreting the range of stimuli which impinge upon our sense organs. Learning cannot be defined as merely experience. The problem is to understand the ways in which different experiences bring about changes in response and behavior in human beings, and to perceive what experiences cause what learning under what circumstances.

If we are to understand the behavior and actions, the interests and attitudes, the ideals and beliefs, the skills and knowledge which characterize any human being, it is essential to understand the learning process, for it and maturation comprise the two major influences affecting human behavior. The fact that learning is subject to environmental manipulation and control makes it essential that we not only understand the process, account for it, and explain it, but also that we develop skill in effective manipulation of the environmental variables which influence learning.

VARIED NATURE OF LEARNING

We shall approach our discussion of the fundamental nature of learning by way of a few typical examples drawn from everyday life and representing different forms of learning by different types of individuals. It will be noted that, despite their diversity, the cases have certain features in common. The isolation of these common features will be the initial step in the formulation of a comprehensive working concept of learning.

An animal learns. A dog wants to leave the house but he finds his way blocked by a screen door. He pushes against the door with his nose, and then with a front foot; he paws at the lower part of the door, but it does not open. He whines and moves about in an agitated manner. Finally, he rears on his hind legs, planting his forefeet against the door well above the floor. As he moves about, one paw by chance strikes the latch and releases the fastening. The dog's weight against the door causes it to swing open, and out he dashes. With a few repetitions of this situation, the behavior of the dog changes. He soon singles out the latch, and when he wants to leave the house, we see him approach the door, rise immediately on his hind legs, release the latch with a direct thrust of a forepaw, and go out. His procedure is now calm, direct, and well adapted to cope with the situation. The useless reactions that were so pronounced a feature of his first performance have disappeared. He has learned how to open the door.

An infant learns. A baby cries because he is hungry. He is taken up, petted, and fed. He enjoys the attention as well as being fed. Soon he cries when he wants to be taken up even when he is not hungry.

Acquiring a motor skill. A boy of eight years has just received a pair of skates for Christmas. He is anxious to try them out. He has never had skates on his feet before, but in his eagerness he assumes that it must be very easy to skate. He observes how swiftly and smoothly the other fellows skim around the pond. With considerable effort he finally gets the skates on his feet. He stands up on the ice. Ankles wobble. He teeters forward. One foot starts off by itself, quite out of control. Hands fly up, but there is nothing to grasp; so down he goes with a bump. Undismayed he tries again. On his feet, he tries to go ahead. Cautiously he pushes one foot forward a bit. His whole body is tense. He teeters. Unsteadily the other foot is drawn up. He is using, or attempting to use, the movements which have served him well in walking. In this awkward and hesitating manner he creeps forward a few feet. He has courage. It is fun even if he does fall down frequently. As he continues his efforts, we see him improve. He discovers how to turn his foot outward so that he can push himself forward on the other foot. Coördination of movements and balance develop. Soon he is skimming over the ice, making rapid turns, playing hockey with the other fellows in what appears an utter forgetfulness of his feet. They just seem to take him around wherever he wants to go as faithful, obedient, efficient, unquestioning servants.

Memorizing a poem. A girl in the eighth grade has been asked by her teacher to memorize a poem. She has brought the book home and is now sitting at the table in the dining room. She has her book open to the poem. She reads over the first two lines three or four times, looks up, and tries to say them without looking at the book.

At the end of the first line she can't think how the second one begins. She glances at the first word of this line. That starts her off.
She completes the line without reading. The next time she gets
through both lines without looking at the book. She repeats them
over aloud three or four times just to be sure she has them so she
won't forget. After these can be recited, she goes on to the next
lines and continues reading, reciting to herself, prompting herself
when she cannot remember, and repeating until she is able to recite
unhesitatingly the whole four stanzas without the book.

Acquiring information. In his home room in high school, a boy
is preparing his American history lesson. He is bent over his book,
reading. His eyes move back and forth as they pass along from line
to line. His lips move a bit. He pauses and makes a few notes with
his pencil. Later when he goes to class, the teacher asks a question
about the reconstruction period in the South just after the Civil
War. She calls on this boy and he tells about the carpetbaggers,
though he knew nothing about them before he studied this lesson.

Developing understanding. In college, a student is listening to a
lecture on genetics. She hears for the first time the word *mitosis*. She
writes it down in her notebook and follows the professor's explanations attentively. She copies the sketches he puts on the blackboard.
A point is not clear; she asks the instructor to explain it. She understands the explanation, and as she leaves the room, she has many ideas
related to the term *mitosis* that make clear to her the nature of the
process of cell division. Later, in the examination, a question calls
for an explanation of *mitosis*. As she sees the word, not all, but many
of the things she heard that day come to her mind, and she is able
to write a passable answer to the question.

Acquiring and reducing a fear. A nine-year-old boy, running
home from the grocery store with a quart bottle of milk in his hand,
trips and falls; he smashes the milk bottle, cuts a deep and jagged
gash in his wrist, and severs a tendon. Hospitalization and surgery
are necessary to repair the injury. The result of the entire experience
is that the boy becomes afraid of glass. When he returns home from
the hospital, he refuses to touch any object made of glass. The suddenness, fright, and associated pain have produced a newly acquired
fear of a material which had previously been looked upon in a matter-
of-fact way: the youngster has learned to fear glass. He has adopted
a response which will insure his protection from future similar in-

jury, but which is maladaptive in light of the extensive use of glass in his environment.

Two different approaches are utilized in efforts to readapt the child's behavior. The child's mother attempts to ease the situation by using plastic glasses for drinking water and milk, hoping that the fear will gradually subside and that the youngster will outgrow his alarm if no issue is made of it. The boy's teacher first becomes aware of the fear when he objects to removing the wire which holds the sanitary cap on the bottles of milk distributed to the children in the classroom at mid-morning. The teacher assists the boy on the first occasion or two, but is tempted to insist that the boy open the milk himself, believing it unhealthy to concede to his fear. Both teacher and pupil find it difficult to modify their established reaction patterns in the situation. Receiving assurance that attempts to reduce the fear and encourage the youngster to discover alternate responses to the situation do not constitute concession to the fear, the teacher proceeds to induce the youngster to modify his fear response. Her first attempt is to assign the boy with another pupil to collect the milk bottles. The boy avoids the task by having the other pupil pick up the milk bottles and place them in the crate which he carries, thus solving the problem of executing a task required by the teacher, while simultaneously satisfying his fear. In the course of the next two or three weeks, the teacher observes the boy on an occasion or two standing in front of the aquarium in the classroom, attracted by the fish, and perhaps propelled by his fear, gingerly reaching out to touch the glass and then quickly withdrawing his fingers. As this is happening one day when school is letting out, the teacher asks the boy if he would like an aquarium on his desk. Prompted by his delighted response, she places a small fish in some water in a milk bottle and puts it on the corner of his desk. For several days the boy makes the same gingerly touching response to the glass, gradually gaining more assurance until finally he can be seen rubbing his fingers on the milk bottle, poking his finger down in the water at the fish, and then engaging in a variety of such actions which involve touching and handling the milk bottle. Taking advantage of this development one afternoon when she has the children cleaning their desks for some repair work that is to be done during vacation by the carpenter, the teacher casually asks the boy to take the bottle containing the fish to her desk. Unthinkingly, he grasps the bottle and carries it to her desk. As he is placing it on the desk, she calls his attention to what he has just done—taking hold of a glass bottle and carrying it. Thus, a fear response which had been learned is gradually being unlearned under the guidance of the teacher.

COMMON FEATURES OF LEARNING

These examples represent some different kinds of learning, although not all of the varieties that we shall have occasion to consider. There are several features common to all of them. *First,* the learning took place during some type of activity in which the organism was engaged with a purpose. *Second,* the organism attempted various responses in an effort to get a solution. *Third,* hitting upon a correct response, whether by accident or by forethought, produced either a new kind of performance or a change from previous performance in that the organism adopted this response as a habitual one. The sequential steps in learning have these common features. Some purpose or motivation directed toward a goal results in varied responses in connection with certain aspects of the environment ultimately leading to the stabilization of a particular response or response pattern. Learning, then, is the process by which an organism, in satisfying its motivations, adapts or adjusts to a situation in which it must modify its behavior in order to overcome obstacles or barriers.

DEFINITION OF LEARNING

Learning is a process by which behavior is modified, but we shall soon see that this definition is incomplete and must be qualified. In each of the foregoing illustrations, the behavior described was definitely and permanently changed as a result of learning. The dog opening a door, the child memorizing a poem, the boys skating, the college students writing during their examinations, the boy eliminating his fear are all examples of newer modified forms of behavior resulting from learning. It is evident, too, that the learning took many different forms.

Process versus product. To make the definition more meaningful, certain modifications and distinctions must be made. One of these distinctions to be made in clarifying the definition of learning is that it is a process, not a product. Human beings learn many things—

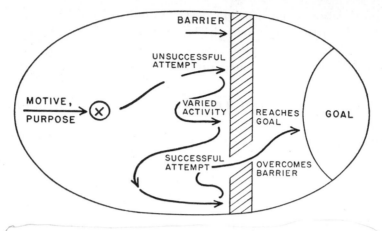

Fig. 1.1. Elements in a learning situation: *purpose, varied responses, selection of successful response, and ultimate stabilization of response.*

attitudes, fears, gestures, motor skills, language skills, etc.—all of which represent changes of performance in some area of human behavior. From the lay point of view, the end product—the particular performance change—is frequently seen as learning. For the psychologist, however, learning is the process by which the changes in performance were brought about, and it is not restricted to such skills as counting, reading, and motor skills, but also includes such functions as perception, emotion, and thought processes.

Learning as improvement. Another common misconception is that learning always results in improvement of performance. This is, of course, a common conception when one is thinking of the learning that takes place in the classroom according to the wishes and intent of the teacher, or where one engages in learning for a definite purpose. As one's performance is molded to approach the goal of excellence or skill toward which his efforts are directed, thinking of the process as the improvement of performance seems appropriate enough.

But improvement usually connotes enhancement of value. It seems hardly possible to conceive of *all* learning as improvement in this sense. If improvement is to be taken as meaning the fixation and consolidation of performance, good or bad, so that the performance is carried through with greater dispatch, ease, and with certainty, then and only then, can we say that all learning constitutes improvement. Change which results in bad habits, the fixation of error, and undesirable attitudes is quite definitely learning, and it seems difficult to consider this kind of learning as improvement. The child learns many things in the classroom that do not fall within the range of the teacher's objectives. He may learn habits of idleness and disrespect for authority. He may learn to write more poorly or he may acquire habits of poor reading. If improvement is to mean an approach toward the more desirable, we cannot restrict our concept of learning to this criterion.

Learning as adjustment. Learning has been described as a process of "progressive adjustment" to the ever-changing conditions which one encounters. To *adjust* means to bring into proper relation. When the individual is out of adjustment with the conditions of life, he is disturbed, unsatisfied, and unhappy; there is lack of harmonious functioning. Through learning, he is able to make adjustments. He acquires new ways of behavior that bring him into harmonious relationship and secure for him the desired satisfactions.

But it must be noted that a child frequently adopts modes of behavior that are definitely maladjustive. He may acquire emotional habits detrimental to his mental health, habits of conduct that get him into trouble with the authorities of the school or state, and attitudes that cause failure in schoolwork. Even in school he may be taught to aspire to goals beyond his ability to attain. When the domestic science course teaches the girl to cook and buy in a manner not suited to the budget within which she must operate, it is maladjustment rather than adjustment for which it is preparing her. There is not much consolation in saying that her learning constitutes an adjustment to the school requirement.

More than any other animal, man must depend upon learning to make adjustments to his environment. But man's environment is so complex that an adjustment to one feature of it is not necessarily adequate for other situations or for life as a whole. As teachers, we must have a broad view of the child's needs and endeavor to promote learning that will enable him to adjust harmoniously to all conditions of life.

Learning versus maturation. Two further aspects of the definition require clarification; the first is the distinction between learning and maturation. Learning is not the only process by which behavior is modified. A second important process is that of maturation, which in view of the scope of its effect on behavior, constitutes a major developmental process on a par with learning in producing behavior changes. Maturation is the process whereby behavior is modified as a result of growth and development of physical structure; it is most easily illustrated by the fact that until a child is ready to walk or talk, i.e. has the neuro-muscular development for making such a performance, no amount of training can bring about these particular changes in performance. Similarly, many higher thought processes are not available to immature humans, i.e. utilization of symbolic notation or algebraic operations. Although such illustrations can be made to clarify the distinction between learning and maturation, it is not as easily made in actual practice because learning and maturation are inter-related, making the actual distinction of the separate contributions of these two processes difficult to determine.

Learning and proficiency. A second distinction to be made is between changes in performance produced by work decrements and those produced by learning. The same practice which makes learning possible can simultaneously produce fatigue and have the opposite effect of learning, usually a decrease in proficiency. Thus all changes in performance are not the result of learning. Practice can produce both increases and decreases in proficiency at the same time, that is, a decrease resulting from fatigue and an increase resulting from learning. Both can occur simultaneously, and both are inferred from changes observed in performance. For example, the effect of a rest period in relation to learning is to produce a loss in proficiency of performance due to the occurrence of forgetting, whereas performance is *more* efficient after a rest period in a case where fatigue or work decrement has been in process.

As a result of the foregoing qualifications our definition now stands: *Learning is the process by which behavior (in the broader sense) is originated or changed through practice or training* (after Hunter, 1934; Hilgard, 1948).

Learning and education. At this point, it is worth while to distinguish between learning and education. From our discussion, we are aware that learning includes the changes in behavior, both favorable and unfavorable, which result from experience, whether in school or out, whether intentional or accidental. Much learning is intentional: when a child studies his multiplication tables in order to be able to recite them, when a college student reviews his lecture notes for an examination, when a golfer drives two hundred golf balls on a driving range in order to improve his golf score. Much learning is unintentional or incidental to another purpose: boys playing a game of football or baseball for the enjoyment of the game can incidentally improve their passing, kicking, or tackling ability. Children and adults also unintentionally learn advertising slogans seen on billboards or television without a conscious desire.

Education, in the formal sense of the word, refers to the systematically organized programs designed to produce certain knowledge, skills, understanding, attitudes and behavior patterns in members of a given social group. Schools are established and maintained for the purpose of securing desired learning outcomes. In a general way, it may be said that organized education seeks to perpetuate the good features of the social order, to secure the continuance of certain social institutions, and to combat the evils that threaten the society, by producing the so-called "educated man" whose behavior theoretically epitomizes the society's best.

Along with this, we seek through education to secure and safeguard the individual's welfare and security in a complex society. These ultimate objectives can be achieved only by developing appropriate forms of behavior in the individual members of the social group. This requires that educational goals be envisaged in terms of individual learning outcomes. Our success in accomplishing the purposes of organized education depends primarily upon the learning that takes place in the classroom under the direction of the teacher.

It is possible to forecast certain types of situations that the individual is likely to encounter. We know with some degree of assurance what kinds of abilities and what forms of behavior will serve the individual to advantage in these situations and at the same time be socially acceptable or desirable. These include certain *skills,* such as writing, reading, and arithmetical computations; certain *habits* of personal hygiene, emotional stability, and social behavior; and a variety of *verbal responses.* They represent forms of functioning which we are quite certain will be useful or necessary. Since we can foresee the need for them, it becomes our task to initiate and fix these functions so that they will be ready when the occasion demands.

It is apparent, however, that we cannot foresee all the situations a child will be called upon to face in his later life. We cannot supply him with ready-made modes of functioning in the form of habits, skills, and memorized materials that will serve all his future needs.

Unpredictable demands and questions are certain to arise. He must therefore be equipped with *knowledge, understanding,* and some *training* in the *art of problem solving* so that he can devise for himself appropriate answers and suitable modes of behavior.

It is also essential that the individual be disposed in a general way so to conduct himself that his own well-being and the interests of his associates will be safeguarded and preserved. It is important that his conduct conform to the ethical standards of society. Therefore, certain general functional trends are to be established that will assure desired features of conduct in even widely differing circumstances and in varied types of activity. *Attitudes* and *ideals* are the learning outcomes that meet this need.

These three types of learning outcomes are the educational objectives toward which the work of the teacher is directed: first, skills and habits; second, knowledge and understanding; and third, attitudes and ideals.

That which does, or should, constitute the formal education of members of any group is a philosophical question dependent upon the values and beliefs held by that particular group. Our particular problem is not concerned with educational objectives, nor exclusively with the learning that occurs in schools, whether intentional or unintentional, but rather with the process by which changes in human behavior are produced and with the variables which contribute to these changes, regardless of the source of the training or practice.

VARIABLES INFLUENCING LEARNING

In the description of the learning process, several aspects were identified: an organism with its motivation, which directs it toward a given goal, a period of varied responses as the organism attempts to reach the goal, and the discovery of the appropriate response followed by stabilization and fixation, retention, and generalization of the response. In the study of learning, we are interested in the many factors which influence behavior in these episodes: (1) how the motives and the goals capable of satisfying the motives are determined, (2) what factors influence the variability of responses, (3) which factors affect the speed of discovery, fixation, and retention of the correct response and what the conditions are under which they operate, and (4) what the conditions or circumstances are under which the learned response is utilized or transferred to new and different situations.

The many variables which affect these different aspects of the learning process may be grouped under three headings: (1) variables associated with the individual, (2) variables associated with the task to be performed, and (3) environmental variables. Although separate chapters will be devoted to each group, they will be briefly identified now.

Individual variables. Maturation, readiness, capacity, motivation, and personality traits are variables—associated with the individual learner—which affect the outcome of learning. The level of maturation of the individual learner plays a significant role in the amount of material, the kind of knowledge acquired, the rate of learning, and the amount of retention. Generally speaking, the more mature the individual, the greater the learning; however, such a generalization does not hold throughout life, e.g. the difficulty of teaching old dogs new tricks. Individuals also differ in their capacity for learning given tasks, and these differences contribute to differences in learning. Differences in capacity may be either physical or intellectual; such differences may be outgrowths of variations in experience. Individual readiness at any given period is a function of both maturation and prior experience, and signifies the degree to which any individual is prepared for learning a particular task.

It need scarcely be said that the more highly motivated the individual, the greater the learning. Personality factors such as perseverance, curiosity, self-confidence, level of aspiration, aggressiveness, etc., are closely allied to motivation in their effect upon learning. Each of these variables may be isolated for experimental purposes in order to measure their separate contribution or effect upon learning under certain circumstances; nevertheless they operate simultaneously and multifariously in any actual learning situation.

Task variables. The meaningfulness of the task to be learned, its difficulty, its similarity to previously performed tasks, its pleasantness or unpleasantness, and the manner in which it is organized or presented are variables which affect the speed of learning and amount of retention obtained.

The more meaningful the task, the more readily it is learned. The more an individual understands the task, the more readily he can select the appropriate response for the particular situation. The de-

gree of meaningfulness is one of the variables which is associated
with tasks and affects learning outcomes. Recognition of this factor
led to the development of nonsense syllables (meaningless materials)
in order to permit exploration of other factors associated with learning. Secondly, the difficulty of the task affects learning outcomes,
and although difficulty tends to vary with the degree of meaningfulness, it is not identical inasmuch as difficulty varies with the length
of material as well as with complexity.

Tasks vary in their degree of similarity and hence, in the amount
of transfer of learning which may occur from one task to another.
Meaningfulness is in part a function of the degree of transfer, i.e. the
extent to which previous learning makes the immediate task easier.
Tasks also vary in the degree of affect which they have for the learner.
Some tasks are pleasant, some are unpleasant, and many are neutral.
The affective reaction of an individual influences the learning situ-
ation.

Environmental variables. In addition to individual variables and
task variables, a number of environmental variables influence the
learning process. The frequency with which a response is practiced
affects the speed with which the response is acquired and fixed and
the length of time it is retained. Closely associated with practice
are overlearning and drill. To overlearn is to practice a response
beyond the first perfect performance, as one frequently does with
many motor skills such as swimming, skiing, dancing. Knowledge
of results is another variable which aids the individual in selecting
the correct response from the sequence of varied responses attempted
in any learning situation. The incentives in play in a given situation
have a marked influence in the learning process. Reward, punishment, competition, cooperation, praise, blame, grades, honor rolls,
etc. all have their influence upon learning. The degree of influence
may be great or slight depending upon the relationship between the
incentives and the motives characterizing the individual learner. In
the classroom as distinguished from the laboratory, factors of a social
nature have to be considered, such as group attitudes and values,
motivation of other individuals in the situation, including the
teacher, and the social restraints in operation.

Interaction of variables. It is possible in an experimental situation
to reduce the number of variables that are operating freely at any
given time, but such is rarely the case in the learning situations that

occur in home or school. In any situation, several of these variables are operating simultaneously and inter-relatedly. To give a simple illustration: an individual's efforts will vary greatly depending upon whether he is alone or in a group situation. Our problem is to understand not only how the many factors operate individually, but more important, their combined operation in the classroom in inter-action with each other.

ORGANIZATION OF THE TEXT

This text has been organized in three main sections. The initial section concerns itself with a study of learning, first attempting to define learning, describing how learning is measured both in experiments and in school settings, and describing the effect of error upon such measures.

While experimental evidence and observation provide facts about learning, it is necessary to explain, account, or organize these facts into some overall scheme or theory of learning. The final chapter in the first section attempts to orient the student to the two main divisions of theory—association and field theory—which not only provide two basically different explanations of how learning occurs and differing sets of experimental data, but more important for teachers, provide two sharply different concepts of teaching method. Preceding the description of learning theories are two chapters, one on research methods, which identifies typical experimental methods utilized in the study of learning, the second on techniques and problems of measurement in the study of learning.

The second section of the book is concerned with those variables operating in learning which have been briefly identified in the foregoing pages — individual variables, task variables, and method variables — and the interaction between them. Experimental evidence related to each of the many variables will be presented in order to illustrate and specify the relationship of each variable to learning. By the end of Part Two, the student should have identified the many factors to be considered and established some general answers to these important questions: what is the relationship of capacity to learning; how does capacity change with age; do individual differences affect learning and vice-versa; what influence does learning have upon individual differences; how do motivation and incentives operate in learning; how do such factors as reward and punishment, cooperation and competition, success and failure operate; what are the differences between massed and distributed practice; what is the relationship of each to various kinds of learning and to retention?

Part Three is intended to relate the many variables affecting learning to the kind of learning tasks with which children are confronted in growing to maturity. It is possible to classify learning in any one of several ways; e.g., learning tasks may be classified according to the kind of experimental situation typically utilized, such as classical conditioning, instrumental conditioning, discrimination-learning, and problem solving. Another scheme is to subdivide learning tasks into sensory-motor skills, perceptual skills, affective learning, problem solving, conceptual learning, and associational learning.

In this text, the classification scheme adopted distinguishes between seven forms of learning: motor skills, perception, rote learning, comprehension, problem solving, emotion, and attitudes. The scheme is adopted, not because learning is intrinsically divided into such categories, but because such a classification seems convenient for the study of learning as it occurs in schools. These forms of learning may be considered the main types of learning fostered in our schools in all of the various subject matter areas. The final chapter considers the ultimate problem of the transfer of learning from school to life situations.

Experimental and empirical knowledge. In acquiring our understanding of the learning process, two main sources of information are available: (1) the results of experimental studies (those which are carried out both in laboratory and in life situations), and (2) the empirical judgments of skilled teachers and observers. It would be desirable, even though it is well nigh impossible, to have conclusive experimental evidence upon which to base our knowledge of the many influences which operate in all learning situations, so that we could be most proficient in manipulating them to produce maximum learning with a minimum of effort. In situations where we are lacking direct experimental evidence, we are forced to make inferences from related experiments, particularly those involving animal learning, or depend upon empirical judgment that is based upon experience. In the pages that follow, the student will find presented both types of information, while at all times we shall try to maintain the distinction between the two and utilize experimental evidence as far as possible for a basis upon which to make judgments.

SUMMARY

Learning is a fundamental process of life engaging much of our waking hours and affecting all forms of human behavior—skills, knowledge, attitudes, personality, motivations, fears, mannerisms, etc. Learning is defined as the process by which behavior is originated or changed through practice. Learning and maturation are the two main processes through which changes in behavior occur.

Learning may occur intentionally or unintentionally, through organized or unorganized activity. Education is the formal procedure through which the attempt is made to develop in individuals certain socially sanctioned behavioral patterns. The study of learning includes not only formal training but all factors producing behavior changes.

The variables which influence learning may be grouped under three headings: (1) individual variables, such as capacity and motivation, (2) task variables, such as meaningfulness and difficulty, and (3) environmental variables, such as practice and knowledge of results.

A consideration of the measurement of learning, research procedures, and theories of learning will be found in the first section of the text, and the variables affecting learning will be reviewed in the second section. The third section is concerned with learning in different areas of behavior: motor learning, perception, memory, comprehension, problem-solving, emotions, and motivation. The final chapter deals with problems related to transfer of training.

Two main sources of information are utilized: experimental evidence and empirical observation.

Chapter Two

Research Methods

Although the systematic, experimental study
of learning is scarcely more than a lifetime old,
man's concern and interest in learning is
undoubtedly as old as man himself, for there has
always been the problem of teaching children
the most rudimentary knowledge for survival
and self-care. We may never know exactly when
the interest in making learning efficient began,
but it is as old as recorded history. In the written
records are many shrewd observations regarding
factors that influence learning and numerous
procedures suggested for making learning
more effective. But until experimental
confirmation and investigation of the circumstances
were made to determine when the judgments
held true and when they did not, they

remained no more or less than judgments of uncertain validity and application.

EXPERIMENTING AND EXPERIMENTS

A common example. We can observe many of these judgments as they operate in daily life. The parent telling the five-year-old who wants to try his older brother's bicycle that he isn't old enough or big enough to ride the bicycle is expressing the conviction that with increased age comes increased capacity or readiness for learning a complex motor skill, and that there is a factor, call it maturation or something else, that makes learning to ride the bicycle either easier or more rapid. Similarly, the parent who teaches his child to use a knife or fork, to keep his fingers out of his food, or to read while still in nursery school makes a number of assumptions about learning: that the child is capable of learning the particular task, that he is desirous of learning, that he has had the necessary prior training, that the parent's procedure for explaining or illustrating the skill is intelligible to the child, that the length of the training period is suited to the task at hand, and that a number of other conditions are being met. If the child learns, both parent and child may be pleased, but if the child fails to learn, the parent is unable to specify which of the several conditions is not being properly manipulated — whether the child lacks sufficient maturity, interest, or motivation, whether the child is capable of learning but the parental demonstration is confusing or meaningless, or whether the practice period is overly long. The parent may attempt to analyze the situation, and by trial and error modify procedures until success is achieved or failure appears inevitable; this occurred in the following situation. A father was attempting to teach his five-year-old son the first steps in swimming (the term "first steps" implies that a preferable sequence of steps exists, in contradiction to the throw-them-into-deep-water school of thought). Following an accepted procedure, the father had the boy put his face into the water, then followed this with instructions to grasp his knees and pull them up to his body so that he would float "like a jellyfish." Repeatedly and unsuccessfully he gave varied instructions on the same theme to the boy. Finally he abandoned his instructional procedure and attempted alternate ways of demonstrating body buoyancy in water. Taking the boy in very shallow water, he pointed at some painted circles on the bottoms of the pool and asked the boy if he could touch his nose on a circle. Attempting this, the boy had to take his feet off the bottom of the pool in order to submerge his head. In doing this and prompted by questions from his father, he suddenly became aware of the way in which the water held him up and made submerging difficult.

In this situation, the father was experimenting with the variables affecting his son's learning — experimenting crudely, but in this instance, effectively. The psychologist is engaged in a similar activity, but with somewhat different purpose and with many more restrictions and refinements. Where the father was interested primarily in the results, the psychologist is interested in the events contributing to the results, particularly in the extent to which manipulating the events produces differences in the results. Secondly, the father was utilizing a crude empiricism, more or less randomly varying his procedure in accordance with the dictates of his analysis. In contrast, the psychologist is especially concerned with systematically studying the effects of different variables, singly and in combination. In doing so, he must utilize a number of procedures for controlling or holding constant the many variables which affect learning, e.g. age of subject, amount of previous training, amount of practice during the experiment, motivation, and instructions to subject, while he systematically investigates the influence of any one of the variables or combinations thereof. Thirdly, while both father and psychologist were using a performance score as a measure of learning (the father was aware of roughly the number of unsuccessful trials or unsuccessful attempts), the psychologist strives to utilize performance scores that are more refined, more subject to precision of measurement, and more clearly related to the learning variable being manipulated. Thus, the psychologist is interested in the systematic, experimental study of learning for the sake of understanding what happens when an organism learns.

The experimental study of learning. Systematic experimenting with learning began in the latter part of the nineteenth century and rapidly expanded during the present century. One of the earliest experimenters in the study of learning was Hermann Ebbinghaus, who was among the first to devise methods for measuring the products of memorizing. In his efforts to determine the relationship between the length of material to be memorized and the amount that a person is able to memorize in repeated trials, and also the effect of the amount of practice upon the material memorized, Ebbinghaus was confronted with a type of problem which psychologists must meet and overcome in their experimental study of learning. It is obvious that certain kinds of material such as poetry are more readily memorized than others, such as series of numbers. This is to say, that the rate of learning is a function of the meaningfulness or familiarity of the material. To secure units of equal difficulty for purposes of measurement, it is necessary to use learning material as free as possible from meaning or previously formed associations. Ebbinghaus met this requirement by constructing many hundreds of nonsense syllables, each one a meaningless combination of three letters consisting of two consonants joined by a vowel. Examples of such syllables are: keb, ruk, meg, cej. The device made possible the building of a series of any desired length with units of approximately equal memory value. With this type of material, Ebbinghaus investigated several problems of memory, retention, and recall. He memorized series of different lengths to discover the relation between the length of the series and the number of repetitions required for learning. He studied the relation of the number of repetitions of a series to the retention of the series. He devised the relearning method for measuring the retention of material that could not be recalled, and by means of it investigated the relation of forgetting to the length of the interval between learning and recall. He discovered many facts about the nature of the associations that are formed in learning. Since his time, his discoveries have been supplemented by the work of many other investigators, but his methods of measuring memory are still standard experimental procedures, and the results of his experiments are regarded as an important contribution to our knowledge of learning and forgetting.

Thorndike and Pavlov. At the beginning of the present century two more chains of experimental studies were begun by Edward L. Thorndike and Ivan Pavlov. Thorndike began a series of experiments on animal learning by placing a hungry cat in a puzzle box from which the cat could escape by operating a latch string in order to obtain food placed outside the box. From the results, Thorndike formulated his theories regarding learning and his concept of learning by trial and error. He saw the need and the possibility of applying experimental methods to the study of learning in the schools, and devoted himself to this task.

Pavlov, a physiologist, began a series of experiments utilizing the conditioning of reflex responses to various stimuli and studied the conditions under which conditioned responses were established and maintained. His procedures and hypotheses about the nature of learning have stimulated extensive experimentation, and have been significant contributions to both procedures for studying learning and theories for explaining learning.

Scientific method and theory. The divorce of psychology from philosophy began when psychological questions were put to experimental tests instead of depending upon logical deduction. Psychology thus shifted from a speculative system to scientific system.

Between the simplicity of the scientific method and the stringency of its application of experimental methods in order to answer psychological questions lie many bewildering details. The logic of the scientific method is fairly simple. One starts with a question. For instance, one may question whether the whole-method is more effective than the part-method in the memorization of poetry. Having established a question which is usually quite specifically limited in its scope, one undertakes an investigation. This may be in the form of controlled field observation or in the form of an experiment utilizing rigid controls in which an effort is made to study the several variables which can influence results. The desired results are those which contribute to, confirm, or refute a scientific theory or explanation. More often, the main result of an experiment is questions rather than answers. An important condition of the scientific method is that results are verifiable by other investigators. The value of this condition is that it makes the results independent of the experimenter.

The subsequent steps in the scientific method are attempts to combine or systematize the result of numerous experiments into a theory which is capable of accounting for or explaining all the observed facts. Theories are inductively built and based upon observed facts. Experimental studies are made in order to answer specific questions which in turn usually suggest further questions for study. Subsequently, generalizations are made upon the basis of groups of related studies. Finally, theories are proposed in order to account for or explain the data and the generalizations. Usually several theories are proposed in different attempts to explain the same data. The theory which stands in the face of the facts will survive, the others are discarded. Sound theories permit deductions which can be tested by scientific experiments to support or refute the theory. The validity of a theory rests upon the kind and extent of predictions that can be made in utilizing the theory. When the prediction fails, or the theory fails to coincide with the observed facts, it is altered or discarded. Thus the scientific method produces a body of verified knowledge from which inferences, generalizations, and explanations are made in an effort to organize existing knowledge into consistent systems.

The problems of using the scientific method in the study of human behavior are not logical but methodological. The fact that human behavior is the complex product of numerous factors acting simultaneously makes it extremely difficult to adequately control these factors influencing experimental results in such a way that the relationships between any single variable in behavior can be systematically investigated. Moreover, the fact that behavior results from the interaction of many variables rather than the singular action of one variable imposes a limitation upon the extent to which generalizations can be established on the basis of laboratory experiments. For these and other reasons, the body of knowledge that has been accumulated in efforts to explain human learning includes data from not only experimental but also nonexperimental sources.

NONEXPERIMENTAL METHODS

Systematic observation of behavior has been and will continue to be a fruitful source of information and deductions regarding human behavior, particularly in supplying clues to relationships which exist between different variables. In nonexperimental methods, little or no attempt is made to control or manipulate the situation. Rather, the purpose of nonexperimental methods is to bring to light the factors, conditions, or relationships present, and essentially to provide a description of the world of behavior.

Differential psychology. In psychology, nonexperimental methods may be subdivided into two main categories called differential psychology and clinical psychology, the former being the study of differences between individuals and groups and the latter the study of individual adjustment. Two studies serve to illustrate the type of investigation undertaken in the area of differential psychology. A longitudinal study of intelligence was completed by Honzik, Macfarlane, and Allen (1948), who administered intelligence tests to a group of children each year from infancy to age 18 in order to determine the stability of intelligence as measured by standard tests and the predictive value of early tests for terminal intelligence scores. In another type of study Anastasi and Cordova (1953) administered Spanish and English forms of the Cattell Culture-Free Intelligence to Puerto Rican children of both sexes in New York. Half the children received the tests in the Spanish, English sequence with an interval of two weeks between tests, and the other half receiving the tests in the reverse order. The investigators were able to compare the influence of such variables as sex, language, and test sequence on obtained scores. These studies illustrate two procedures extensively used in differential psychology: the longitudinal or genetic study and the cross-sectional study. Norms of physical growth and intellectual development have been established by studying groups of children at different age levels and comparing them with respect to such given characteristics as height, weight, mental age, etc., and establishing norms on the basis of results. Cross-sectional methods are continually used in public opinion polls to appraise reactions of differing groups. Interests, fears, preferences, social development are only a few of the many characteristics which have been studied using this approach. The longitudinal method as illustrated by the Honzik, Macfarlane, Allen study is more intensive, for it involves a series of planned and systematic observations of children's behavior over a considerable period of time to discover the nature of their development. Physical and mental tests and examinations are frequently used in addition to observation.

Clinical methods. If a child is a behavior problem, or is maladjusted educationally, socially, or emotionally, adequate treatment calls for an understanding of the factors that have contributed to his particular difficulty. The clinical method provides a diagnosis of the underlying causes of misbehavior or maladjustment. It rests on the conviction that treatment should be concerned with *causes* rather than *symptoms*.

When a child is brought to a psychological clinic, he is given various tests to determine his physical, intellectual, and educational status. The record prepared usually includes a case history. The data for the case history are obtained from a variety of sources. Parents are usually interviewed, in an effort to find out as much as possible about the child's home background and the relations between him and the other members of his family. The record will include whatever can be learned concerning the parents' attitudes toward the child, their treatment of him, his sickness history, his emotional disturbances, and his companions outside the home. The child's teachers probably will be consulted for information concerning his school life. Of particular importance for a case history will be facts concerning his attitude toward his work and toward other children, his success or failure, his conduct in school, and his emotional stability. If he has a court record, that, too, will be investigated. These and any other available facts concerning the child's history that may have affected his personality or his behavior are assembled in his case history.

Although the treatment of individual difficulties is the primary purpose of this method, the data from clinical tests and case histories have thrown much light on many general problems of psychology. Here are revealed the concrete workings of the complex tangle of conditions that determine human behavior. From the mass of evidence gathered by this method, it is clear that misconduct has definite causes and that it can be treated effectively only by discovering and removing the causes. Delinquency is usually the result, not of depravity, but of unwholesome environmental factors and emotional conflicts. Disabilities in school subjects are due not merely to laziness or lack of intelligence, but to a variety of conditions that conspire to prevent the child's normal success.

Studies of the effectiveness of clinical procedures depend upon a before-and-after comparison in order to compare changes in behavior. Many difficulties beset such studies attempting to measure the outcomes of clinical procedures. First, it is difficult to determine what general population any particular group of patients represents, or how typical it is of emotionally disturbed persons. Secondly, it is difficult to identify explicitly the procedure, and even more so to isolate its effects from the host of other influences affecting any individual's life. Finally, the frequent dependence upon the verbal report of the subject as to how he feels or has improved injects additional uncertainty into the validity of findings. Yet, in spite of flaws, such studies will be made and used until more effective procedures are devised. Recent years have seen increased efforts to control more rigorously the clinical studies of personality dynamics.

Figure 2.1 identifies the methods used for obtaining descriptive information in differential and clinical psychology. These methods are subdivided into two main classifications: test procedures including both objective and projective tests, and non-test procedures including observation and report. In general, differential psychology relies more heavily upon test and statistical procedures, while clinical psychology uses non-test procedures such as the case study. Nevertheless, a job analysis of the work performed by the clinical psychologist shows that he not only engages in clinical interviews, counseling, and preparation of case histories, but also utilizes a wide variety of testing instruments — particularly projective tests — in performing his work.

Tests. There are several ways of subdividing tests: pencil-and-paper versus performance, individual versus group, objective versus projective tests. In Figure 2.1 the objective-projective categories are used as a primary distinction in types of tests. Objective tests are so-called because they employ standardized procedures of administration and scoring which produce scores or results that are highly consistent and not dependent upon the examiner's interpretation. Furthermore, the range of response to the items in the test is usually restricted by using such items as multiple-choice, true-false, and short-answer items. Intelligence and achievement tests are usually objective in format. Projective tests are so named because the test situation permits the person being tested to "project" himself into the situation. The person taking the test is presumed to interpret the situation in a way characteristic to his personality structure with the result

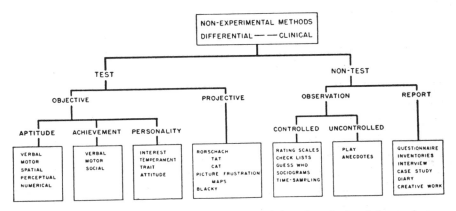

Fig. 2.1. Nonexperimental methods for obtaining descriptive information.

that his responses may be interpreted to provide further understanding of the dynamics of his personality. Obviously the effective use of projective tests is dependent upon the clinical skill and understanding of the psychologist administering the test. Widely used projective tests are the Rorschach Test, which consists of a series of ink-blots, and the Murray Thematic Apperception Test, which is a series of pictures of people and situations. The examinee describes what the ink-blot or situation means to him. This report is then scored and interpreted by the psychologist.

Objective tests in particular have been useful in descriptive research as well as in controlled studies of learning, particularly when statistical methods are utilized in conjunction with the tests. Statistical methods make it possible to reduce large numbers of scores or data to a few simple expressions which are meaningful to the observer.

Statistics. The statistics used in describing groups provide three kinds of information. They describe: (1) the central tendency or mid-point of the group, such as mean, median, and mode, (2) the dispersion or variability of the group, such as range or standard deviation, and (3) the relationship between traits or characteristics, such as a correlation coefficient. These statistics make it possible to draw conclusions regarding differences in the characteristics of one or more groups. Figure 2.2 illustrates two groups which differ in their mid-point—one group being considerably below the other, even though both groups have approximately the same range of scores. Such distributions could be obtained if one were to compare the scores of 3rd with 6th grade children on an achievement test on arithmetic or spelling. Figure 2.3 illustrates two groups which differ considerably in their range of scores: Group A is more variable than

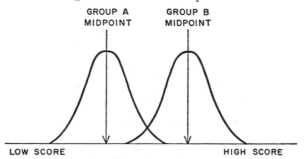

Fig. 2.2. Central tendency differences of two groups.

Group B, even though both groups have the same mid-points or averages. Such a distribution of scores could be obtained if one were comparing the scores of a 6th grade class in reading comprehension with the scores obtained by all 12 grades in the school system. The standard deviation (represented by the symbol σ) is a commonly used statistic for describing the variability of groups. It is a statistic which portrays the extent to which all individuals in a group vary from all other individuals.

A third statistic commonly used is the correlation coefficient (represented by the symbol r) which is used to describe the strength

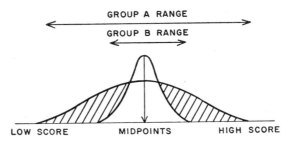

Fig. 2.3. Variability differences of two groups.

of relationship between two variables. If a comparison were made between the intelligence test scores of a group of pupils and their achievement test scores, a diagram like Figure 2.4 would be the likely result. In this figure intelligence test scores range from low to high along the horizontal axis, and the paired achievement test scores range from low to high up the vertical axis. If the correlation between intelligence and achievement were perfect (r = 1.00) that

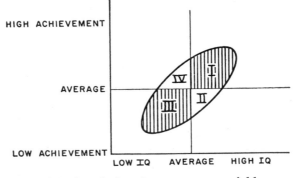

Fig. 2.4. Correlation between two variables.

is, if the highest in intelligence was highest in achievement, and second in intelligence was second in achievement, and so on, the scores would fall along a diagonal line running from lower left to upper right. If there was no correlation (r = 0.00) between intelligence and achievement, the scores would be scattered over the entire grid as shown in Figure 2.5. Inasmuch as the correlation between achievement and intelligence is approximately r = .50, the scores would fall in the egg-shaped distribution shown in Figure 2.4. In general it can be seen that the higher the intelligence score, the higher the achievement score is likely to be; but, that the relationship is not perfect can be seen by observing scores in quadrants II and IV, in which those persons of high intelligence have low achievement scores, and those of low intelligence are high in achievement.

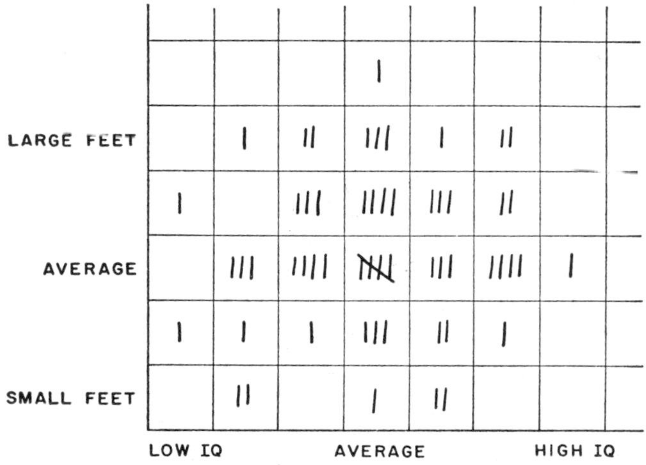

Fig. 2.5. Two variables having zero correlation.

Thus correlation coefficients can range from 0.00, as might be expected if one attempted to correlate shoe size and intelligence, to 1.00 if the correlation was perfect. Near perfect correlation can be obtained if a standard intelligence test is administered twice within a short time to the same group and the scores on the first administration are correlated with scores on the second.

Correlation may be either positive (r.50) or negative (r —.80). The closer to 1.00, whether positive or negative, the higher the degree of correlation.

In positive correlation, high scores on one variable go with high scores on the second. The reverse is true in negative correlation. Here high scores on one variable go with low scores on the second variable. An illustration is found in the correlation between speed and gasoline consumption in automobiles. The faster a car is driven, the fewer miles obtained per gallon of gasoline. Thus high speeds are associated with low miles-per-gallon and produce a negative correlation coefficient.

Correlation coefficients may be used to describe the relationship between two variables within the same group, as in Figure 2.4, or they may be used to describe the relationship of a single variable between two groups, such as the correlation between intelligence scores of brothers or identical twins. Further, they can be used to describe relationships between a number of variables permitting the identification of factors common to several variables.

Observation. This method is valuable because it permits study of kinds of behavior for which no tests are available. It should be performed systematically, however, if it is to be of value. Rating scales and check lists direct observation towards certain aspects of behavior and generally require some discrimination or judgment on the part of the observer. The Guess-who procedure and socio-grams are devices for obtaining information from members of a group about their feelings and attitudes toward each other. In the Guess-who procedure, children are given a list of descriptive phrases such as "the person who is most helpful" and are asked to indicate the classmate who is best fitted by the phrase. A sociogram is a device for plotting the pattern of choices and rejections between members in a group. Each of these procedures provides systematic information about intra-group attitudes and status. Time sampling is a method for making observations at given time intervals and for given lengths of time, thus insuring the observer of a well-balanced behavior sample of the person being observed, rather than merely recording that which happened to attract the viewer's attention. Accidental observations by teachers are not unlike dripping faucets and squeaking wheels. We tend to see what we are conscious of and looking for, and over-look that which does not attract our attention. As a result we develop distorted—or at least highly selective—pictures of a child's behavior.

Reports and questionnaires. A verbal report, both written and oral, is used extensively in the clinical method in obtaining informa-tion. Questionnaires, inventories, and interviews are used to develop case studies and make available intensive background information for understanding the individual. The use of these procedures is not restricted to individual case studies, but may be used also in inventories of interests, vocational preference, samplings of public opinion and attitudes, and market research. These procedures have to be used with skill and discretion if the results are to have any validity.

McNemar (1946) provides a detailed analysis of the difficulties besetting the questionnaire method, which because of its inherent weaknesses, is not considered a first-rate scientific procedure. In addition to vexing problems in formulating good questions, there is danger that the data will be unreliable because the subjects misinterpret questions, answer inaccurately on account of ignorance, or answer untruthfully through desire to make a good impression. Responses of individuals will vary with the status of the person to whom they are reporting. Furthermore, the interviewer may exert influence on the forthcoming response by such means as the following: making negative statements of the question; attempting to balance positive statements; loading by introducing emotionally charged words or phrases; presenting contingent or conditional ideas; juxtaposing questions; inserting suggestive elements; using alternate wording; introducing prestige elements; personalizing the question; stereotyping; and using technical or biased words. Thus many hazards beset the investigator who uses the questionnaire for obtaining data, for the way in which the questions are framed will cause variations in the answers obtained. Another major flaw which frequently results is that of biased returns. In all research it is essential that a representative sample be obtained if results are to be meaningful. Questionnaire methods are particularly susceptible to biased or unrepresentative samples.

In spite of such difficulties, the questionnaire has its place when used with discretion. It has been fruitful in making surveys of opinions and interests and has been the means of collecting valuable data when no other method was available. It is widely used in public opinion polling with reasonable accuracy when sample and questions are carefully drawn, although major errors still occur, as in the 1948 presidential election in which pollsters erred in their prediction.

Diaries and creative work—finger painting, clay modeling, story writing, or poetry—provide material which in the hands of trained psychologists may be interpreted in a manner similar to the projective tests, and probably are most useful in providing clues or leads for further study or investigation by other methods.

EXPERIMENTAL METHODS

The more exact and refined methods of research are to be found in the scientific experiment which differs from the non-experimental procedures largely in the extent to which rigid controls are introduced in order to determine the relationships between independent and dependent variables. The investigator is primarily interested in functional relationship—the extent to which alteration in an independent variable is associated with or produces variations in the dependent variable. For example, how do variations in amount of practice facilitate or hamper the learning of a given motor skill?

The experimenter's task is essentially to establish a procedure which permits him to identify or control the effects or influences which determine the outcomes of the experiment. Generally, three sources of influence have to be controlled in an experiment. They are: (1) those associated with the population used, (2) those derived from the experimental procedure followed, and (3) external influences, including the experimenter.

A practical illustration can be made of the difficulties involved in establishing adequate controls in the complex learning experiment. An investigator wishes to determine whether teaching arithmetic by drill or understanding is the more satisfactory method. The question is broad—too broad for a single experiment—and must be delimited: (1) what arithmetic: addition, multiplication, fractions, etc; (2) at which grade level; and (3) what specifically is meant by "drill or understanding."

Controlling population variables. With respect to the population to be utilized in such a study, there are several factors which could influence the results that would be obtained in the experiment. Age, intelligence, previous experience, motivation, and education are factors associated with population and could produce variations in the results obtained; they must therefore be controlled in some fashion.

It is quite apparent that learning varies with the age of the subject and with differences in intelligence. The amount of arithmetic learned by either method could easily vary with differences in previous experience or education. If some students were more highly motivated than others, they would be likely to learn more. It has been shown both in animal and human experiments that native char-acteristics and previous experience can affect experimental results. In experiments using animals, careful control of the breeding and re-cording of preliminary handling and training experiences have been adopted to counteract these influences. Such controls are not possible with human subjects. Therefore procedures which do two things have been adopted: (1) identify variations in experimental outcomes associated with individual differences by systematically varying the differences, and (2) distribute the effects of individual variation as uniformly as possible by randomly assigning individuals to experi-mental groups. In experimental terminology, "random" does not mean haphazard, but rather, unbiased variation.

In the arithmetic groups, the influence of certain individual differ-ences could be ascertained. Within the experimental groups it would be possible to identify sub-groups of superior, average, and inferior ability, or sub-groups whose prior training had been by drill or understanding methods, or even combinations of these categories. Attitudes and motivation would be more difficult to control by sys-tematic variation. A most important consideration is the selection of representative samples from the stipulated populations. The experimenter must first define the population to be utilized in his experiment, and then, being unable to experiment on all such sub-jects, randomly select a sample of that population for the experiment. If the sample is biased, it is impossible to know if the results hold true for the total population. Unfortunately there are often devia-tions which occur in actual practice and produce unspecified effects; for example, many learning experiments are performed upon volun-teer groups of college students. Considering the variations in student bodies from college to college and even the differences between stu-dents in one college curriculum compared with those in another, it can scarcely be claimed that populations used in these studies are representative of human beings in general, or college students in particular. In the arithmetic experiment being discussed, it would not be uncommon to use entire classes; for example, three entire classes may be selected to provide a sample of 100 4th grade pupils, instead of taking a random sample of all 4th grade pupils in the community, mainly because it is easier to work with intact classes than use a few students from each class. Such a procedure violates the requirement for having representative, randomly selected samples.

A third step in controlling errors resulting from differences in the population samples is the use of large enough numbers to insure some reliability and stability of results. The smaller the sample, the greater the possibility that it is not representative. Large numbers offset this type of error. Unfortunately large numbers do not offset errors resulting from biased sampling.

Controlling experimental variables. Another set of variables arising from the experimental procedure must be controlled. In the case being discussed the amount of practice, the distribution of practice, the subject matter content for various lessons, the measures used to establish gains, the total time period over which the lessons extend, and other details of organization would have to be regulated. It well could be that a drill method would show greater results over a short time period, or that it would show greater gains by the end of the teaching period but greater losses than the "understanding" method over a longer period of time. Conversely the "understanding" method could easily show smaller initial gains but less forgetting over an extended period of time. The subject material would have to be equally susceptible to teaching by either method. Another important consideration would be the criterion established for measuring gains. For instance, if the measure used was speed of multiplication or addition, the drill group would be likely to be superior, whereas if the solving of unfamiliar problems involving multiplication and addition were the test, the "understanding" group would probably be favored. Utilizing several measures is a safeguard against such errors.

Two methods are utilized for controlling the effects of practice. The control group method is a procedure whereby two groups are selected as representative samples from the same population. One of the groups is exposed to the experimental procedure, a second is used as a control group. In the present experiment, it would be necessary to have two experimental groups, one for drill and one for "understanding," and a control group if possible. The effects of practice are established by determining the net differences between the scores of the experimental and control groups at the beginning and end of the experiment. Thus the amount by which the drill group exceeded the control group would be compared to the like gain of the "understanding" group. The conclusions to be made would depend upon which of the experimental groups made the greater gain.

Statistical procedures have been developed for comparing scores of groups, thus making it possible to tell whether the differences in scores of two groups is sufficiently great to be a real difference or whether it is only a chance fluctuation. If the dart-throwing scores of an individual or group of individuals were recorded over several trials, they would have some variation, even though the skill of the throwers remained constant. If many scores on each individual were available, it would be possible to use an average score. But in experiments such as have been described, the experimenter ordinarily has only a single score for each person, with no way of knowing whether that score happens to be a chance low score or a chance high score. In order to make sound conclusions regarding the usefulness of one method over another, he has to know whether the difference obtained is greater than could be anticipated on the basis of chance fluctuation in scores. The experimenter starts by making the assumption that there is basically no difference (the null hypothesis) and that observed differences are merely chance fluctuations. Only when the observed differences become so great that it is improbable to attribute them to chance does the investigator reject the null hypothesis and accept the difference as real, i.e. one method is more effective than the other.

The problems of method control center essentially on reducing errors which arise from differences in the way groups are treated, in contrast to the previous section in which the errors arose from biased or faulty sampling of individuals. Statistical procedures which permit an estimate of the chance fluctuation make it possible for the experimenter to say that a difference between two methods is greater than can be anticipated on the basis of chance, i.e. it is statistically significant. Where differences are small, it is impossible to know whether they are real or chance differences.

A second procedure used in controlling effects of practice is called the counterbalanced presentation method. In situations where limited numbers of subjects are available, where several experimental variations are to be tried, or where the experimental procedure consists of a sequence of conditions A and B, counterbalanced presentation can be used. There are several combinations of order possible. Half of the subjects are given the sequence in the order AB, the other half in the order BA. The results of both halves of A can be compared with both halves of B. Such an arrangement counteracts losses from fatigue or gains from practice, if all were given the same AB sequence. The counterbalanced presentation is useful in experiments involving comparisons of teaching methods and in controlling the influence of teacher skill in a particular method. By rotating teachers, differences in their skill are controlled.

In several kinds of experiments, standardized procedures have been devised and are used. Just as standardized test procedures are employed to prevent testers from providing their subjects with cues as to correct responses, so have automatic devices such as one-way mirrors, pursuit rotors, exposure drums for words, etc. been used to control differences resulting from variation in experimental procedure. Recording and reporting of procedures and results, which permits duplication and verification of experiments, is another scientific safeguard.

Controlling external influences. Finally, external influences have to be controlled; the physical environment can influence outcomes. Extraneous noise or poor acoustics which interferes with attention or hearing must be avoided. The questions of teacher proficiency and personality, and how to control them are difficult even if several instructors are used. If only two teachers are used, one for each method, they can easily vary in their skill or preference for a given method. Several instructors can be used, but still a problem of assignment exists — of guaranteeing that both methods are taught at equivalent levels of proficiency by equally motivated instructors. It is implicit in the scientific method that an experiment should yield the same results if repeated. However effectively the population and method variables may be controlled, a third set of errors derives from unequal characteristics allied with external conditions of the experiment.

Experimental design. No mention has been made of the effects of interaction between the many variables, but it should be evident that no one variable operates singly in human learning, that several or perhaps all are operating simultaneously and in conjunction with each other, and that they are likely to produce different results in different combinations.

The student may marvel that experiments are ever attempted in view of the difficulties involved. Actually there is no shortage of experiments. Unfortunately the results of many experiments are of dubious value because of experimental naivete'. With other carefully performed experiments, comparisons are difficult because of variations in procedure or population. Nevertheless in spite of these difficulties, an extensive body of experimental research has been established which today resembles a partly finished jig-saw puzzle.

There are many areas in psychology and learning in which research is limited. Our knowledge of creative thinking, imagination, forgetting, development of attitudes and emotional responses is rudimentary. Many of our teaching practices are based upon conjecture, logic, and limited experience. To a great extent, our teaching practices are based upon *experimenting* rather than on *experiments*. The results of such empirical judgments can be excellent; nevertheless we do not know the *how* and *why* of what occurs, only the *what*. Controlled experiments are needed to learn the *how* and *why*.

No attempt will be made here to explain the variations in design which are possible, for this is a subject sufficient in itself for a text — and a difficult one. But it should be evident that any experimental procedure utilized should provide control of the three classes of variables — population, method, and external — and of the types of errors associated with each. Still more important to the advance of scientific knowledge is an experimental design which provides information about the variables' interaction with each other. For these reasons, the simpler designs which have been mentioned within each section — two randomly selected groups, each treated by a different teaching method; groups with sub-groupings of different levels of ability; experiments in which all groups receive all treatments whether in counterbalanced order or not; and multiple groups being treated by similar methods to control teaching skill — all have definite limitations in providing scientific knowledge about human learning. The desired experimental design should provide not only information about the operation of single variables, but about their interactions as well. The trend has been to utilize procedures which permit use of combinations of the above methods, using multiple groups in which different treatments can be systematically varied to permit simultaneous observation of the effects and interaction of two or more variables.

SUMMARY

An experimental approach to problem-solving and adjustment to new situations can be found in much of our behavior. Usually the approach is unsystematic, even though based on guesses with respect to solutions. Scientific experiments differ in their provision for systematic procedures for gathering information and testing hypotheses under controlled conditions. Scientific theory results from attempts to generalize regarding a range of experimental data and to explain that data. Further experiments refute, confirm, or force modification of theory. Psychology became a science when an experimental approach was adopted.

Both non-experimental and experimental methods are fruitfully used. Tests, statistics, observations, and verbal reports are used in differential psychology and clinical psychology in surveys, descriptive studies, and investigations of individual and group behavior.

The purpose of experimental studies is to discover the relationships functioning between variables. Controls are essential to eliminate or hold constant the influence from factors other than the variables being investigated. Such influences arise from population sources, experimental procedures, and external influences. Sampling procedures, matched groups, control groups, counter-balanced presentations, statistical methods, standardized experimental procedures, and reporting of procedures and results are methods used in the effort to control variables and carry on experimental investigations.

OVERVIEW

Hilgard, E. R., "Methods and Procedures in the Study of Learning," *Handbook of Experimental Psychology,* S. S. Stevens, ed. New York: Wiley, 1951, pp. 517-67.

SELECTED REFERENCES

Anastasi, Anne and J. P. Foley, *Differential Psychology.* New York: Macmillan Co., 1950, Chapter 2.

Edwards, A. L., *Experimental Design in Psychological Research.* New York: Rinehart, 1950.

Goedicke, V., *Introduction to the Theory of Statistics.* New York: Harper, 1953.

Lindquist, E. G., *Design and Analysis of Experiments in Psychology and Education.* Boston: Houghton Mifflin, 1953.

Chapter Three

The Measurement of Learning

In the investigation of learning in the psychological laboratory, the early experimenters studied forms of learning which were easily observable and measurable, such as typewriting or rote memorizing of nonsense materials. In these situations it was easy to plot the rate of learning or forgetting in terms of such scores as the number of items learned, the number of items retained, or the number of errors made in a series of trials. Initially there was a tendency to underestimate the complexity of learning; the result was that over-generalizations were made from the experimental results. An experimental fact with which many students entering college are familiar is the rapidity of forgetting; forgetting is greatest immediately after learning, but gradually slows.

This generalization, which was experimentally established in Ebbinghaus' studies of retention, is frequently presumed to apply to all situations and all materials, overlooking the fact that the generalization is limited to situations in which the conditions and the materials are similar to those in the experiment.

As psychological experimentation in learning expanded during the last half century, much effort was devoted to determining the circumstances under which particular generalizations regarding learning applied. More important, psychologists strove to develop theories which could reconcile or account for the many divergent facts and generalizations which were obtained in experiments under different conditions, and to develop experimental procedures and measures which permit more refined observation and more sophisticated conclusions regarding the effect of different variables upon learning.

TYPES OF LEARNING

A variety of procedures has been devised for studying learning — both animal and human — under different circumstances. Conditioning experiments, puzzle boxes, discrimination problems, mazes, detour problems, reasoning tasks, and social learning situations have been utilized in both animal and human learning experiments, while the learning of verbal materials, motor skills, concepts, and the solving of problems has been used extensively with human subjects. Usually a particular procedure has been associated with certain types of learning questions.

Conditioning. The study of conditioning originated with Pavlov, who perceived that the salivation which occurs in response to food can also be elicited by a different stimulus, such as a bell, if the ringing of the bell precedes or accompanies the presentation of the food for a number of trials. He called these responses to the substitute stimuli "conditioned reflexes"; in present usage, the term applied is *conditioned response.* A wide variety of responses such as salivation, muscular contraction, eye wink, leg flexion, and others can be conditioned to substitute stimuli in both animal and human subjects.

Instrumental conditioning is a variation of the *classical* conditioning experiment. In instrumental conditioning, the animal must first make a desired response before the reward is given, whereas in classical conditioning the food appears irrespective of the behavior of the animal. A hungry pigeon may be trained to peck at a button, turn his head, or lift his wing to a particular position if he receives a pellet of food each time he makes the desired response. Also, animals may be trained to make a particular response in order to avoid an electric shock or other noxious stimuli. Thus, in the instrumental conditioning situation it is the response which is instrumental in bringing about the reinforcement — the avoidance of pain, whereas in Pavlov's classical conditioning the reinforcement — the unconditioned stimulus, food — appears irrespective of the animal's behavior.

In both classical and instrumental conditioning a response of the animal is connected to a new (conditioned) stimulus whether it be a signal such as a light or buzzer or a total situation such as a cage. The two procedures differ, however, in the manner in which the response is evoked and reinforced. In classical conditioning the response is evoked more or less automatically, as when the presentation of food prompts the salivation or a shock produces a leg withdrawal. In classical conditioning the unconditioned stimulus which evokes the response is, at the same time, the reinforcing agent. In instrumental conditioning, on the other hand, the response is brought about not by an unconditioned stimulus, but must be in the animal's repertoire and occur in the conditioning situation in order to be reinforced. The reinforcement follows, rather than precedes, the response, as in the typical training of pets where a desired response, such as sitting on command, is rewarded. In either classical or instrumental conditioning, the continued omission of the reinforcement for a number of trials results in the gradual disappearance of the conditioned response; this process is termed *extinction*.

Hilgard and Marquis (1940) list four types of instrumental conditioning: (1) reward training in which the animal is rewarded for the correct response, (2) escape training in which the conditioned response terminates a noxious stimulus, as in the situation in which an electric shock builds up gradually over a period of seconds but can be terminated by such a conditioned response as pressing a lever, (3) avoidance training in which making the conditioned response prevents the occurrence of a punishing stimulus, and (4) secondary reward training in which, as a result of previous learning, animals produce the desired conditioned responses for some kind of token, such as chips.[1]

[1] E. R. Hilgard and D. G. Marquis, *Conditioning and Learning* (New York: Appleton-Century, 1940), p. 51.

Trial-and-error learning. The puzzle box was introduced by Thorndike in his studies of learning in 1898, and it was from his experiments with animals that he developed his theory of trial-and-error learning known as *connectionism*. The puzzle box is essentially a cage with a door operated by some type of release mechanism such as a string, lever, or pole as shown in Figure 3.1. In order to escape

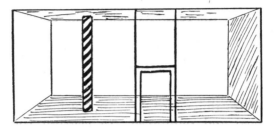

Fig. 3.1. Cage with pole-releasing mechanism.
Used in puzzle-box experiments.

from the box and obtain a reward, such as food placed outside the box, the animal must operate the release mechanism. On early trials the animal engages in a great amount of ineffective movement in his efforts to get out of the cage. Although the efforts may have purpose, they are ineffective in that they fail to trip the mechanism. Gradually, the time required to get out of the cage decreases as the useless movements are eliminated. Thorndike believed that the animal underwent a process of selecting and connecting the correct responses, hence the term connectionism. The extent of the erroneous responses pointed to the concept of learning as a trial and error procedure. The term "trial-and-error" did not imply that the learning was thought to be blind or purposeless, but rather that it was inefficient.

Discrimination learning. In discrimination learning experiments, the organism, animal or human, is presented with the problems of differentiating between two stimuli, one of which requires a positive response, the other requiring either no response or a different one. The situation is analogous to that of the aviation gunner who must identify an approaching plane as friend or foe before deciding whether or not to fire. The situation requires that the gunner be able to recognize what are frequently small differences in shape or silhouette of various aircraft, and respond accordingly. Considering aircraft speed, which makes a decision necessary within a short time, the similarity of aircraft shapes, and the variety of airplanes involved, the discrimination required is a difficult one.

Discrimination problems can vary in degree from gross to fine, and may be utilized in conjunction with other types of learning problems such as conditioning or problem solving. In conditioning experiments, the discrimination is ordinarily between responding or not to the presence or absence of a stimulus, e.g. responding when a light is on and not responding when it is off. The training procedure involves establishing a conditioned response to the positive stimulus, and subsequently presenting the negative stimulus without reinforcement, until the discrimination is learned. In the problem-solving discrimination experiment, the organism usually must make a choice between two stimuli presented stimultaneously, only one of which will be reinforced. A discrimination problem carried out with rats on the Lashley jumping apparatus can be used to illustrate this experimental procedure. This apparatus (Figure 3.2) consists

Fig. 3.2. Diagrammatic sketch of Lashley jumping apparatus. *Used in discrimination experiments.*

of a small platform facing two windows, but separated from them by a short gap; below this gap spreads a net, into which the rat falls if he fails to jump through the correct window. Rats can be trained to jump through the window in which a card containing a white triangle appears, and to avoid jumping through the window in which a card containing a white circle appears. Making this discrimination requires the development of a concept of triangularity. That rats are capable of this can be demonstrated by their willingness to jump to the triangle, regardless of the particular shape of the triangle, and by their resistance to jumping when alternate shapes are introduced.

In the type of discrimination illustrated in the foregoing paragraph, the problem facing the learner differs from that in the conditioning experiment in that the two stimuli are presented simultaneously rather than consecutively, and the learner must choose between two reactions rather than merely reacting or not reacting.

Maze learning. Many kinds of mazes have been used with both animals and humans. Animal mazes range from simple alleys to complex combinations of pathways in three dimensions. The mazes used with humans, although frequently similar in design, are not directly comparable because of size differences which produce a different stimulus basis. Of even greater significance is the difference resulting from the factor of verbal instruction used with human subjects. The difficulty of mazes can be increased by intensifying the complexity of the alternations. Alternation problems which require the organism to make two right turns, followed by two left turns, followed by two right turns can be introduced, with the maze being so designed that the alternating choices have to be made at the same point in the maze each time. Mazes have been widely used in motor and serial learning.

Problem solving. Several different types of experiments may be grouped under the heading of problem solving. Delayed reaction experiments are those in which a stimulus such as food is placed in a container and then hidden from view for a short period of time by interposing a screen, thus forcing a delay in the response of the animal. Particularly in long delays, some kind of learning has to mediate between the presentation of the stimulus and the making of the correct response. Experiments of this type have been used for comparing differences in capacity of organisms to make correct responses after varying intervals.

So-called reasoning problems which require the organism to achieve a novel solution, either on the first trial or after repeated failures, differs from the conditioning and trial-and-error learning tasks: the solution is abruptly made, rather than gradually in the manner characteristic of conditioning and trial-and-error. An illustration may be given from an experiment by Maier (1945) in which two strings were suspended from the ceiling far enough apart so that they could not both be reached simultaneously. The subject was instructed to tie the ends together. This could be accomplished only by tying a weight to one string, starting it swinging like a pendulum, taking hold of the other string, catching the swinging pendulum, and tying the two together. Solving such a problem requires recombining previous experiences into new combinations.

Detour problems which require a subject to move away from the goal in order to finally reach it have been used as problems, particularly with children. The situation ordinarily involves a desired goal-object to which access is blocked by a barrier. The goal can be obtained only by moving away from the goal in order to get around the barrier. For example, candy may be placed within view on the opposite side of the screen from a child, who may try to reach through the screen unsuccessfully. To obtain the candy, the child must overcome the immediate appeal of the goal-object — the candy — and move to one end of the screen in order to get past it and obtain the candy.

Verbal learning. A type of material used extensively with human subjects is verbal material, both meaningful and nonsense. As previously described, Ebbinghaus invented the nonsense syllable (a vowel between two consonants, e.g., QEJ) for the study of the learning of verbal materials in order to control variation in meaningfulness of the verbal material. Subsequent investigation demonstrated that the so-called nonsense syllables varied in meaningfulness, associations being more easily established with some. For instance, the syllables JAN, KEN, MEX are more readily learned than are GUQ, SIJ, YUS. Studies were carried out to establish the degree of meaningfulness of lists of nonsense syllables, in order to provide psychologists with materials of known degrees of meaningfulness varying from those that are completely meaningless to the meaningful words found in language. Nonsense syllables, word lists, foreign words, prose, poetry, etc., have all been used in experiments studying the learning and retention of verbal materials.

Of the several procedures available for studying the influence of practice on the learning of verbal materials, two procedures are most frequently used. The first is called the *anticipation method* in which a list of words, either nonsense or meaningful, is presented for a standard period of time at a uniform rate to the subject. The latter's task is to associate each word with the subsequent one so that he can anticipate its occurrence on subsequent trials by naming it prior to its appearance. The subject is expected to announce his anticipation. Each word serves as the cue for the following word and the subject's anticipation is confirmed or corrected when the following word appears. A typical example from everyday experience is memorizing prose or poetry, or remembering directions.

The second procedure utilizing verbal materials is the *paired associates method* in which the words are presented in discrete pairs to the subject, whose task is to recall the second upon presentation of the first. The order of the pairs of words is usually varied from trial to trial in order to prevent the subjects from using serial anticipation learning of the second words in each pair, rather than associating them with the stimulus word — the first word of the pair. The pairs may consist of two words, a word and a number, two nonsense syllables, or items of other kinds of material. The score consists of the number of appropriate responses given when the stimulus items are presented in the test. To illustrate, the learning series could be: house — 62, leaf — 96, dog — 35, etc. After training, the words would be presented one at a time and the subject would be expected to give the number paired with each. The total number of correct responses is the score. The paired associates method is similar in form to several common learning tasks. Pairing state capitals with their respective states, pairing foreign vocabularly words with their English equivalents, and learning multiplication tables are all everyday uses of the paired associates method.

Perceptual motor learning. A wide variety of perceptual motor-skills may be used as the basis for learning experiments. One of the earliest experiments with motor skills was that of Bryan and Harter (1897) in their study of telegraphy. Since then, mirror star tracing, spool packing, maze drawing, ball throwing, and other motor skills have been utilized as the basis for learning experiments in this area.

In describing the measures that are used with verbal and motor learning, a distinction must be made between the acquisition of the material or skill and its retention. In actual experience, both learning and retention are occurring simultaneously and are interacting with each other. For instance, a child learning to spell words ending in "ought" such as fought, bought, may begin misspelling words which he had previously learned such as caught and taught. If learning occurred on a single trial, then subsequent measures of the event would be of retention. But where learning requires repeated trials, an individual's performance on any trial after the first, includes that which he has retained from previous trials plus that which he has learned during the last trial. In practice it is customary to describe the acquisition of a skill or behavior up to a specified point or degree of mastery as learning, and naming subsequent measures as retention.

METHODS OF MEASURING LEARNING

Response frequency, latency, and amplitude. The frequency with which a response occurs in a given number of trials, the length of time elapsing between presentation of a stimulus and the occurrence of the response (latency), and the amplitude or strength of the response are commonly-used measures of learning in conditioning experiments. Of these three, frequency of response is more widely used. It may be reported either as a given number of responses or as a percentage of a total number of trials.

Memory span method. Different methods have been devised and used for measuring the acquisition of behavior as compared to its retention. The memory-span method was one of the first to be used in quantitative studies of memory. A person's memory-span is the largest number of items he can correctly reproduce immediately after one presentation. The items used may be digits, letters, syllables, words, geometrical figures, or any other kind of material that readily falls into a series of approximately equal units. There is no single fixed memory span, but rather a memory span for each particular set of conditions under which the presentation is made. For example, if we say a person's memory span is seven, we mean that it is seven for a certain kind of material, presented under specified conditions, and scored according to a particular procedure. An individual's memory span for digits may differ from his memory span for words or other types of items. His memory span for digits read by the experimenter may differ from his span for digits presented visually by means of cards.

The typical procedure in memory-span experiments is to present several series, varying in length from three or four items, which the subject may be expected to get every time, up to twelve or thirteen, which is clearly beyond his ability to reproduce. Between these limits is located the number that is correctly reproduced in just 50 per cent of the trials. This number is taken as the measure of the memory span. By keeping all the conditions of the experiment constant save one, which is varied at will, the experimenter can determine the influence of that factor on the memory span for those conditions. By using in turn other factors as variables, he can explore the complex of conditions which affect this relatively simple act of memory.

Various studies on the memory span indicate that it varies not only with the rate and sense modality of the presentation, the scoring method, and materials used (Brener, 1940), but also with the rhythm of presentation, time of day, practice, distraction, attitude, fatigue, the subject's grouping of the items presented, and other influences (Blankenship, 1938). More important, it has been found to increase with age up to the point of mental maturity, and this finding has been put to practical use in the digit tests of the Binet scales for measuring intelligence. With the auditory method of presentation the memory span of college students for digits usually falls between six and eight. The span for meaningful words is greater than for nonsense syllables, and still greater for words related into a meaningful sentence.

When the length of the material exceeds the memory span and the number of trials or presentations is insufficient for complete learning, learning is scored in terms of the number of items the subject can reproduce either immediately after learning or at a later time. This becomes a test of retention. The student will undoubtedly be more familiar with methods used in measuring retention because they are commonly used in school. In 1922 Luh identified five methods of measuring retention in conjunction with verbal materials which he designated as recall, reproduction, recognition, relearning, and reconstruction.

The method of recall. Reproduction may be unaided, as described below, or cues may be given to aid the recall. The latter procedure is followed in the serial-anticipation method of presenting verbal materials, where each word serves as a cue to prompt the recall of the following word which has become associated with it. The completion type of question in which a word or phrase is omitted from a question and the student is asked to fill in the correct answer is another illustration of the recall method. Similarly, the short answer question in which the response is a phrase or sentence, or perhaps a diagram, is another illustration. Many workbook tasks for elementary school children depend upon recall as a measure of learning.

The method of reproduction. This method is similar to the method of recall except that no cues are given, e.g., the typical essay question in examinations. In using this method, learning is usually carried to the point of an adopted criterion of learning, such as one or two perfect recitals. Scoring is in terms of the number of items reproduced. In the carefully controlled experiments in which this method is used to measure retention, care is usually taken to control the degree of learning. Overlearning is usually avoided or made constant unless discovering the effects of overlearning on retention is the aim of the experiment. In that case, an effort is made to secure varying amounts of overlearning while the other factors are held constant.

School testing relies heavily on the reproduction method of measuring retention. The usual classroom, however, lacks the precise controls of the conditions and degrees of learning found in good laboratory experiments. Too often children are rated exclusively on the amount of the lesson they can reproduce or the number of memorized facts they can recall and write down on an examination paper. We should remember that not only may a child know more than he can recall at a given time, but that there are other devices for gauging the persistence of learning outcomes, which in some cases are more appropriate than recall.

The recognition method. The ability to recognize an object depends upon previous experience with it. It is as much an outcome of learning as is recall. Therefore, we are measuring the persistence of the results of learning when we ascertain the extent of one's ability to recognize items previously experienced. The characteristic features of the recognition method of measuring retention are: first, the presentation one or more times of a list of items for learning; second, a test given immediately after this presentation or later, in which the same items are again presented but mixed with a number of other items of the same class; and third, the report by the subject on each item of the test series regarding whether that item appeared in the list originally presented. Scoring is in terms of the number of items correctly recognized. For example, if we let letters represent the items used, we might present for learning M Z D G X B J Y and for the test series K U G Z O N D T J M P X Q Y B F. The subject would be asked to state for each item in the second group whether or not it appeared in the first one.

Recognition is one of the more commonly used measures, at least in achievement tests. Many true false items, though not all, and many multiple choice test items are essentially recognition tests.

It is generally found that higher percentage scores of retention result from recognition testing than from the recall methods, and this is taken to mean that recognition is easier than recall. This is probably true, because in recognition tests the subject actually has before him the identical stimulus-pattern he previously observed. It is to be expected that this would contain more adequate reminders of the earlier impression than something else connected with it. Even if it does result in a higher percentage score of retention, its use can help us distinguish between effective learning, poor learning, and no learning at all. Its use in testing certain forms of school learning seems not only justified but desirable as well. Our testing should be in accord with the desired outcomes. The value of learning is not restricted to the ability to reproduce. In many cases the values of a study are fully realized if one is able to recognize a statement as true or false when he reads it, or if he knows what an object is when he sees it. Apparently, no one has undertaken to determine what proportion of our learning serves its purpose on the recognition level. Certainly a considerable proportion of it does.

Regarding the relative difficulty of recognition tests and recall tests it may be noted that the difficulty of the former depends largely on the extent to which the additional items of the test series are similar to those of the learning list. Greater similarity here means greater difficulty. Moreover, items may be constructed of any degree of difficulty from very simple to very difficult, so that the comparative ease or difficulty of a question is less important than the type of performance that is being measured, and the item that gives the best measure — the most valid and reliable — is to be preferred.

The relearning, or saving, method. Devised by Ebbinghaus, this method has one advantage over all the other methods, and that is: It can be used to measure the degree of retention when the subject has forgotten to the extent of being unable to recall or recognize. In the usual procedure the subject learns a list of items to the point of one or sometimes two perfect recitals. Since the material is not overlearned, it is soon forgotten so that its recall is impossible. After an interval the subject relearns the same list to the same criterion of mastery. Ordinarily it takes less time to relearn than was required for the original learning. The time saved, that is, the difference between the time required for learning and for relearning, is taken as the measure of retention existing at the time relearning was undertaken. It is commonly stated in terms of the percentage of the original learning time. Thus, if it takes a person ten minutes to learn a list of words to the point of one perfect recital, and four minutes to relearn it after five hours, the time saved for relearning as a result of having previously learned the list would be six minutes. This would indicate a saving or retention of 60 per cent, and a loss of 40 per cent for the five-hour interval. The difference between the number of trials required for learning and for relearning may also be used as an index of the amount of retention, when this method is employed.

The length of the time interval that elapses between the initial learning and the subsequent relearning introduces another variable which must be controlled in order to avoid spurious retention scores. Again using the illustration of the person who relearned the list of words in four minutes after a lapse of five hours, it is obvious that only if the person required the original time of ten minutes (approximately) to learn a new list of equally difficult words can it be safely concluded that the saving in time results from having previously learned the original material. If he learns a new list in four minutes, then apparently something has occurred whereby he has become able to learn such lists of words faster, rather than retained a residue from the original list.

The reconstruction method. In testing retention by this method the experimenter first presents to the subject a group of items in a certain order or pattern. He then breaks up the arrangement and turns the materials over to the subject who tries to arrange them in the former order or pattern. The unique feature of this method is that it calls for the reproduction, not of the items, but of the order or arrangement in which they are originally presented. It may be used not only for verbal materials but also for colors, odors, and objects of various sorts. When this method is used to measure learning, the score is usually based on the number of trials or time required to learn the arrangement well enough to reproduce it exactly. When using it to secure a measure of retention over an interval following learning, the degree to which the reconstructed order coincides with the presented order may be taken as the basis for scoring.

A number of practical adaptations of this method may be made. For example, in the domestic science course the teacher may test her students' mastery of the lesson on the proper arrangement of the dishes and utensils on the dinner table by having them set the table. After the members of a class in general science have been shown an electric bell correctly connected with batteries and switch, a good reconstruction test of the knowledge gained would be to separate the parts of the assemblage and have the pupils attempt to put them together again. The soldier in training must learn to take his gun apart and put it together again. In any case where the proper assembling or arrangement of materials or parts is the aim of teaching, this method with suitable adaptations may be used to determine the extent to which the aim has been achieved.

Work scores. The most frequently used measures in the study of the learning of motor skills are work scores (quantity of work accomplished within a given unit of time) and time scores (time required to complete a trial or unit of work). Hilgard [2] cites three reasons favoring the use of work scores in conjunction with measures of motor skill: "(1) Scores can be obtained for the poorest learners (who receive a score of zero if they do not achieve anything measurable); (2) improvement is shown by a rising curve, which produces divergency of scores later in practice, when small differences are of greater theoretical interest; and (3) the experiment is easily conducted in groups because trials are of uniform length for all learners throughout the learning."

MEASUREMENT OF LEARNING IN SCHOOL SITUATIONS

The learning of verbal materials and motor skills, and to a lesser degree, discrimination learning and problem solving, are typical of most school situations. Children are learning to read and spell. They acquire information about the area and the world in which they live

2 E. R. Hilgard, "Methods and Procedures in the Study of Learning," in S. S. Stevens, ed., *Handbook of Experimental Psychology* (New York: Wiley, 1951), p. 538.

and about natural science. They are learning to move their eyes in prescribed fashion and to discriminate small differences in the reading of verbal symbols. They are learning to manipulate a pencil in certain designs in order to print and write letters and words. They are learning procedures and sometimes understanding the principles involved in arithmetical computations. Simultaneously the teacher is engaged in manipulating the variables of motivation, practice, transfer, and others in a variety of procedures just as the psychologist does in his learning experiments, although with a different purpose and without the stringent experimental controls found in the laboratory. Like the psychologist, the teacher is using similar measures of performance in order to appraise learning. The five measures previously described — recall, reproduction, recognition, reconstruction, and relearning — are commonly utilized by the teacher.

The true-false and matching questions utilized in the achievement tests, both standardized and teacher-made, depend upon pupil recognition. The essay question is an illustration of unaided reproduction, while the short answer, in which a preliminary cue is given by presenting the stem of a sentence with the answer omitted, is a recall question. Scrambled sentences which the student has to rearrange are based upon the reconstruction method of measurement. Relearning is used less frequently as a measure of learning, although teachers are aware of summer loss in achievement in certain school subjects such as arithmetic and spelling. Were it not for the gains possible through relearning in a shorter period of time, this loss would produce a very slow rate of learning in such subjects.

Limitations in methods of measuring. Recall and recognition are the two most widely used measures in the classroom; achievement tests depend heavily upon these types of items in the measurement of retention. It may be argued that too great a dependence is placed upon such measures when children are rated exclusively on the amount of the lesson they can reproduce or the number of memorized facts they can recall and write down on an examination paper. Immediate recollection has its limitations as a measure of retention, for it is restricted to a particular aspect of learning and does not include important concomitant learnings such as development of attitudes, problem solving ability, and concept development.

Figure 3.3 shows the percent of retention obtained by Luh when he had subjects learn lists of 12 nonsense syllables to a criterion of one perfect recitation, and subsequently measured their retention at four intervals by the different procedures of measurement described. It can be seen readily that the impression one obtains of the amount of material learned and retained will vary with the kind of measure utilized. This fact suggests that some sophistication on the part of

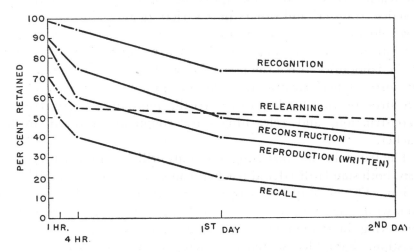

Fig. 3.3. Retention curves obtained by 5 different methods of measuring retention (after Luh, 1922).

teachers is necessary to interpret the meaning of scores obtained on any measure of learning; particularly they must recognize that performance is not absolute, but relative to the measure used.

Reliability of scores. At this point another word of caution regarding the interpretation and use of learning scores by teachers is advisable. Aside from the variation by type of measure, all measurements in general, and psychological measures in particular are subject to error. This is to say that any single measure or score is at best an approximation rather than a true score. If repeated measures of exactly the same object are taken by a number of persons, they will show variation which may be small or great according to the precision of the measuring instrument being used. Any *single* measure, it follows, is incorrect by some amount; the variation in scores or measures is termed unreliability. Thus, when a teacher has a performance or achievement score of a pupil, it is at best an approximation of the pupil's true score. If the same pupil were to be given an identical test immediately thereafter (and if it could be assumed that having taken the first test would in no way affect his score on the second test), in all probability the second score would vary from the first.

In the psychological experiments it is possible to introduce rigid controls in order to insure moderate to high reliability of scores; unfortunately, in the classroom such circumstances are less possible for the teacher. His best protection is to understand the limitation of the scores being used in order to avoid making faulty judgments.

LIMITATIONS OF PSYCHOLOGICAL AND EDUCATIONAL SCALES

One source of inaccurate measurement arises from the nature of psychological measures themselves. We are accustomed to using instruments which measure such physical phenomena as distance, area, and weight; also familiar is a second type of measuring scale, e.g. thermometers for such phenomena as temperature. These two classes of scales have advantages which are denied to psychological measures. Both have equal units of measurement; that is to say, the distance from 2 centimeters to 6 centimeters is the same as from 10 centimeters to 14 centimeters, or the temperature increase from 80 to 82° Fahrenheit represents the same increase in heat as the increase from 105 to 107° Fahrenheit. Thus any unit at any point on the scale is equal to any unit at any other point. In addition, measures of height, weight, distance, and area have an additional advantage in that the scales have a true zero, i.e., zero pounds of weight or zero inches in height. Having a true zero makes comparative measures possible. Thus it is possible to say that a person weighing 150 pounds is twice as heavy as a person weighing 75 pounds, or that a person 6 feet tall is twice as tall as a person 3 feet tall. Such comparisons are not possible unless the scale has a true zero. By comparison, 50° Fahrenheit is not twice as hot as 25° Fahrenheit. It would be true if 0° on the Fahrenheit scale were a *true zero,* i.e., complete absence of heat. One need only to convert the temperatures to a centigrade scale to realize that such a comparison does not hold.

The two types of comparisons that are possible with the physical scales, one with a true zero and equal units of measurements, the second having only the equal units of measurement, are not possible with psychological measures.

In general, psychological measures provide a rank-ordering of individuals or items from high to low in standing. The typical intelligence test, the most widely known of all psychological measures, provides scores called intelligence quotients, which range from approximately 40 to 160. Even though such scores make it possible to rank a group of individuals from most intelligent to least intelligent, they do not permit more refined comparisons. The units on the scale are not of equal size which means that the intellectual gaps between individuals at different points on the scale may not be proportional to the score differences. And, because psychological tests lack a true zero, it is not possible to say that a person with an IQ of 100 is twice as intelligent as a person with an IQ of 50. All that can be said is that he is more intelligent.

Aside from the limitation of scores, there are other sources of unreliability. Different types of tests have differing reliability. For instance, standardized achievement tests usually possess much higher reliability than do teacher-made tests owing to the more careful selection of test questions. A series of environmental factors can contribute to errors in measurement and produce scores which are either too low or too high. The procedure utilized in administering a test may be such that it gives many cues as to the correct answers, or it may favor a person seated in the front of the room where he may hear questions more readily if it is given orally or see them more clearly if written on a blackboard. The amount of extraneous noise or interruptions will affect the scores obtained, as well the mere factor of administering a test in a different setting from that to which the subjects are accustomed. Variations in motivations, fatigue, and misunderstanding of instructions are but a few of the factors which may affect individual performance and produce a degree of error or unreliability in scores. The limitations introduced by unreliability do not make tests valueless, but merely require judgment in interpreting test scores.

Validity of measures. A second major source of error in psychological measures centers around the question of validity. This is the quality or characteristic of a test which makes possible judgment or prediction regarding the performance of the subject. For instance, an individual's speed in running the 100 yard dash provides little information upon which to base a prediction regarding his swimming ability; the running scores would have little validity as far as estimating swimming ability. In contrast, an intelligence test is valid to a degree for estimating school achievement because it apparently measures some of the components that contribute to school achievement; it has, however, little validity for estimating success in salesmanship.

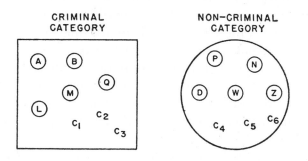

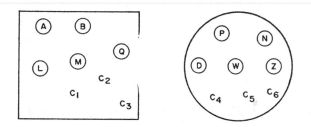

Fig. 3.4. Perfect reliability without validity. *On each trial, subjects are consistently placed in the same category; however, criminals are not predicted better than chance (c_1 to c_6 are criminals; (A) to (Z) are noncriminals).*

Figure 3.4 provides an illustration of a situation in which there is high reliability but no validity. From time to time, it has been claimed without considerable success that it is possible to predict criminals on the basis of their physical characteristics. Let us assume that an individual believes all persons with bushy eyebrows, broken noses, and thin lips are criminal types, and that he proceeds to classify a group of people on the basis of his belief. As is shown in Figure 3.4, it would be possible for him on two successive trials to put the same individual into identical categories; that is to say, on each trial he would put all individuals with bushy eyebrows, broken noses, and thin lips in the criminal category — the square box in the figure — and all other persons in the non-criminal category — the circles in the figure. Thus his measures have high reliability — they are consistent. But do they have validity? Is he distinguishing between criminals and non-criminals on better than a chance basis, or is he no more successful than if he sorted them blindfolded? One criterion of how to validate the measure would be to check the police records. As is shown in the illustration, the distribution of criminals and non-criminals would be no better than could be anticipated on the basis of chance.

Ignoring the scientific findings for the purpose of illustrating simultaneous reliability and validity, let us assume that the people were sorted as in Figure 3.5 and their criminal records checked. In this instance, although the reliability is not perfect, it is high; the classifier is consistent in getting nearly all individuals in the same category on each trial. On both trials, criminals C3, C4, C5, and C6 are placed in the criminal category while C1 and C2 are interchanged on the second trial. Nevertheless, the proportion of criminals in each category remains the same. Similarly, the non-criminals are each placed in the same category on both trials with the exception of W and A, who as a result of inconsistency are interchanged on the second trial. In this illustration, the sorting shows both high reliability — consistency of measurement — and high validity — dependable prediction based on an outside criterion (the police records).

One factor contributing to the problem of validity stems from the distinction between performance and learning. In any learning situation, the observed and scored behavior is a variation in performance resulting from the experimental or classroom procedures. The learning obtained is always an inference derived from the change in performance; it cannot be assumed that the performance change is a direct measure of the learning obtained. A ready illustration of this fact is found in the extent to which changes in motivation influence performance scores. Figure 3.6 is a schematic illustration taken from studies performed by Tolman and Honzik (1930) on latent learning. Three groups of animals were used in the maze experiment.

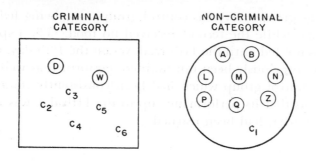

TRIAL 1

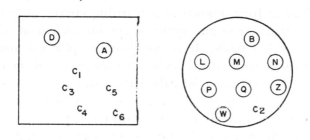

TRIAL 2

Fig. 3.5. **High reliability and validity.** *On each trial, nearly all subjects are placed in the same category; the criminals are separated (although not perfectly) on the basis of the measure used.*

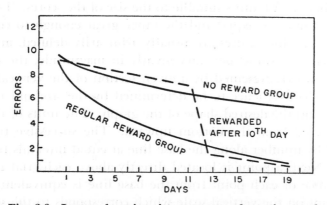

Fig. 3.6. **Latent learning in a maze; schematic graph (after Tolman and Honzik, 1930.)**

Two of the groups served as control groups, one being fed each day in the maze while the second received no food. The experimental group was not fed until the 11th trial, yet on the 12th day, this group which had previously been unrewarded, performed as well or better than the control group which had been consistently rewarded; this fact suggests that its performance up to the 11th day was not a true measure of what had been learned.

LEARNING CURVES

When several trials are given in an experiment and measures of learning or of retention are obtained, these measures may be plotted in the graphical form known as a learning curve — a graph which affords a comparison of the performance on each trial with a performance on other trials. It is customary to plot the independent variable on the horizontal axis, called the abscissa, and the dependent variable on the vertical axis, called the ordinate. The dependent variable is the variable which undergoes changes as a result of the experimenter's manipulations. Scores on the dependent variable are dependent upon or are a function of the experimental factor, and are usually some form of a learning score — errors made, number of words learned, time consumed, etc. In constructing a curve, we first draw two straight lines, a perpendicular one at the left side of the page, and a base line which extends horizontally to the right from the bottom of the first. On the perpendicular line a scale is marked off and numbered with units suitable to the size of the scores. The units of the scale must be equal and the range great enough to cover the largest score. Since scores are usually arbitrarily defined, and since for different measures they vary greatly in magnitude, the number of score points represented by a given section of the vertical line is a matter of convenience to be determined by the size and range of the scores and the desired shape of the graph. The units of the scale are numbered from the bottom upward. The successive trials are indicated by number along the base line at equal intervals from left to right. Next, a point is located directly above each trial number. The distance of each point from the base line is equivalent to that of the point on the vertical scale which corresponds to the score for that trial. Then these points are connected by straight lines. The

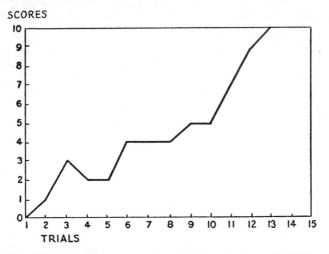

Fig. 3.7. Learning curve showing improvement in ability to reproduce the English equivalents of Hebrew words.

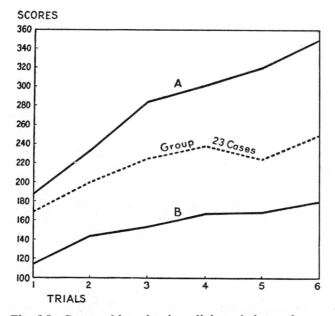

Fig. 3.8. Curves of learning in a digit-symbol experiment. *The subjects were given a sheet containing the digits and were instructed to write, as rapidly as possible, a symbol under each digit, as indicated by a key. The scores are the number of symbols written during a practice period of 5 minutes.*

lines connecting the points constitute the curve of learning. It shows at a glance how the learner has progressed from trial to trial.

An example of a learning curve so constructed is shown in Figure 3.7. The scores are taken from an experiment in which the subject was required to learn the English equivalents of ten Hebrew words. The experimenter first read the Hebrew word and gave the English equivalent. In the following trials, after reading each Hebrew word, the experimenter paused and the subject gave the English word if he could remember it. If he could not do so, he was told what it was, and then the experimenter proceeded to the next word. The score on each trial was the number of correct responses. The criterion of learning was three successive trials in which all the right English words were given. The scores for the fifteen trials were as follows:

Trial:	1	2	3	4	5	6	7	8	9	10	11	12	13	14	15
Score:	0	1	3	2	2	4	4	4	5	5	7	9	10	10	10

Since the highest score was ten, the scale is made up of ten equal units numbered from bottom to top. Each unit of the scale represents one score point. The fifteen trials are represented from left to right on the base line. The height of the curve above the trial points indicates the score for each trial.

Figure 3.8 shows an arrangement of the scale to represent larger scores, and in this graph three curves are presented. A and B are curves of two individuals, and the middle one represents the average scores for twenty-three students. The scores of A and B are included in the averages used to construct the group curve. It is possible here to compare the progress of the two individuals with each other and with the average of the whole group. We see that A was faster than the group average on the first trial and that she gained more with the same amount of practice. We see also that she did not fall back on trial 5 as did most of the group. The lower curve shows that B started off more slowly than the average, and while she gained at about the same rate, she is approximately as far behind after six practice periods as at the end of the first period.

The rate of improvement. One of the things a learning curve reveals is the rate of improvement and the changes in this rate. A uniform rate of improvement is indicated by graphs of the type shown in Figure 3.9. Here progress is indicated by a straight line. Such a graph means that the increment of gain is the same for each suc-

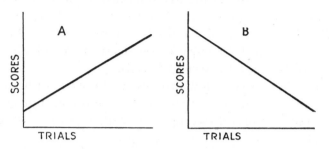

Fig. 3.9. Theoretical learning curves showing zero acceleration, or a uniform rate of improvement.
*In A improvement is shown by an increase in
scores. B depicts those learning situations
wherein decreasing scores indicate improvement,
such as fewer errors.*

cessive trial. When the rate of improvement shows no change, we
have what is known as *zero acceleration.*

Most curves of learning show variations in the rate of improvement.
Curves for motor learning usually show the fastest rate of gain at the
beginning and a slowing up as practice continues. Such a change in
rate is called *negative acceleration.* It should not be confused with a
loss of skill. It refers to those cases wherein improvement is still being
made, but the increment of gain decreases in successive trials. Theoretical curves for negative acceleration are presented in Figure 3.10.

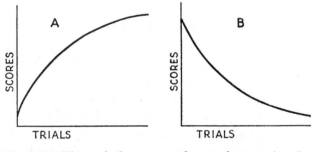

Fig. 3.10. Theoretical curves of negative acceleration
showing a decrease in the rate of gain.

In the cases in which the scores grow smaller (time scores or error
scores on successive trials) as performance improves, negative acceleration is indicated by a downward concave curve. Negatively accel-

erated curves are most frequently obtained in situations in which (1) the learning task is relatively simple, (2) the subjects are of average or above average ability (either well-practiced or bright), (3) there is positive transfer from previous learning, or (4) the tests are given toward the end of a series of trials.

Sometimes there is very slow progress at the start, with an increase in the increments of improvement as practice is continued. This increase in the rate of improvement is called *positive acceleration* (Figure 3.11).

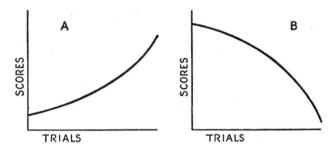

Fig. 3.11. **Two theoretical curves of positive acceleration.**
In both, the rate of improvement is faster in the second half of the learning period than in the first part.

Curves of positive acceleration are frequently found (1) in motor learning, (2) in tests with very young children or children of less than average ability, (3) early in the learning of material that is difficult or meaningless, such as nonsense syllables, or (4) where previous learning interferes with the new learning.

An example of positive acceleration is found in the increase of children's vocabularies during the second year. In an investigation by Smith (1926), the average number of words in children's vocabularies at one year was found to be three words. For children fifteen months old an average of nineteen words was found. At eighteen months old there was an average of twenty-two words. But by twenty-one months, ninety-six words were added, and at the end of the second year the average was 272 words. Thus, the increase during the second six months of the second year was found to be 250 as against an increase of nineteen for the first half of the year. These findings are presented graphically in Figure 3.12.

WORDS

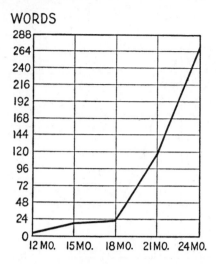

Fig. 3.12. The increase in the average number of words in children's vocabulary during the second year. *The curve for this period is positively accelerated. (Constructed from data by Smith.)*

It is clear that positive acceleration cannot continue indefinitely, for sooner or later the learner reaches complete mastery, or the curve levels off as he approaches the limit of his ability to improve. Which of these two possibilities takes place will depend upon the nature of the learning task and the manner of scoring the performance. In many cases a rate of learning that is positively accelerated at first, changes to negative acceleration as it continues. This provides an S-shaped curve, examples of which are shown in Figure 3.13, which illustrates several variations in rate of improvement; its general form indicates increasing rate in the first few trials, followed by a slowing up.

It is likely that if we were able to plot a complete learning curve from zero to the absolute limit of improvement for any single performance, we should find the S-shaped curve with relatively slow progress at first followed by increasing increments of gain and leveling off with decreasing gains as the limit was approached (Culler, 1928). It may be presumed that a very rapid initial rise in a learning

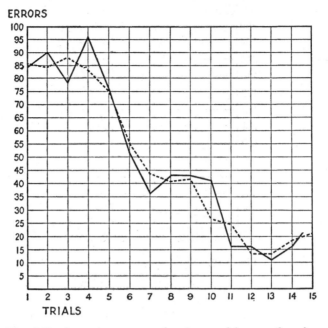

Fig. 3.13. Learning curves showing positive acceleration in the early stages and negative acceleration near the end. *The scores, for one subject, represent errors made in tracing a star outline while looking at its image in a mirror. The solid line is the actual curve; the dotted line is the same curve smoothed by the method of averages.*

curve is due to the fact that the learning task is not altogether new to the learner and that he, therefore, does not begin at a zero point. Initial ability may make some aspects of the total performance easier to master than others. If these easier steps have a direct effect on the score, there naturally will be rapid improvement as indicated by the method of scoring. The harder steps are not mastered so quickly; therefore, the apparent progress becomes slow after the easier initial gains have been accomplished.

The increase in the rate of improvement, or positive acceleration, may be due to the fact that the results of practice are cumulative in their effect on the score. Much of the early practice may be a kind of preparation that makes possible the more rapid advance later. Various aspects of the total performance may be undergoing improvement with comparatively little effect on the score; then, when they are being integrated and consolidated, the curve rises more rapidly. Faster progress may also come with new insight or with mastery of tools of learning. In a first course in science, the progress may be slow at the beginning when the student is becoming accustomed to the terminology of the new field and to the insistence of science upon exact data. After a difficult period of adjustment to new points of view, new methods of study, and new vocabulary, he becomes oriented, acquires confidence, and then goes ahead at a faster pace. When the results of learning in the early stages of practice or study contribute to and make easier the advancements in the later stages, positive acceleration occurs.

The slowing down of the rate of improvement may be caused by several factors. In some cases, part of the effect of continued practice may be consumed in maintaining gains already achieved. As learning advances, this tends to be true to a progressively greater extent. More and more of one's practice is required to keep the performance up to the level of efficiency already attained. Then too, as the limit of improvement is approached, it takes more effort and time to secure an increment of gain. This would cause a slowing down. There are also the influences of such factors as fatigue, loss of interest, a sense of sufficiency, lack of desire for further advancement, and the needless repetition or overlearning of parts of the performance mastered in the early steps of learning. These are some of the varied factors which may produce negative acceleration in the rate of improvement.

Plateaus. Frequently one finds in a learning curve a level stretch in which the scores remain very nearly the same through several trials. It appears from the scores that no advancement is being made even though practice seems to be going on as usual. Such level stretches of the learning curve in which there is no apparent progress are known as *plateaus*. Investigators have pointed out that since plateaus are more likely to occur in complex performances than in simple ones, they may be due to the fact that the learner concentrates on one part at a time. It is suggested, therefore, that if the learner attacks the whole performance as a unit, he is more likely to make steady and continuous progress (Kao, 1937). In a performance measured for both speed and accuracy we may get a plateau in the reduction of errors when the subject sets himself to improve his speed. If he suddenly decides to concentrate on accuracy, his curve of speed may show a plateau.

In general, it may be concluded that plateaus are caused by several different factors. They may be due to: concentration on one part of a complex performance; the fact that the learner is doing as well as he can for the method he is using; imperfectly established elementary habits; poor physical condition, or aspects of attitude or set of the learner, such as loss of interest, discouragement, or divided attention. Since most investigators are inclined to believe that the plateaus are not a necessary feature of learning progress, the teacher should be on the alert to detect any slumps in classroom learning. When they occur, an attempt should be made to discover the cause. and help the learner to resume his progress.

Minor fluctuations in the learning curve. A learning curve seldom rises smoothly from trial to trial. While the general trend may be upward (or downward), there is frequently a great deal of zigzagging.

Figure 3.14 shows the fluctuation in the progress of a learner seeking to reduce his time for sorting forty cards into four compartments. As each card was thrown, its suit was noted, and the next card was thrown into the compartment marked for that suit. The curve is based on the time required for each of twenty sortings. It is to be noted that the subject's progress is marked by numerous setbacks and spurts.

A number of factors affect progress in learning. Some of them tend to better the score, while others operate against improvement. The combinations of these factors vary from trial to trial, and fluctuations in performance result from the variations. With diligent effort and good attention, one makes an excellent score. Then on the next trial he does not do so well because the combination of conditions at the time are not so favorable. A temporary setback may result from poor attention. The learner may be distracted by a noise or by the movements of another person. He may reflect for a moment on how well he is progressing and may perhaps grow a bit careless or relax his effort because of overconfidence resulting from his previous good score. It may be fatigue which in the following trial is offset by adopting a different posture. Possibly these variations in performance are related to other changes in organic conditions. Upon seeing that he has not done so well, the learner sometimes renews his effort and applies himself more diligently the next time. As he does so, his performance reaches a new high. So he goes on, occasionally slipping back, but again advancing to higher levels of proficiency.

Composite curves. The progress of a group of subjects may be indicated by a curve based on the average scores for the various trials.

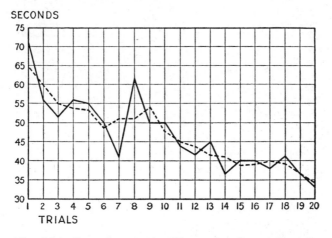

SECONDS

TRIALS

Fig. 3.14. Learning curves illustrating fluctuations in progress. *The scores represent the seconds required to sort a deck of 40 cards in a prescribed manner. The solid-line curve shows the actual scores of a single subject; the dotted line shows a smooth curve based on the same scores.*

In Figure 3.15 are shown the individual curves for six subjects based on their scores in a letter-digit substitution experiment. The individual curves appear in dotted and broken lines. The heavy solid line is the curve for the averages of the group. It will be observed that the composite curve is much smoother than the individual curves. This is because the fluctuations for the various trials tend to cancel out. A drop in one case is offset by a spurt made by one of the other subjects. A curve for a larger group probably would be still smoother. The composite scores are useful in indicating the general course of improvement of a group taken as a whole. Any pronounced dip or sudden rise in a curve based on them reflects a potent factor common to the group rather than an individual peculiarity. A disturbance in the experimental situation which distracted the whole group, for example, might occasion a general slump.

INDIVIDUAL DIFFERENCES IN RATE OF IMPROVEMENT

The improvement or gain resulting from a given amount of practice in a performance varies for different individuals. A child of six may not be expected to gain so much proficiency in typewriting with 100 hours of practice as a high-school student. Even in a group of the

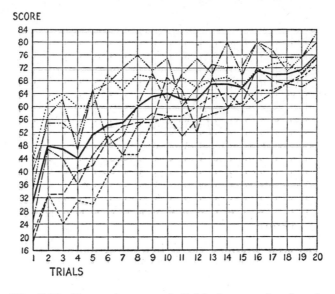

Fig. 3.15. **Composite curve; individual curves for six subjects in a letter-digit substitution experiment.** *The scores represent the number of digits written in one-minute practice periods. The dotted and broken lines are the curves for individual subjects; the heavy solid line represents the mean scores of the group for the various trials.*

same age we find that some advance faster and farther than others with an equal amount of practice. In Figure 3.16 appear the smoothed curves for the performance of six subjects whose individual curves are shown in Figure 3.15. These curves indicate a similar negatively accelerated trend for all six subjects, but they also show that there are differences in the rate of improvement and the amount of gain over the initial score. While A starts with the highest initial score, in the last trial he is tied with F who started with the lowest initial score. C starts third but gains more than A and B to end in first place, while D who starts in fourth place does not gain as much as E and F, so that he ends in sixth place.

The causes of such differences in improvement are difficult to determine. It may be that those who started high and failed to maintain their superiority had some factor of advantage that favored initial performance but did not contribute to gains under practice. Such an initial advantage might be provided by some special previous train-

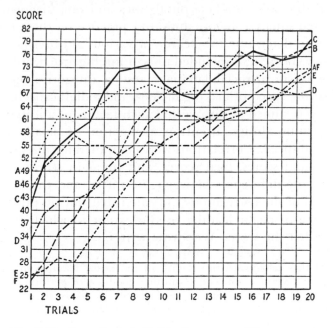

Fig. 3.16. Smoothed individual curves. *These curves, made by smoothing the individual curves appearing in Figure 3.15, show individual differences in rate of improvement and gain over the initial score.*

ing or a particularly fortunate selection of a method of attack in the initial practice period.

Abilities in relation to improvement. A critical experimental investigation of this problem has been made by Woodrow (1938). He sought by careful statistical analysis of the results of several tests to determine whether there was a change during continued practice in the extent to which the score of a performance depended upon the various abilities of the learner. For example, in the case of the practice on letter-digit substitution, does the performance depend on the factor of speed to a greater or lesser degree in the twentieth trial than in the first trial? Fifty-six subjects completed 39 days of practice on each of 7 tests. These tests consisted of adding, letter-digit substitution, reproducing spot-patterns, rearranging letters to make words, canceling certain letters from lines containing all the letters of the alphabet, estimating the length of various sections of a rod, and drawing four horizontal lines and one diagonal line in small printed squares. Before and after practice on these tasks, tests were given to determine the degree of various abilities possessed by the subjects. These tests included tests of intelligence, word and form analogy tests, an artificial language test, a categories test, mental multiplication, speed of making crosses, and a digit-cancellation test. The tests were aimed at discovering such factors of ability as "g" or general learning ability, attention, perception of detail, numerical aptitude, and speed. Correlations were computed for the various tests with the initial scores, final scores, and the gain scores. The gain scores were the differences between the initial and the final scores. The analysis of the correlations indicated that during practice there was a change in factor loading or the extent to which the various factors affected the score. Woodrow writes,

> In general these changes with practice in the factor loadings mean that the quantitative pattern of abilities, determining goodness of performance, changes with practice, i.e., a performance after practice is likely to depend for its success more on one ability or less on another than it did initially. Such a change must mean a change in the mode of operation whereby the subject carries out the task he has been instructed to accomplish.

From these tests there was no indication of an increased dependence on the "g" factor or intelligence, but there was a tendency for the loading of the speed factor to increase. The average correlation of the tests regarded as measuring intelligence with the gain scores was found to be negligible except in the case of the cancellation, and there was no indication that the gain score was related to the speed factor.

Thus, when an individual possesses to a high degree some ability which contributes largely to the initial performance but becomes less important for the score after considerable practice, he may make a relatively high initial score but progress more slowly and gain less with a given amount of practice than another learner who rates lower in this ability but higher in one that counts more in the final score after practice. This may be the explanation of the differences between the gains of A and F whose curves appear in Figure 3.16.

If practice in any function is carried on long enough, the learner sooner or later reaches the limit of his ability to improve under the conditions operating at the time. Different kinds of limits are distinguished on the basis of the conditions which make further progress impossible.

Physiological limits. All activity involves physiological mechanisms, and while the functioning of these mechanisms is subject to great improvement, there are limits inherent in them beyond which any amount of practice cannot produce a faster or more perfect performance. It takes a certain amount of time for the arousal of sense receptors and transmission of the nerve impulse over the fibrous pathways of the nervous system to the effectors. It takes a measurable unit of time for the muscle to contract after the impulse has reached it. Practice can reduce simple reaction times to something like one tenth of a second, but that seems to be about the minimum time required for the simple voluntary motor response. It is a limit for such a performance. Motor performances also may be limited by the capacity of the nervous system for developing coördination of movement, by the strength of the muscles, or by the amount of energy the body is able to supply. Just as no amount of practice would enable a six-weeks-old baby to walk, so no amount of practice would enable a college student to make a broad jump to fifty feet, or run a mile in one minute, simply because such levels of performance are beyond the possibilities of the normal neuromuscular equipment.

The physiological limit is probably rarely reached. To reach it requires a high degree of motivation. It is more easily reached in a simple performance such as flexing the finger as quickly as possible in response to a signal, than it is in the case of complex performances like typewriting or violin playing. In fact, so many factors are involved in the improvement of the more complex performances that it is practically impossible to know when one has reached his physiological limit. There is need for caution in assigning the cause for a final plateau to the physiological limit. This is indicated by cases of further improvement with a change to more favorable conditions when the limit of one's ability was supposed to have been reached. We cannot consider that the individual is approaching his physiological limit until he has discovered and adopted all possible short cuts, eliminated all useless movements, adopted the best possible methods, and is working at maximum motivation.

There are extensive individual differences in physiological limits. The child's limit, for many performances, is below that of the normal adult because his muscles are not so strong, he cannot execute movements so quickly, and he is inferior in ability to coördinate movements. Differences in physiological capabilities also appear among individuals of the same age.

The physiological limits may change from time to time in the same individual. Exercise may strengthen the muscles. Growth increases the possibilities of neuromuscular coördinations. Improvement in health adds to the reserves of bodily energy, and its impairment results in a lowering of physical stamina. In general, the limits of improvement rise from infancy to maturity, fluctuate with changes in health and bodily vigor, and drop to lower levels of achievement in old age.

When one approaches his physiological limit in a complex performance, further increments of improvement require more and more effort. The returns for time and effort expended diminish. In the case of typewriting, for example, an increase in speed beyond sixty words per minute requires a great amount of diligent practice. For these reasons, and because of other limits to be considered, most persons seldom reach their physiological limits of improvement, and in most cases it would be a waste of effort and time to do so.

Practical limits. The absolute limit of efficiency in any function and the degree of excellence which is good enough for all practical purposes are usually quite different. The degree of proficiency sufficient to meet all normal demands is called the *practical limit.* It is frequently very much lower than the absolute limit of improvement. Workers in industrial establishments, clerks, stenographers, and others tend to strike a level of proficiency good enough to get them by, and then go on year after year without making any improvement in their work. That this level is much below their possible achievement is shown by the fact that under the incentive of demands for a better grade of work as the price for retaining their position, or under the stimulus of competition with other workers for a coveted promotion, they apply themselves with greater diligence and thereby increase their efficiency.

Students in college courses probably never do their absolute best. They are usually satisfied with a good grade, and sometimes with a mediocre grade that gives them credits toward a degree. More time and more effort would enable them to accomplish a greater degree of mastery of any subject, but they have to divide their time between several subjects and other activities.

The child might be able to learn to spell all the words in the dictionary, but the cost of such an achievement would be entirely incompatible with its practical value. It is considered a waste of a child's time to require him to learn the spelling of more than two thousand of the most commonly used words. The practice of requiring children to learn scores of historical dates which will rarely be encountered in reading, or of requiring the mastery of problems involving eight- or ten-place decimals is now vigorously challenged by educators. The practical limit of proficiency in the use of decimals is certainly far below the maximum possible attainment. The practical limits of training in any school subject must be determined by a consideration of individual and social needs in relation to the values the subject offers. Subject matter that does not minister to the needs of the child, and that which will be of no use to him, should not be forced upon him. To require a child to learn useless material is to waste his time and deprive him of more essential training.

Motivational limits. Closely related to the limits imposed by practical considerations are motivational limits. A person has reached his *motivation limit* of improvement when he is content with his present achievement and is not interested in doing better. Much poor work in school is due, not to lack of ability, but to lack of application of effort because of insufficient motivation.

Incentives determine in a large measure how far a person advances his skill and knowledge. A comparatively few persons in every field of endeavor rise above the level of mediocrity. A few train dispatchers emerge from the mass of telegraphers. Occasionally a great captain of industry rises from the ranks of common machinists. One boy out of thousands growing up on the sidewalks of a great city reaches fame as a leader in national politics. To become great requires energy, ability, and opportunity, but these essentials, without the *will to succeed,* will not produce greatness. There is probably no case more difficult for a counselor to handle than that of the young man of high-grade ability who does not care whether he makes anything of himself or not. The lack of desire to improve, lack of interest in achievement, and satisfaction with mediocrity prevent a person from reaching the possibilities of which he is capable. There are probably few cases where a person's performance cannot be improved if a sufficiently strong motive is established.

THE TEACHER'S USE OF LEARNING CURVES

As we have seen, learning curves provide a graphic record of the course of learning. They reveal the fluctuations in progress, stages of rapid advancement, periods of slowing down, and the plateaus where no apparent improvement is being made even when practice is continued. The teacher may use them for her own enlightenment and as an impressive means for informing pupils of their progress. Learning graphs based on scores derived from standardized tests may indicate whether satisfactory advancement is or is not being made by the pupils individually or as a class. Plateaus in those curves will serve as a warning that all is not going well. They may indicate the intrusion of some detrimental factor, the need for a change in teaching methods, or the desirability of some new form of incentive.

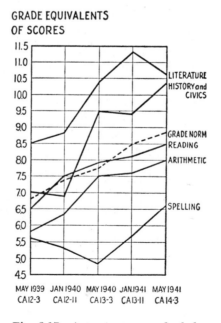

Fig. 3.17. A two-year record of the progress in 5 school subjects made by a pupil of average intelligence.

In Figure 3.17 are presented curves showing the progress in five school subjects of a pupil of average intelligence over a period of two years. They are based on grade equivalents of scores which the pupil made on the Metropolitan Achievement Tests given at the midyear period near the end of January and at the close of the school year near the end of May. This sample record was selected at random from the school's test files.

The standing of the pupil in the five subjects is indicated by solid-line curves. The dotted line shows the grade norm for the pupil's attained age. An examination of this graph reveals many things concerning this pupil's accomplishments. First, we see a marked difference between his achievement in the five subjects as indicated by his performance on these standardized tests. His literature curve is consistently much higher than the grade norm. The curve for history and civics begins near the grade norm but rises considerably above it during the two years. Reading keeps close to the grade norm throughout, but falls off slightly in the second year. Arithmetic is down, but is slightly nearer the norm at the end of the two years than at the start. Before seeing this graph the child's teacher had not realized that he was so much below his grade norm in arithmetic. The curve for spelling shows a marked deficiency in that subject. It reveals that while this child was 1.2 grades below where he should have been in spelling at the beginning of this period, after the two years he was 2.2 grades below the standard for his age. During these two years he made but one year's advance in this subject. The graph reveals the areas in which the child has and has not been making satisfactory progress. It indicates the need for discovering and correcting the causes of his deficiencies in arithmetic and spelling.

As a means of informing pupils concerning their progress, learning curves, if wisely used, may serve as a valuable motivation device. Everyone desires to know what his efforts are accomplishing, and the graphic method of portraying progress is especially effective in the case of children. Learning graphs may be built on the scores from the teacher's own weekly or monthly tests. As each new score is made, the curve is extended, showing how much advance has been made over previous scores. Many teachers have found that children become greatly interested in their curves and try hard to make them go up. An upward swing of the curve brings great satisfaction, while its failure to rise is often effective as a stimulus to greater effort.

Although in curves used for the sole purpose of motivation some lapse from scientific precision may be condoned, it should be remembered that a suitable curve requires that the successive tasks from which the scores are derived should be of approximately equal difficulty and scorable in terms of units of approximately equal value. It is also essential that the tests be given at regular intervals and that they measure the same kind of ability. For example, a curve might easily be constructed to show monthly gains in speed in typewriting by means of scores representing the number of letters written per minute. Gains in accuracy could be plotted by using for scores the number of errors made in typing a given number of words. Improvement in rate of reading could be graphed from time scores derived from weekly tests on passages of uniform length and difficulty. Weekly gains in the learning of the addition facts could be represented graphically by using for scores the total number of such facts mastered after each week's study.

In using learning curves as motivational devices with elementary school children, certain wisdom is necessary on the teacher's part. Even if possible, it is usually undesirable to score each trial in a series, for instance in the recognition of lists of words on flashcards, or in spelling series of words, or performing arithmetic problems in daily sessions. One of the reasons is that fluctuations in the learning curve (which are unavoidable) are a source of concern especially to primary grade children. A drop in score is not likely to be seen by them as a chance fluctuation in performance, but as a failure; this belief creates tensions which impair performance, thus defeating the purpose of the curve. Spaced measures are more likely to insure scores which reflect gains; these in turn encourage the children. This is especially true with children who may be having difficulty learning or who are under pressure from teachers or parents for improved performance. A second drawback in such use of learning curves is that it distracts some children from the main learning task. They concentrate on the graph, not on the lesson. Judicious use of learning curves is suggested.

SUMMARY

Many different procedures have been utilized in experimental studies of learning: conditioning, trial-and-error, discrimination, mazes, problem solving, verbal materials, and perceptual motor tasks. Of these, the last two have been most widely used in studies of human learning. In each procedure, characteristic measures are utilized. With verbal materials reproduction, recall, recognition, relearning, and reconstruction measures have been used; with classroom learnings reproduction, recall, and recognition are most frequently utilized.

Different methods of measuring performance on the same learning task produce different scores. In addition, the limitation of psychological measures permitting only a comparison of relative rather than absolute standing, the lack of reliability due to errors in measurement, and limited validity prompt caution and skill in their interpretation.

The scores from a series of trials of either an individual or a group of individuals may be plotted in graphical form to show a curve of learning which, although ordinarily quite irregular for an individual but less so for a group, reveals the rate of improvement in a given task, and permits an analysis of progress. Individual differences in ability, motivation, and physical capacity influence the shape of learning curves.

OVERVIEW

Stevens, S. S., "Mathematics, Measurement, and Psychophysics," *Handbook of Experimental Psychology*. New York: Wiley, 1951, pp. 1-49.

REFERENCES

McGeoch, J. A. and A. L. Irion, *The Psychology of Human Learning*, rev. New York: Longmans, Green, 1952.

Strang, Ruth, *An Introduction to Child Study*. New York: Macmillan Co., 1951.

Thorndike, R. L. and Elizabeth Hagen, *Measurement and Evaluation in Psychology and Education*. New York: Wiley, 1955.

Chapter Four

Theories of Learning

*The word "theory" conveys a sense of intangibility
which is forbidding to some students. To others,
theory is associated with a sense of impracticality
and unrealism which prompts negative initial
reaction. Yet nearly every one, whether teacher,
parent, employer, or college student, has
and believes his own theory of learning, even
though he may not have stated it
in so many words. Explicitly stated or not,
each person's behavior in attacking learning
problems, whether learning himself or teaching
others, is based upon personal judgment as to
how people learn and retain learning
once acquired. The school principal who states,
"We don't teach arithmetic by drill anymore,"
has his own theory of how arithmetic is learned,*

just as does the teacher who whole-heartily believes that only by repeated drill of basic number combinations can children acquire arithmetic "fundamentals." The teaching of typing by letter combinations implies a different assumption about the nature of learning than does teaching it by phrase and sentence groups. Parents who admonish their children with, "Why don't you pay attention?" or "Didn't you hear me?" are making expressed assumptions regarding the importance of attention or set for performance. Requiring a youngster who is learning to play the piano to practice an hour each day implies particular assumptions regarding the relationship of amount of practice to speed of learning.

In practice, the usual parent is likely to espouse a dual theory inasmuch as he is likely to believe that his child should have immediate insight whenever the parent is giving an explanation, while simultaneously supporting the value of drill in habit formation. For all practical purposes it is not important that either parent or teacher have explicitly explained theories of learning or that they adopt a single point of view. But it is important that teachers be aware of and understand the questions and points which are a source of agreement between proponents of different schools of learning theory; it should help them to a more understanding view of the premises upon which their own teaching methods are based. More important, it may help them obtain a critical attitude with respect to the merits of differing teaching procedures. In view of the extent to which theories of learning have affected educational practice and vice-versa, understanding of the main views of learning is important.

ASSOCIATION THEORIES VERSUS FIELD THEORIES

Theories of learning fall into two main groups, those classified as *field* theories and those classified as *association* theories. The former stress changes in the field and the learner's perception of the field as crucial to learning, whereas in the association theories it is the response of the learner, its association with particular stimuli, and changes within the learner himself that receive greatest emphasis. Even though the terms field theories and association theories are gradually giving way to a new nomenclature, and although the distinction between the two is not always sharply drawn, nevertheless it serves to identify the main line of cleavage between two major groups of learning theories. The field theories are those emphasizing cognition and sign learning. The association theories include those placing emphasis upon contiguity and reinforcement as essential conditions of learning.

Association theory. The concept of association has had a long history and an important influence in psychology. Aristotle formulated certain laws of association and distinguished association by similarity, by contrast, and by contiguity. The English psychologists of the eighteenth and early nineteenth centuries regarded association as the key to the secrets of the mental life. They used it to explain memory, perception, and reasoning. According to this doctrine, when mental processes occur together, they become linked so that if at some later time one of them is aroused, it in turn tends to arouse the others. If, for example, a person sees a boy standing on a bridge, the mental processes meaning boy and bridge become associated so that later sight of the boy calls up the idea of the bridge; or if someone in conversation mentions this particular bridge, the person in whom this association is established is inclined to think of the boy. The sequence of ideas was believed to be governed by the associations formed by previous experiences. The "qualities" from which these associations arise, according to Hume (1711-1776), were three: first, resemblance; second, contiguity in time or place; and third, cause and effect.

Experimental psychologists of the late nineteenth century found this doctrine of association of ideas unsatisfactory. They rejected the notion that ideas are discrete mental entities with a mysterious link binding them together and causing them to be recalled together. The qualities of resemblance, contiguity, and cause and effect were observed to belong to the objects of thought rather than to the mental processes themselves. The belief in a link between the ideas themselves was supplanted by the belief that the sequence of mental events, when not determined by external factors, was due to associative tendencies established in the nervous system as a result of previous activity. A new form of associationism appeared in the *stimulus-response psychology*. According to this psychology human activity was based on associations between stimuli and responses.

The *stimulus-response* psychology of learning built around this concept sees in any activity first, a *situation* which influences or affects the individual, second, a *response* which the individual makes to the situation, and third, a *connection* between the situation and the response by means of which the former is enabled to produce the latter. This connection has been called the *S–R bond*. The term signifies a tendency or predisposition to respond in a particular manner to a given stimulus. In terms of observed behavior it refers to a degree of probability that a certain kind of response will be made under certain stimulating conditions. The bond is said to be strong when this probability is great, and weak when the probability is small.

According to the connectionist's point of view, knowledge, behavior, and personality are systems of bonds, each S–R connection being a unit part of the total. Learning is regarded as a process of building new bonds and organizing them into these systems. A child learns the name of an object by connecting the name with the object, or, more precisely, with his perception or thought of the object. Manual skills are acquired by connecting movements with appropriate stimuli. When the responses are in the form of movements, the connections are called *motor bonds*. Complex skills are believed to involve a great many motor bonds. Knowledge is acquired by building bonds between ideas. These are called *ideational bonds*. Memorizing is a process of building a fixed sequence of responses by means of a series of bonds.

This conception of learning involves the point of view that wholes are developed by compounding parts. Learning is a process of putting together units to form total experiences and complex forms of behavior.

Field theory. Differing from the associationist point of view, the field theories place emphasis upon the concept that learning is a process of discovering and understanding relationships, and of organizing and finding significance in the sensory experiences aroused by the external situation. It has frequently been observed in learning experiments that an animal, child, or adult human subject hits rather suddenly upon the correct solution. This sometimes appears in marked contrast to the slow and clumsy process of trial and error. When a conspicuous change in a learner's method of attack upon a problem occurs in a single trial and leads directly to the solution of the problem, the learner is said to have manifested *insight*.

Although the word *insight* was occasionally used by writers before the time of Köhler's experiments with chimpanzees (1913–1917), **it** is to his work and his use of the term that we owe most of the present emphasis on it in the literature on learning. To Köhler it appeared that the trial-and-error feature of animal learning was due to complexity of the problem and that a better type of problem-solving procedure might be found in animals if suitable problem situations were arranged for them. He arranged and conducted many experiments in which the animals showed a rather direct approach to the solution and in which insightful behavior was attributed to the subjects. He regarded behavior as insightful when, in the face of barriers blocking any self-evident course, it leads by a roundabout path to an immediate solution. If, for example, a dog placed before a fence between a building and a short wall, sees food through the fence and runs directly back around the wall to the food instead of merely running back and forth along the fence or lunging against it, his behavior would be regarded as indicating insight.

As an example of the type of problem used by Köhler (1929) we shall describe one in which a box was used as an implement in reaching the objective. Six young chimpanzees were placed in a room, on the ceiling of which a banana was fastened. The banana served as a lure. On the floor some distance from the banana was a wooden box. In their eagerness to secure the banana all six chimpanzees jumped repeatedly toward it but could not grasp it because it was too high. Now there are individual differences in learning aptitudes among anthropoids as well as among human beings, and one of these chimpanzees, whose name was Sultan, seemed more apt than the others in solving problems of this type. Sultan at first tried leaping toward the banana as did the others. Soon, however, he ceased his jumping and paced back and forth across the room. Then he stopped for a moment in front of the box. Quickly he moved it over under the banana, climbed onto the box, and then jumped from this point of vantage to secure the fruit. Sultan seemed to grasp the situation in such a way as to bring the box into relation with the banana. From the moment of his hesitation before the box his behavior showed unified and continuous action adapted to securing the banana.

In the case of experiments with animals and children, the term *insight* should be understood as referring to the character of the behavior employed in reaching the goal or solving the problem. It is commonly contrasted with trial-and-error behavior. Insightful behavior is marked by an attentive survey of the problem situation.

Sometimes the animal halts his precipitous and miscellaneous assault and, after deliberately sizing up the situation, proceeds directly to the goal or to the solution by a well-ordered series of appropriate responses. During the course of insightful behavior, the attention is persistently or recurrently fixed on the objective. Once the problem is successfully solved by the aid of insight, the adaptive behavior is readily repeated. In the case of crude trial-and-error learning, the situation is not mastered when the successful reaction is first accomplished. The succeeding trials are still full of trial and error. The successful reactions are differentiated only gradually and mastery comes only when, and in so far as, the learner discovers the relation of the successful responses to the solution of the problem. Insight implies that the animal grasps this relationship at once, or at least in a comparatively few trials.

The writer observed a five-year-old child trying to get his coin bank from a plate rail high up on the dining room wall. He climbed into a chair and reached for it, but it was about six inches beyond the tips of his fingers. He paused a moment, ran into the living room, picked up a small hassock. He brought this back, placed it on the chair, mounted the chair, and then climbed onto the hassock. From there he seized the bank and descended with it in his hand. This case resembles in many respects the box problem used with apes, mentioned above. There is one important difference. The child showed insight more quickly than the best of the apes. He was able to bring the hassock into relation with his objective even when it was not within the range of his vision. He remembered or thought of the hassock, and the idea of it was incorporated into the total situation. In the case of human learners, at least, insight may be achieved through memory or imagination. In very young children and animals the ideational element is presumably meager or entirely lacking, and the relations which provide insight are apparently those found in the organization of the perceptual field.

Perceptual organization. Since the organization or patterning of the sensory field is so potent a factor in determining clear perception, it follows that for effective learning through observation, a well-organized perceptual field is important. Learning will be difficult or easy according to the observer's ability to establish a suitable and coherent configuration of the sensory materials at hand. Few persons would be able, for example, to reproduce Figure 4.1 after one quick

glance at it. Yet almost anyone could make a good reproduction of
Figure 4.2 after the briefest sight of it. There are twelve lines in each
design and all of the lines are of equal length. But from one we get
a poorly organized figure; from the other, a very good configuration.
The design of Figure 4.2 has a number of the features favoring good
organization. The parts are similar and contiguous, but they are
also balanced, and arranged in a compact, coherent form. Moreover,
the pattern is familiar, and it makes sense. The parts of the other
design are also similar and they are contiguous. But they are not

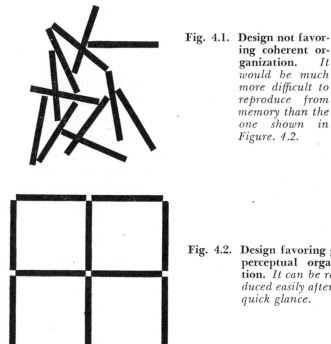

Fig. 4.1. Design not favoring coherent organization. *It would be much more difficult to reproduce from memory than the one shown in Figure. 4.2.*

Fig. 4.2. Design favoring good perceptual organization. *It can be reproduced easily after one quick glance.*

arranged in any definite order or according to any discernible scheme.
This design is nonsensical, unfamiliar, and incoherent, and it is
much more difficult to learn to the point of reproduction than Figure
4.2. A good arrangement of the learning materials favors learning.

Differences between the theories. The differences evident in the
preceding illustrations contrast the two main sets of theories — association and field. The issues around which the differences in field
and association theories may be grouped have been identified by

Hilgard in his "Theories of Learning" (1956) in which he describes in greater detail than is possible here, the basic positions and workings of the individual theories.[1] He identifies the issues as: (1) acquisition of habits versus acquisition of cognitive structures, (2) "peripheral" versus "central" intermediaries, and (3) trial-and-error versus insight in problem solving.

In Hilgard's view, the associationists emphasize the role of prior learning and experience, and they conceive of the whole as being no more or less than the sum of the parts; this means that a complex habit is merely the combination of simple habits which add together to equal the whole. The associationist stresses the significance of the responses or reactions that an organism makes and the association of the responses with the external stimuli, and minimizes the notion that mediating ideas or perceptions may intervene between the stimuli and the responses. The associationist, endorsing an historical viewpoint, sees responses and response patterns being built up gradually through the accumulation of many trials. In problem situations, he sees the learner vary his responses by trial-and-error until he achieves a solution.

In principle, the field theorist's views on these issues would be diametrically opposed to that of the associationist. He believes the whole to be greater than the sum of the parts, just as the melody of a song is more than the musical notes of which it is made. He sees the whole as preceding the parts, and the latter being derived by degrees from the whole. The field theorist places stress upon cognition and insight, and on the development of perceptions and the understanding of relationships between stimuli in the environment. This leads the field theorist to stress contemporary causation and to place emphasis upon the present components of the field.

It will soon be evident that even within these major divisions of learning theory — association and field — there is considerable disagreement and difference with respect to how learning occurs. In part, this is because psychology is still in the process of searching for and describing the variables which determine and account for learning. The behavioral sciences have not progressed as far as the physical sciences in formulating the inter-relationships between the known variables into an integrated theory. As a result there are several

1 E. R. Hilgard, *Theories of Learning*, rev. (New York: Appleton-Century-Crofts, 1956), p. 9.

theories, no one of which can or attempts to account for all of the known facts; rather, each is restricted to a portion of them. As a result, several of the theories are not attempting to account for the same observed behavior, but instead are dealing with entirely different aspects of learning — motor, perceptual, verbal, etc.

Limitations in theory-making. It is possible to compare the situation of theory-making in psychology to the situation which existed during the early exploration of the Western Hemisphere. Anyone who has looked at a series of maps which reflect educated man's idea of the shape and extent of the Western Hemisphere would find that the early maps contained sharp misconceptions regarding the outlines and extent of the New World, and certain disproportions in size between different areas. As explorations progressed, these early misconceptions were gradually eliminated until the cartographers were in essential agreement regarding most particulars. The work of the early explorers tended to be associated with a given area; for instance, most of Columbus' voyages centered around the Caribbean, while the Cabots' explorations were associated with the North Atlantic. It was no accident that being the first voyager to a given area led one on subsequent voyages to extend previously obtained knowledge and information in the same area, e.g., as Columbus did in his remaining voyages. It is also worth noting that, although the explorations were rapidly pushed forward and the early misconceptions were eliminated with general agreement being achieved, nevertheless today, nearly five centuries later, detailed exploration and mapping still continues.

It will probably be some time before a complete theory of learning is developed, for the situation with respect to theories of learning is much the same as the exploration of the New World five centuries ago. Early experimental explorations have been pushed by a number of experimenters who, upon obtaining some fruitful results, have extended their work in a given area while simultaneously attempting to explain their previous results. Thus we have rough maps of certain areas of human learning, with many areas which scarcely have been explored. It has only been in the last twenty years that the explorations have been pushed into common territory.

In order to understand this more fully it might be well to take a brief look at a few of the theories that represent the two groups — association and field theories — in order to obtain some understanding of the current situation. From the association theory we shall include Thorndike's connectionism, Guthrie's contiguous conditioning, and Hull's theory of behavior. Tolman's sign-significate theory of learning and Lewin's topological theory are chosen as representative of the field theories. After briefly attempting to describe the essential position of each theorist with illustrative experiments, the areas of agreement between the theories and the main issues dividing them will be identified along with their implications for education.

THORNDIKE'S TRIAL-AND-ERROR LEARNING

Thorndike's view of learning was that of a trial-and-error process, during which the animal or human gradually selected the correct response and "connected" it with the appropriate stimulus. He based his views upon the observation that when animals, children, or adults are confronted with a new situation in which they do not know how to do what they want to do, they make use of activity patterns they have already mastered. In such a case they may try out various ways of reacting until they hit upon one that brings success. Learning by this method is called *trial-and-error* learning. It makes up a large part of animal and human learning. It is the method employed whenever one is unable to execute the appropriate responses or does not know what they are. It is frequently relied upon in the process of thinking out the solutions of problems.

Characteristics of trial-and-error learning. There are four characteristic features of trial-and-error learning. First, there is some sort of motive that arouses and sustains the activity. This motive may appear in the form of a need, a problem, a goal, a purpose, or some form of discomfort. Essentially, the equilibrium of the organism is disturbed, tensions are developed, and a need or desire for adjustment is felt. This impels the organism to react to the situation in an effort to come to terms with it. In the second place, several different kinds of responses are made to the situation. Here we have our principle of varied activity in operation. Third, we see the progressive elimination of the superfluous, unsuccessful, or wrong forms of activity. Finally, there is a progressive integration and establishment of the reactions by which the goal is achieved.

The student will recognize from Fig. 1.1 several elements in the preceding sequence which characterize learning in general. The essential difference of trial-and-error learning is the second step, the process by which the correct response is identified through trying various responses until a solution which permits the attainment of the goal is achieved.

Thorndike studied the character of trial-and-error learning in a number of experiments on cats. A favorite device was the puzzle-box used years ago by him in his studies of animal learning. The following account is of a similar experiment. It is presented because it demonstrates the essential features of learning at this level.

The subject of the experiment was a cat about eight months old. The apparatus used was a specially constructed puzzle-box two feet long and sixteen inches in width and depth. The sides and top were made of wooden slats $1\frac{1}{4}$ inches wide and set $1\frac{1}{4}$ inches apart. On the floor near the rear of the cage was a six-inch slat hinged at one end and slightly elevated at the other. This served by means of levers as a trip for opening the door. A light pressure on the floor slat released the fastener that held the door closed and then the door was thrown open by a spring.

For each trial, the cat was placed in the box and the door was shut. A dish of salmon was placed on the floor outside the box near the door but beyond the cat's reach from within. The cat was given 100 trials, ten each morning and each afternoon for five days. He was fed at the end of each experimental period and then was given nothing more to eat until after the next session. If, after opening the door in any trial, he went immediately to the food, he was allowed a small taste. A complete record was made of the cat's behavior during each trial.

The outstanding points revealed by the results were:

1. In the early stages there was *a great variety of activity,* and depressing the slat which opened the door was just part of the great mass of activity that was taking place. This activity included: looking around, turning, walking about, sticking paws through the opening at the side of the door, poking at the door with nose and paws, scratching the door on the inside, pushing paws out and scratching the door on the outside, sitting down, biting the levers in the cage, reaching for the food with paws, mewing, clawing at a peg by the door, swinging rear of body from side to side, stepping on the slat which opened the door or sitting down on it, backing into it, smelling the floor,

pushing nose between the slats at the top, and reaching with paws for the lever on the top of the box.

2. *The situation was problematic.* The cat wanted to get out. He was hungry, and the only way to get to the food was to escape from the box. He did not know how to get out. All he could do was to keep trying with all the means available. He had to experiment, and he experimented by doing just about everything a cat could do in such a situation.

3. It was indicated that *the "successes" in the early trials were accidental* in the sense that the cat saw no relation between pressing down on the floor slat and the opening of the door. In the first series he happened to sit down or step on the slat. This had no more significance for him at the time than biting or clawing the door. In some cases he did not even notice that the door had opened for several seconds after he had released the fastener. He opened the door a few times by just falling over the slat.

4. There was *a gradual elimination of useless activity* as the cat was called on to repeat his performance in successive trials. It is significant, moreover, that elimination took place in the case of action that had been repeated dozens of times — an example of the fact that repetition alone does not serve to "stamp in" a mode of response.

5. After the cat had opened the door several times in the early part of the experiment by awkwardly backing onto the slat, sitting on it, or stumbling over it when backing from the door, he apparently *related his backing up with escape.* For trial 23, the record states: "Looked through left-hand corner of box. Looked at the top. Backed around the box and sat on the slat. As soon as he backed into the slat he turned to look at the door." He followed the backing procedure for many trials. At this stage in his "knowledge" he doubtless would have argued stoutly with his feline companions that he knew walking backwards caused the door to open. That he had not yet grasped the relation between pushing down the slat and the opening of the door is shown by the several instances in which he stepped completely over the slat while backing. When he did this, he continued walking backwards all the way around the cage. Sometimes he missed the slat on his second and third backward tours of the cage. In trial 24, for example, he backed over and missed the slat three times, and each time he turned to look at the door. But he kept on backing around the cage and finally opened the door by sliding backwards over the

slat. (One is reminded in this connection that certain theories are defended on the ground that they work out in practice. Some beliefs that have "worked" have been found later to be as unsound as this cat's notion that his walking backwards was what made the door of his cage open.)

6. *The awkward backing method of attack was eventually abandoned,* in spite of its success and repetition, in favor of the more efficient procedure of opening the door by directly pressing on the slat with one of his front paws.

7. As the trials went on, there was *a gradual discovery of the relation between pushing down on the slat and the opening of the door.* This discovery, indicated by the cat's looking toward the door as he pressed the slat down, gave new significance to the slat and the reaction to it. In the 58th trial the subject pawed the slat, pushed it up, and then turned to look at the door. He poked at the slat again, and once more turned to look at the door. It had not opened. He then pressed down on the slat with his front paw, saw the door open, and came out. Behavior of this sort continued through several trials at this stage of the experiment. There was, however, a gradual reduction of the useless activity preceding the successful thrust. In the 65th trial the cat clawed the slat first and looked at the door. Then he turned and pushed down on it vigorously. Toward the end he walked straight to the slat and pushed it down with his paw without any useless activity.

8. There was a gradual *differentiation* and *consolidation,* and to some degree *fixation,* of the movements appropriate for the quickest and most direct solution of the situation. The behavior became effectively organized with respect to the goal.

9. Throughout the 100 trials of this experiment the *cat's behavior was not a response to an isolated stimulus,* but to a whole constellation of factors making up the entire problem situation. The food was a stimulus-object, but the cat acted as he did because the food was outside the box, beyond his reach, and he was inside and hungry.

Thorndike's laws of learning. From such experiments, Thorndike proposed a set of principles to account for the changes he observed in the process of learning. The major principles were his laws of *readiness, exercise,* and *effect.* By readiness he meant that when an animal or a human is prepared to respond or act, giving the response is satisfying and being prevented from doing so is annoying. Secondly, Thorndike believed that repeated exercising of a response strengthened its connection with the stimulus and that disuse of a response weakened it. He subsequently revised this assumption to make the strengthening or weakening of a connection during exercise dependent upon the satisfying or annoying effect derived from making the response. The most important of Thorndike's principles was his *law of effect,* which stated in essence that when a connection is accompanied by a satisfying state of affairs, its strength is increased; by this, Thorndike meant that the probability of its recurrence is greater. Inversely, when the connection is accompanied by an annoying state of affairs, its strength is reduced or weakened. Thorndike's primary law rests upon his conviction that an organism tends to repeat that which has previously been satisfying and avoid that which has been dissatisfying. Thus favorable outcomes strengthen connections between responses and stimuli.

In addition he had several subsidiary principles which are evidenced in the preceding descriptions of behavior in the experimental situations. The first maxim is that an individual *varies his responses* in a novel situation, using different responses until he hits upon a correct solution. Second, an individual's previous experiences, beliefs, and attitudes cause certain *sets or predispositions* which determine what goals the individual will seek and what will satisfy or annoy him. For instance, many Chinese candies are not palatable to occidental taste, accustomed to cream-filled chocolates. Third, Thorndike believed that individuals have the capacity to select the important from the irrelevant elements of a situation in order to *determine the appropriate response* to make. Fourth, he held that one's responses to a new situation are determined by the extent to which that situation is similar to or identical with a previously experienced situation, the result being that one responds as in the previous similar situations. Finally, Thorndike believed that any responses of which an organism is capable can be connected with any situation to which he is sensitive, terming this characteristic *"associative shifting."* Thorndike subsequently added the concept of *belongingness,* which in effect said that a response is more easily learned if it fits the situation or belongs to it. Thus the Spanish word "Sabado" for Saturday would be more readily learned by English-speaking persons than "Viernes" for Friday because there appears to be a relationship between the former pair.

Thorndike's theory of connectionism has proved important to learning for three reasons. First, in his law of effect he called attention to the importance of motivation in learning, heretofore largely neglected. Secondly, the specificity of his theory contributed to the ready identification of the acts or responses to be learned and their gradation from simple to complex for most efficient learning. Thirdly, he placed much emphasis upon experimental verification.

Significance for education. There are few learning theories that have had as marked an effect upon educational practice as Thorndike's, and much of this was due to his prodigious volume of writing. He devoted his attention not only to theoretical aspects of learning, but more to the applied aspects and classroom situations. The specificity of his theory contributed much to its applicability in classroom situations. Thorndike recognized in the learner an individual ready to make certain responses, capable of varying his responses, and trying to respond to the aspects of a stimulus situation which appeared familiar with a response previously successful in a similar situation. He believed that in order to develop these potentials efficiently, it was essential for the teacher to identify the specific elements of the learning task: to determine the particular responses desired to the given stimulus, to gradate the parts of the task from simple to complex, and to present the elements in a way providing the most favorable opportunity for eliciting the correct response, which could then be rewarded. Repetition and rewarding of the correct response would stamp in the desired response and gradually eliminate the inappropriate responses. While Thorndike did not deny that insightful learning occurred, he believed it to be a less frequent form of learning.

It is interesting to pause for a moment and consider the educational program that follows from a literal application of Thorndike's theory of learning. One essential aspect of the program would be knowing the responses the individual is capable of making. The other would be identifying the tasks to be done — tasks within the capability of the individual — and subdividing these tasks into their elemental component parts in order that they may be arranged in a sequence which progresses from simple to complex. The latter point may be illustrated in relation to language development. Thorndike, in order to determine which words should be taught earliest, made a frequency count in order to determine the words most often used in the English language. These high-frequency words he considered the more important — the words which should be taught first. Thorndike established these two component parts for the learning situation: a task to be presented with the least confusion, making certain that the significant stimulus would clearly precede it to increase the probability of the appropriate response; and upon occurrence, the correct response would be rewarded, the reward being either the intrinsic satisfaction derived from making the correct response or an extrinsic incentive such as praise. In either event, the learner would know that he had made a correct response. The situation would be repeated under motivating circumstances in order that the response would be firmly connected with the given stimulus.

The traditional method of teaching arithmetic closely follows such a scheme. The prime numbers are the first to be taught. Then the combining of these basic numbers through simple addition and subtraction follows. The more difficult addition and subtraction are followed by multiplication and division. In each process, the learning task begins with the simple so-called "basic addition facts" and proceeds to the complex. In each response the child makes, the problem is followed by confirmation as to the correctness of the answer. There is little effort in developing meaning or understanding, for instance, of the "place" concept; rather, the emphasis is on specific steps, with the assumption being made that mastery of the simple component parts ultimately provides the essential understanding of the whole.

It would be a mistake to confuse these events with rote learning; it would be more accurate to see them as segmented learning. School should be made as interesting as possible, the learning child's enthusiasm and interest should be cultivated, and the tasks should be presented in as stimulating a fashion as possible. Nevertheless, the task should proceed from the part to the whole, rather than vice versa. Regardless of the limitations of Thorndike's theory with respect to explaining learning, it nevertheless has advantages in actual operation within the classroom, for its very specificity permits a direct attack upon learning problems. The teacher may identify errors and directly proceed to their elimination. Here, diagnosis of errors leads directly to suggestions for correction. Thorndike's theory is utilitarian in the sense that one teaches what is most useful as determined from actual practice. On the other hand, it has a serious limitation in its lack of concern regarding understanding. Thorndike did not consider understanding unimportant, but merely assumed that it would follow as a natural result of well organized learning. He believed that insightful learning, though it did occur, was infrequent.

GUTHRIE'S S-R CONTIGUITY THEORY

"A combination of stimuli which has accompanied a movement will, on its recurrence, tend to be followed by that movement." Upon this statement rests Guthrie's contiguity theory of learning, an association theory based upon the connection of stimuli and responses, but differing radically from Thorndike's connectionism in that the law of effect is rejected. Guthrie's statement could be paraphrased to read, "We repeat what we learn and we learn what we do." Moreover, according to Guthrie, the full associative strength — the pairing of the stimulus and the response — is established on a single trial.

The stimulus-response bond. In Chapter 3 a brief description was given of Pavlov's conditioned response experiment: the response, the dog's salivation, becomes associated with the conditioned stimulus, a bell or buzzer, when the conditioned stimulus is presented simultaneously with the original stimulus, the food, which elicited the response. Using puzzle-box experiments similar to Thorndike's, Guthrie takes the model of the substitution of one stimulus for another as the basis for his theory of learning, when he contends that the responses given in any situation will be reproduced or repeated on any occasion on which the same situation is presented. Thus, if a youngster copying the multiplication table of 9's from the blackboard mistakingly inverts 6 $\times$ 9 = 45, he will tend to respond 45 on the next occasion on which he is presented with the stimulus 6 $\times$ 9. Guthrie's argument is based first upon the principle of substitution and secondly upon the contiguity in time, that is the simultaneous occurrence of stimulus and response. According to this view, any stimulus-response situation — any learning situation — is composed of a variety of stimuli and responses. Some of the stimuli are external to the organism, others are internal. For example, in the preceding instance of the boy learning the multiplication table, the various attracting and distracting visual stimuli in the room, sounds occurring at the instant — the teacher's voice or his own repeating the problem, the movements of his fingers and hands as he writes the problems and answers on the paper, and all the other various stimuli that are impinging upon his sense organs are being associated with all the movements and responses which he is making. All responses the boy makes have the effect of altering or modifying the situation; some furnish cues for further action — getting pencil and paper ready, others sustaining action — looking up at the blackboard at the illustration, while others terminate the stimulus situation — getting the answer to the problem written on the paper. In any situation, particularly a complex one, many responses are being associated with many stimuli. Some may be the correct associations, others may be erroneous or faulty associations. Guthrie contends that learning is complete on each trial, and that all the responses are associated with some stimuli and will be repeated on repetition of the stimuli. In other words, the strength of the association will not gain through repetition, for it attains full strength on the first occurrence. Improvement is brought about not by strengthening the association or the connection of any single stimulus and response, but rather by building up the number of correct associations in the total stimulus-response situation. To give another illustration which will illustrate the application of this idea to a complex learning situation, picture a boy learning to shoot a basketball. According to Guthrie, the act of shooting the ball through the hoop incorporates within it a large number of movements which become associated with all the stimuli present at the moment: the balance of the body, the position of the feet, the feel of the ball, the position of the hands, the visual stimuli being received from all sources such as the reflections of the backboard, the distance and angle from the hoop, and the different sounds occurring. All become associated. On the next trial, the same stimuli will elicit identical responses, but unfortunately some of the associations made on the previous trials interfere with a perfect performance: the boy may have sighted for the front of the hoop, he may have been standing on the wrong foot as he released the shot, etc. Some of the responses will have been correctly associated with the stimuli, for instance, the feel of the ball in the hands, the amount of force, and the trajectory of the ball in making the shot. Improvement comes on subsequent trials not because the correct responses were strengthened but because new learning occurs to replace the erroneous fraction of the response — improper stance and improper sighting — with the result that total performance shows improvement.

In any situation, then, there are many cues and many responses. That which occurs on each trial, the particular combination of cues and responses, is that which is learned. Perfect performance comes from ultimately associating all the correct responses with the appropriate cues. It follows from this also that forgetting occurs, not from disuse or lack of practice, but because of the interference resulting from subsequent learning. In other words, what we learn today tends to interfere with that which we have previously learned.

The appeal of Guthrie's theory lies in its simplicity. Motivation, repetition, and reward are discounted as relatively unimportant to learning; drive and motivation merely arouse the individual and cause him to act and to vary responses. Other than having this initiating effect, motivation is not instrumental in learning. In direct contradiction of Thorndike and the law of effect, which holds that rewarded responses tend to be repeated, Guthrie contends that reward as such does not enter into the learning (association) process. Rather he holds that reward brings about a finale by disrupting the sequence, and as a result, on a repetition of the situation, the response preceding the reward is likely to occur because it was the last response made.

Significance for education. The teacher in Guthrie's classroom would behave in a different manner than the one in Thorndike's classroom. To begin with Guthrie's program would involve activity in an experience curriculum with the child learning that which he is to do in the way in which he is expected to do it. He would not be concerned with motivation, as such, other than that he would want children to be active and engaged in work. In no sense would he be interested in the use of reward or punishment for the purpose of establishing the correct responses. In any learning situation, it would be important that extraneous stimuli be reduced to a minimum, and that the widest association of correct responses with appropriate stimuli be established. This would necessitate rote learning and frequent drill: learning necessitates doing.

Guthrie would have several suggestions to make regarding the appropriate manner for handling faulty or negative learning, e.g., when a boy having difficulty in learning to read develops a dislike for reading and attempts to avoid the task, Guthrie would suggest that the reading be presented (1) in a form that was too faint to arouse the negative response, (2) when the negative response was fatigued, or (3) in combination with other stimuli which produce desired responses. To be specific, one would (1) present reading that was so simple the boy could easily read it, (2) force the boy to persist in the task in spite of all his protests, or (3) present reading material of such inherent interest that he would want to read it in spite of the difficulty.

One of the difficulties in appraising the validity of Guthrie's view lies in limitations in the available experimental data designed to demonstrate the applicability of the theory. Granting the practical wisdom of much of what Guthrie has to say about learning and recognizing the premise upon which he bases it, one must concede, nevertheless that the application of his theory to various learning situations is a logical rather than an experimental extension.

HULL'S REINFORCEMENT THEORY

In the introductory chapter, learning was described as the process by which an activity was originated or changed as a result of practice. In this chapter, we have been considering different theories which attempt to account for what occurs in the process of learning. The two theories we have considered thus far, those of Thorndike and Guthrie, together with that which we will now consider, Hull's reinforcement theory, are classified as association theories. Yet Thorndike and Guthrie could scarcely lay claim to having accounted for the learning process; rather, they defined what they considered to be the essential conditions upon which learning is dependent. Guthrie, espousing a substitution theory of learning, stressed the importance of contiguity in time of the stimulus and the response as an essential condition to learning. Thorndike placed primary importance upon motivation and reward as the important essentials for learning. But naming a condition is not explaining its operation. In contrast, Hull has systematically and explicitly attempted to define the nature of the process we call learning. His theory is a conceptual descendent of Thorndike's inasmuch as he adopts reinforcement as an essential characteristic of learning. On the basis of the experimental variables that have been shown to play a role in conditioning experiments, Hull formulated a series of postulates or laws by which he defined the intervening variables essential to learning. As suggestive of the explicitness and precision with which Hull attempted to define the intervening variables upon which learning is dependent, his fourth postulate is presented in detail: [2] "Whenever an effector activity and a receptor activity occur in close temporal contiguity, and this is closely and consistently associated with the diminution of a need or with a stimulus which has been closely and consistently associated with the diminution of a need, there will result an increment or a tendency for that afferent impulse on later occasions to evoke that reaction. The increments from successive reinforcements summate in a manner which yields a combined habit strength which is a simple positive growth function of the number of reinforcements."

Details of Hull's postulates. Paraphrasing these postulates, it may be said that the strengthening or the establishment of connection between responses of an organism and particular stimulating conditions is dependent upon two events: first, the close proximity in time of the stimulus and the response, and secondly, reinforcement, a rewarding state of affairs which produces drive- or need-reduction. Reinforcement may be primary, relieving basic tissue needs of the organism (hunger, thirst, sex, etc.), or secondary, derived from once neutral stimuli which have acquired reinforcement strength by having been repeatedly associated with primary reinforcement. In addition to this basic premise, Hull's fourth postulate defines the upper limit of habit strength in terms of the relationship between three variables: the magnitude of the need reduction, the time interval between responses and reinforcement, and the time interval between the conditioned stimulus and the response.

Hull saw the learning situation as one in which a motivated organism, seeking to satisfy its needs, responds or reacts to particular stimuli or cues in the environment. Those responses and stimuli which are closely associated at the time of reinforcement are strengthened as the organism learns to make that response in the presence of the particular stimuli. Moreover, the responses and stimuli leading up to the situation in which reinforcement occurred are similarly strengthened, although to a progressively lesser degree, depending upon the length of time they occurred prior to reinforcement.

2 C. L. Hull, *Principles of Behavior* (New York: Appleton-Century, 1943), p. 178.

Hull saw needs as the states or conditions within the organism which result when external conditions deviate from the optimal conditions necessary for survival. Deprivation of water or deprivation of food in the external environment gives rise to physiological changes which produce a state of hunger or thirst and the need for food or water. These needs give rise to certain drive states which arouse the organism. At birth, each organism has the capacity of making certain responses which are capable of satisfying needs and drives. These responses become associated with certain stimuli as the result of their occuring in proximity to need reduction. Moreover, other stimuli which are present at the time of need reduction tend to acquire the capacity to reinforce, i.e., to provide need reduction; for example, the appearance of the mother or the sound of her approaching footsteps frequently has the effect of soothing a crying infant, although initially it was either the feeding or the direct soothing of the baby by holding it which had the desired effect. However, in time the stimuli preceding the event acquired the capacity of reinforcement.

Other variables. In addition to his construct of habit strength as a result of reinforcement, Hull has introduced a number of other intervening variables which, in terms of experimental conditions, have been shown to affect the strength of conditioned responses. One is that habit strength and drive strength interact in a multiplicative manner to produce a reaction potential which governs the strength of response. The strength of response at any given moment is a function of the reaction potential, derived from habit strength and drive strength in relationship to certain inhibitory factors. The first of these inhibitory factors is reactive inhibition, a term for describing the fact that once we perform an act, we are somewhat reluctant to repeat it immediately; secondly, the greater the amount of work involved in the act or the more frequent the number of performances of the act within a given period of time, the greater the reluctance, or as Hull describes it, the greater the reactive inhibition. This inhibition subsides with the passage of time, the so-called spontaneous recovery of conditioned response experiments. Furthermore, Hull adds that organisms vary from moment to moment, showing an oscillation in their capacity to respond, which Hull believes distributes itself according to the normal probability functions. At any given moment, an organism's effective reaction potential for responding is controlled by the sum of reaction potential and inhibitory influences.

It is readily seen that Hull, who devoted the last thirty years of his life to developing a vigorous and systematic model of a learning system, differed from the preceding theorists in that he first established certain fundamental, specifically defined postulates or laws from which theorems subject to verification by experimental tests could be derived; these ultimately yield verification or refutation of the postulates, or correction to account for experimental evidence. This hypothetico-deductive system differs from those of Thorndike and Guthrie in that their's are primarily descriptive.

Limitations. Although Hull's theory is the most rigorous that has yet been devised and is the model for association theory, and although his use of intervening variables holds the promise of a shift in psychological theory-making from those that are purely descriptive to those that are explanatory, nevertheless certain marked limitations exist which are of critical importance to the survival of his theory. One is the restrictive experimental base upon which the theory is built. His experimental verification with human subjects is limited. More important, having placed reinforcement as the central consideration in his system, and having held that strength of habit is a direct function of the number of reinforcements, Hull's theory is challenged by experimental findings which do not support these assumptions. Two kinds of experiments have been carried out which do just this: the experiments on latent learning (Figure 3.6) suggest that under some circumstances reinforcement is not an essential condition of learning, and secondly, the experiments on partial reinforcement (50% instead of 100% of the trials are reinforced) produce conditioned responses which are more resistant to extinction than those resulting from 100% reinforcement. These two sets of experiments, raising certain questions regarding the place of reinforcement and the force of reinforcement in learning, will be discussed later in this chapter.

Significance for education. Systematic order and arrangement would characterize the classroom patterned after Hull's theory. The development of habits and skills would proceed from the simple to the complex with a clear understanding of the stimuli and responses to be associated. The program would have to be dynamic and stimulating in view of the central position that reinforcement holds, inasmuch as aroused drives which can be reduced by satis-fying outcomes are an essential condition of learning. In the early stages of learning, few artificial incentives would be used with young children, but gradually they would be developed for the values to be derived from secondary reinforcement. Practice would be pre-sented for the purpose of building the desired habits and maintain-ing them, but would not proceed to the point at which the increase in inhibition from repeating the same response would make the child reluctant to respond.

In spite of the differences that exist between the theories of Thorndike, Guthrie, and Hull, the similarities far outweigh the differences. The structure of learning which they visualize is like a brick wall, put together brick by brick until the total structure is complete, with the upper courses of bricks resting and dependent upon the foundation courses. For them, learning proceeds in much the same manner, with the responses of the organism becoming associated with the stimuli in the environment, bond by bond, until the entire complex structure in human learning is erected. The process proceeds automatically and mechanically with little, if any, need for thought, insight, or cognition on the part of the learner. Both Thorndike and Hull gave motivation a central place in their theories, implying not that the learner has conscious purposes, but rather that he has needs and seeks their satisfaction, thus creating situations which make reinforcement possible. The desired satis-faction of the learner's motives leads him to repeat responses which previously have been need-satisfying in the presence of particular stimuli. All three stress the importance of contiguity of stimulus and response, and their proximity in time. In fact, Guthrie gives contiguity the central position in his theory, denying the primary importance of motivation.

The difference between the association theorist and field theorist is readily apparent, for the latter adopts a diametrically opposed view on many of the basic issues. He believes that the characteristic form of learning is one involving sudden solutions of problems — insight, as it is called. He disagrees with the concept that learning consists of the gradual association of connections — of stimulus and response — but rather believes it depends upon insight into the relationships existing in any given situation. The whole is more than simply the sum of its parts: it is a unique organization in itself.

The field theorist places considerable stress upon perceptual organization of the stimuli in the environment and upon factors which
affect perception.

GESTALT THEORY

During the first quarter of this century, when trial-and-error learning and behaviorism were predominant schools in American psychology, three German psychologists, Max Wertheimer, Kurt Koffka,
and Wolfgang Köhler were conducting a series of studies and experiments which gave rise to Gestalt psychology, so called because
of the emphasis placed upon configuration, structure, and patterning
in experience. They took specific issue with the concept that all
learning consisted of the simple connection of responses to stimuli,
without recourse to the existence of ideas or thought processes. The
Gestaltists insisted that experience is always structured, that we react
not to a mere mask of separate details, but to a complex organization or pattern of stimuli, some of which may be primary and some
subsidiary. Moreover, we attempt to perceive stimuli in organized
wholes, not in disconnected parts. For instance, in Figure 4.1, the
drawing is perceived as a scramble of lines, not line by line, while
Figure 4.2 is seen perhaps as a window with four panes in it, or four
white squares side by side, or a rectangle with a cross in the middle.

In support of their contention that perception does not occur
piecemeal, and that the processes involved in perception apply to
learning, the Gestalt psychologists pointed out some of the characteristics of sensory fields which influence organization in perception.

Figure and ground. The sensory field in perception is organized
first with respect to figure and ground. The thing perceived stands
out against a background, as when a ship at sea is seen against a
background of an indefinite expanse of water and sky, when a farm-
house stands out against the fields and hills of the landscape, or when
a star shines against the darkened dome of the heavens.

In Figure 4.3 the black area is figure, and the white area is ground
when one sees a black face looking toward the right. When one
sees a white face looking to the left, the white area is figure and the
black portion is ground. It is to be noted that the change in figure-
ground relations appears without a change in the designs themselves,
but with this change comes a different meaning. Something differ-

ent is seen. Thus, the figure-ground aspect of perception is an arrangement of the sensory field, or the way in which the individual organizes the situation for himeslf. It is a fundamental determiner of what one sees and of what one learns by way of observation.

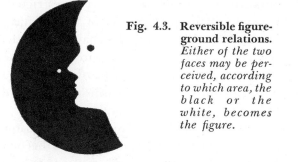

Fig. 4.3. Reversible figure-ground relations. *Either of the two faces may be perceived, according to which area, the black or the white, becomes the figure.*

Certain characteristic differences between the figure and ground are to be noted. In the first place, the figure has more or less definite form. It is compact with fairly distinct boundary lines that mark it off from the ground. The figure may be complex, but its parts in clear perception are always closely patterned to form a unified whole. The ground, on the other hand, is formless and indefinite. The figure seems to stand forth, usually in front of the ground or surrounded by it. Elements of the sensory field not incorporated into the figure lack significance and seem not to belong to anything in particular. Note that when the black portion of Figure 4.3 is perceived as the face looking to the right, the black dot in the white area is not related to the other parts at all, and it has no particular meaning. But when the white part is figure and a white profile is seen, the black dot occupies an essential position in the figure and definitely is an eye. The part is what it is by virtue of its relation to and membership in the whole figure. The common experience of failing to see some object before one's eyes, even when attending to it, is probably often due to failure to incorporate it into a definite figure pattern.

In the case of a puzzle picture, a person may look at a mass of lines and shadings and perceive a landscape with trees and rocks. Then he reads the instructions, "Find the hunter." As he scrutinizes the picture, lines and shadows suddenly snap together forming a new configuration for him and a new object-meaning appears. What

at first were branches and leaves of a tree, now have become clearly
and certainly the picture of a man with a gun. No change took place
in the ink pattern on the paper, but a change occurred in the
observer's patterning of his own experience, and with it a new object
of perception appeared.

Figure-ground relations, moreover, are not restricted to visual perception. They appear in perceptions of sound, taste, smell, and
touch, though in these the boundaries may be less sharply defined.
The grouping of the sound elements into tonal patterns in music
is controlled largely by the stimulus-pattern sent forth by the instruments. Rhythmical units may be established by regular variations
of intensity, pitch, or length of interval.

The stimulus-pattern and perceptual organization. While the
patterning of the visual field is established by the observer himself
and is to be seen as a matter quite distinct from the stimulus-
pattern presented to his receptors, it frequently happens that the
character of the stimulus-pattern influences or even dictates the way
the sensory qualities are organized. The way the dots are printed in
Figure 4.4 makes it almost necessary to see a group of four at the
upper left, a group of six at the upper right, and a line of seven below.

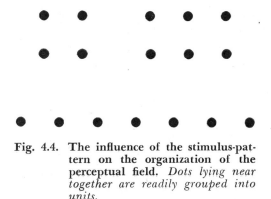

Fig. 4.4. The influence of the stimulus-pattern on the organization of the
perceptual field. *Dots lying near
together are readily grouped into
units.*

Proximity. The parts of a stimulus pattern which are close together or near to each other tend to be perceived in groups. The
proximity of the parts in time or space affects the organization of
the field in perception. To one walking in the woods, trees or bushes
will appear as clusters and groups according to their proximity,
whereas in a nursery field, in which the plants are uniform distance

from each other, the very uniformity makes it difficult to view it other than as a whole.

Similarity and familiarity. Objects similar in form, shape, color, or size tend to be grouped in perception. When we look at the keyboard on a piano, we tend to see the black keys as a group and the white keys as a group rather than octave groups. Familiarity with an object facilitates the establishing of an appropriate figure-ground pattern. When we look at familiar objects or hear familiar sounds, the pattern takes form readily and a clear apprehension occurs at once because perceptual traces have been established by our seeing similar things and hearing like sounds many times in the past. According to the Gestaltists, memory is made possible by the persistence of traces in the brain which allow a carry-over from previous to present experiences. These traces are not considered to be static, but instead are modified by a continual process of integration and organization.

Closure. Individuals strive to reach a satisfactory end-state of equilibrium. Incomplete forms, missing parts, gaps in information, etc., are completed or filled in by the perceiver. Most readers will read the symbols in Figure 4.5 as "Tom," because of their adding missing parts in order to close the stimulus, yet it can as readily be read as "Pam." Perhaps more forcefully, the principle

Fig. 4.5. Incomplete figure.

of closure is illustrated in rumor spreading. The situation is usually one in which some degree of tension and ambiguity exists. The tension is eased and the ambiguity eliminated by the creation of rumor (supposition) amplified by details which will change as the story moves from one person to the next as each attempts to achieve and maintain a perception which provides a satisfying end–state.

As far as perception is concerned, closure is to Gestalt psychology what reward is to association theory. It produces the satisfying, tension-relieving end-state which terminates activity.

Anticipatory set, expectation, and motivation can all play a significant role in the closure that results in a given situation. Mark Twain provides a ready illustration of this in Tom Sawyer, whose Aunt Polly was ever ready to attribute any mischief that occurred to Tom, even though his cousin Sydney was frequently the perpetrator. Magicians rely upon induced audience sets to successfully carry out their tricks.

Good continuation is another aspect of organization in perception, and is closely allied to the principle of closure. Not only does the perceiver tend to see stimuli as complete, but on repeated reproduction he tends to shift distorted perceptions in the direction of greater symmetry and balance. Imperfect figures are seen to improve with the passage of time, to show "improvement" as it were toward more stable and symmetrical forms. Good figures, such as circles, squares, lines, etc. tend to remain stable and continue as good figures.

Gestalt psychology in relation to learning. The preceding discussion contrasts a difference in emphasis between association and field theories of learning. Gestalt psychology is concerned primarily with factors influencing perception and not as specifically with the learning process. Nevertheless the Gestaltists insist that the laws of perception which they have observed apply to learning. Koffka, in particular attempts to demonstrate the relationship of the foregoing principles of organization to learning.

The best illustration of these principles is seen in situations in which insightful learning occurs, situations in which a restructuring of the field relationships permits sudden solutions to problems. The previously described behavior of the chimpanzee, Sultan, in using the box to obtain fruit, shows insightful behavior. After an unsuccessful period of trying and failing in different attempts to obtain the banana, the relationship of the box to obtaining the suspended fruit was understood. This led to immediate success which could be readily repeated as well as transposed, e.g., used in new situations. The question is not whether insight occurs, but rather if it is the model of learning, a model best explained by the application of the Gestalt principles of perceptual organization.

The configuration or structuring that occurs with the operation of the Gestalt principles persists in the memory as traces. These traces are presumed not to decay or fade with the passage of time, but instead to shift towards a more stable organization — toward a better Gestalt — in which certain features of the perceived figures are sharpened and accentuated, and some levelled in a shift to greater symmetry. The hypothesis assumes that the trace is initially a somewhat unstable product of the field forces which slowly changes internally toward a more stable organization. The aggregate of traces persists from previous experiences and can be activated in the present. In any present situation, there exists in perceptual response to external stimuli a process which selects or reactivates a given trace or traces which then enter into the present field of forces.

The essential difference between the trace theory of the Gestaltists and the views of the associationists is not that memory occurs, but rather that the traces are not merely stimulus-response connections which decay in time or are inhibited by new learning. Instead, Gestaltists conceive of traces as being in a condition of dynamic change until an equilibrium is reached; following this change, dynamic entry is accessible to them into the present field, in which both past and present traces are in a state of transformation according to the principles of learning organization.

Significance for education. The teacher's task is to help the child see significant relations and so to manage the instructional situation that the child will be able to organize his experiences into effectual functional patterns. The teacher does not organize the child's experiences, nor does he establish relations for him any more than he learns the child's lesson for him. But in verbal explanations, showing pictures, putting words on the blackboard, presenting reading matter, and in many other teaching activities, he is arranging and providing stimulating situations. Now, since the stimulus-pattern may and often does determine the character of the experiential configuration, it follows that the arrangement of the subject matter and materials of instruction, and the order in which they are presented will affect greatly the child's observations, his comprehension, and, in general, his learning.

For this reason, careful lesson planning with due regard for suitable arrangement and orderly presentation is essential for good teaching. Practices conducive to the establishment of appropriate relations and organization include starting with the familiar, basing each step on those already taken, putting together facts which belong together, grouping items according to their natural connections, placing subtopics under the topic to which they belong, using illustrations based on the learner's experience, giving major emphasis to essentials, centering supporting details around the main points, and avoiding irrelevant details.

Furthermore, effectual classroom learning requires the integration of all the divisions and topics of each subject. Previews, outlines, and reviews reveal relations between the various parts of a subject and promote the organization of a subject as a whole. When a reader begins a new book, an examination of the table of contents will often provide a degree of orientation which facilitates comprehension because it helps him to see each part in relation to the whole.

Just as the material of each subject should be organized into a coherent whole, so also all the various subjects of a course of study should be integrated. As reading should be tied to spelling, arithmetic, and the social studies, so every subject should be related to all the others. Projects or activity units which call for the use of reading, writing, spelling, arithmetic, geography, and oral expression in a single undertaking provide excellent opportunities for binding together the substance of different subjects.

LEWIN'S TOPOLOGICAL THEORY

A derivative from Gestalt Psychology is seen in Lewin's topological psychology, which like Gestalt theory contends that the total pattern or field of events determines learning but differs in the greater emphasis that is placed upon motivation. Lewin saw each person as existing within a field of forces. The field of forces to which the individual is responding or reacting is called his "life space." The life space includes features of the environment to which the individual is reacting — the people he meets, the material objects he encounters and manipulates, and his private thoughts, fantasies, and imaginings. In addition to the external aspects of his environment of which he is aware, each individual is responding to certain internal tensions, some of which are the basic physiological drives for food, water, etc., and others the tension systems of a psychological nature which cause the individual to seek certain goals, objects, and situations in the external environment.

Life space. The concept of life space can be illustrated by a U.S. weather map, which is a diagram representing the dynamic interplay of high and low pressure areas across the continent; shown is the resultant field of weather forces — cold fronts, occluded fronts, sun, wind, and rain being experienced in different areas as the result of the interplay of the high and low pressure areas, which in turn are the outgrowth of still greater forces within the solar system. Like the weather in any one spot, an individual is caught up in vast networks of forces. At the moment of this writing, it is cold in the midwest, unseasonably warm in the southeast, and snowing and sleeting in the middle Atlantic and the New England States. Yet each individual is only reacting to a fraction of this and all of the other physical characteristics which constitute his total physical environment. For instance, yesterday, aside from a few moments of clearing snow from the steps and sidewalk, I was relatively oblivious to the physical presence of snow which began about midday. Today, however, is a different matter, inasmuch as a 20-mile trip to the University is necessary even though the weather is considerably worse. Today the snow and sleet are very much a part of my life space, in contrast with their small significance to me yesterday.

The forces acting in a person are considered as psychological, not physical, forces. Lewin's system sees behavior as resulting from the interplay of forces, both those from tension systems within the individual and those external to the individual. He placed considerable emphasis upon the present, insisting that past events do not exist now and therefore cannot have effects now. Instead, for Lewin, individuals possessed different degrees of organizational complexity and personality differentiation as outgrowths of past experiences, and it was these differences of complexity and differentiation which contributed to behavior differences in the present field.

According to Lewin, learning occurs as a result of a change in cognitive structures, which is to say that one develops a more highly differentiated life space. These changes in cognitive structure result from two types of forces, one from the structure of the cognitive field itself and the other from the internal needs or motivation of the individual. Changes in the cognitive structure may occur suddenly, or they may require repetition if the structure is to be changed; however there is not such a one-to-one relationship between repetitions and performance as we observed in the association theories. The repetition may produce either a change in the cognitive structure — a more highly differentiated knowledge of the relationships between facts in the environment — or a change in needs — the tension system. Attractive goals may lose their attractiveness as a result of repetition. For instance, one who works in a candy store gradually becomes much less enthusiastic about candy. Secondly, unattractive goals may become attractive through repetition, as in the proverbial "learning to like avocados," or through a change in meaning, as is observed frequently in the previously disheveled adolescent when he begins "going steady" for the first time.

Motivation. Perhaps as a result of his emphasis upon the immediate field of forces, Lewin was much more sensitive to the factors affecting motivation and involved in motivation than any of the theorists we have been considering. Motivation involves more than mere reward, irrespective of whether it is need-reducing or situation-terminating. Lewin recognized that it is the individual who is motivated and who possesses the tension systems which give rise to his responses. These motives are related to specific goals which are established by what the individual learner is trying to do or wants to do, and the satisfaction of the motive is determined by changing the goal or achieving it. Such a success is different from reward, for it is defined not by what is given by such an external authority as the teacher, but by what the learner seeks. Closely related to success and failure is the individual's level of aspiration; this is the temporary goal established as a result of an estimate of his own capabilities in the present situation.

Significance for education. Much of what has previously been said regarding the implications of Gestalt psychology for educational practice holds for Lewin as well, particularly with respect to the process of increasing differentiation of life space. Lewin would go further to point out the importance of recognizing the forces in play in any individual's life space and to emphasize that the teacher must effectively understand the relationships between the learner, his environment and his behavior. Particularly important is the distinction between goals and incentives, and between success and reward. Success consists of reaching goals, which in turn depend upon individual motives. The teacher's task consists of aiding the learner to establish attainable goals and then assisting in his attaining them by reducing or helping overcome the barriers that block achievement. Particularly the teacher should be sensitive enough not to interpose unnecessary barriers by over-managing the environment or by arbitrarily establishing or creating unattainable or artificial goals through the use of such incentives as rewards or praise.

TOLMAN'S SIGN-GESTALT-EXPECTATION THEORY

If the Gestalt psychologists' formulations apply mainly to perception, and Kurt Lewin's topological psychology to behavior, Edward Tolman's theory of sign-learning applies primarily to learning. Although Tolman may be grouped with the Gestaltists as a field theorist, he nevertheless proposes that more than one kind of learning may occur, and that these different kinds of learning may be explained temporarily best by a particular theory. This view results from his recognition that psychological theory-making is still in swaddling clothes, and that the ultimate theory or theories, while derived from current points of view, will probably, if not certainly, be more complexly organized. Yet, of the field theories of learning, Tolman's is the most highly developed.

Response-learning. Fundamentally, Tolman rejects the ideas that a person learns "to do something" and that learning is the association of responses to particular stimuli. From the associationist viewpoint, it is the response or sequence of responses resulting in reward which are learned. In contrast, Tolman believes it is the route to the goal which is learned. The animal or human, seeking to satisfy needs, learns to recognize certain cues or signs and the relationship of these signs to particular goals. In other words, he learns *what leads to what*. Compare this with the associationist viewpoint, which sees needs as leading to arousal of activity in the organism, permitting performance to be stamped in by repeated rewards.

Tolman conceives of behavior as being purposive in nature, directed toward goals capable of satisfying needs. He thinks that organisms, at their respective levels of ability, are capable of recognizing and learning the relationships between signs and desired goals; in short, they perceive the significance of the signs. This perception permits behavior that is purposeful and which gets to goals with the least effort. Learning consists of recognizing the signs and understanding their meaning in relationship to goals — in short, the forming of cognitions.

The sequence of events resulting in learning is sign-behavior-significate. The organism's perception of a stimulus, a sign, is followed by behavior which results in the reaching of particular goals; these goals Tolman refers to as significates in the memory of the organism. The result of this sequence is the learning of a means-end relationship, so that on a repetition of the same situation the organism responds with expectations of what leads to what. In Tolman's words: [3]

> The process of learning any specific maze is thus the building-up of, or rather a refinement and correction in, the expectations of such specific (sign, significate, and signified means-end relations) wholes, or, as we may hereafter call them, sign-gestalts.

Tolman's theory is referred to as a sign-Gestalt-expectancy theory because of his supposition that the organism forms maps or Gestalts of the relationships between signs and goals, and that its behavior is directed by expectations of how to get to a particular goal.

One of the crucial points of difference between Tolman's sign-Gestalt theory and the association theories is concerned with the role of reinforcement in learning. As we have seen in both Thorndike's and Hull's theories, reinforcement holds the key position. Learning is directly dependent upon the reinforcement of responses; this stand is consistent with their concept of learning as the association of response (performance) with stimulus. To understand Tolman's position, one must distinguish between the roles that reinforcement plays in relation to performance and in relation to the acquisition of cognitions. Rewards and punishment are related directly to performance. Hungry animals seek food. The performance of the animal is regulated by the need for obtaining food to satisfy its motivating conditions. But if, as Tolman contends, learning consists of acquiring a knowledge of means-ends relationships, then it is not the satisfying of hunger by reward that is important, but the effect of the reward upon the map or cognition of means-end relationship. Tolman contends that the extent to which pleasant or unpleasant experiences (rewards or punishments) accelerate learning is dependent upon how they emphasize or make vivid the relationships between signs and goal objects, and confirm or refute the expectation held. In this setting, reward or punishment is not essential to learning, although either can contribute to learning.

[3] E. C. Tolman, *Purposive Behavior in Animals and Men* (Berkeley: University of California Press, 1949), p. 136.

Experimentation. To support this distinction, Tolman relies upon three types of experiments: latent learning, place learning, and intermittent reinforcement experiments. Reference to the latent learning experiments has already been made in Figure 3.6, in which a group of rats was run in a multiple T maze for ten days without receiving food at the end of the maze. Food was introduced on the eleventh day. The performance on the twelfth day and thereafter was as good as that of a group which had been fed each day from the beginning, suggesting that in spite of the absence of reward, learning had occurred, being demonstrated in the immediate improvement on the twelfth day. Under a reinforcement theory, improvement should have been gradual from this point forward, paralleling the rewarded group.

In a series of experiments in which place learning was opposed to response learning, Tolman and his associates further attempted to demonstrate that the learning of cognitions was demonstrable and took precedence over the learning of responses. The first experiment (Tolman, Ritchie, and Kalish, 1946, 1947) utilized an elevated maze, shaped like a cross.

Rats were started at either the north or south ends of the cross and fed at either the east or west end. Both the place-learning group and the response-learning group were randomly alternated in starts between north and south. The response-learning group always had to make a right turn to get food. Thus, if they started at the north end, food was to be found in the west wing of the maze. When they were started at the south end, the food was located at the end of the east wing of the maze. A particular response, a right turn, was always required to get to the food. For the place-learning group, the food was always at the same place, irrespective of whether they started at the north or south ends. They had to learn to go right or left, depending upon the end at which they had started, in order to reach the food which was constantly in the same wing of the maze. The results of the experiment confirmed Tolman's position. All eight rats in the place-learning group learned within eight trials, but none of the response-learning group learned as quickly, and several were unable to learn the response.

The second experiment utilized a maze consisting of three paths to a goal. The first was a straight run to the goal which passed a choice point at which the animal could turn left into the second path or right into the third path. Both the second and third paths were longer than the first; the second path returned to the first approximately half-way to the food box, while the third and longest path returned to the first at the food box. The arrangement of the pathways made it possible to block the direct run to the food box (by inserting the block between the choice point and the re-entry of the second path) in such a way that the second way was the best alternate (shorter) route to the goal. In a second arrangement, the direct run could be blocked by inserting the block beyond the re-entry of the second route in such a way that both the direct run and the second route were closed with the result that the third route, the longest of all three, was the only route open.

In preliminary trials, a preferential hierarchy for the differing routes was established. With all paths open the animals preferred the direct route. With that blocked, they preferred the second, and only when both the first and second were blocked did they choose the longest of the routes, the third. In establishing the preference hierarchy, the block had been placed between the choice point and the re-entry of the second route, so that the rat had to back out of the direct path, then turn left into the second route.

Having established the preference order for the different routes, the test consisted of placing the block in the direct run beyond the re-entry of the second path, so that the longest and least preferred route was the only one open. The question was whether the rats could perceive that both the first and second routes were closed, or whether they would perform in order of their preference. The rats most frequently rejected the second pathway and chose the longest but open route. Apparently they had formed a cognition which permitted the selection of appropriate pathways, rather than being habituated to a given sequence of responses.

The third set of experiments which supports Tolman's position includes the experiments in which intermittent instead of 100% reinforcement is used in the conditioning of given responses (human eyelid conditioning). Humphreys (1939) showed that random alternation during conditioning led to as rapid conditioning as did 100% reinforcement, and further that the response established showed greater resistance to extinction. The results, according to Humphreys, support a preparatory set or expectancy hypothesis; this is to say that it is not the frequency of reinforcement that is responsible for the learning that occurs or its resistance to extinction, but the effect that the reinforcement has in confirming or refuting the expectations of the learner.

In conjunction with his position, Tolman like Hull, attempts to explain what is happening when learning occurs. To do this, he defines a series of intervening variables which are operative in learning. Unlike Hull, no attempt is made by Tolman to describe rigorously the quantitative relationships between the variables, because he believes such action would be premature.

To begin with, Tolman recognizes three sets of factors which are operative in learning: those of individual differences in the capacity of the organism, those related to variations in the nature of the material or learning task, and those related to variations in the manner of presentation. These are the factors that are known to affect learning outcomes. To account for their influence, Tolman conceives of two kinds of determinants or intervening variables: cognitive variables and demand variables. The cognitive variables relate to the perceptual organization of stimuli by the organism, and operate under Gestalt laws. The demand variables refer to the motivational states existing, such as sex, hunger, thirst, etc. The interaction of these variables leads to certain expectations in the organism with respect to the goal-objects or significates which produce the observed behavior.

Although both Hull and Tolman hypothesized the presence of intervening variables to explain the learning process, Hull was more explicit in definition and in his attempt to specify the quantitative relationships. Simultaneously, he restricted the type of learning situations which he attempted to apply experimentally to verify his hypothetical constructs. Attempts at extending the theory to cover all forms of learning were usually by logical analogy. Tolman doesn't restrict himself to a single type of learning; instead, he suggests that several different kinds of learning probably exist and need different theoretical approaches to explain them. Similarly, he does not attempt to define and explain the various ramifications which are implicit in this theory; rather, he is content to treat learning on a broad basis.

Significance for education. The fact that Tolman accepts different forms of learning makes it more difficult to infer how an educational program which followed his theory literally would operate. Among the different kinds of learning which Tolman (1949) presumes to exist are what he terms: cathexes and equivalence beliefs, field expectancies and field cognition modes, drive discrimination, and motor patterns. A cathexis is the attachment of a specific goal-object, e.g., the preference for a particular food, to a basic drive, such as hunger. All organisms have the basic drives of hunger, thirst, fright, etc., and they learn that certain objects, in either a positive or negative manner, satisfy them. They also learn they can obtain equivalent satisfactions from various sub-goals. Tolman gives the illustration of how the obtaining of A grades may provide the equivalent of parental approbation, provided the individual did not directly continue to seek the approval of the parent; in the latter case, the A grade is a means to an end, not an end in itself, and thus is not an equivalence belief. Tolman expresses the thought that cathexes and equivalence beliefs are best explained by a reinforcement doctrine.

The suggestion for education would be that parents and teachers clearly define the type of goal-objects they desire children to seek in the satisfaction of their motives, utilizing reward and punishment to establish them. Tolman would probably go further and suggest that an analysis be made to determine whether the goal-objects which are being established by children, consciously or unconsciously, are those desired by parents and teachers, particularly because he believes these are not subject to the usual forgetting as are field-expectancies and field-cognition-modes. It is with the latter that the teacher's task is primarily concerned — the creating of stimulus-conditions which make it possible for the learner to perceive clearly what leads to what, and to understand the different means by which a given goal can be reached. Emphasis would be placed upon making vivid the relationships between the parts and the whole, thus following Gestalt principles. Because of variations in capacity with age, previous experience, etc., it would be necessary to select learning tasks which can be perceived as wholes. Field-cognition-modes is the term by which Tolman describes the established memory-perception-inference patterns which play an important, but undefined, part in the expectancies or perceptual set of the organism in any situation, particularly a novel one. If in each new learning situation the field-expectancies had been clearly established so that a minimum of ambiguity in the sign-Gestalt existed, then the probability of appropriate memory, perception, and inference in a new situation would be at a maximum. Ambiguities or confusion would reduce the probability of appropriate memories or inferences being made.

Drives. Tolman has little to say about drive discriminations. By inference, however, it would appear that any way in which an individual can learn to discriminate between his own needs as they operate and to demand certain actions would make possible more satisfaction, particularly where a choice exists between different equivalences, many of which are arbitrarily attached to basic drives. Much of pyschotherapy or re-education would consist of helping individuals make such discriminations, for instance in the breaking of compulsive-obsessive behavior. Another aspect of drive discrimination would be the importance of the teacher's recognizing high-drive states and the extent to which they may interfere with the desired learning. A crude illustration would be the case of attempting to teach a child a given arithmetic skill at a time when he was extremely hungry. The demands of his high-drive state would make it difficult for him to learn a task involving a lesser drive — that of maintaining teacher approbation. In view of the relatively neutral aspect of much learning, particularly as children became older, the recognition and prior satisfaction of such high-drive states would be important.

POINTS OF AGREEMENT BETWEEN THEORIES

It is readily apparent that some of the differences between the theories result from the different tasks that the several theorists choose as learning problems: e.g., motor responses versus perceptual responses and the different emphases placed on such features of learning as whole versus parts, or present situation versus past experience. The situation is not unlike the four blind men describing the elephant, each basing his description on the different part which he happened to be touching. Several attempts have been made to evaluate the similarities which exist, although one must keep in mind the full gamut of learning and not confuse the basic differences between theories.

Dashiell (1935) reviewed the major emphases of conditioned-response, trial-and-error, and Gestalt theories with the intention of establishing their common components. Very briefly, the points he found emphasized were (1) the complex motivation of the subject, (2) the hyperactivity resulting from obstruction of motivated activity, (3) the multiple and varied responses to stimuli relationships, the most important being between means and objective, (4) the selection occurring among the multiple responses and resulting in the elimination of extraneous responses, (5) the selected responses, originally occurring fortuitously and confirmed or reinforced by their effects, and (6) the gradual to sudden improvement in response.

McConnell's (1942) synthesis is similar to Dashiell's, although ordered somewhat differently. Learning situations are (1) a complex of both stimuli and responses and must be (2) described in terms of mutual relationships. (3) Motivation initiates and directs behavior and (4) leads to particular responses, organized for the attainment of a particular end, which, (5) if resulting in the satisfaction of the motives, becomes established. (6) The crux of learning lies in the learner's recognizing the appropriateness of his response and modifying future tries in the light of previous experience. This action is dependent upon the ability of the organism (7) to discriminate between differences and (8) generalize between similarities. Only the last three steps are not common to both lists.

POINTS OF ISSUE BETWEEN THEORIES

While the foregoing efforts demonstrate the existence of considerable consensus among the different theories, it is largely a consensus on the descriptive rather than the explanatory level of behavior, as to what is happening when learning occurs; it thus fails to reconcile the fundamental differences. These differences hinge on whether (1) learning is essentially a change in perceptual organization or a change in stimulus-response connections, and (2) whether or not reinforcement is an essential condition for the occurrence of learning.

The support for the position defending perceptual organization as the explanation of learning centers around so-called "insight" experiments, experiments on latent learning, place versus response learning, and partial reinforcement. The support for stimulus-response learning comes from the classical and instrumental conditioning experiments, and the trial error experiments. The S-R theorists do not deny that insight occurs in some experiments; at least they recognize that sudden solutions to problems occur. They question, however, whether an apparently sudden solution as far as performance is concerned implies that insight has occurred inwardly as suddenly, and they question the value of insight as a concept explaining learning. Instead they ask, "What are the factors or variables which produce insight of perceptual reorganization?" On their behalf, the S-R theorists argue that the experimental situations in which insight occurs are open situations wherein the results of a response can be anticipated or deduced without actually making the response. This process stands in contrast to many of the typical S-R experiments in which the subject works blindly. They suggest that trial-and-error learning occurs in the open situations, but that it isn't as obvious because it involves sensory-organ adjustments instead of overt motor responses. For example, give a person a pencil-and-paper maze with instruction to draw a line through to the middle of the maze. He may begin to draw his line through the maze, making mistakes and correcting them, retracing lines and taking correct turns until finally he reaches the center, or he may make no lines until he has visually explored the maze, then proceed to make a perfect or near perfect path. Both may have made the same number of incorrect turns, but only the first were observable.

In contrast, the field theorists do not deny that reinforcement speeds behavioral changes, but they contend that although reinforcement really affects the rate of acquisition of behavioral responses, it is not crucial or essential to the perceptual organization of the stimuli, which to them constitutes learning.

Essentially, the S-R position is that learning occurs gradually and continually, and is not characterized by sudden breaks in learning curves. Those favoring a cognition theory take the opposite view, that learning can occur suddenly and that such learning is reflected by abrupt dislocations in learning curves. This divergence in views creates a conflict regarding the continuity versus the non-continuity of learning. Illustrative of experiments utilized to test the hypotheses are discrimination experiments, e.g., learning to respond to a black rather than a white visual stimulus, following preliminary training trials during which the reverse discrimination had been rewarded (the positive cue is made negative and vice versa). According to a noncontinuity hypothesis, the reversal should not effect the subsequent learning of responding to the black stimulus, while according to a continuity hypothesis, the learning of the reversed discrimination should be retarded when compared to a control group. In situations where the trials are spaced and the discriminations are not difficult, the results favor a continuity hypothesis, but the reverse appears true under massed conditions and difficult discriminations.

At first presentation, the experiments on latent learning, place-versus response-learning, and partial reinforcement appeared to be critical refutations of the reinforcement theory. They were responded to as such by those favoring an S-R position. Several experiments (Kendler, 1947; Kendler and Mencher, 1949; Walker, 1948; Mac-Corquodale and Meehl, 1949; Walker, Knotter and DeValois, 1950) show that latent learning occurs only under restricted conditions. Animals operating under strong drive conditions, e.g., hunger, but exposed, freely or forcibly, to the presence of water during their seeking of food, fail to demonstrate any latent learning regarding the whereabouts of water as evidenced by their subsequent behavior under thirst motivation. Apparently, conditions of satiated drive favor latent learning, whereas strong drive conditions interfere with it. Thus a modification of the sign-Gestalt theory is necessary to account for these differences. On their behalf, S-R theorists still have to face the fact that under some conditions, latent learning occurs. This they do through the introduction of the notion of secondary reinforcing stimuli. The reader will recall that Hull described primary needs of the organism (hunger, thirst, etc.) which give rise to drive states. Primary reinforcement occurs when there is a reduction in drive level, e.g. the sating of hunger with food. It has been further postulated that neutral stimuli which regularly occur in conjunction with primary reinforcement acquire reinforcing powers of their own right. This has been termed secondary reinforcement. Thus, in experimental situations in which primary reinforcement character-izing much of human learning cannot be demonstrated, the assumption is usually made that secondary reinforcement has occurred. This explanation is given to account for latent learning under satiated conditions of primary drives.

The place-learning experiments, which first appeared to provide vital support to a cognition theory, have become a field of important exploration in their own stead. On repetition of the experiments, it became apparent that many extra-maze cues contributed to the results obtained, and that results varied when the training was spaced over a longer period of time (Thompson and Thompson, 1949), or when kinesthetic cues were controlled (Ritchie, Aeschliman, Pierce, 1950). At present, more knowledge regarding the variables affecting place-versus response-learning and partial reinforcement is needed before implications of the results for either cognition or S-R theories can be considered.

For some students, the total result of such controversy is confusion and dissatisfaction, for none of the results are final and neither side wins the argument; characteristically, we find it difficult to tolerate uncertainty. It should be noted, however, that each set of controversial experiments produces new knowledge regarding different conditions and variables affecting learning and forces modification and extension of alternate theories to account for the observed facts. A theory which cannot account for the experimental facts must either deny them or discount them as unimportant, or else cease to exist as theory. The pathways of all sciences are littered with discarded theories, and psychology does not differ in this respect. Defending and strengthening a theory is probably most productive from the theoretical viewpoint, but another possible solution exists for the student; he may adopt a pluralistic attitude in which he assumes that all learning cannot be explained by a single existing theory, and that each is useful to account for certain aspects.

More important for the teacher is consideration of the significance of given theoretical positions for educational practice and, perhaps, questioning the justification of strong adherence to given concepts regarding teaching method. If, in the described experimental situations, which are far simpler than most of those involving human learning, there are questions to be raised in accounting for the learning itself, certainly simple or eccentric explanations of human learning are scarcely justifiable.

SUMMARY

The essential characteristics of six learning theorists have been described: Guthrie, Thorndike, and Hull representing the association or stimulus-response theories, and Lewin, Tolman, and the Gestalt psychologists representing the field theories. Guthrie's contiguity theory, and Thorndike's and Hull's reinforcement theories are similar in their emphasis upon the effects of the environment, the development of the whole from the parts, the importance of previous learning upon present behavior, and particularly the association of responses with stimuli. In contrast, the field theories, placing emphasis upon perception and cognition, believe that learning consists of discovering what leads to what, that the whole is greater than the sum of its parts, and that insight into the relationships between the parts is vital. The interplay of the present field forces, which influence learner's motivation, is important and is stressed by field theorists.

At present no single theory is adequate to account for all forms of learning. The key issues between the two sets of theories center on whether learning is a change in perceptual organization or a change in stimulus-response connections, and whether or not reinforcement is an essential condition for the occurrence of learning. Solutions are being sought to the question of perceptual organization versus response learning in place-learning experiments, to the question of continuity versus discontinuity in discrimination experiments, and to the question of reinforcement in latent learning and partial reinforcement experiments.

OVERVIEW

Spence, K. W., "Theoretical Interpretations of Learning," *Handbook of Experimental Psychology*, S. S. Stevens, ed., New York: Wiley, 1951, pp. 690-729.

SELECTED REFERENCES

Estes, W. K., S. Koch, K. MacCorquodale, P. E. Meehl, C. G. Mueller, Jr., W. N. Schoenfeld, and W. S. Verplanck, *Modern Learning Theory*. New York: Appleton-Century-Crofts, 1954.
Hilgard, E. R., *Theories of Learning*, 2nd ed. New York: Appleton-Century-Crofts, 1956.
Stone, C. P., ed. and others, *Annual Review of Psychology*. Stanford, Calif.: Annual Reviews, 1950-1956, Vols. 1-7.
Thorpe, L. P., and A. M. Schmuller, *Contemporary Theories of Learning*. New York: Ronald Press, 1954.

ORIGINAL INVESTIGATIONS

Stolurow, L. M., *Readings in Learning*. Englewood Cliffs, N. J.: Prentice-Hall, 1953.

Part 2

Variables Influencing Learning

Chapter Five

Individual Variables

Where the psychologist speaks of variables which influence learning, the teacher usually refers to individual differences, a term which ordinarily denotes the numerous ways in which the children in a class differ from each other. More broadly used, individual differences sometimes denote the varying responses which children give to different approaches used by teachers in organizing their lesson plans and presenting their materials. In either the laboratory or the classroom, psychologists and teachers are concerned with the factors which influence learning and with knowing how to manipulate these factors. Our knowledge with respect to these

variable factors—these individual differences in the broadest sense—
is derived from two main sources, experience and experiment. Both
sources are needed to provide the teacher with skill and understanding. As valuable as experiments are in testing and verifying our
knowledge and conclusions as to how people learn, they have two
limitations. First, there are areas in which little work has been accomplished: thinking, problem solving, attitude development, and
character development. Secondly, the results of experiments represent a kind of average outcome. Individual children do not
behave by laws of averages. A high degree of artistry is essential in
the teacher who successfully utilizes the results of experiment and
experience in applying them to individual children.

The variables influencing learning fall into three categories: *individual* variables, *task* variables, and *method* variables. These are
listed in the order in which they will be considered.

Individual variables	*Task variables*	*Method variables*
Maturation	Length of material	Practice, amount and
Age	Difficulty of material	distribution
Sex	Meaningfulness	Degree of learning
Previous experience	Retroactive inhibition	overlearning
Capacity	and interference	drill
mental age		Recitation
intelligence		Knowledge of results
aptitude		Whole versus part method
Physical handicaps		Sensory modality used
Motivation		Temporal relations
		Set
		Guidance
		Incentives

Each group will be discussed in a separate chapter, followed by a
consideration of the relationship of the variables to educational
practice.

It takes a rare degree of "tunnel-vision" to overlook the variations
in ability, achievement, family backgrounds, personality, and behavior present in any group of school children. Yet, our concern with
the subject matter we teach, aided by the similarity of the garb and
grooming of children and abetted by their docile acceptance of
school routines, encourages us to overlook their wide individual
variation. To provide some idea of the range of differences, consider a typical fifth grade class. Ages are likely to range from 9.5 to
12 or 13 years of age, and heights from 48 to 66 inches, with some

girls among the tallest members of the class because of the advent of the adolescent growth spurt and attendant sexual maturation. Weights may range from 55 to 125 pounds with physical coordination and athletic skills as greatly different. And these are only the grossest physical attributes. Vision, hearing, energy output, metabolism, and nutrition will show differences as great. IQ scores from the most frequently used and misused measure of learning ability, intelligence tests, will range from 70—150, relatively meaningless numbers unless one converts them to mental ages. Based on ten as an average age, the mental ages in this class would range from 7—15, in many respects a staggering difference. In various aptitudes, which is to say the potential for development in specific areas—verbal, numerical, mechanical, musical and artistic—the range is as great as in mental ages.

The achievements of the children, whether scholastic or non-academic, will be no less diversified. Reading achievement is likely to range from second to ninth grade levels. Fortunately for the teacher, two-thirds or three quarters will probably be between fourth and sixth grade level, with approximately a tenth above and below this middle range. Achievement in other school subjects may be nearly as great, depending upon the amount of practice or experience that children have out of school as well as in. In special accomplishments — sports, music, crafts, and hobbies — the children will range from almost complete inexperience to considerable skill.

Family background, as identified by such factors as occupational differences of parents, ethnic characteristics, social attitudes, travel experiences, number and variety of books, tools, equipment or other objects in the home, number and ages of children and adults, or any other index, will be as heterogeneous as the other variables. Sometimes the fact that the children within a school come from a fairly restricted geographic area which is somewhat homogeneous as far as economic or welfare level will make for less divergence socio-economically. But in spite of this the gamut of the out-of-school experiences of the children will be great. The goals, the values, the attitudes, and the personalities will be as manifold as the more measurable attributes listed in the preceding paragraphs.

Although the differences between children may sometimes be overlooked, they cannot be ignored if one would have children learn. Whether one is confronted with a group of children or a single child, the concern with individual differences in learning is ever present. Our tendency to label a given child as bright or dull has behind it the erroneous and unfortunate assumption that all the aptitudes and achievements of a given child are highly correlated. Again, it would be a convenience for teachers if children who were capable in a given way such as reading or arithmetic were equally capable in all other matters — music, social studies, sociability, motor skills, etc. One has only to recall how few decathlon champions are found, much less individuals who are also highly skilled simultaneously in golf, cricket, archery, basketball, football, lacrosse, and swimming, to be aware of the fact that the range of abilities within an individual is nearly as great as that between the individuals in a classroom.

The work of the teacher, then, is to select tasks of suitable difficulty and to organize and present them in ways which make it possible for children of different abilities to acquire and retain the necessary skill and understanding. To do so requires knowledge by the teacher of the influence upon learning of the task, the method, and individual variables.

To this point we have been concerned primarily with definitions and limitations. In Part 1 the description of the learning process, the discussions of the problems of measurement and experiment, and the introduction to the several existent theories of learning represent an attempt to establish a frame of reference within which the student recognizes the restrictions imposed upon interpretation and application of the available data by virtue of limitations of method and conceptualization. As comforting as absolutes may be in the use of logic, we must learn of necessity to operate effectively in their absence in this area of human learning. Lacking such absolutes and lacking so-called laws of human learning does not mean that the existing knowledge is inconsequential or relatively useless. Rather it means that students need to be alert to and accepting of known limitations.

NATURE OF LEARNING

Acquisition versus retention in learning. In common usage, little distinction may be made between acquisition and retention in discussions of learning. Especially in schools, learning is frequently thought to be synonymous with the amount of information or skill acquired, overlooking the generally known fact that the amount retained does not equal the amount learned. All of us recognize areas of former proficiency in which, for lack of practice or other reasons, we have lost our former skill. Thus acquisition of new knowledge, skill, or information is not the only measure of proficiency in learning. In looking at learning curves, we observed that learning could be measured by improvement of performance shown by increase in score or reduction of error. The improvements could be related to either the number of trials or the amount of time required to attain a given level of skill. Even though any number of trials greater than a single trial involves both retention of former skill as well as gain of new skill, nevertheless, any series of trials or experiences given in a sequence, whether in the course of a day, a week, and sometimes months is considered acquisition. Measures of learning subsequent to the termination of the trials are considered measures of retention. And for all practical purposes retention is the more important measure of proficiency in learning.

Transfer of training. This term is used to identify and describe the process by which a mental or motor function shows improvement without direct practice but as a result of practice at some other related activity. A person with some skill in tennis should adapt to the game of squash more quickly than would a person with commensurate skill in volleyball, and would more quickly acquire skill at squash even though it is quite different from tennis. Having learned tennis facilitates learning squash, just as Latin shows a greater transfer of training to the learning of Spanish than to the study of German. Fundamentally our entire arrangement for education of children in schools is based on transfer of training. Presumably the skills, knowledge, information, and behaviors obtained in school are directly transferable to out-of-school life to such a degree that one's life outside of the school is the better for the education. Were transfer of training non-existent, each person would have to have direct training in every activity in which he would participate during his life. As simple an act as getting on a bus or a subway in a strange city would require separate training if the arrangements for paying fares, etc. were different from those with which one was acquainted. The absence of transfer of training would impose tremendous restrictions upon our lives. A third index of proficiency in learning, then, is the amount and kind of transfer of training that occurs as the results of different variables operating in learning.

In describing the functioning of the variables and reporting their effect upon the learning process, consideration must be given to their effect upon acquisition, retention, and transfer of training. Because verbal and motor learning have been more exhaustively investigated than many aspects of learning such as thinking, problem solving, and attitude development, the discussions to follow will reflect these biases.

Table 5.1.

	IMMATURITY	MATURITY
Emotional	Impulsive, uninhibited, easily upset, cries easily, fearful, anxious Gives full expression of all feeling, easily angered, sensitive, inconsistent, easily hurt by criticism	Able to control impulses and work toward deferred goals Avoids unnecessary worry Able to express wholesome feelings without embarrassment Consistent in responses toward others; can take constructive criticism
Social	Shy, withdrawn, isolated from groups Self-centered Unable to co-operate with others Acts solely to satisfy personal needs Prejudiced or disdainful towards some social groups Forces others to comply with wishes or refuses to participate in groups Extremely docile or submissive in groups	Understands and accepts group goals and values Able to work effectively with groups Able to maintain status and individuality in group without infringing on others Accepts responsibility
Sexual	Unable to reproduce species Antagonistic toward opposite sex Promiscuous in love-making activities Prudish, disgusted regarding sex Body build characteristic of childhood	Capable of reproduction Able to establish friendly relationships with opposite sex Romantic interest with single person Accepts sexual role without embarrassment Body build with primary and secondary sex characteristics associated with adulthood
Physical	Lack of bladder or bowel control Incomplete skeletal development Unable to learn complex motor skills Partial intellectual development	Control of body functions Complete dentition Neuromuscular development Peak intellectual development

MATURATION

The amount of learning occurring in any situation is dependent upon the child's level of maturation. Level of maturation refers to the person's stage of development in size and complexity of function with respect to maximum physiological development. Before elaborating on the foregoing generalization, we should consider the different meanings associated with the word maturation. We think of maturation as the process of attaining full development of all abilities and capacities; emotional maturity, social maturity, sexual maturity, physical maturity are terms descriptive òf certain states of human development. In each the term, maturity has a different meaning. A glance at Table 5.1 will illustrate the difference in the meaning of these terms in common usage. Social and emotional maturity describes an idealized concept of behavior which is almost completely dependent upon learning. Sexual maturity can be used in either of two ways, with reference to the attainment of physical capacity for reproduction or as regards the learned ability for effectively relating to members of the opposite sex. Physical maturity describes the attainment of a condition of full physical growth and development. Sexual maturity occurs in mid-adolescence, while physical maturity is attained five to ten years later. Emotional and social maturity are achieved no earlier than physical maturity and are frequently delayed much longer. The size of the prison and state hospital population permits the conclusion that many never attain emotional or social maturity.

In distinguishing between the two processes of learning and maturation, the latter is used in the restricted sense associated with physical maturation. Changes in behavior resulting from physical growth and development are attributed to maturation. The actual course of human development shows a continuous process of change over the entire span of life from conception to death. One does not suddenly become an adult and is no longer a child. Within the gradual sequence of changes that occur are many trends both in rate and direction, trends which vary with different aspects of human development.

Differentiation of development. One characteristic of maturation based on experimental evidence is *differentiation*. Gross movement precedes specific movement; simple movement precedes complex movement. Differentiation begins in the germinal stages following the fertilization of the ovum. In the early stages, growth takes place rapidly by an increase in the number of cells through cell division; in the later stages, growth is accomplished almost entirely through enlargement of the cells. By the end of the first month, the eye-cup has taken its initial form and the heart begins to function. By the fifth week the main parts of the central nervous system are outlined. Limb buds appear between the fourth and eighth weeks, and by the eighth or tenth week, the typical human form has been assumed and the general bodily structure laid down. From the tenth week to birth, the body of the fetus increases many times in length. About the end of the second month, the limb buds make slow movements. Then reflex movements appear, gradually being differentiated out of mass movement and becoming more specific. Crying occurs among infants born at six months. During the seventh month, the structures are much the same as at full-term birth. During the eighth and ninth months, there is a large amount of mass movement with further development of the specific character of the reflexes.

When the baby is born, his receptor-neuromuscular system is developed sufficiently to provide for a great many essential activities, such as breathing, feeding, crying, digestion, and elimination. He yawns, hiccoughs, sneezes, pulls his hand away from painful stimuli, grasps a small rod placed in his hand, and turns his big toe upward when the sole of his foot is stimulated. Besides these comparatively specific reflexes, there is a great amount of mass activity in the form of wriggling, twisting, waving arms, and kicking of legs.

It has been generally assumed that all this activity results from maturation alone, and that the essential neuromuscular connections are formed in the process of growth and not through learning. It has been taken for granted that there could be no opportunity for learning prior to birth; hence, behavior at birth must be innate and unlearned. However, in recent years there has been a growing tendency to attribute the specific character of complex behavior patterns less to pure maturation determined by hereditary factors and more to environmental influences and learning. The concept of instincts as inherited, growth-determined patterns of behavior has been found wanting and has been abandoned in human psychology. Now the question arises whether the reflexes — those simple forms of reaction present at birth — may not have been differentiated from mass activity of the fetus by a process more properly regarded as learning than as maturation.

According to one view (Kuo, 1932), the movements occur first simply as part of the generalized mass activity of the fetus aroused by internal stimulation. If some form of external sensory stimulation occurs at the time of a movement, an association is made in the nervous system between this sensory stimulation and the process producing the movement. Because of this association after the manner of learning known as conditioning, this sensory stimulation becomes adequate for the production of that particular movement. In this way, a new reflex is formed or differentiated from the mass reactions of the fetus. To illustrate, let us assume that as a part of the mass reaction the fist is clenched. This produces a pressure on the palm of the hand, causing a sensory stimulation at that point. According to this theory, pressure on the palm becomes, by conditioning, an adequate stimulus for producing the grasping response. If this version is correct, the grasping reflex and possibly many others are differentiated from the mass reaction and take on the specific character they manifest at birth through the reactions of the individual before birth; hence, they are learned.

Although the process of differentiation of responses is clear, the evidence for specific learned changes during the prenatal period is inconclusive and equivocal. Spelt (1935) using a mild electric stimulus paired with a buzzer attempted to establish conditioned responses in infants in utero. Only unstable, transitory responses which were quickly extinguished could be established. Wenger (1936) obtained similar results in efforts to establish conditioned responses in newborn infants. That learning probably has limited influence is suggested by the relatively constant environment of the fetus in the uterus, wherein the range of stimuli to which the fetus is exposed is at best restricted. Furthermore, if learning is dependent upon cortical functioning which in turn depends upon myelination, then learning is not possible until after birth.

That gross changes in environment before and after birth alter development is shown by studies by Sontag (1935), Corner (1944), and Spitz (1945). Marked deficiencies in maternal diet, infectious diseases such as measles at given stages of pregnancy, and gross deprivation of human contact after birth contribute to marked deficiencies in development. Spitz's studies of children in foundling homes showed that infants deprived of the stimulation of human contact were slower to develop physically, socially, and emotionally, and were subject to a higher incidence of death and infant diarrhoea.

In general it appears that the younger the child, the greater the influence of maturation upon ability to modify behavior; inversely, the greater the age, the greater the influence of environmental stimuli.

Sequence of development. One observation resulting from a number of longitudinal studies of growth and development is that a strikingly uniform sequence of behavioral changes occur. In infancy and childhood, development is characterized by rapid change, both in size and complexity of function, with increasing stability and gradual decrement in function occurring with advancing age. But regardless of the rate, the sequence of changes follows fairly constant patterns.

The behavior of the newborn infant is largely reflexive in nature. During the first few weeks, the cerebral cortex matures rapidly and, judging from the baby's more adaptive responses, begins to influence behavior. The baby's initial responses to stimuli are total responses involving the whole organism, but gradually more specific voluntary responses occur. Emotional response is similarly undifferentiated, at first involving a general state of excitement, thrashing, and crying alternating with quiet and sleep. Gradually more specific responses of fear, rage, and pleasure develop. The smiling response, at first general, becomes associated with specific people or objects as the infant's capacity for visual discrimination increases and he becomes able to recognize and respond appropriately to family and strangers.

Shirley (1931) has made a thorough study of the developmental sequence in 25 babies through the first 2 years. Postural and locomotor development were found to follow a fairly uniform pattern. At about the third or fourth week, the child holds up his chin when placed on his stomach. A little later, when lying in this position, he raises his chest. At about 4 months he sits with support, and by the seventh month he generally manages to sit alone. Next he stands with help or by holding on furniture. Then follow in order creeping, walking when led, pulling up to a standing position beside furniture, climbing stairs, and standing alone. Finally at about 15 months, he walks alone. Shirley found considerable variation with respect to the age at which the traits appeared in different children. But since the children were free to engage in as much activity as they desired, she felt these differences could not be accounted for on the basis of differences in practice. The uniformity in the sequence of motor development points significantly to a maturational factor. The effects of practice are manifest, but they do not acount for the uniform order of development in these infants.

Individual differences in maturation. The studies by Shirley and those of Gesell (1924, 1934) and Bayley, (1935) as well as the review of research prepared by Bayley and Espenschade (1941) demonstrate not only the sequential development of behavior but also the wide individual differences between children in rate of growth and development. No two children grow alike. Not only do children differ in the age at which they pass through different stages of development and in their native talent for various skills, but apparently they also differ in their activity levels and their willingness to spontaneously participate in different activity. These longitudinal studies have been useful in setting up norms for various ages. Against these norms we are able to compare a child with others of his own age, but we cannot be certain that his status at any subsequent time will be constant. Children vary in the way in which they progress toward maturity with wide differences in timing. Some children maintain a fairly constant status, while others are highly variable. The growth of some functions is closely correlated so that certain predictions are possible; others are not. Youngsters who score high in verbal aptitude are likely to be above average in mathematical aptitude. Prediction of art or musical or motor aptitude from verbal aptitude is little better than chance. Rate of development and level of development in early childhood is of limited value in predicting later status. This is mainly due to the fact that observations and tests of infant ability are largely sensori-motor in character and have low positive to negative correlation with later intelligence tests which are highly verbal in content.

The effects of these variations in growth are twofold: the curbing of predictions with respect to individual progress, especially with younger children, and the necessity for charting each child's development in order to estimate probable progress from his individual growth trends.

Maturation and sensori-motor skills. The acquisition of sensori-

motor skills is of primary importance to children, particularly during preschool years. Acquiring skill in managing the body and
manipulating objects in the environment are major aspects of early
development. Crawling, walking, running, and manipulating objects by hand develop out of the child's untutored activity and appear
to result mainly from maturational changes rather than from formal
training. In fact, one of the chief occasions in the first 2 years in
which formal training is undertaken — toilet training — indicates the
relative ineffectiveness of formal training, especially if begun before
appropriate level of neuromuscular maturation has been reached.
Early studies on maturation confirmed these observations.

Gesell and Thompson (1934) gave one of a pair of identical
twins daily practice in climbing stairs for a period of 6 weeks. During this period the other twin was not trained in this activity. At
the end of the 6 weeks, when the twins were 52 weeks old, the trained
twin climbed the stairs in 26 seconds. At 53 weeks of age, the twin
who had not been trained climbed the stairs in 45 seconds. But
at the age of 55 weeks, this twin, after 2 weeks training, climbed the
stairs in 10 seconds. The second twin did better at 55 weeks than the
first did at 52, even though the first one had been trained 3 times as
long. These authors concluded that the superiority of the second
twin was due to the fact that she was more mature at the time of
training.

Hicks (1931) gave one of 2 equal groups of young children practice once a week for 8 weeks in hitting a moving target. Then both
groups were tested once a week for 2 weeks. The difference in improvement made by the 2 groups was too slight to be significant. He
concluded that "for the development of complex motor skills in preschool children, maturation and a general environment in which
many experiences are possible are much more important than
systematic practice."

Hilgard (1932) gave a group of 10 children 24 to 36 months old
practice in buttoning, climbing, and cutting with scissors for a
period of 12 weeks. A control group, equated for chronological age,
mental age, sex, and initial abilities, was also tested in these skills
at the end of this 12-week period. The performances of the trained
group were superior in all tests at the end of the practice period. But
after one week of practice, the performances of the control group
were as good as those of the practice group after its 12 weeks of train-

ing. The fact that the control group gained more rapidly was believed to be due to factors of maturation and general practice in related activity.

More recently Gesell, Ames, and Ilg (1946, 1948, 1951) have collaborated in several studies of developmental trends in handwriting and associated behavior, such as posture and directionality of writing. By obtaining repeated samplings of writing and drawings of given figures of small groups of children at 6-month intervals, and by taking samples of writing of children of different age levels and comparing the production at various age levels for amount, accuracy, size, slant of letters, and direction of movement, fairly consistent developmental trends were observed. Not only can children write more letters, figures, and words more accurately with increase in age, but also they tend to form their figures in characteristic ways at a given age, e.g., making circles counterclockwise at age three and clockwise at age three and a half. The authors attribute these sequential trends to maturation occurring in spite of the difference in environments and instruction experienced by the children.

Without minimizing the importance of maturation, the early studies in this area tend to overgeneralize from the results obtained in stressing the significance of maturation. The lack of control groups, the failure to include complex tasks, the overlooking of variability in performance, and the use of selected samples of children, usually from more favored socio-economic levels, limit the certainty with which all early acquisition and retention of motor skills can be attributed to maturation.

Rarick and McKee (1949) administered a test of motor skills, including running, jumping, balance, agility, catching, and throwing, to 172 children, and selected the 20 boys and girls with highest and lowest scores and investigated previous history. The superior group came from a more homogeneous family educational background, had more and better play facilities, and had showed an earlier preference for large muscle activity, for more active games, and for companionship of older children. While it may be argued that such earlier preference may suggest earlier maturation, the reverse effect of varied stimulation upon maturation cannot be rejected. It suggests that extrinsic factors have to be considered.

The most conclusive study of the relationship between learning, maturation, and complexity of task is Mattson's (1933) in which an experimentally trained group and a control group were tested on rolling-ball mazes of differing complexity. The simpler the task, the more results conformed to those reported above in which the control group with increased maturation acquired the same skill in less time than was required by the experimental group in which training was begun earlier. With tasks of greater complexity, the trained groups demonstrated significantly better performance, and the greater the complexity of the task the greater the advantage. The task was to roll a ball through a maze by tilting it in various directions. Simple, intermediate, and complex maze patterns were used. The children, of average IQ, ranged from 58 to 72 months in age.

Fifty children of both sexes were divided into experimental and control groups, matched for age, sex, IQ, and maze scores after 4 days of training. Following the initial 4-day training experience, the experimental group received 9 trials per day for 26 days. All 3 mazes were used in training in equal proportion and in counter balanced order. At the end of the 26 days' training, both groups were tested on each of 8 days with progress being measured in time and error scores. After an interval of 60 days, both groups were again tested for 8 days for retention. Thus the control groups had a total of 20 days experience in the 3 test periods, in addition to which the experimental group had the 26 day training experience. The performance of the trained group was superior to the control group on error and time scores both at the end of the training and after the retention period, and the differences were statistically significant on all but 2 retest error scores on the 2 simpler mazes. Most striking was the fact that the greater the complexity of the task, the greater the difference in favor of the experimental group. This study suggests that the simpler the task (and this would apply to many of the earlier studies of relationship betwen maturation and motor skills), the greater the likelihood that the gains from maturation, and possibly from incidental practice, will be as great as from specific practice. However, the more complex the skill, the more persistent the advantage derived from training.

Maturation and intellectual functions. Bühler (1930) and Allen (1931) have used delayed reaction experiments with children during the first year of life to test memory, and Skalet (1931) has similarly tested children between 2 and 5 years of age. A typical procedure is to hide a toy in one of 3 boxes, or place a cookie under one of 3 plates in the presence of the child. Delays of varying duration are introduced by screening the objects from the child for specific lengths of time. After the interval, the child is presented with the objects to see if he can locate the toy or cookie. Children of one year of age show maximum delay possible associated with correct response of between 30 seconds and one minute, depending upon the method used. With the older children, longer delays are possible; in delays of 1-3 days, in Skalet's experiment accuracy was 65% and 46% with delays of 3 to 4 weeks. Longer delays reduced accuracy to the chance level.

Gates (1928) conducted an experiment to determine the effect of practice on the immediate memory for digits. After practice spread over a period of 5 months, his practice group showed a gain of 2.07 digits while the gain of the control group was 0.73 digit. However, after 4½ months, the scores of the 2 groups were practically identical. The superiority of the practice group was only temporary. There was soon a recession to the normal maturational level.

Jersild (1932), using 2 equated groups of 6-and 7-year-old children, gave one group 31 practice trials in color-naming distributed over a period exceeding 3 months. The children were presented a sheet containing 100 colored squares. Five different colors were used, and these were arranged in rows of 10 each. Each child was asked to name the colors as rapidly as possible. The score was the time required for naming the 100 colors. The score for the practice group at the end of the period of training was better than that of the control group which received no practice, but after 3 months had elapsed, when both were again tested, it appeared that the advantage of the practice group had disappeared.

The foregoing study included also a comparison with adults, who were given training similar to that of the practice group of children. The final score for the adults after training showed a gain of 22 per cent, while the final score for the children showed a gain of approximately 24 per cent. While the adults made better scores, it appears that in proportion to their initial performance, the children and adults made practically the same gains. The results indicate that the improvement derived from training is definitely limited by the child's level of maturity.

In general, the data concerning the influence of maturation upon various intellectual functions is limited. Much more attention has been given to the relationship between maturation and motor skills because motor skills are more easily observed and experimentally controlled and are not plagued with the problem of definition or validation — a difficulty with measures of intellectual function. The distinction between environmental and maturational influences is more difficult to discern with intellectual functions, largely because both are inextricably interwoven in the functioning of intelligence. In recent years, the research trends in child psychology have been shifted markedly to studies of personality dynamics and development, with less than 20% devoted to intellectual functioning and few of these to the influence of maturation, provided that the Children's Bureau Bulletin reviewing research is a representative sampling (1953).

The exact nature of the mental growth curve is not precisely established, but the evidence points to rapid growth in early childhood with annual increments which are fairly uniform, followed by a gradual slowing. The increments from year to year in mental growth are sufficiently great in childhood that reliable measures can be made. From mid-adolescence on, the annual gains are small, making reliable measurement more difficult. Exact point of termination of mental growth is uncertain, being estimated to occur between ages 14 and 20, perhaps later. One of the difficulties is that gains in test scores occurring during this period may reflect growth in information and knowledge rather than growth in mental capacity, inasmuch as greater gains occur in areas in which greater training occurs, e.g., vocabulary and language ability. A second difficulty centers in the nature of intelligence test scores. They represent a composite of a number of specific abilities — verbal, numerical, spatial, perceptual — intermixed in varying proportions in different tests. Even where the test components are constant, the contributions of the separate abilities to total score varies at different ages because of differential growth rates for the separate abilities. Several studies, of which Bayley's (1935) is one, show the correlations between scores of children tested in infancy and in childhood to be negative, thus suggesting either marked reversals in rate of intellectual maturation or different abilities being tested at different levels. The latter interpretation is the favored one, infant tests being largely sensori-motor tests whereas later tests incorporate more and more tasks of mental functioning.

The concept of mental age is the criterion ordinarily utilized in gauging intellectual development. *Mental age* is defined in terms of the average performance of children of a given chronological age. Any child, irrespective of chronological age, whose responses in an intelligence test situation correspond to those of the average ten year old is assigned a mental age of 10. If at the time he is tested his chronological age is 8, he is intellectually advanced for his age. This advancement is indicated by the intelligence quotient which indi-

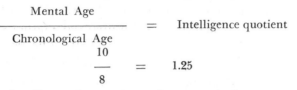

$$\frac{\text{Mental Age}}{\text{Chronological Age}} = \text{Intelligence quotient}$$

$$\frac{10}{8} = 1.25$$

cates *rate of intellectual growth to chronological age.* The quotient is reported as a whole number — 125 — as a convenience (obtained by multiplying by 100). If a child with the mental age of 10 had a chronological age of 15 his IQ would be 67, suggesting that his rate of intellectual growth is approximately ⅔ of normal.

Early studies showed that children who scored below a mental age of 6.5 on admission to the first grade showed a higher frequency of reading failure in the first grade than did children who scored above this mental age. From such studies the conclusion was made that intellectual maturation equivalent to mental age of 6.5 was required for success in reading. Subsequent investigations have shown that success in reading is more dependent upon the presence of given skills in visual and auditory discrimination than upon mental age, and that training designed to produce the visual and auditory discrimination necessary to word recognition reduces the failure rate. Such investigations have resulted in a shift of emphasis from the search for the given level of maturation necessary for acquiring given skills to consideration of the hierarchy of skills essential to the acquisition of proficiency in complex skills such as reading, which involves visual and auditory discrimination, eye movements, perceptual speed, persistence, experiential backgrounds, etc.

Maturation and readiness. Studies of the relationships of maturation to sensori-motor and intellectual development indicate without question that natural physiological growth and development regulates the ability to learn. Children so immature that they lack the sensory or neuromuscular capacity for performing a given task find it impossible to learn it at that time. With additional growth the task may be accomplished with ease. If the learning task is not entirely beyond reach but is too advanced, improvement may be obtained with great effort or with slow, clumsy, and irregular progress. Such gains are usually temporary, being quickly forgotten. If the task is wholly suited to the maturational level, the first requirement of efficient and effective learning has been met.

Failure to consider the maturation level of the child, however crude the standard for gauging it may be, can have serious detrimental effects. An unusual illustration involved a father's attempting to teach his 4½ year old son to play baseball. The father, once an outstanding college athlete, was extremely eager to have his son achieve an equally illustrious athletic career. He purchased his son a baseball glove and ball and proceeded with his son's athletic training. The training sessions were filled with impatient criticism and fault-finding. In spite of his efforts to learn and especially to please his father, the little boy could not acquire the skill. He could not because it was physically impossible for him. It is virtually impossible for children of this age to make the visual corrections necessary to follow a rapidly moving small object and coordinate and time their muscular movements to meet it. The results in this case were particularly unfortunate. A murmur was discovered in the boy's heart when he was six. For several days the boy was literally ill, not because of the heart murmur itself but because to him it meant that he could never live up to his father's expectations which were important to him.

One of the primary implications for educational practice of the studies of maturation has been the question of learning readiness. Initially the concept of readiness was restricted to maturational levels necessary for given tasks. In relation to motor skills, such a concept held greater validity; however, increasing awareness of the role of experience in complex motor skill as shown in Mattson's study and even more in intellectual development has resulted in a modification of the concept of readiness to include not only the maturational but also the essential prerequisite experiences necessary for the learning of any task. This has been especially true with advancing age and grade in school, for with each added year and grade it is the prerequisite experience which takes precedence over the neuromuscular development. More attention has been given to the most effective placement of learning tasks at appropriate age-grade levels and to pacing the material to the development of children at points where probability for learning is greatest. For instance, the instruction in formal grammar has been largely abandoned in the lower grades because young children are not ready to benefit from such instruction.

In the case of arithmetic it is felt that certain aspects of the subject have been taught too early. Wilson (1926) claims that when young children are forced into the mechanical phases of arithmetic, they waste time and develop errors that hinder their work later. The tendency in this subject is to simplify the course of study and to postpone the teaching of some operations until later years. For example, Wilson maintains that there should be no formal number work in the first two grades, and that the work of these grades should be devoted to experiences and activities which will develop the number concepts. It has been found that a large proportion of the errors in solving problems are due to the child's inability to understand the problem situations. Perhaps it would be desirable to defer all formal instruction in arithmetic to the later grades and junior high school.

AGE

If the adage "You can't teach an old dog new tricks" were true, this section could be concluded with this sentence. Unfortunately the adage applies to only certain dogs, and perhaps recalcitrant rather than incapable dogs; facts suggest that even with the decline in certain abilities found with advancing age, learning of many varieties of tasks is quite possible. Knowledge of the relationship between age and different kinds of learning abilities is important in determining which tasks shall be assigned to which age-grade levels of instruction. What differences in learning ability exist between young and old, and are the differences of degree or the kind? Are they qualitative or quantitative differences?

Although a distinction between perceptual-motor learning and skills of the symbolic-conceptual type is necessary, certain generalizations can be made. The majority of studies shows that older children and adolescents exceed younger children in superiority of performance. The older child is stronger, has more endurance, is willing to persist longer at given tasks, is able to direct his energy and attention more effectively and for longer periods of time, and has better motor coordination, work habits, and memory. He can follow verbal instructions, explore more methodically, and generalize more effectively. The younger child tires easily, makes more errors, has less motivation, poorer work habits, and poorer motor coordination. The advantages of the younger child lie in being less cautious, more responsive to stimulation, and more active. In general, studies comparing children at different ages with adults show similar results on both motor and ideational learning with regard to the form of the learning curve, trials for relearning, spacing of practice, interference between learning tasks, and transfer of training. Adults and older children have an advantage in initial attack upon problems, in the ability to generalize, and in the ability to synthesize isolated experiences in obtaining solutions to problems. Presumably these advantages are associated with greater intelligence, broader experience, and greater verbal facility.

Age and sensori-motor learning. At first glance it would appear reasonable to assume that ability to acquire motor skills improves with age up to maturity. The young child is limited by lack of maturation. As he grows older his coordination, control, and steadiness of movement improve, he becomes more resistant to fatigue, and he is more capable of sustained attention and interest. In comparison with a 5-year-old, an average child of 7 years of age can run faster, throw a ball farther and more accurately, kick harder, and jump farther (Jenkins, 1930). A young child's reaction time is considerably slower than an adolescent's or a college student's (Goodenough, 1935).

When children of different ages are compared with each other or with adults in ability to master an experimental task in motor learning, the older individuals are found almost invariably to be superior in the degree of skill attained under similar conditions of practice. For example, Gould and Perrin (1916) found a group of college students to be superior in maze learning to a group of children whose average age was 11.6 years. Likewise, high-school pupils surpass elementary-school children in maze learning. In an experiment with a pursuitmeter in which the problem was to keep a stylus on a moving electrode in order to keep the machine running, three age groups between 7 and 17 years were compared by Langhorne (1933). For both boys and girls the rate and limit of improvement was higher for the older groups. Willoughby (1929) found that the ability to make a good score on the digit-symbol test improved sharply from childhood to about age of 22 and then declined gradually toward old age.

A more careful analysis of the facts discloses that the differences that occur between younger and older children are the result of initially higher starting scores in the older children rather than the result of more rapid learning. Munn (1954) has thoroughly reviewed the evidence and concluded that there is no clear evidence that the same amount of practice produces greater improvement in performance with older than with younger children. McGinnis's (1929) experiment with 3, 4, and 5-year-old children may be cited as an illustration. Twenty children at each age level of both sexes were given 50 trials at pushing a stylus through a slot maze. Error and time scores were recorded. At both beginning and end each older age group was superior to the younger groups, but the gains made by all 3 groups during the 50 trials were equivalent. Thus the youngest group gained as much as each of the older groups during the same number of trials. Most noticeable was the difference in variability. Variation was greater on initial than on final scores, and the older groups showed the greater decrease in variability by end of the 50 trials. An unanswered question is whether or not the mazes had sufficient progression in difficulty to permit the better learners to increase their scores.

Several studies done with elementary and secondary school children corroborate the foregoing conclusions with respect to the relationships of age to learning. Seels (1951) investigated the relationship of height, weight, age, and skeletal maturity (determined by X-rays of the bones of the wrist) to large muscle motor skills involved in running, jumping, throwing, balancing, agility, striking, and catching. The highest correlation coefficients (between .40 and .50) were obtained between skeletal maturity and performance. Height, weight, and age showed low coefficients. McCloy (1935) in cross-sectional studies and Jones (1949) and Espenschade (1942) in longitudinal studies of adolescent children came to the conclusion that strength, rather than chronological age, appeared to be an important determinant of degree of motor ability.

In comparing infants and school children in their acquisition and retention of motor-skills, the inferiority of the younger children

resulting from their neuromuscular immaturity is strikingly evident.
In comparing school children at different ages with adults in the
learning of motor skills it appears that the differences are not so much
those of neuromuscular immaturity as differences in strength, experience, and motivation. Age in itself is not the crucial factor,
inasmuch as marked differences in learning rates of motor skills do
not appear with difference in age. Beyond the early years practically all differences — especially the higher initial starting scores —
may be attributed to the greater range of experience accumulated and
to differences in motivation. The older person has greater ability to
sustain attention, follow instructions, and maintain a given set, especially in delayed-reaction type problems. Where gross motor skills
involving the large muscles are involved in the task, the lesser
strength of the younger subjects handicaps their performance. It
should be apparent that it is difficult to devise tasks which are comparable in difficulty, sufficiently motivating, and equally novel for
a wide age range. As tasks become more complex, they tend to incorporate abilities other than motor skill, e.g., remembering instruction and perceptual or symbolic skills. In some instances the previous
learning of the older subjects may interfere with the new learning.
Foreign language instruction provides a good example. Younger
children can learn to pronounce a foreign language more rapidly
because they have less interference resulting from the much practiced, familiar sounds of one's native language, but the total advantage goes to the older subject because his greater understanding and
knowledge of language offsets the advantage in pronounciation held
by young children. Similarly, in typewriting, a motor skill which incorporates perceptual-symbolic skills, e.g. spelling, grammar, vocabulary, etc., we cannot expect a child of 10 years to improve as fast with
the same amount of practice as a student of 16 or 18 years of age.

The illustrations just given disclose the difficulty in making generalizations with reference to age differences in learning without
taking into account the level and type of learning task. Unless one
stops to consider the differences between the tasks presented in the
laboratory and the greater complexity of the learning tasks in and
out of school, there is danger of overgeneralizing from the results of
experimental studies.

Age and verbal learning. The available evidence on the relationship between age and verbal learning or problem solving shows a

progressive improvement in learning with increase in age. Yet there is the same limitation as posed above: is it improved learning ability or difference in experience and motivation?

Memory span for digits (Terman-Merrill, 1937) and objects (McGeoch, 1928) nonsense syllables and poetry (Straud and Maul, 1933), problem-solving ability (Harter, 1930; Gellerman, 1931), reasoning ability (Maier, 1936), ability to generalize (Heidbreder, 1927, 1928), and ability to learn school subject matter (Thorndike, 1928) shows progressive improvement with age.

The rather popular notion that childhood is the golden age for memorizing is contrary to the findings of systematic investigations of age differences in ability to learn. Evidence from many studies shows that the ability to memorize increases from its earliest manifestation in the young child to the late 'teens or early twenties.

The age norms of the Revised Stanford-Binet Tests of Intelligence for the number of digits to be repeated after one hearing is a good indication of the increase of memory ability with age up to maturity. With the standard in each case being one correct repetition in 3 trials, the child at $2\frac{1}{2}$ years repeats 2 digits; at 3 years he repeats 3 digits; at $4\frac{1}{2}$ years, 4 digits; at 7 years, 5; and at 10 years he repeats 6. The superior adult repeats 8 or 9. The sentences to be repeated as memory tests are longer for the upper age levels than for the earlier years, and the standard is higher for passing the memory-for-designs test in year 11 than for year 9.

When children of various ages are given the same learning tasks, the older ones learn in fewer trials and retain better than the younger ones. In a study by Stroud and Maul (1933), 226 subjects ranging in age from 7 to 18 years learned lists of nonsense syllables for 10 minutes and selections of poetry for 15 minutes. The learning was measured in terms of the number of syllables and lines of poetry learned within the time limits. The results in averages for the various groups were:

Average age		Lines of poetry	Nonsense syllables
7.7		9.71	4.73
8.5		11.16	5.12
9.4		13.15	5.82
10.4		16.02	6.43
11.7		17.55	6.47
14.4		21.31	7.39
18.1		22.14	8.71

A regular increase in scores for both kinds of material accompanied the increase in age through the range studied.

The correlation coefficients of chronological age and poetry (r = .61) and nonsense syllables (r = .49) were lower than of mental age and poetry (r = .67) and nonsense syllables (r = .61). When the variation in learning associated with mental age was partialed out (deducted) the authors found that the correlation coefficients with age were reduced to zero (because of the very high degree of relationship, r = .90, between mental age and chronological age). As a result the authors concluded that mental age was of primary importance, not chronological age.

Thorndike (1928) reports several experiments on adult learning which show that learning ability in childhood is inferior in many respects to learning ability in the twenties and thirties. Studies on learning Esperanto indicate an increase in ability from age 8 to 20 or later, with a continuance of the high level until about 25 or later. Then there is a slight decline to about age 35, followed by a decrease to 45 and after. Thorndike estimates that the ability to learn Esperanto drops about 22 per cent between the ages of 22 and 42.

It has frequently been stated that childhood is the ideal time for education because the child's mind is more plastic than the adult's. Since the child's habits and ways of thinking are not so fixed as the adult's, it was assumed that he could be more easily trained along desired lines. Thorndike,[1] commenting on this point, writes:

> . . . If there were nothing in favor of early schooling save the greater mental plasticity of the youth, in the sense of youth's ability to learn, we might better replace "Childhood is the time for learning" by "The time for learning anything is the time when you need it." For there are great advantages which occur when learning satisfies some real need, benefits some cherished purpose, and is made use of at once and so kept alive and healthy for further use.

Generalizing from his findings, which are based not only on learning foreign language but also on code learning, learning new motor skills, and school subjects, Thorndike suggests (see Fig. 5.1) that the curve showing the relationship between learning and age shows a steep rise through adolescence, attains a peak in the twenties, and then gradually declines.

[1] E. L. Thorndike, *et al.*, *Adult Learning* (New York: The Macmillan Company, 1928), p. 183.

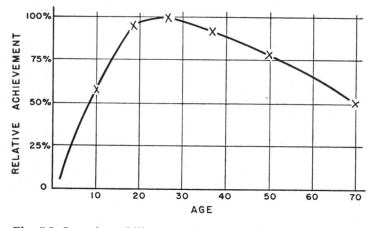

Fig. 5.1. Learning ability as a function of chronological age (from Thorndike, et al., 1948).

The tasks in which the greatest decline with age occurred were:

> learning a code
> drawing a line of prescribed length
> associating numbers with nonsense syllables

The tasks in which the least decline with age occurred were:

> typewriting
> addition
> various school subjects

The least decline occurs in the most meaningful and most familiar material. Furthermore the more intelligent and better educated the subjects, the less the decline.

Research on the symbolic processes such as thinking, problem solving, and imagination has been too limited to be very conclusive, but the available data supports the generalization of increase with age. Using 10 subjects at each of 4 age levels (3, 4, 6-10, adult), Heidbreder (1928) presented them with 3 discrimination problems of increasing difficulty involving the selection of a doll in a box which could be the left or right, near or far, plain or marked, or combinations of them. Scores were in terms of the number of persons in each age group solving the problem and the number of trials necessary. Not before age 6 did all subjects of a group solve all problems, and progressively fewer trials were needed by older subjects.

Adequate verbal explanation of the solution was not found under 6 years of age.

In a study of reasoning ability in children, Maier (1936) utilized a swastikashaped maze with a booth at the end of each arm in which children ranging in ages from approximately 4 to 9 years were first allowed to explore for a brief period. After being taken out of the maze, the child was walked by a devious route around the maze to another of the four booths in which he was shown a toy house which played a tune when a penny was inserted. For the second time the child was taken out of the maze, ostensibly to go find another penny to play another tune, but actually to disorient the child. Having found the penny, the child entered the maze. The problem was to find the correct booth which could be identified by the size of the chair and the position of the light within it. A solution could only be obtained if the child were able to synthesize his 2 past experiences to solve the problem, which process Maier believes to be the basis of reasoning. On an accidental basis a child could get to the correct goal once in 3 trials. Only when the proportion of correct solutions for repeated trials was significantly greater than 1 in 3 could reasoning be attributed to the children. It was not until age 6 that the proportion of correct trials went far above chance (59%).

Such data is in agreement with observation of the development of space and time concepts in children, whose understanding of temporal and spatial relationships does not approach adult concepts until well along in elementary school. Similarly, children are inferior to adults in both range and reliability of reports on what they have seen and heard. This is due to the child's more limited experience, immature judgment, imperfect understanding, and greater suggestibility. As he grows older the range of his report increases faster than its accuracy. The reports of very young children in picture tests are usually mere enumerations of objects. Later, the ability to describe in terms of relationships develops, and at the age of 10 or 12, children are usually able to evaluate and interpret. Through adolescence there is growth in the ability to analyze and organize experiences.

A study which incorporates the least disparity in task and motivation for different age levels is that of Holaday and Stoddard (1933) who tested the retention of items recalled at different intervals after viewing a motion-picture. The per cent of items retained by different age groups at 3 intervals after viewing are as follows:

	Per cent of items recalled at stated intervals after viewing of motion picture		
Age group	*1 day*	*6½ weeks*	*12 weeks*
Adult	88	72	73
15-16	81	71	65
11-12	66	59	56
8-9	52	47	48

The evidence offered in this section on the relationship of age and learning indicates that there is a progressive increase in learning of complex skills with advancing age, and although there do not appear to be learning rate differences in motor skills at different ages, the performances of the older person will begin and end at a higher level. The inability of younger children to perform more difficult tasks only emphasizes the necessity of grading tasks to children's level of readiness—sensori-motor, intellectual, experiential, and motivational. Variations in instruction and motivation may make it possible for children to learn given tasks at earlier ages than customary, but in general, if ease and rapidity are the standards for determining age-grade level of instruction, much of the instruction offered at given grade levels such as reading, arithmetic, geography, etc. could well be deferred. However, usefulness—not ease or rapidity of learning—is the standard for determining level of instruction. Even though the illiterate adult can learn to read more quickly than the illiterate 6-year-old, both individuals profit from earlier instruction. Neither the adult or child is likely to be asked, "How rapidly do you read?" or, "How long did it take you to learn to read?" but rather, "Can you read"? The earlier the skill is obtained, the more valuable it is, provided it is of sufficient use to be maintained through incidental practice (which recalls Thorndike's words that the time for learning something is when you need it and can use it). Undoubtedly, some differences between experimental and control groups which disappear in time and as a result are attributed to maturation would continue to exist with continued equal amounts of practice. The earlier a skill can be acquired, the greater an asset it becomes, provided it serves some useful purpose, some increase in the child's life-space or in his control over his environment.

SEX DIFFERENCES

There are few readers of this section who do not already have definite and frequently strong convictions about differences between

the sexes with respect to many skills, attitudes, interests, temperament, aptitudes, and behavior patterns, and not a few are equally
convinced that such differences are innately derived from the difference in sex. It would be pleasant, at least for those who favor the
status quo, to confirm such beliefs, but fortunately or unfortunately
the evidence prevents it. This is not to deny that there is a physiological sex difference, nor to contradict the fact that there are associated differences in attitude, interest, and occupation. But this is
to deny the fallacious deduction that the relationship establishes the
physiological difference as the cause and the difference in attitudes,
etc. as the effect. Enough evidence has been accumulated from an-
thropological studies of different societies to show that the ways of
behaving which are called masculine or feminine in any society are
the result of cultural customs and conventions which evolve over a
considerable period of time. Margaret Mead's (1935) study of 3 New
Guinea tribes of the same racial stock showed that in one tribe both
men and women tended to be gentle, submissive, and cooperative;
in the second both were aggressive, competitive, and antagonistic;
while in the third the women were aggressive and performed the
tasks usually thought of as masculine, and the men behaved in a
manner which would be called feminine in the Western World, engaging in the arts, performing the dances, being easily offended or
slighted, and becoming emotionally upset quite easily. It was evident
that the manner in which men or women acted was the result of
traditions that evolved over a long period of time rather than the
result of innate sex differences. Again this is not to deny that differences in attitude between the sexes in interests and in occupations
are observable, but to caution against attributing the cause to physiological differences. The contribution of physical structure, basal
metabolism, pulse, strength, etc. to attitudes, interest, etc. is little
known, but from the available evidence it appears that most differences are learned behavior patterns resulting from social tradition.

Sex and motor learning. There is no clear-cut evidence of significant differences between the sexes in motor-learning ability. Some
reports favor men while others indicate a slight superiority of women.
It is commonly supposed that motor activities involving great endurance or muscular strength can be handled better by men, while
women are likely to excel in skills requiring close coordination of
small muscles and strict attention to detail. It is doubtful, however,

whether there are any innate differences other than possibly that of muscular strength. Watchmaking, surgery, and violin playing are examples of skills requiring delicate coordination of small muscles and close attention to detail, and in these it cannot be said that women surpass men. Moreover, there are comparatively few skills depending so much upon brawn that women may not become as competent in them as men.

The same results are obtained with children. Of the studies which have been done with motor learning by children, no consistent difference favoring either sex has been found. Occasionally the boys will be found to have higher starting scores; nevertheless, the amount of gain made by both sexes as a result of specified amounts of training has been equivalent. Presumably the difference in initial scores may result from differences in previous experience.

Sex and verbal learning. It is frequently stated that girls surpass boys in ability to memorize; Jordan (1942), for example, writes that only 40 per cent of the boys do as well as or better than the median for girls in memory for words. On the other hand Stroud (1935) cites a study in which no sex differences were found for memorizing nonsense syllables and poetry. For reproduction after one presentation of a list of nonsense syllables, 15 unrelated monosyllabic words and 15 related words, the writer obtained the following averages for five groups of students making up a total of 106 men and 161 women:

	Nonsense syllables	*Unrelated words*	*Related words*
106 men	4.36	9.94	13.63
161 women	4.34	10.09	13.08

It will be noted that there is practically no difference between the scores for the men and women. These data are based on one impression, and the learning is incomplete; they do not speak for complete mastery or for learning under other conditions.

If such a difference exists, it is small in comparison with the differences likely to occur with variation in interest and familiarity with material to be memorized. Again in evaluating sex differences in learning, caution must be exercised in distinguishing between that which is associated with a given sex by social custom and training and that which is sex-linked by birth. Earlier students of the problem fell into the same trap. Comparing famous men in history to famous women, one finds the men out-numbering the women on roughly a 10-to-1 ratio. From such data a conclusion could be (and was) made that men are innately more capable than women, if the matter of equality of opportunity or differences in training derived from social tradition is overlooked. The fact of the matter is that no primary sex difference in average intelligence exists. A number of studies have been completed which give a slight advantage one way or the other, apparently depending upon the particular test being used. The two most thorough samplings have been Scottish Mental Surveys (1933) and MacMeeken (1934). In the first a verbal group test was given to all children (87,000) born in a given year and in the second all children born on a given day were given the 1916 Stanford-Binet individual intelligence test. In both studies the means for boys and girls were almost identical.

Where aptitude tests based upon factor analyses have been used so that single relatively pure tests of a given aptitude are available (in contrast to the general intelligence test which is a mixture of items—vocabulary, numbers, analogies, etc.—in different proportions in different tests), specific sex differences are observed. Hobson (1947) administered the Thurstone Primary Mental Abilities Tests which measure 6 factors—number, verbal, spatial, word fluency, reasoning, and rote memory—to approximately 2400 eighth and ninth grade boys and girls. Although some bias in sampling occurred because of students leaving the public school either to drop out of school or transfer to private schools, the particular community utilized has a very high proportion of its students in public schools. The girls showed significantly higher mean scores in word fluency, reasoning, and rote memory. The boys were higher on the spatial and verbal meanings tests. Interestingly enough, the boys were not higher than the girls on the number factor which would be anticipated from obtained differences in school achievement.

In vocational aptitude tests and scholastic achievement tests, boys obtain superior scores on mechanical aptitude and in science and mathematics, while girls obtain superior scores in clerical aptitude and all kinds of language skills (Stroud and Lindquist 1942; Edgerton and Britt, 1944; Burt, 1941).

With respect to these differences it is important to note that they are usually not great enough to be statistically significant with preschool and primary grade children (Bergen, 1943; Buckingham and MacLatchy, 1930). It is possible that the tests may be insufficiently sensitive at the earlier ages, but it is more probable that experience and interest—which become progressively self-generating—contribute to the sizeable differences. Some confirmation of this is found in the fact that mechanical aptitude scores of Chinese males receiving pilot training in this country during the last war were comparable to American girls, both being significantly lower than American boys Perhaps the natural habitats of the Chinese males and the American girls are equally non-mechanical.

PREVIOUS EXPERIENCE

Two classes of data are available for evaluating the influence of previous experience upon learning: the first are a series of studies which resulted from attempts to determine whether heredity or environment contributed the greater share to intelligence test performance; the second are studies on the transfer of training, the process by which any motor or mental functioning is improved (without direct training) as a result of prior experience or practice in some similar or related activity. The heredity-environment studies reviewed in this chapter are generally concerned with the effects over a long period of time of such influences as rural-urban residence, parent education, foster-home placement, etc., whereas the transfer of training experiments discussed in the final chapter deal with facilitating or inhibiting effects over a short period of particular experiences such as individual school subjects upon subsequent learning.

The nature-nurture controversy. Two decades ago a major concern of a number of investigators was to discover whether heredity or environment played the greater role in the determination of intelligence. Were individual differences in mental ability due to hereditary or to environmental influences? Were they susceptible to modification through change in environment? Were there genetically superior racial stocks? The questions could not be answered with any finality for three reasons: first, and most important, is the fact that hereditary and environmental influences are constantly interacting with each other to produce a human organism which, at any stage of development, is the product of this interaction. The two forces are inseparable. Secondly, it is impossible to achieve complete experimental control of either the hereditary or environmental variables affecting human behavior. Thirdly, most of the studies have used the intelligence test score as the dependent variable; this score is susceptible in an uncontrolled manner to variation from other influences as well, making it difficult to determine which change in intelligence test score is associated with which factor. Perhaps the dilemma of attempting to resolve the controversy is best illustrated in "Twins, A Study of Heredity and Environment" (1937) by Newman, Freeman, and Holzinger, representing a biologist, psychologist and statistician. Discussing the same data, the biologist thought the influences of heredity were well demonstrated, the psychologist thought the same for environment, and the statistician agreed with both.

In spite of the unanswered question, the accumulated data provide some interesting evidence concerning the effects of previous experience upon intelligence test scores. At this point, the students may question the authors' using intelligence test scores as a measure of learning by arguing that the scores represent differences in native ability. While partially true, an investigation of the content of most intelligence tests will show that they measure performance in skills or information in which the subjects have had direct or indirect (transfer of training) experience, and only if the previous experiences of those being tested is equivalent (and it rarely is) can intelligence tests be said to measure differences in native ability. Instead they may be said to measure those differences in capacity which result from whatever combinations of nature and nurture are useful in predicting future performance in some tasks, particularly school subjects. For our purposes, by taking subjects of known differences in background, a rough estimate of the effects of these differences upon test performance is useful information. In general the studies depend upon the administration of two intelligence tests before and after a given set of experiences of one or more groups of children or adults. Care must be taken to inquire if the behavior sampled by the two tests is the same, if the groups being compared are similar and representative samples, and if any extrinsic factors such as coaching or practice are influencing results.

Circumstances contributing to variation of test scores. As mentioned previously, factors other than the experiences of an individual will produce changes in test scores from one testing to the next, and a review of these factors is pertinent at this point, prior to consideration of the available data.

Test composition. IQ scores may differ if two different tests are used, the variance resulting from differences in content in the two tests. Even where the same test is used, but at different age levels, the content may differ noticeably. This disparity is particularly true between items suited for infants and older children.

Instability of early IQ's. Intelligence test scores of children under 4 have generally negative correlation with later test scores, thus suggesting possible changes in functions being measured or differential growth rates effecting changes in variability. To a large extent, this instability reflects the inadequacy of the tests designed to measure intellectual functions of infants and young children.

Errors in norms. Because one's IQ is determined by comparison to the performance of the group of children selected for standardization of the test, any failures to obtain a representative sample of children at a given age will produce apparent changes in IQ even though one's performance has not changed.

Motivation. Attitudes of subject taking intelligence tests can have a detrimental effect upon score, particularly with younger children. Mayer (1935) reports the number of negativistic responses from pre-school children being testing by highly-trained examiners ranging from 4 to 7. The extent to which negativism can influence scores was shown by Rust (1931) who repeated on successive days the items which 100 children had refused to perform, until they passed or failed them. A quarter of the group gained 15 or more points; two-thirds of the total group showed some gain.

Administration of test. Intentionally or unintentionally, the attitude and skill of the examiner in administering the test can and does produce differences in scores. Goodenough (1940) reports a correlation of .40 between ratings of personal attractiveness of children and number and direction of errors made by teachers in scoring spelling papers. Under conditions in which teachers were attempting not to make errors, their errors were in favor of those children they rated as attractive and opposed to those rated unattractive.

In another illustration taken from one of the studies on the effect of nursery school attendance upon intelligence, on the second test the examiner administered only the items which the child had previously failed. Obviously, the scores could go nowhere but up.

Statistical regression. When groups being studied are selected from either the high or low ends of the distribution of intelligence test scores, the second test score tends to regress closer to the mean,

showing a loss for the above average groups and a gain for the below
average groups which is due not to changes in intelligence but to
fluctuations in error factors inherent in mental tests.

Practice effects. Depending upon the test, age, education, and
test-wiseness of the subjects, small to great differences in test scores
result merely from taking the same test twice in succession. Terman
and Merrill report an average gain of 2-4 points on successive administration of the same test or of a comparable form of the Stanford-
Binet (1937 revision). Dearborn and Rothney (1941), in the Harvard
Growth Study, report gains in median IQ of 11 points on successive
tests which dropped when a different test was substituted. However,
other data is available which shows gains occur not only on the same
tests but on different tests. Generally in tests in which a principle
can be learned, e.g., maze problems, the greater gains are shown,
whereas the more specific the test in terms of information or speed
required, the smaller the gains.

Practice effects, while representing a limitation of tests, nevertheless constitute an illustration of valid learning. The greater gains are
obtained in those areas which tend to be most susceptible to practice
in daily life. In general, the greatest gain in score occurs on the
second trial. The gains, of course, may result from a difference in
speed of taking the test, in different work methods in attacking the
test problems, or in memory or insight into the solution. Particularly
in "test-wiseness" and its effect upon gains between first and second
trials, the practice effects are not unlike the results obtained by Harlow in his experiment related to "learning how to learn," to be discussed in the chapter on transfer of training.

Keeping the foregoing limitations of test results in mind, we can
divide the studies providing information about the effects of previous
experience into two types: those dealing with variations in family
background such as parent education and social class status; and those
dealing with the effects of schooling.

Family background. That differences in the environment in
which the family lives can produce differences in intelligence test
scores is seen in the numerous comparisons of children living in rural
and urban environments both in this country and Europe. The rural
children consistently attain lower scores on both intelligence and
achievement tests. Some of the variation in the results of particular
tests is a function of vocabulary content, which favors urban children

and is partly due to the tendency of rural children to be slower and more deliberate in their work methods. Nevertheless, some of the differences are probably associated with marked variations in the range of stimulation available throughout libraries, museums and the like; in the lesser educational opportunity for the rural areas in terms of books, school facilities, training of teachers, and length of school term; in the kinds of recreational activities pursued; and in the kind and extent of social stimulation. Typical of a series of studies which show a progressive retardation in intellectual develoment are one by Baldwin (1930) and others in which children in four rural Iowa communities were compared with urban children. Scores of rural infants were comparable to urban infants, but beginning with 5 to 6-year-olds the intellectual retardation became progressively greater and was more noticeable in those children attending one room schools. Pressey and Thomas (1919) have shown the existence of differences within rural areas in Indiana in favor of children residing in better farming districts. Oxendine (1953), using a standardized lecture demonstration of the principle of sound with fourth and sixth grade urban, suburban, and rural children in New England, found that the proportion of rural children at both grade levels who could learn the principle was significantly less than urban or suburban and that the deficit was approximately equivalent to one grade.

Three explanations have been offered for the differences: (1) the depressing effect of poor homes on intellectual development, (2) selective migration and resultant differences in hereditary strains, and (3) test unsuitability. Jones and Conrad (1932) compared the responses of urban and rural New England children (ages 4-14) to different test items and identified differences in responses to specific items which could be associated with cultural differences. They estimated that about half of the point difference between rural and urban children could be attributed to social and economic factors. Several studies have shown also that selective migration of the more intelligent from rural to urban areas occurs in areas adjacent to cities and in badly depressed areas, but that it is not uniform for all rural areas. Undoubtedly, the explanations differ according to the particular area.

Another distinction besides the rural-urban which is commonplace is between "working-class" or "blue-collar" and "white-collar." Sometimes the terms "lower class" and "upper class" are used. They identify recognized distinctions in attitude, behavior, privilege, and status between members of the same community. Early studies by the Lynds (1929) and Warner (1945) stimulated a series of investigations of these phenomena in modern communities. Nearly any community of any size will have its preferred residential sections with their greater exclusiveness. Furthermore there will exist second-best and third-best and the "wrong-side-of-the-tracks" areas. Ask the residents in these areas who their friends are, with whom they participate in different activities, and with whom they hold beliefs in common; you will observe distinct groupings. Ask the members of these groups whom they look up to and whom they look down on; differences in the status of the various groups and in the amount of prestige they command in the community will be noticeable. Having identified these groups, check on such characteristics as property owned, occupations held, education obtained, church and club membership, amount of income, attitude on unionization, etc.; definite differences will be observed.

Warner found he could subdivide the community into three major groupings which he called upper, middle, and lower class on the basis of their prestige or social status and which included approximately 3, 38, and 59 per cent of the community respectively. These three social strata could be subdivided again into upper and lower fractions. These six strata are identifiable ranging from upper-upper to lower-lower. Of special interest is the fact that people who are members of a given social class differ from the other classes in intelligence, educational achievement, home life, recreational pursuits, occupations, religious observance, child-rearing practices, sexual behavior, personality, and attitudes (Warner, 1945; Kinsey, 1948; Davis, and Havighurst, 1946; Maddy, 1943).

When a comparison is made of the mean IQ's of children classified according to their father's occupation as in Table 5.2, higher mean IQ's are found to correspond to higher occupational status.

A difference of nearly 20 IQ points is noted between children of professional workers and children of day laborers in this study in which painstaking efforts were taken to obtain a large and representative sample of American children for the standardization of the 1937 Revision of the Stanford-Binet Intelligence Test. It is interesting to note—and this has been confirmed by other investigations—that the differences are observable as early as age 2½-4. Some interpret this fact as supporting a hypothesis of hereditary causation, suggesting that the differences are observable before environmental influences can have marked effect.

TABLE 5.2
MEAN STANFORD-BINET IQ's OF 2757 CHILDREN CLASSIFIED
ACCORDING TO PATERNAL OCCUPATION *

		Chronological age of child		
Father's Occupation	*2-5½*	*6-9*	*10-14*	*15-18*
Professional	114.8	114.9	117.5	116.4
Semi-professional and managerial	112.4	107.3	112.2	116.7
Clerical, skilled trades, and retail business	108.8	104.9	107.4	109.6
Semi-skilled, minor clerical, and minor businesses	104.3	104.6	103.4	106.7
Rural owners	97.8	94.6	92.4	94.3
Slightly skilled	97.2	100.0	100.6	96.2
Day labor, rural, and urban	93.8	96.0	97.2	97.6

* From McNemar (1942), p. 38.

Correlation coefficients between social status and scores on the Thurstone Tests of Primary Mental Abilities ranging between .21 and .42 were obtained by Havighurst (1947) in a study of the relationships with 10 to 16-year-old-children, confirming the preceding results obtained by McNemar. Highest coefficient (.42) was that between verbal comprehension and social status. Number ability and word fluency were .32 and .30 respectively, while spatial, reasoning, and memory abilities were all in the low .20's. Mechanical aptitude tests show the least correlation with social class. It is possible that the foregoing relationships may be the outgrowth of different environments in which the children living in the most favored environment, e.g., professional homes, show greater development, particularly in verbal areas, than do children living at poorer socio-economic levels. It is also possible, as Allison Davis (1951) points out, that the tests are loaded in favor of upper socio-economic levels. In other words, the items contained in the test pertain to vocabulary, objects, and experiences which are characteristically obtained in middle-class families, and thus children from lower social classes are at a disadvantage in taking such tests and are penalized as a result.

Davis contends that such tests underestimate the learning ability of children from lower social classes. He argues that the obtained differences are the result of faulty tests rather than being due to genetic differences in social classes. The opposing argument, of course, is that by a selective process in operation in the selecting and qualifying for different occupations, the more capable people rise in the social scale.

Davis' argument that standard intelligence tests underestimate the learning ability of children from lower social classes finds some support in Klineberg's studies of negro children migrating from rural to urban areas and from southern to northern United States. Klineberg (1935) tested negro children who had been resident from 1-7 years in New York City and found that the longer the city residence, the higher and closer to average the mean intelligence score was. When the argument was advanced that this could be true if migration was selective, i.e., the more capable families moved first, Klineberg showed that the gains occurred when given groups were retested after given intervals of residence. Gains were greater on verbal tests than on non-verbal tests, supporting the hypothesis of environmental influence.

But before an environmental hypothesis can be accepted, one would have to account first for the fact that foster children's intelligence correlates more closely with their natural parents' than with their adopted parents', and secondly for the fact that differences found in IQ's of children when comparison is made on the basis of paternal occupation do not increase with age as would be expected under circumstances of continuing exposure to favorable environment. In other words, differences at age 2-3 are practically as great as at age 18. The point that is most significant in consideration of the effect of previous experience on learning is Davis' demonstration of the differential effect of family background and associated experiences upon capacity to satisfactorily answer certain kinds of tests items, particularly those having to do with verbal comprehension. Children from middle and upper social classes, whether of superior ability or not, apparently have an advantage in verbal learning (which is characteristic of much schooling) as a result of previous experience.

A further comment is needed, however, regarding Davis' (1951) contention that the differences observed in IQ's of children at different socio-economic levels are the result of unfair and inadequate tests, and that the appropriate solution is to adopt "culturally-fair" tests. This concerns validity of tests. The purpose in the use of tests is not fairness but prediction. Unless the "culturally-fair" tests can predict some kind of performance at a higher level of confidence than standard intelligence tests, they are not as useful, in spite of being "fair."

Present intelligence tests are extremely useful in various kinds of prediction: performance in school, occupational selection, job performance, military classification, etc. It has yet to be demonstrated that "culturally-fair" tests provide more accurate predictions, and until they do, they are not as valuable. We should note, as Davis correctly points out, a limitation in present tests. With certain populations the scores are not highly dependable but are subject to noticeable change in a given period of time. In such instances, long range predictions are not in order. The entire controversy could be avoided if we gave up any notion that our present tests are measuring innate intelligence, innate reasoning ability, capacity to learn from experience, or any other definition of intelligence you may wish to substitute here. Most tests measure rather limited aspects of behavior. The term general intelligence is a misnomer as far as tests are concerned, for in most instances the items being answered are specific rather than general and provide measures of particular abilities or combinations thereof. Granting the charge that currently used intelligence tests are "culturally-loaded" and may contribute to underestimates of the educability of children from "lower" social strata does not mean that they are useless or that a "culturally-fair" test is more useful. An important measure of the goodness (i.e., the validity) of a test lies in its predictive powers. The "culturally-fair" tests will have to show a higher degree of correlation with various criteria such as academic performance, job performance, etc., to be preferable. Several considerations mitigate against such an event—one related to test construction, a second to society and a third to the effects of social stratification upon individual development. It is difficult to devise new items for tests which surpass carefully selected items in standardized tests. Secondly, culture exists and societies change slowly. Tests, like people, are immersed in the matrix of culture and must make predictions within the matrix. Finally, the relationship between the particular experiences associated with a given social strata and the resulting effects upon intelligence test scores or academic achievement is probably not as great as between personality, motivation, attitudes, and the like. In a recent investigation by Woodbury (1952) of the relationship between social status and scholastic achievement, the correlation was barely statistically significant, appoximating .20

at each of three grade levels, 4th, 6th, and 8th, in an entire community containing all the previously mentioned social classes as identified by the use of the scaling procedures devised by Warner.

Effects of schooling. Attempts to appraise the influence of formal school experience upon intelligence test scores have been made by administering intelligence test scores before and after formal schooling of a given type and by sampling the intelligence scores of the similar populations a generation apart. Both types of studies have shown gains in intelligence as a result of school experience, but both are subject to question as to the meaning of the results.

In a series of studies at the University of Iowa, Wellman and her associates (1940) have compared the effects of nursery school experience upon intelligence test scores and school achievement by comparing matched groups of children, some having nursery school and kindergarten training, others not. Age ranges of the children studied were from $1\frac{1}{2}$ to $6\frac{1}{2}$ years of age and school experience was from 1-3 years in duration. In general, the pre-school attendance group showed mean gains of 2-8 IQ points, although not all children showed individual gains, some gaining and some losing as much as 30 IQ points. Gains at the end of the first year of pre-school training were the greatest, with smaller gains recorded with additional years' experience. The differences in IQ scores were greater than in subsequent school achievement. In general, slight but statistically insignificant differences in favor of the pre-school group were found at elementary, high school, and college level. McNemar (1940) has critically reviewed the Iowa studies and found them wanting in sampling procedures, experimental controls, and statistical technique. The groups were small in number, were volunteer rather than randomly selected in that parents had entered them in school, came from above-average homes, and were not constant during the period of the study.

In Lorge's (1945) study of an original group of over 800 eighth grade New York Public Schools boys who received tests in 1921, a representative sample of 131 was retested 20 years later and comparisons of changes in IQ scores made. Lorge found that greater gains in IQ were shown for greater amounts of schooling. Groups that had the same IQ at the eighth grade showed differences of 10-20 IQ points when those having the least education were compared with those having the most. Table 5.3 shows the differences for a single group having an initial score falling between 79-88 but differing in amounts of education.

TABLE 5.3

A TWENTY-YEAR FOLLOW-UP ON THE EFFECTS OF SCHOOLING UPON
INTELLIGENCE TEST PERFORMANCE *

Highest school grade completed	Increase on Otis Score on retest	N
8 – 10	28.9	21
11 – 14	31.4	13
15 or more	42.5	11

* From Lorge, p. 487.

Representative of a different set of studies is Tuddenham's (1948) comparison of World War I draftees with a sample of World War II draftees using the Army Alpha test. The 50th percentile of the World War II draftees was estimated to be equivalent to the 82nd percentile of World War I draftees. In other words half of the former group surpassed all but 18 per cent of the World War I group, a significant difference. There was a two-year educational difference on the average between the two groups. Again questions must be raised regarding the data. During World War I, group testing was in its infancy and may have included more persons for whom group tests were inappropriate. For instance, it has been shown that group tests administered to a prison population which includes a large percentage of males of limited educational experience provide a marked underestimate of intelligence. Secondly, the World War I draft was not uniformly administered, thus bringing about marked variations from state to state in draftees.

The weaknesses in the foregoing representative studies have prompted Jones (1954) to maintain that the question of whether or not educational experience increases intelligence test scores can be more effectively answered by conducting an experiment using carefully matched control and experiment groups from selected rather than accidental populations; these should receive stipulated educational experiences, with resulting changes in intelligence test scores being carefully assayed.

Even with these limitations in mind, the weight of the evidence is that gains in tested performance do accrue from school experiences. The little evidence available suggests that the gains are associated with differences in amount of schooling rather than in kind. Wesman (1945) grouped 643 tenth and eleventh grade New York City High

School students according to their major area of academic study and compared the groups on gains made on general intelligence test scores and on verbal, numerical, and spatial aptitude test scores. The evidence indicated that there was no greater gain in intelligence associated with any one course of study more than another, nor were gains on specific aptitudes, such as numerical, greater for science or mathematics majors than gains made by students in other courses of study.

CAPACITY

At any given moment each individual is possessed of certain abilities, that is, available and developed skills for performing acts of varying complexity, and certain capacities or potentials for development of future skills. Abilities are measured by achievement and performance tests; capacities are measured by intelligence and aptitude tests. Because the tests available fail to measure all one's abilities and capacities, we are frequently forced to resort to less reliable guides. With respect to abilities, we can use observation to inform us whether an individual is able to perform given tasks successfully, and, lacking the opportunity to observe (as is typical in employment interviews), we depend upon questions during interviews or reports of previous observers. Capacity presents greater difficulty than ability inasmuch as it involves a guess or prediction as to future level of performance. The greater the experience of the predictor and the broader his acquaintance with the individual and skill under consideration, the better his predictions are likely to be; but they are still fraught with error, as anyone who has attempted to predict the performance of race horses can tell, in spite of lengthy genealogy and field performance data. Betting odds represent a ready estimate of the margin of error involved in the prediction. Another illustration from human performance may be had from spring training camps of professional baseball teams. Many promising prospects attend spring training, all estimated by professional observers to possess considerable capacity and promise; only a minority, however, fulfill the promise of major league careers. The reasons lie not only in shortcomings in capacity as such, but also in differences in opportunity, motivation, temperament traits, and so on. The influence of these several variable factors necessitates ascertaining the degree to which capacity controls ultimate performance and its relationship with the other important factors contributing to successful acquisition of any given skill—in short, the relationship between capacity and learning. We can begin with the concept that a person's capacity—his potential for learning various skills—is at present only partially measurable, and proceed to a distinction between capacity and intelligence.

Ask a lay group what intelligence is, and the responses will include: learning ability, ability to adapt to the environment, ability to do abstract thinking, problem solving ability, etc. These definitions simultaneously combine both ability and capacity with respect to an individual's general goodness of response in meeting the conditions of life. Although psychologists would not disagree with the definitions presented except to ascribe some vagueness to them, they would reject any notion that this is what intelligence tests measure. They would have to say that intelligence tests do not measure intelligence as defined above.

Psychologists began with similar definitions of intelligence, and went further in stating that intelligence was in large degree innate and subject in minor degree to variations resulting from environmental influences. The nature-nurture controversy referred to in previous pages was an outgrowth of the concept of intelligence as an inherited capacity of the individual and of the attempt to ascertain the influence of environment upon biological attributes. Intelligence tests were developed in this frame of reference as devices which, it was hoped, would provide measures of innate learning ability. It was soon apparent that regardless of the standard of goodness of "adapting to environment" or "problem solving" being utilized, persons with high intelligence tests scores did not always perform best. One found persons with high intelligence test scores in prisons and mental hospitals, institutions provided for those who have not adapted or solved problems well. While it is true that studies such as Terman's (1947) showed that the gifted made a more successful life adjustment than those less capable, nevertheless correlation was far from perfect. The problem shifted from identifying how much innate learning ability was being measured (as far as test performance is concerned it is impossible to distinguish the innate aspects from the learned) to what sort of predictions can be made and what degree of relationships exist between test performance and behavior in other systematically defined situations. In other words, what do intelligence tests measure, if it is not intelligence?

Correlational techniques have provided an answer to this question. By correlating intelligence test scores with various external standards of judgment such as success and failure in different occupations, external validity coefficients that provided knowledge regarding the kinds of predictions which could be made from intelligence test scores were obtained. By intercorrelating scores on different tests and subtests, certain common components of tests could be identified, especially through the use of factorial analysis techniques; with this information, homogeneous tests of single factors could be constructed to serve as measures of single aptitudes. This can be illustrated by comparing aptitude and intelligence tests currently in use.

Since their inception, intelligence tests have been composed of a variety of items: vocabulary, arithmetic computation, identifying missing parts of objects, memory span for numbers, digit-symbol substitution, and the like. They tapped a variety of human capacities. Through the use of factor analysis it was possible to group together those segments of tests which had much in common (as shown by high intercorrelation) with each other and little in common with other segments. These constitute aptitude tests, which in general measure a single primary aspect of human behavior. More than a score of such aptitudes have been identified, but the more commonly recognized and used aptitudes are verbal comprehension, abstract reasoning, numerical reasoning, spatial visualization, perceptual speed, rote memory, word fluency, mechanical aptitude, and motor dexterity.

Verbal comprehension and abstract reasoning are two aptitudes which comprise significant portions of most intelligence tests. Verbal comprehension pertains to the understanding and use of words and is tested by such items as vocabulary, synonyms, and definitions of words; abstract reasoning is usually tested by geometrical, pictorial, number series, or verbal items which involve analogies, sequential or logical analysis. The fact that most pencil-and-paper tests are dependent upon reading skill and vocabulary, and that even oral or performance tests are dependent upon verbal instructions results in this factor being found in some proportion (however small) in nearly all aptitude tests. This fact plus the further one that aptitude tests show greater than zero correlation with each other supports an argument that there is a general learning ability. Table 5.4 shows the interest correlations of certain of the aptitude tests in the Chicago Primary Mental Abilities battery. It will be noted that the correla-

TABLE 5.4

INTERCORRELATIONS AMONG CHICAGO PRIMARY MENTAL ABILITIES TESTS (AGE 7-11)

	V	S	R	P	N
Verbal	....	.24	.63	.33	.25
Spatial		....	.40	.37	.10
Reasoning			....	.45	.32
Perceptual				....	.35
Numerical					....

tion coefficients range from .10 between reasoning and numerical aptitude, to .63 between verbal and reasoning aptitude. Spearman, a noted English psychologist, has proposed a two-factor theory of intelligence to account for the correlations, suggesting that a general learning ability exists which underlies all human abilities and that supplementing this general ability are specific aptitudes. Opposed to this theory is a multi-factor theory proposed by Thurstone, whose primary mental abilities test intercorrelations have been cited in Table 5.4. Thurstone's viewpoint is that the aptitudes are discrete, unitary factors, and that the intercorrelations occurring are an arti-fact of test construction in which the pencil-and-paper techniques used depend upon words for communication. Supporting this stand are several studies which show that low intercorrelations between learning tasks are the rule, and that gains made in learning tend to be fairly specific to the particular task. Moreover, the intercorrelations between test scores tend to diminish with increasing age, being greater in childhood and smaller in the older groups being tested; the result is that in fairly homogeneous populations such as college students it is possible to construct separate aptitude tests between which the correlations approach zero.

Numerical aptitude involves the ability to work with numbers and to compute elementary quantitative problems such as adding and multiplying rapidly and accurately. Such quantitative reasoning ability is commonly used in test batteries for college admission, particularly in engineering and scientific schools, and in simpler form in elementary school tests predictive of achievement in arithmetic. It is frequently found combined with verbal comprehension and abstract reasoning items in so-called general intelligence tests.

Spatial visualization involves the ability to conceive objects in two or three dimensions, such as one does in looking at a blueprint which presents several two-dimensional views of an object, thus requiring the viewer to visualize the appearance of the object in three-dimensional form. Perhaps a simpler explanation would be that it is the ability one uses when looking at a parking space to estimate whether or not the automobile will fit in it. Perceptual speed involves the ability to identify similarity and differences in symbols or objects quickly and accurately. Clerical aptitude tests which require the comparison of groups of numbers or letters for likeness or difference utilize this aptitude.

Memory is apparently an ability which may be subdivided into several different components, judging from the research reports produced by the U. S. Air Force Aviation Psychology program. Several of the components which have been identified are rote memory, perceptual memory, and memory span. Word fluency is a factor measured by the capacity to recall words quickly and by spelling and grammatical construction items. Games such as Scrabble and Anagrams utilize this aptitude.

Mechanical aptitude appears to be a composite of several aptitudes, rather than a singular factor, involving verbal comprehension, abstract reasoning, and acquired mechanical knowledge. Scores on tests of mechanical aptitude also appear to be more susceptible to modification from learning. Motor dexterity, like memory, is a factor which can be subdivided into several aspects involving speed of reaction, fine and gross motor coordination, and other components.

It should be evident that the term capacity has been used to avoid the connotations of innate and general learning ability generally associated with intelligence tests, which do not measure this quality. There are varied human capacities, some of which are measured by aptitude tests in a fairly singular form and several of which may be tapped in intelligence tests in composite form. The factorial analyses of tests give them some psychological meaning, judging from the kinds of items which are highly correlated with each other. Validation studies of tests provide a second external standard for determining what a test is measuring and more important, provide a basis for predicting future development. It is in this sense that intelligence tests and aptitude tests are useful, not that any inference is made regarding genetic or environmental source of ability, but rather that they sample aspects of behavior which can be used to estimate performance several years hence, e.g., ability to succeed in college, to perform adequately at certain jobs or professions, etc.

The relationship between intelligence and sensori-motor learning. As far as younger children are concerned, there appears to be little relationship between intelligence test score and sensori-motor learning. This generalization applies in either direction. Although children differ in the ages in which they pass through the various stages of motor development, their age of walking and attainment of other motor skills of early childhood are not predictive as far as future intelligence is concerned. Nor is the intelligence test score valuable in predicting sensori-motor learning. Mattson's study reported earlier in this chapter showed no relationship between intelligence test-score and performance with the rolling-ball maze. These findings have been confirmed on other tasks such as throwing quoits, hitting targets, and mirror drawing.

Conflicting results have been obtained in studies using adolescents and college students. Knotts and Miles (1929) and Thompson and Witryol (1946) have obtained correlation coefficients ranging from .17 to .75 between intelligence and performance on high-relief finger mazes.

The relationship between physical capacities and sensori-motor learning. Paralleling the work done with intelligence and aptitudes tests, numerous efforts at factor analysis of motor tests and motor skills have been made with the hope of isolating motor aptitudes and a general motor ability which might be comparable to general learning ability and the different mental aptitudes. The results of several studies (McGraw, 1948, Larson, 1941, Seashore, 1942) have classed the fundamental elements underlying the performance of motor skills as:

a) Strength	*f*) Body size
b) Speed	*g*) Reaction time
c) Accuracy	*h*) Steadiness
d) Endurance	*i*) Balance
e) Agility	*j*) Control of voluntary movements

The fundamental skills in physical education were identified as:

a) Running	*e*) Kicking
b) Jumping	*f*) Climbing
c) Vaulting	*g*) Catching
d) Throwing	*h*) Pronograde locomotion

These lists do not exhaust the factors but present the most typical, for it must be recognized that the factors revealed by analysis are those contained in the tests used by investigators. Differences in the number and kind of tests used produce variations in the factors that can be identified. Unlike mental capacity, in which primary mental abilities and possibly a general learning ability can be identified, the factors in motor capacity which have been isolated do not appear to be distinct and separate primary factors. Instead each may be subdivided into minor abilities, which in turn may be subdivided. Strength, for instance, may be subdivided into "abdominal strength," "static strength," "dynamic strength," etc. Similarly, the intercorrelations of performance in different motor skills are much lower than those given earlier illustrating the relationship between primary mental abilities.

Seashore (1942) administered a battery of fine motor abilities tests such as the Koerth Pursuit Rotor, the Minnesota Rate of Manipulation Test, and several steadiness tests, plus gross motor abilities tests such as punting a football, standing broad jump, 440 yard run, balancing, and chinning to large groups of athletes and non-athletes. There was little difference in strength and athletic skill. The intercorrelations between the fine motor abilities tests averaged .31 and those between the different gross motor abilities averaged .26; but the relationship between the two sets was close to zero. All told, the studies of motor learning support a theory of specific characteristics in which motor learning depends largely upon specific abilities related to their specific motor areas, bearing little relationship to skills in other areas. Skills in one motor ability apparently have a low transfer effect to other abilities. In performances which are relatively free from intelligence, learnings seem to be dependent upon the general development of the specific musculature involved in the activity.

The more complex the motor skill or particularly the sport skill which is to be learned, the greater the likelihood that it will involve abilities other than pure motor learning. The ability to follow directions, to visualize spatial relationships, to perceive small differences, or other mental capacities are more likely to be involved in the more complex skills in addition to strength, speed of reaction, balance, coordination, and other motor abilities. In these instances, performance in the skill is more likely to correlate with particular aptitudes, which fact may account for the observed correlation between intelligence and sensori-motor learning in adolescence. Additional support for this possibility may be found in Tuddenham's (1948) study of World War II draftees which showed a positive correlation between intelligence and vocational skill. Associated with the learning of complex trade skills such as cabinetmaker, machinist, tool-and-dye maker, electrician, and the like are higher degrees of tested intelligence. Granting the argument that there are undoubtedly social factors other than intelligence operating in the assortment of persons into occupations, nevertheless, minimum levels of ability are necessary for the acquisition of increasingly complex vocational skills. When intelligence test scores of Army draftees were classified as superior, high, average, and low and a comparison made between the men's occupational status in civil life and their intelligence rating, the professions such as physician, accountant, engineer, teacher, business executive fell in the superior category; stenographers, photographers, electricians, tool-and-dye makers, telegraphers, and other highly skilled occupations fell in the high category; the skilled trades such as plumber, mechanic, carpenter, printer, butcher, tailor fell in the average category; while the low category included the semi-skilled and unskilled occupations such as fisherman, cook, day laborer, and truck driver. There was a great amount of overlapping in intelligence scores between groupings. The professional group had the narrowest range of intelligence, ranging from high average intelligence to superior, but in each subsequent category an increasingly greater range of intelligence was found. In the low category were laborers whose intelligence was as high as a few professional workers, thus confirming the fact that considerations other than intelligence—personality, educational opportunity, motivation, and the like—enter into vocational achievement.

In training feeble-minded individuals in manual tasks, it has been found necessary to fit the task to the level of intelligence. A boy with a mental age of 7 can sew a broom, but it takes a mental age of 9 or 10 to build up the shoulders of a broom. Girls with a mental age of 6 can learn to crochet, but high-grade fancy embroidery calls for a mental age of 9 to 12. An imbecile can tear off the soles from old shoes or pick apples which are to be used for cider, but he cannot operate a burnishing machine nor pick apples for packing without bruising them. The higher grade idiot can be trained to pick up stones and do a few very simple tasks under supervision, but he cannot wash dishes. For dishwashing, the minimum IQ of approximately 26 to 30 is found in the low-grade imbeciles. A man with a mental age of 7 can paint a barn under supervision, but he cannot estimate costs or mix paint. An imbecile can learn to milk a cow but, the minimum IQ for general farm work is about 65 or 70. In general, it has been found that the more complex the task, the higher is the minimum mental age needed to master it.

The relationship between mental capacities and verbal learning. Stephens (1951) has compiled and summarized a number of studies reporting the relationship between intelligence test scores and academic achievement. These are shown in the three tables, 5.5, 5.6, and 5.7 which show, respectively, the correlations at elementary, secondary, and college level.

The median correlation coefficient is higher for the elementary grades than for either the high school or college level, probably because the range of ability is greater at the elementary level than at the other levels where the less capable tend to be eliminated from school. One of the characteristics of the correlation coefficient is that its size is affected by the range of talent in the group. The smaller the range of talent, the smaller the correlation coefficient is likely to be. As would be expected from the content of most intelligence tests, the correlations with verbal and arithmetic phases of the curriculum

TABLE 5.5

CORRELATIONS BETWEEN INTELLIGENCE AND ACHIEVEMENT IN DIFFERENT SUBJECTS
AT ELEMENTARY SCHOOL LEVEL *

Size of Correlation	Reading	Spelling	Arithmetic	Handwriting
.90 – .99			2	
.80 – .89	6	2	1	
.70 – .79	7	3	6	
.60 – .69	12	7	2	
.50 – .59	5	5	10	
.40 – .49	4	4	6	1
.30 – .39	4	5	6	1
.20 – .29	6	3	1	1
.10 – .19		2		
.0 – .09		1		3
−.10 − −.01	2			1
Median r	.60	.51	.55	.08
Number of r's	46	32	34	7

* J. M. Stephens, *Educational Psychology* (New York: Holt, 1951), p. 228.

TABLE 5.6

CORRELATIONS BETWEEN INTELLIGENCE AND ACHIEVEMENT IN DIFFERENT
SUBJECTS AT HIGH SCHOOL LEVEL *

Size of correlation	Average marks	Science	Math.	English	Latin	Commercial subjects
.70 – .79		1		1		
.60 – .69	2		3	2	1	
.50 – .59	13	2	12	2		
.40 – .49	12	1	16	6	1	
.30 – .39	11	4	12	2	3	
.20 – .29	6		4	2	4	
.10 – .19	1				2	2
.00 – .09						2
Median r	.44	.40	.45	.46	.29	.10
Number of r's	45	8	47	15	11	4

* *Ibid.,* p. 229.

are somewhat greater than with other aspects such as science and Latin. It is interesting to note that the courses involving the greatest degree of motor skill — handwriting and commercial subjects — produce the lowest correlation coefficients. The size of the coefficients reported has prompted the suggestion that intelligence tests be renamed scholastic aptitude tests because they are most predictive of academic achievement.

TABLE 5.7

CORRELATIONS BETWEEN INTELLIGENCE AND ACHIEVEMENT IN DIFFERENT
SUBJECTS AT COLLEGE LEVEL *

Size of correlation	General college grades	Science	Math.	English	Foreign language	Social studies
.70 – .79	1					
.60 – .69	4		1			
.50 – .59	26	4	2	3	1	1
.40 – .49	44	6	2	3	6	2
.30 – .39	24	5	5	4	10	4
.20 – .29	4	3	2	1	2	2
.10 – .19					3	
.00 – .09						
Median r	.46	.42	.38	.42	.36	.36
Number of r's	103	18	12	11	22	9

* *Ibid.,* p. 230.

Correlation coefficients between aptitude and achievement tests are presented in Table 5.8 Table 5.8 shows the relationship between the Thurstone Primary Mental Abilities Test and tested reading and arithmetic achievement (Thurstone, 1954, page 5).

TABLE 5.8

Achievement in	No. in Group	Verbal	Spatial	Factors Perceptual	Numerical
Reading	177 age 9 to 9.5	.75	.34	.43	.53
Reading	213 age 10.5 to 11	.85	.40	.40	.48
Arithmetic	463 fourth grade	.50	.30	.37	.44

On the whole, the correlations are not greater than those reported for intelligence tests, and particularly interesting is the fact that the numerical aptitude test correlated no more highly with arithmetic than with reading. For purposes of predicting scholastic achievement, an intelligence test is as useful as aptitude tests, probably because of the highly verbal content of most school curricula. For identification of special aptitudes, factor-type tests are more useful. It is also possible to combine the results of such tests statistically to produce higher accuracy in prediction of performance; but as far as most teachers are concerned, intelligence tests will suffice.

THE EFFECTS OF PHYSICAL HANDICAPS UPON LEARNING

All learning depends upon integrated physiological functioning. There are no special organs or structure of the body developed exclusively for the acquisition of skills and knowledge. The physical equipment which serves all human behavior serves learning as well. The receptors, the muscles, the glands, and the nervous system constitute the somatic bases of learning.

Receptors. The environment presents certain forms of energy called *stimuli* which impinge on the organism. These, acting as irritants, disturb the equilibrium of the organism, and initiate activity through the neuromuscular system. But a stimulus can initiate activity only if the organism is sensitive to it. Certain structures of the body are highly sensitive to particular forms of energy. They render the specialized service of receiving physical stimuli, and for this reason are known as *receptors*.

There is considerable specialization among the receptors themselves. Each is sensitive to at least one kind of energy but not to all. The eye contains cells which are receptors sensitive to light energy. In the inner ear are receptors which are aroused by air vibrations. In the nose are sense cells which are stimulated by gases and volatile particles. In the skin are the receptor cells for heat, cold, pressure, and pain. Because they receive stimuli from outside the body, these receptors are called *exteroceptors*.

Inside the body there are many receptors which receive internal stimuli. On the tongue are receptors sensitive to chemical substances in solution. Others are found in the throat, intestines, stomach, and lungs. These are called *interoceptors*. Those located in the muscles, tendons, and joints, and stimulated through movements of these parts are the *proprioceptors*.

Man is dependent upon this receiving set for his contacts with the world about him. It determines and limits his range of response. If some of the receptors are defective or missing, as in the case of the blind or deaf, the range of functional contact with one's environment is correspondingly diminished. Without the visual receptors we would have no world of sight or colors. Without them nothing could be learned about the appearance of objects, and none of the many skills for which sight is essential could be developed. Likewise deficiencies in the other organs of sense handicap or preclude certain kinds of learning.

The receptors condition the various forms of sensory experiences; sensory experience is essential to perception; and perception is the basis for memory, imagination, and thinking. Thus, our knowledge rests directly or indirectly upon impressions received by way of our receptors. Our skills and habits could not be maintained or even developed without the services of these receiving mechanisms.

Effectors. In all animal life, movement is a vital factor in adjustment and survival. The bodily mechanisms for movements are the muscles. The contractions of the skeletal muscles execute the voluntary movements and certain reflex responses. The smooth muscles of the internal organs take care of involuntary movements of these organs. The muscles are called *effectors*.

There is probably no learning activity that does not involve the muscles, for the action of muscles is an integral feature of the psychological activities. The roles of these effectors in the case of the action and the motor skills are matters of common observation. But the muscles also lay an important, though less universally recognized, part in perceiving, remembering, imagining, comprehending, and thinking.

The nervous system. The receptors and muscles play their parts only in connection with the nervous system. This somatic system links together all the organs and structures of the body into a working unit. Nerves connect the receptors and muscles with the central nervous system, which consists of the spinal cord and the brain. The brain has been called the "great central adjuster" because the integration and smooth performance of the psychological functions depend upon its services.

It is commonly assumed that the functional modification that takes place through learning is due to some kind of change in neural structure and that this change is effected by the nervous system's own operations. These operations are the neural processes involved in carrying on the learning activity. It is supposed that they leave their mark in the form of structural changes in the great central adjuster, and that these changes determine the altered character of the functions when they are renewed. What the nature of these changes is, nobody seems to know. The microscope reveals no difference in the appearance of the brain cells before and after learning has taken place. The evidence in favor of the view is found chiefly in the loss of the effects of learning through damage to brain tissue, and deductions from the generally accepted principle that the central nervous system governs the functional effects of stimulation.

Glands. Mention should be made of the glands, though their connection with learning is probably less direct than that of the neuromuscular system. The glands are classed with the muscles as *effectors*. Their activity is governed by the autonomic nervous system. Under stimulation they secrete certain fluids that stimulate and sustain the vital processes of the body. The secretions of the *duct glands* pass through little tubes, or ducts, and are discharged into internal chambers of the body, such as the mouth or stomach, or on the outer surface of the body. Examples of duct glands are the sweat glands, which help to maintain uniformity of bodily temperature, and the salivary glands, which assist in the digestive processes.

The *endocrine,* or *ductless, glands* make up an intricate and integrated system of regulators of the bodily functions. Under stimulation they secrete powerful hormones which are discharged directly into the blood stream. These hormones promote growth, physical vigor, energetic action, and mental alertness. Because the normal action of the glands is essential to the full effectiveness of the psychological functions, glandular dysfunction or imbalance may produce states highly detrimental to learning.

Energy. Any activity requires and uses energy. This is as true for the so-called "mental activities" as for physical activity. The body furnishes the energy as well as the mechanism for the learning activities. Serious loss of physical energy means a loss in the ability to learn.

For a more complete description of the bodily mechanisms of action and reaction and how they operate in support of the psychological functions, the reader is referred to chapters on the nervous system and sense organs in textbooks on general psychology or physiology. The aim of this short section on the bodily basis of learning has been to emphasize the fact that learning is dependent upon the normal functioning of the somatic systems. This means that an intact and healthy body is essential for the best results in learning.

Although it is generally assumed that physical defects tend to retard school progress, definite evidence in substantiation of this view is difficult to find. It appears that some defects do not interfere with school progress while others seem to be serious handicaps. Apparently the retarding influence of defects depends upon several factors, such as their nature, number, severity, and the attitude the pupil takes toward them. In many cases the effect on schoolwork is indirect, as when a defect produces a sense of inferiority or leads to habits of dependence upon others or to the practice of using it as a means of escape from responsibility.

The estimates of the prevalence of defects made by investigators vary widely, probably due to different methods of examination and to differences in views regarding what types and degrees of deviation from perfection are to be considered defects. Several studies have indicated that between 50 and 75 per cent of the children in our schools are the victims of some kind of physical defect. The need for thorough physical examinations and remedial measures is evident.

One of the best objective studies of the relation of physical defects to school achievement was made by Mallory (1922). His findings, based on standard achievement tests and physical examinations, led to the conclusion that physical defects contribute to retardation and that some defects, particularly of hearing and vision, are greater handicaps to progress than others.

Defects of vision. The eyes are used so constantly in school learning that any serious impairment of vision is certain to prove a handicap to the pupil. This handicap cannot be adequately measured in terms of actual retardation because many pupils may compensate for it by extra effort, although in so doing they suffer added strain, discomfort, and fatigue. Visual defects appear in many forms and in varying degrees. Estimates of their prevalence in the school population vary from around 10 or 12 per cent to about 25 per cent, no doubt depending upon what degree of deviation from perfect vision the examiner considers a defect and upon the thoroughness of the examining procedures.

When an exacting definition of visual defect is used, few people are found completely free of defect. Dalton (1943) made a survey of the vision of more than 5000 public elementary and high school children using the Keystone Telebinocular, a refined diagnostic instrument. Less than 20 per cent of the pupils passed all the tests given. When the relationship betwen normal and defective vision was compared with reading ability and academic achievement, no significant difference was found. The probable explanation for this result is that all kinds of visual defects do not have a like effect upon learning and that in minor degrees, visual defects may not impede learning.

Errors of refraction. Among the more common forms of visual defect are the errors of refraction, characterized by faulty focusing of the light upon the retina. In myopia, or nearsightedness, the rays of light entering the eye focus before they reach the retina. Near vision is less likely than far vision to be impaired by a myopic condition. Thus, the myopic pupil may be able to see fairly well by holding his book or other objects very close to his eyes. He is likely, however, to be unable to see things on the blackboard. Myopia is rarely found in young children, but it appears more frequently in the middle and upper grades. Hypermetropia, or farsightedness, is a condition in which the distance from the lens to the retina is too short for a clear retinal image, or in which the refractive power of the lense is insufficient. This means blurred vision. Hypermetropia is common among young children and appears less frequently in the upper grades and high school.

In astigmatism the curvature of the lens or cornea of the eye is irregular; this causes uneven focusing of the light on the retina. The child who has astigmatism sees more clearly in one meridian of his visual field than in others. Astigmatism may be either myopic or hypermetropic. The latter is by far the more common among school children.

Muscular deviations. For clear vision there must be sufficient co-ordination of the eyes to bring about convergence of the lines of vision on the object to be seen. This convergence is controlled by muscles external to the eyeballs. In a study of 350 poor readers, Eames (1938) found incoördination difficulties at the reading distance in about one half the cases. This defect was marked in more than a fourth of all the cases. For distant vision, deficient coördination was found in about one tenth of the poor readers. Many persons suffer from slight incoördination of the eyes without noticeable effects, though there may be impairment of their binocular vision and strain occasioned by the effort to secure clear vision. In serious cases there may be inability to fuse the images from the two eyes into single vision. This may lead to the suppression of one and the eventual loss of sight in one of the eyes.

Aniseikonia. The condition known as *aniseikonia* is one in which the "ocular images" are unequal in shape, in size, or in both shape and size. It is believed by those who have studied this defect exten- sively that many persons who have such symptoms as headaches, dizziness, or nervousness associated with the use of their eyes and who do not exhibit the ordinary ocular defects may have aniseikonia. It has been found to have a significant relation to reading disability (Dearborn, 1938) and anomalies of visual space perception.

In a typical elementary classroom, one can expect to find three to four children in need of special attention because of visual disabili- ties—visual acuity between 20/40 and 20/70. An equal number are likely to have minor disabilities which can impair efficiency of learning.

Visual defects and learning. Blindness restricts the person's ability to get about in his environment, directly restricting the range and variety of experiences obtained as well as reducing the ability to manipulate and control objects and events in the environment and the self in relation to it. The difficulties imposed are of two kinds, first, limitations in opportunity for normal development and second, frustration, particularly in social relationships which produce a preference in the blind for retreating from reality. It is a reasonable, though unprovable, assumption that such experiences would have a retarding effect upon intellectual development. It is a fact as Hayes (1938, 1941) has reported that when tested on intelligence and achievement tests adapted for use with the blind, a smaller portion of blind children are of average and superior intelligence than the general population, and that a greater proportion of intellectually retarded children is found. Young blind children were on a par or superior to sighted children in information on language, literature, and social sciences, but inferior in nature study. With advancing years in school, the sighted children surpass the blind, the latter dropping two grades below in general achievement. Undoubtedly, the educational programs for the blind are not as adequate in all instances as for the sighted. Even more difficult is the task of building reading skill in Braille and providing Braille materials for reading. Teaching Braille to children is like teaching shorthand in the elementary school, but it is more difficult than shorthand, for Braille must be written from right to left in the way words would appear if a book were held up to a mirror and the image copied.

Many studies have indicated the relation of defective eyesight to poor reading. In the study of 350 poor readers by Eames, mentioned above, about one third had defective vision when both eyes were used. About two thirds of the right eyes, and three fourths of the left eyes exhibited defective vision. This writer states that incoördination of the eyes is the defect most frequently encountered among poor readers and that this factor appears much more frequently among pupils with reading difficulties than among unselected controls. He writes, "It results in the early onset of fatigue, insufficiency of convergence in reading, impaired fusion, irritability, and inattention." Other conditions which Eames finds related to poor reading ability are: farsightedness, anomalies of eyedness, and low fusions of the images from the two eyes. He finds very few astigmatic reading cases, and nearsightedness is reported as an "infrequent offender" with respect to reading. He suggests that a low degree of myopia may even favor reading, as the child will need to exert less than the usual amount of effort to secure adequate accommodation for near vision (1935).

These findings are in substantial agreement with those of Farris (1936) who found that hypermetropia and muscular deviations were associated with poor reading progress but that myopia and myopic astigmatism were associated with better than average progress. Correction lenses aided achievement in the cases of those defects associated with poor reading. Imus (1936) reports from a study of 100 first-grade children by the Dartmouth Eye Institute that approximately 25 per cent had defective vision to a degree that warranted corrective measures and that some of these cases were probably handicapped in reading by their defects. Schwartz (1940) reports improvement in 71 per cent of the cases of poor readers after correction was made for ocular defects. In a study of fifty unselected cases of reading failure Eames (1943) found that 80 per cent had visual trouble of some kind. These were given glasses or treatment. Half of them, those with IQ's below 90, did not gain any more in reading during the year following treatment than they did the year before. But the 40 per cent who had eye trouble and whose IQ's were above 90 gained thirteen months in reading age during the ten months following correction or treatment as against a gain of seven months for the year before treatment. Twenty per cent of the total group of reading failures had no eye trouble. It is recognized that poor reading may be due to several conditions other than defective vision; but that such defects often are the primary cause of reading disability seems clear (Durrell, 1940; Gray, 1936), and the need for professional examination and ocular therapeutics is definitely indicated.

Teachers should understand that glasses do not always free a child from visual handicaps. Of such cases Eames writes:

When a child has low vision which is only partially improved by glasses or which cannot be improved at all, the teacher should not expect the pupil to compete with normally seeing children. He should be given a seat in a good light, be given frequent rest periods, be permitted to look out of the window whenever he wants to (because looking out of the window rests the focusing muscles), and be provided with textbooks having large, boldface type. He should be allowed to use a heavy, soft pencil and to write script large enough for him to see clearly. If vision is markedly low, placement in a sight-saving class should be considered.

Sato (1937) compared the achievement of 3300 nearsighted, normal, and farsighted children in Tokyo elementary and secondary schools. Markedly near-sighted pupils without glasses showed lower perform- ance on the whole, while few poor students had normal vision. Far- sighted students were inadequate in subjects in which use of text- books was greatest, e.g., language and history. In physics and algebra, where less dependence is placed upon texts, the achievement of the farsighted approximated that of the normals, as it did in such sub- jects as drawing and gymnastics.

Hearing defects and learning. Although there is no sharp line of demarcation between the hard-of-hearing and the deaf, the latter are those children who are unable to acquire language because of inability to hear and whose hearing is of no practical value in com- municating with others. These individuals may range from the totally deaf to those with considerable sound perception, but in all cases their hearing is of little practical value in the ordinary affairs of life. Those who fall between this range and normal hearing con- stitute the "hard-of-hearing," children whose hearing, though de- fective, is functional. Deaf children are classified into those who are congenitally deaf and those who are adventitiously deaf — as the result of events occurring after birth, such as injury or illness.

Hearing disability presents an even greater handicap than visual defects, for sound is basic to language and language is basic to learn- ing. A child who cannot hear directions cannot act intelligently. Estimates of the intelligence of deaf children vary acording to the type of test used as a measure. In general, the intelligence of deaf children is lower than that of normal children, and there does not appear to be a difference between those congenitally and adventi- tiously deaf. The deaf appear to be approximately two years re- tarded intellectually by age 10-11. Pintner (1941) reports the IQ of deaf children to be in the mid 80's in a 1928 study of the National Research Council, thus corroborating a more recent survey of Eng- lish children by Hood (1949) who found one-third of the deaf children fell below IQ 85 compared with only one-fifth of normal children. This retardation is most noticeable with respect to abstract intelligence and verbal comprehension; for non-verbal performance scales, deaf children apparently perform as well as normal children (Hood, 1949; Springer, 1938; Oleron, 1950).

Similar findings are reported by Pinter and Lev with respect to the hard-of-hearing school child. Comparing verbal intelligence test scores of 1556 normal hearing children with 1404 hard-of-hearing, the mean IQ of the former was 100.6, the latter's 94.7. For marked hearing defects, the mean IQ was 92.4. On a non-language intelligence test, the mean IQ of 372 normally hearing was 102.2 compared to 99.3 for 315 hard-of-hearing children, a difference that was not statistically significant.

The progressive mental retardation noted with respect to intellectual development is paralleled in the academic achievement of the deaf and hard-of-hearing children. Heider (1940) reports a 1.5 year retardation in educational achievement at 10 years of age progressing to a 6-year retardation by 18 years of age in an analysis of achievement test results obtained over an 8 year period at the Clarke School for the deaf. The accelerated retardation in achievement is probably associated with the fact that the subjects of the study were institutionalized children who tend to show greater retardation than those living outside of institutions. This is confirmed by two studies which, though showing educational retardation among hard-of-hearing children, indicate a lesser degree of severity with what is also undoubtedly a more representative sample of hard-of-hearing children. Sprunt and Finger (1949) screened 692 pupils in grades 3-7, retested those showing marked hearing loss, and then compared a sample of 28 children with deficient hearing with a matched sample of 28 normally hearing children on a non-verbal intelligence test and on educational achievement. The children with hearing deficiency showed a half-year retardation in academic achievement but no difference in non-verbal test score. In a survey of 1000 children representative of Toronto children in grades 5-8, Conway (1937) found 8% hard-of-hearing in one ear, 2.7% in both ears. Where the hearing loss was greater than 20 decibels the retardation in school was between 10-15%. A survey of the elementary school pupils of New York City indicated that 3.17 per cent of all the children had impaired hearing in both ears, and approximately 42 percent of the hard-of-hearing children were retarded one year or more (Caplin, 1937). That poor hearing is a handicap to achievement under ordinary classroom procedures can scarcely be doubted, particularly if the deficiency is severe enough to cause a child to fail to hear much of what is said. Adequate hearing tests should be given to all children in order to discover those whose hearing is deficient. When cases of defective hearing are found, the necessary treatment should be secured not only for the sake of better schoolwork, but also to prevent the development of serious deafness. Diseased conditions of the nasal passages and the throat, which tend to block the Eustachian tubes, are credited with being the most prolific sources of impaired hearing. These include diseased and enlarged tonsils and adenoids, and chronic catarrh. Scarlet fever and measles frequently cause inflammations of the middle ear. Aching or discharging ears are indications of trouble and should receive prompt attention. Too frequently, children who have defective hearing are treated as stupid or annoyingly inattentive.

Other handicaps. Cerebral palsy, spastic paralysis, cardiac problems, poliomyelitis, osteomyelitis, bone tuberculosis, and epilepsy handicap a much smaller percentage of children than do visual and hearing defects. Zintz (1951) found that approximately 1 child in 200 had a serious physical handicap in a statewide survey of 11,142 pupils at the 6th to 8th grade levels in Iowa. Not only were the handicapped children retarded 4, 6, and 10 months respectively at the 6th, 7th, and 8th grades, but those having multiple handicaps showed greater retardation. Handicapped children showed a significantly greater degree of withdrawing behavior. The educational achievement of these pupils was similar to a group of 835 crippled children in a special orthopedic school; these children progressed about .8 of a grade per year. This group (Lee, 1943) included some children with non-orthopedic difficulties (teeth, tonsils, vision, nutrition, speech) as well. Each child averaged two non-orthopedic defects in addition to the orthopedic difficulty. Frequently the assumption is made that a regular academic program can be followed equally well by orthopedically handicapped children, provided that physical and speech therapy is included. When one considers that the mean IQ of crippled children has been placed between 82 and 87 (Lee, 1931; Fouracre, 1950), that the orthopedically handicapped tend to be over-age for grade (Fouracre, 1950) with an average educational retardation in the elementary school of 10 months, and that a consistently higher percentage of below average intelligence is found than with normal children, it is questionable if the typical academic curriculum is adequate for these children. The problems become even more acute at high school level when problems of vocational choice and non-dependence must be faced.

MOTIVATION

As important as capacity in the learning process is motivation, the combination of events which serve to activate the child and regulate his behavior in connection with goals. Teachers as a group, when asked to designate topics connected with learning which they wish to study, invariably rank motivation and discipline high in importance. Motivation is recognized as important because without it, learning progresses slowly; discipline is important to teachers because it represents behavior motivated towards goals other than those which the teacher has selected or designated or deemed proper. A common fallacy which teachers express is their desire "to motivate" students to learn, thus confessing failure to recognize that children *are* motivated. They are exceedingly active, curious, and enthusiastic, all of which indicates motives in operation, but the motives may have no affinity for the arithmetic lesson or the chemistry experiment or whatever the item on the daily schedule of the teacher. Furthermore, the desire "to motivate" implies as often a desire to regulate behavior—to be able to turn it on or off as the teacher desires. Each person's and child's motives are intrinsically his own, useful if they can be tapped, malleable if guided, but resistant if thwarted.

Although the motives of mice and men are recognized as important by learned and laymen alike, it is difficult to find experimental studies on the human level in which motivation is directly related to learning. Most direct studies of motivation have been done with various sub-human species because it is possible to control the propagation, feeding schedules, cage experience and the like with animals; this cannot be done with humans. A still greater difficulty lies in attempting to isolate a single motive on a human level. One man's desire for dominance may be satisfied by being a professor, another's by operating a bulldozer, a third's by simulating a heart attack when threatened. The very pervasiveness of motives makes it difficult to delimit them in ways which satisfy rigorous experimental design. The same behavior in different persons may derive from entirely different motives. Caring and fondness for animals may be a substitution for childlessness in one, an escape from inadequacy in social relationships for a second, and a directly satisfying vocational interest in a third. A review of several typical experiments concerned with motivation on the human level will quickly illustrate the complexity of the problem and make clear why so much of our discussion must depend upon sources other than these experiments, such as clinical psychology, observation of child behavior, and inference from animal experiments.

Illustrative of several early experiments on motivation concerning the influence of incentives such as praise and blame, reward and punishment, and success and failure upon school work was Hurlock's (1925) study of praise and reproof. One hundred and six fourth and sixth grade children of both sexes were divided into four matched groups on the basis of intelligence test and arithmetic skill. A 15-minute daily practice period in addition was given to the groups for 5 consecutive days and progress recorded. One of the four groups served as the control group and recéived its tests separately without comment as to performance. The remaining three had their tests together but under different incentive conditions. Irrespective of score obtained, each of the three remaining groups received consistent praise, reproof, or was ignored. The children in the praised group were called by name and told of their excellent results and encouraged to improve. The reproved group was called out and criticized for poor work, careless mistakes, and lack of improvement. The ignored group received no recognition, merely heard what occurred to the other two groups. Figure 5.2 provides a diagram of the results. The praised group showed the greatest gain, with the reproved group second. The ignored group improved only slightly more than the control group. The praised group was the only one to make consistent gains. When the results were compared for other individual differences, it was observed that girls in the praised group showed greater gains than boys, but the reverse was true in the reproof group. The less capable pupils made the greater gains. Superior pupils were more affected by reproof. These latter results were confirmed by later studies by Forlano (1936). He showed that the effects of given incentives were related to personality differences as well; shy and inadequate pupils, for instance, respond more favorably to praise than criticism.

An entirely different type of study of motivation has been that involving the reactions of subjects of different ages to frustration.

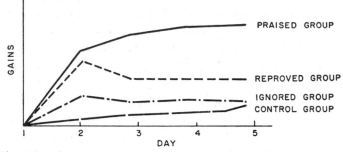

Fig. 5.2. Schematic diagram of gains made in addition by 4th
and 6th grade pupils under different incentive conditions
(after Hurlock, 1925).

Zeigarnik (1938) tested the effect of interruption during the performance of a task in which a person was engrossed in his memory for
the task. Students of different ages were given a variety of tasks to
perform, such as solving puzzles and matching blocks to given designs. On half of the tasks the subject was interrupted. After the
series of tasks were completed and put away, the subject was asked
to recall the tasks upon which he had worked. A higher percentage
of the interrupted tasks were recalled than of the completed tasks.
The important practical consideration here is not that the teacher
should interrupt children to improve their memory, but rather that
the importance of the desire to carry work through to completion
when one is engrossed (ego-involved or strongly goal-directed) be
recognized. Zeigarnik found that the presence of certain conditions
prevented the occurrence of what has come to be known as the
Zeigarnik effect. As might be expected, fatigue prevented it, time
dissipated it, and emotional disturbance disrupted it. Interrupted
tasks which were too difficult tended to be forgotten, giving confirmation to the level of aspiration studies to be discussed later
which show that a task has to be seen as offering some likelihood for
success if subjects are to become involved with it. The satisfaction
or dissatisfaction of the subject with the solution, irrespective of
what the experimenter thought, influenced its retention in memory.
And if a single task were seen as endless, or if all the tasks were seen
as part of a whole rather than as separate tasks, the effects of interruption were lost. There is significance in the fact that the subjects
tended to remember what appeared to them to be their failures or
their not attaining a successful completion. In view of the reluctance

of children to generally persist with eagerness in a task at which they appear to be failing, and in view of the high frequency with which attention is called to errors during the course of the school day, it would appear wise to minimize this effect by making subtasks the parts of a whole having a definite terminal point at which success can be experienced.

In a different vein, Barker, Dembo, and Lewin (1941) have measured the effects of frustration upon pre-school children by first involving them in a play situation in which they rated the child's "constructiveness of play"—the ability to integrate a few toys into an imaginary play situation of his own creation. For instance, a child was brought into a room in which several sets of toys were available, one set consisting of a cup and saucer, a toy iron, a doll, and a toy car. The child was allowed to play with the toys and was rated as to the complexity of the play situation he created. Then a screen was lifted which revealed a much more desirable play environment. There was, for instance, a doll house with doll clothes and an ironing board, table and chairs with teapot and silverware with which the child could play, using his previous set of toys much more enjoyably. After permitting the child sufficient time to become deeply involved in the new situation—about 5-15 minutes—the child was removed from the scene and returned to the other side of the room with his original sets of toys. A wire barrier was interposed between the child and the doll-house which permitted him to view it but prevented access to it. The effect of this frustration upon the child's behavior was observed. One effect was a regression in constructiveness of play. Approximately 5 out of 6 children regressed to a type of play that was typical of a younger age level, with the regression amounting to approximately 18 months on the average. A second effect was the occurrence of a variety of behavior symptomatic of frustration: attacking the barrier directly or the experimenter verbally, crying, thumbsucking, whining, etc. Another study involving experimental frustration with adolescent subjects involved 196 naval radar operator trainees during the performance of test situations involving rapid discrimination (Allee, et al., 1951). After an initial period of performance in which each operator set his own rate without interference, the tasks were continued but with an interruption at the end of each half-minute, when it was indicated to the subjects that they were failing to meet standards of performance.

When performance under pressure which was derogatory was compared to normal performance, it was found that two patterns of response occurred: the majority speeded up their performance at the expense of accuracy while a minority showed stable performance, and under speeded conditions the group as a whole showed greater variability of performance.

It is readily seen that none of these studies make any attempt to specify what given motivation is operating in the experiment, nor do they indicate in what way the experimentally produced frustration is affecting the subjects so as to produce the observed changes in behavior. It may be said that the subjects were motivated, and that when motivated, given changes in behavior occurred upon exposure to frustrating external events.

A restriction in the particular motivational variables in action has been achieved in two studies involving college students described as anxious. Both studies involved experimental groups designated as "high-anxiety" and "low-anxiety" on the basis of scores on the Minnesota Multiphasic Personality Inventory. The first by Hilgard, Jones, and Kaplan (1951) involved the conditioned discrimination eyelid response. During the first period, the conditioned eyelid response was established to an increase in illumination in one of two windows, and was based on an unconditioned eyelid response to a puff of air. This simple conditioning was established for both the "high-anxiety" and the "low-anxiety" groups. During the second period a discriminatory conditioning was established by following the illumination of one window with an air puff, but never when the illumination occurred in the other window. A significant positive correlation was obtained between anxiety and the ratio of negative to positive conditioned responses, and between anxiety and frequency of negative responses; this supported the authors' hypothesis that anxious students could not learn the discrimination as well as less anxious ones, possibly being more prone to perceive neutral stimuli in the environment as threatening.

It cannot be inferred that anxiety will operate in all situations to impede learning. In a more complexly designed study, Deese, Lazarus, and Keenan (1953) established a control and two experimental groups, each including 15 anxious and 15 non-anxious students. The task was learning 12 consonant nonsense syllables. One group was given an electric shock for wrong responses and were told they could avoid the shock through correct responses, while the second experimental group was shocked at random. The third group was informed that they were a control group. In all groups, the anxious students scored higher than the non-anxious, and the difference between them was greatest in the shocked-wrong response group. It is evident that in the Hilgard experiment the anxiety impeded learning, while in the Deese experiment it had the opposite effect of facilitating learning; in both situations it apparently was working to avoid what appeared as threatening. These two experiments represent investigations of the relationship between a single drive, as anxiety is in some ways considered, and the learning of given responses.

In a more recent study, which in sequence with the foregoing experiments shows consistent development in research design, Wendt (1955) administered a modified Thematic Apperception Test—or picture-story test—in which the stories created in response to pictures are scored according to the strength of the need to achieve, and a Critical-Flicker-Fusion test which indicates the frequency at which a flickering light fuses for a subject and provides a measure of attention or effort. The subjects were high-school students. The results showed that the higher the need for achievement, the better the output and quality of performance on arithmetic tasks, the better the ability to work under unscheduled conditions, and the less tendency to fatigue or boredom. This conclusion may seem to be a confirmation of the obvious to the reader, but its value lies in the potentiality of the measures of motivation utilized.

As interesting as these studies may be, they fall far short of explaining what we know or guess about man's unique and oftentimes bizarre motivation. Consider a few examples: the college student attends a college to further his education but as often as not can't decide about education on or for what. He avoids eight-o'clock classes like a plague, in fact avoids as many classes as possible, preferring contract-bridge, coffee, and chit-chat in the "commons" to study. He will join a fraternity not because the accommodations are any more comfortable or less expensive but for status, subjecting himself voluntarily to a variety of indignities during "hell-week." Just prior to examinations he will voluntarily work day and night long after all other higher and lower forms of life have retired to rest (with the exception of rats, bats, and burglars), smoking and drinking coffee endlessly to stay awake in order to cram sufficient information into his memory to pass an examination which will be forgotten within a fortnight—unless failed. Or take man en masse. He lives in cities and commutes to factories in the suburbs. He lives in the suburbs and commutes to offices in the city. He grows more food than he needs, then stores it in bins while other men starve. He spends half or more of his wealth building armaments to destroy other men's wealth, fearful all the time that they will destroy his own. He reduces death-rate and increases birth rate and ignores over-population. He writes symphonic and folk-music for his pleasure, invents tools and machines to make work easier, then fears being made idle by his inventions. He dies from heart attacks from over-work and by dysentery from under-sanitation, yet permits both to continue. He employs psychologists and psychiatrists to study himself, but is unimpressed by their findings. In short, man is a unique and oftentimes strange creature, for with all his bizarre behavior he accepts himself as normal. And the explanation of his behavior lies in the origin and development of the socially sanctioned behavior systems (the province of the anthropologists and sociologists), in the process of learning by which he adopts these systems, and in the motives he develops and acquires and which push him inexorably along.

Motivation and learning. It is no secret that activity is basic to learning and that motivation is basic to activity. The first step in the diagram is, for example, a baby's crying.

Activity or
varied behavior —————→ Event —————→ Cessation of activity

He then is fed and ceases to cry; or he continues to cry and his diapers are changed, following which he ceases to cry. When asked to account for the change in behavior, one reasons backward from the observed events, saying that something must have caused the activity—some drive which was satisfied by food—for after feeding, the activity came to an end, and so it must have been a food-seeking drive. Or, it didn't come to an end with food, so it wasn't hunger; but it ended with a change in diapers, suggesting an avoidance-of-discomfort drive. The diagram thus appears:

Drive —→ Behavior —→ Goal —————→ Behavior Ceases —→ Drive reduction
Inferred →|←————— *Observed* —————————→|←*Inferred*

The inferred drive in the diagram finds verification in the innumerable animal studies in which the subjects are deprived of food or water for periods of time in order to provide them with sufficient drive to perform countless tasks. But the questioning pushes still farther: what produces the drive, what arouses it? Early studies suggested that stomach contractions were the signal because they became more frequent after specified intervals without food. This explanation was inadequate because the question of what caused the stomach contractions was unanswered. Further research disclosed that tissue changes produced variations in the sugar content, density, and salinity of the bloodstream, and these in turn triggered glandular responses which produced hunger and thirst drives. Thus was born the homeostatic or equilibrium concept of motivation, that needs basic to survival give rise to drives which produce activity with the purpose of satisfying the drive. Responses could be learned (where to find water) to reduce the variation in activity. When satisfied, the drive ceased, and equilibrium was restored. The concept could as easily, but with much less dignity, be called the hungry-dog model. The dog sleeps in the sun until hunger or thirst stirs him; when he is satisfied, he returns to sleep. The model is intriguing in its simplicty, but is too simple for man. He doesn't stop eating when filled, or wait until hungry to begin to eat. Some will eat or drink themselves to death, others will refuse to eat during a hunger-strike until dead. In other words, certain of man's motives will on occasion outweigh the presumed basic motive of survival. Nevertheless, the concept of equilibrium has pervaded explanations of motivation in many areas. A recent article concerning economic psychology by Katona (1954) discusses this point:

> The notion of "saturation" of the market is based on old-fashioned psychological assumptions which in turn rest on the analogy of biological drives: for example, if an animal is hungry, it is motivated to search for food; after it has eaten, the motive disappears or becomes weak. The saturation concept has resulted in dire predictions about the future of the U. S. economy. Some people point to the large proportion of U. S. families that already possess major goods, such as refrigerators (over 80%) or automobiles (about 70%), and they argue that in the future, sales will be limited largely to replacement needs.
>
> But social motives are different from biological ones. Levels of aspiration—in sports, for school grades, for position, for income, and for goods—mostly rise with achievement. A beginner in golf, for instance, may strive hard to achieve a score of 100; when he has achieved his goal, he invariably raises his sights. We give up aspirations when we have failed, not when we have succeeded. . . . .
>
> We translate our needs in demand when we are optimistic, confident, and

secure. We are "saturated," on the other hand, when we are pessimistic, insecure, and especially when our past endeavors have been unsuccessful.

The distinction which Katona[2] makes between biological and social motives is a valid one. Man has biological motives which operate similarly to those of animals, but his behavior is more highly variable and the biological needs are so overlaid with acquired response patterns and motives that the equilibrium concept is an incomplete explanation. McClelland[3] (1953) has aptly pointed out that biological drives do not suffice as an explanation of how animal behavior is directed and controlled; much less do they explain the "extraordinary strength characteristic of learned human motives."[4]

This was dramatically demonstrated in a classical study by Roethlisberger and Dickson (1939) in their Hawthorne studies of the relationship between working conditions and productivity. This is one of the few studies in which every effort possible was made to control factors influencing production. A team of girl telephone-relay assemblers was put at their work in a room in which different aspects of the physical environment could be controlled—humidity, temperature, light, rest periods, etc. The variables were manipulated with the desire of ascertaining the optimal combination of working conditions as far as maximum output was concerned. With each improvement in light or temperature, production increased. The work week of the girls was reduced first from 48 to 44 hours, then from 44 to 40 hours. With each change, production increased. Rest periods and snack periods were introduced. Production increased. It appeared that improving working conditions improved production. But investigation of production records revealed that when one of the group of five girls was absent for a day, production did not fall off as would be expected if output were near the maximum per person. Puzzled by this, the investigators reversed the experimental conditions, eliminating rest periods, lengthening the work period, and

---

[2] G. Katona, "Economic Psychology," *Scientific American*, 1954, 191, p. 35.

Drive and motive are used with different meanings by different authors. One distinction made is between drive as a generalized state of activity and motive as being specifically related to a given goal; a second is between drive used with reference to physiological motivation and motives with reference to personal-social (acquired) motives. In this chapter, the two are used interchangeably. Other terms frequently synonymous are needs, predispositions, and purposes.

[3] D. C. McClelland, J. W. Atkinson, R. A. Clark, and E. L. Lowell. *The Achievement Motive* (New York: Appleton-Century-Crofts, 1953), p. 17.

[4] *Ibid.*

reversing the improvements in illumination and humidity. Production did not fall off as expected; it increased. This began a monumental shift from looking at working conditions and time and motion studies, to looking at workers and their attitudes and motivations. The girls on the relay-assembly team liked the novelty associated with the experiment; it provided an interest and appeal which their work had lacked; they wished it to continue. As the experimenters made their modifications in working conditions, the girls obligingly improved their work. It made little difference to them the direction of the modification. They wanted to continue the project as long as possible. One thing the study did reveal was the intricate nature of motivation and its inevitable relationship to behavior.

As Mowrer[5] points out (1952) it would be convenient if man operated like a temperature thermostat, responding to only two stimuli, hot and cold, with two responses, on and off. However, man not only can make a wide variety of responses to a single stimuli or drive, but he is also capable of separating those acts which work best from those which do not. The basic pattern of motivation is subject to modification by learning in three of its aspects.

Aspects Modified by Learning

Need ——┬—→ Drive ————→ Behavior————→ Goal ————→	Need reduction
Acquisition of drives and direction of behavior	Modification of behavior; selection of appropriate behavior; selection of goals

Under some circumstances the basic tissue needs may be modified, as is found to occur with some drug addictions; in general, however, the modification occurs through the acquisition of drives which direct behavior toward given goals, toward the learning of behavior and habit patterns which work successfully to attain goals, and toward the identification and establishing of selected goals.

Most of the work on acquired drives and rewards has been done with animals and is based mainly on experiments involving fear as an acquired drive and fear-reduction as a reward, and studies using hunger as a basis for learned rewards. If the test of a drive or a reward lies in its ability to produce learning or behavioral changes,

5 O. H. Mowrer, "Motivation," *Annual Review of Psychology*, Calvin Stone, ed. (Stanford, California: Annual Reviews, Inc., 1952), p. 434.

then fear is a strong, acquired drive. Miller (1948) has demonstrated how rats placed in one compartment of a cage and shocked on repeated trials quickly acquired a conditioned fear of the compartment, so that on subsequent trials they showed immediate agitation and fright on being placed in the compartment, even though not subsequently shocked. They had acquired a fear of what were previously neutral cues. The fear drive was sufficiently strong that they learned to operate a wheel to open a door permitting escape into an adjoining compartment. Their learning curve on manipulating the wheel showed steady improvement. Moreover, when the wheel device was blocked, the rats learned a second response of pressing a bar to escape. Some animals operated the device for several hundred trials without need for further shock, so powerful was their acquired fear. Fears play an important role in human behavior, mainly in safeguarding the individual from real danger, but also in protecting him from the discomfort associated with situations perceived as dangerous or threatening. Some persons possess a marked fear of speaking in public. They avoid it if possible, but when unable to do so their behavior prior to the event exhibits many symptoms comparable to our friends, the rats. They become extremely tense, nervous, and emotionally upset. One can't help but wondering if the frequent errors and embarrassment incurred while reciting before classes during many years of school has any relationship to this fear.

The foregoing studies show acquired drives; experiments using hunger and food show the acquisition of learned rewards or goals. Chimpanzees, for instance, have been trained to work for tokens which they could exchange for food, then to perform a variety of tasks in order to obtain the tokens, thus showing that the tokens had acquired reward value. We are all familiar with the lengthy process of training in which humans learn "the value of money." The student will recall from the discussion of Hull's learning theory that he considered reinforcement essential to learning. When behavior results in the attainment of a goal capable of satisfying the drive conditions, drive reduction reinforcing the behavior results. Moreover, Hull and his students believed that secondary reinforcement also occurs and that neutral stimuli associated with the reinforcing state of affairs acquire reinforcement value themselves, as do tokens or money. To illustrate, a child may acquire a drive for affection from a previously acquired secondary drive to be held, fondled, and cuddled; this is based on conditions associated with feeding and the resultant primary drive reduction. The explanation is attractive, but it also contains a paradox: how can the same object be simultaneously drive-increasing and drive-reducing, as money or tokens appear to be, acting as both incentive (spurring drive) and reward (satisfying drive) simultaneously? It is probable that the drive-reduction explanation is overly simple. Possibly in younger children drive-reduction serves to reinforce responses and terminate behavior, but with increasing age humans develop deferred as well as immediate goals, and also aspirations that are relative to the accomplishment of other persons as well.

Our desires may focus on certain objectives, such as college graduation, not only because it is (1) a way station to a particular vocation or to a higher degree, but also (2) because it may satisfy parental aspirations of importance to us, and (3) it simultaneously satisfies a desire to surpass the achievement of a neighbor, cousin, brother or sister. The football team, having scored a third touchdown over an opponent, thus providing a comfortable margin (drive-reducing) may return to the kickoff line saying, "All right, let's get another one!" (drive-stimulating). The problem of developing a theoretical explanation which is consistent and applicable to all situations is difficult.

Mowrer (1952) contends that a distinction must be made between (1) solution learning and (2) sign learning, the former providing the basis by which organisms acquire acts or means which are instrumental in satisfying drives, and the latter being the basis on which they acquire emotions, secondary drives, and meanings. In (1) instrumental learning, an act which contributes to drive-reduction becomes attached to the drive through reinforcement. In (2) sign learning, fears and desires depending upon whether the cue signifies an increase in drive (fear) or a decrease in drive (desire) are acquired.

The pattern of motivation so modified appears as follows:

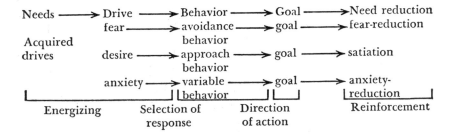

Anxiety has been added as an acquired drive, as distinguished from fear. Although the two are related in that both refer to events which appear dangerous or threaten harm or pain to the individual, fear is commonly considered as being more specific and segmental in nature. We fear dogs, high places, insects, or the like. Anxiety, when allied with fear, is more ambiguous and vague. In more frequent usage, however, particularly in clinical psychology, anxiety refers to a general all-inclusive state of feeling continually apprehensive and threatened.

Earlier it was pointed out that drives are acquired. Responses which are capable of satisfying drives, e.g., reaching rewards or avoiding harm, and given goals or rewards are learned. The process of learning can be shown in our eating habits. A balanced diet is attainable in many forms, but different cultures establish preferences for specific foods and aversions for others. Raw meat, rancid fat, squid, snails, rattlesnake meat, sea urchins, to name but a few, are foods which some peoples relish in contradistinction to the preferences of most people in this country. These preferences have been learned as a result of training experiences. The mode of eating is learned as well – the socially approved manner of holding one's fork or one's chopsticks, or using nothing but hands, of belching politely or not, singing during the meal, etc.; all are learned rituals to be performed as necessary or are corollary acts to obtaining and eating food. Our drives, as well, have been modified and added to as a result of learning. Our preferences for given foods and anxieties about tabooed foods, as well as our seeking of money as a means to food, are all acquired drives.

The diagram also points out the three functions of drives: energizing the organism into activity, directing it toward an appropriate goal, and selecting the responses instrumental in reaching the goal. Some learning theorists (Brown, 1953) hold that the concept of motivation should be restricted to the energizing functions, and believe that the directing and selecting functions can be adequately explained by habit patterns; this again points up the need for extensive research in the relationship of motivation to human behavior. McClelland and his colleagues have provided new impetus by suggesting that the distinction that has long been made between primary (biological) and secondary (social) drives or motives be discarded, and that all motives be handled as learned. They define a motive as

a recall of a change in affect (emotion) by a cue established by association. This view differs from Mowrer's (mentioned above) in
placing the emphasis upon the association of a cue to a change in
emotional state rather than viewing emotions as acquired drives.
According to McClelland (1953), changes in emotional states result
from discrepancies between the adaption level and the expectation
level of the organism. Small discrepancies produce no emotional
reaction, moderate differences produce a positive emotional reaction,
and large discrepancies between adaption level and expectation level
produce negative affect. Negative affect leads to avoidance behavior;
positive affect yields approach behavior. Two quotations from
McClelland[6] will illustrate the hypothesis: "U.S. and Indian populations as groups should show different color preferences according to
the principle that moderate discrepancy from different skin color
adaptation level bases will yield pleasure in colors of different wave
length composition . . . . in India red is the most preferred color and
white the color for mourning, whereas in the United States blue-
green is the most preferred and black is the color of mourning, and
"Johnny may develop expectations as to what a model airplane
or a solved arithmetic problem looks like, but he may be unable to
confirm these expectations at all, or only partially. The result is
negative effect, and cues associated with these activities may be expected to evoke avoidance motives. To develop an achievement approach motive, parents or circumstances must contrive to provide opportunities for mastery which, because they are just beyond the
child's present knowledge, will provide continuing pleasure. If the
opportunities are too limited, boredom should result . . . . if the opportunities are well beyond his capacities, negative effect should result, and he may develop an avoidance motive as far as achievement
is concerned."

The proposals are intriguing, promising for research in human
motivation, and have many implications for educational practice.

Motivation and educational practice. Inasmuch as the problem
of motivation in educational practice will be considered more extensively in chapters 15 and 16, only brief consideration will be
given here.

By the time children reach school, few of their drives are being
satisfied on solely an elementary basis. Already a complex hierarchy

[6] D. C., McClelland, *et al., The Achievement Motive,* (New York: Appleton-Century-
Crofts, 1953), pp. 46, 65.

of goal preferences, response patterns, and approach and avoidance drives, fears, desires, and anxieties will have been established. The tasks which the child meets in school are usually abstract and intangible, and being plagued by constant evaluation of goodness of performance by teacher, parents, and classmates, he can easily establish neutral or negative emotional reactions. More important still is that many of his acquired motives are social in nature: affection, belonging, acceptance, and the like. To be satisfied, these motives involve interaction with other people, particularly teachers. Children's motives can be satisfied only if the motives of the teacher permit and tolerate the motivational and learned behavior pattern the child has established prior to beginning school. The teacher's own motivations — her fears, anxieties, and desires with respect to discipline and control, authority and school, brightness and stupidity, neatness, and cleanliness — must be such that she is capable of satisfying the social motives of children through herself and her arrangements for the class by guiding them in the acquisition of motives that will contribute to a satisfying life.

SUMMARY

Each of the individual variables — maturation, age, sex, previous experience, capacity and motivation — has been considered, and its relationship to the acquisition, retention, and transfer of training of sensori-motor and verbal learning has been reviewed. Most significant are the individual learner's readiness for any learning experience as determined by his maturational level and previous experience, his capacity or potential for development, and the acquired motives which give direction to his energies. All of the individual variables must be considered simultaneously by the teacher in planning learning activities for individual children, for the rate of progress is a product of the interaction of the combination of particular capacities and motivation occurring.

Tests of intelligence, aptitude, and achievement can be valuable to a degree in estimating possible progress. The value of tests will vary with their validity for any single subject, intelligence tests, for instance, being useful predictors of verbal achievement but not of art achievement. Tests must be supplemented by individual observation and judgment in deriving estimates of capacity. Physical defects and impoverished environmental backgrounds contribute to unreliable test scores.

Essential to the learning process is motivation, which energizes the organism, gives direction to activity, and selects the goals deemed valuable. The teacher is concerned not only with utilizing existing motives for educational ends but also with shaping the motives in desirable directions, inasmuch as the results achieved in striving for given goals operate to modify the motives themselves. The end of learning is not only a skill or knowledge but also the acquisition of motives, attitudes, and interests which serve individual, educational, and social needs.

OVERVIEW

Monroe, W. S., *Encyclopedia of Educational Research*. New York: Macmillan Company, 1950, pp. 137-207.

SELECTED REFERENCES

Anastasi, Anne and J. P. Foley, *Differential Psychology*. New York: Macmillan Company, 1950.

Humphreys, L. G. and P. L. Boynton, "Intelligence and Intelligence Testing," *Encyclopedia of Educational Research*, W. S. Monroe, ed. New York: Macmillan Company, 1950, pp. 600-12.

McClelland, D. C. *et al.*, *The Achievement Motive*. New York: Appleton-Century-Crofts, 1953.

Mowrer, O. H., "Motivation," *Annual Review of Psychology*, C. P. Stone, ed. Stanford, Calif.: Annual Reviews, 1952, 3, pp. 419-39.

Munn, N. L., "Learning in Children," *Manual of Child Psychology*, L. Carmichael, ed. New York: John Wiley & Sons, 1954, pp. 374-458.

Wechsler, D., *The Range of Human Capacities*. Baltimore: Williams and Wilkins, 1935.

ORIGINAL INVESTIGATIONS

Barker, R. G., Tamara Dembo, and K. Lewin, "Frustration and Regression: Studies in Topological and Vector Psychology: II," *University of Iowa Studies in Child Welfare*, 1941, 18, No. 1.

Mattson, M. L., "The Relation Between the Complexity of the Habit to be Acquired and the Form of the Learning Curve in Young Children," *Genetic Psychology Monographs*, 1933, 13, pp. 299-398.

Mead, Margaret, *Sex and Temperament in Three Primitive Societies*. New York: William Morrow & Company, Inc., 1935.

Chapter Six

Task Variables

A second important group of variables affecting the course of learning includes those associated with differences in whatever task is to be learned. Tasks vary in length, in difficulty, and in similarity to other tasks. They also differ in their degree of meaningfulness to each individual learner, as well as in their degree of pleasantness or unpleasantness. The major part of the experimental work that has been completed to date on these characteristics of tasks has utilized verbal materials, nonsense syllables, word lists, various kinds of poetry, and prose. A few experiments have been concerned with motor skills.

LENGTH, DIFFICULTY, AND MEANINGFULNESS OF MATERIAL

Length of material. The form of the learning curve is relatively uniform for acquisition of new material of differing lengths. When the total time required to learn verbal tasks of different length is divided into fractions, the per cent learned during given fractions of time is comparable (Robinson and Heron, 1922; Robinson and Darrow, 1924). Some variation occurs in relation to the type of material and the criterion of learning employed, whether memorization of nonsense syllables, verbatim reproduction of word lists or poetry, or learning of the logical meaning of materials.

When the length of the list exceeds the memory span, a noticeable increase in difficulty occurs. Ebbinghaus, for example, was able to recite seven nonsense syllables after one reading, but seventeen readings were required for learning a list of twelve, and thirty readings were necessary to master a sixteen-syllable list. As the number of syllables in the list was increased there was an increase in the number of readings per syllable. Similar results are reported by Lyons (1914). When difficulty is judged in terms of the amount of time required per item, a similar disproportionate increase is usually found. Beyond the region of immediate memory span additional increases in length do not produce disproportionate increases in difficulty. If anything, the longer lists are more readily learned.

The school situation to which the foregoing evidence may be most applicable is learning to spell. The conventions adopted for the spelling of words are in many respects similar to nonsense syllables. The latter make little sense in either form or meaning. Similarly, the spelling of words, though associated with words and meanings comprising part of the child's vocabulary, is inconsistent in many cases with common pronunciation. The rules are of little value because of the numerous exceptions. Consider first the sounds of the following words, then the spelling: "ideeut," "idyut," and "ijut" are common pronunciations of the word spelled *idiot*. "Cooja" and "jeetchet" are spelled *could you* and *did you eat yet*. "Nupshul" and "nupchooal" present no problem to anyone married, but they are strangely spelled: *nuptial* and could as easily be "nuptual." Then consider *bleed, mead,* and *Reid,* and *stead* and *bead*. Different spellings are pronounced alike; identical spellings are pronounced differently. Learning the conventional spelling of words is largely rote memory of forms that are frequently as meaningless as nonsense syllables and is better served by short lists within the memory span, with provision for overlearning to increase retention.

This problem is complicated by other factors besides the magnitude of the lists compared. The increase in difficulty with an increase in the amount of material to be learned is apparently influenced by the kind of material and by the distribution of practice. Lyon's study indicated that during continuous learning at one sitting, the time required for memorizing digits and nonsense syllables increased at a proportionately faster rate than the length of the series; but at one reading per day (distributed learning), the increase in time corresponded roughly to the increase in the series. Henmon (1917) reports that in memorizing poetry, the number of repetitions increased proportionately less than the increase in the number of lines or stanzas. Greater economy for the longer passages was also indicated by the greater saving found for them in relearning after 24 hours. This difference in retention in favor of the longer selection was relatively greater for poetry than for nonsense syllables. For prose, the number of repetitions remained approximately constant for passages of different lengths. Prose passages of 100, 200, and 300 words required an average of 6.1, 7.3, and 7 repetitions respectively.

Cofer (1941) compared the time and trials required to reach mastery of prose passages of different lengths for both verbatim and logical learning. For logical learning, the learner had only to master the essential ideas of the passage. It was found that verbatim learning not only required more time and repetitions than logical learning, but that it was also more affected by increases in the length of the passages. With increases in the amount of material to be learned, difficulty increased at a greater rate for verbatim than for logical learning.

To explain the disproportionate increase in difficulty of learning with an increase in the amount of material to be learned, some writers have suggested that it may be due to the greater fatigue effects and needless repetitions of parts already learned in memorizing the longer lists. The most satisfactory explanation, however, seems to be that in the longer lists there is more interference between the members within the series due to remote associations. This view is in keeping with the findings of better retention for the longer series, because the remote associations drop out or are forgotten more quickly than the associations between adjacent members; hence, they offer less interference at the time of recall than at the time of learning.

Length of task and retention. Are longer lists or longer lessons remembered better than short lists or short lessons? The answer seems to be "Yes," provided the longer material is learned to the same degree. Ebbinghaus learned lists of nonsense syllables of different lengths and computed the saving when the same lists were relearned after 24 hours. The 12-syllable list was relearned with a saving of 35 per cent, the 24-syllable list with a saving of 49 per cent, and the 36-syllable list with a saving of 58 per cent. The greater savings for the longer lists indicate that a relatively larger amount was retained. This may be owing in part to the fact that the longer lists required more readings. The 12 syllables required 17 readings, the 24 syllables required 45 readings, and the 36-syllable list required 56 readings. Thus, each syllable in the longer lists was seen many more times.

These results have been verified in principle by other investigators who have used other materials and other methods. Robinson and Heron (1922) experimented with lists of nonsense syllables, and Robinson and Darrow (1924) with three-place numbers. Their results indicated the tendency toward a greater percentage of retention for the longer lists with both the recall and relearning methods. When controls have been used to prevent overlearning of various units of the longer lists by eliminating them from the series as soon as they are learned, the recall and relearning scores have been found to be approximately the same for lists of differing lengths. This was the finding in an experiment on paired-associates learning where each pair was removed as soon as the subject had responded correctly with its second member three times (Sand, 1939).

That the larger number of presentations in the case of the longer lists is not the full explanation of the higher retention rates found for longer materials is indicated by a study made by Woodworth (1938). To a group of 25 students he read lists of words arranged in pairs at the rate of one pair every six seconds. The subjects were instructed to learn each pair so that when the first one of the pair was presented, they could recall the second. The lists varied in length, containing 5, 10, 20, and 30 word-pairs respectively.

The prompting method was used, and each list was read three times. A recall test of retention was given two days later. For immediate recall, the percentages were higher for the shorter lists, but after two days the percentages of the various lists recalled were as follows: 5-pair list, 4 per cent; 10-pair list, 16 per cent; 20-pair list, 36 per cent; 30-pair list, 34 per cent. Thus, retention was higher for the longer lists even though they were presented the same number of times as the shorter ones and the same time was allotted to each word-pair in all of the lists. The fact, however, that the 30-word list fell short of the 20-word list suggests that there is probably a limit beyond which the returns begin to decrease. Woodworth suggests that in the harder tasks, the subjects were stimulated to a greater degree to find meaningful relations between the paired words.

Position in a series. It is well known that the first of a series of experiences is likely to have high memory value. As a rule, we easily recall our first day of teaching, our first visit to a particular city, and our first airplane ride after we have forgotten later ones. In memorizing, the beginning and the end of a series are usually learned before the middle part.

In an experiment, three series of fifteen items were presented once to a group of 68 students. The first series consisted of nonsense syllables; the second, of unrelated words; the third, of related words. The number of correct reproductions for each item in the three series is shown in the following table:

Serial position of item:	1	2	3	4	5	6	7	8	9	10	11	12	13	14	15
Nonsense syllables	56	35	24	22	24	8	12	9	6	3	7	3	18	26	51
Unrelated words	65	68	45	37	58	18	44	32	36	15	46	31	49	49	58
Related words	66	68	67	54	67	58	59	58	58	56	52	52	62	52	62

It will be noted that the first and the last nonsense syllables were reproduced with far greater frequency than the others in the series. A similar trend is found in the two meaningful series, although to a lesser degree.

It is probable that the effect of primacy and finality varies for different learning and testing methods (Raffel, 1936). Where the learner can glance back or review the early items during the presentation of the series, the added frequency for these items might account in part for the primacy effects. There is for the first item in most experimental situations an expectant attitude and alert attention, which is conducive to a good impression, while later items suffer from the interference occasioned by the crowding or piling up of impressions. Novelty, zest, and freedom from interference by preceding impressions favor first impressions, and lack of interference by succeeding impressions favors the final impressions.

Difficulty of material and learning. Krueger's data (1946) reproduced in Figure 6.1 shows the learning curves for eight series of nonsense syllables of increasing difficulty, both qualitative and quantitative. The student may question the relevance of experiments dealing with nonsense syllables to human learning, particularly in conjunction with school. Consideration will lead one to the conclusion that many tasks at all grade levels are non sense-making in the respect that the material is novel, abstract, and comparatively foreign to any of the previous experiences the subject has had. Figure 6.1 shows a negatively accelerated acquisition curve for easy material (rapid early gains gradually slowing). Rate of learning is linear for intermediate difficulty and positively accelerated for the

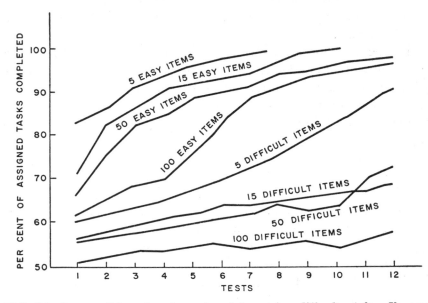

FIG. 6.1. Curves of learning for tasks of increasing difficulty (after Krueger, 1946).

most difficult material. Few comparable studies have been made of the difficulty of school tasks.

Gunborg (1939) checked the difficulty of the arithmetic processes of addition, multiplication, subtraction, and division when appearing in combinations of two processes in a single problem. He attempted to answer the questions of what effect being the first or second step in a problem had upon each process, and what effect being combined with the other three processes had upon difficulty. For instance in this problem: Alice picked 13 quarts of cherries. Her sister picked six times as many. How many quarts did they both pick together? Multiplication is combined with and precedes addition. The problems were graded to a sixth grade level of difficulty and administered to 3831 pupils. Addition and multiplication were easier when the first step in a problem, and division and subtraction when the second step. For all processes in the first position, the order of increasing difficulty was addition, multiplication, subtraction, and division; in the second position, the order was subtraction, addition, division, and multiplication. This held true for all levels of ability. Whether these results are inherent in the processes or are an outgrowth of the method of teaching is not clear, although the number of children involved in the study, taken from six states, would indicate that a wide range of procedures were probably represented in the sample. It has been shown with reading material that the frequency of difficult words is related to progress of reading with primary grade children. When the portion of difficult words exceeds 20 per cent, the task of reading becomes too difficult and progress is retarded, probably as a result of reduction in motivation as well as difficulty in comprehension. Between 5 per cent and 20 per cent of difficult words in the reading material appears to be optimal as far as learning of reading is concerned.

Hildreth (1941) emphasizes that children and adults attempt to simplify a problem which is too difficult for them or beyond their comprehension by reducing it to a level at which it is coherent; in the process however, they produce errors or distortions which are not chance errors but the product of attempting to give meaning to the problem, and as such are clues to the mental processes of the individual. In reading, a child attempting to make sense out of the visual and auditory symbols may perceive them incorrectly. Observational study of the responses and substitutions provides useful analytic material for evaluating mental development, understanding thought processes, and diagnosing learning problems.

The learning curves for motor skills are similar to that shown in

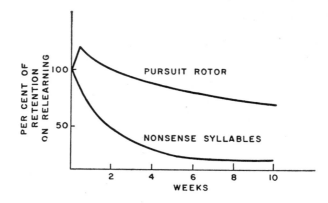

Fig. 6.2 Comparison of retention of motor (pursuit
    rotor) and verbal learning (nonsense syllables).
    After Leavitt-Schlosberg, 1944.

Figure 6.1 for verbal materials, judging from a compilation of studies
by Davis (1935). A more rapid initial rise occurs in simple motor
tasks than in complex tasks, with fluctuations and plateaus more frequent in the latter. Retention curves for motor skills have typically
shown less forgetting than occurs with verbal material, as Figure 6.2
illustrates. Most adults would estimate that their performance in the
Sunday picnic baseball game is better after a lapse of several years
without practice than their recollection of historical events, although
performance at the picnic table probably surpasses both in speed and
dexterity. An ingeniously designed study by Van Dusen and Schlos-

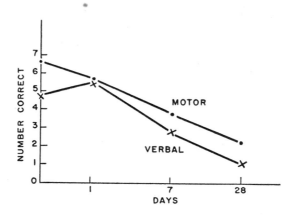

Fig. 6.3. Retention of verbal and motor learning
    after equal practice (after Van Dusen and
    Schlosberg, 1948).

berg (1948) which controlled the differential practice effect, produced the highly similar curves shown in Fig. 6.3. Two sets of switches were labelled with nonsense syllables. Subjects were then given paired association learning tasks that involved the simultaneous learning of pairs of switches and pairs of nonsense syllables. Retention was similar for both, suggesting that the usual greater retention of motor skills over a period of time is probably a function of overlearning and degree of organization and integration within the task.

The transfer effects of complex versus simple motor skills were investigated by Jones (1952) in a study involving a complex and simple two-hand coordination tracking task. Four groups of 41 men learned one of the four possible combinations of the complex and simple tasks (simple-simple, simple-complex, complex-simple, complex-complex). Data showed that the transfer of training from the complex to the simple task was as great as the effect of direct practice on the simple task and was greater than the reverse transfer of simple to complex. Direct practice on the complex task gave greater learning than the transfer from simple to complex, suggesting the possibility that with adults it may be more advantageous to tackle the complex skill directly, e.g., one may learn more golf starting on the golf course, than on the driving range. With children, these results would undoubtedly have to be qualified in terms of the restrictions imposed by differences in neuromuscular development.

Meaningfulness of material and learning. The youngster coming to school for the first time has been hearing and speaking and experiencing his native language for some years. Measures of his spontaneous vocabulary indicate a usage of between 2500 and 3000 words by grade one and possibly a total vocabulary five to ten times as great. These are 2500 sound-words, not symbol-words. The process of learning to read requires the recognition and association of arbitrarily chosen symbols with sounds and concepts acquired through previous learning. The task seems eminently simple to anyone who can read. Written words are an inescapable and practically constant part of the environment, more numerous in our daily lives than automobiles. For the illiterate, however, these minutely differing symbols are a meaningless hodge-podge. To give you the impression once again of the confusion that goes with learning to read, a series of shorthand symbols has been printed below. Your task is to learn to read them by associating the symbols with the words al-

ready known to you, so that you can recognize them when you see
them again.

The shorthand sentence reads, "In the primary grades book is the
symbol for a word already very familiar." Now turn to page 217 and
without glancing back at the original, see if you can read the sentence
which appears there. (See footnote 1, page 218 for transcription.) The
only change is that which is typical in first grade readers — the same
symbols are re-arranged in different order.

If you have had the experience of memorizing nonsense syllables,
you can appreciate what it means to children to be required to
memorize material that has no meaning for them. Experimental
evidence clearly indicates the greater ease and facility for memorizing
meaningful as compared with meaningless material. Being meaningful means that there has been some previous experience with the
material and that some associations have been formed with it. In
other words, meaningful material is already learned to some extent.
It was for this reason that Ebbinghaus devised and used nonsense
syllables in his experiments. He wanted to avoid the uncontrolled
variables of previous experience in the interest of more reliable
quantitative measures of associative learning.

The importance of meaning for the formation of new associations
is revealed by comparing the learning of a list of nonsense syllables
and a list of familiar words. In an experiment by the writer, three
lists differing in meaning were presented to 348 students. The first
series consisted of 15 nonsense syllables, the second was a list of 15
three-letter sense words, and the third contained 15 words meaning-
fully related to each other. These items were presented one-by-one
on large cards at the rate of one every two seconds. After a single
reading, reproductions were made in writing. The mean number
of correct reproductions for each of the three series was:

I.   Nonsense syllables 4.47
II. Unrelated words 9.95
III. Logically related words 13.55

In the experiments just cited the series were presented only once; hence, learning was incomplete. The measure of the degree of learning for purposes of comparison was made in terms of the number of members reproduced. Similar differences between meaningful and non-meaningful materials can be demonstrated by the method of complete mastery. Here the subject continues to repeat each series until he can recite it correctly. Learning is measured in terms of the time or the number of repetitions required to reach complete mastery. For the same three lists used in the experiment just described, Guilford (1934) reports the following as the mean number of trials required for complete mastery by 117 subjects:

I.	15 nonsense syllables	20.4	trials
II.	15 unrelated words	8.1	trials
III.	15 related words	3.5	trials

It should be remembered, moreover, that there is a rather wide range of individual differences in the case of all of the measures of learning mentioned here.

There is probably very little learning without meaning. Even in learning nonsense syllables, the learner finds various ways of making meaningful associations, and it is very difficult to avoid doing so. Sometimes these associations, which afford a meaningful grip on the syllables, are found between the members of a series, and often they involve bringing in something from the outside. The learner may observe that *muh* and *kuh* are alike except for the first letter, and that they rhyme; that *kef* was encountered in another series; or that *cug* is the same as *guc* backwards. When one is memorizing lists of unrelated sense words, the words themselves are already meaningful units. The learner therefore does not find it necessary to resort to the devices used to make nonsense syllables take on meaning. The clever learner here builds up meaningful connections between the various words. This integrates the members of the series into larger units, and the more closely they are integrated in learning, the surer will recall run on from one member to the next. One subject, for example, tied together the words *pet, son, cat,* and *box,* by making the sentence, "The *son* put his *pet cat* in the *box.*" A few constructed a story, which tied together in a meaningful unit a large number of the words. Such relations of belonging together greatly facilitate this kind of learning.

In the series of logically related words all the words of the list were names of parts of the human body. They started at the head and proceeded downward to the toes. Here the relations between the words, which had to be devised by the learner for the lists of unrelated words, were ready-made. The effect of these relations on learning is revealed by the consistently larger score for lists of this type. Sometimes in reproducing these lists, the subject inserted a term that was not presented in the learning series because it was associated with some of the presented items in previous experiences. For example, in the list of names of parts of the body the words *hip, wrist,* and *elbow* were not included, but these words were often added to the words reproduced.

The practical importance of the influence of meaning is indicated. No pupil should be asked to memorize something he does not understand or in which he is unable to find meaning. All material should be made as meaningful for the child as possible. Number experiences should precede the learning of the combinations in addition and subtraction. A child should know definitely what words mean before attempting to learn their spelling. Poems should be thoroughly comprehended before one undertakes to learn them verbatim. Dates and names of persons and places should not be memorized as isolated bits of information but should be incorporated into larger units of understanding.

In order to meet these requirements for economy in memorizing, the teacher should seek to widen the child's range of associated experiences. Particularly, the material to be learned should be related to his own needs, welfare, and interests. This may be accomplished in various ways: by discussion, by explanations, and by stories of related events. Questions are useful in bringing the child's former experiences into relation with the new material. Meaningful organization may be promoted by a consideration of likeness and differences, the bearing of one fact upon another, group membership, and the answers to such questions as: Who was involved? When did this incident take place? Where? What were the causes? What were the consequences?

1 Book is a word already familiar in the primary grades. (See page 216.)

Adults are prone to confuse facts and generalizations. For example, the statements that a plucked violin string vibrates, or that the air temperature is 65 degrees, are both facts. In contrast, the statements that sound is caused by a vibrating instrument, or that condensation results from the cooling of air, are more than facts. They are generalizations which can only be sense-making if one understands the hidden meanings and relationships involved. Memorizing of the generalization makes it possible to reproduce it like a record, but does not guarantee any understanding of meaning.

Swenson's (1949) study of the comparative effectiveness of teaching arithmetic to second grade children by the meaning and drill methods substantiates the foregoing views. The experiment involved 332 pupils in fourteen classes, half taught by drill method, half by the meaning method. The one hundred arithmetic facts, $0 + 0$ through $9 + 9$, were divided into three sets. In the groups taught by the generalization methods, the facts which centered around a generalization were presented together and the children were encouraged to discover and formulate their own generalizations, e.g., when you add 0, the other number stays the same; if the numbers are upside down the answer is the same. Practice exercises were given after the generalizations had been achieved to aid understanding. In the drill groups the addition facts were presented as isolated facts, speed of response was emphasized, using fingers was discouraged, errors were corrected immediately, and drills were varied and made interesting. The total length of the experiment was 20 weeks. The fact that the addition facts were presented in three sets permitted not only measures of initial acquisition, but also of retention, interference and transfer of training between sets. In this study the advantage went to the group which learned by the generalization method; the initial learning was greater, and there was greater transfer and less interference between sets. In relation to amount learned, the amount retained was equal for both methods.

RETROACTIVE INHIBITION

The fact that activities of the interval following learning may, and often do, impair retention has been demonstrated by many experiments. This interference with retention by activities, in which a person engages between learning and the test of retention, is known as *retroactive inhibition.* In controlled experiments the activity of the interval is usually some other learning, and it is called the *interpolated* activity.

The usual procedure in the study of retroactive inhibition involves a control group in which the learning is followed by a period of rest. At the end of this period retention is tested, usually by recall or relearning. The *rest* is usually some form of relaxation with perhaps light reading, an interesting game, or physical exercise designed to occupy the subject sufficiently to prevent his reviewing what he has learned. In the experimental group a second learning task is inserted at some point in the interval before retention of the original learning is tested. Since the other conditions are alike for the two series, the differences in retention may be ascribed to the presence of the interpolated activity in the one case and its absence in the other.

The first systematic study of retroactive inhibition was published by Müller and Pilzecker in Germany in 1900. They presented to their subjects lists of pairs of nonsense syllables. The interval between the presentation and the test of retention was occupied either by studying a second series of syllables or by rest. They found that the retention was better when the subjects rested after learning and concluded that the poorer retention of the lists followed by learning a second list was due to retroactive inhibition produced by the specific activity of the interval.

Since this early study, experiments have shown that retroactive inhibition may be deleterious to the retention not only of nonsense syllables but also of prose, poetry, words, and motor skills. Persistent efforts have been made to discover the conditions governing this phenomenon, for the conviction that retroactive inhibition is the main cause of normal forgetting has become general. To know the conditions of retroactive inhibition is to understand better why we forget. In the following paragraphs we shall consider some of these conditions and the experimental findings regarding them.

Similarity. *Materials and operation.* It early became apparent that the amount of retroactive inhibition is related to the degree of similarity between the original learning and the interpolated task. Skaggs (1925) used interpolated activities having different degrees of similarity to the original learning and found that as the similarity increased, the retroactive effect increased. But in some other experiments he found less retroactive inhibition with a high degree of similarity. From his results he concluded that retroactive inhibition tends to increase with increases in similarity up to a certain point and that beyond that point further increases in similarity approaching identity bring a reduction in the amount of inhibition.

Robinson (1927) reached a similar conclusion. He believed that if we begin with an interpolated task identical with the original and make it dissimilar by increasing degrees, there will at first be an increase in retroactive inhibition until a maximum is reached, and beyond this point further increases in dissimilarity will result in decreases in retroactive inhibition. He tested this hypothesis by an experiment in which he used lists of eight consonants for learning material. He regarded the learning of the first four consonants of each list as the original task and the learning of the last four as the interpolated task. The degree of similarity of the two tasks was varied by including in the second half of each list zero, one, two, three, or four consonants that were presented in the first half. Thus, the degree of similarity here was a matter of the number of common elements in the learning material of the two tasks. The results showed an increase in retroactive inhibition with the reduction of similarity or number of common elements. Owing probably to the limitations of his learning materials, there was no indication of a reversal of the trend.

Other experimenters with different methods and materials and with other ways of securing different degrees of similarity have tried to test this hypothesis. Results have varied. It appears that the Skaggs-Robinson hypothesis does not hold for all relations of similarity in that under some experimental conditions a decrease in similarity (percentages of identity) produces a corresponding increase in retroactive inhibition, while under other conditions the amount of retroactive inhibition increases with an increase in similarity (Britt, 1935).

Harden (1929), for example, in an experiment somewhat similar to Robinson's, used a list of four consonants (original learning) followed by four other consonants for the condition of maximum similarity. Here the last four consonants were different, but as units they were of the same class. Decreasing similarity was arranged by replacing one to four consonants in the second half of the list by digits. With four consonants in the first half and four digits in the second half of the list, the maximum degree of dissimilarity was attained. The results showed better recall of the first half of the list when the second half was all digits. This indicated that greater dissimilarity produced less retroactive inhibition.

Gibson and Gibson (1934) had 26 subjects study a list of ten pairs of consonants for two minutes. After a three-minute interval spent on an interpolated task, the subjects were tested for recall of the original material. Five groups were employed, and their interpolated tasks differed in materials, in operation, or in both. The five tasks were: first, learning another list of consonants; second, learning ten pairs of digits; third, canceling paired consonants; fourth, canceling paired digits; fifth, looking at pictures. The recall scores for the groups improved in the order in which the tasks were listed. The conclusion was that similarity between the interpolated task and the original learning in either operation or material produces poorer retention than similarity in neither of these aspects of the tasks.

In an experiment by Buxton and Henry (1939) a study was made of the influence of various interpolated tasks on the gains made in scores on pursuit rotor performance as a result of growth or other processes during the interval of no practice. Four groups were employed. The interpolated tasks were: first, another form of pursuit performance; second, spool packing; third, learning a simple stylus maze with mirror control; and fourth, reading. All four groups showed gains in their pursuit performances after the interval, but their gains differed. On the basis of correlations between the pursuit performances and the performances of the interpolated tasks as an index of similarity, there was some indication that the amount of retroaction varied with the degree of similarity between the two tasks. The smaller gains made by some of the groups were regarded as evidence of the retroactive effect of the interpolated activity.

Meaning. That similarity of meaning as well as of operations and materials is a factor conducive to retroactive inhibition has been shown by McGeoch and McDonald (1931). They used a list of adjectives for the original learning, and then compared the retroactive effects of learning synonyms and antonyms of these words, unrelated adjectives, nonsense syllables, and three-place numbers. The highest retention scores for the original lists were obtained with the numbers, the lowest with the synonyms. The scores with the other materials fell between in the order of their similarity to the original list. When the synonyms were arranged in three groups according to degree of similarity of meaning, it was found that the interpolated list with meanings most similar to the meanings of the words in the original list produced the greatest amount of retroactive inhibition. Similar results were obtained by Johnson (1933), who used lists of nouns for the original learning and synonyms of three different degrees of similarity in meaning for the intervening learning. In a later study, McGeoch and McGeoch (1937) used lists of paired associates and found that there was more loss in retention when the interpolated material was similar to the original list in the first or in both members of the pairs than when it was unrelated or synonymous only in the second members.

Methods of learning. When the materials of the original and interpolated tasks are learned by similar methods, the amount of retroactive inhibition is likely to be greater than when different methods are employed in the two tasks. A demonstration of this fact was made in an experiment by Waters and Peel (1935). Their subjects learned lists serially and by the method of paired-associates. The retroactive effect of the interpolated learning was greater when paired-associates learning was followed by paired-associates learning and when serial learning was followed by serial learning than when one of the forms of learning was followed by the other form.

Degree of learning. *Original task.* Thorough learning of the original material tends to minimize the adverse effects of the interpolated activity on retention. In one of the earlier studies on this problem, Heine (In Britt, 1935) compared the retroactive effect of interpolated activity on the retention of nonsense syllables that methods are employed in the two tasks. A demonstration of this had been repeated a different number of times, and found more inhibition for the lists repeated fewer times.

Later Pyle (1919) had two groups of subjects, A and B, sort decks of 150 cards into 30 compartments numbered to correspond to the numbers on the cards. The subjects practiced for about one hour daily for 30 days. There were two arrangements of the numbering of the compartments. Group A alternated daily from one arrangement to the other. Group B practiced 15 days on the first scheme and then spent 15 days on the second. Group B surpassed A both in gains over initial scores and in the final speed attained. Pyle believed that practice on the second scheme inhibited the learning of the first, and that the inhibiting effect was less for B because the first arrangement was more thoroughly learned at the time practice on the second was undertaken.

The influence of the degree of learning of the original task on retroactive inhibition was clearly demonstrated by McGeoch (1929). Lists of 9 nonsense syllables were presented 6, 11, 16, or 26 times. For the experimental series, the learning was followed by a rest of 30 seconds, and then another list of 9 syllables was presented 11 times. The results indicated a tendency for retroactive inhibition to decrease as the number of repetitions of the original list was increased. The inhibition fell from 108.5 per cent at 6 presentations to 5.3 per cent at 26 presentations.

Interpolated task. Regarding the interpolated activity, it has been found that in the early stages of learning, an increase in the degree to which it is learned increases its retroactive effect, but that when the learning is carried to a high degree of mastery, there is sometimes a decrease in the amount of inhibition caused by it (Melton and Irwin, 1940). McGeoch (1932) obtained results indicating that after the interpolated task is completely mastered, additional repetitions do not increase its retroactive effect. In a study in which the interpolated list was presented 2, 5, 10, or 20 times, retroactive inhibition was found to increase with the increase in the number of repetitions up to the tenth repetition; but for the additional 10 repetitions, when the number was stepped up to 20, there was no further increase in the retroactive effect (Thune and Underwood 1943). The greatest amount of inhibition is believed to occur when the degrees of learning in the two tasks are about equal.

Bunch and McTeer (1932), in a study of human maze learning, used 110 subjects who learned two stylus mazes, one for the original task and the other for the interpolated activity. The experimental condition tested for its effect on retroactive inhibition was the administration of electric shock on the hand for errors. The retroactive effect of learning the second maze on the retention of the first was less than half as great when the original learning took place with punishment for errors as when it was done without shock. Retroactive inhibition was also greatly reduced when the second maze was learned under punishment conditions. Since the administration of shock for errors was conducive to faster learning with fewer errors, it seems likely that these results are related to those considered in the preceding paragraphs. Punishment for errors may reduce retroactive inhibition because it facilitates learning.

Amount of material learned. *Original task.* Some of the earlier studies showed a decrease in susceptibility to retroactive inhibition as the amount of material of the original task was increased. This may have been due not simply to the amount of the material itself but to the fact that the longer lists require a higher degree of learning and are retained better. In a more recent experiment, in which lists of 6, 8, 10, 12, and 15 pairs of nonsense syllables were used, an attempt was made to control the degree of learning by removing each pair as soon as it had been correctly reproduced 3 times. The groups that learned the four longest lists recalled almost identical percentages of these lists. It appeared, therefore, that increases in length from 8 to 15 pairs of syllables did not produce decreases in retroaction (Sand, 1939).

Interpolated task. In one of McGeoch's studies (1936) it was found that the interpolation of 16 adjectives after an original list of 16 had been presented 8 times produced more inhibition for relearning after 20 minutes than did the interpolation of lists of 8 adjectives. His data indicated that the amount of retroactive inhibition was determined by the relative lengths of the original and interpolated lists.

Another study bearing on the influence of the length of the interpolated task was reported by Twining (1890). He used lists of 8 nonsense syllables. After the original list was learned to one perfect trial, he presented, during the 30-minute interval before relearning, 1, 2, 3, 4, or 5 lists ten times each. The recall scores for the original list decreased and the number of relearning trials increased directly as the number of interpolated lists increased. Thus, the length of the interpolated task appears to be one of the factors determining the amount of retroactive inhibition produced by it.

Temporal position of the interpolated task. There has been considerable interest in the question of whether the retroactive influence of the interpolated activity varies with its position within the interval between the original learning and the test of retention. Müller and Pilzecker (1900) and Heine (1914) believed that the sooner the interpolated activity was introduced after the original learning, the greater would be its inhibiting effect. Robinson (1920) introduced the interpolated task at four different temporal points of a twenty-minute interval and found no relation between the position of this task and its inhibiting influence. Skaggs (1925) concluded that the retroactive effect is greatest when the interpolated activity comes immediately after the original learning. The results of later experiments have not been in agreement on this point. In some experiments the greatest amount of inhibition has resulted from interpolation immediately after the original learning (Sisson, 1939); in others it has resulted from activity placed just before the recall or relearning of the original material (McGeoch, 1933; Whitely, 1927). The results have sometimes shown no consistent differences in inhibition for different temporal positions of the interpolated task (McGeoch and Nolen 1933).

In view of the fact that the experimental data suggested two distinct points at which the interpolated learning produced maximum retroactive inhibition—immediately after learning and immediately before recall—Postman and Alper (1946) tested the effect of nine different temporal conditions upon recall. Twenty unrelated word-pairs were learned by 63 college students, using the anticipation method. They were tested for recall on the list after a 16-day interval. At 9 different points in the interval between learning and recall—immediately after learning, 1, 2, 4, 8, 12, 14, 15 days, and immediately before recall—an interpolated list of 20 word pairs was learned, in which the first word of each pair was the first word in the original list. A new association was learned for it. The maximum retroactive inhibition occurred when the second list was interpolated one day after original learning, with two other high points at 8 days and 15 days. The authors interpret their results as showing that the retroactive effects are greatest one day after learning because that is the point by which maximum unlearning had occurred. The interpolation at 15 days was construed as most disturbing to recall, with the 8-day interpolation being a combination of both effects.

Sisson (1939), obtaining results similar to Postman's and Alper's, believes that the "confusion between constellations of associations and memory traces" is greatest just after learning and just prior to recall and least in the middle of the interval. He points out that in the case of the first position of interpolation in his study, both lists were equally well learned and were probably equally disintegrated over the interval prior to recall. The conditions would be conducive to cross associations and confusions between the two lists. When the interpolated list is presented immediately before recall of the first, its members, being newly learned, would be more closely knit together into a consolidated system, which would minimize interlist confusion. The position in the middle of the list should be conducive to the least amount of interference and confusion between the two lists. In the last point Sisson differs from Postman and Alper, but his experimental design did not provide for as many interpolated intervals as the latter, and as a result could easily have missed the overlapping of the two effects.

Organization. Considerable evidence points to the degree of intraserial integration as a matter of importance in determining the extent to which retention may be impaired by the activity that follows learning. By *intraserial integration* is meant the organization of the unit members of the learning material into a unified whole or pattern by means of the various associations formed between them.

In an attempt to secure gradations in similarity throughout the scale from maximum to minimum similarity, Watson (1938) used 10 groups of subjects and 10 variations of the interpolated task in an experiment on card sorting. Each group first sorted a deck of 80 cards 10 times into 16 compartments numbered to correspond with the numbers on the cards. Then followed an interpolated sorting with changed arrangement and the final sorting with the original arrangement. For group I the interpolated task was exactly the same as the original. This meant that the group simply had additional practice on the same performance. Here was complete similarity, and the effect of the interpolated practice was a slight improvement in the performance. For group II 4 compartment numbers were changed for the interpolated sorting. This meant that the cards bearing these numbers had to be thrown into compartments different from the ones in which they were placed during the original practice. Group III had 8 numbers changed; group IV, 12; and for group V all 16 numbers were changed. In terms of materials the first five patterns were completely similar, for numbers were used throughout, but from group I to group V there was increasing change in the organization of movements required. For groups VI to IX letters were substituted for numbers to the extent of 4, 8, 12, and 16 letters respectively. Here was increasing dissimilarity in terms of materials, while the movement patterns remained the same as in V. The results showed an increase in retroactive inhibition through groups II to V. The change to 4 letters in group VI did not appreciably diminish the retroactive effect of the interpolated sorting, but from group VI on, there was consistent decrease in retroactive inhibition with the least amount appearing in group IX where all 16 numbers were changed to letters.

Watson believed that the factor of similarity is insufficient to explain the results and suggested that compatibility also is a factor determining the retroactive effect of the interpolated activity. In his pattern I there was complete similarity and complete compatibility in the identity of the original and interpolated tasks. In V, where all numbers were changed, there was complete incompatibility and complete similarity. The same numbers were used, but each one was associated with a different response. In IX he found complete dissimilarity and complete compatibility because here the interpolated task was entirely different from the original both in materials and in organization of movements. There was, therefore, no necessity for unlearning the original task in order to learn the interpolated task. He points out that when compatibility and similarity are both high, the retention is high; when compatibilty is low, even though similarity is high, retention is low; and that when similarity is low and compatibility is high, the retention is relatively high.

This investigator found, moreover, that his subjects did not learn the original and interpolated patterns as entirely separate units, but that they tended to organize them into a comprehensive pattern that included the two. In cases where some of the numbers were changed, the subjects apparently reorganized the original pattern to include the needed changes in response. When letters were substituted for the numbers, the original pattern was not repeated (the pattern being the same as for V) and so, with the increase in the number of letters in the interpolated task, the material of the two tasks became less similar. There was then a decrease in the extent to which the interpolated task would disrupt the original organization. These observations led Watson to conclude that "the factor of organization determines the conditions of transfer and inhibition."

Studies by Sisson (1938) have thrown light on this problem. In one of them he used nonsense syllables. Some of the lists were made up of syllables known to have high associative value. Others were composed of syllables known to have low associative value. By *associative value* is meant the ease with which subjects are able to find meaning in a syllable by means of some form of association. It was found that when both the original and the interpolated lists had low associative values, there was less retroactive inhibition than when both lists had high associative values. When the two lists differed in associative values, there was less retroactive inhibition than when they were similar in this respect. It seems reasonable to assume that when the associative values are different for the two lists, there would be a greater tendency to organize each into a separate pattern, and that the resulting isolation would lessen the chances for interference from the interpolated list at the time of recalling the original. When the lists permit the easy formation of inter-list associations, a high degree of retroaction is to be expected because of the greater possibilities of confusion at the time of recall. Sisson suggests the hypothesis "that where two activities are mutually isolated in the total organization of behavior, by whatever means this isolation can be achieved, retroaction will be reduced to a minimum."

For the purpose of testing this hypothesis, Sisson conducted another experiment (1938 A) in which the learning material consisted of lists of 10 adjectives. Two methods of presentation were tested for their bearing on retroactive inhibition. In one the words were presented 5 times each and always in the same serial order. In the second the words were presented 5 times, but in random or jumbled order. For the rest conditions the subjects read jokes; for the work conditions the original list was followed immediately by a second list of the same kind. The results from the recall tests showed that the percentage of retroactive inhibition was 46 for the words presented in serial order and 55 for those presented in jumbled order. There were more cases of overt transfer for the jumbled lists than for the serial lists. *Overt transfer* means the shifting of words from one list to the other during recall. It was believed that serial presentation favored a closer intraserial organization of the words, and that the jumbled order made it more necessary to form associations with "the subjects' total memorial organization," including inter-serial associations. According to Sisson's hypothesis, this latter condition would result in greater retroactive inhibition.

Other factors. *Age of the associations.* When the degree of retention is about equal for two sets of material and one of them has been retained over a longer period of time, the retention of the older material will be impaired less by an interpolated activity than the retention of the younger. Thus, there appears to be a connection between Jost's law and retroactive inhibition (Britt and Bunch, 1934).

Mental set. An experiment by Lester (1932) showed that instructions given to the subjects tend to reduce the retroactive effects of the interpolated actvity when those instructions lead to expectation of recall, to expectation of the interpolated material, and to an understanding of the possible effects of the interpolated material. An even greater reduction of retroactive inhibition resulted from urging the subjects to make an effort to avoid letting the interpolated material interfere with their retention of the original lists.

Affective toning. Memory value has usually been found to be greater for pleasant than for unpleasant materials, and also greater for unpleasant than for affectively indifferent materials.

The investigation of this problem has been difficult because of the many complicating factors involved. One of these is the factor of vividness. It is known that the vividness of an impression enhances its retention (Van Buskirk, 1932). Affective experiences are usually more vividly impressed than indifferent ones, and this would tend to increase their frequency of recall. Another fact to be taken into account is the greater frequency for most persons of pleasant experiences than unpleasant ones (Flügel, 1925). The very fact that one has more pleasant experiences would account to some extent for the greater number of pleasant than unpleasant experiences recalled. Then, the degree of affectivity varies for both pleasant and unpleasant experiences, a fact which makes reliable measurement difficult. Also the affective toning of an experience tends to change with the lapse of time and under repetition.

Because of these features of the problem, the method of free recall of experiences often used in earlier studies is not considered dependable. In this method, individuals were asked to list all the experiences of a given period which they could recall and then rate them as pleasant, unpleasant, or indifferent. In most cases this method has shown more affective than indifferent memories and more pleasant than unpleasant ones. But the results are obviously determined not by the factor of affectivity alone.

A more satisfactory method of dealing with this problem is one in which the subjects learn a list of terms judged to be pleasant, unpleasant, or indifferent; then after an interval they are tested to determine the differences in retention for the three kinds of items. This method, however, is limited by the following facts: words in an experimental list may not have the same affective values as in other situations; a word may have a pleasant or unpleasant meaning without actually arousing the feeling (Young, 1937); and the words in such a list may differ in degree of familiarity or number of associations. In the light of these complicating influences it is not surprising to find some disagreement among investigators. The gist of the evidence, however, seems to justify the following tentative conclusions: first, pleasant material is usually retained better than unpleasant material: second, the greater retention value of pleasant material tends to increase as time passes, but eventually it decreases as complete forgetting of both kinds of material is approached; third, for children this difference between the retention of pleasant and unpleasant material is much less than for adults; fourth, unpleasant material is usually retained better than indifferent material; fifth, both pleasant and unpleasant experiences tend to lose their affective toning and to approach indifference as time passes, but this tendency is greater in the case of unpleasant experiences; sixth, the factor of vividness plays a part in the recall of affective material, but compared with feeling, its influence is greater for immediate recall than for delayed recall (Beehe-Center, 1932; Cason, 1932; Dudycha, 1941; Gilbert, 1938; Meltzer, 1930).

A study of Bunch and Wientge (1933) of the relative susceptibility of pleasant, unpleasant, and indifferent words to the retroactive effect of interpolated indifferent material showed the least amount of retroactive inhibition for the pleasant words. Frank and Ludvigh (1931) used pairs of nonsense syllables for the original learning and then a series of odors was presented to the subjects. The odors were grouped as "pleasant," "unpleasant," and "indifferent" according to results from previous experiments. Recall was tested after an interval of 10 minutes. There was better retention when the learning was followed by pleasant odors than when it was followed by unpleasant ones. It appears that the unpleasant odors had a greater inhibiting effect on the recall of the syllables learned prior to the presentation of the odors. These results are in keeping with other studies that show better retention for pleasantly toned materials than for those regarded by the learner as unpleasant.

Order of presentation. McGeoch and McKinney (1937) used lists of nonsense syllables paired with nouns as learning material and compared two procedures of presentation with respect to their bearing on retroactive inhibition. In one procedure the order of the pairs within the series was the same in all five of the presentations. In the other procedure the serial order of the paired items was changed from one presentation to another. The results showed the greatest retroactive effect when both the original list and the interpolated list were presented in constant order. The retroaction was less when the order in both lists varied, and it was slight or absent when one of the lists was presented in a changing order while the order of the items in the other list was kept constant.

Methods of measuring retention. Several studies have shown that the indicated impairment of retention by interpolated activity is greater when retention is measured by recall than when it is measured by relearning trials (Britt, 1935; Lester, 1932). The retroactive effects of the interpolated activity on the retention scores tend to diminish as relearning takes place, and after a few trials there may be no difference with respect to retention between the work and rest conditions. How quickly the retroactive effect disappears seems to depend on such conditions as degree of learning and the similarity of the two tasks (McGeoch, 1942). These findings indicate the practical importance of reviews as a means of counteracting the impairment of retention by the activities that follow learning.

When the recognition method has been employed for measuring retention in experiments designed to investigate retroactive inhibition, it has revealed in some cases no difference in retention between the work and rest conditions. When this method has yielded evidence of retroactive inhibition, the amount indicated has usually been small. This is in keeping with the fact, mentioned in an earlier section, that higher percentage scores of retention are usually obtained by the recognition method of testing than by the method of recall. It appears that recognition is affected in essentially the same way as recall, though to a smaller degree, by the activities of the interval (Britt, 1935; McKinney, 1935; Zangwill, 1938).

Forgetting during sleep. In one of his studies of retention Ebbinghaus found that the amount forgotten between the twenty-fourth and forty-eighth hours after learning was about three times as great as that lost during a 15-hour period falling between 8.8 and 24 hours after learning. This was not in line with the usual findings that indicated a slower forgetting rate for the intervals farther removed from learning. It was observed that the proportion of time spent in sleep was greater for the earlier 15-hour period than for the later 24-hour period, and it was suggested that sleep might favor retention. This explanation was not accepted by Ebbinghaus, who considered forgetting a function of time. He attributed these exceptional results to experimental error. But later on, experiments were undertaken by other investigators to discover the relation of sleep to retention.

Jenkins and Dallenbach (1924) made the first real test of the hypothesis, rejected by Ebbinghaus, that forgetting takes place at a slower rate during sleep than during waking periods. Two college seniors served as subjects. They learned lists of ten nonsense syllables to the point of one correct reproduction, some in the morning and some at night just before going to sleep. Tests for recall were given after intervals of from one to eight hours. The results indicated a striking difference between the amount forgotten during periods of sleep and of waking. More than twice as many syllables were correctly recalled after intervals of sleep than after the intervals in which the subjects were awake. Considerably more were reproduced after one and two hours of sleep for the corresponding intervals of waking. The amount retained continued to drop during the day, but for the periods of sleep there appeared to be no further loss after the second hour. These results led to the conclusion that forgetting is the result of the interfering or obliterating effects of experiences, impressions, and activities which follow learning. This conclusion was in opposition to the view, prevalent at the time, that forgetting is a matter of deterioration of the effects of learning with the passing of time because of disuse.

Later, Van Ormer (1932) investigated retention during sleep and waking by means of the relearning method with the experimental refinement of making corrections for differences in learning efficiency at different periods of the day. It was found that more readings were required to memorize lists of nonsense syllables at night than in the morning. His results were in substantial agreement with the findings of Jenkins and Dallenbach. For the first hour, the rate of forgetting appeared to be about the same, as determined by relearning, for the waking and sleeping intervals; but after that, retention was definitely better during the periods of sleep.

Since the results from nonsense materials do not always apply to meaningful materials, a more recent study by Newman (1939) is particularly significant for educational practices. His subjects were 11 college students, and he used for learning materials 3 short stories equated for number of points essential and nonessential to the plot. The stories were read at different times of day and reproduced after intervals of approximately 8 hours. It was found that the essential points were reproduced much better than the nonessential ones, and that there was practically no difference between the number of essential points reproduced after 8 hours of sleep and after an equivalent day interval. But for the nonessential points there was a difference, and the results were in accord with the findings of the previous studies in which nonsense materials had been employed. After the 8-hour interval of sleep, the subjects reproduced on the average 47 per cent of the nonessential points, while after the 2 waking periods only 25 per cent and 19 per cent were recalled. Newman concluded that forgetting is due to interference produced by the events of the interval, but that the meaningful organization of the learned material tends to counteract this action.

Theories. Several theories have been advanced to explain retroactive inhibition. The first, known as the *perseveration theory,* was offered by Müller and Pilzecker (1900). According to this theory the neural activity involved in learning perseverates, or continues for a time after practice has ceased. This perseverating process, it is assumed, strengthens retention by consolidating and fixating the neural residues of learning. The activities following learning would tend to suppress such a consolidating process, or prevent it from running its full course; while rest would favor perseveration and make possible a more complete realization of its advantages. The fact that activities coming immediately after learning have often been found to produce more retroactive effect than those coming later in the interval is cited as evidence in favor of this theory.

However, the perseveration theory does not adequately explain the retroactive effect of activities that follow learning by several days or weeks, nor the detrimental effect on recall produced by activity placed just before the test and after a relatively long interval. It does not account for the amount of retroactive inhibition being greater when the materials and methods of the original and interpolated tasks are similar than when they are dissimilar. Against this theory also, is the fact that some forms of activity, even though fairly strenuous, when placed immediately after the learning, do not produce any appreciable amount of retroactive inhibition (McGeoch, 1931).

Two tenable and related theories to explain retroactive and proactive inhibition (the latter differs from retroactive in being the interference of old learning in new learning — just the reverse of retroactive inhibition) are McGeoch's competition-of-response theory and Melton and Irwin's unlearning theory. In our daily life, we are continually learning new responses to the stimuli previously associated with other responses. MeGeoch suggests that the result is a competition between responses to a given stimuli — an interference of new learning with old and vice versa. The fact that less forgetting occurs during sleeping hours than with the intervening activity of waking hours lends support to the hypothesis that forgetting is not the result of disuse but rather of interference between new and old learning. The interference may be viewed as a case of negative transfer of training, with previous learning inhibiting present learning and the latter interfering in the recall of previous learning. The product of the interference is a confusion of the old and the new. The findings on the relation of the degree of similiarity between material to the amount of retroactive inhibition and the effect of different temporal relations support an interference theory.

Melton and Irwin (1940) extended the interference theory to include what they designate as active unlearning. In a study of the intrusions between lists of nonsense syllables presented as original and interpolated learning, Melton and Irwin came to the conclusion that the competition of responses — the direct interference — was inadequate in accounting for all of the retroactive inhibition. Using lists of 18 nonsense syllables of low associational value, and varying the number of trials on the interpolated list, retroactive inhibition was greater for interpolated lists practiced for 5 and 10 trials than when the amount of practice was greater. The authors concluded that the number of intrusions is insufficient to account for the amount of retroactive inhibition, and suggested that an additional factor which may constitute active unlearning occurs by causing the original learning to become disrupted during the process of learning the interpolated list. This unlearning apparently lessens as the degree of learning of the interpolated and original list increases, suggesting that the higher the degree of organization of material learned the smaller the degree of interference. Further investigation of the factor of unlearning is needed, but it is not unlikely that retroactive inhibition involves more than the direct knocking out of one response by another and that a more dynamic change may occur. McGeoch and Underwood (1943) have provided some experimental corroboration of Melton and Irwin's hypothesis, but Osgood (1948) contends that even the two-factor theory is not adequate to account for all the retroactive inhibition; he suggests that the reciprocal inhibition of antagonistic responses needs investigation.

SUMMARY

The difficulty of material and the meaningfulness of the task are of significant importance in their influence upon learning. The shape of the learning curve varies with the difficulty of the material to be learned, difficult tasks showing a slow rate of acquisition, and verbatim learning requiring more repetitions than the learning of generalizations. The same task varies in difficulty for different children as a result of their capacity and experience differences. Even with this variation, there are tasks more suitable to given age-levels than others. Although experimental evidence describing the difficulty level of various school tasks is limited, it is possible for the teacher to empirically arrive at valid judgments by checking the rates of progress of several children within the class, selected at different levels of ability. Tasks which are too simple fail to challenge children, while tasks too difficult discourage them. Learning curves as seen in the middle of Fig. 6.1 are desirable. By periodic checks of rate of progress on different material, a teacher can assure herself that it represents an appropriate level of difficulty.

The practical importance of meaningfulness to learning has been pointed out. Rote memorization of meaningless material is a useless waste of the time of teacher and pupil. One of the justifications of a curriculum that is coordinated with the life experiences of children is that it achieves greater meaningfulness by utilizing the daily experiences of children. Words from the child's vocabulary can be read and spelled more readily than words which are strange to his vocabulary, for the latter lack meaning because of inexperience. It is obviously impossible to relate all learning to past experience, but one of the keys to teaching is still available in providing experiences which lend meaning to tasks. This is the function of pictures, exhibits, field trips, and the like—to provide the pegs of meaning upon which abstractions and generalizations may be hung. The teacher of the sixth grade class who lifted a boy out of his seat and turned him upside down in order to teach the class to invert the fraction and multiply when dividing by a fraction had a penchant for vivid illustrations which the class didn't readily forget.

The importance of discovering meaning for oneself cannot be overlooked. As with almost all discovery, it is not the number of errors that counts but the ultimate solution. Errors made in the process of discovery of solutions and generalizations are to be encouraged, for the modification of performance as a result of experience is an essential aspect of learning. One of the main problems with children is to narrow the field of search sufficiently that a solution is likely. Even in Easter egg hunts, children have to have some idea of where to look. Certainly, in discovering mathematical, scientific, and social generalizations, some clues are necessary as to where to look or what particular aspects of the problem demand attention.

There is no lack of evidence that today's learning interferes with yesterday's and tomorrow's. The smaller the interference the more substantial the learning. Interference between learning tasks is greatest when the meaningfulness of the material is low, when the degree to which the sequential tasks are learned is low, and when tasks have low degrees of organization and near similarity in content, processes involved, and method of presentation. The evidence suggests that a sequence of tasks during the school day should avoid juxtaposition of subjects that are somewhat similar, such as French and Spanish, or Latin and English. Addition and subtraction, and multiplication and division of numbers involve similar processes which may be confused, particularly when aspects of the learning may be incomplete or of insufficient degree. Differences in methods of presentation which contribute to distinction and contrast between present and previous learning serve to reduce interference.

OVERVIEW

Stroud, J. B., "Experiments on Learning in School Situations," *Psychological Bulletin*, 1940, 37, pp. 777-807.

SELECTED REFERENCES

Deese, J., *Psychology of Learning.* New York: McGraw-Hill, 1952.
McGeoch, J. A. and A. L. Irion, *The Psychology of Human Learning,* rev. New York: Longmans, Green, 1952.
Stephens, J. M., *Educational Psychology,* rev. New York: Holt, 1956.

ORIGINAL INVESTIGATIONS

Krueger, W. C. F., "Rate of Progress as Related to Difficulty of Assignment," *Journal of Educational Psychology,* 1946, 37, pp. 247-49.
Melton, A. W. and Jean Irwin, "The Influence of Degree of Interpolated Learning on Retroactive Inhibition and the Over Transfer of Specific Responses," *American Journal of Psychology,* 1940, 53, pp. 173-203.
Swenson, Esther, G. L. Anderson, and C. L. Stacey, "Learning Theory in School Situations," *University of Minnesota Studies in Education.* Minneapolis: University of Minnesota Press, 1949, pp. 9-39.
Van Dusen, F. and H. Schlosberg, "Further Study of the Retention of Verbal and Motor Skills," *Journal of Experimental Psychology,* 1948, 38, pp. 526-34.

Chapter Seven

Method Variables

The discussion in the preceding two chapters has centered on the learner and on the nature of the task to be learned. We have ignored the function performed by the teacher: the systematic organization of materials for presentation to individuals. Knowledge of individual differences and of the meaningfulness and and difficulty of tasks presented is essential in any attempt to initiate and maintain learning with children; however, the ways in which given tasks may be presented are varied, and the teacher must understand the effects of different presentations or arrangements upon the learning process. Many times, each of us has heard or used the maxim, "Practice makes perfect." It is used to justify continued repetitions of given acts, such as practicing musical scales, rehearsing dramatic plays, drilling in multiplication and addition tables, and practicing football plays, apparently on the assumption that repetition in itself is useful. What purpose does repetition of responses play in learning? How much and how often should practice be given? Does practice function differently in acquiring a skill than in retaining the skill once it is mastered? What factors other than amount of practice should be taken into account in organizing learning tasks? All these questions concern the teacher in her work of facilitating learning.

In the first place, we must bear in mind that where learning is actually taking place, there is modification of response. This does not mean simply the repetition of a performance in the sense that the learner does the identical thing over and over. The response does not recur in identical form because each time it is carried through, a change is produced in the learner, and this change in the learner brings a change in behavior. Thus, in learning we do not merely repeat a performance; we alter it. Otherwise we would not have improvement, and the acquisition of new modes of response would be impossible. When there is no longer any change being made in the response, learning has ceased.

As a result of his early studies in learning, Thorndike (1916) proposed a law of exercise based on his conclusion that the connection or association between a stimulus and a response is strengthened by mere exercise — the repetition of response in the presence of the stimulus. Thorndike's prolific writing made a profound effect upon educational practice, and his recommendations for organization of learning tasks — arrangement from simple to complex, the use of frequency of occurrence of events as a criterion of importance for learning, and frequent repetition in the process of learning — were widely adopted. Subsequently, after further experimentation, Thorndike changed his opinions on the value of exercise in learning. Unfortunately, many teachers were not aware that Thorndike had shifted his views as a result of his continued studies (1931, 1932), for their chief technique continued to be endless repetition. In *Human Learning,* Thorndike refers to the former acceptance of the view that the mere repetition of a situation in and of itself produces learning, and then states that this is not true. In an experiment involving

3,000 attempts to draw with eyes closed a line four inches long, the lines drawn in the last two of the twelve sittings were not drawn appreciably better than those in the first and second sittings. The repetition of the situation was not sufficient in itself to cause learning. Here the learner had a task, a goal, but no way of knowing how far he fell short of it each time, and no way of knowing in what way to change his performance in order to improve it. The need for some kind of check or appraisal of achievement in terms of the desired outcomes is indicated by the results of this experiment.

Thorndike reported another experiment in which a long list of two-letter combinations was presented to the subjects who were instructed to regard these letters as the beginnings of words that they were to complete. Some of these beginnings were repeated 28 times. The subjects did 240 completions each day for a total of 14 days. For completing the word beginning with *el,* one subject wrote "ephant" and "evate" twice in the first 7 trials. For all of the last 8 completions, this subject wrote "f." In spite of the early repetitions of the longer completions, they disappeared in favor of the shorter and more easily written "f." Here again is shown the inability of repetition to perpetuate a particular response. A shift and a substitution are made in the interest of completing the task more quickly and with less effort. Repeated encounters with an external situation or part of a situation are not likely to produce learning when they bear no relation to the individual's purpose, interests, task, or problem, and, for that reason, do not claim his attention. This fact may be demonstrated experimentally by instructing our subjects to watch for one thing and then later to recall something else not mentioned in the instructions. Such a demonstration is made by presenting to a group of students a series of cards, each bearing a printed word, a number, and a strip of colored paper. The subjects are instructed to observe closely the word and the number on each card so that later when each word is presented alone they may supply the number which goes with it. No mention is made of the color to be presented with each word. After several presentations, the students are asked to give the color that was presented with each word as well as the number. The score for colors is found to be much poorer than for numbers. Frequently, some of the subjects will protest that they were not told they would be asked about the colors and so did not pay any atten-tion to them. They did not learn them as they did the numbers, not because of a difference in frequency of presentation, but because they were not set to observe them. Usually, a few students in such an experiment assume that the colors do have something to do with it and instruct themselves to watch them. Such students may make a good score on the color test.

The result of such experiments was a shift in emphasis from repetition and drill to such factors as distribution of practice, knowledge of results, overlearning, whole learning versus part learning, incentives, and set, and the relationship of all to learning. Nevertheless, the evidence we have been considering points clearly to a fact every teacher should bear in mind, namely, that the mere frequency of a situation or of a response is not sufficient, in and of itself, for successful practice, drills, or reviews. A child may write a list of words many times without learning to spell them. He may do his penmanship exercises without improving his handwriting. He may do a series of exercises by following the steps indicated in the sample without mastering the principles involved. We sometimes forget or fail to realize that teaching means more than simply placing educational materials before our pupils.

Practice gives the learner a chance to discard false motions or needless and awkward reactions, and to try out short cuts and more efficient methods. It gives him a chance to correct errors and to profit by his experiences. Such opportunity for improvement is essential for most forms of classroom learning. It is necessary, therefore, that the teacher provide practice which invites and encourages improvement. Whether these opportunities for improvement mean anything to the learner depends upon the motives with which he encounters them. Without interest, attention, or purpose on the part of the learner there is likely to be little accomplished. Skillful teaching calls for the clever management of these subjective factors quite as much as the manipulation of environmental conditions.

DISTRIBUTION OF PRACTICE

Practice, like medicine, may be presented in small or large doses. It may be concentrated into relatively long unbroken periods of work or spread over several short sessions. It is possible, for instance, to organize college curricula so that one studies nothing but psychology one semester, political science the next, and so forth; or it may be arranged so that a student takes a variety of courses in each semester. When practice is concentrated in long unbroken periods, it is referred to as massed; when it is spread out over a period of time, it is referred to as spaced or distributed practice. Almost without exception, the studies concerned with the relative effectiveness of spaced versus massed practice, whether with motor or verbal learning, show that practice should be spaced for best results. A few words in spelling each day for a week will be mastered better than a large number bunched in one lesson.

Three variations may be introduced in distribution of practice. The length of the practice period may be varied with rest periods constant; the length of the rest period may vary with amount of work constant; and varying arrangements of work and rest periods may be combined.

Length of the practice period. In general it appears that the shorter the practice period, the greater the learning that occurs. Typical of the experimental findings is Starch's (1927) study in which two 10-minute, one 20-minute, and one 40-minute practice periods per day at letter-digit substitution were carried out until a total of 120 minutes had been completed. The shorter work periods were all more effective than a single 2-hour session, and the two 10-minute sessions per day were most productive of all. At the same time, it appears that there is a limit below which it is not profitable to reduce the length of time spent at one sitting. Pyle (1928), for example, compared the results from practice periods of 15, 30, 45, and 60 minutes in a substitution experiment, and found the 30-minute period to be the most effective for gains in speed on the basis of the total time spent in practice. The 15-minute period was too short for best results in this task, and the 45 minute and one-hour periods were too long. The results for the longer periods indicated very little gain after 30 minutes of practice, presumably because of fatigue in the latter part of the hour.

Hovland (1940) has conducted a series of research studies on distribution of practice. In one he compared the effectiveness of massed and spaced practice in learning three lists of nonsense syllables of differing length, and found that distributed practice was superior to massed practice for all lengths of lists and that the superiority was greater the longer the list, particularly in the central portions of the lists where acquisition is slowest.

The results obtained with verbal materials occur as well in motor learning. Travis (1939) compared the efficiency of practice periods of different lengths when the rest intervals were kept constant. The experiment was a study of improving eye-hand coordination. The apparatus used was a manual pursuit-oscillator. The learner's task was to keep a hinged stylus on a moving target. Three groups of college men served as subjects. The length of the practice periods was 1 minute, 2 minutes, and 4 minutes respectively for the three groups. The interpractice rest period was 3 minutes for all three groups. There were 6 practice periods; hence, the total time was 6 minutes for the first group, 12 minutes for the second, and 24 minutes for the third. The 4-minute practice group made the poorest percentage score, despite the fact that its total time spent in practice was 4 times that spent by the 1-minute group. The 2-minute practice group made the best score. The experimenter concluded that, since the second group which practiced a total of 12 minutes made the highest score, the second 2 minutes of each practice period for the third group was a waste of time and deleterious to learning.

In a more recent experiment, Duncan (1951) compared unequal amounts of practice under two conditions. Calling attention to the fact that when the amount of practice is the same for both groups, the distributed practice group requires a greater elapsed time from beginning to end, Duncan held the time for both groups equal to 20 minutes. Each group had two 5-minute work periods separated by a 10-minute rest period. During the 5-minute work period, one group practiced continually; the other worked 10 seconds, then rested 20, with the result that it had only one-third the amount of practice. Nevertheless, the distributed practice groups were superior in both pre-test and post-test sessions. The pre-test massed-practice group produced superior performance when switched to distributed practice in the post-rest session.

The evidence supports a conclusion that the shorter the work period, the better, provided it is not too short. Most tasks and activities require an initial period for warm-up. If the work period is too short, the learner probably fails to become oriented to the nature of the task.

But just how long should the periods be, and how long should the intervals between these periods be? The optimal length and spacing of the periods appears to depend upon the nature of the learning task and upon the age of the learner. It is safe to assume that in memorizing large blocks of material the learning should be spread over several periods, that for difficult material the periods should be shorter than for easy material, and that for young children there should be shorter periods than for older learners. In attempting to secure the advantages of distributed effort, we must guard against making the periods either too short or too long.

Reed (1924) compared the gains made from 60 minutes spent in practicing addition of two-place numbers under 4 different procedures with respect to the distribution of the total time. One group worked for 60 minutes continuously. A second spent 20 minutes a day in practice for 3 days, a third group worked 10 minutes a day for 6 days, while a fourth group practiced for periods of 10 minutes twice a week for 3 weeks. His results indicated that the greatest gains were obtained from the 20-minute periods once a day spread over 3 days.

Hahn and Thorndike (1914) found that for a total of 90 minutes of practice in addition, $22\frac{1}{2}$-minute periods brought greater gains than periods of $11\frac{1}{4}$ minutes for pupils in the seventh grade. For the sixth grade 20-minute periods were equivalent to periods of 10 minutes; in the fifth grade $7\frac{1}{2}$-minute periods were almost as good as periods of 15 minutes; and for fourth graders 10-minute periods were better than 5-minute periods.

The effectiveness of the distribution of learning depends to a large extent upon what one does during the intervals. In a laboratory study in which 520 subjects were given the task of learning the names of thirty pictures, Eaton (1937) used intervals of 20, 30, 40, 50, and 60 seconds between the presentations of the items. He found that learning efficiency was greatest for the 40-second interval when the subjects rested during the intervals. Learning efficiency was reduced, however, when the intervals between presentations were filled with such activities as working out problems in arithmetic, checking letters of pied type, memorizing, or learning the names of other pictures. The greater the amount of attentive concentration demanded by these interpolated activities, the more was learning efficiency reduced.

Length of the rest period. How long should the interval between practice periods be? In general, the length of the interval does not appear as important as the fact that rest periods occur, for the variations which occur between rest intervals of different length are smaller than occur between having or not having periods of rest. The optimal length of the rest period varies with the type of task or skill being learned. For instance, in an experiment by Dore and Hilgard (1937) utilizing the Koerth pursuit-rotor—a target tracking task— three groups practiced for periods of 1 minute with rest periods of 1, 3, and 11 minutes respectively. The task was to hold a hinged stylus on a small brass target mounted on the disc of a phonograph turning at the rate of one revolution per second. Within an equal number of trials, the group that rested 11 minutes between trials made the greatest gain. The group resting 3 minutes was second best, and the group with the 1-minute intervals was third. A fourth group, which worked 3 minutes and rested 1 minute, made the poorest showing of the four groups.

Results reported by other experimenters indicate that for a given task there is an upper limit to the advantage of spreading practice out in time. It is possible to have intervals that are too long for best results. In a study of eye-hand coordination with a pursuit-oscillator, Travis (1939) compared the results obtained under different interpractice intervals while the practice periods were kept constant at 5 minutes. Rest intervals of 20 minutes were found to produce better results than rests of 5 minutes, and intervals of 48 hours, 72 hours, and 120 hours. Here it appears that for a working period of 5 minutes on this task, 5-minute rest periods were too short for maximum gains, while intervals of 48 hours and over were too long. It seems that the most effective length of interval varies not only with the nature of the learning task but also with the length of the practice period. Within limits, the longer practice period calls for longer rest periods.

Relationship between work and rest interval. Several studies are available regarding the interaction between work and rest periods of different length. Kimble and Bilodeau (1949) used 4 combinations of 10-second and 30-second work periods with 10-second and 30-second rest periods to determine which was the most important variable—work, rest, or interaction between the two. The task used 300 seconds total practice time on the Minnesota Rate of Manipulation Test which requires the rapid turning and placing of circular blocks. The subjects were 48 men and 48 women evenly divided between the four groups. The groups with the shorter work period had the higher output, and the shortening of the work period rather than variations in rest period appeared to be the important variable. Interaction between the two was insignificant.

In a more elaborate experiment, Ammons (1947) utilized combinations of $\frac{1}{3}$, 1, 5, 8, and 17-minute work periods with $\frac{1}{3}$, 2, 5, 10, 20, 60, and 310 minute rest periods. All combinations of work and rest periods were followed by a continuous 8-minute work period. Thirty-four groups with 14 subjects in each practiced a rotary-pursuit task in which they were forced to work at a faster than normal rate. Ammons was interested in the rate at which work decrement occurred during the initial work period, was dissipated during the rest interval, and reoccurred during the post-rest continuous practice. On this task, the work decrement reached a maximum during the 8-minute practice group, dissipated rapidly during the first 2 minutes of rest, reaching a maximum at 20 minutes. Five-minute rest intervals appeared optimal for this task. Again the crucial factor was the length of the work period.

Theories explaining distributed practice. Several explanations have been offered to account for the superiority of distributed practice: perseveration, fatigue, motivation, rehearsal, maturation, reactive inhibition, and differential forgetting. The perseveration theory assumes that neural processes continue for a time after the activity ceases, thus assisting in the fixation of responses; fatigue and motivational explanations are allied in the assumption that continued work increases fatigue and decreases motivation, thus having a negative effect upon learning. In massed practice, both fatigue and decreases in motivation presumably would occur more rapidly. If no activity is introduced during the rest period, it is possible for subjects to rehearse the task implicitly, facilitating improvement of response. Snoddy (1938) maintains that the advantage of distributed practice is due to growth that takes place during the intervals in practice. According to Snoddy there are two distinct processes of growth involved in learning. One, called primary growth, is said to be a positive function of both repetition and the interpolated time intervals, while the other, called secondary growth, is the sole result of the stimulation afforded by practice. Primary growth comes early in the practice series and is a setting or stabilizing process that establishes a base upon which the effectiveness of later practice depends. Short initial practice periods are believed to stimulate primary growth, which continues through the rest intervals.

Reactive inhibition is a term used to describe the tendency to avoid repetition of a response once given. The student will recall that Hull developed the concept of excitatory potential and inhibitory potential. Excitatory potential results from drive states and reinforcement. One of the factors in the inhibitory potential is reactive inhibition, a theoretical construct postulated to account for decrement in work resulting from a negative after-effect of responding. Reactive inhibition is believed to dissipate proportionally to the amount of time allowed for rest; this process would account for the improved performance observed in distributed practice when compared to massed practice.

The final theory proposed to account for the advantages of distributed practice is one of differential forgetting (Easley, 1937; McGeoch, 1942). According to this theory, we learn wrong responses as well as right responses during practice, but the wrong ones are not learned as well as the correct ones because the latter are more often repeated. Since the wrong responses are not learned as well, they are forgotten more rapidly during the intervals of no practice. The rest periods between practice sessions afford an opportunity for the progressive elimination of incorrect responses.

The available evidence supports the reactive inhibition, the differential forgetting, and to some degree the motivational explanations. Ammons' study, reported earlier, and a study by Kimble support the occurrence of a rapid increase in reactive inhibition early in practice. Kimble (1949) divided 474 subjects into 8 groups, 6 experimental and 2 control, which were presented with an alphabet printing task in which the letters are printed upside down from right to left, so that when the work sheet is rotated 180 degrees the letters appear in proper form. All groups had 40 trials of 29 seconds. One control had massed trials, the other had 30-second rest intervals between trials. The experimental groups had a single 10-minute rest occuring after the fifth trial of the first group, after the tenth trial of the second group, and so forth. Each group showed a marked increase in performance after the rest, which was smaller for the groups in which the rest was longest postponed.

In an experiment similar in design to Kimble's (Wasserman, 1951), high and low motivated groups were added by inducing an ego-oriented set in the former by the instructions given them and a task-oriented set in the latter. The results which favored the high motivated group supported the hypothesis that increases in motivation raise the critical level of reactive inhibition.

Hovland (1938, 1939, 1949) and Underwood (1951, 1952) have carried out a series of experiments designed to check the variables influential in the greater effectiveness of distributed practice. Hovland (1938) presented nonsense syllables at different rates, 2-second and 4-second and found distributed practice markedly superior at the faster rate of presentation. In analyzing the results, the advantage of distributed practice was more closely related to the amount of work—that is the number of trials—than to the degree of learning. Perseveration, rehearsal, and fatigue could not be used to explain the differences: there was no reason to assume that perseveration is greater at a 2-second rate; color-naming during the rest period was used to prevent rehearsal; nor could fatigue be explained as occurring more rapidly.

The findings, which shed no light on motivational changes, support the reactive inhibition and differential forgetting theories. Hovland (1939, 1949) has shown that distributed practice is more effective in serial learning than in paired associates learning (less interference would be expected on the latter), and is more effective the faster the paired associates are presented. Underwood (1951) and Oseas and Underwood (1952) have tested the effectiveness of distributed practice, on learning of concepts where massed practice would be anticipated as better, and on learning of partially learned material where the advantage of distributed practice should be less. The experimental results were inconclusive.

From a theoretical viewpoint, motivation, reactive inhibition, and differential forgetting appear to have the greatest support in explaining the effectiveness of distributed practice, although it is more difficult to isolate motivational effects. Increased motivation and decreased reactive inhibition and differential forgetting during the rest periods operate to facilitate performance, if not the learning itself.

Educational significance of distributed practice experiments. From the foregoing studies, it appears that when the amount of work involved in a task is great, when the task is complex or not particularly meaningful, when the frequency of error responses is likely to be high, or when motivation is low or amount of effort required high, the practice sessions should be spaced with primary attention devoted to the length of the practice period rather than of the rest period.

In contrast, when the task is highly meaningful (Ash, 1950) or when insightful learning is possible, when the material has been previously learned to a high degree of proficiency but during a prolonged intervening interval the forgetting has been great, when peak performance is required on tasks already well known, or when prolonged warm-up periods are necessary to becoming involved in the task, then massed practice periods are favorable.

New tasks generally should be introduced to school children in small quantities with short initial practice periods and short rest intervals; gradual lengthening of the practice period should follow. The fact that the length of the rest period is less important than the length of the work period permits teachers considerable flexibility in scheduling practice periods. For peak performance, massed practice on well-learned material is usually desirable.

DEGREE OF LEARNING

Retention of learned materials is increased if practice continues beyond the point of the first errorless reproduction, for consistently higher degrees of retention have been shown for corresponding higher degrees of learning. Overlearning works to reduce forgetting and undoubtedly accounts for the retention of skills in some degree after long periods of disuse. Recollection of college songs, game skills, poetry, and various motor skills, even after long periods without use, results from the fact that they were originally oft-repeated well beyond the point of initial learning.

That overlearning improves retention for rote learning of meaningful words was demonstrated experimentally by Krueger (1929). The learning material consisted of lists of 12 one-syllable nouns. The anticipation method of learning was used. Each list was considered learned to 100 per cent when the subject could anticipate correctly all of the words during a single presentation. Two degrees of overlearning were employed. In one (50 per cent overlearning) the lists were shown one and one-half times the number of presentations required for 100 per cent learning. In the other (100 per cent overlearning) the number of presentations was twice that required for 100 per cent learning. Tests for retention were given after intervals of 1, 2, 4,

7, 14, and 28 days. Both the recall method and the relearning method were used for measuring retention. The scores indicated that for the one-day interval retention for 50 per cent overlearning was about 50 per cent better and that the longer the interval, the greater was the superiority of retention from the overlearning. The 100 per cent overlearning brought higher test scores after each interval with both recall and relearning than were obtained from 50 per cent overlearning, but the superiority of 100 per cent overlearning over 50 per cent overlearning was less than the superiority of 50 per cent overlearning over initial learning. Thus, there appeared to be a diminishing advantage as the degree of overlearning was increased. This study indicates that overlearning, at least to the extent of 50 per cent, increases retention, and that the longer the interval, the greater is its value. These findings are significant for memory drills and for all other cases where retention for a long period is desired. It should be noted, however, that to be effective, the repetitions beyond the threshold of recall require the same high degree of attention as those which precede the first perfect recital.

As might be anticipated following the discussion on retroactive effects, less interference or negative transfer accrues from material which is learned to a higher degree. As the amount of training increases, the amount of positive transfer tends to increase; this was revealed in the experiment by Bruce (1933) involving nine relationships of similarity and identity between the training and test lists of paired nonsense syllables studies. When the training list was presented twice, there was negative transfer in 6. With 6 presentations of the training list, 3 of these negative cases shifted to positive transfer, and the amount of negative transfer was less for the remaining 3. With 12 presentations, only 2 of these conditions showed negative transfer, and the amount was less in these cases than it was for 6 presentations. In the case of 2 conditions which showed positive transfer after 2 presentations, the amount of positive transfer was increased as the number of presentations was increased to 6, and to 12.

Other studies have shown negative transfer (interference) when the training was meager and positive transfer when it was more extensive. In the submerged target experiment by Hendrickson and Schroeder (1941), the explanations of light refraction differed in completeness for two experimental groups. The group that received the fuller explanation showed greater gains from transfer. These findings led to the definite conclusion that partial or superficial learning is more likely to interfere with other learning than is complete mastery, and that, for maximum returns in the way of positive transfer effects, thorough training is needed.

The studies on overlearning have one or two practical implications for educational practice. The first is the distinction between practice and drill. In the popular conception of the terms there is little difference in meaning, except, perhaps, a different occasion for use. One practices the piano and drills in arithmetic, practice perhaps being done singularly and drill in groups; but the meaning of both terms incorporates the repetition of given acts. Psychologists give a different meaning to practice which might be described as a condition of learning involving the repetition of an act as a means to a change (presumably improvement) of performance. This is quite different from repeating an act for purposes of fixating or stabilizing the performance. The student will recall that in the original discussion of the process of learning, two aspects were mentioned: the identification of the correct behavior, and the subsequent stabilizing of the correct behavior. Practice is the condition under which one learns the correct response, and, as can be seen from the studies on distributed practice, it is desirable to provide situations in which variability of response, continued motivation, and differential forgetting are possible. Once material is correctly learned, drill or overlearning is desirable to stabilize the response. Premature drill produces greater negative transfer as well as stabilization of erroneous responses. The second implication is that drill is desirable, properly located in the learning cycle. In one sense, drill corresponds to massed practice, and consequently is desirable later in practice. It should be apparent also that prolonged drill has diminishing returns, for gains in retention are not proportional to increases in overlearning. In addition, they are likely to suffer from diminished motivation on the part of the learner.

RECITATION DURING LEARNING

It has been reliably demonstrated that reading combined with recitation is superior to reading alone for memorizing both meaningful and non-meaningful material. This combining of reading with recitation is known as the *recitation method*. In practice it means that after a few readings or presentations, the learner attempts to recite the material without looking at it. When he is unable to proceed, he refers to the printed material again to prompt himself. Then he continues reciting what he can, glancing at the book or lists only when necessary. A number of experiments have indicated the advantages of such a procedure.

One of the most widely quoted studies on this subject was made some years ago by Gates (1917). He had children and college students memorize nonsense syllables and biographical material. The time devoted to study was divided for different groups so that different amounts were devoted respectively to reading and recitation. The material to be learned was printed on a sheet of paper. This each subject read until he was given a signal to recite. Then he began reciting to himself and referred to the paper whenever necessary. It was found that for the nonsense material, the amount reproduced was much greater for reading with recitation than for reading alone, that the difference increased as the proportion of time devoted to recitation was increased, and that it was greater for delayed recall than for immediate recall. The difference was not so marked for the meaningful material, although it was sufficient to indicate the value of recitation in memorizing.

Similar results were obtained from a study on this problem by Forlano (1937). His subjects, children in the fifth and sixth grades, learned spelling, arithmetical facts, and vocabulary material under normal school conditions by the recitation method and by reading without recitation. The recitation method was found to be superior to the all-reading method in each of the experiments for both immediate and delayed recall. The superiority of the recitation method was generally greater for delayed recall than for immediate recall. In the case of spelling with one-fifth and two-fifths of the time devoted to recitation, the results were only slightly better than for reading only. But with three-fifths of the time spent in recitation, the superiority over all reading was significant and only slightly less than for putting in four-fifths of the time reciting.

Granting the superiority of the recitation method over the all-reading method, Skaggs (1930) devised an experiment to discover the relative value of grouped and interspersed recitations. After two preliminary readings of a selection of poetry, his subjects—college students—tried four different procedures with regard to reading and recitation. According to the results of this experiment, it is better to have one recitation or attempted recitation after each reading than to have the readings and recitations grouped by twos or threes.

The practice of attempting to recall during the course of learning is conducive to an active attitude, vigorous effort, and concentrated attention; but perhaps the most important reason for its superiority over the all-reading method is that the individual actually practices what he is trying to learn. Just as we learn to write by writing, so to learn to recite, one should practice reciting. It gives the learner an immediate goal, shows him the progress he is making, and reveals the imperfections in his performance that need to be remedied. After a few readings, nearly everyone tries to test himself in some way. This was found to be true more or less in the experiments using the all-reading method.

A practical question arises about when the recitation process should be started. This naturally varies with different types and length of material. Except for every short selections, it will first be necessary to read the material through a few times without recitations. Four to 8 times has been suggested as optimal for relatively short materials (Skaggs, *et al.,* 1930). Recitation must not be guessing (Forlano and Hoffman, 1937).

It will probably be comforting to many teachers to know that the time-honored classroom procedure of assigning reading and hearing recitations is experimentally justified. Unfortunately the typical procedure of serial classroom recitation in which students report one-by-one assumes that *hearing* recitation is as valuable as giving it. In view of conflicting motivations and varying levels of attention, this assumption is hardly tenable. Fortunately, recitation need not be oral to be effective. Spitzer (1939) investigated the effectiveness of the test reviews as a method of recitation. He divided 3600 children drawn from the sixth grade in nine Iowa cities into 10 groups of approximately 400 each. Each group was tested at a different interval after initial learning—1, 7, 14, 21, 28, and 63 days—on reading material about peanuts and bamboos designed to be relatively new, highly factual, authentic, and of adequate difficulty. Both articles were approximately 600 words in length. Twenty-five item tests having reliability coefficients of above .75 were used as measures. The results showed that review in the form of a test was an effective method of aiding retention and that they can serve as learning devices. It is possible for them to fix errors as well, and it was important that corrected tests be returned. The earlier the test was given after initial learning, the greater the review value. These findings were confirmed by Tiedemann (1948) who advocated that review tests should be administered immediately after learning and at less frequent intervals as time elapses. He found more forgetting in one day when retention is not aided by review than is forgotten in 63 days when two intervening review tests were used as aids to retention.

The important consideration for educational practice is that written review can be effective and has the advantage of providing a group procedure which permits everybody in the class to review the material. The review need not be as formalized as a test, with possible negative affect on the part of the students, but may be incorporated into small group procedures in which pupils check one another, one pupil having the answers. Review may be in the form of simple recognition or recall, or may involve higher levels of organization, depending upon the ingenuity of the teacher in developing her questions for review. This procedure can be especially valuable with pupils of below average ability, with whom Spitzer found the most rapid forgetting.

Jones and Stroud (1940) checked the comparative effectiveness of both test review and reading review at intervals of 1-17 days and found that test review is most effective between 1-3 days but is progressively less effective the longer the interval of time. At intervals of 15 and 17 days, reading review was superior to test review. When one considers the form of the forgetting curve—with the initially sharper drop gradually levelling off—it is understandable that early test review permits recall when the amount retained is still comparatively great, but that after the major forgetting has occurred, the residue to be tested for is small. Reading serves to promote relearning, which of course progresses more rapidly than the initial learning.

KNOWLEDGE OF RESULTS

Earlier in the chapter mention was made of an experiment, reported by Thorndike, in which the subject attempted 3,000 times to draw a 4-inch line with his eyes closed. No improvement was made as a result of all these trials because the subject did not know the extent of his error in the various attempts. It seems unlikely that anyone in such a situation would be able to make any real gains. But suppose the subject were informed after each trial just how far short or how much over 4 inches he had drawn his line. We would then have a different sort of situation, and an essential condition for improvement would be provided. This was demonstrated in an experiment carried out in the writer's laboratory.

Three groups of students were used as subjects. Seven subjects in group A_1 were asked to close their eyes and draw a line 4 inches long. This was repeated until each subject had drawn 400 lines without opening his eyes or once looking at his drawings. No information was given at any time regarding the success of the attempts. The average error for the first ten trials for all seven subjects was $15/16$ of an inch, and for the last 10 trials of the 400, it was $13/16$ of an inch. The variations were so great, however, as to make this slight gain wholly insignificant. Some subjects drifted a bit nearer the goal while others were making larger errors at the end of the 400 trials than they made at the beginning.

The members of this same group (A_2) were then given 25 more trials, but after each attempt they opened their eyes and placed a 4-inch strip of cardboard along the line they had just drawn. It showed at once just how much the line was too short or too long. Under this procedure, the improvement was rapid during the first few trials. It will be noted that this group had just had the 400 trials without check on errors. Therefore, the first trial of this series was actually their 401st attempt. In this, their mean error was 21.4, while in the first of the 400 trials their average error was only 16.1, the unit of measurement being $1/16$ of an inch. After 400 trials with no check on errors, they were doing worse than when they started. But after only four visual checks on their performances they reduced their errors to only 2.9.

To avoid possible complications due to the effects of the first series of 400 checkless trials, and to compare two different methods of informing the subjects concerning their errors, two additional series of trials were conducted with two other groups. After each line was drawn, the members of group B opened their eyes and checked their errors with a four-inch strip of cardboard. Members of group C kept their eyes closed but after each line was drawn, the experimenter measured it and announced the extent of error in sixteenths of an inch and stated whether it was more or less than 4 inches.

The mean error scores in sixteenths of an inch for the 1st, 5th, 10th, 15th, and 20th trials in the four series were as follows:

Group Check	A_1 *None*	A_2 *Visual*	B *Visual*	C *Auditory*
Number of subjects	7	7	14	15
Mean scores				
1st trial	16.1	21.4	21.6	22.0
5th trial	15.9	2.9	6.2	6.7
10th trial	11.4	2.7	4.4	4.1
15th trial	13.0	4.7	3.1	5.3
20th trial	17.3	2.2	2.0	3.7

It will be observed that the average score of the group that had no check on the nature and extent of its errors (A_1) was actually poorer for the 20th trial than for the 1st, while with a clear and definite check on errors after each attempt all three groups made rapid gains during the first 5 trials. A slight advantage appears in favor of the visual check, in which the subjects checked their lines themselves, over the auditory check, in which the experimenter measured the lines and informed the subjects of their errors. The results of this experiment were confirmed by Trowbridge and Cason (1932) with the additional observation that the degree of improvement was directly related to amount of information provided. The more specific the knowledge regarding the nature of the error, the greater the improvement.

Some faults are not easily apprehended. In the experiments described above the deficiency of each performance could be definitely observed and precisely stated. The mistakes in typewriting due to striking the wrong letter may be seen easily by the pupil himself. In shooting at a target, the exact deviation from the bull's-eye may be measured. In the mirror-drawing experiment, the errors, being defined as touching either line bordering the path to be traced, can readily be noted. In many skills, however, the imperfections in one's performance may not be so easily discernible. In some cases it may be difficult for the teacher to get the child to see in what respects his performance falls short of the desired standard. There may be faults due to lack of coordination or deviations from the goal that the learner, because of his inexperience, cannot detect or even see when the teacher attempts to point them out to him. Such may be the case, for example, with the young violin player. He goes through the required motions but his music lacks the refinement of good timing, or some other less tangible quality. For such conditions, the teacher must have patience and the pupil must have the benefit first, of good examples and adequate demonstrations given repeatedly in order to refine his conception of the goal, and secondly, of sufficient practice to provide the opportunity for improvement.

A distinct shortcoming of most college courses is that final examinations are seldom returned to students to provide them with essential knowledge of results regarding their performance. Immediate, meaningful, specific, and, as far as possible, automatic knowledge of results, besides providing the information requisite to improvement of performance has further advantages in that awareness of progress serves as an incentive toward increased effort. Still more important, knowing what one doesn't know permits more effective distribution of effort during practice, because time isn't wasted rehearsing what is already known; instead it is allocated to what isn't known. This is probably most true for those students performing at lower levels, for self-information regarding performance is less likely to be a reliable guide. Ross (1933) found no difference in performance in a college course in tests and measurements between groups with differing knowledge of results. The author attributes the lack of effect of knowledge of results to the fact that experiments conducted in the laboratory can't be relied upon to predict classroom results. It is equally likely that the control group was self-informed on its performance.

Brown (1932) obtained results in favor of providing knowledge of results regarding arithmetic work given daily for 20 days in fifth and seventh grade classes (N of 138) as did Plowman and Stroud (1942) with 250 tenth and eleventh graders. In both studies each group served as its own control, working under both conditions of receiving results and not, with both conditions presented in counterbalanced order.

WHOLE AND PART LEARNING

Considerable attention has been given in the literature on learning to the relative efficiency of memorizing by *parts* or by the *whole method*. By the whole method one reads and rereads the entire block of material to be learned, be it a list of terms, a selection of prose, or a poem, and continues until the whole block can be recited. By the part method the material is learned one section at a time. The learner takes not the whole, but a part of the list or a stanza of the poem, and completely learns it. Then he takes up the next section and studies it until he can recite it. Then the third division is learned, and so on from part to part until each of the divisions has been mastered.

The results of the experimental studies on the relative merits of these two procedures have not established the forthright superiority of either method for learning under all types of conditions. Some studies have found the whole method better, others have obtained better results by the part method, while a number have found no clear-cut difference between them. The weight of the evidence and competent opinion seems to favor the whole method, particularly with adults, but under some conditions the whole method is not superior to nor as good as the part method.

Jensen and Lemaire (1937), including ten experiments on this problem, found that the whole method was superior to the part method in six experiments. For memorizing chemical information one group did better with the whole method, another did better with the part method. With some other materials the part method was found slightly but not significantly better than the whole for one group. The report on these experiments claims that 34.3 per cent of 504 children learned better by one or the other of the two methods, and that of these, half did better with the whole method, while half learned better by the part method. These children did not always do better by the method which was habitual with them. For about a third of them, their habitual method proved to be less effective in the experiments. The suggestion made here is that a child left to his own selection cannot be depended upon to choose the method which for him will be more effective, and that the method more effective for one child will not necessarily be superior for other children.

The general advantage of the whole method lies in the fact that from the start it puts the items to be associated in their proper order, and binds them together in the sequence needed for correct recital. It utilizes the consolidating values of meaning for the whole selection, and this favors good retention. Some experiments indicate that *practice* with the whole method is necessary before some persons can do better with it than with the part method. Steffens (1900), who found that the whole method required less time for learning poetry and syllable lists, observed that the advantages of the whole method sometimes did not appear at first and showed up only after the learner had become accustomed to using this procedure.

There is no doubt that the *attitude* of the learner toward the whole method is an important factor in determining how well it works. Children often prefer the part method, and unpracticed adults are often skeptical of the advantages of the whole method. With the whole method, much more time and work is required before any results of learning are manifest. One may read a long poem through a dozen times without being able to recite a single line, while with the same amount of work by the part method the learner would probably be able to recite several stanzas. For this reason a learner gets the feeling of success sooner with the part method. The recitation of parts become sub-goals, which provide a series of steps toward the main goal, the ability to recite the whole. These intermediate goals and the satisfactions derived from reaching them no doubt favor the part method, particularly with children and with adults unaccustomed to rote memory work. The whole method is likely to be discouraging because the learner has to work so long before he can see any returns for his effort.

Finally, the *character of the material* itself has much to do with the relative advantages of these two methods. The superiority of the whole method depends largely upon how compact a meaningful unit the entire selection is. If it is not too long and the material is closely knit together on one theme, the whole method will probably bring better results. Studies by Northway with school children, for example, indicated that for memorizing poems, the whole method is advantageous for poems understood as a whole (1937). When the parts themselves are more closely integrated than is the whole selection, we may expect the part method to be superior (Seagoe, 1936).

It appears, therefore, that under the right conditions the superiority of the whole method can hardly be questioned. In actual practice, however, we seldom have together all the conditions that make this method superior to the part method. For best results in memorizing, a combination of the two methods, which will avoid most of the disadvantages of both and at the same time secure as far as possible the advantages of both, is to be recommended. In one form of such a combination of the two procedures, the learner first reads the selection through entirely several times to get the thought of the whole clearly established. Then the selection is divided into suitable parts and learned by the part method. Finally, the whole is reviewed to secure adequate organization of the parts into the total associative train. This procedure is regarded as desirable for offsetting the principal drawbacks to the whole method.

SENSORY MODALITY

There are several different possible modes of impression: visual, aural, kinesthetic. If a poem is to be learned, for example, it may be read to the child while he listens, the printed poem may be given to him to read silently or aloud, he may write it down as he hears or reads it, or he may read it aloud with other children. These and other possible variations, it will be noted, make use of different sense impressions and different combinations of sense impressions. Here we have another variable in the complex of conditions affecting the efficiency of memorizing. Our concern is with the relative effectiveness of the various modes. It seems to depend upon the individual learner what particular method is best. Some persons learn better by hearing, others by seeing, and others by combinations of seeing, hearing, and responding verbally. At present we cannot say that any one method is best for all. Even the method best for one person in learning one kind of material may not be the best method for him in learning other kinds of material. The practical course for the best interests of all when dealing with a number of children would be to use different modes of impression and procedures in order to bring into play different senses and various combinations of the senses.

A study of the relative effectiveness of twelve different modes of presentation has been made by O'Brien (1921). His subjects learned nonsense syllables and meaningful words. While his results showed that no one mode was best for all, the group averages were distinctly in favor of the reading-aloud procedure, which combines visual, auditory, and vocomotor impressions.

Winch (1913, 1914) conducted experiments on learning to spell for the purpose of finding out whether silent study or spelling aloud in concert with the rest of the class would produce better results. Concerted oral repetition helps the young and backward pupil, while the silent method seems better for the brighter and more mature student who has no difficulties with reading and who is habituated to individual silent work. Winch points out that since most learning must be done silently and alone, the school should train children to learn efficiently by the silent, visual method.

An experimental study was made by Russell (1928) to determine whether pupils learn better by having the material read to them by the teacher or by their own silent reading of the materials. Over 600 pupils from grades 5, 7, and 9 took part in the experiment. Three procedures were employed with groups equated for ability by means of an intelligence test. In the first procedure the teacher read the material to the group twice. In the second the members of the group were handed the material and told to read it at their normal rate. The time allowed them was the same as that used by the teacher for two readings. In the third procedure, the pupils were told to read the material twice at their normal rate. The second method kept the time the same as the first, while the third kept the number of readings the same, regardless of time. The results differed for the three grades. In the fifth grade the children learned more from having the material read to them. For the seventh grade the two procedures were about equally effective. For the ninth graders the reading method proved to be somewhat superior. It appears, therefore, that the relative efficiency of learning by hearing and learning by reading is dependent upon the factors of maturity and training.

Audio-visual education. The use of audio-visual materials in the classroom is justified on the basis of a multi-sensory approach, but the mere use of a multi-modal stimulus does not insure greater learning. An enthusiastic but naive use of recordings and films, silent or sound, can produce as much confusion as learning. Extensive research completed during the past decade in conjunction with military training programs has demonstrated that audio-visual devices, most notably sound films, can provide as much learning as a teacher using a variety of teaching techniques—e.g., lecture, discussion, etc.—and further that an effective teaching film can surpass a poor teacher. A number of limitations to the use of films have been observed and bear repeating. The influence is greatest when the film content reinforces and extends previous knowledge and attitudes.

It has the least influence, particularly upon attitudes, when previous knowledge is inadequate or when content is antagonistic to prevailing attitudes. Films are most effective where the skill or knowledge concerned is specific rather than general. Variations in audience reactions which are functions of age, intelligence, education, sex, and attitude influence the nature of the learning that occurs, particularly if the film content is general. For audio-visual aids to be most effective, they should be supplemented by desirable conditions of learning: appropriate set, opportunity for recitation and review, examination, knowledge of results, etc.

THE ROLE OF SET IN LEARNING

The intent to learn is an important factor for successful memorizing. While it is true that associations are formed in many cases without intent to learn, little progress in mastering the memory material of the school situation may be expected from mere exposure to that material. A teacher may read a poem to children several times for the purpose of having them learn it verbatim and find that he cannot recite it himself after the children are able to do so. In giving an intelligence test, we tell the child to listen carefully while we read a passage so that he will be able to tell what it says. The child listens with the intent to remember what he hears. As examiners, having no such purpose, we do not retain what we read and are a bit shocked to realize that the child is reproducing the content far better than we could.

The influence of the learner's *task* or goal-set on his learning has been demonstrated in an experiment previously referred to. A series of 10 cards, each bearing a word and a number, was presented 8 times to a group of 10 students. Below the number on each card was a strip of colored paper, the color being different for each card. As the cards were presented, the students were instructed to observe carefully the word on each card and the number appearing with it, so that they would be able to reproduce the words together with the correct number for each. Nothing was said about the colors. Following each presentation of the whole 10 cards, the students were asked to write down as many of the word-number pairs as they could recall. After the series had been presented 8 times, they were asked to name the color which was presented with each word. The means of the reproductions for the 8 trials were as follows:

Trials:	1	2	3	4	5	6	7	8
Word-number pairs	3.7	5.6	7.0	7.2	8.3	8.7	8.8	9.7
Word-color pairs	—	—	—	—	—	—	—	2.9

It will be seen that more word-number pairs were recalled after a single presentation than word-color pairs after 8 presentations. After the eighth presentation, all but one of the group gave correctly all 10 word-number pairs. The one who had not reached complete learning reproduced 7 correctly. Yet the mean number of word-color pairs reproduced was only 2.9. When allowance for successful guessing is made, it is evident that there was very little learning of the word-color combinations.

Another and more general form of set which affects the learning process in a vital way is the *attitude* of the learner. Lack of confidence in ability to memorize, dislike for such work, dislike for the teacher or the school in general, feelings of distrust for the teacher, unwillingness to coöperate, antagonisms, and the feeling that there is no sense or value in learning the material are some of the attitudes which may affect unfavorably the child's efforts to learn. Necessary for best results are a spirit of coöperation between pupil and teacher, confidence in ability to learn born of past successes, and the feeling that the ability to recite this particular material will be definitely worth while. The teacher should strive to secure the eager and active kind of attitude that comes from a real desire to learn.

Attention. An indispensable condition for successful learning is *attention*. It is well known that unusually vivid and novel impressions have strong memory value. The heightened attention which attends such impressions is probably the main reason. It is also well known that one does not remember things to which he fails to give attention. The securing of adequate attention on the part of the learner is an essential feature of accepted laboratory techniques. In experiments on learning, lapses of attention or serious distraction during the presentation of a series of items to be learned would be due cause for considering the results invalid. Without the sustaining effect of interest, the child's attention is likely to shift readily from the task at hand; he is easily distracted. It behooves the teacher, therefore, to secure adequate interest in the material and to prevent so far as possible all distracting influences. Negative adaptation should be developed for unavoidable noises or other factors to which children are prone to shift their attention. Drills and exercises should be short to prevent attention lapses resulting from fatigue.

GUIDANCE AND CUES IN LEARNING

The question of how much guidance should be provided and at what point in learning is important in defining the function of the teacher. At what point should the teacher step in and show children the correct responses; when should she allow children to search for themselves? The evidence is sufficient to provide definite guide-lines. Carr (1930) and his students investigated the question of guidance with respect to motor learning using both animal and human subjects. Carr's results showed that guidance given in small amounts early in practice was beneficial, but that if it was deferred, its effectiveness decreased the farther it occurred from initial practice. Two to four guided trials in maze-learning were sufficient. More guidance impeded learning. The evidence suggests that if a learner is to acquire a skill, he must perform the required tasks with little outside help. The findings undoubtedly apply as much to parents and assistance with homework as they do to teachers.

The available evidence suggests that the same generalizations apply to learning which involves higher mental processes (Swenson, 1949; Stacey, 1949). Stacey distributed 100 sixth grade pupils into five equated groups and presented them with learning material consisting of 50 items in which one of the 5 words composing each item did not belong with the other 4. The five groups were given different amounts of information regarding the task ranging from the brief instruction that one of the words did not belong with the others up to being told what the word was and the basis or principle as to why it did not belong with the other 4. The latter group, the most informed, had the greatest opportunity to practice without error, the opposite being true of the group given the least information. Stacey concluded from his results that the process of active participation involved in self-discovery made for more effective learning than a process which involves mere identification of information previously given. Although the least informed group made a greater number of errors in the process of discovery, their errors were eliminated more quickly and with less detrimental effect than those of the highly informed group, which tended to perseverate in their errors once made.

Such findings suggest that guidance plays a less important role in learning than does knowledge of results, and that too much and too late guidance can have a detrimental effect. It should be pointed out, however, that the subjects in these experiments had knowledge of what the task or goal was which served to direct their behavior. It is very likely that guidance is effective in the degree to which it helps establish the appropriate sets.

A possible qualification to the preceding generalizations regarding guidance is suggested in a study of Maier and Klee (1945). In studies concerned with the effectiveness of trial-and-error and guidance in changing fixated behavior which the animal was unable to modify even though aware of the correct response to be made, Maier and Klee came to the conclusion that trial-and-error procedures are more effective in learning new responses, and that guidance was effective in breaking old, fixated responses but ineffective in the learning of new responses. Guidance should be discontinued as soon as the old response is broken, i.e., when the new adjustment has been successfully made. Undoubtedly the limited effectiveness of guidance is related to the problems in complex learning of discriminating between relevant and irrelevant cues and external and internal stimuli— external physical environment, posture, self-instruction, and the like — all of which are part of the stimulating conditions during learning.

A simple experiment frequently used in the laboratory to demonstrate the development of perception reveals various fairly typical changes in the sensory patterns. A dozen small cardboard boxes are used. These boxes are alike in appearance, and each one contains some small and familiar object, such as a penny, nail, or paper clip. The subject is asked to lift and shake each box and tell, if he can, what is in it. In naming the object, he reports the meaning he attaches to the sounds and tactual pressures. He is also asked to report on his attention, sensory experience, and mental imagery. After this, he is shown the object or told what it is. This procedure is followed through with each of the boxes, and the whole series then is repeated as many times as is needed for the subject to learn to identify all the objects correctly from the sounds and tactual impressions. The boxes are presented in a different order in each trial to prevent serial learning of the names of the objects. The most easily observed change is in the meaning that the sounds and pressures have for the subject, but careful observation reveals a number of coincident changes in the experiential components and their integration.

In the process of learning in this experiment, we have the elimination of those sensory elements that are of no value in identifying the object or that do not contribute to the subject's ability to distinguish between objects. This is the case for those sounds and pressures that are so similar for the various objects that no difference can be detected. Also, new elements are added as learning goes on. Some peculiar quality of sound, overlooked in the early trials, assumes a place of prominence in the field because it is just what enables the subject to distinguish a particular object. It might be a slight scratching noise or the distinctive pitch of a sound which emerges to take an important place in the new configuration. That which is unique about the sounds and pressures in each case becomes the significant feature for correctly identifying the object in auditory-tactual perception. These unique features are sooner or later selected, isolated, and integrated into a new and unified pattern that means *penny, nail, paper clip,* and so on, through the list.

Changes in the context or changes in the cues serve to reduce recall and impede performance, for evidence suggests that incidental cues as well as relevant ones become associated in learning. Perhaps in some degree, such factors explain the advantage that is evident in a team playing on its home court or home field.

INCENTIVE CONDITIONS

Motivation has been separated from incentives to emphasize a distinction which is more artificial than real in actual practice, yet of practical concern to the teacher. Motives are those conditions within the individual which cause him to seek particular goals. The student will recall that in Chapter 5, the development of motivation and the acquisition of acquired drives was traced. Motives and goals, as well as the appropriate behavior for reaching the goals, are established and modified as a result of learning.

Incentives are those objects or situations external to the individual and capable of satisfying a motive. In many instances, goal and incentive are identical; in some they are not. It is the differences in the two situations which are of especial interest. An incentive may be objectively described; a goal can only be defined in terms of the motive conditions, and as such is more speculative. More important, the incentive which an individual seeks may not be the goal. We commonly strive for money — a few persons for the sake of the money itself, but most for different reasons — to provide economic security, to satisfy various appetites for a new automobile or boat, or to achieve the prestige of being wealthy. Money may be an incentive sought by many, but their motives for seeking it, the why of seeking it, and thus their goals may be quite different. A pupil in a class may strive for a perfect mark in an arithmetic or spelling lesson not because that is his goal, but because it may symbolize teacher approval, which is what he basically desires; or, he may wish to avoid parental criticism for less than perfect work. The incentive of the perfect paper is not his goal.

It is also possible for the incentive to be synonymous with goal. A youngster may work hard sanding, glueing, and painting a model airplane for the sole satisfaction he derives from the completed model. The distinction that has been made between incentives and goals is an important one for the teacher because she manipulates incentives — praise and blame, reward and punishment, sarcasm and ridicule, gold stars and grades, competition and coöperation. Not infrequently, these incentives are manipulated in ways which *satisfy the teacher's motivation* by the results which are produced. A junior high school teacher who sarcastically ridiculed individual pupils in her English class was thought to be very humorous by her students — until one by one nearly all of them became the butt of her ridicule. The few who escaped still thought her humorous, but most of the others developed a strong dislike for the teacher because her approach conflicted with their personal motivation.

Incentives may be classified into two kinds: *intrinsic* and *extrinsic*. Intrinsic incentives are those which operate to functionally relate the task and the goal. Extrinsic incentives are those which have no functional relationship to the task. Taking again the arithmetic or spelling lesson, successfully spelling words which had been previously missed, indicating improvement or correctly answering all the arithmetic examples are satisfying ends in themselves and are functionally related to the task being performed. Having a teacher put a gold star on the paper, or receiving a grade of A at report time has only an arbitrarily established artificial relationship, and as such is an extrinsic incentive.

We are so accustomed to grades and accept them as an apparently inherent part of schooling, that calling them artificially related to learning tasks may be a surprise. Ask yourself for a moment what C means. Your answer is probably that it is average. Investigate the meaning of the letter "C" in a dictionary; no connotation of average is given. At best, the dictionary will say that it may be used as a symbol to arbitrarily designate a class or group, usually third in order. For the moment let us accept the meaning of average and ask, "Average in what? In relation to a particular group of students? But are they capable students?" If so, the average is different than if they are retarded. The symbol as used is not only artificial, but relatively meaningless. A teacher might as well give a ten-penny nail for average work and a 20-penny nail for superior work. In either situation it is by the authority of the teacher that a given symbol is chosen; some prefer cowboy stickers or flowers to gold stars; to know the meaning of the symbol requires knowledge of the teachers' standards, which vary considerably. The author has met three teachers who would not give any A's, the first because she couldn't stand to give F's and wanted to be "fair," the second because she thought only God was perfection, and the third because he didn't want any pupil to think he was really that good.

In considering the effect of various incentives, it is well to keep in mind that many at the disposal of the teacher are extrinsic — rewards, punishment, praise, etc. In time, by the process by which motives are acquired, the reward or praise or A's may become a goal of itself. Moreover, most situations are more complex in that they involve a combination of several incentives, extrinsic and intrinsic.

Reward and punishment. The role of reward and punishment in learning has been described in some detail in earlier chapters and need not be repeated here except to acknowledge the obvious effect of reward upon learning, thus serving as a cornerstone of many of the association theories of learning. Rewards are not only directly reinforcing but, it will be recalled, they have secondary effects as well; these are important in view of the teacher's concern not only for utilizing existing motives, but also for modifying them in ways that are socially desirable.

In the case of rewards and punishment, we frequently have out-comes or aftereffects that are not relevant to the motive responsible for the activity but that nevertheless serve to reinforce or eliminate an activity or response which they follow (Thorndike, 1935). Ex-periments with animals have shown that if a response made because of one motive is followed by an effect that satisfies some other motive, the effect, though irrelevant to the first motive, serves to reinforce the response. Thus, the scratching by a rat is relevant to irritation but not to escape or eating. Yet, when rats were released from a problem box and rewarded by food following the activity of scratch-ing, the tendency to scratch was reinforced by the reward. The rats thus rewarded learned to scratch as a means of escape (Lorge, 1936). The strengthening effect of irrelevant satisfying aftereffects has also been experimentally demonstrated with human subjects (Thorn-dike, 1933). A considerable amount of learning appears to result from outcomes which are irrelevant to the motive prompting the activity. When a child completes his arithmetic assignment, and then is rewarded for accuracy and neatness by a special privilege or honor, the satisfying effects of the reward will tend to reinforce his efforts to secure neatness and accuracy in his work.

The effect of punishment appears to be less direct than that of reward. The rat enters a blind alley because of his food-seeking set. But when he receives a shock, he quickly retreats. The recoil due to the shock is a recoil from the blind-alley situation. The pathway becomes something to be avoided, not merely a place where no food is found. An avoidance set is added to the tendency to stop entering the alley merely because it does not lead to the food and fulfillment of the motive. Hence, we observe a more rapid elimination of false runs when punishment is attached to them.

In a study with adult human subjects, one experimenter used a maze so constructed that a shock was received at the end of blind alleys. A group who received the shock for errors learned the maze with fewer trials, in less time, and with fewer errors than another group who learned without punishment for errors. Shock for errors increased the time per trial, indicating greater caution, but since fewer trials were necessary to reach the criterion of learning because of the smaller number of errors, the total time required was less than for learning without the shock (Bunch, 1928).

Other experiments have shown the accelerating effect of shock for errors in maze learning, in mirror drawing, and in rational learning (Bunch and Hagman, 1937). When the number of trials is constant, the total time is usually increased by shocks for errors while the errors are usually reduced. One investigator found in a mirror-drawing experiment that shocks for errors on one side of the path reduced errors on the other side where shocks were not received, due presumably to the greater caution induced by the shock (Barlow, 1933).

In the realm of human conduct, the pattern of motives is often complex and conflicting. Here the influence of reward and punishment may sometimes extend over rather long intervals of time by means of memory and imagination. Punishment promised or foreseen on the basis of the consequences of one's own previous behavior or consequences known to have been suffered by others for certain deeds may influence one's choices or his formulation of a task with respect to a certain action. The individual knowing or fearing that the outcome will be annoying may decide to refrain from a particular course of action or alter it in order to avoid the unhappy consequences. A conflict may arise here. The individual may wish to avoid punishment, but at the same time may value certain other fruits of his projected exploit so highly that he will go ahead with the conviction that the satisfactions to be derived will outweigh the possible or inevitable suffering. Then it is that punishment fails as a deterrent. Hilgard and Russell (1950) have aptly pointed out several limitations to punishment as an incentive to learning:[1]

1. Punishment tells what *not* to do, rather than what to do.
2. The effects of punishment as an aid to learning are of shorter duration than those of reward, possibly because of simultaneous emotion effects which may interfere with learning.
3. The effect of punishment upon the subsequent attitude of the child toward the teacher may be negative.
4. In some instances, the punished behavior becomes more resistant to change, e. g., thumbsucking and bedwetting.

Praise and reproof. Hurlock's (1925) study has been cited earlier to show the different effects of praise and reproof upon performance in arithmetic over a short period of time, although it must be remembered that the praised, reproved, and ignored groups were in the same room and observed all treatments; this fact may have produced effects that would not occur if a group were given a con-

[1] By permission of E. R. Hilgard and D. H. Russell, "Motivation in School Learning," *Forty-ninth Yearbook of the National Society for the Study of Education*, Part I. (Chicago: University of Chicago Press, 1950), p. 49.

stant diet of praise. Furthermore, it has been demonstrated that differential effects occur in relationship to personality traits of the recipient, with those having feelings of inadequacy responding more favorably to praise and those who are self-assured working harder after criticism.

Knowledge of results as an incentive. There is a considerable amount of experimental evidence that indicates the stimulating value of the learner's knowledge of his score, his successes and errors, and the progress he is making (Fay, 1937). There is satisfaction in bettering one's previous score, in seeing the errors disappear, and in watching one's curve of accomplishment rise to new heights; that is, of course, if one is trying to improve. Pointing out to a child his errors or other deficiencies in his work is the classroom analogue of the laboratory announcement of "Wrong" for incorrect responses or electric shock at the end of a blind alley. Through their informative value, they both accelerate learning. Likewise, being informed of the good points in his work and the gains he has made is equivalent to mild shock or "Right" for correct responses in the laboratory. The critical evaluation of a pupil's work will be more effective as an incentive to improvement when it is specific with respect to particular defects, errors, and good points than when it is general and indefinite, as in such comments as "Your work is poor," or "That is very good." Forlano (1936) compared the effectiveness with fifth grade pupils of immediate and delayed knowledge of results as an incentive when it was combined with a monetary reward. The gains in achievement with knowledge of results alone were as great as those obtained with a supplementary reward.

Competition and cooperation. Many a teacher has been able to secure enthusiastic effort by means of a competitive enterprise when other methods of motivation have failed. For such motivation to be effective, a child must have a fair chance of winning. If a child knows from repeated experiences that he does not have a chance, he not only will not be stimulated to exert himself, but he may develop an attitude of hopelessness and a sense of inferiority or a resentment against the whole classroom situation. While generally considered more desirable from the standpoint of wholesome social attitudes, group competition appears to be less effective as an incentive than individual competition (Maller, 1929; Sims, 1928).

In one experimental study on rivalry 155 fourth- and sixth-grade pupils were divided into two approximately equivalent groups for each grade on the basis of initial ability, sex, and age. The experimental group then was divided into two subgroups who were told that they were to try to surpass each other. The work consisted of addition exercises in arithmetic. Rivalry was further stimulated between the two subdivisions of the experimental group by putting the scores of each on the board and calling out the names of the members of the winning group. This procedure was continued over a period of one week. The results indicated clearly that the rivalry had been a strong incentive, for the experimental group made considerably higher scores than the controls. Here the effect of rivalry was greater for the younger children, and for those less gifted intellectually (Hurlock, 1927).

The use of organized competition and rivalry in the classroom, while it no doubt does provide a strong incentive, is not generally regarded as a first-rate teaching procedure. It may work when other and better means fail. But it has numerous disadvantages. Aside from the fact that it is conducive to antagonisms and other undesirable social attitudes, it is probably the most artificial of artificial incentives. The interest is in beating the other fellow or the other group, not in the studies or in improvement. When the competitive conditions are removed, there is little likelihood of any transfer of interest or continuance of effect thus artificially aroused. A case in point is that of a teacher whose pupils had been coming to school without being properly washed. Urging and coaxing had failed to secure the desired handwashing. So she arranged for competition between boys and girls. Boys were lined up in one row, girls in another. Hands were held out as the teacher walked down the rows to see whether boys or girls had the cleaner hands. After a time the practice was discontinued. Then one morning one of these boys started off to school without his usual washing of hands and face. His mother caught him just in time and said, "Here, you haven't washed up yet." "Oh, we don't have to wash any more," was the youngster's reply.

In interpreting the value of competition, one must bear in mind its acceptance in our society. In other groups which do not sanction competition, such as the Arapesh in New Guinea or the Zuni in the United States, experimentally induced competitive situations would very likely produce different results. Competition, like soup-spooning, is learned. It can be of value in providing considerable zest to classroom activities on a number of occasions, provided the individuals on competing teams are evenly matched. As a long term procedure, however, it can have disastrous results, unless one is concerned only with the winners. Those who constantly lose (and some are almost certain to be constant losers in academic competition) ultimately, in self-defense, reject the competition and, in rejecting it, they cease trying.

Sarcasm, ridicule, and fear of punishment. The merits of any incentive must be judged by its effect on the pupil as well as on his effort. No pupil should be shamed or humiliated before his fellows. Sarcasm and ridicule are the devices of a weak teacher. They may have their place, but that place is not in the classroom. They breed attitudes of contempt, antagonism, and resentment, and these attitudes are not conducive to learning. They may impair the mental health of a timid or nervous child.

Fear of punishment and fear of failure are unwholesome for the child's emotional adjustment and their effect on learning is deleterious and inhibitory. A child needs security and self-confidence in order to make satisfactory progress. Punishment may be necessary in some cases of persistent misconduct but the threat of it should never be used to stimulate learning.

Success and failure. If A's, honor rolls, and victory in competition are attainable by only a few, success is available to all, provided that success is defined as achieving one's goal. Success has the advantage of coming in degrees, in contrast to rewards, which are more likely to be an all-or-none affair. One at least derives satisfaction from progress towards a goal which is having success in degree. The mere setting of a goal is satisfying, as any college student who has spent two to three years at college without a definite objective can aver. Progress towards a goal and attaining proximity to the goal region are still more satisfying. The Sears' have carried out several studies of the effects of success and failure upon motivation. In one study (1937) Sears demonstrated that in an experiment in which half the group received consistent failure in attaining the goals which had been set in a speed of card-sorting task, they showed progressively slower progress than the success group which made consistent gains. In another study of the level of aspiration of academically unsuccessful students, Sears (1940) found that their failure resulted in unrealistic goal-setting. They either set goals so low that no hazard was involved (note that a too-easy success is not satisfying) or so high that success was impossible. Academically successful students were realistic in estimating their improvement. Other related studies have shown that successful atttainment of goals contributes to realistic levels of aspiration.

Levels of aspiration are modified not only by the attained results, success or not, but also by certain group influences. Few college students will acknowledge before an examination that they are well-prepared even though they may believe they are, because to do so would be to invite the disfavor of the group. Neither will they acknowledge that an excellent score was the result of preparation; rather they will dissemble, attributing the result to "luck."

The effect of a steady diet of failure is easily seen in pupils held in school against their wishes because of minimum-age laws for leaving school or in non-promoted students whose goals shift from learning to getting out of school. Few teachers will say that such pupils are incapable of learning more than they know; rather, they complain about the lack of interest or motivation which prevents their learning and makes the teacher's life difficult. One solution offered is to change the law; another that should be considered is changing school practices—to encourage pupils to progress to the limits of their own abilities by aiding them to set attainable goals, which would have to be short-range goals in the elementary school for the period, the day, or the week. This would require teachers to see value in progress itself, not solely in excellent scholarship. It would necessitate a realistic estimate of what progress she can expect a pupil to make, not what she would like to see made by all. It would mean seeing that school children are not too often discouraged nor too easily satisfied.

Placing the emphasis upon success and failure to reach goals realistically set would tend to overcome other disadvantages of incentives. The first is the limitation found in the arbitrarily established standards of adults. Maturation requires the attainment of independence from parents and teachers—the adult authority figures in children's lives. With the coming of adolescence, the struggle for independence is usually intensified, and in the struggle it is inevitable that symbols the adults hold dear—such as grades and similar incentives—should become subject to some degree of rejection. It is usually junior high school teachers who first complain of the indifference of pupils to grades. Secondly, incentives tend to lose their appeal in the absence of satisfaction of motivation. Secondary rewards need periodic strengthening unless they become goals in themselves. The operation of this in practice is easily seen in the giving of monetary rewards for good report cards, which in a sense constitutes bait for a bribe for learning. Interestingly enough, in a study conducted by the author among 700 students in a junior high school, it was the students having poorer academic records whose parents used the giving and taking away of monetary rewards and allowances to a significantly greater extent. Thirdly, unattainable incentives lose their appeal except under unusual drive conditions. When incentives such as grades and honor rolls and teacher praise are so rigged as to be accessible to only a few—the students having the advantage of greater ability, superior academic achievement from grade to grade, etc.—it is these few who alone will continue to strive for them, while the remainder gradually lose interest in attaining the impossible.

SUMMARY

The methods of the teacher can make a considerable difference in the learning that occurs. The tasks she presents, the amount of practice given, the distribution of practice, provision for drill and recitation, furnishing knowledge of results, and adopting effective incentive conditions fall within the available methods by which the teacher can influence the course of learning. Fortunately for class schedules, it is the length of the work period rather than the length of the rest interval which is of greater significance in the distribution of practice. With few exceptions, the advantage in learning goes to distributed practice. The exceptions are where peak performance of material already well-known or relearning of material once well-learned is desired, or where insightful learning is possible or prolonged warm-up periods necessary. Otherwise, practice should be spaced, with shorter periods of work and rest at the beginning being gradually lengthened. Practice periods should be long enough to permit warm-up and short enough to avoid the decrement in work which comes with fatigue, reactive inhibition, and lowered motivation. It follows that the younger the child or the more novel the task, the shorter the practice period should be.

Continuing learning beyond the first perfect trial (overlearning) is desirable up to 50 per cent more. But overlearning should come after learning. Drill, presented before the task or skill has been acquired, is as likely to fixate error responses. Recitation or review during the process facilitates learning, promoting more effective grouping and better distribution of practice, and providing knowledge of results. Guidance is of greater value in correcting faulty performance than in establishing initial responses, and where used early in training should be done sparingly.

The incentive conditions used in the classroom are of considerable significance not only because they determine the direction of immediate effort, but more because they determine in degree the future motivation of the learning. Because drives and motives are to a large degree learned—at least the major portion of personal-social motivation—the effect of differing incentive conditions upon the kind of motives acquired should be carefully considered. The typical incentives used of grades and similar devices, which permit only a few to experience success, create artificial goals in those who can attain them and a rejection of such incentives by those who cannot. Repeated failure to obtain the incentive produces increasing feelings of inadequacy accompanied by negative motivation, and hostility and aggression towards others. The creation of sound personal and group mental health in the classroom is closely allied with the incentives employed by the teacher. Realistic goals—those which are attainable—towards which one can progress and ultimately achieve with the related sense of success are preferable to the run of praise, punishment, competition, reward, cooperation, ridicule, and the like. However, it cannot be denied that the latter incentives can be effective in producing and prompting learning.

OVERVIEW

Melton, A. W., "Learning," *Encyclopedia of Educational Research,* W. S. Monroe, ed. New York: Macmillan Co., 1950, pp. 668-90.

SELECTED REFERENCES

Bugelski, B. R., *The Psychology of Learning.* New York: Holt, 1956.
Deese, J., *Psychology of Learning.* New York: McGraw-Hill, 1952.
McGeoch, J. A. and A. L. Irion, *The Psychology of Human Learning,* rev. New York: Longmans, Green, 1952.
Stephens, J. M., *Educational Psychology,* rev. New York: Holt, 1956.

ORIGINAL INVESTIGATIONS

Hovland, C. I., "Experimental Studies in Rote Learning Theory, I-VII," *Journal of Experimental Psychology,* 1938-1940.

Plowman, Letha and J. Stroud, "Effect of Informing Pupils of the Correctness of Their Responses to Objective Test Questions," *Journal of Educational Research,* 1942, 36, pp. 16-20.

Sears, Pauline, "Levels of Aspiration in Academically Successful and Unsuccessful School Children," *Journal of Abnormal and Social Psychology,* 1940, 35, pp. 498-536.

Chapter Eight

Individual Differences and Educational Practice

In the preceding three chapters, the relationships of individual, task, and method variables to learning have been described. The majority of the studies have been concerned with the operation of a single variable or, sometimes, the interaction between two variables. In actual practice, all variables are functioning simultaneously in any single individual; and, further, by virtue of the administrative arrangement of schools in which children are taught simultaneously in groups, there is the additional influence of social interaction between members of the group. The problems resulting from such arrangements were foreshadowed in

279

Chapter 5 in the description of the range of individual differences occurring in a fifth-grade class in which one would find mental ages spanning a 7-year range, the spread of individual aptitudes and scholastic achievement as great, and as wide a variation in personality, physical, socio-economic, and experiential factors. The greatest task of any teacher is to organize her work to provide for the tremendous range of individual differences encountered.

GROUPING

It would be convenient if each pupil were uniform in degree of aptitude and ability in all areas. Under such circumstances it would be possible to establish fairly stable and homogeneous groups for purposes of instruction and standardize teaching practices for the different groups. When intelligence tests were first developed, a certain naive faith ensued that at last we had a magic mirror in which we could see all. By obtaining intelligence test scores, it would be possible to group children with others of like ability, all of whom could be taught by standardized procedures utilizing standardized materials; educated persons could be mass produced in the same manner as automobiles. The rude awakening came all too abruptly. Intelligence tests provided no magic key to analyzing human capacity; instead, they proved to be crude measuring devices of a restricted aspect of human capacity. When children of the same mathematical aptitude are grouped together, they are heterogeneous (highly varied) for any other aspect of aptitude such as language, art, music, etc. They are not even homogeneous (similar) as far as achievement in mathematics is concerned. To test this statement, compare the range of *achievement* in mathematics or reading ability of any group of youngsters having average mathematical or verbal aptitude; the range of their achievement will be found to be nearly as great as for the entire unsorted group. Unfortunate as this outcome may be for educational practice — for it makes the task of teaching by groups more difficult — it redounds to the benefit of society. Man's evolution has become dependent upon establishing new ways of behaving, individually and socially, rather than upon the selection of organically better adapted species. To this end, a homogeneous populace of uniformly trained people is ill-suited.

In spite of the non-homogeneity of so-called homogeneous groups based upon any single criterion such as intelligence tests, the practice of homogeneous grouping has persisted in educational practice, particularly at the junior high school level. While it is true that it is a convenience to be able to teach a group of children who approximate each other in aptitude and achievement, mainly because the instruction can be carried on with less diversified materials, it should be apparent that the frequently observed junior high school practice of subdividing children into groups on the basis of intelligence, achievement, or any other criterion, and leaving them in these fixed groups for all subjects, fails in its purpose. What often occurs is that the groups become more homogeneous in attitude and motivation, negative or positive; the inferior groups become less motivated, and the superior groups become anxious about maintaining their status.

The elementary school organization in which the classes are heterogeneous provides the teacher with the necessary flexibility in arranging her subgroups so that she can have comparatively homogeneous subgroups for a particular subject or activity, whether it be reading, singing, spelling, auditory discrimination, or other tasks. This permits her to adapt methods and materials to a particular task for particular groups of children. The student who investigates the question of the relative superiority of homogeneous versus heterogeneous groupings will find the results of the many research studies favoring one as much as the other. Like the many studies investigating differences in teaching method, it will be found that favorable results can be obtained by many methods. The question is not which method is superior, but rather which method should be used with what group of children under what circumstances. In the question of grouping, the extent to which the teacher can adapt her materials and procedures to the particular grouping arrangement appears to be the important consideration.

Another problem of educational practice associated with the variability in learners is that of making adequate provision for exceptional children —those who deviate markedly from the average of the group in intelligence, physical development, etc. It is apparent that individuals learn at different rates and that it is desirable to have all individuals learning at an optimum rate. Gifted children learn more rapidly, while intellectually retarded children learn more slowly; both differ in qualitative aspects as well as quantative aspects of learning. Physically handicapped children have special problems to be faced in overcoming the degree of isolation that handicaps impose, just as children with personality disturbances encounter an isolation resulting from their difficulty.

The solutions in educational practice for the problems presented by such individual differences are of three kinds: *adaptation, segregation,* or *acceleration.* Adaptation is merely the provision of specially suited tasks within the regular classroom organization. Adaptation for the gifted child consists of enriching the program by providing special opportunity for investigating and learning at a more intensive level or in more extensive areas than for the average child. Adaptation for the less intelligent consists of simplifying and reducing the degree of abstraction.

Segregation is a procedure for setting up special classes or special schools. Some school systems have established schools or special curricula within schools for either the gifted or retarded. These children are separated from the average children and are provided with special programs. Such a solution is more difficult for a small school system than a large one, for if the intellectual deviates constitute between 2 and 5 per cent at either end of the distribution curve, a school system would need a minimum of 200 pupils entering school each year to fill special classes, and a larger number for special classes for other handicaps.

Acceleration consists of advancing or retarding children to the grade level at which they are capable of performing. The gifted children would be advanced and the intellectually retarded children would be held at grade level and advanced more slowly through the educational program.

A variety of arguments favoring and opposing all three procedures can be advanced. To mention a few: special classes can be adapted to individual needs providing a special program impossible in the regular classes; enrichment provides a wider and deeper range of experiences and at the same time permits a youngster to participate with other children who are at his same level of development both socially and emotionally; and acceleration challenges a youngster to work up to capacity, avoids his wasting time, permits him to

complete lengthy academic training sooner and become a contributing member of the community at an earlier date. In the opposite
vein: special classes create artificial cleavages between children —
the gifted become vain and the dullards discouraged — thus defeating
a basic democratic principle of mutual respect; enrichment is so
difficult to attain in the regular classroom that it can be had only
at the expense of the majority of the children; and acceleration
and retardation places individual children in groups in which they
are unable to participate because of differences in maturation.

The arguments all have some degree of validity. No educational
program can be adopted without having some defects and disadvantages. Teaching children by groups has faults. Individual tutor-
ing would eliminate some faults but would substitute others. The
essential task is to arrive at the most workable solution, given certain contingencies. One set of contingencies is the acquired knowledge from experimental psychology about learning. A second set
is the interaction between individual children and teachers in
group situations. A third set of contingencies is the community,
its size, number of children, and available resources. A fourth set
is the social objectives and value systems of the community and the
society of which it is part. Any of the procedures mentioned for
providing for exceptional children can be made to work while the
disadvantages can be minimized by careful effort.

GRADING AND PROMOTION

Grading and promotion are two aspects of educational practice of
much concern to the teacher because of their relation to motivation. Three or four times during a school year, teachers go through
the ritual of grading. Few derive any satisfaction from the practice
and many have their misgivings. Concurrently, the children work
harder, pretend to be better than they are, apple-polish, and resort
to other devious tactics to insure favorable grades. Few will be
satisfied, many disappointed, and all can well question the procedure. For all practical purposes, grades and report cards could
be dispensed with today without serious loss. College admission
programs would not suffer, parents would not know less, and

teachers could devote their time to educational activity. But like many rituals, grades and report cards will persist.

Grades and report cards have three main features: (1) they are measures, (2) they constitute a communication system, and (3) they serve as incentives affecting motivation. As measures they provide information on individual and group progress and knowledge of results to children and parents. As measuring systems, they suffer the usual problems of validity and reliability: what do they measure and how consistently do they measure it? In the total sense, the composite average of teacher grades is as good a predictor of scholastic achievement as is available — as good as tests. The sum total of all the grades a child receives constitutes a composite measure of aptitude, achievement, motivation, deportment, study habits, initiative, et al. But taken individually, it is difficult to determine what a grade represents. Each teacher establishes her own basis for grading. Seldom do two teachers have the same basis. Some base their grades on achievement, some on achievement relative to ability, others on effort, others on gain, others on attitude, etc. Worse, only a few tell children the basis upon which they are grading, with the result that the learner doesn't know the direction his efforts should take, much less what the grade means when he receives it.

The first step in grading is to make clear what it is that is being judged or measured — quality of work, quantity of work, effort, or whatever — and to recognize that, for each aspect to be measured, a separate grade is needed (if it is to be meaningful without further explanation, inasmuch as a grade is no more than a symbolic representation of standing in some characteristic). The teacher and the pupil should both be clear on the meaning of the grade. Secondly, once the attribute being judged has been selected, the basis of comparison should be established. Three such bases are possible: (1) comparison with the performance of others, (2) comparison with the potential performance of the individual, e.g., degree of improvement, (3) comparison with some absolute external standard. Adopting the foregoing steps in establishing criteria for grades will increase both validity and reliability.

Grades are part of a communication system informing the pupil and his parents on his progress. As a communication system, it is only as good as the amount of information conveyed in relation to the amount of energy expended. Previous comment has been made on the relative meaninglessness of letter grades. In spite of this, the conventional A-F grading system has two advantages in conserving energy: the first is that parents think they know what the grade means and ask for no further information; the second is that if grading is unavoidable, this method is as convenient as any. As for the pupil, his information is more accurate in spite of the grades, for he knows from daily performance how he is progressing in arithmetic, spelling, history, physiology, etc. To improve grades and report cards as communication systems requires providing more explicit information, possibly in the form of check lists, letters, parent-teacher conferences, and the like — no small task.

It would be helpful if pupils and parents could divorce the informational aspects of grades from their motivational aspects, utilizing grades purely for knowledge of performance. But grades are incentives and operate with the effects described in this chapter. From the viewpoint of educational practice, it is important that the grades do not become a deterrent to motivation. Considering the central position of motivation in learning, any losses in motivation are mutually defeating to the purposes of both pupil and teacher.

Promotional policy similarly influences learning by virtue of its effect upon motivation. In general, two choices are available: holding the pupil at the grade level of the tasks he is capable of performing, which necessitates retaining the pupil at a given grade until he succeeds in the tasks; or, keeping him with the pupils of his same physical-social-emotional development, irrespective of his performance on tasks. The former is called non-promotion or retention, the latter, social promotion. Research shows that a policy of non-promotion does not assure any more mastery of subject matter or any faster progress than social promotion (Collinson, 1940; Cook, 1941), but that it (non-promotion) does have a negative effect upon motivation (Sandin, 1942; Trainor and Rogers, 1955) in that non-promoted pupils, when compared with socially promoted pupils, show more symptoms of maladjustment, are more hostile towards schools, are more often socially rejected by their new classmates, and are more often viewed unfavorably by their teachers. While this evidence strongly favors a policy of social promotion, it does not justify a conclusion that social promotion can be depended upon for learning. In either case, learning only proceeds if capacity, task, and method have been adequately considered. A child can remain illiterate under either procedure if suitable provision for learning is not made.

CLASSROOM ATMOSPHERE

Certainly more significant in the total environment of the classroom and the interaction of the multiple factors which have been considered in the preceding chapters is the classroom atmosphere created by teachers. Differences in the style of leadership produce differences in the amount of interaction among children, in the attitudes towards the tasks and skills to be performed, in the amount of aggression expressed — either verbal or physical, and in other aspects of behavior important in learning (Lewin, Lippitt, and White, 1939). The teacher, by action or default, creates the classroom environment in which learning is to take place. Although research to date has been limited because of the complexity and subtlety of the questions along with the limitations in research techniques, nevertheless it has been sufficient to point out the varied climates in which learning can progress. Lectures, discussions, audio-visual devices, teacher-centered classes, student-centered classes, demonstrations, and so forth all have their value. The problem for the teacher is not the adoption of a particular method, but the understanding of the scientific bases upon which the various methods depend, amplified by an experimental approach in the classroom. A double meaning is intended in using the word experimental: (1) trying different approaches to solve teaching problems and (2) being objective about results. The teacher may not conduct controlled experiments in the scientific sense, but she can be scientific about the results of her teaching. Instead of blaming the stupidity or the laziness of a given child for his failure to learn (both are intangibles, and if they exist, they are beyond the reach of the teacher), it is better to ask how the task can be varied, what differences can be introduced into the arrangement for practice, and what incentive conditions, set, etc., can be established to provide more favorable results. An experimental approach by an enthusiastic teacher can lead only to learning outcomes which are mutually more satisfying to both teacher and learner.

OVERVIEW

Monroe, W. S., *Encyclopedia of Educational Research,* New York: Macmillan Co., 1950. Selected topics: School Progress, Marks and Marking Systems, Curriculum Development, Social Climate of Classrooms.

SELECTED REFERENCES

Barker, R. G., J. S. Kounin, and H. F. Wright, eds., *Child Behavior and Development.* New York: McGraw-Hill, 1943.

Coladarci, A. P., *Readings in Educational Psychology.* New York: Dryden, 1955.

Seidman, J. M., *Readings in Educational Psychology.* Boston: Houghton Mifflin, 1955.

Part 3

Learning in Behavioral Areas

Chapter Nine

The Objectives of Education

*Education is fraught with much con-
flict. There is first the question of whom
should be educated and at whose
expense. There are some who would
educate only the gifted, although, considering man's relations to his fellow man,
"gifted" may be misconstrued to mean
those from a given social class rather than
those of a given capacity. There are those
who would educate all, on the premise
that the successful development of
democratic society depends upon an educated
citizenry. Whatever the preference of people, there
is no unanimity of opinion, and even those
who espouse the cause of universal education aren't enthusiastic about its*

cost. It is reasonably safe to say that the general philosophy within the United States is that all children shall at least have equal opportunity for education; and if at times the boundary lines of what constitutes "equal" are stretched, the acceptance of the philosophy justifies efforts to make "equal" mean the same. This leaves the questions of what the education shall be, of what studies shall be incorporated, of whether or not personal or social development of children shall have equal place with academic and scholastic development, of what values shall be stressed, and of whether or not religion shall be incorporated in the curriculum, and, if so, whose religion. In general, this is a philosophical question which in modern societies is decided by some agency of government to which the general public has varying degress of access. In the United States, the authority as to what shall be taught rests with locally constituted school committees, directly elected by the constituency served. That conflict can exist in this area of decision can be seen in the controversies that have arisen in recent years regarding world government, the United Nations, and the United Nations Educational and Social Organization, and their appropriate place or lack of place in a course of study.

If groups of adults are asked to identify the skills, achievements, and competencies which they would like to have their children attain by the end of twelve grades of school, the list they prepare will usually include:

1. Able to read, write, speak effectively
2. Able to think and reason
3. Able to get along with others
4. Able to appreciate art and music
5. Able to select a suitable vocation
6. Have some knowledge of history, government, and science
7. Have a hobby, and leisure or sport skills
8. Have a working philosophy of life
9. Have the ability to lead a happy, well-adjusted life

The lists vary from group to group, being sometimes longer or shorter, and sometimes phrased in different terms, just as lists of educational objectives prepared by various committees over the past 50 years have varied in the number of items in their lists; but, in essence, they say much the same thing. The foregoing list of items may be grouped under three headings:

1. Cultural
2. Social
3. Personal

Cultural items are those which involve learning to live in the man-made part of the environment, that is, using the language and the customs, the tools and utensils, and the machinery and equipment that a particular group of men have adopted for their use. The so-called fundamental skills are fundamental only to a particular society; they are far from being universal. The fundamental skills desired in a Samoan boy and in an American boy are quite different, one including fishing, boating, swimming, the other reading, writing, and arithmetic.

The items grouped under the second heading—social—are those related to living successfully with other human beings in a given society. This involves certain formal knowledge about the customs and institutionalized procedures — how the government operates, when to pay taxes, what accepted religious procedures are, and the informal procedures involved in maintaining satisfactory relationships with those persons met on a face-to-face basis—one's family, friends, and fellow-workers. Again, these vary from social group to social group even within a country; witness differences in the groups discriminated against in northern and southern United States. The third group of personal items includes those concerned with personal adjustment—having a philosophy, a way of working, knowing one's assets and liabilities and accepting them for what they are, and knowing how to satisfy one's motives without infringing on the rights and privileges of others: in all, being personally well-adjusted.

Each of these groups of behaviors is sufficiently important that a science has been developed for each one—anthropology for cultural characteristics, sociology for social behavior, and psychology for personal behavior. The lines between the three are not sharply drawn, for obviously personal behavior involves objects and persons, and thus psychology overlaps sociology and anthropology. Whether from the interests of its practitioners or the necessities of science, this overlapping is recognized in practice, as may be seen in the study of social psychology or social anthropology, which in a sense are dual sciences tapping two fields of knowledge.

If any of these fields can absorb the lifetime energy of a man without his encompassing the entire field, then teaching dwarfs them in comparison, for the teacher transects not only all three fields in the skills and knowledge she promotes, but additional fields as well, in her attempt to understand human behavior: biology, physiology, psychiatry as well as sociology, anthropology, and psychology contribute knowledge which the teacher utilizes in daily practice. This is not to suggest that the teacher is superhuman in her skill, but merely that her job is more complex.

In relating the psychological variables to education, one may view the objectives of education in several organizational schemes. A distinction may be made between content and process. The content of education may be divided into such categories as knowledge and understanding, skill and competence, attitudes and interests, and action patterns; this implies that learning consists of an informational aspect, an application aspect, a motivational phase, and a behavioral phase. Teachers are trained to consider these different aspects of education in order to avoid too narrow a concept of their teaching objectives. Frequently, these four categories are specifically related to given areas of knowledge. A school's curriculum may specify its objectives as the development of knowledge and understanding, skill and competence, attitude and interest, and action patterns related to physical health and development, the physical world, the social world, communication skills, quantitative skills, ethical behavior, social and emotional development, and esthetic development.

In Part 3 of this text, a different classification scheme is utilized, one that is more psychological in that the categories are more concerned with the processes involved. The chapters in sequence are concerned with motor learning, perception, rote learning and memory, comprehension and understanding, problem-solving and thinking, emotional development, attitudes and ideals, and transfer of training. The categories established are not mutually discrete, for it is virtually impossible to avoid some overlapping of functions, no matter what scheme is used. The purpose is to provide a framework within which the individual, task, and method variables reviewed in Part 2 can be related to the work of the teacher.

An unfortunate outgrowth of concern with the methods of teaching is an impression that a specific, approved technique exists for meeting any problem which arises and for providing immediate and easy solutions. It can be said only that there are better and worse techniques, but that for any immediate educational problem, there are probably several avenues to a successful solution, just as there are several procedures by which one may add a column of numbers and obtain a correct answer. The skill in teaching lies in being able to select the knowledge pertaining to a given situation and to adapt and apply it. Just as frequently, the skill lies in knowing that a procedure doesn't apply and feeling free to depart from convention.

Children are individuals, like others in the main but unique in part. Psychological experimenting, at best, provides guide lines for action, not specific answers for given individual children. The results of experiments depend upon averages. One can almost make the generalization that there are no average children—no children who are exactly average in all characteristics. The experimental result provides a useful anchoring point upon which to base decisions, but variations must be allowed for. It is in this ability that the art of teaching is distinguished from the sciences of education and psychology. The reader will find more empirical information, more anecdote, more specific instances used in illustration in Part 3 than in the preceding parts, which incorporated more of the experimental aspect. In approaching the following chapters, the student may well consider the following questions:

1. Can motor skills be learned blindly, automatically? What part do perception and thinking play in motor learning? Can motor skill be increased without direct practice? Are the usual practice periods for piano, football, or other motor skills too long? Would as much be learned in less time?

2. How do perceptions develop? How are they modified? How does motivation affect perception? Does learning proceed slowly in initial phases because it is more often organized on a logical basis rather than on a psychological basis? How can tasks be presented so that the learner perceives clearly what is to be done and what to be learned? How can the teacher sharpen the differences and the similarities and make clear the discriminations that have to be made?

3. Can rote learning be really considered learning by the teacher? In a classroom where rote learning is the vogue, could we not eliminate the teacher and do a more effective job with television teaching and self-checking devices? Could children recite to each other in small groups in preference to the teacher? Where memorizing proceeds without comprehension, is anything ever retained for more than a short time?

4. What are the relationships between comprehending and perceiving? Does correct usage of words indicate comprehension? Can abstract ideas and concepts be developed in the absence of actual

experience? How can audio-visual aids be used as a substitute for direct experience? Does television provide a base for developing comprehension? Can the teacher teach children how to learn?

5. What are the essential characteristics of problems? Do pupils react to "problems" with a need to solve them or as tasks to be performed? To what extent can problem solving ability be developed? To what extent do teaching methods defeat the development of problem solving ability? Can one think without using words or symbols? Are children capable of solving problems and thinking?

6. What role does learning play in emotional development and behavior? Do understanding and insight play significant parts, or do conditioning and reinforcement predominate? Was emotion better suited to a more primitive life with direct dangers than to a complex urban society with indirect frustrations? How do children acquire fears? How can they be met and controlled?

7. How are attitudes learned? How changed? Can ideals and values be taught directly, or are they acquired indirectly? How does group behavior affect attitudes? How does appreciation for art, music, literature develop? To what extent should the teacher regulate her own attitudes and values in the classroom? Should she make her attitudes explicit or covert? Can she be neutral about attitudes? To what extent is the teacher justified in attempting to develop ideals?

8. To what extent does schooling make a difference in the lives of children? Are the skills learned in school carried over into the out-of-school life? How much transfer of training occurs and how can it be increased? Do some subjects have greater transfer value than others? How do memory and reasoning ability develop? Do certain subjects develop such abilities?

Chapter Ten

The Development of Motor Skills

*An individual's ability to meet the
demands made upon him by his environment depends upon the acquisi-
tion of a great many motor skills — skills
that involve bodily movement. To possess
such skills means to be able to act with dexterity
and proficiency. Every normal individual acquires a large number of motor skills,
some quite incidentally as various acts are
performed again and again, others by
dint of much effort and time spent
in practice to achieve high levels of expertness
for their monetary or social values. Their possession
is an asset in many ways. They mean greater
efficiency in one's work; they enhance self-
esteem; they bring social recogni-*

tion, and are the source of rich satisfactions and pleasures. Among the activities associated with making a livelihood and involving motor skills are operating machines of various sorts, painting, carpentering, drafting, weaving, surgery, plumbing, masonry, and dramatic performances on the stage. For recreation and enjoyment, we have skills such as swimming, baseball, tennis, ping-pong, skiing, rowing, dancing, singing, and playing musical instruments.

Not only does one find satisfaction in being able to do things with dexterity, but most persons enjoy watching feats of skill performed by others. The clever handling of a huge steamshovel soon draws a crowd of interested spectators. The juggler and the acrobat have a secure place in the entertainment world. A cleverly executed football play is admired even when it is made by the opposing team.

In school every child is expected to learn to write. So important as a tool for further learning is the ability to write that he is started on the skill in the first grade and his training is continued throughout the elementary grades. In high school we have typewriting and the manual arts. Other school activities in which the motor functions are paramount are sewing, drawing, singing, pronunciation of words, athletic games, and gymnasium exercises. Training in mechanical arts, drafting, shopwork, and the trades is a matter of developing motor skills. In the kindergarten are found such motor activities as singing, bouncing balls, sewing designs on cards with yarn, marching, cutting paper with scissors, and coloring pictures with crayons. Skill in reading requires, among other things, the ability to make finely coördinated eye movements in order to keep on the line, to move forward in rapid sweeps, and to shift back and catch the beginning of the next line quickly.

PROGRESSIVE CHANGE IN ACTION UNDER REPETITION

Repetition of an act normally brings about habituation. It does so by producing progressive change in various aspects of the total function. At various stages of learning and with various amounts of repetition, we find different degrees of habituation. In considering the modifications which result from repetition we shall be concerned with changes in the following features: 1. the task, 2. perception, 3. accessory responses, 4. feeling tone, 5. integration, 6. speed and accuracy, and 7. fatigue effects.

Changes in the task. At the beginning, the individual sets up general, specific, and secondary tasks. This means that he thinks of what he is to do in a general way, consciously selects particular movements to be made, and as he proceeds to carry out his task, he chooses and plans details and executes steps with reference to the anticipated end result. As the act is repeated, the tasks appear in various forms, due to revisions, abbreviations, and fractionations. Before long, they tend to dwindle and eventually drop out altogether. Longwell (1938) found that the general task tended to disappear first, while the secondary task taking care of the various details in the course of the action persisted until a further degree of habituation was reached. In time, however, the secondary task also was eliminated.

The "dropping out of the task" means that the subject does not have to formulate the act in his mind. He does not have to design consciously the pattern of movements. He does not, as he confronts the situation, have to think, "Now I'll do this particular thing." The perception of the situation touches off without conscious intent or purpose the sequence of movements previously made. Thus, attention is freed from the details of the process of carrying out the act. This effects an enormous economy for the individual in getting things done, because his attention may be given to other matters while the habituated performance goes forward. In the case of writing a letter, the movements of the fingers and hand do the writing quite automatically while the writer's attention is free for the nonhabituated activity of thinking what to write. The habituated activity contributes to the total enterprise, which involves also nonhabituated performance.

Changes in perception. In nonhabituated activity, perception plays an important role. As indicated above, it leads to the formulation of the task, and through it the learner is made aware of various objects involved in the course of action, of the various movements made, and of the changes in the situation effected by the movements. In the course of habituation, however, perception diminishes. First, it narrows to those aspects of the situation most vital to the action. The perception of irrelevant factors tends to drop out fairly early. Then it is reduced with respect to those features of the situation of vital concern to the performance. In learning to play the piano, the novice sees each individual note. But with practice comes a reduction of perception

In many skills where one's sequence of movements must be suited to changing aspects of the situation, as in automobile driving or in baseball, a residuum of attention is indispensable. One must watch the traffic and curves in the road. But the extent to which perception drops out in this activity can be seen by the fact that one may drive under familiar conditions with his mind absorbed in conversation or the topics of the day. The vaguest kind of perception, with reduced cues and obscure reference to the sides of the road or the traffic lines, enables the driver to keep his car on the road and in the right lane. Without conscious intent he turns the steering wheel upon approaching slight curves and depresses the accelerator as he comes to an upgrade. These movements, which were initiated by sub-tasks, issuing from clear perception of curves and hills when he was learning to drive, now follow the barest flash of perceptual meaning. Clear perceptions may emerge again as active participants in the performance when the driver encounters a traffic snarl or unusual road conditions, for here he is thrown back to a less practiced level of activity.

Because of the great amount of repetition of the acts involved in driving a car, the whole process tends to become automatized, and yet one cannot drive safely without being attentively alert. Lapses of attention, the normal result of automatization, constitute a threat to safe driving. They are responsible for many accidents.

Changes in accessory responses. The novice usually displays a number of responses which are more or less accessory to the action. Superficially, these appear to be irrelevant and to mark the behavior of an inexperienced performer. Yet they are integral features of the course of resolution. They reflect the status of the performance at the moment and sometimes appear to effect changes in the procedure. The accessory factors include various comments, facetious remarks, giggling, squirming, sighs, exclamations, emotional reactions, self-instructions in the way of admonitions to be more careful or to try for speed and let the errors take care of themselves, and flashes of reference to self indicated by such questions as "How am I doing?" To illustrate these features of untrained action we quote from the record of the first trial by a subject in the mirror-drawing experiment. The drawing made by this subject in this trial is shown in the first star of Figure 10.1.

Trial No. I. At the beginning S smiled, then laughed in embarrassment. "It's awful! I can't start to go in the right direction. Now, if I push it that way. . . . Oh, I'm only going back and forth. How do I ever go forward?" The hand of

S, grasping the pencil tightly, shook as it bore heavily on the paper. Leaning over in a hunched, cramped position, S exhibited marked attention. Exclamations of disgust were frequent. Having gone around the first point, she remarked, "A little better!" There were sighs as she went along the side of the second point, making many errors. After tracing around the third point, she said complainingly, "Oh-oh, stuck again!" Her mouth was closed tightly. Just before the fifth point she crossed the line several times, exclaiming, "Oh, dear! I'm slipping out again!" According to her own introspective report, she felt "awfully hot!" Her attention, she said, was not steady because part of the time she was trying to think out the process; then she decided to pay attention. Her thoughts also dwelt on the instruction to keep between the lines. She was conscious of the fact that she was making many mistakes.

Under repetition, these accessory responses tend to drop out. As this experiment went forward, fewer comments were made by the subject. In trial 14, the drawing of which appears in Figure 10.1, there were no comments at all. There was a calm, businesslike demeanor, with uniform attention on the image of the star in the mirror. The subject reported that her hand was just "going of its own accord," and that she was "not being of much help to it." Accessory factors sometimes persist. In the thirteenth trial of this experiment, for example, the subject decided to take more time and try to make the tracing as perfect as she could (self-instruction); a contortion of the face occurred during the tracing. Longwell (1938) reports that accessory factors did not drop out altogether but that they tended to disappear or to become stabilized as a result of repetition.

Changes in feeling tone. Actions are frequently toned by feelings of pleasantness or unpleasantness, by satisfaction and annoyance. These feeling tones, like other features of action, tend to change under repetition. In general, the feeling which accompanies an action shifts from the unpleasant and disagreeable to the pleasant and agreeable. The tensions, uncertainties, misgivings, awkwardness, and mistakes of the earlier tries are annoying, as are the distressing frustrations due to inappropriate sub-tasks, miscalculations, getting off on a wrong course, running into blind alleys, or the chagrin occasioned by one's ineptitude and the fear of being compared unfavorably with others. To be sure, a new action is not always unpleasant. Its novelty may provide the exhilaration of a new adventure, or the delight in being able to take the initial step toward a skill which brings happiness or monetary reward may outweigh the disagreeable elements. As a rule, however, a person finds it more satisfying to do what he is accustomed to doing or what he has practiced and knows he can do well, than to engage in an untried form of action or to struggle with a task that is unfamiliar. This is probably why our lives become so ruled by habits, why we get into ruts. We tend to do things day after day in the same manner. The adoption of new ways is too disturbing to our comfortable complacency. With practice, training, and the resulting cleverness come confidence, self-assurance, pride in ability, satisfactions of success, and sometimes even the sense of superiority.

Integration of movements. Under the influence of repetition, the movements undergo considerable transformation. In the beginning, as one undertakes to develop a motor skill, his movements are likely to be jerky, hesitant, clumsy, and awkward. The individual fumbles in his attempts. He tries out various movements to see whether they will help. The movements vary from trial to trial. As practice proceeds, the useless movements drop out and digressions are eliminated. Those movements that prove useful in bringing the person to his goal are made with greater promptness and precision, and become coordinated into a smoothly flowing sequence. The performance becomes unified, stable, and highly integrated.

In learning to send messages by telegraphy, improvement depends largely upon developing *higher units* of action. The learner must begin by learning to make the movements that produce the dots and dashes standing for each letter. These at first are made as discrete movements, but the constant repetition of the series for each letter soon enables the sender to tap out each letter as a unit. He does not have to think of each movement, but only of the letter. Here the letter unit is a higher unit when compared to the separate movements involved in tapping out the letter. The learner may continue for some time on the letter-sending level, spelling the words and tapping out each letter as a separate act. As the letter units become familiar and more automatized through practice, they are made with greater ease and while the movements for one letter are still in progress, the sender's attention reaches ahead to the next letter. The second letter-unit of action then is actually begun before the first is completed. We then have overlapping. Soon the letter habits are tied together into action units incorporating all the movements for whole words. Then the sender does not have to think of each letter as he taps out his message. He has passed from letter habits to word habits. Thinking the word "arrived" sets off the rhythmical unified pattern of finger movements for the whole word.

This process of integration of simpler action units into higher units is seen also in learning to shift the gears of a car. Here the same order of movements is repeated time after time. The beginner has to think of each movement to be made. He must first memorize the sequence so that at each step he can think of what to do next. But the skilled driver has only to note that the traffic light has flashed green to have the whole series of gear-shifting movements run off automatically while he keeps his eyes and attention on the other cars.

In considering this matter of the integration of the discrete units of a total action function, it should not be assumed that there is no framework to hold these units together at the beginning of practice. Building a skill is not merely the adding of one movement to another. There is at the start the purpose, or the general task, which envisages the goal of the total performance. The various units of action are steps taken to reach this goal. The selection and integration of certain movements and the elimination of others is a matter of their congruity or incongruity with the individual's aims. Repetition affords the opportunity for developing better methods of accomplishing that which is to be done.

Speed and accuracy. As a consequence of the changes we have been considering, there is usually an increase in the speed and accuracy of performance. The typist writes faster and with fewer mistakes. The tennis player lets the high balls go by and thereby wins a point, where the novice tries for them and loses. The driver reacts in an emergency quickly enough to prevent the threatened crash. The mail dispatcher does not require so long to sort his letters and throw them into the right sacks. The skater glides smoothly and swiftly without losing his balance. The trained worker gets more done with less effort and does it better. The smooth and rhythmical movements of the skillful dancer flow on in charming gracefulness.

An example of reduction of errors in motor learning is presented in the reproductions of the tracings of star outlines by a subject in the mirror-drawing experiment. Mirror drawing provides a good example of sensorimotor learning, and it is well suited to experimental study. It presents a novel task, and, in a conveniently short period of time, one can observe the stages and changes characteristic of this

form of learning. Since it is easy to record the time required for
each drawing and the number of errors made in each, we are able
to evaluate the successive trials in terms of speed and accuracy and
thus obtain a definite measure of the improvement that takes place
through practice.

In the experiment from which these drawings were selected, the
star forms were placed on the baseboard of the apparatus and a shield

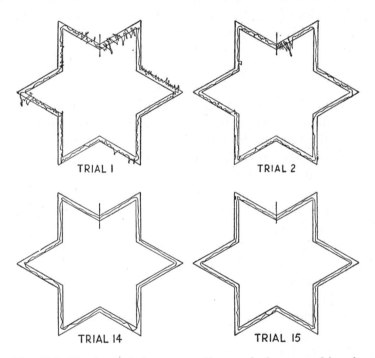

TRIAL I   TRIAL 2

TRIAL 14   TRIAL 15

Fig. 10.1. Tracings of the star outline made by one subject in
the mirror-drawing experiment. *The drawings for the
first 2 and the last 2 of the 15 trials are shown. The
stars were 5 inches from tip to opposite tip, and the
distance between the lines was one eighth of an inch.*

was adjusted so that the subject was able to see the star only by looking into the mirror. He was instructed to trace the star outline by
drawing a line along the path between the lines of the star. An error
was defined as touching or crossing the line on either side of the path.
Fifteen stars were traced. The first two and the last two are shown
in Figure 10.1. A comparison will show the extent of improvement
in the subject's ability to keep within the lines. The error scores

for the first, second, fourteenth, and fifteenth trials respectively were 92 ,51, 10, and 4. The time scores in seconds for these trials were 440, 276, 70, and 75.

The reduction of time and errors with practice is shown graphically in Figure 10.2. The curves are based on the average scores for each trial made by 50 students. The dotted line is the curve for errors; the solid line is the curve for time scores. Improvement in both speed and accuracy is indicated by the steady decline of the curves throughout the 15 trials.

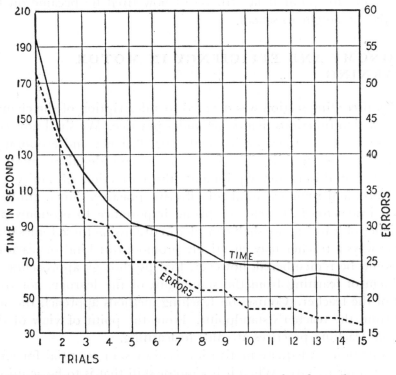

Fig. 10.2. Learning curves for time and errors, based on the mean scores of 50 subjects in the mirror-drawing experiment.

Changes in fatigue effects. As a rule, practice reduces the amount of fatigue resulting from performing a given task. We refer here, of course, to the fatigue produced by a single performance, not the cumulative effects of a long series of trials. Early trials are sometimes very exhausting. One is likely to begin with a great deal of muscular tension; nervous energy is dissipated and effort is wastefully expended in surplus motion. Energy is consumed by anxiety and fear. In the practiced performance, energy is expended more economically; there is less wasted effort, and futile digressions are not so likely to appear. The skilled performer is less subject to loss of energy through distractions and emotional disturbances. He takes his work more calmly and performs it with greater ease. A person's first day's work on a new job is likely to leave him pretty well worn out. It is difficult for a teacher to realize how fatiguing are the child's first exercises in penmanship. The experienced teacher will appreciate this point if he will recall how tired he became on the first day he taught in school.

ECONOMY AND EFFICIENCY IN MOTOR LEARNING

The preceding section was devoted to a description of the changes in the action functions that occur under practice. We shall now consider some of those factors that make for efficiency and economy in acquiring a motor skill. The factors to be considered are motives, working conditions and equipment, the correction of faulty performance, and some essentials of effective practice. Since guidance by an instructor is a factor of prime importance to economy and efficiency of learning, we shall consider in discussing these topics some of the ways a teacher may effectively promote this kind of learning. It should be remembered, however, that psychology approaches the problem of learning from the standpoint of the learner, not from that of the teacher. Courses on teaching methods approach the subject from the teacher's standpoint. From the point of view of this volume teaching practices are aids to learning.

Motivation. Adequate motivation is always an essential for effective learning activity. When it is a motor skill that is to be acquired, probably the best motive is the desire to possess the skill. Before he can desire a skill or feel a need for it, the learner must appreciate its value. When there is no such desire, the teacher's first concern is to create it if possible. In many cases, it will be sufficient to point out the benefits to be derived from the skill. If the learner is a younger child and the advantages offered by the skill are so remote that they do not appeal to him, then other motives must be enlisted. Among these are the desires for social approval, prestige, and play. The enlistment of these motives calls for the use of incentives. If, for example, a young child is learning to write, he might apply himself earnestly in order to take home specimens of his work to show his parents how well he is doing. The resourceful teacher will think of many ways to arouse interest and secure active effort.

The contribution of instruction. It is important that we see clearly just what instruction does and does not contribute to the efficiency and economy of learning. It is a valuable source of information regarding what to do and how to do it. It gives knowledge but not skill. The skill must be acquired by the learner through his own practice. A child will never become a good writer merely from listening to the teacher's explanation of the way to hold the pencil or how to form this or that letter. The student of violin will never become a great player by merely reading books on how to play a violin. Skill in teaching does not come from taking education courses in a university. One acquires skill in teaching, as in other skills, by practice — by actual teaching. But instruction shows one what to do and ways of doing it, and thereby aids in the acquiring of a skill. It may prevent wasteful and harmful experimentation. As a colleague once put it in addressing his class in a course on education, "We are trying to keep you from doing more harm than is necessary while you are learning to teach." Good instruction in motor learning helps the learner to formulate appropriate tasks and sub-tasks. These determine what he does and how he learns.

Self-instruction and motor learning. In the absence of knowledge of how to proceed when one undertakes to develop a new type of skill, and with no one to give the learner directions, it would seem that an individual might in some cases be able to think out the proper procedure and thereby save himself from the less efficient manipulative exploration of a trial-and-error attack. Perhaps this is sometimes done, though it is probably safe to say that it is rarely done. To think out the best method of performing a task requires a certain amount of knowledge or experience relevant to the task, an acquaintance with principles involved, and the ability to restrain the impulse to experiment blindly. It is probably more often the expert or a person who has already acquired more proficiency than the novice who actually thinks out a better way doing a thing. Repeatedly, students have reported that prior to their start on the mirror-drawing experiment, they thought that they could manage the tracings easily by simply going in the opposite way from that which was normal because they were aware of the fact that the mirror reverses the image of the star outline. Here is an example of trying to solve the problem of procedure by thinking. But the actual benefit of such reflections is invariably slight. Usually the subject soon becomes baffled and finds that his deductions lead only to confusion. He then casts aside his logic and plunges into a try-this-and-try-that method.

When reflective thinking is helpful, its contribution is of the same sort as that made by the instruction of a teacher or of a book. It provides suggestions of how to proceed. Of itself it can never yield a motor skill. It is, in fact, a source of self-instruction out of which grows the task or sub-task which governs the learner's reactions. It may, if good, foreshorten trial and error and thereby contribute to the efficiency of learning. The development of skill, however, requires practice on the part of the learner, although mental practice can assist the process. Vandell, Davis, and Clergston (1943) divided 12 males from each of three school levels, college, senior and junior high school, into matched experimental and control groups. The groups having actual practice or mental practice showed improvement in basketball shooting, with the groups having actual practice making the greater gain. Control groups showed no improvement. Although the study suffers from the small size of groups, it suggests that mental rehearsal can contribute to motor skill improvement.

GUIDANCE OF LEARNING

Initial instruction. In order to acquire a motor skill efficiently, a correct start is of great importance. One is fortunate if he has a good teacher or coach to direct his efforts at the beginning. Proper initial instruction not only will save the learner's time but will help to prevent the development of bad habits, which may be formed by the untutored. Wrong habits established as a result of faulty methods employed in the early stages of learning prevent the attainment of a high degree of proficiency and are often overcome only with great difficulty.

Adequate instruction for a good beginning involves more than placing before a child a perfect model or completed sample of a product of the skill he is to acquire. A child may desire to write and may have as his goal the acquiring of the ability to write. But when he begins, he must start by making particular letters. His ultimate goal must be reached by way of achieving sub-goals. In order to become a good writer, he must learn to make the letter *a,* and the letter *h,* and all the rest. Now suppose we hand him a well-written copy of the letter *a* and merely tell him to reproduce it. He may draw a rough likeness of what he sees but his methods may be altogether bad as a foundation for skill in writing. With a specimen of writing before him and with no direction except to copy it, there is no particular reason why the child should not begin to write at the right-hand side of the page and work backwards. He might build up his reproduction in sections, making a figure *8* by drawing two small circles one above the other, or the letter *R* by drawing a circle and putting two legs on it. These are only suggestions of the many faulty habits a small child might form if left to learn to write without instructions about how to form his letters. For a good start, he must be taught what movements are necessary and the sequence in which they should be made. This calls for directions with explanations and demonstrations.

In some cases of motor learning, a clear verbal explanation, simply telling the learner what to do and how to do it, may be sufficient, depending upon the learner's ability to grasp and retain the instructions. This will require a background of experience or knowledge sufficient for comprehension of what he is told, adequate attention to the explanation, and a memory for the essential details of the instructions. Thus, an eighteen-year-old who has ridden with others in a car might be able to fix in his mind the necessary procedure for starting a car from verbal directions either oral or printed. But an adult who has had no acquaintance whatsoever with the language of golf would probably be baffled if his instructor in his first lesson in golf tells him he must play his iron shots off the center of the body and that he should keep his stance slightly open. The essential purpose of the initial instruction is to give the learner a clear idea of what he must try to do. If verbal explanation and directions are not sufficient to accomplish this, the instructor must show the learner. Since a young child is less capable of strict attention than a mature person and since his ability to comprehend and remember what he is told is more restricted, he, more often than an adult, will need to be taught by means of demonstration.

In giving a demonstration of the performance to be learned, the instructor must take care that his pupil is in a position to observe the essential details of the demonstration and that his attention is being given to it. It must not be hurried, but should be given slowly enough for each step to be witnessed and understood. In the case of a demonstration involving several steps, it may be necessary to repeat it several times. In most cases, explanation should accompany the demonstration.

Common mistakes of an inexperienced teacher are to cover too many details in a single explanation, to give too many directions all at once, or to demonstrate more than a beginner can possibly assimilate at one time. The instructor should remember that the role of his instruction is to establish a set in the mind of the learner — a task — and that the capacity of any person is limited with respect to the number of steps that can be incorporated into a single task. It is poor teaching, for example, to take a young person out for his first lesson in driving a car, and proceed to tell him all you know about handling a car. He will not be able to remember more than four or five items of instruction at a time. The complex processes must be taken up a few steps at a time. As these are practiced and mastered, new steps can be added and the whole process integrated by practicing all the steps together.

Reversed view of the demonstration. A demonstration of a motor performance may be very confusing if the instructor and learner face each other. The reason for this is that the learner, in such a position, sees the movements in a right-left reversal of the way he must make them himself. The reader may observe this difficulty if he faces someone who is trying to show him how to tie a new kind of knot. It will be much easier to see how the knot is tied if he stands beside the demonstrator; thus he can see the movements from the direction from which he will see his own movements when he attempts to tie the knot himself. An instructor of surveying reports that his students learn to use the surveying instruments more readily if he has them stand behind him and look over his shoulder as he gives his demonstrations.

Manual direction. Sometimes in teaching a motor skill, manual guidance of the learner's movements is employed by the instructor. This procedure involves taking hold of the learner's hands, feet, or whatever part of the body he is to use in the skill to be acquired and pushing them through the desired movements in the proper sequence. In the case of handwriting such a procedure would be to take hold of the child's hand and push it through the movements required to make various letters. Piano teachers sometimes use manual guidance in placing a child's hand in position and pushing his fingers down to strike the keys. For beginners in manuscript writing, the letter forms cut from emery paper are sometimes used. The child traces these forms with his fingers. In the first trials, his hand may be guided manually by the teacher.

The merits of such practices must be determined from results obtained. Any practice which will help the child realize more clearly what movements he is to make would appear to be psychologically sound if it does not encourage faulty habits. In the first place, the actual contribution of manual guidance should be clearly understood. What we have here is a form of demonstration. It is a way of showing the learner what to do and how to do it. As a form of demonstration, it has certain advantages over merely observing the teacher's performance. It avoids the difficulties of a reversed demonstration described in the preceding section. The learner sees his own members moving in the manner in which he must make them go himself. This should be helpful in selecting and identifying the proper movements and in determining their rightful significance.

There is another possible advantage of this kind of demonstration: the kinesthetic element involved. The child not only sees his hands or other members in the various positions but also feels them there and feels the movement from one position to another. The value of this is somewhat uncertain since the kinesthesis involved in having someone else move your arm about cannot be identical with that which comes from your own execution of the movement. Some individuals seem to depend on kinesthesis more than others in learning movements. A student in the writer's laboratory was found to be entirely lacking in visual imagery according to all our tests. She was given a learning problem that consisted of reproducing a nonsense design after a five-second exposure. Most students have been found to make a reasonably good reproduction after four or five trials. This student was unable after many trials to make any headway in learning the design well enough to reproduce it. Finally, she adopted the scheme of tracing the design in the air with her finger during the exposure period. By doing this she was able after three trials to make a very good reproduction of the figure. It is possible that such persons, more than the visually minded, might profit by manual guidance. This question calls for more adequate research.

It has been claimed, moreover, that manual guidance may be helpful for little children who have a particularly difficult time in trying to copy a performance they observe in another. Of course little children should not be called upon to do things which are too difficult for the level of maturation attained. But apart from this, their first attempts may be so far from the standard set by the teacher's demonstration as to be extremely discouraging. The teacher must avoid creating a sense of inadequacy or hopelessness in the initial stages of learning. If, for a young child, the manual guidance of his hands in showing him how to do something helps to promote a sense of security or confidence, it will be worth while as a temporary expedient.

It should be remembered, however, that while manual guidance may be, in some cases, a good way of showing the learner how to carry out the performance, it does not take the place of the individual's own efforts and practice. To learn a skill is to modify the controls or determination of movements involved in the action. The center for these controls is in the central nervous system, and the modification of them is brought about by the learner's activity, not by the activity of the teacher.

Direction should be positive. Experimental evidence and teaching experience indicate that when a child is being directed concerning the form his activity is to take, he should be told what *to* do rather than what *not* to do. From the instructions arises the task which determines the course of action. The instructions, therefore, should be aimed at the results desired. Negative instructions may serve to inhibit undesirable responses, but when imposed upon the child as he is about to enter upon a new kind of motor performance, they may serve to distract and divide his attention and lessen his chances of success. Direct measures must sometimes be taken to block error and break up faulty methods, as we shall consider later; but, in the beginning when we are trying to help the child to a good start, his attention should be directed to his goal and the movements to be made in order to reach it rather than toward the undesirable or forbidden modes of response. The best way to prevent the formation of faulty habits is to have a strong set and undivided attention directed toward the correct means of gaining one's end.

The matter of form. The best procedure for acquiring a motor skill usually involves certain matters of bodily adjustments, posture, and ways of grasping the instruments. These features of a performance are called *form*. Good form is essential for attaining the highest possible degree of excellence. A learner may know what he is supposed to do and he may have the right objective in mind, but, with poor form, his performance is likely to be poor and improve little under practice. In typewriting, one may acquire some degree of skill by watching the keys and by tapping with only two or three fingers. Experience of experts indicates that the use of all five fingers of each hand is conducive to a greater degree of efficiency and that it is good practice to use certain fingers to strike certain keys. Most skills can be developed more rapidly and to a higher degree of proficiency if the learner knows and follows certain rules of form which have been developed from the experience of experts. In ignorance of these matters, the learner, if left to his own devices, must discover them as best he can through trial and error; or failing to discover them, as is often the case, he must struggle along on a plane of achievement far short of the skill which he might have reached had he known and practiced the best form. Fortunately, the knowledge of the best ways of doing a thing, gleaned from experience of experts, may be taught by a teacher or coach to the great advantage of the learner.

In learning to play the violin, the pupil is instructed to keep his left wrist curved. The beginner at the piano is taught to hold his hand in a position parallel with the keys. The handler of freight finds advantageous ways of tilting and gripping heavy boxes. The juggler who keeps several balls in the air at once knows the trick of throwing the ball from a position to one side of its line of fall in order to keep it from colliding in the air with the others coming down. And so on, in tennis, basketball, ping-pong, swimming, fly casting, painting, dancing, bandaging wounds, and all the various skills, there are important matters of form which, if mastered at the beginning through the aid of one who has been through the process, will greatly increase the effectiveness of the learner's efforts.

Working conditions and instruments. Favorable working conditions and good tools or instruments have much to do with efficiency and economy of motor learning. Room temperature and humidity should be conducive to bodily comfort. Lighting should be adequate for clear vision without strain. The height of chair, desk, or table used should be adjusted to avoid fatiguing positions. Instruments should be placed within natural reaching distances and, where several are used, arranged so that a minimum of effort is expended in shifting from one to another.

Poor working tools may retard learning or, because of necessary adjustment required to offset their defects, they may even be the source of habits that may later have to be overcome. In learning to write with a pen, a child should not have to contend with a scratching or blotting pen. The beginner in typewriting should have a machine that responds normally when the keys are struck, and the child learning to play the piano should have an instrument that is well tuned.

EFFECTIVE PRACTICE

The effectiveness of practice will depend largely upon the manner in which the practice is conducted. From the great amount of work done on this subject, it is possible to state a few generalizations that should be helpful to one who desires to secure the best possible returns for the time and effort expended. It should be borne in mind, however, that any generalization can be usefully applied only with such adaptations or restrictions as may be indicated by a consideration of all the requirements of the particular situation. Some of the variables which affect the applicability of the principles are age and interest of the learner, the nature of the learning task, the grade of proficiency needed, and the amount of time available for practice. The points mentioned below are those which have been found to apply in a general way to most motor-learning situations.

Conditions under which practice should be conducted. *Practice should be conducted under conditions similar to those which will attend the use of the skill, and the procedures practiced should be those in which skill is desired.* One learns what one practices. After the steps necessary for a good beginning have been taken, attention during practice should be directed toward the desired results. If it is skill in throwing a ball that is sought, the eyes should be fixed upon the target when throwing. While some useful bits of information regarding what to do in the water may be acquired on land, one must, to become a skillful swimmer, practice in the water. To be able to tackle well, the football player requires practice in real game situations. In the shop, the student should have real machines and make real things. Since the fountain pen has come into general use, children should be allowed to practice writing with a fountain pen. To learn to handle a car well in traffic, the learner must have repeated opportunities to drive under traffic conditions. He will not learn this if his practice is restricted to lonely country roads. So with all skills; for best results, one should practice under conditions which resemble as closely as possible those under which the skill will be used.

Older methods of drill for students of typewriting called for a great amount of drill on nonsense syllables. Various combinations of letters were used for the purpose of having the students acquire dexterity in tapping out these combinations. It was thought that since these movements were used extensively in actual typewriting, the dexterity acquired in them would be readily transferred to the writing situation in which they would be used. No doubt some transfer does take place in such cases, but there is not full transfer of the results of practice in one situation to another type of situation. There is, therefore, a certain amount of wasted effort in such kinds of practice. Modern methods call for the student to start practicing on sentences just as soon as the keyboard is learned. It is claimed that better results are obtained by this newer form of practice. This is to be expected, since in working on sentences, the student is practicing in accord with his goal, which is to be able to type sentences skillfully.

Experimental evidence bearing on the point under consideration is found in studies made on the comparative value of different modes of practice for learning to write. Gates and Taylor (1923) had one group of children trace letter forms on transparent paper placed over the letters, while another group of approximately equal ability and maturity practiced actual writing by means of a model which the children were told to copy. The tracing group improved during 10 five-minute practice periods in their ability to trace letters on tissue paper, but when tested later for their ability to write with only a model as a guide, it was found that the amount of transfer from the tracing exercises, to writing was negligible. The children were confused and some were wholly unable to produce a legible letter. The performance on paper with no letter underneath to trace was quite a different performance from the one they had learned. The children who had practiced copying from a model did much better in their tests. The tracing children were reported to have gained some knowledge of where to start and in what direction they were to proceed in making letters, but they could not write as well as those who practiced actual writing. Other studies have also shown that direct practice in writing is more effective in developing ability to write than practice in tracing letters by means of grooves, transparent paper, or sandpaper outlines (Hertzberg, 1926).

Knowledge of results. One of the most effective guides to improvement of performance is having knowledge of results. This has been discussed in greater detail in a preceding chapter, but an additional study will re-emphasize its value. Helmstadter (1952) divided 100 college undergraduates into four groups and compared their performance curves on the Minnesota Rate of Manipulation Test (a block-turning test) under 4 different conditions. One group received immediate knowledge of its performance; each of the other three groups had performance goals set by one of three different procedures: a self-set goal, an externally established goal, and a goal of improvement. All groups showed similar performance curves, in contradiction to the hypothesis that goal-setting procedures would provide stronger motivation. Knowledge of results provided as great an incentive as the varied goal-setting procedures. It would be more accurate to say that knowledge of results alone was as effective as knowledge of results plus an established goal. The simplicity of the task may have induced only limited amounts of ego-involvement restricting the effectiveness of goal-setting procedures, yet, if true, the situation is not unlike many learning situations in which the participant's interest is comparatively slight.

One advantage which many motor-skill learning situations provide is immediate knowledge of results. The baseball is hit or missed, the golf ball lands on the fairway or in the rough, the paint-brush drips or splatters paint. Knowledge of results is immediately apparent, and self-instruction directed at correcting and improving performance follows. It is essential that the self-instruction be accurate and that the analysis of behavior lead to improvement, not to further distortion in performance. This is precisely one of the main functions of a teacher.

Punishment, emphasis, and extraneous cues. It is a common practice in training animals and children to punish undesirable forms of behavior. The belief behind this practice is that the unpleasant after-effects of an act tend to prevent its recurrence. As noted in Chapter 7, many experiments have been performed with animals to determine the effect of punishment for "errors." It has been found that an electric shock accompanying wrong responses generally serves to hasten the elimination of errors. The explanation in terms of the law of effect was that the tendency to make the wrong responses was weakened by the annoying result. This explanation has been proven inadequate by recent studies, which have shown that shock on right responses or in an alley between turns also tends to facilitate learning. These findings have led some writers to believe that the effect of the shock is not to inhibit the wrong responses but rather to make the learner more alert to the significant cues and to emphasize the fact that the response is either right or wrong (Reed, 1935). Muenzinger concluded that the effect of the shock was general rather than specific (1934).

Bernard and Gilbert (1941) report an experiment on maze learning with 52 college students as subjects; it was designed to determine whether the effect of shock on entering blind alleys was general or specific. They found that the alleys in which shock was received were eliminated more readily than those in which no shock was received. From this they concluded that the shock did have a specific effect in modifying the reactions it accompanied as well as the general effect on the learner's alertness demonstrated by other studies.

These writers also point out that the use of the words *reward* and *punishment* may be misleading in considering the effect of extraneous stimuli on learning. For a stimulus which may be annoying as a signal that an error has been made may be satisfying when it means that a right choice has been made. Shock, when used to announce errors, usually has punishment value, but it has been found to have about the same effect as a reward when used on right responses. Bernard and Gilbert (1941, pp. 184, 185) make the following significant comments on this point:

From the evidence available it seems reasonable to postulate that any well-defined stimulus introduced consistently in connection with either right or wrong responses will tend to favor their repetition if they are right or their elimination if they are wrong, provided that the stimulus is not of such a type or strength as to introduce a distracting effect. In other words, any stimulus which is not highly distracting may act either as a "punishment" or a "reward," depending upon whether it accompanies responses which are arbitrarily designated as right or wrong. . . .

In human subjects, knowledge of a "punishment" stimulus appears to mean much more than direct affective reactions to the stimulus. In the present investigation most of the subjects reported that they tried to avoid shock mainly because it signified error rather than because it was disagreeable, in spite of the fact that they all reported the shock to be decidedly uncomfortable. Their reports also indicated that they tried to avoid un-shocked blind alleys as instructed, but that they tended to forget where these alleys were in the maze and that they often failed completely to perceive that they had entered a blind alley. On the other hand, the shock which was given in the "shock" alleys announced the errors in a definite and clean-cut manner and enabled the subjects to mark the location more accurately.

If an extraneous stimulus serves to facilitate learning by way of emphasizing right or wrong responses, is it better to emphasize the right responses or the wrong responses? An answer to this question is provided by an experiment reported by Silleck and Lapha (1937). A punchboard maze, containing 30 pairs of holes, was used. One hole of each pair had an electric connection with a bell which rang when the stylus was inserted. One group of subjects was instructed to place the stylus only in holes which rang the bell, while another group was instructed to place the stylus only in the holes which did not sound the bell. For one group, the bell meant an error, for the other group it signaled success. The mean number of trials required for an errorless performance was 11.7 for the Bell-Right response, and 15.7 for the Bell-Wrong response group. The findings are in accord with other experimental data in indicating that emphasis on right responses is more favorable for learning than emphasis on wrong responses.

Criticism. Evaluation of a student's performance is an essential part of any teacher's work. This includes the pointing out of errors and faults. Its purpose is to promote improvement. Good criticism is a valuable means of helping the learner see and correct his deficiencies. To accomplish its purpose criticism should be specific, constructive, and encouraging. For example, it will not help the child very much to tell him merely that his writing is poor and that he should do better. The specific faults in his writing should be brought to his attention, with suggestions about how to overcome them. An analysis of his writing may reveal that his trouble lies chiefly in one or a few features of his writing. It may be found that particular letters are poorly formed, or that his spacing is faulty. Lack of uniformity in letter size, or poor alignment may be the principal defect. In any case, the first step in correcting faults is to locate and determine as definitely as possible what they are. Criticism should be constructive, not merely faultfinding. It must, to be effective, point the way to a better performance. We shall not make satisfactory progress simply by trying to inhibit the undesirable response. The best way to get rid of the undesirable response is to substitute for it the desirable one. The detection of error should serve to emphasize the need for special attention and effort on the form of response that will serve to correct the fault.

In offering criticism, the teacher should seek to avoid discouraging or antagonizing the learner. Some sensitive persons cannot take graciously even the kindest and most constructive kind of criticism. In dealing with little children we should be careful when criticizing their work that we do not discourage them or make them feel that they are incapable or less capable than other children. Some children who are not doing well simply need to be told that they can do better. The teacher should show appreciation of good work, should commend the child for advances he is making. If adverse criticism is preceded by a recognition of merit, it will be easier to take, and it will be more likely to stimulate effort to improve. The effort of criticism will depend largely upon the spirit and manner in which it is given.

One possible way to avoid the negative effects of criticism is to encourage the learner to criticize his own work, to find the errors he has made, and to locate for himself, where possible, the weak points in his performance. Binet considered the ability for self-criticism to be an essential aspect of intelligence. It is well-known that it is less painful for one to speak of his own faults than to have someone else mention them. The practice of autocriticism should make for self-reliance and initiative in promoting one's own progress.

Too much guidance. While the services of a teacher in directing learning may serve to hasten it and prevent much waste effort on the part of the learners, it sometimes happens that guidance is overdone. This may occur when the teacher, in her zeal to prevent all errors, dictates precisely just what is to be done step-by-step. Too much guidance may destroy initiative of the pupil and thus deprive him of the opportunity to learn. When each step is dictated, the child may learn to perform the steps, under dictation, but fail to develop the ability to perform the whole task without aid. The end sought should be the child's ability to carry out skillfully the whole performance by himself, not the ability to follow step-by-step the teacher's directions.

The goal and improvement. Instruction, as was pointed out above, should serve not only to establish the child's goal, but should cover the ways and means for reaching the goal. A child with a goal and no knowledge of the steps necessary to achieve it must resort to trial-and-error methods of discovering how to accomplish his purpose. But emphasis on steps to the exclusion of emphasis on the goal is fully as bad as emphasis on goal with no instruction regarding the necessary steps. After a proper start has been made, practice should be aimed at the end to be achieved. Practice on difficult parts may require definite attention to the steps, but the steps should be regarded as the means for achieving the final goal. The goal gives meaning to the steps.

As an example of emphasis on steps without due regard for the final goal we cite the case of a friend, who is now past 70 years of age. When she was about 10 years old, the aunt with whom she lived wanted her to learn to make a quilt. Her task, set by her aunt, was to sew together small pieces of calico cloth to make one "square" every Saturday morning. The child's goal, therefore, was not to make a quilt, but to piece a square every Saturday morning. After she had completed a square, the task for that day was done. Now, at 70 years of age, she still has the collection of completed squares, but she has never put them together to make a quilt. Here was emphasis on steps to the neglect of the real and ultimate goal. The goal is needed to secure the integration of the steps into the total performance.

Speed against accuracy. Effort should be applied in the direction of speed and accuracy, according to the requirements of proficiency. In some skills, such as dressmaking, cooking, drawing, dressing wounds and applying bandages, painting portraits, and cabinetmaking, where quality of performance is far more important than speed, the effort in practice should be primarily directed toward doing the task as well as possible. Where speed is an important factor in the skill, practice at a rapid pace is desirable. This, in most cases, will not be possible or advisable at first, when the appropriate movements are being selected and when the correct form is being acquired. But after these are pretty well under control, one's tempo in practice should be his best for advancement in speed.

Where both speed and accuracy are important, as in typewriting or handwriting, to meet the requirements of expert performance, effort must be directed in such a way as to secure advancement in both. In the mirror-drawing experiment, in which subjects are instructed to work as rapidly and at the same time as accurately as possible, it has been found that some students improve more in speed while others improve more in accuracy. A comparison of the gain in speed and in accuracy for a group of 50 subjects reveals than 27 gained more in accuracy, while 23 made greater gains in speed. Reports of the subjects indicate that self-instruction frequently operates to shift effort from speed to accuracy or the reverse. In the case of the 50 subjects mentioned, the coefficient of correlation between the gains in speed and the gains in accuracy during the 15 trials was —.24 ±.004. This indicates a slight tendency for high gains in speed to go with relatively poor gains in accuracy and vice versa. The correlation is so low, however, that it does not warrant prediction in individual cases. While it appears that large gains in one were made frequently at the expense of gains in the other, this was not always the case.

An experiment that throws light on the relation of the speed of practice to efficiency of learning has been reported by Sharp (1939). In the usual type of maze learning and in the case of the mirror-drawing experiment, the trials vary both in time and in the number of errors. In this experiment, however, a special form of maze was constructed so that the time for each trial could be kept constant and controlled. This maze was made on a circular band, $9\frac{1}{2}$ inches wide, around a 26-inch bicycle wheel. As the wheel was rotated, the maze passed at a constant speed beneath a 5×8-inch opening through which the subjects worked. Data were obtained from three groups of subjects. For one group, the time for a complete revolution of the maze, or one trial, was 50 seconds; for the second group, 60 seconds; and for the third group, 70 seconds. A comparison of the results from the three groups revealed that more trials were required and more errors were made as the speed per trial was increased; but, for the faster speed, less time was required for complete learning. The averages for the 50-seconds group were 45.1 trials, 277.2 errors, and 37.58 minutes for total learning time. For the 70-seconds group, the averages were 39 trials, 226 errors, and 45.5 minutes.

In another experiment bearing on the same topic, Solley (1952) gave three groups of 40 randomly-selected subjects different instructions during an initial training period and studied the effects on subsequent performance. The experimental equipment involved a twelve-ring target, a striking instrument, a 1/100 second clock, a photo-electric system, and a scoreboard for timing and scoring thrusts at the target. Each group had 90 training trials distributed on 6 days over a 3-week period, one stressing speed in striking the target, one stressing accuracy, and the third placing equal emphasis on both. Subjects' scores were computed and they were informed of performance after each day. At the end of the initial training period, statistically significant differences in speed and accuracy demonstrating the effectiveness of the sets obtained from verbal instruction were obtained between the three groups. During a second 3-week period, all groups were instructed to place equal emphasis on both speed and accuracy. The results showed that the initial training period had a pronounced effect upon subsequent performance. Speed developed under initial emphasis of speed readily transferred into performance during the equal-emphasis period, whereas accuracy gained at low rates of speed was lost almost immediately when the rate of performance was increased. The result indicates that in motor skills where speed is to be a significant factor in ultimate performance, the emphasis should start on speed, with accuracy secondary; but, where both speed and accuracy are to be combined in performance, the initial training should incorporate both.

Part and whole learning methods. *For complex and difficult skills, use a combination of the part and whole or the progressive part method of practice.* In acquiring a skill, will it be more advantageous to practice the operation as a whole or by parts? Theoretically it should be an advantage to practice by the whole method, for in so doing, the various steps would be exercised in their proper sequence. In a comparatively short and simple task such as learning to slip a belt on a pulley, it would not seem reasonable to break the operation up into parts with separate practice on the parts. But in the case of complex and difficult skills, the evidence indicates that some practice on parts is more efficient than a strict adherence to the whole method.

Distribution of practice. For the more difficult and complex skills, practice should be liberally distributed. The length of the practice period should be short when new motor tasks are being introduced for the first time. This is especially true with elementary school children whose differences in maturation, attention span, and interest span are noticeable. Many motor skills not only involve complexity in the physical movements involved but also depend upon complex mental or social processes which increase the learning difficulty, thus augmenting the need for spaced practice. For example, handwriting involves intricate thought and grammatical processes, as well as minute finger-movement; team games such as volley-ball, baseball, and basketball embrace complex group actions and detailed rules of action, as well as highly coordinated motor movements.

Rhythm. The development of motor skills involves both spatial and temporal coördination of movements. Rhythm is an aid in establishing temporal coördination. The playing of music with lively rhythm will help to speed up the slow worker. Since it operates to reduce tensions in muscles not directly used in the task being practiced, rhythm tends to lessen the fatigue effects of practice. It is desirable to have children practice their writing exercises in rhythm. Music may be used to set the pattern of rhythm. The rhythm of music, counting, or tapping is used to advantage in pacing the strokes for typewriting drills, in direction calisthenics, in establishing the proper timing of movements needed for giving artificial respiration, and in promoting graceful dancing.

But to secure the advantages of rhythm, one must know at what stages to use it. A reasonable familiarity with the task, ability to make the various movements, and proper form are essential prerequisites to the use of rhythm drills. A young teacher who had been working in her first position only a few weeks complained that she could not keep her pupils together in group drills in typewriting because they had to stop and look for the keys. Students will not be able to type rhythmically until they have learned the position of the keys. Children will be able to write rhythmically only when it is no longer necessary for them to stop to think of the various movements required to form the letters or of the correct position of their fingers and hands. According to Freeman (1914), writing becomes rhythmical for most children at the age of 9 or 10. He suggests that this is the age when writing drills requiring rhythm may be suitably given.

Moreover, group drills in which rhythm is used will not in the later stages of practice be suitable for developing maximum speed. There will be individual differences in capacity for speed which will render any pace unsuitable for all members of the group. If the tempo is suited to the average, those who could go faster will be held back, while certain slow ones will not be able to keep up or will work under too great a strain in doing so. In order to attain the greatest possible speed, the individual must practice at his own best speed.

Tests of motor ability. It seems reasonable to suppose that one who has a quick reaction time, can maintain good speed in a series of movements, and has good motor coördination and good motor control will be able to make better progress and reach a higher level of proficiency in skills for which these abilities are essential than one less gifted in these respects. Several tests of these motor abilities have been in use for a long time in psychological laboratories. These, with other tests, have proven useful in gaining a clinical picture of an individual, and in some cases their use is valuable in guidance counseling.

Among the simpler tests of motor ability are those which measure rate of tapping, accuracy of aiming, steadiness of the hand, and eye-hand coördination. In a number of cases, a battery of tests has been set up for the purpose of determining an individual's chances of success in a given skill or vocation. Many have been developed in the field of physical education, while others have been devised to predict success in industrial occupations. Sometimes, tests of interests, perceptual alertness, judgment, and manipulative ability are included in the battery in an attempt to determine mechanical, musical, or artistic aptitudes (Guilford, 1936; Bingham, 1937). Some of these tests have not been very reliable or valid owing to emphasis on factors bearing little relation to success. For example, some of the earlier tests for ability in athletic skills placed too much emphasis on strength and size, whereas neuromuscular ability, as indicated by motor performance, appears to be more significant.

One of the difficulties in developing motor performance tests has been the specificity of individual motor skills. While it has been possible, on the basis of factor analyses, to devise tests for aptitudes such as verbal, numercial, and spatial aptitudes, which underlie a number of intellectual tasks, research efforts have failed to disclose group factors of motor abilities. Motor skills appear to be highly specific, lacking the overlap that would make it possible to predict performance in many areas from a few tests of motor aptitude. Instead, individual tests for specific skills have to be devised.

A good example of this problem in the use of motor tests in educational research is the study by Rowley (1938). Her problem was to find out whether or not slow writers in grades 4, 5, and 6 were inferior in motor coördination to the fast writers. On the basis of suitable speed tests of handwriting, two groups of children were selected, one made up of the slowest, and the other of the fastest writers. Each group included 25 children. The members of the two groups were paired for sex, C.A., M.A., and I.Q. These children then were given the tapping test for the right and left hands. By means of special apparatus, a test was made to determine the speed for making short vertical finger movements similar to those used in writing. Tests were also made for speed in making similar movements with the arm. The scores of the slow writers on these tests were compared with the scores made by the fast writers. There was no signficant difference between the scores of these two groups on any of the tests. It was concluded that the difference between these slow writers and these fast writers was due mainly to training factors, not to a difference in native endowment with respect to capacity for speed or motor coördination. The findings indicated the possibility of successful remedial instruction for improving the speed of slow writers.

SUMMARY

Maturation. A number of generalizations can be made with regard to the influence of such different factors as maturation and capacity, on motor learning. Studies of the motor achievement of individuals in different stages of growth have indicated the important relationship between motor development and maturation. In the studies considered, the term maturation refers not only to chronological age, but embraces also skeletal and physiological advancement.

1. It is possible to predict the stage of growth at which an individual can acquire certain motor skills. This is particularly true in infants and young children.

2. There is noted wide variation in the motor achievement of individuals within any age range. This is most apparent in adolescence.

3. The degree of motor attainment of the child is influenced by his social and psychological maturity.

4. Strength, rather than chronological age, intelligence, or school grade, is a primary determinant of the degree of motor ability.

5. The increase in strength is not a constant one but has a characteristic curve related to physiological maturation.

6. Motor skill development tends to coincide with the growth curve. Early or late physiological maturation effects motor performance.

7. Although gross motor skills are better performed at adolescence due to the strength increment during puberty, those motor skills dependent on flexibility, coordination and control appear to be less ably performed during the period of rapid growth.

8. Until puberty, boys and girls compare favorably with one another in many motor skills; after puberty, however, boys tend to excel, especially in the gross motor skills.

Capacity. The capacity of an individual for the learning of motor skills may be divided into physical and mental capacities, which have been analyzed through factor analysis techniques. The result has been the identification of a large number of separate factors which may be classified into three general categories: fundamental elements underlying the performance of a skill such as strength, speed, and accuracy; fundamental skills in physical education such as running, jumping, and throwing; and complex skills such as basketball or football.

1. The efficiency of physical factors increases with age up to maturity; age influences are equivalent to maturational influences. This means that it is possible for a child to learn a new motor skill with greater efficiency and with less practice as he approaches maturity.

2. The requirements for intelligence are dependent upon the complexity of the skill to be learned and the instructions to be understood.

3. Individuals with higher intelligence generally learn new motor skills with greater ease and speed than individuals with lower intelligence.

4. It is doubtful whether there are any motor skills which do not require some intelligence, although some studies seem to suggest that there are some "pure" motor activities, independent of intelligence.

Practice. The effects of practice can be summarized as follows:

1. Spaced practice is more efficient than massed practice.

2. Rest periods facilitate learning, although the optimum length of rest periods has not been determined. It is probably comparatively short but varying with the activity.

3. Progress in the learning of a motor skill is dependent upon error reduction. Motivation and knowledge of results are usually the determining factors.

4. The latter part of the practice period is not as effective as the first part. Efficiency decreases as fatigue and boredom increase. Individual capacity and the degree of previous training have been known to affect persistence. Also, this may be a factor of motivation, since it has been found that the initial level of effort is higher at the beginning and decreases as the magnitude of the task is increased.

5. There are great individual differences in the amount of practice required to learn a specific skill. This probably is due to differences in physical and mental capacities, motivation, etc.

Motivation

1. Reinforcement of the learning of a motor skill will facilitate learning whether the reinforcement is in the form of reward or punishment, although emphasis on right response is more effective.

2. As a general rule, motivation is greater at the beginning of a practice period than during the latter part of the practice period.

3. An important motivating factor for the direction of the learning activity (practice) is knowledge of results.

Retention and transfer

1. Verbal guidance appears to play an important part in transfer and retention of a skill.

2. The importance of retention is shown by the fact that growth or improvement in skills, knowledge, and attitudes is dependent upon the learner's retention of the effects of previous experiences.

3. In skills in which speed is the predominate factor for successful performance, the most efficient results are attained by early emphasis on speed. In skills in which both speed and accuracy are important to successful performance, emphasis on both speed and accuracy yields the most desirable results.

4. Transfer in motor skills tends to be highly specific.

OVERVIEW

Trow, W. C., "Perceptual Motor Learning Skill," *Educational Psychology.* Boston: Houghton Mifflin, 1950, pp. 579-630.

SELECTED REFERENCES

Ammons, R. B., "Acquisition of Motor Skill: Quantitative Analysis and Theoretical Formulation," *Psychological Review,* 1947, 54, pp. 263-81. 263-81.

Barker, R. G., Beatrice Wright, and Mollie Gonick, *Adjustment to Physical Handicap and Illness: A Survey of the Social Psychology of Physique and Disability.* New York: Social Science Research Council, 1946, Bulletin No. 55.

Watson, E. H. and G. H. Lowrey, *Growth and Development of Children.* Chicago: Yearbook, 1951.

ORIGINAL INVESTIGATIONS

Dore, L. R., and F. R. Hilgard, "Spaced Practice and the Maturation Hypothesis," *Journal of Experimental Psychology,* 1937, 27, pp. 303-12.

Leavitt, H. J. and H. Schlosberg, "The Retention of Verbal and Motor Skills," *Journal of Experimental Psychology,* 1944, 34, pp. 404-17.

Solley, W. H., "The Effects of Verbal Instruction upon the Learning of a Motor Skill," *Research Quarterly,* 1952, 23, pp. 231-40.

Tuddenham, R. D. and Margaret Snyder, "Physical Growth from Birth to Maturity," *Review of Educational Research,* 1947, 27, pp. 371-79.

Chapter Eleven

The Development of Perception

A large part of our learning is ac-
complished through perception. In the first
place, we learn directly about
things by observing them. In addition
to this, perception often plays an im-
portant part in other learning activities. It fuses
with action; it is a frequent source of
the task; it is essential to learning by limita-
tion; it furnishes the experiences that promote
understanding and augment reflective
thinking. Without it we could have
no memories, no imagination. It is the initial
step in most of our emotions. Through perception
we learn, and without perception there could
be no learning except possibly that of the
most primitive and meager sort. But

what is probably not so fully realized is the fact that we also learn to perceive.

The perceptual skill that is involved in daily performance is easily overlooked. Not until someone challenges us with a perception which we are unable to make do we become aware of the discrimination which occurs in perception. The city-bred person has difficulty making the fine discrimination needed to see a wild animal, such as a deer, hidden among the brush on a hillside when his woodsman companion points at the animal. The difference is not one of visual acuity but of perceptual training. Driving an automobile in traffic involves a gamut of perceptions impinging in a steady stream upon different sensory organs and involving perception ranging from literal to highly-enriched interpretations. The judgments of speed, direction, and angles of movement of other automobiles on the highway involve the literal perception of objects in space. In some instances, the perception may be impoverished by limitations of stimulation, as when an unusual sound occurs in the motor, but is so blurred by the accompanying sounds that we have difficulty in sensing it; or, in contrast, many of the perceptions may be highly enriched by previous experience. The green and red signal lights have meaning because we have learned green means "Go" and red means "Stop." The westerner arriving in New England for the first time doesn't know how to respond when he observes both red and yellow showing simultaneously, a signal meaning "Pedestrians move, automobiles stationary." More skillful discriminations are involved in anticipating the movements of the car ahead from slight changes in speed, shifts in position in the traffic lane, or other varia-tions foretelling a left or right turn or the intention to pass or stop. In fact, in recent years a gadget having red-yellow-and-green lights has been introduced into the rear window of automobiles to reduce the error in interpreting cues as to the intentions of the preceding driver. A common misinterpretation of stimuli is imagining that one sees water lying in a dip in the road when the reflected light is right. Lapses in attention or concentration on matters irrelevant to driving frequently produce failures to observe stop signs or the entry of other vehicles, occasionally with fatal results.

Perception ranges from a minimal level of barely sensing stimuli through the literal interpretation of cues as to size, shape, motion, texture, distance, and the like, to those which involve a wealth of past experience and training in order to provide the appropriate interpretation of a stimulus. The tobacco-buyer who can identify the particular area from which a batch of leaf tobacco came by its texture, color, and shape, or the wine-taster who can identify the vineyard and year of production of wines from their body and flavor have learned to respond to and interpret stimuli which others do not perceive. The processes by which perception develops and the influence of attitudes, sets, motives, and group norms upon perception are of prime importance.

THE GENERAL NATURE OF THE PERCEPTIVE FUNCTIONS

Perception is a fundamental psychological activity. It is something the individual does. It is not, as we consider it, a faculty of the mind, nor merely a cluster of sensations. Sometimes it is described as a process of getting knowledge of the physical world or as a means of making adjustments to the environment in which we operate. Knowledge and adjustments are important outcomes of perception, but to understand the role of learning in the development of this function it is necessary to consider the nature of the process itself. In perception, we apprehend objects or events. When we perceive, we translate impressions made upon our senses by the stimuli from our environment into awareness of objects or events. Moreover, the temporal reference is to the present, for the objects and events of which we become aware are regarded in perception as present and as going on. This activity of perceiving is such a universal and intimate feature of our mental life that it is often difficult to realize that objects of the physical world do not merely present themselves and that we do anything more than open our minds to receive them as they really are. It is easy to overlook the fact that we construct our world of things and events out of our sensory processes and that physical objects as we know them through sight, sound, taste, smell, and touch are the products of our own perceptions.

Essential features of perception. *1. Sensory experience.* All perceptions are characterized by the presence of sensory experience. This includes the various qualities of experience derived from the stimulation of the sense receptors by the appropriate physical stimuli.

Visual sensory experience consists of many thousands of different
visual qualities. These include all shades of grays and the colors—
reds, yellows, greens, blues, and their intermediates in all degrees
of saturation from the richest colors to grays and in all tints and
shades from lightest to darkest. In hearing, we have tones and the
various kinds of noises. The tones vary in pitch, and a good ear
can distinguish approximately 11,000 differences in the range from
the lowest to highest. Sweet, salty, sour, and bitter are the primary
taste qualities. In the olfactory group are a great variety of odors.
The sense of smell provides the odors of flowers, fruits, spices, de-
cayed flesh, burnt cloth, and many others. From the receptors in
the skin and in the internal organs we get such qualities of experience as sensory pressure, pain, warmth, and cold; and from the
proprioceptors in the muscles we get the strains and pressures of
kinesthetic experience. These widely differing qualities of sensory
experience depend upon the organs of sense and upon the nervous
system. They are the basis of our knowledge of the world about us.
Without them there would be no awareness of anything.

2. *Meaning.* The mere experience of a particular color, sound,
taste, smell, or touch appears without learning. We do not have to
learn in order to sense the color blue, the rumbling sound of thunder, the odor of violets, a salty taste, or a pain. But we do have to
learn what the color is a color of. We have to learn to identify one
noise as that of thunder, another as the roar of an airplane, and
another as the report of a pistol. We learn to perceive objects, but
we have sensory experience directly as the result of the impact of
environmental forces upon the bodily mechanisms of perception.

When the qualities of conscious experience refer to an object
or event in the physical world, they are said to have *meaning.* All
perceiving involves the factor of meaning. When we see a chair, a
tree, or a house, we perceive the objective fact. The thing-out-there
is the meaning that the pattern of colors and lights has for us. The
relation between sensory experience and meaning is mainly the
product of learning.

Meaning and the components of sensory experience are two distinct aspects of perception, admitting of separate consideration. A
particular set of sensory components may take on new meaning.
Note, for example, the forms shown in Figure 11.1. We see at first
four squares, one with a dot in the center, the second divided into

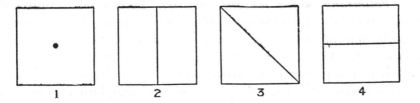

Fig. 11.1. When you learn that 1 represents the letter *B*, 2 the letter *O*, 3 the letter *A*, and 4 the letter *T*, the group of four squares means the word *boat*.

halves by a vertical line, the third divided into two equal triangles by a diagonal line, and the fourth divided into halves by a horizontal line. If we now find that these are the symbols of a code in which the first square represents the letter *B*, the second *O*, the third *A*, and the fourth the letter *T*, the four squares take on the meaning of *boat*, which they did not have for us at first. The weird sounds made by a loon in the night on a lonely lake may be, to one who has never heard them before, the alarming cry of a person in distress or the whooping and wild laughter of an intoxicated bathing party. But after one has learned the true source of this queer complex of sounds, it is the delightful and unique call of a beautiful bird that flies, swims on the water, dives, and swims long distances under the water.

Also, meaning may be stripped from sensory experiences. This sometimes occurs under repetition. Take almost any word and repeat it aloud rapidly for two minutes. By the end of that time the vocal sounds will probably have little meaning for you or anyone listening to you. Moreover, there are times when the meaning lags behind the experience, as when we hear a sound which at first has little or no meaning for us, and then suddenly we realize that it is the sound of a distant steamboat whistle. Again, the same meaning may attach to different sensory items, and different meanings may be carried by the same items of experience. The meaning of *five* may be presented visually by five single marks, the symbol 5 or V, or by five fingers held up. It could be indicated in auditory experience, as well, by the sound of the spoken word "five," or by five taps. The same meaning could be attached to taste, smell, or touch qualities. The vocal sound "tu" may mean "two," "to," or "too," according to context.

3. Patterning of the sensory qualities. Perceptual meaning depends upon the patterning of the sensory field. The matter of organization of the sensory field has already been discussed in Chapter 4. There it was pointed out that in perception, the sensory field is primarily organized on the basis of figure and ground. Certain sensory components are relatively closely knit together and marked off by more or less definite boundary lines from the surroundings which constitute the ground. These components make up the figure and usually represent what is perceived. As the figure-ground relations change, the meaning changes; that is to say, as the figure changes, the object perceived changes, as seen in Fig. 4.2.

4. Sensory discrimination. In order to have patterns of sensory qualities, the individual must be capable of sensory discrimination. To have visual patterns, the individual must be sensitive to different colors and grays. For tonal patterns, such as we find in music, there must be the ability to discriminate tonal differences. The same is true for all the senses. Thus, sensory discrimination is also an essential for perception. The efficacy of perception depends in no small degree upon the range of distinguishable sensory elements. Certain color-blind persons, for example, are not capable of sensing the difference between stimuli that yield the colors red and green for normal vision, and they find it impossible to distinguish between red and green objects that are alike except for the color. Things that look exactly alike cannot be distinguished in visual perception. If a distinction is made, other senses are used. If a person's hearing were so dull that he could not distinguish more than ten tonal pitch differences, his perception of music would lack most of the fine variations and harmonies we normally know as music. If one could hear only one quality of sound, he could distinguish sound objects only on the basis of variations in intensity and duration of that sound. Thus, the greater the range of noticeable differences in the qualities of sensory experiences, the greater will be the possibilities of making fine distinctions in perception.

Can sensory discrimination be improved? If this question is interpreted as referring to perception, the answer is "Yes." If we interpret it to mean the improvement of the capacity for sensing, or sensory acuity, the answer is "No." If a person is dull in hearing, training will not improve that hearing capacity. Color blindness cannot be cured by practice in looking at colors. Perhaps, in some instances, certain exercises may help to minimize certain sensory defects, but these do not come under the term *training*, as used here. The sensory mechanisms are limited regarding the variety of experimental qualities they can provide. Training does not change this capacity, but it may greatly improve the use of one's sensory capacity in distinguishing small differences. Children improve in their ability to distinguish between letter patterns in learning to read. In experiments on conditioning, animals and human subjects have learned under training to discriminate between similar stimuli so as to respond to one and not to the other, when before training they reacted to both.

The various objects of perception. The objects of perception are not all concrete and particular, space-filling, material objects. We perceive sound objects, for example, music, melody, and rhythm. We apprehend events, work, or study. We note the material of which a garment or a piece of furniture is made. We sometimes perceive an object not merely for itself alone, but as a representative of the class to which it belongs, the meaningful reference in such cases being not to the particular thing at which we are looking but to the whole class. Thus, the thing is perceived as a sort of generalized object.

Then there are perceptions through which we realize the moods, emotions, and motives of other persons — valuable perceptions for getting along socially. We perceive complacency, indifference, happiness, and sorrow in our friends. There are also esthetic perceptions, which afford the realization of beauty and the enjoyment of good humor. Relationships are often important objects of perception. We perceive the height of a building, the width of a river, the distance to school. We observe that one event invariably precedes another, or that John is taller than Henry. We note the passing of time and realize that some events transpire quickly, while others run on and on. We observe that the apples are ripe, that the coffee needs sugar, that the potatoes are cooked, that the room is too warm, that the ring is made of brass, or that the man is old.

Moreover, we perceive objects not for what they are themselves but for what they stand. When an object stands for or represents some other thing or fact, it is a symbol. The meaning of a symbol is *symbolic meaning*. A sign is a symbol because it signifies a fact beyond itself. Thus, the arrow on a trail tells us which path to take.

The red flag is perceived as more than simply a red flag: it indicates danger and the need for precaution. Printed and spoken words, numbers, and code signals are symbols, and for the initiated they bear a meaning of a higher order than that of vocal sounds or of printed forms.

MODIFICATION OF PERCEPTION THROUGH ACTIVITIES

Our perceptions do not come ready-made. Neither are they fixed and immutable processes. They grow, and in growing they change. They are enriched in detail and become more definite, refined, and specific. Like action, they tend toward economy of performance under repetition by the elimination of superfluous adjuncts. These modifications, like all learning, are the results of activities. Various functions leave their traces in the form of trends, predispositions, and tendencies that control the course of our perceptions and determine the nature of their outcomes (Neff, 1937). It is customary to refer in a general way to these traces of antecedent functions as the influence of past experiences. The principal modifications are alterations in the sensory patterns, changes of meaning, reduction of cues, and greater adroitness in detecting small differences.

Changes in sensory patterns. Whether or not there is some innate predisposition which causes a newborn babe to see unit forms against a background without learning, there is no doubt that the way older individuals organize their sensory field is influenced by tendencies and predispositions resulting from their earlier activities. The establishment of a particular pattern inclines the observer toward such an organization of his perceptual field on subsequent occasions. Once we have discovered the hidden figures of a puzzle picture, these figures are usually very persistent and compelling in later perceptions of the picture.

In an experiment by Siao-Sung (1937), a series of 12 simple, irregular figures formed by dotted lines were first shown to a group of subjects. Later, these figures were presented again, but as parts of larger and more complex figures, the larger figures thus "masking" those of the original series. To a control group, the larger figures were presented without the previous showing of the simple figures. It was found that the experimental group tended to see readily the masked figures as units in their respective complexes because they had previously observed these figures in isolation. The control group saw the masked figures much less frequently because no predisposition had been established for them in previous experience as in the case of the experimental group. The latter saw the masked figures as units in the larger figures 20 times more often than did the control subjects. It is evident that what we see depends upon the organization of our visual field and that this organization is greatly influenced by previous experiences.

Changes in meaning. As experiences increase, perceptual meanings change, tending, as a rule, to become more definite and more effective as a means of adjustment. An acquaintance walking along a dimly lighted street on a rainy night came to a crossing where the pavement was broken. He saw a dull, irregular patch of gray which he took to be a piece of the broken cement pavement. It appeared high and dry, so he proceeded to step on it. To his consternation his food splashed into a puddle of muddy water. The experience of hearing the splash and feeling his foot slipping into the mud quickly changed the meaning of his visual pattern from *cement* to *mud puddle*.

In some cases, the pattern of learning involved in the development of perceptual meaning is similar to that of conditioning. A child who is learning to read is shown the word *house*. He does not know what it means, but the teacher says, "House." He knows the meaning of the spoken word. By the association of the spoken word with the printed symbol the latter takes on the meaning of the former. As one handles an apple, he sees its color and form, feels its smooth waxy surface, and if he eats it, gets the odor and taste of the apple. Later, the visual stimulus-pattern alone sets off a perception, the meaning of which encompasses all of these features. The individual gets only a pattern of color directly from the stimuli, but he apprehends an apple; because of all his various past experiences with apples, he sees an edible fruit with a characteristic texture, odor, taste, and smooth surface. He does not think of each of these qualities of the apple in separate thoughts, but includes them in his meaning; he has learned that an apple is that kind of thing, and the visual stimuli now set off the perception of an apple, not merely of a disc of color.

Cue reduction in perception. A special case of the change of meaning in perception is cue reduction. From the name, it might seem to be more appropriate to describe this as a change in the perceptual pattern without change in the meaning. There is a change in pattern because certain parts of it are dropped out and the meaning carried by the original pattern is now attached to the remaining portion. On the other hand, we have a change of the meaning borne by the part which remains. You hear a voice over the telephone and do not recognize the person speaking. He must tell you his name. Later you get well acquainted with this person. He calls you on the telephone, and you recognize him by his voice at once. The quality of this particular voice is now sufficient for the apprehension of the person calling. It has taken on a meaning which at first it did not have.

In cue reduction, a part stands for the whole, or at least renders the same service for perception as it rendered earlier only in conjunction with other stimuli. Thus, the sight of a human foot means that a whole person is present; a particular noise indicates an airplane overhead; and a scorchy odor reveals that the potatoes have boiled dry. The role of past experiences with a larger range of stimuli is recognizable in these cases and in countless others which the reader can readily bring to mind.

Cues in visual space perception. The stimuli from objects of our environment make impressions upon our sense organs, and the unique features of the various impressions become significant cues for apprehending and distinguishing the various objects. A good example of this principle is found in the visual perception of distance and the tridimensionality of objects. The mosaic of colors and grays resulting from light patterns on the retina is not of itself sufficient to enable us to see an object as solid or one object as farther away than another. Persons who are born blind and who later in life have been given sight by an operation have found it necessary to learn to judge distances in visual perception. The visual stimulus-pattern provides cues that make this possible. But we must learn to use them. The learning activities involved are believed to be mainly touching, handling, and exploratory movements of various sorts.

Of primary importance in our perception of the three-dimensional nature of objects is the difference between the stimulus-patterns received by the two eyes. If an object is not too large and not too far away, we see more of its left side with the left eye and more of the right side with the right eye. Therefore, the two ocular impressions are not identical, and the difference becomes a cue for the apprehension of the spatial character of the object. We learn to see the object as solid or extending from us in space because normally only three-dimensional objects could yield disparate impressions in binocular vision. A perfectly flat surface would yield like impressions. Hence, we learn to translate retinal disparity into depth.

The way this operates may be seen in the following example. If one holds up his two index fingers before his eyes, one about 18 inches from the nose, the other about 12 inches away and one inch to the left of the line from the nose to the farther finger, and looks at them first with the right eye and then with the left, he discovers that the fingers appear closer together for the left eye than for the right. This is because the retinal images of the two fingers are closer together in the left eye, owing to the nature of the eye, to the actual position of the fingers, and to the way the light travels from the fingers to the retinas. Now, if we reproduce artifically this stimulus-pattern on the retinas by means of a stereoscope and a stereograph with a pair of vertical lines on each side — one pair for the left eye to see and the other pair for the right eye — but have the lines on the left side closer together, we see not 4 lines but 2, and one of them is seen farther off in space. Looking at the stereogram without the stereoscope we see 4 lines, 2 on each side, but all on the same surface and equidistant from the eyes. The stereoscope reproduces the retinal conditions normally produced by two vertical objects when one is farther away. The stimuli, the receptors, and the nervous system provide an experience-pattern corresponding to conditions in the external situation, and we learn to use this experience-pattern as a sign in apprehending objects and events.

Other signs or clues used in visual depth perception are available in monocular vision and give the meaning of relative distance of objects in a picture, where the light is reflected from a flat surface. These are: size, distinctness of contour, convergence of parallel lines, height in the visual field, covering, and distribution of light and shade. An object of a given size makes a smaller impression on the retina the farther away it is. Distant objects usually make less distinct impressions than near objects. Parallel lines appear to converge in the distance for the same reason that a far object appears smaller than a near one. Distant objects usually appear higher in the visual field than near objects because of our own upright position. Near objects sometimes cover or shut off in part our view of the more distant ones. Uneven surfaces produce shadows. These physical conditions produce their corresponding effects in our perceptual field; by learning their significance, we visually perceive the relative farness or nearness of the objects about us.

Auditory perception of distance and direction. Sound stimuli grow weaker the farther they travel from their source. If the sound waves come from points in the median vertical plane between the two ears, they strike the ears with equal intensities; if they come from one side, the intensity will be slightly greater for the nearer ear. Also sound waves from the left side will strike the ear on that side a fraction of a second sooner than the right ear, the reverse being true for sounds from the right side. The individual learns to use these binaural differences in apprehending the distance and direction of sources of sound. If the approximate loudness of a sound at its source is known, the weaker it is heard, the greater will be the apprehended distance of its source. If the stimulation is slightly more intense on the right side, that small difference is interpreted to mean that the sound is coming from the right. Greater intensity for the left ear leads to localization of the sound to the left. If there is no cue from vision, without bias from previously acquired knowledge regarding the source, a sound originating in the vertical plane between the ears is likely to be incorrectly localized. In addition to differences in intensity and wave phase (time) for the two ears, knowledge of the probable source of the sound contributes to the perception of direction and distance of sounds.

Perception of movement. Moving objects within our field of vision produce changes in the stimulus-pattern on the retina. This applies whether the eyes remain fixed on a stationary object or follow the moving object. In the former case, the stimulus-pattern from the object moves across the retina; in the latter case the whole background pattern shifts. These changes in retinal stimulation provide the cues for our perceptions of movement. It is apparent that previous experience has a lot to do with the apprehension of movement, especially in those cases where the awareness of changes in location depends upon the cues mentioned above. If an object is seen now in one place and the next instance in another, we are likely to perceive it as moving from the one position to the other. An object that appears to grow steadily smaller in the absence of surrounding points of reference may be seen as receding; one growing larger may be perceived as approaching. Predispositions and knowledge of what is probably happening greatly influence our perceptions of movement.

Illusions. The role in perception of trends and predispositions acquired from former experiences is revealed by many false perceptions where the established ways of interpreting sensory cues prove inadequate. Movement is likely to be perceived with a change in spatial relations within the visual field. Sometimes it is referred to the non-moving object. Suppose you are seated in a train standing at a station and looking at another train on the next track, headed in the opposite direction. If the other train starts, you may get the illusion that your own train is moving forward. Your expectation of starting would no doubt be a factor in causing the incorrect perception. Standing on a low bridge looking down on a swiftly moving stream may give one the illusion of moving rapidly upstream. Placing a pencil between the tips of two crossed fingers gives the tactual illusion of two objects instead of one. Under ordinary circumstances the fingers are not crossed and it would take two objects to stimulate the outer sides of the two adjacent fingers. The patient reports pain in the amputated foot because he is localizing the pain, derived from the nerves which formerly brought impulses from the foot, according to his established habits of localization. The building across the street appears unusually large in a fog, because the haziness has come to mean distance, and a distant object makes a relatively small retinal impression. Here a hazy object makes a large impression. A distant object must be very large to make a large impression. Hence, we get the appearance of unusual size because the cues are contradictory. Likewise, the unusually clear atmosphere makes a distant mountain seem nearer than it really is, because usually the distant objects are less clear than those nearer.

First sight at eighteen years of age. The part that learning plays in perception is difficult to realize because much of the learning takes place so early in life. A baby cannot tell us how his perceptions develop. Perceptual habits are so well established before one is able to reflect on them that the process of identifying objects by our senses seems wholly natural. There are, however, several cases on record in which persons born blind have been given sight by means of surgery after many years of experience without vision. Upon receiving sight, these persons have at first a confusing array of colors, strange shapes, and shadows which they are not able to understand or interpret. One such person who had congenital cataracts on both eyes making him 97 per cent blind during his childhood was given sight at the age of 18 by a surgical operation. He reported that when the light first flooded his eyes, everything seemed hazy, with no definite forms, or arrangement, and with no perspective. The room seemed full of objects new and strange. He did not recognize anything about him at first. The doctor took him to the window and asked him if he saw the hedge across the street. He replied, "No, Sir," for, as he said, he had no idea which among the many strange forms was the hedge. He had to learn what a hedge looks like. Then he asked the doctor where the curb of the street was. The doctor explained which form was the curb. He could see it then. Later he went to a motion-picture theater. He found it very confusing because so many things were portrayed that he did not recognize. When he came from the theater he saw the stars for the first time. He was so amazed and delighted that he thought it strange that other people were not looking at them too. When he returned to school and old friends came up to congratulate him, he could not tell who they were until he heard them speak. He misjudged distances at first. He had experiences such as reaching for an object and having his hand go beyond it. There was much trial and error in his learning to judge distances from shapes, shadows, and angles (Campbell, 1941).

Activities by which perceptions are modified or developed. The "experiences" which contribute to the development of perceptions are actually functions or activities of the organism. These activities are to a large extent themselves perceptual. Just as we acquire motor skill through repeated action, so we acquire skill in perception by repeated perceiving. Our observations of today are the result in a large measure of our past perceptions, and what we observe tomorrow will be governed in part by today's perceptions.

In the infant, motor activity is an important source of perceptual development. Swinging arms and kicking legs make contacts that provide experiences out of which concrete objects emerge. Placing objects in the mouth yields a combination of impressions — tactual, gustatory, kinesthetic, and visual — that become organized into perceptions of specific things. Nursing, crying, feeling comforting pats, and hearing the vocal efforts of adults trying to attract his attention lead to the differentiation of persons from inert things. Later, handling things, exploring with eyes and hands, lifting, shoving, walking, running, jumping, climbing, tearing, breaking, bumping, falling down, getting hurt, reaching for things, twisting, pulling, clawing, kicking, rolling, and romping all help to build up the child's ability to discern the nature of his physical surroundings through his senses. As the years advance, action continues to contribute to the development of perception. The perception of a gang of men working at hard labor cannot be the same for a person who has never done a hard day's work as for the man who has earned his living by arduous toil. The man who has lifted heavy things can see weight; he can feel the strain as he watches another struggling with a heavy load. Perceptual meanings are enriched by action.

Perceptions are enriched also by inspection. The sight of the earthworm carries a fuller meaning to the student who has dissected one in the biology laboratory and has examined it in systematic, piecemeal fashion. Search contributes to the alteration of perception. Having been asked to find an obscure object in a picture and having done so, the observer is likely, upon being shown the picture later, to apprehend at once the part previously discovered through the search.

Studies indicate that perception is influenced by needs, motivations, value systems, social perceptions, and reinforcement. Proshansky and Murphy (1942) found that perceptions of college students which were rewarded by money during a training period (longer lines, heavier weights, and lighter movement in a given direction) produced a significant shift in perception when the responses were compared after training with perceptual responses given before training. The difficulty exists in determining whether it was the affective component of the reward or merely its informational aspect which was an appropriate response derived from receiving the money and which produced the change, for it has been shown that perceptual learning can occur without reinforcement. Hamilton (1929) found that discriminations on the Galton bar showed that improvement was greater when reward was included with knowledge of results, as compared with the latter alone.

Operating on the premise that the need and value systems of poor children differ from those of rich children and that such differences should result in observable differences in perception, Bruner and

Goodman (1947) and Carter and Schooler (1949) asked fourth grade pupils to adjust a light spot on a screen until it matched the size of objects — coins, cardboard discs, and aluminum discs presented to them. Bruner and Goodman found that the poor children as a group made a statistically significant constant error of overestimating the size of coins. Carter and Schooler observed the same tendency to overestimate coin size, but only in the absence of the coin. When the coin was present in view of the children, they found no difference in their estimates. In both experiments, the conclusion was reached that the need systems influenced the perceptual judgment of socially valued objects. Some degree of caution is necessary in accepting these particular studies as verification of such a hypothesis, for at least Carter and Schooler's results can be accounted for on the basis of the greater practice of richer children with coins producing more accurate memory for size. A related study by Bruner, Postman and McGinnies (1948) provides further support of the influence of needs and attitudes in perceptual organization. When words of equal familiarity from the Allport-Vernon Study of Values (which provides scores on six scales of values, theoretical, economic, esthetic, social, political, and religious) were exposed in a tachistoscope for .01 second to a group of college students of both sexes, those words which represented a student's highest ranking value on the scale were recognized more rapidly than others. College students deprived of food for intervals of 1–9 hours showed an increase in number of food responses given to ambiguous pictorial stimulation; this suggests the influence of physiological motivation on perception (Levine, Chein, Murphy, 1942). The studies reported probably oversimplify the influence of motivation and attitude upon perception and cause it to appear as a linear relationship. Postman and Crutchfield (1952), in a large scale study which included 724 college students as subjects and involved 5 conditions of experimentally induced set and 3 conditions of stimulus words which varied in respect to the probability of food-responses, found that intensity of need is but one variable influencing perceptual responses and that the interaction of the variables influencing perception involves more than a simple desire for the fulfillment of a wish.

Children's perceptions. Another approach to the problem of the development of perception is through the consideration of differences in perception at the various age levels. In general, the child's perceptions are meager, vague, indefinite, and lacking in detail. They involve, for the most part, reactions to gross and unanalyzed wholes. The infant first becomes aware of certain elements of his environment that stand out as strikingly different from the rest of the surroundings. A loud noise against the otherwise comparative quiet of the room, an abrupt tug on the blanket that covers him, a face that comes into view, or the contact of his lips with the nipple set off certain reactions. At first these things are fused with the general situation. As he reacts to these in different settings, they gradually become disentangled from the mass situation, take on the quality of individuality, and become more or less distinct items of the objective world. The sequence of development, like that of the motor activity, is from mass to specific. Upon looking at the books in the psychology section of a library, for example, an infant probably would experience only a broad, loosely patterned, variegated expanse; the five-year-old would see a lot of books; the high-school student would see many books on psychology; while the college student of psychology would see the particular works of several well-known psychologists.

In the first weeks of life, the sense organs appear to be capable of effective functioning, but the experiences arising from them are indistinct and poorly organized. The perceptual ability of the infant develops rapidly during the first year. His behavior reveals his growing awareness of objects. In the first few months he acquires the ability to distinguish persons from inanimate objects. His eyes follow an object moved in front of his face. He reaches for and grasps small objects, inspects and manipulates them, and turns his head toward the source of sound. The ability to recognize his mother is manifest about the third month. When first her face is singled out as an object of perception, it appears that he sees it as a whole. Later the eyes, nose, and mouth are distinguished as discrete parts. By the fifth or sixth month he discriminates between strangers and familiar persons, and begins to show fear of strangers. About this time he first distinguishes between a friendly voice and an angry or threatening voice. The ability to learn to distinguish between simple geometric forms, such as circles, squares, and triangles, has been found in children as young as six months (Ling, 1941). By the end of the first year the child's world contains many objects known and recognized by him through perception. His needs and the outcomes of his reactions are important factors in determining what perceptions develop during this period.

During the preschool period, the perception of objects continues to develop in the direction of distinctness and precision. Spatial and temporal relations are, however, discerned very imperfectly. Three-year-old children have very imperfect notions of the meaning of "near" and "far." Even four-year-olds have not completely learned to use the spatial cues of relative size, shadows, and converging lines. Children's perception of size is frequently faulty because they have not learned to allow for the factor of distance. Curti (1938) reports the case of a little boy at the age of three who thought horses seen at a distance were tiny horses, and of a little girl four years old who thought her father was getting smaller as he walked away from her. Early space perceptions in children appear to depend mainly on touch and exploratory movements. These are gradually transferred to vision. The ability to localize points touched on the skin is well developed before the age of three, and school children are as adept as adults in two-point tactual discrimination.

A number of studies have revealed that young children are woefully ignorant of the most commonplace things. It appears that much that passes before their eyes is never seen. They usually know best the things they handle and the things they encounter in their home life. Their knowledge of things encountered in their walks and travels is less exact. New experiences are interpreted in terms of former experiences; hence, observations for which there is inadequate preparation or background are likely to be unreliable sources of knowledge. After about the third year, children's imagination becomes very active. This often colors and distorts their perceptions, sometimes making them fantastic. They may see the clouds as strange beasts, or perceive thunder as noise made by God rolling barrels about. A little girl seven years old had heard about a vaudeville performance in which colored lights were used in such a way as to produce changes in the color of the performer's costume. Later the girl reached home breathless, and excitedly related that she had seen a man coming down the street with a red dress on, and that as he came toward her the dress turned from red to green, then to yellow, and to blue. It had frightened her, and she had run all the way home. She was sure that what she had seen was real.

Individual differences restrict the value of generalizations here as in all matters of human development. Yet, certain general trends of perceptual growth may be observed. By the end of the second year the perception of objects is fairly well established, but throughout early childhood, objects and persons are likely to be apprehended as more or less isolated or disconnected items. A child of three years can enumerate objects seen in a picture, but description and interpretation require a higher degree of mental development. Perceptions of size, distance, and form are relatively crude in the preschool child, and spatial and temporal relations are imperfectly grasped at this age. The ability to apprehend relations improves as the child grows older and learns to interpret the various cues commonly employed.

As the child grows to maturity, his perceptions become richer and more definite in detail, his past experience playing an ever-increasing part in his observations. This gives stability to the perceptive functions. The small child's perceptions are much influenced by his present mental set, his emotions, and suggestion. This is true of an older person's perceptions also, but to a lesser extent because of the greater weight of past experience. If, for example, you were walking along a dark street with a small child and pointed out the dark form of a bush and said, "See that bear over there," he would probably see a bear. But if you tried that on a high-school boy or girl, it would probably not provoke the perception of a bear.

As adolescence is approached, the qualitative analysis of objects appears and perceptions become more abstractive in character. A further development, which comes as the child moves toward maturity, is the acquiring of symbolic perceptions in which the object is perceived, not for itself, but for what it represents. Examples are found in the meanings of words acquired as language is learned and in the meanings of various signs. The acquiring of these prepares the way for creative thinking and the solving of problems on the level of thought.

THE IMPROVEMENT OF PERCEPTION

From the foregoing discussion it will be seen that perception develops pretty well without special training through the various activities of the child. Without schooling and without tutors the child will learn to perceive. Given a normal equipment of bodily organs, he cannot help learning to perceive. His survival requires reactions to the objects in his environment, and out of these reactions perceptions take form. Yet, without guidance and the assistance of instruction, there may be many deficiencies and inadequacies in this function, which is so fundamental to the whole mental life of the individual. Perception is of such basic importance to the individual and his educational progress that its improvement becomes a part of the task of every teacher. Because it does attain a considerable degree of respectability before the child comes to school and because it develops to such a large degree through incidental learning, it is too often accepted as a ready-made vehicle for stocking the child with information. However, the facts revealed by the study of perception make clear the need for serious attention to the deliberate cultivation and training of this function. Probably the best work in this type of training has been done in the kindergarten and in our schools for the feeble-minded. Here, the need for such work is more easily appreciated because the lack of perceptual development is more apparent in the very young and in the mentally deficient. But much can and should be done at all levels of the educational program to foster better habits of observation and more effective use of the sensory equipment provided by nature. To be educated means to have eyes that see and ears that hear.

Perceptions are made keener and more reliable by training. The unreliability of ordinary observation is due to a variety of causes. Faulty vision or hearing may be a contributing cause. Mental sets, biases, prejudices, anticipations, moods, and emotional states of the observer color and channel the course of his observations and determine in a large measure what he sees and hears. The event observed, as in the case of an automobile accident, may occur so quickly that one does not have time to see all that takes place; or, the situation may be so complex that one sees only a part. These sources of error or incompetence may be overcome to a large extent by adequate training.

The most exact and reliable knowledge derived from observations is found in science. Here, special measures are taken to overcome or offset the factors that cause error. In the first place, the scientist is a trained observer. In making observations, he must maintain an attitude free from personal bias. He seeks to discover the facts, not to prove a point. He knows how to proceed in order to make a careful and systematic survey. He repeats and checks his observations. He uses instruments to extend the limits of his own organs of sense. His training steers his observations. He is not infallible, but the products of his perceptions are more exact, more verifiable, and more dependable than most nonscientific information.

The results of perceptual training may be seen also in the alertness of the proofreader in detecting mistakes in printing. The trained professional buyer for a clothing store is especially adept at distinguishing the various qualities of cloth. Expert tea tasters are noted for their acute perceptions of minute differences in the quality of the brew. The experienced hunter knows by the tracks in the snow what game has passed. The musician detects in tones the slight defect which passes unnoticed by the untrained listener. In every field of human art and endeavor, the perception of the expert — the well-trained and the fully experienced — is keener, more critical, and more analytical than is that of the novice or the uninitiated.

Gibson (1953), after making an extensive summary of the experimental studies pertaining to the effect of training upon perceptual judgment, concludes that the studies confirm the influence of practice upon improvement of judgment over a wide range of relative and absolute discriminations of visual and auditory stimuli. Several factors were reported to be influential in improvements of perceptual judgment. Although few learning curves are reported, improvement varies with amount of practice. The role of reinforcement is less clearly defined, as has been pointed out earlier in the chapter, but there is no question that verification and checking of responses through knowledge of results is an essential variable for increased proficiency. Apparently, practice which provides initially easy discrimination and a progressive reduction in difference is most valuable. Periodic practice appears necessary to the maintenance of perceptual skill. The developed skills in perceptual judgment appear to be relatively specific and show but little transfer. An illustration of this will be found in the transfer of tachistoscopic training in reading discussed later in the chapter.

Fostering the development of perception in children. The young child should have freedom to run about, to explore his environment, and to handle, taste, and smell the things he encounters. Reactions to objects are essential for the growth of his ability to perceive adequately. They take on meaning in proportion to the activity con-

nected with them. Being shut up in a pen day after day is hardly
conducive to his best interests. If this should be necessary at times,
the mother should see to it that he has a sufficient supply of toys,
blocks, and "bangable" things to manipulate — things that squeeze
easily, that make noises, and that can be pushed — so that he may
have the opportunity to learn. He should have the opportunity to dig
in the dirt, tear up paper, and play with other children. Every young
child should have the pleasure and educational experience of splash-
ing in water, watching the honeybee, feeling the soft fur of a kitten,
touching the hard, smooth, cold surface of ice, smelling the fragrance
of flowers, and tasting the things he can get to his mouth. His questions about the things he meets should be answered in a manner that
will enrich their meanings for him. He should be told the names of
things, for this will not only help build up his vocabulary, but will aid
in the process of differentiating specific objects.

The kindergarten is well adapted to contributing experiences that
have excellent developmental value. Here, the child's perceptual
possibilities are drawn out by his play with other children, by making
forms in sand or clay, by weaving — which calls for the discrimination
of colors, by singing, by finger painting, and by the many other interesting activities that afford direct sensory stimulation and the opportunity to respond, explore, and manipulate.

Developing perceptual trends. By perceptual trends we mean
the sets, predispositions, or tendencies derived from former activity
which govern the course of our perceptions. They may be thought of
as habits of perceiving. Just as we secure the establishment of a
motor skill or a habit of doing a certain thing at regular times by
telling a child what to do and how to do it and by providing appropriate incentives, so we secure the establishment of perceptual trends
by instructing the child to watch for certain things, by directing his
observations, and by seeing to it that the experience into which he is
led brings satisfaction. Instruction is the source of a temporary set
which determines the immediate perception.

To develop perceptual trends, the first step is to secure appropriate
perceptions. The objects and materials to be observed are important
factors. Natural objects, models, charts, and other concrete materials
are most suitable. The child may be asked to describe what he sees,
draw pictures of it, or write a composition on it. Questions give a
definite incentive and direction to perception. A child may be led

to see many details which otherwise might entirely escape his attention if questions are asked. Another means is to show a group of objects or a page of several pictures for a few seconds and have the children later tell how many things they can remember. This may be made into a sort of game. Group discussion of a picture or of what is seen on a field trip may be made stimulating. In all of these procedures, the teacher has the opportunity for correcting wrong impressions or faulty observations, and, in so doing, helps the child to become more accurate in his perceptions. For this reason also, conversations with children about their experiences are recommended.

Children naturally seek adventure and new experiences. They like to explore. One teacher succeeded in arousing the interest of a boy who was indifferent to his schoolwork by telling him he was to describe to her every morning one interesting thing he had seen on the way to school. This assignment included the subtle suggestion that if he noticed things around him, he would find interesting things. This boy was soon reporting to his teacher not one but several interesting things he had seen, and his attitude toward his work quickly improved.

Field trips and movies. The observations on a field trip or of a classroom motion picture — excellent means of instruction — need to be directed. Preparatory instruction about what to look for should be given to secure best results. One of the disadvantages of these devices is the danger that attention may be diverted from the important things to some trivial and irrelevant, though to the child interesting, detail. It is well, also, to announce that a report on the subject of the trip or picture will be expected. This will tend to make the pupils more alert and stimulate them to make careful observations. This report may be either oral or written. In either case, the excursion or the movie should be followed by a discussion in which false or erroneous impressions are brought to light and corrected.

Perception and language. Perception plays a fundamental part in the acquisition of all the language skills. First, there is learning of the names of various objects. A child learns the name of an object by hearing it spoken by another. The vocal sound becomes associated with the object in his experience and thereby comes to mean or represent that object. The mother, for example, says, "Doggie," as she hands the child the toy dog. After a few repetitions, "Doggie" means the toy dog. As he strokes the kitten he hears someone say, "Kitty," and by this association the sound means that little soft, furry, moving thing. He learns in this way the names of many objects before he can say the names himself.

The next step in the development of language is the emergence of speech. About the end of the first year, the baby begins to utter his first words. As he sees the kitten come into the room, he says, "Kitty." Having heard "Daddy" many times in connection with seeing his father, he says, "Daddy" when his father appears. At first, the meaningful reference of these words is not very specific for him. He may call a fur coat "Kitty" or say "Daddy" to any man he happens to see. This indiscriminate use of names is like the generalization of the conditioned response. It is overcome by further learning through which is developed the ability to make appropriate distinctions.

The child's auditory perception at the age when he is learning to talk is very imperfect. He may have normal hearing and the pronunciation he hears may be faultless, yet his own pronunciation may be faulty because he fails to hear the fine variations and delicate shadings of sounds characteristic of good speech. Children often need special training to improve their ability to hear various word sounds accurately. This imperfect auditory perception of word sounds may affect not only the child's pronunciation unfavorably, but may be responsible for confusion in the next language steps and his learning to read and spell. For example, in a composition by a seventh-grade girl appeared the following errors in spelling: *hunerds,* for hundreds, *Washinton,* for Washington, and *witch* for which. The relation of these errors to faulty pronunciation is obvious. This child wrote these words as they sounded to her and as she herself pronounced them. Her difficulty was not due to home influence, nor to bad pronunciation by the teacher. Her parents were well educated and spoke plainly. Failure to hear properly was a basic cause here of bad spelling. This child needed "eartraining" to help her hear the word sounds correctly.

In order to learn to read successfully, a child must be capable of good auditory and visual discrimination. Reading begins with the child's oral vocabulary. He knows the spoken word first. This is associated with the printed word. Then, after the pattern of learning by conditioning, the visual form takes on the meaning carried by the speech sound. If the learner does not hear the essential and distinguishing elements of the spoken word, he may have trouble in making this shift to the printed form. A large proportion of the children referred to the Boston University Educational Clinic as reading-difficulty cases have shown lack of ability to notice similarities and differences in the sounds of spoken words (Murphy, 1940).

In a carefully controlled study, Eames (1947) compared the speed of object recognition and word recognition of 329 children between the ages of 6 and 13. Seventy-five children were passing in all school subjects, 254 were failing. The speed of object and word recognition was the same for succeeding students, but markedly disparate for failing students, with speed of word recognition falling behind object recognition between ages 6 and 12. Eames explains these results in terms of an artifact of the educational program which places emphasis upon sight vocabulary and oral reading during the elementary grades, thus permitting the lack of speed of recognition of words to go unnoticed.

Several studies have shown a correlation between perceptual span, perceptual speed, and speed of reading, but they have failed to show that improving perceptual span or perceptual speed produces a concomitant improvement in reading (Sutherland, 1946; Smith and Tate, 1953; Freeburne, 1949). The three studies mentioned have utilized such devices as flashmeters, ophthalmographs, tachistoscopes, and reading rate controllers with which the reader could progressively advance his reading rate. Marked increases in perceptual speed of recognition have been shown in all instances (using college students as subjects), and also, (where the reading-rate controller was used) in reading speed as a result of training. Unfortunately, the increases transferred in such small amounts to normal reading situations that direct work at increasing reading speed appears equally if not more beneficial.

Visual discrimination is essential for reading, for if the learner does not distinguish relatively small differences in word forms, he will confuse such similar letter patterns as *house, louse,* and *horse.* To distinguish between *new* and *mew,* for instance, requires rather keen perceptual discrimination, and it is not surprising, in view of the fact that perceptions are so imperfectly developed at the first- and second-grade levels, to find that these words look alike for some children. Durrell (1940) has stated in reference to this matter that, "Children learn to recognize words by the general appearance of a word rather than by exact letters. Often a part of a word stands out and serves as a cue for the recall of the whole. Cues used by children to recognize words often lead to errors. The word *dog* is commonly misread as *girl* probably because the *g* is the cue for the latter word." He gives inadequate perception of the printed word as one of the causes of reading difficulties, and in his chapter on word meaning and recognition, he presents a number of exercises designed to train children to observe differences between words that are similar in appearance. Murphy has developed a series of exercises for training the auditory and visual word perception of young children, and has demonstrated that their use facilitates the process of learning to read (Murphy 1941, 1943).

ATTENTION AND PERCEPTION

Attention as a selective process. The activity of perceiving starts with the excitation of the sense receptors by physical stimuli and runs on its course with the transmission of neural impulses to the cortex and the organization of the resulting sensory qualities into meaningful patterns. At any moment, however, the organism is assailed by a multiplicity of stimuli too great to be utilized in perceiving. The perceptive functions are limited with respect to the area of stimulation they can manage. Hence, a selection must be made with respect to the stimuli assailing the organism at one time. The process of selection is attention.

Attention is not a mental power that does the selecting. It is the organism itself that selects. It favors certain stimuli and disregards others according to its own needs, inclinations, state of being, and its activities at the moment. Some of these conditions which determine the selection are transient, as, for example, the activity in progress or sets induced by a command or a suggestion from the teacher; others, which have their sources in the history of the organism and its racial development, are more constant factors. These sets, biases, and habits give orderliness to the apprehending of our surroundings by providing a right-of-way for clarity of perception in one area of stimulation while other areas are disregarded or are made to wait their turn.

Studies of the attention aspect of perception have been largely concerned with three problems: first, the relation of attention to clearness of the experiential pattern; second, the number of things that can be attended to at one time; and third, the factors which determine attention.

Clearness. Through introspection, one may observe the effects of attentive selection on conscious experience. If the reader will for a moment observe his patterns of experience, he will note that they are constantly shifting and that at any given moment, some parts of the conscious field stand out clearly while other parts are obscure. As you look at the clock on the mantel, the visual pattern is dominant. As you attend to the clock, you are only vaguely aware of other objects in the room. The radio sounds are unclear and you fail to hear what the announcer says. If, as you gaze with eyes fixed on the clock, your attention shifts to the speaker's voice, the vocal sounds become focal and clear, while the visual qualities become obscure. Perceptual experience is organized with respect to different degrees of clearness into a foreground-background pattern. The constant shifting of the foreground gives emphasis now to one, then to another part of the general scene.

The range of attention. Regarding the second problem, we find that one really attends to one thing at a time. Quick shifts of attention may enable a person to observe several things in a few seconds, or to carry on two operations that require attention. Where several things occupy attention at the same moment, they are taken as a unit. One may apprehend clearly a group of five dots, a flock of chickens, or a forest. In such cases, one does not attend to the individual dots, chickens, or trees.

Determiners of attention. Regarding the factors which determine attention, we stated above that they were factors of bias or habit within the individual. We must now examine the conditions more fully. First, although the factors controlling attention lie within the individual, this does not mean that factors in the external situation have no influence. Just as the instructions from another person may give rise to a task-set, so commands or suggestions from another person may give rise to sets that govern attention. When the teacher says, "Look here," "Notice the band on the pigeon's leg," or, "Tell me what you see in the man's hand," his words serve to direct the attention of his pupils to things he wants them to observe.

1. Primary determiners of attention. There are certain characteristics of objects or stimuli that usually are potent for securing attention. Large, moving, novel, unusual, or isolated objects in contrast with their surroundings are usually favored items of attention. Intense, continuous, repeated, or changing stimuli make a strong bid for attention. These factors appear to dominate the attention of animals and play a relatively larger part in controlling attention of children than of adults.

The individual's needs, organic and otherwise, exert a powerful influence on attention. If one is hungry, he looks for a restaurant and notices signs of food. Thirst causes one to notice wells, pumps, faucets, or any other indicator of drinking water. The need for security causes one to be on the alert for danger signals.

2. *Acquired determiners of attention.* In general, we attend to those things that have significance or value for us. Acquired determiners of attention develop out of experiences, and as the child advances toward maturity, they assume an ever increasing role in the control of attention. From the need for security grows the desire to please others and to be liked by one's associates. This desire is an important determiner of attention. The child listens to the teacher to please her or to avoid her displeasure. One may give his attention to a speaker in order to show that he has good manners. Also, potent factors in attention are acquired interests. An interest in flowers, birds, music, or airplanes inclines one to select these things out for observation. To develop new interests is a most effective way of improving the student's perceptions and habits of observation.

Attention and search. There is something forward-reaching about attention; it may be observed in the alertness for what is to come. Woodworth (1940) speaks of attention as the exploratory phase of observation, and of perception as the discovering phase. This is seen in the expectant attitude of attention aroused by the words "Look!" "Listen!", by the straining to hear the words of a whispered conversation, by the craning of necks to see the passing parade, and by the various motor accompaniments and adjustive postures of an attentive attitude.

Attention in children. One of the practical problems of a teacher is that of sustaining the attention of the members of a class. Little children are sometimes said to be incapable of sustained attention, but this is hardly an accurate statement. As stated above, the attention of a little child is more completely governed by the characteristics of the things that appeal to his receptors than is the adult's. His attention is likely to shift rapidly from one thing to another in his environment. He is readily distracted by noises, bright colors, moving things, and bodily discomfort — more so than the older child or adult. This is as we should expect in view of the fact that he has not had time to acquire the strong social motives and the controlling interests that play so important a part in the determination of attention in the adult. Nevertheless, under the right conditions a child can give attention over a considerable period of time. It is largely a matter of motivation. At the movie, at the circus, or in hearing an interesting story, the child will have little trouble in keeping his attention from wandering. Attention is so important a matter for learning that it must be aroused, directed, and sustained by the teacher if he is to meet with any degree of success in his work. It is futile to disregard the nature of children in attempting to accomplish this. It will do little good merely to demand attention and then proceed with a dull, monotonous, and meaningless presentation of facts. The secrets of securing and maintaining attention are change, novelty, interest, and meeting a need.

WHAT PERCEPTIONS SHALL WE TRAIN?

No attempt will be made here to list all of the perceptions which the school should endeavor to develop. The needs of various individuals are so diverse and the demands of different vocations so varied with respect to effective perception that only general principles can be stated. There are certain needs which are well nigh universal. These must be our guide.

Perceptions of natural objects. Every individual must get on in a world of natural objects. The perception of *natural objects,* their nature, qualities, and form, is a basic necessity. A good start in this direction has been made by the time the child enters school. But the imperfections and limitations of object perception at this age are so great that the school has both an opportunity and a duty in enrichment, extensions, and refinements. Through nature study and science, on the field trip, and in the laboratory, the pupil's eyes may be quickened to see more penetratingly into marvels of nature.

Space perception and orientation. Because adjustments of various kinds must be made to the spatial aspects of the contents of one's environment, the individual needs a well-developed ability to apprehend spatial relationships. He must learn that a man walking away is not really getting smaller and that railroad tracks do not actually draw closer together in the distance. Since nearly everyone today drives a car, the ability to make quick estimates of distance and speed is most essential for the welfare and safety of the driver and of the pedestrian. An important form of space perception, which should receive attention in the school, is orientation with respect to the points of the compass. All children should know how to get their bearings with respect to north, south, east, and west. One youngster, when asked what direction is Australia from India, replied that he knew how it looked on the map, but he could not answer, "South-east" because he did not know the names of directions on the map. The geography class should foster correct orientation perception.

Esthetic perception. Every child should learn to see the beauty in his surroundings. The enjoyment of a beautiful sunset, land-scape, picture, or music depends upon the degree to which perception has been established. To appreciate good music one must be sensitive to the figures and patterns of tones that make it good. To appreciate art the pupil must be able to see the shadings, rhythm, and balance by which the artist has expressed his purpose. The domestic-science class should be taught to see the pleasing details of an artistically arranged dinner table, and the fine points of good taste and design in clothing. The botany class should learn to see the beauty of the color patterns of flowers, not merely stamens, pistils, and petals. The literature class should be taught to see the beauty of the total pattern of the poem, not merely to tear good literature to pieces in a search for similes and metaphors.

Social perceptions. The school should contribute to the refinement of the child's social perceptions. It is important in getting along with people to realize their moods, attitudes, and motives, and to see quickly the effect of one's actions or words on others. Some persons are sensitive to social stimuli, while others are callous to them. Even a dog learns to watch his master's face for cues of approval. The successful husband learns to notice his wife's new dress or "permanent." The good teacher is sensitive to the attitudes and responses of her pupils.

Vocational training. Besides these perceptions, which should be developed in all pupils, there are those which are particularly essential for success in the various fields of study, in the vocations, and in the professions. The doctor, for example, learns the diagnostic significance of the appearance of the patient's skin; the fisherman knows the meaning of the tug on his line; the scientist sees more in his microscope than the untrained observer does; the carpenter distinguishes readily different kinds of lumber; and the farmer can tell when the grain is ready to cut.

SUMMARY

Perception is an activity upon which most of our learning depends. It is the apprehension of things as present and of events as taking place. It is modified and developed through learning. All perceptions involve sensory experience and meaning. The meaning depends largely on the patterning of the sensory qualities, and sensory discrimination is essential to patterning. Besides material objects, we perceive sounds, materials, events, work, motives of others, relations, and symbols.

The modifications accomplished through learning include changes in the sensory patterns and in meaning. Distance, size, direction, and form are apprehended by means of cues that have been learned. When the customary use of these cues is not appropriate, we may have illusions or inadequate perceptions. Any of the psychological functions may serve to modify and enrich perception, but the development of perceptions in the early years probably results mainly from exploratory activity and perceiving.

The perceptions of young children are meager, crude, indefinite, and lacking in detail. Wholes are usually perceived before parts, and discrete objects are apprehended earlier than their spatial and temporal relations.

The keenness and reliability of perceptions may be improved by training. The school should give serious attention to the development of adequate perceptions. Children should be given opportunity to explore and manipulate, and should be provided with a variety of stimulating experiences. To develop desirable perceptual trends, the child's observations must be directed. A question is a good means for guiding perception.

Perception plays an important role in the mastery of the language arts. Good auditory discrimination is necessary for speech development, and fine visual discrimination is essential for learning to read.

Attention is a process which selects the stimuli for perception. It provides clarity and dominance in the shifting sensory patterns. One really attends to one thing at a time, but grouping makes it possible to incorporate several items into one object of attention. Some determiners of attention are innate, others are acquired; some are permanent, others are transient. Basically, one attends to large, novel, isolated, and moving things, and to stimuli that are intense, changing, or repeated. Purposes, interests, habits, and social motives are acquired determiners of attention. Attention is forward-looking and exploratory. It may be directed by questions, commands, or suggestions. Compared with an adult's, a child's attention is more controlled by intense stimuli and novel, moving things. The child is easily distracted, but with sufficient interest and variety his attention may be sustained.

Education should seek to improve perceptions of natural objects and their spatial and temporal relations. Training should be given for the development of esthetic and social perceptions. The various vocations call for specialized perceptual training.

OVERVIEW

Hilgard, E. R., "Perception," *Introduction to Psychology*. New York: Harcourt, Brace, 1953, pp. 281-310.

SELECTED REFERENCES

Blake, R. R. and G. V. Ramsey, eds., *Perception: An Approach to Personality*. New York: Ronald, 1951.

Gibson, Eleanor, "Improvement in Perceptual Judgments as a Function of Controlled Practice or Training," *Psychological Bulletin*, 1953, 50, pp. 401-31.

Gibson, J. J., "The Study of Perceptual Phenomena," *Methods of Psychology*, T. G. Andrews, ed. New York: Wiley, 1948, pp. 158-88.

ORIGINAL INVESTIGATIONS

Gage, N. L. and G. Souci, "Social Perception and Teacher-Pupil Relationships," *Journal of Educational Psychology*, 1951, 42, pp. 145-52.

Helson, H., "Adaptation Level as a Basis for a Quantitative Theory of Frames of Reference," *Psychological Review*, 1948, 55, pp. 297-313.

Postman, L. and R. Crutchfield, "The Interaction of Need, Set, and Stimulus in a Cognitive Task," *American Journal of Psychology*, 1952, 65, pp. 196-218.

Chapter Twelve

Rote Learning and Retention

*Perception, as we have seen, is an
activity through which the individual becomes aware of objects about him
and of events that are taking place. It
depends upon physical stimuli from the
environment and the excitation of receptors for
the essential sensory qualities of experience. Frequently, however, by means
of other modes of functioning the individual
slips away from the present. Through his
memories, he reviews past scenes
and relives to a certain extent his former experiences. The meaningful reference in remembering is to some past experience or to some
object or situation previously encountered.
When we remember a thing, we*

apprehend it as past. In imagination we anticipate the future, we make plans, we forecast, we suppose what has been, we daydream, and we think of certain kinds of things with reference only to the general characteristics of those things.

ASSOCIATION

The appearance and sequences of our memories and the various imaginational experiences are determined by functional trends that have already been formed and by other factors of set which we shall consider later. A perception sets off a memory; one memory leads on to another; and ideas run their serial course in daydreaming. A picture of an old friend sets off memories of experiences shared with him and the odor of new-mown hay brings to mind scenes of childhood days on the farm. Sometimes a perception sets off imagination. The doorbell rings and we anticipate the appearance of an expected guest. As we look at the package marked "Not to be opened until Christmas," we imagine various things it may contain. The relations found in the sequences of such centrally aroused and sustained experiences are known as *associations*. To understand these associations, we must go back to the organization of perceptual experiences and consider that ordinarily our perceptions are not isolated events. They usually are linked with other perceptions. We see the boy in the cart drawn by the pony. We see the train drawn by the locomotive and running on steel rails. We hear the factory whistle at twelve o'clock and see the crowd of workers coming out. We hear the author's name followed by the title of the book he wrote. We hear the thunder after the flash of lightning. In many ways the relation of belonging is here established.

The series may be longer. As our eyes pass over the landscape viewed from the top of a hill, we notice, in turn, a cluster of trees, broad fields of grain, farm buildings, and cattle on the distant hillside; and all of these experiences are combined to make up the "wonderful view." They belong together as integral parts of the rural scene. We enter a grocery store and observe in succession the boxes stacked on the counter, the shelves laden with canned goods, and the pleasing display of fresh vegetables and fruits. Here again, the various perceptions are joined together as successive phases of our visit to the store. Likewise the successive experiences of a week-end trip are combined into the unit which we regard as the trip.

Moreover, the organism is capable of rehearsing these events and scenes in memory without the original stimuli and receptor processes, and the memorial rehearsal tends to follow the order of the original perceptual trains. However, so many and varied are the impressions from former experiences that there are likely to be alterations and breaks in the chain. Deviations from the original patterns may come from the blending and interference of traces from countless other antecedent functions. There may be omissions and there may be filling in and substitutions from other earlier experiences. Breaks may be caused by the intrusion of potent stimuli from the present situation. Still, the general fact remains that things experienced together in perception are likely to be thought of together in memory and in imagination.

Previously established associations also govern the appearance and sequence of the imaginational functions in revery, anticipation, mediation, and creative thinking. Because of repeated associations the thought of boy is followed by the thought of girl; table suggests chair; house suggests barn; grocery store, canned goods; pony, cart; dog, cat; and so on. In these cases we have objects that have been experienced together in spatial contiguity. The associative trends are established also by such relations as part-whole, cause-effect, opposites, and similarities. The principle of establishment is the same. The part is experienced in connection with the whole, effect is seen to follow cause, opposites are known as opposites only as they are apprehended in connection with each other, and in the case of thoughts of similar things, the sequence is secured by the common features of the experiences.

Verbal associations. Words in spoken and written language stand for the various sorts of objects of experience. As carriers of meanings they render a great service in thinking. Here the distinction often made between action as a physical process and thought as a mental process breaks down. Talking aloud is a form of action; but is talking to yourself, without uttering a sound, action or thinking? The associative processes serve many different functions. Distinctions between the functions must be based on differences in modes of operation and their products. The early behaviorists claimed that thought is internal speech based on muscular habits learned in overt speech. There is no doubt that much we call thinking is carried on in such a manner. The unuttered words here carry the meanings of rich and varied experiences. Especially in thoughts where the reference is general or where the meanings are abstract, words serve as effective bearers of meaningful experience. A very large part of our associative processes is verbal in character.

Memorizing is largely a matter of forming verbal associations. To memorize a poem means to acquire the ability to recite it in exact order without recourse to the book and without any other form of perceptual prompting. The principles governing the formation of the associations of memory and imagination already described apply also to the establishment of the verbal associations. In paired-associates verbal learning, we see or hear two words which are connected in perception; later, the first is presented to us as a "stimulus word" and we respond with the second. Our response may be in inner speech, in audible speech, or in writing, but it is evoked in the same manner as a memory that is touched off by a perception. In the case of serial verbal learning, the recital is carried through by associative tendencies derived from the perceptual trains established during the learning.

There has been some tendency to think of an individual's memory span as being constant for all kinds of materials. True, it has been recognized that one's span of memory increases with age, as is seen in the capacity to repeat digits in different individual intelligence tests; but, irregardless of these changes in time, the memory span has been thought to be similar for different kinds of materials. Quite the opposite is true. The kind of material being presented and the method of presentation produce marked differences in memory span. Brener (1940) presented a variety of materials — digits, nonsense syllables, meaningful words, sentences, geometrical designs, etc. — to a group of college students using both visual and auditory methods of presentation and testing for recall and reproduction. Sizable variations in memory span were observed, with smaller spans associated with lower degrees of meaningfulness.

Associative tendencies regarded as neural trends. Just as the ideational experiences themselves depend primarily upon the central neural processes, with mental images taking the place of the sensory patterns of the antecedent perceptions, so it is the nervous system that determines the sequence of these ideational experiences. We shall, therefore, not think of association as a kind of magnetic force that binds together two or more mental entities called "ideas," and by means of which one, upon appearing in consciousness, is able to pull in the other. By association we mean the temporal course of events in memorial rehearsal, in imaginational trains, and in verbatim recital, resulting from the tendency of the nervous system to carry through its renewed operations on the lines previously established. The associative tendencies bear the same relation to the thought processes as habit tendencies bear to action. They are observed as are habit tendencies in the sense that repeated performances indicate an inclination toward certain types of response. They are regarded by hypothesis as neural trends.

Rote memorizing. Most of us have formed a great many associations with the things which we meet frequently in the course of our daily living. Thus, *church* may suggest: worship, preacher, building, bell, sermon, hymns, usher, pew, aisle, wedding, music, congregation, deacon, contributions, or Sunday school. Now, the chances are that on different occasions with different attitudes and sets, the mention of *church* will bring to mind different ones of these associated experiences. If you are worried over money matters, the thought of church may make you think of your pledge to contribute a dollar every Sunday. If you are hungry, you may think of the church supper. At Christmas time you may think of the music of your church. In other words, the total situation governs associative recall, and the response to a stimulus made in one situation may be altogether different from that made to the same word in another situation. From a large number of possible associations which may recur there is selection, and the favored item may not be the same under different circumstances. What appears depends upon the relative strengths of the tendencies, the purpose, problem, attitude, mood, and other sets.

In such cases as we have just mentioned, our associations are, for the most part at least, formed incidentally. There is no forthright attempt to insure particular forms of reproduction. In rote memorizing, however, there is normally a definite purpose to acquire the ability to recite or reproduce in a fixed manner. An attempt is made to form a particular associative train and to strengthen it by repetition, so that the recurrence of a particular item of experience or verbal reaction will invariably be succeeded by the one that followed it in the learning situation. So, the poem is read and reread until every word in every line can be recited in the precise order in which it is read. Spelling must be learned so that for each word the exact sequence of letters can be reproduced. A deviation from the order experienced in learning is considered an error, and the learning in that case would be regarded as imperfect or incomplete.

In paired-associates learning, where two items are learned together, the pair is repeated until the learner, upon experiencing the first member, will be able to recall the second. Such, for example, would be the learning of the dates of historical events, the capitals of states, the names of the authors of books, the foreign language equivalents of English words, and the answers to simple fact questions, such as "Who is the Mayor of Chicago?" Memorizing is, then, the process of developing associations strong enough to make it probable that when certain perceptions or ideas appear, they will prompt specific responses.

QUALITATIVE CHANGES IN TIME

A number of qualitative changes in the retained material take place during the interval prior to recall. In recitations and examinations, children show not only a loss of much that they have learned but also various imperfections and deviations from the original material in what they reproduce. From the standpoint of school learning, it is obvious that this feature of retention is quite as important as the quantitative loss. The facts of quantitative decline are significant for all cases of rote learning, such as the memorizing of the arithmetic combinations, spelling, and verbatim learning of poems and rules. But the qualitative changes which include insertions of new elements—transpositions, distortions, substitutions, omissions of particular details, and the like—are common, and for the teacher who is trying to build up topical understanding they are of vital concern.

Interference and intrusions. The studies on retroactive inhibition have shown that the insertion of a second learning activity between the original learning and recall results in interference, which impairs retention. But besides this it is found that sometimes items from the interpolated lists or learning materials appear as erroneous responses during the recall of the original material (Melton and Irwin, 1940). Thus, we find that from experiences occurring during the interval, various elements may be blended with what has been learned so as to cause errors in reproduction. A classroom illustration would be the case of a child who reads two stories in succession, and then into his reproduction of the first inserts characters or events from the second. An example from every-day life would be the case of a person who sees an automobile accident and afterwards hears another witness tell something about it which he himself did not observe, and who later in court testifies to having seen what he only heard from the other witness after the accident.

One of the factors influencing intrusions is the similarity of the interpolated and original material. Early research treated the similarity factor alone, but a study by the Gibsons (1934) systematically modifies both method and material. Five matched groups of 26 college students learned lists of 10 pairs of consonants for 2-minute periods. After a 3-minute interval spent on an interpolated task which was alike or different in method of operation and material, the subjects were tested for recall of the original material. The control group which spent the intervening interval looking at pictures had the highest percentage of recall. In the other four groups, the interpolated task was alike in both method of operation and material, dissimilar in one but alike in the other, or unlike in both. The interference resulting from the interpolated task was at a minimum where both operation and material were dissimilar, but was greater where either operation or material was similar.

Twining (1940) systematically varied the amount of interpolated material learned and the length of the interpolated interval, and found that the amount of interference (serial anticipation memorizing of nonsense syllables) was related to the amount of interpolated memorizing, with greater forgetting associated with greater amounts of interpolated mental work. As would be anticipated from the typical shape of retention curves, the time interval was of progressively less importance.

Stories and other comprehended materials. When children or older subjects are asked to reproduce stories or other topical material, a number of discrepancies are usually found when their reproductions are compared with the original. Omissions, alterations, and additions are frequent. Points not essential to the plot as understood drop out. Uncomprehended elements are omitted. The general meaning of the story or topic dominates the reproduction, and elements that were not incorporated into the general meaning structure are not recalled. Where gaps occur in recall, the subject fills in from his own general fund of experience. Thus, his account is more than reproduction; it is in part a creation (Bartlett, 1932).

When a story is passed along from person to person, the accumulation of alterations sometimes produces a remarkable transformation that bears little resemblance to the original. In one study of story-remembering the experimenter submitted the story by the method of serial reproduction to 6 boys and 6 girls in the seventh and eighth grades. The first boy read the original and reproduced it after 5 minutes. His reproduction was read by the second boy, who in turn passed his reproduction on to the third, and so on through the group. Titles and names of persons and places were found to be the most unstable elements of the story. The story shortened as it passed along. Minor details dropped out first, incidents and events were transposed, and the language was changed to patterns more familiar to the members of the group (Morris, 1939).

Objects. The memory changes for a particular object tend to follow a course similar to that found for stories. Minor details tend to drop out rather early. The recalled object tends to become less distinctive and to approach a type according to the individual's general experience with many objects of the class to which the particular one belongs. Certain essential features become stereotyped. For example, one sees an elephant at a circus; as time passes, the particular characteristics of this elephant disappear from memory and the features common to all the elephants one has seen remain. If, however, the object possesses some unusual feature that receives special attention and arouses interest, this feature may not only persist in memory but it may dominate the recalled structure. A young boy had noticed for the first time the front sight on the end of a gun barrel and was much interested in its purpose. Later he made a drawing of the gun from memory. The sight was drawn altogether too large in proportion to the other parts.

Pictures and nonsense figures. In a number of studies on this problem, pictures and nonsense figures have been used as learning materials, and retention has been tested after an interval by means of drawings. As in the case of retelling stories, this test is not a measure of retention alone. In addition to what is actually recalled, such drawings represent the creative activity by means of which the subject fills in the gaps in his recall in order to complete the picture. The results of such studies indicate that the details tend to drop out sooner than the main outlines of the picture or figure, and that with the lapse of time there is a drift toward a schematized type. Sometimes the figure changes so that it comes to resemble something else. This appears in some cases to be due to verbal labeling or to an associated idea. For example, if the subject sees a nonsense design and thinks, "It looks like a cat," his reproductions are likely to look more and more like a cat as time passes (Crosland, 1921). Under repeated reproductions, an irregular or unsymmetrical figure tends to become more regular or to shift toward symmetry (Perkins, 1932). Figures resembling to some degree a more familiar form tend to be drawn more like the familiar form. Lines that in the presented figure are fairly close to parallel, vertical, or horizontal tend to be drawn as parallel, vertical, or horizontal. A peculiar feature of the picture may be exaggerated, and certain writers partial to the Gestalt point of view hold that under repeated reproductions figures tend to improve through structural change (Wulf, 1922).

It is clear, therefore, that qualitative changes in the material learned, as well as changes in the amount retained, take place during the interval following learning. These changes are due to previously acquired knowledge, to experiences which precede learning, to verbal description and analysis, and to various events or experiences of the interval.

The range and accuracy of report. The range and accuracy of the report are influenced by several factors. In the first place, in order to get a full and reliable report, the individual's observation must be thorough and accurate. His perception of the scene or incident may be defective because of failure to attend adequately, or because of emotional excitement or an indifferent attitude. His report may be erroneous because of his poor judgments with respect to spatial and temporal relations, it may be incomplete because of forgetting, and it may be distorted by what the individual hears or sees between the incident and his report. Its accuracy and completeness are, moreover, influenced by the form of the report, by the character of the questions the individual is called upon to answer, and also by the factors of age and training.

The report may be made in *narrative* form, in which the individual lists all the objects he can remember, or recounts, without prompting and in as full detail as possible, the story of what he saw. A second form of report is the *interrogatory* type. Here the individual is asked a series of questions, or is presented with a list of questions about the scene or incident. The narrative form is usually more reliable than reports given by answering questions. On the other hand, the interrogatory form is suited to bring out more details. The range is usually greater for the interrogatory report because of the prompting value of the questions, but this form of report is less reliable than the narrative because of the misleading suggestions often contained in the questions (Cady, 1924). With the lapse of time, there is a decrease in both the reliability of the report and in the amount reported; but for both the narrative and the interrogatory reports, the decrease is more rapid for accuracy than for amount (Dallenbach, 1913).

The manner in which the question is phrased may greatly influence the subject's response. Some years ago Muscio (1916) made a systematic study of the relation of various types of questions to caution or uncertainty, suggestiveness, and reliability of the answer. Among other things, he found that the use of the definite article *the* in place of the indefinite *a* tends to make the individual less cautious, and the answer less reliable. The use of the negative *not* gives a question greater suggestiveness, and decreases caution and reliability. Example: "Didn't you see a dog?" A question that simply asks whether certain things happened, or were present, is conducive to less caution in answering and to less reliability of the answer than one that asks the individual whether he saw or heard them. Of all the forms of questions studied, the implicative type, such as "Was the dog black?" which implies that there was a dog, was found to be least conducive to caution and reliability. This investigator concluded that for the most reliable answer, the question should not contain the definite article or the negative, and that it should be specifically directed toward what the individual actually observed.

Children are inferior to adults in both range and reliability of reports on what they have seen and heard. This is due to the child's more limited experience, immature judgment, imperfect understanding, and greater suggestibility. As he grows older, the range of his report increases faster than its accuracy. The reports of very young children in picture tests are usually mere enumerations of objects.

Later the ability to describe in terms of relationships develops and at the age of 10 or 12, children are usually able to evaluate and interpret. Through adolescence there is growth in the ability to analyze and organize experiences (Whipple, 1909, 1910).

The reliability of report may be increased by means of practice. The training of children for accuracy in reporting should be suited to their developmental level and involve both instruction in observation and practice in making reports. In training the child to observe more effectively, an adequate motive or interest must be secured. Attention should be directed to important features and essential details of the situation. Questions that stimulate discovery by the child are useful and effective for this purpose. In report training, the child's attention should be called to his errors or misstatements. Children usually are uncritical of their statements and often make incorrect ones with a high degree of assurance. They are prone to fill in the gaps in their memory by their own imagination. Young children often confuse the product of their imagination with the objects of perception. They are easily influenced by suggestion. They need to be taught to be more critical of their reports — to distinguish fact from fancy— by the teacher's refusal to accept erroneous statements and by having pointed out to them the discrepancies between their reports and the facts presented for observation. In the interest of accuracy of statement, they should be taught that it is better to admit that they do not know than to guess.

Defects of memory. Forgetting is a perfectly normal process, but there are abnormal losses of memory and conditions under which an individual is unable to recall events which normally would be recalled. The general term for abnormal losses of memory is *amnesia*. Several forms of amnesia have been distinguished. These and other defects of memory appear as: first, defects of learning; second, defects of retention; third, defects of recall; and fourth, defects of recognition.

Defects of learning are marked by an inability to learn anything new. They are associated with senility, arteriosclerotic and toxic conditions, and sometimes are connected with head injuries. Having been told and asked to repeat simple things, such as the doctor's name or the time of day, the patient is unable to repeat them again after a few minutes.

Defects of retention can result from diseases of the brain or brain injuries which destroy the neural bases for memory. In such a case, there may be a total or partial loss of memory. In cases caused by accident or sickness, a person loses all memory for events of a limited period. There are also cases in which the amnesia is for a short period prior to an injury to the brain. This particular defect is accordingly known as *retroactive amnesia.* Where the cause is organic there can be no restoration of the lost memory. Recall of the events for the period concerned cannot be made in dreams or in hypnosis, nor can the memories be recovered by psychoanalytic procedures.

Defects of recall may be due, not to the destruction of the brain traces, but to some condition that prevents them from functioning normally. That the neural trends for recall are still present is indicated by the fact that the events sometimes are rehearsed in the patient's dreams, or recalled in hypnotic states. These defects are *functional* forms of amnesia. They are sometimes *general,* in which case the patient is unable to remember anything of his past life, sometimes belonging only to a certain period of time; this is called *localized* amnesia. There are other cases, known as *systematic* amnesia, in which the loss of memory is restricted to objects and events belonging to a particular group or class. Since in these forms of amnesia the retention has not been impaired, the patient may recover his memory under appropriate treatment; sometimes recovery occurs suddenly as a result of some experience that serves to break up the inhibitions which have blocked recall.

Deviations from the normal process of recognition appear in several forms; three of the more distinct types are mentioned here. First, there are cases in which a person fails to recognize objects and places which, under normal conditions, would be familiar to him. This may occur in nervous disorders, such as hysteria, or under conditions of great fatigue. A second form of defect of recognition is the false recognition of strange places or persons. Many persons have had the experience of being in a place for the first time and having it seem so familiar that they feel as though they had actually been there or looked upon that scene before. This is called *paramnesia,* although the term is sometimes applied to all of the defects of recognition. It is believed to be due to elements in the new situation which are similar to elements in situations previously encountered, and possibly also to fatigue or emotional disturbance dulling the individual's sensitivity to the new and strange elements.

Imagination is sometimes transformed into what for the individual is a memory, though from the standpoint of objective fact it is a false memory. This comes about when the object of imagination is falsely recognized. The individual is convinced that he remembers actually having done or seen something he has only imagined. This probably occurs as a result of repetition and confusions with partially deteriorated memories. Repetition causes the idea of imagination to become familiar and thus paves the way for its false recognition.

Some persons tell "tall" stories so many times that they come to believe them. A student once told the writer that she "remembered" attending a wedding that took place before she was born. She was aware that it was a false memory and that it was based on hearing the account of the wedding repeated many times in her early childhood and on her own vivid imagination of the event. It is believed that many of the alleged memories for events of the first two years of life are false. Reports by adults of their early memories have been found to be a very unreliable means of investigating the memory of children.

QUANTITATIVE CHANGES IN TIME

Detailed consideration was given in earlier chapters to the variables influencing the form of the curve of retention, so that a brief review and some elaboration will serve to point out their importance with regard to remembering and forgetting.

Mode of impression. Several different modes of impression are available for rote learning — visual, auditory, kinesthetic, vocomotor. Material may be memorized silently or aloud from listening or reading. Material may be written as an aid to learning, and several combinations of the modalities may be combined.

It is quite probable that individuals differ in the modality through which they perceive best. Whether or not such differences are innate or learned is unknown. The author recalls a boy in the first grade who could repeat the words in a vocabulary drill perfectly when the entire list was written in several widely spaced columns on the blackboard, but could not recognize the same words presented on flashcards. The repetition of the words on the blackboard was not dependent upon the serial order of the list because the boy could name the words in mixed order. The discrepancy in performance prompted the author to ask the boy if he could recall the words on the black board if blindfolded. The boy tried and succeeded, because he had associated the sound of the word and the position of the word on the blackboard. Such individual differences in modes of learning exist even though there is limited experimental confirmation. In general it may be said that as far as groups of children are concerned, no single modality is superior to others, but that a multi-modal approach combining auditory, visual, and kinesthetic stimuli is likely to surpass a unimodal presentation.

Attempts have been made to facilitate the recognition and retention of new vocabulary by such different means of isolating the new words as printing them in larger size or in a different color style of print. The device is effective in helping children identify the new vocabulary when the words appear, due to the isolating effect, but it does not facilitate the essential learning which is to discriminate between a given word and others when all are in the same size, color, or print. In a serial learning task of two syllable adjectives presented to 165 college students, Smith (1949) found that total immediate recall of words was equivalent irregardless of whether all words were in the same color or one word in the list was isolated by being printed in a different color. Whatever gains accrued to the isolated word were offset by losses among the others.

Meaning. Meaningfulness of the material learned and the degree to which it is related to earlier learning are important factors in retention. In one study, the retention curve for nonsense syllables fell considerably below the curve for poems and appeared to drop faster between the second and tenth month (Woodworth, 1938). Experiments on the retention of words, poetry, and factual prose in which the recall method was used have not shown as large a percentage of loss during the first few hours after learning as was found by Ebbinghaus for nonsense syllables by the relearning method. There is little question that we remember better what we understand than what we do not understand. English and Edwards (1939) showed that retention tested immediately, 30, and 90 days after hearing and reading an unfamiliar passage was greater for substance learning than for rote learning. Significantly greater amounts of material learned by rote were forgotten than with sense or substance learning, even when the items were equated for differences in difficulty. The argument for the use of concrete rather than abstract materials, and direct experience rather than second or third-hand experience, particularly with young children, rests upon such studies showing the greater learning and retention of meaningful materials.

Overlearning. Associations once learned are stabilized and habit-uated by memory drills. Reviews preferably should be frequent at first because forgetting is greater in the initial stages, but they may be scheduled at progressively greater intervals. Several studies have shown that verbal material will be retained as well as motor skills if initially learned to the same degree.

Drills should be staged at times when the pupils are actually over-learning in order that they serve to consolidate and fix performance changes which are permanently desirable. Brownell and Chazal (1935) inquired into the effects of premature drill on the learning of third grade arithmetic. When they analyzed the procedures used by a group of 63 third graders who had been taught addition and subtraction by the drill method in grades 1 and 2, they found that only 49 per cent based their answers to addition combinations on immediate recall; nearly half used counting or guess to obtain an-swers, while the remainder obtained a solution by indirect methods. After a month of daily drill in the third grade, the proportion using immediate recall and indirect solutions had increased to 64 per cent at the expense of counting and guessing. Following another month in which no special drills were provided, the recall and indirect solution group had reached 71 per cent. The study illustrates the limitation of drill as a teaching method and especially as a procedure for developing the higher mental processes involved in quantitative thinking.

Distribution of practice. From the evidence available on practice the repetitions in memorizing should be distributed rather than massed unless the material has been previously learned. In general, several half-hour periods spent in memorizing will accomplish more than the same amount of time spent at one sitting. A few words in spelling each day for a week will be mastered better than a large num-ber bunched in one lesson. Ample support for these generalizations has resulted from numerous studies. The collegiate practice of cram-ming for an examination is an inefficient and time-wasting procedure for acquiring or retaining knowledge. The same amount of time dis-tributed over the month preceding examinations or in review of lecture notes shortly after lectures would produce greater learning and provide more time for extra-curricular activities of possibly greater interest.

The length of the practice period is the major determinant in the greater effectiveness of spaced practice, rather than the length of the rest interval. Short rest intervals appear to be as effective as longer ones. The length of the work period will vary with the task to be learned, but in general the less meaningful the task, the shorter the desirable work period. It is possible to have a work period so short that the learners never get fully warmed up to the task.

In instances where distributed practice isn't possible, the evidence suggests that the part-method of learning may be preferable to the whole. Stroud and Ridgeway (1933) compared the number of trials needed to learn three poems (meaningful material) in massed practice by three different procedures: part, progressive-part, and whole. The whole method was inferior to the other two.

Review and retention. For some time it has been advocated, in view of the negative acceleration of forgetting, that to secure the best results in the way of retention one should review frequently at short intervals soon after learning and then after longer and longer intervals as the temporal distance from the original learning increases. This appears to be a sound principle in general, particularly for rote learning. But if a child has just read and clearly understood a story or a lesson in history, an immediate rereading may be rather dull and less stimulating than a multiple-choice test over the materials read. A review may be made by recall as well as by rereading. Tests provide review by recall.

It has been found that the most advantageous temporal position differs for these two forms of review. Sones and Stroud (1940) made a comparison of the effectiveness of review by multiple-choice testing and by rereading for three different temporal positions within an interval of 42 days following learning. About 1,300 seventh-grade pupils spent 20 minutes studying an informational article on the history and methods of making paper. Ten-minute reviews were given by testing or by rereading for different groups on the first and third, on the eighth and fifteenth, or on the fifteenth and seventeenth days after the original learning. When the reviews occurred on the first and third days, the review by testing was significantly more effective than the review by rereading; but for the reviews placed later in the interval, the advantage was in favor of the rereading. The difference in favor of rereading was, moreover, greater for the positions farther removed from the original learning. It appeared that the effectiveness of rereading was affected very little by its temporal position, while for testing, the effectiveness was greatest in the early positions and decreased as the time between learning and review testing increased. The farther the review is removed from the original learning the more, of course, will forgetting have taken place; therefore, less and less of the content will be available for review by testing as the elapsed time increases. Tests and examinations have a salutary effect on retention, both as a means of stimulating reviews in preparing for them and for securing recall while taking them.

A study of retention under various testing procedures was made by Spitzer (1939) with 3,605 sixth-grade pupils as subjects. The learning material consisted of a printed informational article, which was studied for 8 minutes. Some groups were tested immediately after learning and retested later. Others were tested at intervals varying from one to 63 days. The groups tested immediately made definitely higher scores on the later tests. Without recall, forgetting was rapid during the first day. Pupils of superior ability did not forget as rapidly as those of lesser ability. The data clearly indicated that the recall in tests given immediately after learning was a distinct aid to retention. The immediate tests used in the studies mentioned above provided a vigorous form of review. Coming immediately after learning, their effect on retention is in line with the earlier findings of Gates, whose data showed that memorizing is more efficient when part of the time is spent in reciting than when all of the time is spent in reading the materials (1917). These investigators have demonstrated that the advantages from practicing recall for memorizing found by Gates may be secured for substance learning by the use of objective tests. Frequent use of tests in school is a means of promoting better retention of what is learned.

In the course of review and recitation, learning can be facilitated by providing immediate knowledge of results. It is inevitable that some guessing should occur, and this, lacking immediate correction, interferes with learning. Forlano and Hoffman (1937) found that foreign language words were better learned when the meanings of the words were given immediately, rather than permitting the student to guess at it. Empirical evidence obtained with elementary school children also suggests that guessing at word recognition or at the spelling of new words is less desirable than giving immediate information regarding the unknown word. Errors made during guessing, even if corrected, frequently recur to confuse the pupil.

Set. Often, one has many possible responses for a given stimulus. In such cases, the individual's set and other subjective conditions may affect the course taken in recall. Hunger is likely to steer recall toward food. Thirst makes one think of water or places where it may be obtained. One's desires, ambitions, and purposes exercise a directive influence. Fatigue is detrimental to recall and may prevent it unless the associative tendencies are very strong. Students need their usual amount of sleep and recreation prior to examinations in order to do their best on them.

Sets are more often psychological than physiological, being established by prior experiences, by attitudes, by instructions, and even by the task itself. An investigation by Levine and Murphy (1943), even though it suffers from the small number of subjects involved, clearly illustrates the effect of a set in the perception of controversial material and its subsequent effect upon recall and forgetting. Two, small, homogeneous groups of students of college age, one pro-Communist, the other anti-Communist, were selected. Each subject was presented with two prose passages, one anti-Communist, the other pro-Communist and instructed to read each twice. After 15 minutes, subjects were instructed to reproduce the passages as accurately as possible. Again, at weekly intervals, the subjects were asked to reproduce both paragraphs. Sharp differences in both learning (first reproduction) and memory (subsequent reproduction) were shown. The differences in learning approached the .01 level of statistical significance and the differences in retention reached the .01 level, with the anti-Communist group showing marked superiority on anti-Soviet material and vice versa.

Abom (1953) showed that material acquired with a set to learn was more resistant to forgetting under an ego-threatening condition than was the same information acquired incidentally. The materials used were color plates, from standard color vision tests, which one group learned with a set to learn, the second incidentally. Under the circumstances of experimentally induced failure, which was presumed to be ego-threatening, the incidental learning group showed significantly lower memory scores than its counterpart group. The author concluded that the lack of set resulted in less effort to counteract the effects of threat by rehearsal, overlearning or increased motivation.

Affective toning. Among the experiences most easily recalled are those emotionally toned, or markedy pleasant or unpleasant (Dudycha, 1933). The question arises regarding what influence the affective qualities may have upon learning. Experimentation on this problem is difficult, for one can never be sure what feeling-tone may be aroused by a particular situation, nor can one assume that material, pleasant for one subject, may not be indifferent or unpleasant for another. There is always need for report on this feature of the experience by the subject himself. Regarding the material itself, it appears that affectively toned materials tend to make a more lasting impression than indifferent material. In an experiment by White and Ratliff (1934), college students learned a list of pleasantly toned words, such as *flower, smile,* and *home,* and a list of unpleasantly toned words, such as *vomit, disgrace,* and *insult.* After complete learning, the two kinds of words were recalled about equally well in a test given shortly after learning and then one week later.

If one pauses to recall outstanding memories from earlier schooling, invariably the situations that are spontaneously recalled are those which in the main were markedly pleasant or unpleasant. Favorite subjects are as frequently associated with favorable relationships with a given teacher as with the pleasure derived from the subject itself. Perhaps more significant as far as retention of learning is concerned is the comparative indifference possessed by many students towards their studies. At best, their motivation is mild and the affective toning of the material being learned is neutral, neither of which factor constitutes the most desirable circumstances. Apparently it is the intensity of feeling tone rather than the quality that affects the extent of recall (Postman and Murphy, 1943).

Motivation. The importance of motivation has already been stressed and the relationship of various incentives to learning described. Children who have the desire and intent to learn and confidence in their ability to do the work learn more quickly and better. Emphasis has been given to the desirability of using intrinsic incentives as stimuli to motivation and to the use of success and failure in relation to attainment of goals as criteria of performance. The fact that differences in motivation may be reflected in differences in retention is especially noteworthy. Groups of college students learned nonsense syllables no more effectively when asked merely to cooperate in an experiment (Heyer and O'Kelley, 1949) than when told their performance would count toward their course grade, but the retention a week later on a surprise retest showed significantly better retention for the latter group.

IMPROVING RETENTION

In the foregoing sections we have considered a number of factors that influence forgetting. We cannot control all of these at will, but the findings of many studies on retention point to certain practices which may be relied upon to aid retention. It is noteworthy that these, for the most part, have to do with the methods and procedures of learning. About all that can be done to promote retention after learning is to avoid the interferences that operate against it. The following are some of the procedures for securing good retention:

1. Make the material to be learned meaningful. Help the pupil see what it means to him. Relate it to his experience, to other topics studied, and to future use.

2. For permanent and exact retention, secure an adequate degree of overlearning. Drill is essential for permanence, and overlearning prevents the material from dropping below the threshold of recall during the early period of rapid forgetting.

3. Apply the principle of distribution of effort. Avoid cramming. This helps to prevent the deleterious effects of fatigue and interferences due to the piling up of too much material at a single sitting. It allows for the effective operation of any processes of consolidation which may continue after practice is discontinued.

4. Make liberal use of reviews. In general, reviews should come fairly soon after learning and be repeated after increasing intervals. In the case of substance learning, tests of the multiple-choice type may be used effectively if placed immediately or soon after learning. For reviews after several days or weeks, the rereading form of revival is indicated. Tests should be regarded and used as means for promoting retention and not merely as instruments for measuring it.

5. Prevent retroactive inhibition by periods of rest after learning, or by shifting to a different type of work.

6. In the case of substance learning, stress generalizations and summarize at the end of lessons, divisions, or lectures.

RETENTION OF SCHOOL LEARNING

It is sometimes felt that the use of nonsense materials in the labora-tory precludes application of the findings to school learning. However, a comparison of the results of school learning with those obtained from laboratory experiments shows that the same fundamental prin-ciples apply in both situations. After all, the materials presented for learning in school are nonsense materials until some learning has been done on them. The fact that they are meaningful simply means that they have already been learned to some degree and the study of them means additional learning. The use of nonsense materials enables us to start nearer the zero point and makes possible a more exact accounting of the many factors that contribute to learning and retention. The writer agrees with the suggestion made by Stroud "that differences in the materials employed in the two fields of re-search (the laboratory and the classroom) are not so serious as those involving the use that is made of them. The fact that lists learned in the laboratory are usually made up of nonsense syllables does not present so great an obstacle to applicability in school as does the fact that the learning activity is memorization" (1940).

Studies on the rate of forgetting of school subjects usually show a negatively accelerated rate of forgetting of the same general form as the typical Ebbinghaus curve. This has been found in studies on the retention of history, physics, chemistry, botany, and zoology. Of course, as we have already noted, one usually retains a greater per-centage of meaningful material than of nonsense material; the curve of retention does not drop so swiftly for meaningful material.

When children or students are tested after a considerable period with no formal instruction in a subject, a big loss is indicated for factual content. In a study by Greene (1931) 1,064 university students were given in October the same examinations they had taken at the end of three courses the previous June. The repeated examinations showed a loss for the four months of about half of the information that had been reported correctly in the June examinations. Similar results have been reported by other investigators.

Eikenberry (1923) gave standardized tests to college seniors on sub-jects studied in high school but not continued in college. The results were best for American history, ancient history, and geometry, fol-lowed in descending order by Latin, chemistry, and physics. It was believed that the better showing in history and Latin was due to the fact that the work in college afforded more instances of review, addi-tional learning, or use of materials in these fields than for other subjects. The relatively high performance in geometry, Eikenberry suggests, was probably due to the fact that the test was not merely a test of information, but also of ability to reason.

Retention during the summer vacation. Children have been tested in various subjects in a number of studies at the end of the school year and again after the summer vacation. The results sometimes show losses, sometimes no change, and sometimes they actually show a gain. Reports on reading for the first three grades vary from slight losses to slight gains, and for the intermediate grades the trend toward gains appears to be stronger than toward losses. Gains have been reported for history and literature. A study of the retention of American history by junior high school pupils indicated a loss of about 13 per cent after four months, approximately 19 per cent after eight months, and about 23 per cent after one year (Brown, 1928). Losses are found for spelling and arithmetic, particularly for the computational skills. Bright pupils have been found to gain more or lose less than their less intelligent classmates (Schrepel and Laslett, 1936; Swenson, 1941). The gains reported probably may be attributed to practice or additional information picked up during the summer, since they are found most often in the subjects which may most easily be reviewed, practiced, or supplemented by incidental learning. Where actual losses occur, it sometimes requires several weeks after school reopens to recover from the setback caused by forgetting.

Factual information compared with other learning outcomes. There is a considerable amount of evidence which indicates that factual information is forgotten faster than the ability to explain, interpret, and apply general principles. Computational skills in arithmetic have been found to deteriorate more over the summer vacation than the ability to solve problems in arithmetical reasoning. College seniors who had not studied geometry since high school did better on a geometry test that was in part a test of ability to reason than they did on tests in chemistry and physics (Eikenberry, 1923). Results of a test in zoology, given to 82 students at Ohio State University 15 months after the completion of the course, showed the greatest loss in technical material or information and no apparent loss in ability to apply to new situations principles that had been learned (Tyler, 1933). In terms of percentages of the gains made by boys and girls during a course in high-school chemistry, retention after one year for 5 selected objectives of the course was found by retest to be as follows: application of principles, 92 per cent; selection of facts, 84 per cent; balancing equations, 72 per cent; symbols, formulas, and valence, 70 per cent; and terminology, 66 per cent (Frutchey, 1937). Other studies have shown that retention of the substance of paragraphs, as measured by recognition of sentences that summarized the meaning of the paragraphs, is superior to verbatim retention as measured by the recognition of sentences drawn verbatim from the text (Edwards and English, 1939).

Attitudes, also, are apparently more permanent acquisitions than factual material. The evidence that a number of important learning outcomes are more stable and lasting than factual information and verbatim learning is encouraging to the educator. It should not, however, be construed to mean that factual teaching is altogether unnecessary, for such teaching has its place in fostering the development of concepts and the comprehension of principles. These findings bring to our attention again the need for clearly defined teaching objectives, and suggest that our tests, as well as our teaching, should be suited to these objectives.

SUMMARY

The aim in this chapter has been to place before the teacher the findings of careful studies on memorizing so that when he attempts to direct this kind of learning, he may be able to select or devise the most effective methods possible under the conditions of the particular situation. There is no one procedure that can be considered best for all conditions. Good teaching requires suitable adaptations to the conditions at hand. The following suggestions are based on the facts and principles surveyed in this chapter. It is intended that they be considered as guides in formulating suitable procedures, not as rules or laws.

1. The best procedures for directing memorizing vary with the age and intelligence of the learner, his former experience, and the nature of the material to be learned.

2. Things to be recalled together should be presented together and in the order in which they are to be recalled.

3. Use the whole method for short and easy passages and a combination of the whole and part methods for long and difficult passages. Give special attention to the more difficult parts.

4. Use precaution to insure accurate first impressions. Avoid errors so far as possible, and check them on their first appearance.

5. Let the pupils practice some form of recall during memorizing,

for this is conducive to a favorable attitude and provides practice on the functions which the learning is supposed to develop. Such recital, however, should not come so early as to encourage guessing. Errors made by guessing may seriously interfere with correct learning.

6. Secure the advantage of rhythmizing when possible. For very young children this may be accomplished by the method of reading or reciting aloud in concert.

7. Make use of artificial memory aids or mnemonic devices sparingly and only in the case of very difficult associations.

8. Provide for a sufficient number of repetitions or rehearsals to insure an adequate amount of overlearning. Learning to the point of immediate recall only is not sufficient for schoolwork. For permanent retention, review often at first. The length of interval between reviews may be increased as time passes.

9. Distribute the repetitions liberally. Make memory drills short and stop at the first signs of fatigue. In selecting the most appropriate length of learning periods and intervals, consider the age and ability of the child, the difficulty of the task, and the stage of learning.

10. Secure and maintain a desire to learn. Help the child to appreciate the value for him of mastering the material.

11. Commend earnest effort and inform the learner of his progress.

12. Secure and maintain full attention by starting promptly, by varying methods, and by using novel devices to make the work pleasant and interesting.

13. See that the child understands what he is to learn before he starts. The learning of meaningless material is sheer drudgery and an absolute waste of time for the school child.

14. Do not require children to memorize anything that will not serve some useful purpose or provide some pleasure or satisfaction for them. We cannot justify rote memorizing on the grounds that it improves the "faculty of memory."

15. Have the children make use of what they learn. Spelling-words should be used in sentences and compositions and the arithmetic facts in problems; gems of poetry may be recited on programs or quoted by the pupils in their own writings.

OVERVIEW

Hovland, C. I., "Human Learning and Retention," *Handbook of Experimental Psychology*, S. S. Stevens, ed. New York: Wiley, 1951, pp. 613-89.

SELECTED REFERENCES

Blankenship, A. B., "Memory Span: A Review of the Literature," *Psychological Bulletin*, 1938, 35, pp. 1-25.

McGeoch, J. A., *The Psychology of Human Learning*. New York: Longmans, Green, 1942.

Stroud, J. B., "Experiments on Learning in School Situations," *Psychological Bulletin*, 1940, 37, pp. 777-807.

Swenson, Esther, "Retroactive Inhibition: A Review of the Literature," *University of Minnesota Studies in Education*. Minneapolis: University of Minnesota Press, 1941.

ORIGINAL INVESTIGATIONS

Edwards, A. L. and H. B. English, "The Effect of the Immediate Test on Verbatim and Summary Retention," *American Journal of Psychology*, 1939, 52, pp. 372-75.

Hovland, C. I., "Experimental Studies in Rote Learning, VI., Comparison of Retention Following Learning to the Same Criterion by Massed and Distributed Practice," *Journal of Experimental Psychology*, 1940, 26, pp. 568-87.

Krueger, W. C., "The Effect of Overlearning on Retention," *Journal of Experimental Psychology*, 1929, 12, pp. 71-78.

Chapter Thirteen

Comprehension: The Development
of Understanding

*Interrelated with the perceptual proc-
esses discussed previously is the development
of understanding and comprehen-
sion. Both depend upon complex, highly
developed responses, but comprehension
goes beyond perception in being an organizing,
synthesizing process in which experiences are integrated into compact, meaningful units which can be utilized symbolically.
Comprehension is a cognitive activity
involving the attainment of con-
cepts which in themselves represent abstractions
from perceptions. Perception is tied to the objective world of stimuli; comprehension is tied
to cognitive processes in which concepts
are abstracted from their various*

contexts and organized into unitary constructs.

THE DEVELOPMENT OF UNDERSTANDING

Our concepts are the understanding we have of certain generalized and abstracted aspects of many experiences. Our understanding of what we hear others say or what we read involves more than the meanings of the various words as perceived. These various meanings are important to understanding, but in the process of comprehending they fuse; the fusion yields a larger total meaning for the sentence, paragraph, or lecture as a whole. Comprehension is an organizing, synthesizing process that integrates experiences into larger meaningful units.

The outcomes of comprehension. Through comprehension, the student acquires in the history class an understanding of such topics as *the causes of the American Revolution* and *the westward movement*. In studying algebra he learns the meaning of *quadratic equation* and *radicals*. In the English class he comprehends *the principles of good writing* and *the nature of the sonnet*. In biology he studies the subjects of *protective coloring* and *evolution*. In geography the child learns of *the relation of climate to modes of living* and *the industrial products* of the various states. The outcome is an organized, coherent unit of knowledge. It is a comprehended subject, and as such it may be any generalization, such as a rule, a definition, a law, or concept. It usually involves a constellation of ideas, all of which are connected and organized around a central core or idea which incorporates the meaning of the whole topic. These associated ideas constitute what we know of the particular subject and are the ideas that come to mind as we think about the subject. They are not set in a fixed train as are the verbal responses of memorized material, but rather in the form of an aggregation. Comprehending as a form of learning is the process of building these organized concepts.

Comprehension in the classroom. No other psychological function is used more in the classroom for purposes of learning than is the one we are now considering. Without it, no reading could be worth anything, no study could be successful, no explanation or demonstration by the teacher could accomplish its purpose, and every lecture would be a waste of time. Without comprehension, no assignment would set the pupil for the performance of the learning exercise planned by the teacher. Whether we teach in the lower grades, in the high school, or in the university, we spend a large part of our time explaining, lecturing, and prescribing reading with the expectation that through comprehension, our pupils will become better informed and acquire an understanding of the subject we teach.

How comprehension takes place. Concepts are developed by the enrichment of experience, by the differentiation of details, and by the synthesis of these details into a structural unity. The process of comprehension proceeds from vague gross impressions to clear-cut distinctions, and from a poverty of association to an abundance. Take, for example, the concept of *automobile*. For a young child and for many drivers, the automobile is just a mechanical contrivance to ride in. If you do certain things to it, you can expect it to operate in a satisfactory manner. But when some delicate part gets out of adjustment and the motor refuses to start under the usual procedure, the person of such limited knowledge is helpless and must call for a mechanic. To the expert automobile mechanic, the car is a very complex assemblage of parts. He knows all the parts, the purpose of each, the way they work, and the relation of each part to all the others. His knowledge is far more detailed and coherent than his customer's. The growth of scientific knowledge is a process of making finer and finer differentiations and more detailed classifications. Special terms often have to be invented to designate the delicate distinctions to the specialist. To the uninitiated these minute differentiations sometimes appear to be useless academic hairsplitting, but for the scholar they mean a deeper penetration into the subject and more exact understanding.

In acquiring knowledge, we may build up entirely new concepts or enrich those we already possess. A class demonstration of the former process was made in the following manner. The instructor asked the class whether anyone knew what an *esthesiometric compass* is. No one knew, so he proceeded to secure the development of a new topic. In asking the question he had presented for auditory perception the name of the topic. He next wrote the word on the blackboard so that the class could see it. First came analysis. What meanings were to be obtained from an examination of the various parts of the term? *Compass* was a familiar word. Someone volunteered, "It's some kind of an instrument." But there are different kinds of compasses. Distinctions were necessary. Attention was directed to the word *esthesiometric,* and someone picked out *metric* and said, "That refers to measurement." Putting together the two suggestions they got, "An instrument for measuring." But further differentiation was necessary. It was an instrument for measuring what? Then the first part of the term was examined. It provided a clue. Someone said, "Esthetics, that refers to beauty." This did not satisfy. Someone else recalled that this came from a Greek word and that it appeared in other words familiar to him. He thought of *anesthetic,* and *kinesthetic,* and ventured that, "It refers to feeling, or sensibility." Then this was combined with the idea of a measuring instrument to produce the topical meaning, "An instrument for measuring sensitivity." But another differentiating step had to be taken. To prompt this step, the question was asked, "What kind of sensitivity does it measure?" Since no one in the class could tell, the instructor explained that this instrument is used in the psychological laboratory for measuring on the skin the distance between two contact points necessary for the perception of two points instead of one. The topic was further clarified by producing one of these instruments for the class to see. It was elaborated by a demonstration of its use on one of the members of the class, by statements about the differences in sensitivity for two-point tactual discrimination on different parts of the body, and by explanation of the uses of esthesiometry in studies of fatigue. The members of the class then understood what is meant by the term *esthesiometric compass.* A new topic was developed. The process included analysis, differentiation, and integration.

LANGUAGE AND COMPREHENSION

Language is a means of expression. It is also a means of communication. But for communication to take place, the recipient must comprehend what the speaker says or what the writer has written. Concepts are passed along from speaker to listener, from writer to reader, by way of language. The knowledge, information, or understanding, which the speaker or writer wishes to impart to others, is put by him into words. The recipient must translate the words into ideas. Each person, in communicating, must always create his own concepts from the verbal materials supplied by the speaker or writer. Because of this indirect means of communication, it is sometimes difficult for one to make himself understood. Teachers sometimes take too much for granted and assume that if what they say is clear to them, it will be readily understood by their students. They sometimes skip steps through which the child must be led to reach a clear grasp of the subject because they no longer remember the steps they had to take at one time. The possession of expert knowledge does not of itself make one a good teacher. This knowledge must be presented so that the student can correctly comprehend it.

Sources of misunderstanding. Spoken language is a vehicle of communication, but each person builds his own understanding of what he hears in terms of his own previous experience and conditioning. His constructions are, moreover, subject to his own mental set, interests, biases, and moods of the moment. Mutual understanding requires a common background of experiences. When the hearer's *experience background* differs from that of the speaker, the former may put an entirely different construction upon the words of the speaker than that which was intended. A newspaper report told of two bandits who entered the office of a firm in New York, covered the employees with pistols, and demanded the payroll. "Let 'em have it," said the proprietor to his employees, meaning that they should hand over to the holdup men the $550 payroll. But these words carried a different meaning for the bandits. They thought the proprietor was telling someone to shoot them, so they opened fire. Two bullets struck and killed the man. The bandits fled without the payroll.

A statement may be misunderstood because of an inappropriate meaning conveyed by some key word. This misunderstanding may be traceable to differences with respect to the *word meaning*. A man who was seeking employment was told that a job was open at the Eagle Laundry, but he did not think he could qualify because he had never washed an eagle.

Words that sound alike but that have various meanings are frequently sources of faulty comprehension, particularly when the child is more familiar with an inappropriate meaning than with the one needed. This type of confusion is shown by the student who wrote on his geometry paper, "A hole is equal to some of its parts." Children often reveal their misconceptions in drawings made to illustrate the poems or other matter read to them. After reading the poem "Barbara Frietchie" to a group of young children, a teacher asked her class to draw some pictures to illustrate it. One little girl produced the sketch shown in Figure 13.1, and explained that it was a picture of "Stonewall Jackson riding a head."

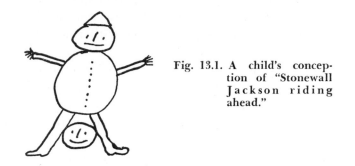

Fig. 13.1. A child's conception of "Stonewall Jackson riding ahead."

Figure 13.2 shows a school child's pictorial representation of "The Old Oaken Bucket." The child's explanation was as follows: "The cot of my father, the dairy house nigh it, the deep tangled wildwood, every loved spot which my infancy knew—these are the spots; here are the buckets." "But," the teacher remarked, "you have three buckets." "Well, there are three," replied the child, "the old oaken bucket, the ironbound bucket, and the moss-covered bucket." Here the child used the meaning of the word *spot,* which she had acquired through experience. She had not learned that it could also mean a place.

Fig. 13.2. A child's drawing to illustrate "The Old Oaken Bucket."

Words frequently do not have the same meaning for a child as for the teacher or for the parent because the child's interests or values differ from theirs, and consequently the child does not clearly comprehend the question or remarks addressed to him. To "miss something," for example, may mean one thing in the child's way of thinking, and quite another thing to an adult. This was indicated in the reply of a little girl who had been absent from school for three days because of a minor illness. When her mother inquired after the child's first day back at school whether she had missed much during her absence, she answered, "Oh, no, not much. One boy threw up, and another bit the end off the thermometer. I guess that's all I missed."

Children acquire word meanings according to the usage in the community where they live. When they move to another locality where usages are different, they frequently encounter difficulties in comprehending what they hear. This was a major difficulty for children evacuees from England. Catherine Coyne tells of a little girl who wrote to her mother that in this country a *jumper* is called a "sweater," a *lorry* is a "truck," a *tram* is a "streetcar," and a *lift* is an "elevator." The following account of a conversation between a boy from England and an American boy outside a suburban garage is quoted from Miss Coyne's article (1941).

. . . .The Briton had been startled by a placard reading, "Flats fixed here."

"That's a strange thing," he remarked to his friend. "Why should a garage be interested in flats"

"That's their business," the American explained patiently.

"How can a garage be interested in flats?"

"Because an automobile can't run if the tire is flat, so the garage fixes it."

"Oh, I thought—Oh, I'm sorry, I thought it meant a real flat, you know, what you call an apartment."

The two boys continued to inspect the sign, and the Briton volunteered that in England a flat tire was called a puncture. Then he said, "But why should they fix it?"

The American exasperated by the cross-purposes of their conversation, asked tartly, "Well, what would you do with it?"

"I'd repair it," the Briton said calmly.

"Well, what does the sign say?" the American asked warily.

"It says they would fix it, and that means they'd stick it, or keep it the way it is."

Another source of error in comprehension is *inadequate perception* of certain key words. A friend was standing by the elevator shaft waiting to go down. As the elevator came down from the floor above, the operator called out, "Going down?" The young man sprightly replied, "Yup." As the elevator passed by him he shouted "Down!" The operator stopped the car, brought it back to the floor where the fellow was standing, and remarked apologetically, "I thought you said, 'Up.'"

Faulty perception of the words may be due to either of two causes. It may be due to an inadequate sensory impression, or to giving the wrong kind of meaning to the word sounds. Defective hearing, lack of attention, interfering noises, or faulty enunciation by the speaker may be responsible for inadequate sensory impressions. Giving the inappropriate meaning to the verbal sounds is a matter of conditioning and perceptual trends derived from antecedent training and experience.

Glasgow (1943) compared the comprehension of prose and poetry when read by tenth grade high school girls first, when it was distinctly enunciated and secondly, when enunciation was deliberately made indistinct. Comprehension was reduced 57% with prose and 42% with poetry by indistinct enunciation.

Comprehension and set. The construction a person puts on the words of another is often determined by his present mental set, desire, interest, bias, or mood. The superintendent of one of our state schools for the feeble-minded gave a lecture on feeble-mindedness to one of the writer's classes. He had described the various clinical types of mental deficiency including the mongoloid. Later on he spoke of the various forms of treatment and mentioned *euthanasia*. After the class was over, one of its members reported that when she heard that word she wrote in her notes "Youth in Asia." She quickly realized her error. But the first reaction had definitely been caused by the previous mention of the characteristic appearance of the eyes of the mongoloid. Later it was discovered that several other members of the class had reacted to this word in this manner.

A teacher said to a child, "You may sit here for the present." After sitting expectantly until he could no longer restrain himself, he asked, "Well, where is the present?" It could be that this child's reaction was due to his not having learned the time meaning of the word *present*. More than likely his concern for receiving a gift was responsible.

Reed (1946) carried out a series of studies concerned with concept learning, one of which involved the relationship of set to concept learning. He concluded that a set to learn meanings yields a higher rate of learning and retention. The task equipment consisted of cards having 4 English words on one side and 6 nonsense syllables on the reverse side, each representing a logical category to which one of the English words belonged. The college students learned the paired association by prompting and anticipation, one group learning only names, the other names and meanings. Furthermore, Reed observed that concepts logically formed are learned more quickly and retained better than illogical concepts.

Our own feelings bias our comprehensions. A depressed mood makes us take a casual remark by a friend as a reflection on our integrity. A guilty conscience makes us see an accusing slur in words never intended as such. An irritable mood makes us see implied criticism when the speaker had nothing of the sort in mind.

Written language. The signs we comprehend may be graphic or pictorial. A cartoon sometimes delivers a timely message. Our alphabet is a convenient device for constructing visual symbols to represent any object or thought within the range of human experience. Such symbols comprise our written language. In reading, there must first be the *perception* of the word or printed symbol. This requires a clear sensory impression. Defective eyesight, inadequate illumination, or distractions may block the reading process at this point. Since reading involves a rapid succession of visual perceptions of word patterns, good eye-movement habits must be established.

Next, there must be *word recognition*. A person recognizes a word when upon seeing it he is able to speak the word, to pronounce it, or to point it out when he hears it spoken. One might be able to perceive a word as a word and not be able to recognize it. For example, we might observe some writing in the Russian language and realize that before us were words, but not be able to select from the group the word we hear someone speak.

Beyond the recognition of the word there must be *word meaning*. When the meaning of a word is grasped, the perception is symbolic and the word is a symbol. A person may be able to recognize a word and not know its symbolic meaning. This is the case when we locate a word in the dictionary in search of its meaning. A child might select a word from a printed list by sounding it out or as a result of having memorized it without knowing the meaning of that word. After learning how to pronounce the various syllables, a beginning student in Latin or German may be able to recognize and pronounce the various words and still have no conception of their significance.

In learning to read, the child usually acquires word meanings by associating an object or its oral symbol, the spoken word, with the printed symbol. When the association or conditioning is complete, the printed word carries for him the same meaning as does the spoken word. Later he may be able to derive the word meanings from printed definitions, explanation, or context.

Finally, the reading process involves *sentence and paragraph comprehension*. Without this there is no true reading. The process of comprehending the meaning of a sentence or paragraph in reading is essentially the same as for comprehending speech. From the word meanings the reader formulates the topical meaning of the whole. Correct word meanings are essential for adequate comprehension in reading. We understand what we read in terms of our previous experience and according to our present attitudes. To be understood, the reading matter assigned to children must deal with things within the range of their experience. If it does not, the teacher must provide the experiences necessary for comprehension. Explanations of new terms, allusions, figures of speech, principles involved, or the use of pictures, diagrams, specimens, and the like may serve to give the child the necessary background for comprehending a passage that transcends his past experiences.

The experience background of children in our schools varies widely. Through newspapers, movies, and home experiences, pupils are often better informed concerning such topics as divorce, alimony, and bail money than they are on topics taught in the schools. The economic status of the home is an important factor in determining the kinds of experiences a child has outside the school. The income tax, for example, is likely to be better known by children in higher income levels. The adult conversations in the home, extent of travel, and the character of the community in which the child lives are all potent factors in determining the character of the child's experiential background. The diversity of these experiences from home and community life presents a real problem of adjusting instruction to the individual pupil's need.

Vocabulary. In any field of study, the lack of a sufficient knowledge of the special vocabulary of that field impedes progress. Until we know the meanings of the special terms of a science, a business, or an art, we cannot read the literature in that field with adequate comprehension. Experimental studies have shown the value of systematic vocabulary training as an aid to the comprehension of subject matter. Ninth-grade algebra students, for example, who were given special instruction designed to help them understand the mathematical terms and expressions with which they were unfamiliar, made better records on achievement tests than did pupils of a control group who were not given such instruction (Drake, 1940). Likewise, special training on the meaning of certain geographical terms encountered in historical matter served to improve the comprehension of this material (Tormey, 1934).

Various attempts have been made to secure better comprehension of the meaning of content by simplification of the vocabulary. In the case of some literary selections, this has been successful. It should be remembered, however, that simplification of vocabulary will not be helpful unless it involves the substitution of words known to the reader for those that are not familiar. The mere substitution of shorter words, or of words selected from a list derived from counting those occurring most frequently in printed matter, will not necessarily make the material easier to grasp. In an attempt to discover the merits of simplifying vocabulary as an aid to comprehension, Nolte (1937) revised selections of reading matter by substituting words taken from the Thorndike Word List, and also by translating them into "Basic English." Care was taken to preserve the original meanings. This investigator concluded that such simplification did not make the passages significantly easier to understand.

While a knowledge of the meaning of the words is a primary essential for reading comprehension, there are other factors involved. One might know the meaning of every single word in a sentence and still not be able to grasp correctly the meaning of the sentence as a whole. Besides the subjective factors of set, there are the arrangement and complexity of sentence structure and the relations of the idea expressed to the experience of the reader. A sentence made up of easy words may express an idea which cannot be grasped by the reader because of its remoteness from his experience, or the sequence of phrases and a multiplicity of clauses may cause confusion.

New words must be learned for intellectual growth, but there is need for introducing them gradually. They should be learned definitely as they are encountered and the load of new words should never be too heavy. They should be graded in terms of child experience and ability. The memorizing of definitions or one-word synonyms for new words is not sufficient. Real mastery requires associations with one's own experiences and a recognition of the relation of the new term to the context in which it is used. To make the new term a part of his permanent equipment, the child should be given opportunity to use it appropriately both in his oral expression and in his written work. But beyond vocabulary itself, the thought expressed by sentences and paragraphs in reading material should also be suited to the reader's level of experience.

Verbalism. The term *verbalism* connotes the use of words without a knowledge of their meaning. All too frequently, the student, unable to understand what he reads and faced with a test of recitation, proceeds to memorize statements from the textbook in order to have something to present to the teacher. He then reproduces words or passages he does not comprehend. This educational evil is fostered by bookish teaching, by asking questions framed in the language of the textbook, by accepting as answers words lifted from the book, by assigning material to be memorized without first seeing that the pupil understands it, and by failure to relate the material to the child's own experience.

A child of twelve in the eighth grade of a junior high school of good repute was doing her homework in arithmetic. It was memory work, and after she had studied for a long time, she asked her father to take her book to see whether she could recite her assignment. The father was surprised to see that the assignment was the flat memorization of six tables of weights and measures. They were in the back of the book under the heading, "For Reference." They included measures never heard of by most adults, much less used by them. But aside from the utter waste of time and energy involved in memorizing them, they were absolutely foreign to the child's understanding. After passing grams, grains, gills, the number of square yards in a square rod, and the number of square rods in an acre, the child came to the table of cubic measure. She recited "1728 cubic inches equals one cubic foot, 27 cubic feet equals one cubic yard." Then her father interrupted and asked what that meant. She said she did not know. The father then explained the meaning of a *cubic inch, cubic foot,* and *cubic yard.* The child understood that readily. Then he asked her if she knew how to

figure out how many cubic inches there are in a cubic foot in case
she should not remember the number. She did not, and so was
shown how to compute the cube of a number. When shown that all
she needed to remember was to multiply 12 × 12 × 12 to get the
number of cubic inches in a cubic foot, or to find the number of
cubic feet in a cubic yard all she needed to do was to take 3 × 3 × 3,
she grasped the principle at once. But it was a new idea to her. The
teacher had said nothing of the meaning of the word *cubic,* nor
had she mentioned the procedure for finding the cube of a number.
Two things were wrong with the teacher's assignment. In the first
place, there was no sense in having the child memorize this material.
In the second place, no child should be asked to memorize material
that is meaningless to him.

That the salute to the flag and the routine concert recital of the
pledge of allegiance is but an empty sham and devoid of meaning
to a large portion of the children of whom it is required is indicated
by what children write when they are asked to write out the pledge.
A revealing study was made of such written pledges collected from
children in grades 5 to 8. In a group of 30 fifth-graders who recited
the pledge twice a week, 16 wrote, "I pledge a (or the) legion. "The
word *indivisible,* in "one nation indivisible," was written in 25
different ways, but not once was it written correctly. The following
are some of the ways it was written:

"in the verble," "in diblise," "into besinble," "in vissilta," "into viszable,"
"intervisbul," "inda vevsable," "in vestable," "invisible," "in the visble," 'and
davisable," "in the Vizbee," "into visable," "inves abull."

The phrase "for which it stands" was frequently distorted, and
"justice for all" was quoted as "just for all," "just as for all," "just
is for all," and "busted for all." The following are exact reproductions of the whole pledge as written by three of these fifth
graders.

"I brith the flage of the United States of dismed and to the spries and it stands
one monton in the besble with hevties and gustees and all."

"I pledge the legion to our flag of the United States of America, and to the
republican for which we stand one nation and davisable with liberty of and
justice for all."

"I blidge a legion to my Amiacan flag and which it stand one nacion in the
vizble and libdy of busted for all."

While the sixth, seventh, and eighth graders did somewhat better, so
many errors appeared in their papers that it was evident that many

of them did not know the meaning of the pledge. A large number, even of the eighth graders, wrote "I pledge a legion," and the word *indivisible* was frequently written, "invisible," "individual," or "intervisable." Yet this salute to the flag is required by state law, and children have been expelled from school for refusing to comply because of religious scruples of their parents.

Comprehension and the assignment. A teacher asks: "How can we get a child to follow directions as given? No matter how simply or briefly given, there is always someone who through either carelessness or misunderstanding fails to carry them out. How can we judge whether it is due to misunderstanding?" This teacher's problem is a difficulty encountered by all teachers. Failure to carry out an assignment may be due to lack of comprehension, or as the question implies, it may be due to other causes. Failure to comprehend the teacher's directions may be due to any one of the following factors:

1. Lack of attention. Here, the words of the teacher would not be clearly perceived.

2. Sensory defects. If the assignment is given orally and the child's hearing is defective, he may not hear the words clearly enough to get the correct meanings. If the assignment is written on the blackboard, poor eyesight may prevent adequate perception.

3. The child may not know the meanings of some of the words used in giving the assignment.

4. The child may know the meaning of each word and still, through some bias or inappropriate mental set, fail to grasp correctly the meaning of the directions as a whole.

Probably the best way to find out whether the child has understood the assignment is to ask him to tell what he is to do. If he shows that he understands, it may be assumed that his failure to do as instructed is due to forgetting, inadequate motivation, faulty attitude, or lack of time or ability. Only if the source of this difficulty is located can adequate steps be taken to remedy it.

COMPREHENSION BY MEANS OF DIRECT EXPERIENCE

Perceptual aids to comprehension. For centuries, education in our schools has been predominantly verbal and bookish. The revival of interest in early Greek and Latin classical writings in the fifteenth century and the invention of printing established the educational tradition that to be educated was to be well read, and this conception of education has prevailed in spite of the protests of educational realists who have repeatedly pointed out the need for learning about things from firsthand experience with them. With the invention and use of such modern devices as the motion picture, film strips, radio, and television, a new insistence on the use of concrete materials has developed.

We have seen that comprehension rests on experiences which the individual has already had, that concepts grow from concrete experiences, and that the meaning of a word is clear only when one knows the thing it signifies. Perception of concrete things is basic to all understanding; yet, ignoring this or remaining in ignorance of it, we have too often taught words without the experiential background necessary to give them real meaning. One way to promote comprehension is to enrich the child's experience by bringing him in contact with the real object he is studying. The student can get a far better concept of the amoeba by observing through a microscope a live one squirming around than he can from simply reading about it. He gains a better understanding of the nervous system of the earthworm by dissecting a specimen than he can get from a purely verbal description. The school excursion is a valuable aid to instruction when it gives the child the opportunity for observing firsthand the situations or processes he is studying (Fraser, 1939). A visit to a museum may provide the necessary experience to clarify a topic in history. Models and specimens in the classroom may make a point clear where words alone would fail.

Next to the object itself in point of directness of experience are pictures of the objects. Besides giving a more accurate impression of the thing being studied, pictures and real objects have greater interest and attention value for children than their verbal representatives. This makes for more vivid impressions and better retention than can be secured from verbal discussions. The motion picture has the added attraction of movement. It can be used to portray action and a continuous sequence of operations. Listening to a radio address by the President presents a much more vital and realistic situation than reading about it in the newspapers or having the teacher tell about it. Other perceptual aids which may be employed in certain cases with profit to the pupil are blackboard drawings, graphs, diagrams, maps, globes, bulletin boards, stereopticon slides, demonstrations, and dramatizations.

The presence of a television set in practically all homes in the urban areas and over half in rural areas presents a window to the world for children in developing understanding and comprehension in a variety of areas. In spite of fears that television was a monster likely to violate the sanctity of the home, the 20-30 hours that elementary school children spend in viewing each week and the 10-20 hours spent by high school students have not lowered their scholastic achievement. Nor, aside from reduction of time spent on movies, radio, and sleep, has it seriously reduced participation in recreational activities. If anything, academic achievement has improved (Garry, 1953). The facts are that the television experiences of children have scarcely been tapped by the teacher as adjuncts to the classroom in concept development, with the result that children undoubtedly possess many semi-organized concepts in need of clarification. Concept development needs not only assistance from the teacher, but also the critical evaluation of the observed programs.

The proper role of such materials of instruction is to supply experiences needed for comprehension. They serve as supplements to verbal instruction, not as substitutes for it. Such perceptual experiences as they provide must be directed toward the formation of concepts and generalizations in verbal terms. Meaningful experience naturally begins with the perception of the real object, but learning should move toward the level of comprehension where more varied and richer meanings can be assimilated from books and oral discussions.

Numerous experimental studies have shown the values for classroom instruction of motion pictures and other perceptual aids. They have also shown the unwisdom of indiscriminate use of them. In general, their use has been found helpful in those cases where the experiential background of the pupils is insufficient to enable them to comprehend verbal discourse. By means of pictures, children can get a better idea than from words alone of the appearance of people and of scenes in foreign countries or of ancient times, although these differ considerably from the peoples and scenes familiar to them.

The effective use of classroom films or of the field trip calls for careful preparation of the pupils in what they are to notice and for the direction of their observations. Without such direction, attention may be focused on some interesting detail which has no significant connection with the topic to the exclusion of more important matters. Also, some kind of follow-up work or discussion is usually needed in order to emphasize important points, to correct erroneous conceptions, and to place the observations in their proper relations to the subject being studied.

Laboratory experience. The laboratory method of instruction is another means of providing firsthand experience. It has proven its value as an aid to the comprehension of principles of science. Under the microscope the student sees what his textbook tells about. In the laboratory he witnesses the chemical change taking place in the test tube, measures electrical current, obtains water by the explosion of hydrogen, and sees the effect of air pressure on the tin can from which air has been expelled. His observations provide the basis for clear and accurate understanding of scientific generalizations and the procedures that have developed our scientific knowledge. What he learns by his own experiments, he is not likely to forget.

On the other hand, merely going through the motions of an experiment and blindly following the directions of the manual, with no real appreciation of the problem and without discovering the true significance of the results by seeing them in relation to other facts, is waste of time. Moreover, the very simplification of the conditions in the common laboratory exercise gives it an artificial character and a detachment that may be fatal to the achievement of its purpose as an aid to comprehension. The laboratory exercise may become abstract in its efforts to be concrete. In using this method, the good instructor will endeavor to secure a full appreciation of the aim of the experimental exercise, and will make every effort to see that the results are viewed in the light of the general body of facts they exemplify.

Participation in group activities. In recognition of the necessity for actual concrete experiences as a basis for learning, many modern schools have adopted a plan of instruction known as an "activity program." This plan conforms to the view that through engaging in various forms of activity, physical, mental, and emotional, the child develops an understanding and an appreciation of his environment and a knowledge of the society in which he lives. In the early grades, the activities usually pertain to the child's immediate social environment, such as the means of obtaining food, clothing, and shelter for the family. Later they may deal with the lives of people more remote from their immediate environment, extending to the peoples of other lands and other times.

Such a program usually consists of a series of "units of activity" in each of which the children, often working in groups, contribute according to their talents and interests to some undertaking, such as building a toy city, making a circus, keeping a grocery store, building a train, making wax candles, constructing an Eskimo village, making an aquarium, or gathering a collection of cocoons. As an example of this realistic form of learning, let us look in on a third-grade group whose activity is centered around the topic of colonial life. Some of the children are dressed in the costumes of the Pilgrim colonists. A corner of the room is fitted up like the interior of a colonial home with a spinning wheel and iron kettle. A child in Indian costume is showing some other children how to plant corn, using a fish for fertilizer. Preparations are under way for a class-written play about an adventure of a Pilgrim child with an Indian. Around the room is a border showing Pilgrims going to church, turkeys, and pumpkins. On the wall is a picture of Pilgrims watching for the return of the *Mayflower*. The room fairly breathes the atmosphere of the old Plymouth of 1630. Several books on colonial life are to be found on a table. But these children not only read about Pilgrims, they actually are living the life of the early colonials in a most realistic manner. Through their active participation in this absorbing enterprise, the hardships of the cold winters, the difficulties of building homes on a desolate coast, and the dangers from Indian attacks become a reality to these children. These vivid experiences bring to them a much fuller understanding and appreciation of colonial life than could possibly be obtained from reading alone.

Similar advantages for comprehension are found in the "full-expression" plan, which has been used with excellent results in teaching the social studies in the junior high school. In this plan, as described by Powell (1940), the work of the course centers around a few major topical units. As each of these topics is taken up, the pupils are asked to name some of the large fields of interests covered. These are written on the board and each pupil selects from the list one or two topics for a more complete study. The pupils are then organized into committees on the basis of their selections. Each committee gathers material on its special subject and makes a report to the class as a whole on the results of its investigation. The committees employ a variety of procedures in placing their findings before the class in novel and appealing forms. These procedures include: dramatizations, panel discussions, group discussions, debates, original drawings, cartoons, movies, still pictures, slides, manual projects, graphs, maps, music, original poems, stories, and book reports. Committees in a unit on Sectionalism *vs.* Nationalism, for example, were formed for the following topics: Cotton, Life in the Old South, The South Today, Negro, Lincoln, Biography, Tariff, Civil War, Reconstruction, and Music. The activities of these committees in gathering information and planning their presentations before the class have stimulated great interest in the topics. For developing an understanding and an appreciation of the meaning of the various topics of the social studies the plan has proven highly successful.

THE DEVELOPMENT OF CONCEPTS

While the meaning of a sentence is ordinarily comprehended in a few seconds, the development of a concept may extend over a period of months or years. However, the process is similar, for in both cases a topical meaning emerges from a series of related experiences. The meaningful reference of the concept is not to a particular object but to a class of objects or to some common feature of many different experiences. Our concept of *rain,* for example, carries a broader meaning than that derived from perceiving a particular rainfall. It is what we know about rain in general. It is derived from seeing rain, from having it wet our clothing, from feeling it on our faces, from hearing its patter on the roof, and from observing its connection with dark clouds, flooded streets, dripping eaves, and the growth of plants. From these varied experiences with rain, that which is common to them all — water falling from the sky in a vast multitude of drops — emerges as the universal property of rain. So, in the development of any concept, the qualities or properties common to a variety of experiences are detached or isolated from those other features which vary from one of the experiences to another, and these common qualities or universal features are organized into a new unit of understanding.

The development of concepts is related to the ability to perceive analytically, that is, to observe the various properties of an object or to apprehend the various features of a situation. Since the young child's perceptions are usually not analytical, he tends to take objects as a whole and without much regard to details. For this reason, his first knowledge usually consists of gross concepts of broad and un-differentiated aspects of the world. He overlooks differences between objects of his large classes and reacts to these objects in approximately the same manner. He knows all automobiles as big things to ride in before he distinguishes different makes of automobiles. He knows dogs as four-legged, furry animals before he is able to identify differ-ent kinds of dogs. Knowledge advances with increased ability to notice details and differences, and concepts are refined and elaborated by distinguishing sub-groups on the basis of special properties belong-ing to each.

Language is an important factor in the development of concepts, for it furnishes a label for each newly differentiated aspect of experi-ence. This label helps to mark off the newly distinguished feature from other aspects of experience and makes possible the social correc-tion of erroneous concepts. A child may have a few limited concepts of objects before he has names for them. These concepts consist of what knowledge the child has of these objects as a result of various contacts with them — principally what he does to them and what they do to him. But when language develops, most concepts bear a name. The meaning the child attaches to this name when he hears it as a word spoken by another person depends on the nature of his own concept.

A child normally forms a number of concepts before he enters school. These are usually gross concepts including only the broader classes of things such as houses, trees, chairs, and so forth, without clear refinements of sub-classes. They are ordinarily taken for granted by the teacher when the child begins to learn to read. If, however, a child does not have a concept for a particular printed word, it will be difficult for him to learn to recognize that word, and he will not be able to comprehend correctly sentences in which it is used. A child should know the meaning of the spoken word before any attempt is made to teach him the corresponding visual symbol.

Promoting the development of abstract ideas. Objects or situa-tions which appear very different when taken as a whole are frequently found under inspection or analytical observation to have some property or quality in common. Take, for example, the property of redness. This color may be encountered in the perception of a blazing sunset, a lady's dress, a man's necktie, lips, fingernails, blood, flowers, and of many other widely differing situations. As redness is experienced in connection with many different things, it tends to become dissociated from them all; it then becomes an abstract concept because it is detached in thought from the many different concomitants or elements which appear with it in the perceptions of the particular objects of which it is the color. The meaningful reference is generalized because redness is known to be the property of many different things.

For promoting the development of abstract concepts in children, two steps are indicated: first, the *location* of the property to be abstracted by an examination of concrete objects or situations possessing it; and second, the *isolation* of that property by varying its concomitants and by contrast.

Location. Location involves the apprehension of the property to be abstracted in the midst of other features of the particular cases used for illustrations. It usually calls for careful inspection or "piecemeal examination." Let us take as an example the concept of loyalty. To teach children this abstract concept, we must help them to realize the nature of this quality or state and to develop the ability to think of it apart from particular persons or situations. Location of this quality is secured by presenting numerous and varied illustrations of loyal conduct. The examples should be examined thoroughly so that the children will see both the relevant and the irrelevant elements in the illustrations. They might be told the story of a dog that was loyal to his master. If we stopped there, however, the children might think that loyalty means a dog's devotion to his master. Since loyalty is to be found in very different situations and because many of the details of this illustration would be irrelevant to the meaning of loyalty, we must isolate loyalty from the irrelevant factors appearing with it in this and other particular cases.

Isolation by varying the concomitants. Isolation is the process of singling out or detaching the essential property or quality so that it will be comprehended as an independent topic. To accomplish this, several examples of devotion, faithfulness, and constancy should be given, and these should present different kinds of situations with different types of people. We should indicate not only what is meant by loyalty between persons, but also the meaning of loyalty to a cause, to one's school, and to one's country. The varying of the situations and connections in which loyalty is manifest will tend to separate the essential quality of loyalty from the irrelevant or incidental factors of the cases cited and to make it stand out by itself in the thinking of the pupils. To prevent any possible confusion with respect to the irrelevant factors, however, the employment of contrast is usually desirable. As would be expected, the more complex the stimuli to be discriminated, the greater the amount of effort needed to acquire the concept and the greater the difficulty of learning it (Reed, 1946a).

Isolation by contrast. We complete the process of isolating the essential nature of loyalty by presenting examples of disloyalty. Here, factors appearing in the examples of loyalty will appear in the absence of loyalty. This should make clear to the pupils that these irrelevant concomitants are not included in what is meant by loyalty.

In arithmetic, a child acquires abstract number concepts. The steps through which they are developed are described above. The child must perceive the number aspect of groups of various kinds of objects. To learn the meaning of *five*, he must observe the number in a group of five things. We may show him five pencils. But we cannot stop there for he might think that five always has to do with pencils. So we isolate this number factor by varying the concomitants. We show him five apples, five boys, five chairs, five books, and so on. Each time he must notice how many things there are. Then, to avoid any possible confusion with the irrelevant concomitants, we show him by way of contrast groups of these same objects containing less or more than five. He must see that the number making up the groups is different from five. When the child can think of *five* without reference to particular things, he has acquired its meaning as an abstraction.

Promoting the development of generalizations. A large part of our teaching is devoted to the development of generalizations. First there is the development of the meaning of nouns which stand for classes of objects, such as *river, tree, horse,* or *sentence.* The process by which these general meanings are developed is the same as for the development of abstractions, except that here, instead of isolating a single feature common to many different situations, we isolate and incorporate into the concept the several characteristics which are common to the various members of a class and which mark an object as belonging to that class. Other forms of generalizations are: rules of grammar or spelling, laws of science, definitions, axioms, and principles. A statement of any of these applies to many different particular situations and it presents a fact common to all the situations which the generalization covers.

In developing a general concept, the first step is to *locate* the essential features; the second is to *isolate* these from incidental and irrelevant features of particular cases by varying the concomitants and by contrast. Suppose, for example, we wish to build up the concept of *river*. The child must first observe the essential features of a river. This calls for a detailed examination of some typical rivers. The child should note that each one examined is a natural stream of water, that it has a source, that it runs its course between banks toward some larger body of water situated at a lower level, and that it is part of a great drainage system. These features common to all rivers must then be dissociated from those characteristics of particular rivers that are not found in all rivers. We vary these irrelevant concomitants by the study of many different rivers. It will soon be discovered that some rivers flow north, some south, some east, some west, and many meander in various directions. Particular direction is then eliminated in favor of *any* direction. In like manner the essential features are to be divorced from particulars of location, sources, depth, length, width, and outlet. Isolation by contrast calls for a comparison with brooks, lakes, bays, and oceans, with a recognition of differences between these and rivers.

For the development of general ideas and an understanding of principles, rules, and laws, the use of a number of illustrations or examples is usually necessary. To serve their designed purpose, these illustrations themselves must be readily understood. The use of a single illustration is frequently insufficient to secure the isolation of the essential features common to all cases covered by the rule, definition, or law. Such a failure to generalize from a single example is seen in the following case. A lecturer had described a form board test as an example of performance tests of intelligence. When asked later to explain performance tests, a student wrote, "A performance test is a test given with little blocks." Apparently other types of performance tests had not been incorporated into his concept.

Sometimes illustrations or analogies convey misconceptions because the related experience of the pupil is not what the teacher assumes it to be. A man in teaching a group of newsboys at a Y.M.C.A. was attempting to clarify the concept of God and was using the "father" analogy. A twelve-year-old boy in the back row jumped up and exclaimed, "If God is like my father, I don't want to have anything to do with Him." The teacher discovered later that this boy's father was a cruel drunkard. To be effective, illustrations must be related not only to the child's experience, but they must be related also to the appropriate kind of experience.

In developing generalizations, it will not be necessary to start at the primitive level of concrete experience in every case. Explanations framed in general terms already familiar to the student may be effective. It may be expected also that the children of relatively high intelligence will require fewer concrete examples to reach a generalization than less gifted children (Ray, 1936).

Harding and Bryant (1943) illustrate how simple personal experience projects, which incorporate concrete number experiences and assistance in abstracting and generalizing, promote number concepts. Using equated control and experimental groups of fourth grade pupils who at the beginning of training were five months below grade level in achievement, Harding and Bryant found that providing the experimental group with functional activities produced a significantly greater gain in arithmetic reasoning and a gain in computation equal to that of the control group which had a textbook-drill procedure. These results occurred in spite of the fact that the experimental group had little or no drill. It is also interesting to observe that the range of individual differences in skill in the experimental group was greater than in the control group at the end of the study.

The development of time concepts is an understanding that comes slowly. Friedman (1944) showed that children do not obtain a full understanding of our conventional time system until they are about 11 years old. Concepts of the immediate past and subsequently the more distant past appear to develop before concepts of future time. Marked gains are seen at the fifth and sixth grade level, but many inadequacies in time concept exist through high school, particularly in translating pre-Christian dates. Pistor's (1940) study has shown little improvement in time concepts resulting from history instruction in the sixth grade, but Friedman and Marti (1946) have shown that history instruction of itself is of little value in developing comprehension of time concepts unless it incorporates specific instruction regarding time lines, historical sequences, time concepts, etc. The latter study was completed with 12th grade students. Whether or not the same result will occur at a sixth grade level is not known. But the foregoing studies confirm Katona's report (1939) that students who learn by understanding develop greater ability to transfer their skills to the solution of new problems than those students who acquire knowledge by mechanical memorizing.

STUDY FOR COMPREHENSION OF CONTENT

The term *study* is used to cover a wide variety of learning activities and various forms of learning. In this section we shall consider those forms of study which are aimed at comprehension of the larger units of subject matter. Such study involves the organization into topics of meanings obtained from reading matter. In reading for comprehension of content, we seek to clarify our understanding and to extend our knowledge; in rote memorizing, the aim is to be able to recite words in a fixed order. The reading assignments in such subjects as history, geography, social studies, and psychology should be comprehended, not memorized.

Study habits. A number of investigations have shown that the study practices of students in high schools and in colleges differ widely (Dynes, 1932; Parr, 1930). It appears that many do not know how to study efficiently and that a great amount of time and effort is wasted through ineffectual procedures and poor study habits. The methods used by a large proportion of students have resulted from a trial-and-error process of striving to meet the demands made upon them. Instruction in study procedures has for the most part been sporadic or incidental.

Experiments on training for effective study. The results of a number of studies indicate the value of special training in methods of study. Some of these studies have dealt with particular procedures in connection with a particular subject. For example, Newlun (1930) found that training in the summarization of historical material in the fifth grade improved the learning of history. Barton (1930) found that training in outlining and selecting the important points of content was an effective aid to comprehension.

An experiment is reported by Wagner and Strabel (1935) in which groups composed mainly of high-school juniors were given extensive training in how to study. Some of the groups met five times a week for one semester, others met twice a week for one semester and three times a week throughout the second semester. The training was aimed at improvement of reading, vocabulary, memory, problem solving, note taking, preparation for examinations, and use of the library. In addition, each student was given encouragement and guidance in a personal conference. During the junior year, the work of the trained pupils was significantly superior to that of the untrained control pupils with whom they were matched for intelligence, age, grade, sex, curriculum, and previous school record. While the trained groups lost some of their advantage after the training period, they continued to make higher marks than the controls. They also carried more work and failed fewer subjects than did the members of the groups that were not trained in study methods.

The effects of emphasizing methods and principles of effective study in a course in psychology were studied experimentally by Edmiston (1937). The subjects were college freshmen students. Two groups of 50 each were equated in terms of intelligence and achievement. The two groups studied the same material, but the instruction of the experimental group stressed "how to learn." For the control group, no special emphasis was given to this matter. At the end of the semester, the experimental group showed a significant average improvement in grades, both in psychology and in other courses, but no significant change appeared in the grades of the control group. The superiority of the experimental group, however, largely disappeared during the following semester after the special training had been discontinued. In a second study, a selected group of low ability was given special instruction in how to study. Their grades in psychology showed marked improvement, but in other courses there was no significant improvement. Some who made relatively high grades in psychology showed a loss in other subjects. A study of the data from the first experiment also indicated that effects of the training carried over to other subjects only in the case of students who ranked relatively high in ability.

Study practices of good and poor students. The experiments described above have indicated the possibilities of improving scholastic achievement by training students in the art of studying. The next question to consider is that of the procedures which make for success in study. Several attempts have been made to discover what constitutes effective study by comparing the methods and working habits of good and poor students. It seems reasonable to suppose that methods used by the most successful students are the ones toward which training should be directed.

Douglass and Bauer (1938) gathered, by means of a questionnaire, data from 395 high-school students in Minnesota. The questionnaire included 50 questions on study activity, note taking, and the ability to concentrate attention. The practices found to be associated with the better marks were: looking up new words in the dictionary, skimming before reading carefully, reading silently without moving the lips, preparing lessons day by day rather than cramming, studying just before class, and, in the case of the group of least intelligence, reviewing before an examination.

In a study of the differences between good and poor students reported by L. C. Pressey (1927), 125 questions were submitted to some 250 students, and the results were studied in relation to their marks for the previous term. Elimination of students for whom data were incomplete left 200 whose records were used. The papers of the 50 students whose marks were lowest and the 50 whose marks were highest were selected for comparison. Of 30 items listed for which there was a difference of 20 per cent or more between the two groups, the following are of special significance to the present discussion. A larger number of the best group had a regular place for study, had a daily study plan, lived where study hours were observed, made charts and diagrams to represent essential points, skimmed over a chapter, glanced at paragraph headings, or read the summary before studying the chapter, took notes on reading in outline form, and wrote summaries of material read. A larger number of the poor students had things on their desks which were likely to distract their attention, skipped over graphs and tables in their reading, and studied late the night before an examination.

The problem of determining best study procedures is complicated by a multiplicity of other factors which contribute to the success or failure of study. Among these factors we have intelligence, health, time devoted to study, distractions, emotional disturbances, previous experiences or study, social habits, and attitudes. This means that some persons may succeed with a study method generally regarded as poor, while others will fail with methods usually found to bring good results.

In a study by Reeder and Newman (1939) of the relation of employment to the scholastic achievement of university students, the data for 246 students showed slightly lower academic records for the working students than for the nonworkers. The small difference was not statistically significant. But, two thirds of the workers were below the average on the university intelligence tests, and the coefficient of correlation between hours of work and standing on the intelligence test was —.21. Workers also were found to come from homes of lower income and occupational levels than the nonworkers. These findings suggest that intelligence has more to do with the quality of a student's academic work than with the amount of outside work he does, and that, with sufficient ability, a student may earn a part of his expenses without detriment to his school record.

Wilkins (1940) reports that at Oberlin the students who participated most in extracurricular activities were, on the whole, the ones who made the best grades and scored highest in scholastic aptitude. There was no evidence that such activities were a cause of poor work.

Time spent in study. No matter how intelligent a student may be or how effective his study habits are, it takes a certain amount of time to accomplish worth-while results through study. Insufficient time devoted to study may be related to poor budgeting of time, to lack of planning for study, to an overabundance of extracurricular activities, to employment outside of school, to illness, to an excessive amount of social activities, to plain indifference, or to any number of things which rob one of time which should be given to study.

Ryans (1939) found a correlation of .37 between the time reported spent in study and college marks for 40 junior-college sophomores. Other investigations have found these variables to correlate .32, .00, —.06, and —.28. It seems that the best students are not always the ones who spend the most time in study. How effectively one uses his time is, of course, a matter of considerable importance. Ryans reports that the time spent in study correlates with good work habits and persistence.

Suggestions for effective study. It is possible to state, in a general way, certain principles of effective study in the light of the results of many different investigations made on this subject. The teacher will realize in the light of the foregoing discussion that these are not absolute rules, that they will not guarantee excellence under all conditions, and that it will be necessary to make adaptations to the requirements of particular cases and special circumstances.

1. *Time.* An adequate amount of time must be provided for the study of each lesson if satisfactory progress is to be made. The planning and budgeting of one's time with a suitable apportionment for each essential task will help one to meet this primary requirement and will promote the efficient use of available time.

2. *Place.* Efficiency is promoted by regular work habits. For best results from study one should have a regular place for study, free from all unnecessary distractions. The desk or table should be clear of things that tend to divert attention from the work to be done.

3. *Set.* The time required for settling down to work is reduced and concentration is encouraged by the following practices: a prompt and determined start with the purpose of the assignment clearly in mind, a quick preliminary survey of the chapter by skimming or by glancing over the division headings, and reading the summary at the end of the chapter before undertaking the intensive reading of the chapter. Having in mind at the start what the chapter is about in a general way helps the reader to select the most essential points and makes it easier to organize them into topics.

4. *Practicing recall.* The practice of attempting at the end of paragraphs or sections the recall of the main points presented in them is an aid to the mastery of content. It is a good practice also to summarize in one's own words at the end of the chapter the main points of the whole chapter.

5. *Organization.* The ideas obtained from reading should be related and organized. In longer and more difficult material, this may be promoted by outlining. A good outline will make the principal ideas stand out and show the relation of secondary or minor points to the major ones. Meaningful associations with previous experiences are helpful both to comprehension and to retention. Their number may be increased by thinking of original illustrations, by relating the new material to previous study, by using what has been learned in other courses to verify or evaluate the statements of the author, by making comparisons, and by thinking of possible practical applications of the principles presented in the text.

6. *Dictionary.* When new words are encountered, if their meaning is not clear from the context, the dictionary should be used.

7. *Application of effort.* Best results call for the application of whole-hearted effort to the task at hand. Intensive work, however, requires an occasional pause for relaxation. The length of period

during which full effort may be sustained will vary with the nature of the subject matter. In fairly heavy reading, one hour is probably as long as most high school or college students can apply themselves efficiently without a change. The value for efficiency of interspersed rest periods has been amply demonstrated, and this holds true for study as well as for other work. There are emergencies in life where a person must drive himself beyond the fatigue point, but this is unwise and seldom necessary in the sphere of study.

8. *Cramming*. One cannot accomplish in a few hours of intense and continuous effort what should have been spread over several weeks. Cramming is not an efficient method of study. Good students, more than poor ones, keep their work up by daily study. When this is done, there is no need for cramming. The habit of letting work pile up through neglect is found more often among poor students. They, more often than high ranking students, sit up late and study long hours before examinations. This practice leads to confusion and fatigue, both of which are unfavorable to a good performance in examinations.

9. *Review*. For retention, reviews are usually necessary. But reviews also have value for comprehension. Frequently, a second reading brings to light points missed in the first. In the light of the thought of the whole chapter as grasped in the first reading, new meanings may be found or more accurate interpretations may be given to various paragraphs.

10. *Notes*. The taking of notes is a good practice when it serves as a stimulus to the selection of the most important points, and when the notes are used for making a quick review of these points. If notes do not serve in either of these two ways, their value is questionable. Note-taking on a lecture or on reading should be selective. It has been found that poor students more often than superior students take notes on lectures as fast as they can write. (Pressey, 1927).

11. *Study questions*. Study is more effective when the student has a definite objective. For the less mature learner, this advantage may be secured if the teacher will supply questions to be answered from the material to be studied. Such questions will serve to guide the pupil's efforts toward the discovery of the points which the teacher wishes to stress. As intellectual maturity is approached, the student must learn to work independently. To do this, he must acquire the art of following certain learning threads which will lead him directly

to the heart of his subject. These threads consist of certain basic questions which may be asked concerning any topic of a given subject. In studying events of history, for example, the learning threads would include such items of information as the nature of the event, where it took place, the date, persons involved, its causes, and its consequences. Only when a student knows the learning threads for the topics in his field of study and when he can ask himself the essential questions for which his study should find answers is he ready to do effective, independent study.

12. *Written exercises.* The writing of a theme, term paper, or thesis on a topic is a good exercise for the promotion of comprehension of that topic. This is true for the following reasons: it calls for the gathering of information; it requires the systematic organization of one's ideas; and it brings to light hazy conceptions and stimulates the writer to clarify his own thought. This applies also to writing reports on field trips, laboratory experiments, collateral reading, or topics discussed in class.

SUMMARY

Comprehension is the process through which we acquire an understanding of concepts. A large part of school learning takes place through comprehension. Concepts are developed through the enrichment of experience, the differentiation of details, and the organization of these details into new structural units.

We comprehend both oral and written language in terms of our own previous experience and training and according to our attitude or set. When an individual lacks the proper experiential background, he is incapable of clearly comprehending what he hears or reads. Faulty perception of words precludes adequate comprehension. To understand the meanings of paragraphs and sentences, one must know the various word meanings. Learning the special vocabulary of a new subject is essential for successful study in that field. Learning to recite words without knowing what they mean is called "verbalism." It is a common evil due mainly to poor teaching.

The development of concepts is an important form of comprehension. Our concept of an object includes all that we have learned about it from many different experiences with it. When some quality or feature common to many different situations becomes dissociated from all concomitants of particular situations and becomes an object of thought in its own right, we have an abstract idea. Abstractions emerge from particular experiences through location of the common quality or characteristic in the midst of its concomitants, and by the isolation of this feature through variation of concomitants and by contrast. Generalizations are developed in much the same way. A general idea refers to the characteristics common to a group or class of objects. Rules, laws, definitions, and principles are generalizations which apply to many different particular situations. The teaching of abstractions and generalizations usually calls for the use of several illustrations. A single illustration often results in incomplete isolation of the essential features of the concept from irrevelant features of particular cases.

Some classroom practices which facilitate or improve comprehension are: the employment of such perceptual aids as field trips, real objects, and pictures; laboratory exercises; and the participation in group activities centered around a topic of study.

Investigations have shown that students differ widely in their study practices, and a number of experiments have indicated the value of special training in effective study procedures. Studies of the differences between good and poor students indicate that academic achievement is influenced by a large number of factors. Important among these are intelligence, time spent on study, study habits, and emotional disturbances. Recommendations for efficient study for comprehension of content include: provision for sufficient time, a regular place for study, preliminary skimming or reading of summaries, practicing recall, organization of as many meaningful relations as possible, looking up new words, working intensively but not too long at a time, day-by-day study as opposed to last-minute cramming, reviews, taking notes on long and difficult material, and using study guides.

OVERVIEW

Brownell, W. A. and G. Hendrickson, "How Children Learn Information, Concepts, and Generalizations," *Forty-ninth Yearbook of the National Society for the Study of Education.* Chicago: University of Chicago Press, 1950, Part I, pp. 92-128.

SELECTED REFERENCES

Durrell, D. D., "Development of Comprehension and Interpretation," *Forty-eighth Yearbook of the National Society for the Study of Education.* Chicago: University of Chicago Press, 1949, Part II, pp. 193-204.

Leeper, R., "Cognitive Processes," *Handbook of Experimental Psychology,* S. S. Stevens, ed. New York: Wiley, 1951, pp. 730-57.

Piaget, Jean, *The Child's Conception of Physical Causality.* New York: Harcourt, Brace, 1930.

ORIGINAL INVESTIGATIONS

McKillop, Anne, "The Relationship Between the Reader's Attitude and Certain Types of Reading Response," *Teachers College Contributions to Education,* 1952.

Reed, H. B., "Factors Influencing the Learning and Retention of Concepts," *Journal of Experimental Psychology,* 1946, 36, pp. 71-87, 166-79, 252-61.

Serra, Mary C., "How to Develop Concepts and Their Verbal Representations," *Elementary School Journal,* 1953, pp. 275-85.

Chapter Fourteen

Solving Problems by Thinking

*The most exalted of all the psycho-
logical functions is the thinking out of the
solutions of problems. Through
it, under the directive and selective
influence of the problem, the individual
draws upon his knowledge and observations to
produce for himself some new bit of
knowledge, or to formulate some new conviction, opinion, or doubt. Through it he
devises new ways of settling accounts with
a problematic situation for which
established methods are insufficient. The other
functions — perception, memory, imagination, comprehension, and action — are basic to this
activity, for the search for the solution of a
problem may involve the use of any or all of them.*

419

The term thinking, as commonly used, incorporates more than problem solving. We often speak of thinking of or about something, in which case the behavior involved may depend primarily upon memory or recollection. Imagination is a form of thinking to which we refer in artistic form, e.g., creative imagination. Daydreams, reveries, and musing are promoted by internal dynamics and motivations; they represent aspects of thought processes, unrestricted by external demands and more or less an unrestricted flow of associations. In this chapter, we shall restrict ourselves to the aspect of thinking and behavior referred to as problem solving. Parents and educators alike stress its importance and emphasize the responsibility of the school in developing skill in this area. Problem solving can be carried out at both concrete and abstract levels. Children function on the concrete level more effectively than on an abstract level because of their inability to use symbolic processes as skillfully as adults.

Much of our thinking is done by means of words. Concept names are important symbolic materials. Words that carry topical meanings are especially effective resources for thinking. Their symbolic reference may cover a whole class of objects or only some abstracted feature of many different situations. The words we find so helpful in thinking may be spoken or they may be carried in inner speech by subvocal movements of the speech mechanisms.

Some writers have been so impressed by the large part inner speech plays in thinking that they have maintained that all thinking is simply a matter of contractions of the muscles of speech. It seems evident, however, that for many persons symbolic meanings may be carried by mental images, bodily postures, and movements of the body. The writer has on a number of occasions asked members of his class to think out the problem of securing a practical substitute for the stairway in their home. When the suggestions begin to come, a point we shall take up later, nearly always someone thinks of the possibility of using a rope ladder. This suggestion is usually discarded almost immediately. When the student is questioned, he almost invariably says that he had a visual image of his mother or grandmother dangling on a rope ladder between the floor and the ceiling. The literal meaning of the image was of minor importance. The real significance borne by this visual imagery was its symbolic meaning of inconvenience and that the rope ladder would not be adequate.

The problem. The problem motivates the thinker. It initiates the thinking and directs the process toward the solution. It is not the situation encountered that is the problem, but rather the individual's sense of difficulty or his desire to find out something. It may, as in the case of the task, arise from the occasion, from instruction given by another person, or from self-instruction. The first of these sources of the problem is illustrated in the case of the difficulty a man feels when, on driving through a strange part of country, he comes to a place in the road that is flooded with water too deep to allow his car to pass. Since there are no detour signs to point out the way for him, this situation arouses the problem of getting through to his destination at the appointed time. The second source of the problem is illustrated by the teacher's asking a thought question. This sets the stage for the problem. The child who thinks out the answer formulates the problem which he solves. In the third place, the problem arises from one's own interests, desires, or curiosity. This may be seen in the case of the scientist who formulates a problem to give definite point to a piece of research, or in the case of the man interested in fishing who puts to himself the question of the best kind of artificial bait to use in the lake at which he is to spend his vacation.

Problems do not always initiate thinking. They are often met in other ways. We frequently avoid hard thinking by recalling the products of former thinking and by taking over uncritically the opinions and judgments of other persons. We sometimes imagine a possible answer to a thought question without really troubling ourselves to reason it out. In many cases, a problem situation is attacked blindly by trial and error in overt action. It is usually only when such methods fail or will not provide an adequate solution or satisfactory answer that we really apply ourselves to the more arduous procedure of thinking out our problem, a procedure which calls for the assembling of data, putting details into new relations, and evaluating suggestions critically. Problem thinking involves the use of signs, symbols, or clues in reaching a solution.

Stages in the course of thinking. While the course of thinking out the solution of a problem varies somewhat for different cases, in general, examination reveals the following characteristic stages in the process: first, a difficulty is felt; second, the problem is clarified and defined; third, a search for clues is made; fourth, various suggestions appear and are evaluated or tried out; fifth, a suggested solution is accepted or the thinker gives up in defeat; and sixth, the solution is tested.

1. *The difficulty felt is the problem.* It may appear as a perplexity, a bafflement, or a need for which established habits and ready knowledge offer no escape or means of adjustment. Expenses are found to exceed income; a child is ill; the car will not start; a tire goes flat before the spare is repaired; a skunk is digging holes in the lawn; water appears on the bathroom floor from an undisclosed leak in the plumbing; the opposing army puts into use a new and deadlier weapon; a crime is committed; or there is not enough fuel oil to meet consumer needs.

2. At first, the nature of the difficulty may not be clearly grasped. Before a person can proceed successfully with the search for a solution, *the problem must be clarified and defined.* One must understand his problem in order to solve it. Failure to size up the situation carefully and to take account of all the significant facts is likely to lead to disastrous results or defeat. This is, in some respects, the most critical of all the steps. Scientific research grows out of clearly defined problems. The expert automobile mechanic locates the reason for the car's not starting before attempting to make repairs. The physician diagnoses the illness before he considers the type of treatment to be given. Unless the conditions of the problematic situation are adequately analyzed, false assumptions which preclude a successful outcome of one's efforts to resolve his difficulty are frequently made.

3. *The search for clues or symbolic materials* is a quest for data that will throw light on the problem and point the way to a solution. It may include an inspection of objects for such signs as fingerprints, an examination and comparison of maps, and the gathering of relevant information from other persons or books. It may also involve a search within one's own associative resources by way of reflection on related past experiences. If the problem is clearly established and maintained, it serves as a guide in this search, preventing futile digressions and random excursions. Successful search turns up evidence and reveals significant relations between factors in the situation.

4. Out of the evidence and relations discovered by the search come various *suggestions for a solution to the problem.* From the data assembled through observation, recall, or imagination, inferences are

made. Here the thinker passes beyond the facts at hand and ventures a guess, a supposition, or a hypothesis. The good thinker is both courageous and cautious in taking this step. For him it is not a random guess or a wild supposition but an inference based on an analysis of all available facts. For him it is not the end of his thinking, for it must be evaluated and tested by the development of its implications in the light of knowledge and experience. He passes judgment upon the propriety of each suggestion before he accepts it as a conclusion. When, through the exercise of critical judgment, a proposal is found wanting, it is discarded and the search is resumed for another. When another appears, it too is evaluated. This proposing and discarding of suggestions continues until the individual either finds a suggestion which meets the requirements of the problem or until he gives up in defeat.

The able thinker is one who can produce a large number of suggestions, knows a good one when it appears, and can see the defects of a poor one. Extensive knowledge of the field in which the problem falls is conducive to fertility of suggestions and good judgment with respect to the propriety of them. The presence of rival hypotheses encourages postponement of the final conclusion until an adequate check has been made; this lessens the danger of hasty and unwarranted conclusions.

When students are asked to think out the problem of finding a practical substitute for the stairway in their homes, the following suggestions frequently appear: ramp, fireman's pole, rope ladder, wooden ladder, and airplane. It will be seen that all of these are related to the problem and are derived from experiences with means of getting up to higher places. The directive influence of the problem is seen in the fact that, while working on it, no one thinks of such irrelevant matters as the current political campaign or the dance he attended the night before. In evaluating these suggestions, the ramp is found to take up too much room; the fireman's pole might provide a quick way to come down, but it would not provide a satisfactory way of getting up; the rope ladder would be very difficult for grandmother to negotiate; and the wooden ladder would be unsightly, and inconvenient when carrying things. The idea of an airplane does not indicate a wholly irrational mind, for it is definitely associated with the various means by which we are carried up. However, the judgment of a person might seriously be questioned if he accepted the airplane as a final conclusion and attempted to put this conclusion into actual practice. The solution for this problem finally adopted by most students is some form of simplified elevator.

5. *The problem is solved* when a suggestion is definitely accepted. Such an acceptance may come when inspection or reasoning reveals that the proposal meets all the conditions required by the problem and when all rival suggestions are found to be wanting or less desirable. In some cases, the suggestion or hypothesis is adopted as a conclusion only after it is tried out under practical or experimental conditions. Occasionally, after a period of bafflement, a complete solution appears with marked suddenness. This may be due to a new bit of evidence that throws new light on the whole situation and makes the solution clear at once or to a new alignment of the details of knowledge already at hand revealing new relations and meanings. This sudden grasping of the means to a solution, as we have seen earlier, is called *insight.*

6. *The solution is tested* by checking its applicability to the problem and by verifying the fact that it is a real solution. In the process of accepting a solution, several possibilities may be considered, the most likely one being tentatively accepted. The test of the actual goodness of the solution lies in trying it. The ultimate test of understanding of the problem and its solution lies in being able to solve similar but not identical problems — id., to generalize from the solution. Gestalt psychologists refer to this stage as transposition — being able to perceive similar relationships in another situation and thus reach a satisfactory solution.

Thinking and learning. The process of thinking out the solution of problems is linked with the subject of learning in two ways: First, we learn by means of thinking; and second, we improve our ability to think by means of learning. Thinking considered apart from its connections with learning is an operation through which one achieves a certain type of goal — the solution of a problem — in a special sort of way (Duncker and Krechevsky, 1939). Thinking is an activity which affects other aspects of learning. Through thinking, we amplify our fund of memories, enlarge the scope of imagination, acquire control over emotional responses, and change our way of acting. In the chapter on perception, we observed that thinking sometimes serves to develop perceptual meanings. The ability to think, on the other hand, is improved through functions other than thinking itself.

Since problem thinking makes use of various other functions, such as perception, memory, and comprehension, the improvement of any of these may serve to enhance the ability to solve problems by think-ing. We shall do well in considering the improvability of thinking to keep in mind that it is an activity — something the individual does. Thinking is not a "faculty" which is improved by mere exercise. As an activity, it is improved by acquiring the tools to think with and by learning how to proceed in order to employ those tools in the most effective manner.

Problem solving by children. The young child's behavior in experimental problematic situations indicates that he learns by his own exploration and manipulation the possibilities of using various instruments or objects in such a way as to secure desired results (Richardson, 1932). When children two or three years old attack new problems, such as those involving the stacking of two boxes or the joining of two sticks, the method employed is usually of the trial-and-error type. If, then, another problem is encountered similar to one already mastered, there may be some transfer of experience bringing an immediate solution (Alpert, 1928). Older children, having a greater fund of experience, solve more difficult problems and, in solv-ing them, manifest more insight. Their behavior in problematic situations indicates a greater ability to formulate and maintain a problem. Their attacks are more deliberate and systematic.

Oakes (1947), utilizing an interview procedure with groups of children between kindergarten and sixth grade, inquired into their explanations of natural phenomena and observed a steady increase in physical explanations grade by grade. Cause and effect explana-tions were characteristic of the brighter children. The steady growth of conceptual developmental and logical reasoning was demonstrated in a field study by Strauss and Schuessler (1951) who followed an interview technique with a group of children between the ages of $4\frac{1}{2}$ and 11. The questions pertained to money and its use and were asked during a sequence of interviews of 15 to 30 minutes. Children's concepts were seen to develop by stages. The typical 5-year-old, for instance, could distinguish one or two small coins, but was unable to identify the remaining coins, whereas with increasing age they understood the function of a storekeeper.

Thinking ability develops gradually. The ability to think out the solutions of problems develops gradually and increases with age (Heidbreder, 1928). There is no specific point in the child's development where trial-and-error ceases to be the method for discovering solutions and where thinking takes over. Some degree of insight appears in young children when they see a significant relation between some object in the situation and their goal, as in the case where a stick is apprehended not merely as a stick but as a means for drawing a toy within reach. This has been observed in the behavior of apes and in children about two years old. A little later, memory and imagination may be brought to play upon the problem. First it may be an object not present in the perceptual field that is thought of as a means for reaching the goal. As understanding develops, concepts are used to advantage and we see the gradual emergence of more abstract forms of reasoning. Symbolic materials become available through the functions of memory, imagination, and comprehension. Suggestions for solutions may be derived more and more from past experiences and the need for the exploratory manipulation of objects grows less. The appropriateness of the suggestions, also, is weighed and estimated more by thinking of their implications rather than being discovered through precipitous attempts to act upon them.

Sporadic bits of associative thinking are sometimes observed in young children. They are limited in each case to the child's range of experience and interests. A child four years old, while watching the water run off from the kitchen sink, asked, "Is it like a little hill?" Though we cannot be sure just what the remark indicates, it appears that this child was bringing his knowledge to bear on the question of why the water was disappearing. A boy of six years asked his grandmother what *double* means. She replied that it means *two*. The boy came back with the remark, "Then Grace is double because she is two." Grace was his two-year-old sister. The outcome was faulty, but it was a clear case of inference, and the error was due to inadequate concepts rather than to the process itself. The effective use of general principles demands a clear understanding of the principles. An adult, when trying to reason with insufficient knowledge, makes errors similar to those found in the thinking of children. In novel situations, when he is unable to find in what he has learned anything to help him out, he frequently reverts to trial-and-error in attempting to solve his problem.

Piaget (1950) describes the intellectual function of a young child as being primarily at a sensori-motor level, at which time, however, he is making the discovery of signs and symbols so that he is able to recognize and use them representatively as well as organize and classify groupings of thought. Nevertheless, his thinking and problem-solving functions mainly on the concrete and representational level. Only gradually does logical thought which is independent of concrete thought develop, so that not until the "teens" does formal logic reach fruition.

Adults, in general, can do better at thinking out the solution of problems than children. They are able to take a more objective attitude toward problems. Having greater emotional stability and control, they are likely to have less interference from emotional reactions. They can usually keep their attention on the problem over a longer period of time and hence are less likely to be thrown off course by the intrusion of a new interest. The most important reasons for the greater thinking ability of adults, however, are their greater range of experience, better understanding, larger fund of well-developed concepts, and the fact that they have acquired certain general procedures for meeting and working out their difficulties.

A young child's needs are comparatively simple and, for the most part, are satisfied by other persons. The responsibilities of adults are often sources of problems. Lacking these, the child does not encounter problems as often. Ignorance may be bliss by shielding us from problems, but when it prevents us from recognizing a difficulty that should be recognized and thought out, it precludes the first essential step toward a successful adjustment. Not only is the child often blind to difficulties which present problems to more mature persons, but his limited knowledge makes him less able to comprehend the nature of the difficulties he does realize.

In the next stage of the thinking-out process, the child's comparatively limited range of experience and his meager fund of generalizations place restrictions on his ability to arrive at a successful solution. Excellence in thinking of this kind requires a fertility of suggestions for solution, and this depends upon the thinker's associative resources. The child is usually not able to bring to mind as many possibilities for solution as one with greater understanding and more extensive experience in the field of the problem.

Finally, the child generally lacks critical judgment. He is less capable of developing the implications of a suggestion and of determining its propriety by reasoning. This, too, is due to his limited range of information and understanding. It requires knowledge to be able to evaluate and judge correctly.

The problem method of teaching. The good teacher will provide opportunity for children to learn by thinking out problems. There are certain definite advantages in this method of teaching. First, it is conducive to an alert, active attitude favorable to learning. A good problem is a good motive for learning. Second, it is conducive to the building up of confidence in one's ability to work things out for himself. This has definite value for the individual's mental health, for one of the first principles of mental hygiene is that difficulties should be regarded as problems to be solved rather than as emergencies to be evaded. Third, the memory value is exceptionally good for results obtained by solving a problem, and, if these results are forgotten, they may be thought out again in most cases more easily than the first time. Finally, this method of learning provides valuable training in facing and working out solutions of problems. Through it, with wise direction by the teacher, the pupil may learn the art of sound thinking. To secure a transfer from a particular field of instruction to problems in other fields, however, it is essential that the student be made aware of the general aspects of the methods and procedures which bring good results (Ulmer, 1939).

A number of experiments have been done on different teaching techniques — lecture versus discussion, teacher-centered versus student-centered and the like, usually with equivocal results. Several comparisons of the lecture-demonstration method with the problem-solving method were made utilizing college students as experimental and control groups. Although the differences obtained usually were not statistically significant as far as determining which is the preferable method, qualitative differences occurred. For instance, on specific information learned, the lecture-demonstration group surpassed the problem-solving group; the latter, however, had greater understanding of generalizations. While the lecture method tends to be superior for informational gains, the utilization of problem-solving techniques in teaching is necessary if the teacher is to develop problem-solving skills.

Reviewing educational research on problem-solving approaches used in conjunction with the teaching of social studies, Broadhead and Dimond (1950) reported that high school students using a problem-solving approach showed greater development in critical thinking as well as in subsidiary research and study skills.

Knowledge is essential to good thinking. By supplying information and fixed associations, we provide the child with equipment for dealing with problematic situations. But the child needs to be taught how to use this equipment. We commonly place too much stress in our teaching on memory work and on the comprehension of lectures and readings, to the neglect of training in thinking. To promote the development of the ability to think out the solutions of problems, instruction must provide first, information and memory materials, and second, training in the procedures for using effectively the factual materials so that pupils will be able to solve their own problems and arrive at conclusions of their own.

DIRECTING AND TRAINING PUPILS IN PROBLEM SOLVING

1. Creating the problem. First of all, in securing and directing problem-solving activity, the teacher must set the stage for the problem. One of the simplest ways in which this may be done is to ask a thought question. Such a question is not one that can be answered directly by repeating something that has been read, heard, or otherwise learned but one that calls for the production by real thinking of a new bit of knowledge, a new opinion, or a new belief. Problems also may be aroused by the assignment of exercises or tasks that bring the child into new situations for which his established modes of response are inadequate. It could be the problem of finding an effective means for raising funds to buy a new flag for the schoolroom, how to secure suitable costumes for the class play, or the need for making the school paper more appealing to the pupils.

Whatever its source, the problem must be adapted to the pupil's level of experience and understanding. For young children, it should be comparatively simple and related to a concrete situation and familiar materials. More difficult problems may be introduced to older children. For them imaginary situations and more abstract propositions may be employed.

While the teacher may suggest a problem, it must become the child's own problem if it is to motivate thinking on his part. The teacher's assignment or question has aroused a real problem only when the child or student himself feels a need or desire to find the answer or solution. It is for this reason that the most effective thought questions are those that appeal to the learner's curiosity or are related to his own interests and welfare. A thought-provoking question is one that delivers a challenge, not one that strikes down a child and leaves him with a sense of failure or incapacity.

It takes more skill and originality on the part of the teacher to ask good thought questions, to arrange thought-provoking projects and activities, and, on the higher levels, to direct research, than merely to ask questions of fact based on a textbook or pass out information by way of telling or lecturing. An investigation, in which the number and kinds of questions asked by 56 sixth-grade teachers of history were compared with the scores these teachers made on intelligence tests while in college, revealed that the teachers with higher intelligence asked a smaller total number of questions but more thought questions than did the teachers who rated lower in intelligence (Haynes, 1936). When the teachers were divided into four groups from lowest to highest according to their intelligence scores, it was found that the percentage of thought questions asked varied directly with the intelligence of the teachers. Assuming that thought questions stimulate thinking, we see that these results indicate that the more intelligent teachers secure a greater amount of thinking than the less intelligent ones.

2. Comprehending the problem. When the problem is established and the difficulty felt, the pupil is ready for the next step, which involves the clarification of the problem, its definition, and precise location. The significance of the question may be but vaguely grasped or the nature of the difficulty may be incompletely comprehended. A vaguely defined problem leads to mental fumbling and floundering. If a pupil is to learn how to think, he must be made to realize the need for determining, at the start, the nature of his problem. He should be warned of the danger of making false assumptions. He may need to be told to reread the statement of the problem and to examine its conditions more carefully. His attention may need to be called to some condition that he has overlooked. Sometimes a well-put question may help him to see more clearly the essential features of the problem. In some cases, as in a proposed research undertaking, it will be helpful to have the student write out a precise statement of the problem which he intends to explore.

Hildreth (1942) demonstrated the importance of having some understanding of the nature of the problem by dividing 100 boys and girls between the ages of 7 and 10 years into two groups, one of which had the opportunity to see the jig-saw puzzle whole before working on it, the other having no idea of the puzzle-solution. Time scores and number of moves made were recorded. The "uninstructed" group was significantly slower than the "instructed" group and engaged in more trial-and-error behavior. Interestingly enough, the children tended to be in action all the time they were working, very few stopping to *think* without making moves. Although it may be argued that jig-saw puzzles are not problems in the usual adult understanding of the word, they are appropriate as tasks for children, who function more effectively on a concrete than on an abstract level.

3. Searching for clues. Superficial thinking and erroneous conclusions are the penalty for trying to solve problems with insufficient information. The discovery of relevant data frequently demands exploration and search. If the problem falls within a field in which the person has an abundance of experience or concerning which he is well informed, he may call upon his associative resources to great advantage. He may be able to solve the problem at once by recalling relevant facts and by reorganizing them in such a manner as to meet the requirements of the situation. In many cases, it is necessary for one to collect and organize new material bearing on the problem. Here, the teacher may render valuable assistance without depriving the pupil of the opportunity to work out his own solution and provide training that will extend beyond the particular exercise at hand.

In the first place, the teacher can acquaint the pupil with the various sources of information and the proper way to consult them for securing needed material. He may suggest procedures for reaching and consulting the most suitable and reliable sources of information. These sources may include such firsthand contacts as a trip to a store, factory, publishing house, the city fire department's headquarters, or a talk with the town treasurer, selectman, policeman, doctor, or minister. The teacher's task will also include instruction in the consultation of printed sources. He may suggest books or magazine articles to be read. The pupil should be taught how to use the resources of the library — how to consult reference works, dictionaries, and the catalogue — so that he will be able to look up material for himself. He should be instructed in the use of books as sources of information on a particular subject. He should be taught the advantages of consulting the index and table of contents and of skimming in order to locate quickly the material bearing on his problem. If the sources consulted contain tables, graphs, or statistical data which he is unable to interpret, he should be given the assistance necessary to enable him to get from them what he needs.

Besides knowing where and how to find material pertinent to his problem, the pupil should be taught to evaluate the sources. He should be able to distinguish between original and secondary sources and between statements of established fact and intepretations or opinions. He should be sensitive to the particular biases or viewpoints of the author consulted.

Finally, in order that the collected material may be most provocative of suggestions for solving the problem, the material must be organized or arranged according to a meaningful pattern.

Although research in the area of thinking and problem solving is limited, more provocative studies are being carried out and the neglected area of the higher mental processes undoubtedly will receive more systematic exploration. Birsh and Rabinowitz (1951) and Saugstad (1952) have shown that the experience preceding the presentation of a problem can interfere with problem solving. Saugstad reasoned and found some verification that students having higher recall for isolated or incidental facts (unorganized in memory) would not perform as well in solving problems. McNemar (1955) selected college students who obtained high and low scores on logical reasoning tests — tests having high variance of the logical reasoning factor and low variances on verbal, numerical, and perceptual factors determined by results of a factor analysis (Guilford, 1954). The tests used involved false premises, syllogisms, and problem solving. These two different groups were then administered tests of word association, deduction and induction, and experimentally induced set. The two groups differed on speed of association, accuracy and speed of deduction and induction, and on ability to overcome set. Cowen and Thompson (1951) found that rigidity of personality, as determined by projective and objective personality inventories, was related to inability to overcome experimentally induced sets and limited productivity. Problem solving apparently necessitates not only the bringing of salient information to bear on the problem but also flexibility in not being bound by previous experience and solutions.

4. Securing suggestions for solution, and their evaluation. The good teacher will avoid both the giving of too much help and the mere exhortation to think. The pupil should be allowed to do his

own thinking, but the teacher can be of service by directing his attention to significant elements in the situation which he has failed to
notice or by asking an appropriate question to stimulate the recall
of some principle or fact which has an important bearing on the problem.

If inferences do not appear readily, the pupil should be encouraged
to search diligently for the right clue. His suggestions for solution or
his hypotheses depend upon the relations he discovers among the
facts and principles organized around the problem.

If the pupil seems blocked by a false assumption regarding the
requirements of the problem, he should be asked to re-examine the
problem.

If he persists in repeating a fruitless attack, he should be encouraged to vary his procedure and try out new leads. A good thinker
is one who can readily change his approach.

If he is inclined to give up too easily, the teacher should urge him
on and point out some of the possibilities which he has not explored.
To become a good thinker, the pupil must learn to be persistent.

If he appears tired, confused, or emotionally disturbed, he should
be allowed to drop the matter for a while and return to it later. After
a period of rest, one is often able to pick up a new lead or see a clue
which before had escaped his attention.

The teacher should point out to the pupil the need for an open-
minded attitude and freedom from prejudice, for biases and precon-
ceived notions are often fatal to sound thinking.

A willingness to venture a guess should be encouraged, not a random guess but an assumption made deliberately with all the available
facts in mind. Such an assumption is a hypothesis. Its merits will be
determined by studying out its implications to see whether it meets
the requirements of the situation. No harm is done if it proves to be
a false lead. It can be abandoned if it proves to be inadequate, but
it might turn out to be a satisfactory solution. Great thinkers sometimes try out hundreds of leads before they find the right one.

The effective direction and training of pupils in problem-solving
activity will foster a critical attitude toward the suggestions for the
solution of a problem. To become a good thinker, the child must
learn that when an idea for a solution comes to his mind, it should be
regarded as a possibility to be tested out before it is accepted as final.
He should be taught the importance of suspending judgment until
all the available data on the subject are examined for evidence and

of seeing the merits and disadvantages of the proposed solution
in the light of all the information at hand.

There are a number of things to consider in dealing with faulty
proposals for a solution or an erroneous answer to a thought question. If a sensitive child happens to give a ridiculous answer and is
laughed at or made to feel ashamed because of it, he is likely to
"close up" and refuse to attempt any further suggestions. Repeated
authoritative rebuttals or denunciations by the teacher are likely to
produce the same results. When a pupil suggests an absurd answer
in good faith, his efforts should be met with a respectful request to
tell why he thinks it is a good answer or by questioning that will lead
him to discover its defects. If he appears to be merely guessing at
random, he should be reminded that he is supposed to find the answer
by thinking over what he knows about the subject. In some cases
where the child lacks sufficient information to see why his answer
or proposal is inadequate, it may be necessary for the teacher to
explain why his offering is not correct or sound.

Failure to detect the shortcomings of a proposal for solution may
be due to faulty conception of the problem, lack of sufficient information, misinformation, biases and prejudices, unwillingness or lack of
desire to exert further effort, or a false assumption of relationship.
In helping the pupil to detect the weakness of his hypothesis or the
error of his answer, the teacher should take notice of its source and
make the attack from that point.

SUMMARY

Thinking is an activity through which an individual arrives at the
solution of a problem. The problem is a felt difficulty, and the solution is a new bit of knowledge or a new belief. An important feature
of this form of thinking is its employment of symbolic materials. Symbolic meanings provide clues, evidence, and flashes of insight. Just as
all thinking is not problem solving, so all problems are not solved
by thinking. We tend to avoid hard thinking by accepting solutions
provided by imagination or memory. When experience or knowledge
is lacking, we are prone to resort to overt trial-and-error. It is often
not possible to tell from a person's response whether or not it is the
result of elaborative thinking.

The characteristic phases in the process of thinking out the solution of a problem are: first, a difficulty is felt; second, the problem is clarified and defined; third, a search for clues is made; fourth, various suggestions for solution appear and are evaluated or tested; fifth, a solution is accepted or the thinker gives up in defeat; and sixth, the solution is tested.

The ability to solve problems by thinking can be improved by training. This improvement results from acquiring the means (knowledge and symbols) to think with and also from learning the best procedures for using these materials effectively. Learning and thinking are linked in two ways: first, we learn by thinking, and second, we improve our ability to think by learning.

Young children solve problematic situations mainly by overt trial-and-error exploration and manipulation. The ability to solve problems by thinking develops gradually with growth in experience and understanding. Children are inferior to adults in problem thinking principally because of their smaller range of experience. They are less sensitive to problems, have fewer concepts to work with, lack critical judgment, are less capable of sustained attention, and are less able to take an objective attitude toward their problems.

The problem method of teaching secures learning through the solving of problems. Its advantages are: first, it promotes an active attitude; second, it fosters confidence in ability to work things out for one's self; third, the memory value is especially good for things learned in this way; and fourth, it provides training in the procedures for thinking out solutions to problems.

In directing and training pupils in problem solving, the teacher's task is: first, to set the stage for the problem by asking thought questions and by devising and assigning problem exercises; second, to assist the pupils in clarifying and defining their problem; third, to stimulate fertility of suggestions for solution and direct the pupil to sources of data bearing on the problem; and fourth, to foster a critical attitude toward the suggestions so that they will be properly evaluated and tested before being finally accepted as solutions.

OVERVIEW

Reitz, W., "Higher Mental Processes," *Encyclopedia of Educational Research,* W. S. Monroe, ed. New York: Macmillan Co., 1950, pp. 540-48.

SELECTED REFERENCES

Harlow, H. F., "Thinking," *Theoretical Foundations of Psychology,* H. Nelson, ed. New York: Van Nostrand Co., 1951, pp. 452-505.

Thorndike, R. L., "How Children Learn the Principles and Techniques of Problem Solving," *Forty-ninth Yearbook of the National Society for the Study of Education.* Chicago: University of Chicago Press, 1950, Part I, Chapter 8.

Vinacke, W. E., *The Psychology of Thinking.* New York: McGraw-Hill, 1952.

ORIGINAL INVESTIGATIONS

Burach, B., "The Nature and Efficacy of Methods of Attack on Reasoning Problems," *Psychological Monographs,* 1950, 64 (7), No. 313, p. 26.

Cowen, E. L. and G. C. Thompson, "Problem Solving Rigidity and Personality Structure," *Journal of Abnormal and Social Psychology,* 1951, 46, pp. 165-76.

Guilford, J. P., et al., "A Factor Analytic Study of Navy Reasoning Tests with the Air Force Crew Class," Battery, *Educational and Psychological Measurement,* 1954, 14, pp. 301-25.

Maier, N. R., "Reasoning in Children," *Journal of Comparative Physiological Psychology,* 1936, 29, pp. 357-66.

Oakes, M. E., "Children's Explanations of Natural Phenomena," *Teachers College Contributions to Education,* No. 926, 1947, p. 151.

Saugstad, P., "Incidental Memory and Problem Solving," *Psychological Review,* 1952, 59, pp. 221-26.

Taylor, D. W. and W. L. Faust, "Twenty Questions: Efficiency in Problem Solving as a Function of the Size of the Group," *Journal of Experimental Psychology,* 1952, 44, pp. 360-68.

Chapter Fifteen

The Development of Emotional Activity

Personality consists in a large measure
of a person's emotional predispositions and
the character of those highly en-
ergized forms of activity which he
manifests when he encounters frustration,
insecurity, and emergency situations. Extensive
differences between various individuals
are to be found with respect to their pro-
pensities for fear, anger, jealousy, joy, and
other forms of emotional upset. Persons
differ also in the depth of their
emotional stirs, the range and nature of the
conditions that arouse emotions, and the manner
in which they conduct themselves when in the
grip of emotional excitement. An indivi-
dual's happiness, his mental health,

social adjustment, and conduct are directly related to his emotional life.

THE EMOTIONS AND PERSONALITY

Wholesome personalities do not lack strong emotions, but they differ from the weak, unstable, and poorly adjusted personalities with respect to the source of emotional disturbances and the manifest behavior on occasions which give rise to them. Today, more than ever before, the possibility and the need for training the emotional activities are recognized.

Three aspects of emotion. Emotional activities are complex psychological functions. In approaching the study of emotions, one discovers that they present many facets. Some students of emotions have concerned themselves with one aspect of them and have neglected others. If we consider the total emotional event, at least three major aspects are to be taken into account. These are skeletal or overt behavior, visceral behavior, and the emotional experience.

1. The skeletal behavior consists of the kind of activity we observe in another when he is angered, frightened, jealous, surprised, joyful, bitterly disappointed, disgusted, or grieved. We note, for example, the shrieks of fear, the threatening fist, scowls, smiles, laughter, sobs, the defensive attitude, shrinking, attack, and flight. Such behavior often, though not always, serves to reveal to others the character of the emotion which has seized the victim of inadequate adjustment to a difficult situation. The effectors for this behavior are the striated or skeletal muscles.

2. The visceral behavior, being internal, is not readily observed in another. Some of the observable effects of the visceral components are the reddened or paled face, changes in breathing, dryness of the mouth, loss of appetite, urination, or defecation, all of which may occur in times of strong emotional excitement. Experimental studies have revealed that the internal changes in emotion include a stepping up of the pulse and breathing rates, an increase in blood pressure and blood sugar, increased activity of the adrenal glands and the sweat glands, and a cessation of the churning movements of the stomach. These changes are produced involuntarily through the agency of the sympathetic division of the autonomic nervous system and the smooth muscles. While this widespread visceral activity is

a characteristic part of the general emotional disturbance, many of these reactions occur in other circumstances, such as violent exercise, exposure to cold, painful experiences, and loss of blood. The activity of the sympathetic nervous system serves to maintain the essential uniformity of the internal environment, including the bodily temperature, and the physical and chemical properties of the blood. In the raw state of nature, emotions are aroused by those situations which, for survival, require flight, defense, or attack. In such situations, there is survival value in the effects produced by the sympathetic nervous system. But for man, whose life must be lived on a plane of respectability far removed by culture and conventions from the animal instincts, the emotions can seldom serve their normal biological purposes. The internal changes, when not used according to the designs of nature, lead to internal turmoil which is often detrimental rather than helpful to successful adjustment.

3. The third aspect of emotion is the experiential accompaniment of these visceral changes and the overt behavior. This is not open to direct observation by anyone except the one who is passing through it, but for him it is the most significant thing about the emotion. It consists chiefly of a complex of organic and kinesthetic sensations toned by a high degree of unpleasantness or pleasantness together with the awareness of the emotional situation. Some psychologists have regarded this complex of sensory experience as the emotion and the manifest behavior as its expression. On the other hand, certain behaviorists have regarded the overt and visceral behavior as the emotion and have ignored the facts of emotional experience because of their bias in favor of strictly objective methods of observation. It seems more appropriate to consider the total emotional event as the emotion. As such, emotion is a function which is touched off by the external situation. It runs its course according to the nature and predispositions of the organism. It embraces both the emotional experience made up of sensations, the feelings, and perceptual meanings, and the emotional behavior consisting of the bodily reactions, overt and visceral.

The general course of the emotion. The first phase of the emotional event is perception of a situation. The specific character of the emotion depends upon the manner in which the situation is apprehended and upon the impulses which the perception arouses. Typically the situation is perceived as threatening, frightful, disgusting, or delightful; as one calling for defense, submission, attack, or escape. The subject experiences a more or less violent surge of feelings. Widespread reactions take place throughout the visceral regions. Skeletal muscles are tensed. Next follow attempts to escape the predicament, to meet the impending crisis, or to ward off the threat of danger. In the more extreme cases, these attempts are sometimes chaotic, as when the individual finds himself unable to muster an adequate form of response. He may be overwhelmed by excitement or bafflement; his consciousness may be deluged by a rush of bewildering and confusing sensations. In his distraught state he strikes out blindly. Sometimes he dissipates his energy in ineffective and disorganized efforts to break the situation or escape from its clutches. Sometimes his acts are so unfortunate that his deeds cause lifelong sorrow or regret. Sometimes he is so overwhelmed that he is aptly described as "paralyzed by fear," "choked with rage," "prostrate with grief," "overcome with joy," or "dumb with astonishment." Finally, there is the stage of recovery. The upheaval slowly subsides, and gradually the individual regains his mental and organic equilibrium.

Emotionalized action. There are, however, cases in which the action trends are established so strongly as to withstand the shock of emotional excitement or in which the emotional stir is not so violent as to prevent adaptive response. Here the individual's response to the sitiuation is dominated by the action trends and is energized by the emotional stir. It is emotionalized action. The individual displays unusual strength and endurance. The frightened boy runs faster, the angry fighter strikes harder, and the anxious mother displays greater resistance to fatigue.

This extraordinary strength and endurance displayed in emotionalized action is believed to be due to the organic changes produced by the sympathetic nervous system and the secretions of the adrenal glands. Blood sugar is released in greater amounts, the pulse rate is increased, and the breathing rate is stepped up. These reactions provide an extra supply of oxygen and combustible materials for the muscles. Thus, reserves of energy are tapped and, at the same time, fatigue is momentarily overcome by the faster removal of fatigue toxins through the accelerated action of the sweat glands and by the increased rate of respiration.

The secret of adequate adjustment through an appropriate form of action, however, lies in the fact that the individual has a ready-made response for the emergency situation. A well-established habit, a reaction which has been trained, or a plan of attack already carefully worked out, provides a determination of action that withstands the emotional disturbance. The disruptive effects of the emotional stir are greatest in cases where the individual is not prepared, where a new form of response is required, where habits are inadequate, and where clear thinking is needed. In public places of entertainment, the patrons are accustomed to leave by way of the front entrance through which they enter. In case of fire, their impulse is to hurry out that entrance. When several hundred frightened persons try to do this at the same time, the entrance becomes blocked and their customary action fails to provide an escape. It is then that panic seizes the crowd and tragedy reaps its toll of lives of the trapped victims. If the front exit does not become blocked, escape is achieved. In that case, an adequate adjustment to the situation is provided by the habitual form of response. The inexperienced driver is more likely to "lose his head" and put his foot on the accelerator when he should put it on the brake for a quick stop than one who has practiced driving for many years. An adjuster for an automobile insurance company tells of a collision between two cars. When the drivers saw the cars coming together, they let go of the steering wheels, threw up their hands, and let the cars crash. A prompt application of brakes by both drivers could have prevented the accident.

Preparing for emergency situations. It is possible to prepare for many emergency situations in such a way as to insure prompt and adequate action and to prevent the disastrous consequences of panic. There are cases where an individual is so well prepared that when the dangerous situation is encountered, he reacts successfully before the emotional seizure arises. An acquaintance of the writer, for example, was driving a car in the wintertime. The streets were icy, so that it was impossible to make a quick stop by applying the brakes. As he approached an intersection, a car suddenly shot out from a side street directly into the path of an oncoming car. To avert a collision the latter car swerved to the other side of the street and was bearing down directly onto the friend's car. The use of the brakes could not prevent a collision. Our friend could not possibly dodge to the right of the oncoming car, for by momentum it was being carried too far toward the right side of the street. He jerked the steering wheel to the left, and escaped the crash by a narrow margin. This all happened in a flash. After the danger was passed, our friend experienced the emotional seizure. He found it difficult to breathe and waited a few minutes until he had gained his equilibrium. He had acted before he was upset by fright.

It is the situation for which one cannot muster an adequate response that overwhelms and produces panic. The emotional upset blocks clear thinking, precludes deliberation, and destroys the ability to formulate an appropriate course of action. This is why it is essential to have fire drills in our schools. To prevent panic, children should be trained in the course of action to be followed in the case of fire. The training maneuvers for soldiers not only serve to give the fighting men skills of warfare but also prepare for cooler heads in the heat of battle. To prevent the breakdown of suitable action in emergencies, we should train or practice the appropriate action as far as possible before the emergency arises. This, of course, depends upon our ability to anticipate the emergency. When it is our responsibility to provide such training for others, our emphasis and the learner's attention should be focused on the action to be carried through and not on the dangers involved. While it is generally desirable to face situations realistically, we should not pave the way for panic by picturing horrible possible consequences. The teacher in charge of the fire drill should not frighten children by harrowing accounts of fire disasters.

It is clear, of course, that we cannot practice the appropriate activity for all emergency situations which can be anticipated. Where actual practice is impossible or not feasible, the next best thing is to decide in moments of calm deliberation what one would do in case a certain emergency arose. Upon entering a theater, for example, one can look around and locate the nearest exit to be used in case of fire. An emergency situation will be less likely to overwhelm the person who has thought out a plan of action for it than one who is suddenly plunged into it with no preparation at all.

Emotional reactions of infants. The complex emotional activity we observe in a child or an adult is not an unlearned pattern of behavior laid down by heredity. It has a history of growth and development under the influence of consequences, social pressures, failures, and successes. Like other forms of activity, it is shaped by learning, and the process involves modification by way of experience.

Inasmuch as the emotional response is based on perception and the significance which the situation has for the individual, it appears unlikely that the young infant is capable of what we know as emotion in an older child or adult, since the perceptions of the infant are relatively undeveloped. Like the other activities, however, the development of the emotions starts with something provided by nature—an "unlearned nucleus." Certain situations such as a sudden loud noise, being pricked or pinched, being removed from the mother's breast while feeding, being deprived of food, being prevented from moving, and the like, call forth in the infant energized reactions commonly regarded as emotional. They include crying, starting, thrashing of arms, and kicking of legs. There is evidence also of the visceral type of behavior. But the overt reactions are diffuse and generalized. They are non-adaptive except for the fact that they are frequently useful in securing escape from discomfort by way of the ministrations of older members of the household.

There are no clear-cut differences in behavior patterns to suggest distinct forms of emotions in the first few days of life. This primitive, undifferentiated antecedent of emotions is probably best described as a state of excitement. It is marked by a general heightening of the infant's activities and may be aroused by a pinprick, hunger, uncomfortable clothing, or any form of overstimulation. From it, as the child develops, are differentiated the various forms of emotion which we recognize in the more mature individual. While the maturation of physical structures may be a factor in this process of emotional differentiation, it appears reasonably certain that learning plays the predominant role.

How different emotions are distinguished. The fact that we detect different kinds of emotion in children and adults leads us to the question of how we distinguish one emotion from another or tell what sort of emotion we have before us. In the first place, we find few differentiae in the visceral reactions. These components have been found to be similar in fear and anger, the emotions in which they have been most thoroughly studied. For the other emotions, such as sorrow and elation, little is known about them.

The character of the overt behavior of another person furnishes us with a clue regarding the nature of his emotion. The rising voice, violent words, and threatening gestures commonly indicate anger. Convulsive sobs and weeping suggest grief. Laughter, smiles, gleeful exclamations, and shouts are associated with joy. The pale face, shrinking, trembling, and fleeing are common signs of fear. Studies of the ability of persons to judge emotions from facial expressions as shown in photographs have generally revealed better than a chance percentage of successful responses. Yet, the hazards involved in diagnosing another's emotion from its outward manifestations alone are apparent to anyone who has reflected on the matter. The overt behavior does not always reveal the true emotion. The various emotions often contain similar kinds of behavior. For example, crying appears in anger, grief, joy, and fear. There are individual differences with respect to behavior under the same conditions of emotional stimulation even in infants. As the individual grows up, he finds it socially expedient or even necessary to conceal and disguise his emotions. A person may smile to conceal his anger or laugh to disguise his sorrow or fear. He may manifest a serious demeanor when courtesy demands it even though actually he is amused, or appear to be delighted when unwelcome guests arrive. At a dull party he must, to be polite to his hostess, give the appearance of having a good time.

In a study by Sherman (1927) infants were subjected to various forms of stimulation to arouse emotional reactions, and observers were asked to name the resulting emotions displayed by the infants. Stimulation consisted of dropping a short distance, hunger, needle prick, and restraint of movement. One group of observers were shown motion pictures of both the stimulating situation and the ensuing behavior. In the case of hunger, the observers were told what the stimulating condition was. For another group, the parts of the film showing the stimulating conditions were deleted so that the observers saw only the resulting behavior. Members of a third group were shown motion pictures presenting a stimulating situation followed, not by the behavior that situation actually aroused, but by the responses evoked by one of the other forms of stimulation. For a fourth group, the child was stimulated behind a screen which was immediately removed so that the observers saw the behavior without knowing the antecedent stimulating conditions.

The results indicated that the judgments of the observers were dependent in a large measure on seeing the conditions which aroused the reactions. When the observers did not see the stimulation, they were unable to agree on the nature of the emotion. When they saw the true stimulating conditions, they agreed very well in naming the emotion, and did so in accordance with what one would expect as the result of such conditions. When dropping was observed, the emotion was named fear. When the baby was restrained, the response was called anger. But when the stimulus conditions and the responses were interchanged by means of the film, the judgments followed what would be expected from the situation. Thus, the reactions which actually followed restraint were called *fear* because what the observers saw as the apparent cause was the dropping of the infant instead of restraint of his movements.

We may conclude that, while we distinguish the emotions of others partly by their behavior, we do so mainly on the basis of what we know about the situations which have aroused them. A certain amount of differentiation and patterning of emotional activity takes place as the child grows older, but even in adults, the behavior patterns for different kinds of emotion have a great many similar components.

DEVELOPMENTAL CHANGES IN EMOTIONS

Widely spread differences exist in the concepts of the development of the emotions in children. Watson (1930) believed that a trained observer could detect neonatal differences in the reactions patterns of infants for the three emotions of fear, love, and rage. According to the psychoanalytic school of thought, the child comes into the world lonely, helpless and afraid, stunned by the event of birth, and made anxious by the change from a placid to an unstable environment. Though incomplete in all other respects, the child was thought capable of adult emotional experiences. The evidence suggests that the initial state of emotion is one of general excitability from which results a gradual differentiation of emotional reactions influenced by maturation and learning. Bridges (1932) describes the emotional development as a process of differentiation, the first stages being distress and delight states; these occur in the first three months, the distress state being differentiated into fear, aversion, and anger by the middle of the first year, while affection is distinguished from elation by the end of the first year. Following this, still greater refinements occur until the adult emotional response patterns are established.

As development goes forward, many varieties of fear, love, and anger appear. Probably there are as many variations in emotions as there are different ways of perceiving emotional situations and different impulses to react to them. Yet, the familiar terms *fear, anger,* and *love* represent fundamental types and provide a convenient form of grouping for purposes of discussion. We may, therefore, consider the developmental changes in these as fairly typical of what takes place in the development of the emotional life. Modifications of the emotional trends are indicated by changes in conditions which arouse the emotions and by alterations in the mode of reacting when emotionally stirred.

FEAR

Careful observations and experiments with infants indicate that fear is naturally aroused by very few forms of stimulation. It has been quite definitely established that without conditioning, an infant does not fear the dark, fire, furry animals, or snakes, although fear of these things is commonly acquired rather early. The stimuli which elicit fear without previous experience are those which come suddenly. Quite generally, sudden, intense, and strange stimuli evoke fear reactions in infants, and these are presumed to do so apart from previous experience. In experimental studies by Watson and others, the fear reactions were aroused by a sudden loud noise, by jerking the sheet on which the infant was lying, and by dropping the infant a short distance. It is noteworthy that the element of *insecurity* found in these situations is the critical feature of all fear situations throughout life, though it appears later in different situations.

Changes in the sources of fear. During the preschool period, the number of fear stimuli is rapidly increased. At about the age of five or six months, a child sometimes shows signs of fear at the approach of strangers. This manifestation presumably is directly related to his growth in ability to perceive. A careful investigation of children's fears by Jersild and Holmes (1933, 1935) revealed that the most common fear objects of children under seven years of age were animals, noises and events previously associated with noises, falling or danger of falling, pain or persons and things which have been connected with painful experiences, strange persons, strange objects, and strange situations. During these first six years, there is a decline in some fears and an increase in others. The percentage of children five and six years of age showing fear of noises, pain, falling, and strange persons and things, was smaller than for the younger children. But the older children exhibited more fears of bodily injury, darkness, being left alone, and imaginary creatures such as ghosts.

Whether or not a given object will elicit fear depends greatly upon the general surroundings and the condition of the child. For example, a child does not fear a dog if his mother is present, but is terrified if the dog comes upon him suddenly when he is alone. A loud noise does not frighten a child who is making it for fun. A child who enjoys being tossed up and caught again by his father may show fear if this is done to him by someone else.

As the child passes into later childhood, he continues to fear many of the things that frightened him in his early years. Sudden noises and threats of bodily injury, for example, are likely to continue to be provocative of fear responses. But there is, in general, a change in the character of the situations causing fear, and this change results in the elimination of many useless fears. The child discovers, for example, that many loud noises are harmless, and they no longer frighten him. Normally he is not afraid of a dog unless the dog is barking, growling, or threatening to attack him, or unless he knows the dog to be vicious. He may be afraid of all dogs because of parental warnings or because of some terrifying experience with a dog. Normally, he will not fear all strangers, but only those who are too aggressive toward him. Normally, he will not fear all forms of falling, but only those occuring unexpectedly and for which he is not prepared.

At this age, however, a new kind of fear situation appears, one that is most troublesome. It is the imagined situation which is not limited by the boundaries of space, time, or objective reality. One constructs by means of his own thoughts terrifying and dreadful situations, which produce worries and anxieties. These emotional reactions have about the same unwholesome effects on one's efficiency and conduct as do the fears touched off by perception. They may even be worse in their effect on the personality, for they easily become habits and are not restricted to the circumstances of the external environment. They may be elicited at any hour of the day or night and they may continue their devastating work for days, weeks, or months at a time. The list of fears in the form of worries and anxieties suffered by children in the primary grades is a long one. The results from one study showed that the worries most frequently reported by sixth graders were concerned with matters of health, bodily suffering or injury, school marks, and grade promotion.

At the period of adolescence, physical violence and suffering continue to be important sources of fear, but to a lesser extent than in the pre-adolescent period. Boys and girls of the "teen" age are extremely sensitive about what others think of them, especially members of their own "crowd." Their fears center largely around social situations and relationships. Clothes, appearance, lack of poise, money enough to do as other young folks do, invitations to the right parties, the family's social standing, hurting other people's feelings, and the impression they make on others, are some of the more common causes of anxiety and worry for them. They appear also to be the greatest sufferers from discrimination due to racial prejudices.

Although studies of children's fears made in the school setting probably produce an exaggerated number of concerns regarding school work, it is safe to conclude that fear and anxiety about school work is important from the intermediate grades on. One-third of a large group of high school students report fears and worries regarding school tests and grades, one-quarter about class recitation and teachers (Noble, 1951).

Jersild, Markey, and Jersild (1933) compared children's fears and children's description of the "worst happenings" that they could remember and discovered that children's fears center on different aspects of life than the day-to-day vicissitudes. The main fears of children aged 5-12 were (1) supernatural and mysterious events, (2) attack by animals, (3) being alone, lost, in a dark or strange place, etc., and (4) of being injured by accident. Almost exclusively, the worst event in children's lives was described as an accident, injury, or other physical hurt. It is, of course, possible to place several different interpretations on such data. They may be taken literally. They can be interpreted as a product of increasing conceptual development and consequent awareness of the environment. They can be interpreted as symbolic evidence suggesting greater insecurity, anxiety, and the like.

Adults worry mostly about their health, their financial security, and about possible harm to loved ones. The mother fears the danger which her soldier son must face or the marriage which her daughter contemplates. The father worries about a possible accident when his son takes the family car. Adults are often subject to fears which beset children and adolescents, but in general the normal development releases them from most of the ill-grounded fears of childhood. Their fears are, as a rule, based on experience and relate to tragedies and misfortunes which they have seen overtake other persons. The emotionally maladjusted and immature adult, however, may have all sorts of irrational fears to beset and torment him.

Fears acquired by conditioning. The fear reactions, like other forms of response, are subject to modification by conditioning. Some of the earliest experimental studies of infant emotions were concerned with this problem. The procedure was, in general, to combine a fear-provoking stimulus, call it A, with some other stimulus, B, for which the child showed no fear. It was found that, after being subjected to such a double form of stimulation, the child displayed fear when B was presented without A. It seems that in this manner the child acquires a great many fears.

In one of Watson's early experiments, the subject was an eleven-month-old boy named Albert. Before the experiment, this child showed no fear of white rats. He did show fear when a loud noise was produced by striking a steel bar with a hammer. The rat was presented to Albert, and just as he touched it with his hand, the bar was struck. In response, he "jumped violently and fell forward." After five combined stimulations, the rat was presented alone. The child "puckered" his face, "whimpered, and withdrew body sharply to the left." After two more combined stimulations, the rat was again presented alone. As soon as he saw the rat, the child began to cry, "turned sharply to the left, fell over, raised himself on all fours and began to crawl away . . . rapidly." After a five-day interval during which he did not see the rat, Albert "Whimpered . . . withdrew right hand and turned head and trunk away" when the rat alone was presented. After he had played with some blocks, the rat was again presented. This time he "leaned over to the left side as far away from the rat as possible, then fell over, getting up on all fours, and scurrying away as rapidly as possible." Next in turn, a rabbit, a dog, and fur coat were presented to Albert, and in response to each, he displayed the same agitated negative behavior as that elicited by the rat. Here appeared the same kind of transfer of the conditioned response to similar stimuli which had been observed in experiments on conditioning of other forms of response.

The picture is drawn here of at least one way in which new fears are acquired. Watson believed all the complex elaborations of the emotional life are built up by the operation of this principle. To many of us, this seems to be assuming a bit too much for conditioning. It seems likely that other forms of learning operate to produce many of the changes which occur in the development of the emotional activity. It does appear, however, that many objects become provokers of fear by being associated or identified with something which causes fear. A high-school teacher became frightened whenever a door or drawer stuck when she was trying to open it. Her trouble originated with a fright she had when a child. She was playing with her younger sister in the attic of their home. The younger child climbed into an old trunk, the lid of which fell down and became fastened. The older sister was terrified when she could not open the trunk, for she thought the child in it would smother to death before help could be summoned.

A little boy was brought to the school psychologist for a mental test. The child seemed afraid of her and all her efforts to secure his coöperation were futile. The examiner, realizing that there was no use in insisting, arranged for the boy to be brought back again in the afternoon. When he came in the afternoon, he behaved like a different child. He was most cheerful and coöperative. The examiner asked him why he would not do the things she asked of him in the morning. The child replied that he was afraid of her. When asked why he was afraid of her in the morning and not now, he pointed out that she had worn a white dress in the morning. He was not afraid during the second visit because the examiner had changed her dress during the lunch hour. A painful hospital experience had conditioned a fear of women dressed in white.

Another small child, after being taken on an elevator to the operating room at a hospital, screamed and struggled whenever his parents tried to take him into an elevator. The fear which some children have of the water may be due to their being lowered too swiftly into their bath when babies. Things associated with loud noises and things connected with bodily injuries that have been received are frequently feared by children. A child is not naturally afraid of the dark, but when a child is frightened in the dark by a loud noise, the dark easily becomes a conditioned fear stimulus. A child is not naturally afraid of dogs, but after he is bitten severely by one, he may be afraid of all dogs. Thus, the principle of conditioning operates to increase the range of objects and events which arouse fear.

Fears acquired by threats, suggestion, and imitation. It is likely that before the child learns to understand spoken language, most of his specific fears are acquired by conditioning. But when language is acquired, a new source of fear is opened. Suggestions of danger and dire consequences carried by casual remarks which a child may only partially understand, threats implied or directly made to the child, and stories of disaster and tragedy often serve to implant fear of a situation which had previously been faced with calm or even feelings of pleasure. The electric storm, for example, may become a frightful thing to a child as a result of hearing his elders tell of some person being killed by lightning. One child developed a great fear of death because an older boy had said as they gazed upon the worm-eaten carcass of a cat, "We'll be like that some day." Accounts of horrible suffering by persons in automobile accidents may make a sensitive child afraid to go in a car. Stories of ghosts and goblins may make being left alone in the dark a harrowing experience. Fear of negro men may result from the threat of having "a black man take you away, if you aren't a good boy." To threaten a child with such forms of punishment as locking him in a dark room, tying him up, or putting him in the furnace is to provide the sources of unwholesome fears. The hint by the teacher that "this is a very hard lesson," may be an incentive to a child with lots of self-confidence, but for a less fortunate one, it may arouse fear of failure. Warning not to go near any strange dog "for you might get bitten," may make a child afraid of dogs. Telling a child to be careful when he goes downstairs because "if you are not careful, you may fall and break your legs," is likely to make a child afraid of going downstairs alone. Holding his hand and saying, "Now don't be afraid. Mother is right here with you. She won't let anything hurt you," can hardly be expected to develop courage in any child. It is significant in this connection that children in countries subjected to bombing by air have shown much greater fear in anticipating the raids than when subjected to the real thing. The source of their anticipatory fear is probably the talk of the dangers and hazards by their elders.

A child is, moreover, sensitive to the fears of others and tends to adopt them. If the first time he sees a snake, his companions show fright, their fear may cause him to perceive the wriggling reptile as a frightful thing, and he will probably react to it as they do. Children tend to imitate the fears of their parents. Hagman (1932) found a correlation of .66 between the number of fears of children and those of their mothers as reported by the mothers. Mothers tend to pass their own fears along to their children. Reports on the conduct of children during air raids indicate that the youngsters tend to reflect the emotional reactions of the older folks around them. If the adults remain calm and quiet, the children are less likely to become terrified than if their elders become panicky. As a result of suggestions, chance remarks, threats, and observing anxiety or panic in others the child learns to perceive situations as harmful or injurious, and the list of his fears grows longer.

Loss of self-esteem and the school as a source of fear. That the conduct of some teachers contributes to the increase of children's fears cannot be denied. In a study of the worries of school children, Pintner and Lev (1940) found that most of the worries of children in grades V and VI were about matters connected with the family and the school. These writers characterized the school worries as "excessive" and stated that their results indicated that there was too much emphasis in school on failing a test, not passing, tardiness, and poor report cards.

An elementary school in the Middle West followed the practice of giving all the children of any room Friday afternoon off if no child in that room was tardy during the entire week. As a device to reduce tardiness, it worked, but how it worked! If a child happened to be tardy, regardless of the cause, he was attacked by the other children, slapped, bullied, and ostracized. The result was that when a child saw he was in danger of being late, rather than face the chastising by his fellow pupils, he turned back and went home. Too often in the past we have been concerned only with whether or not a management or teaching device works. The mental hygiene point of view is concerned with the way a practice works and its effect on the individual child's personality.

Fears may be engendered by harsh criticism, ridicule, sarcasm, blustering, and displays of temper on the part of the teacher; also by unwise punishments or threats of punishment, by threats of failure, and by humiliating experiences in the presence of other children. Some teachers frighten children by shouting at them; others do so by putting down grades while the child recites; and others by ill-chosen remarks which tend to undermine the child's sense of security. One of the most devastating fears is that of failure or the fear that one is inferior in ability. This is often caused by setting up standards of achievement incommensurate with the ability of the child, by unfavorable comparisons with other children, and by using the threat of not passing to stimulate the child to do his work.

The school is a major influence in the self-esteem and the social acceptance held by a child. Children in the classroom reflect the values and attitudes of teachers in judging the worthiness of other children and in deriving a concept of their own worth. That teachers value excellent scholastic performance and submissive behavior can scarcely be questioned. Few children can be "excellent scholars" when they are judged competitively, for we must accept the fact that half of the population is "below average" in intelligence (by definition) and this obviously precludes the winning of competitive honors. Yet, persistently falling short in attaining the teacher's warmest approval promotes a lowered degree of self-esteem and an increase in susceptibility to anxiety and fear. Lazurus and Erickson (1952) demonstrated the deleterious effects of ego-threatening stress based on failure upon college students. When two matched groups repeated a sub-test of the Wechsler-Bellevue, the group placed in the stress situation showed a greater spread of scores than the control group which decreased in variability. The greater spread resulted from the improved performance of students having the higher scholastic standing and from the worst performance of those having lower scholastic standing. Keep in mind that both groups, by virtue of being in college, have probably experienced more success than failure during grade school.

The unwholesome effects of fear. In certain emergencies, fear tends to promote escape from dangers, and this is about the only good thing that can be said for it. The great bulk of the fears which torment children and adults are needless and detrimental. Fear is the enemy of mental and bodily health. It destroys courage and self-confidence, and undermines morale. It weakens and suppresses purposive action, distorts perspective, and inhibits clear thinking. It lessens the chances for success, and is often the cause of mediocrity and failure.

It is sometimes asserted that fear is valuable because it prevents action that would lead to harmful results and promotes the avoidance of danger. This reflects the inhibiting effect of fear. It is far more wholesome to establish positive impulses for beneficial action than to try to hold back action of the wrong kind. As a factor in adjustment, fear is negative. It is not a wholesome means of motivation. Its presence means failure, at least temporarily, to make an adequate adjustment. Habitual fear means habitual failure. Because of these unfavorable results of fear, the teacher's responsibility with respect to children's fears is threefold: first, he should avoid making the school situation a source of fears; second, he should promote courage and self-confidence, and help the child to acquire adequate responses to the situations which confront him; and third, he should help the child to overcome unwholesome and persistent fears.

Comprehension and fears. The modification of fears on the arousal side is also brought about by the growth of understanding. The process of the development of understanding moves from the apprehension of gross situations to the refinements of reacting to various aspects of details of these situations; in the development of concepts, common elements of many different situations are isolated from the concomitants with which these elements appear in the various situations. In like manner, the fear reactions of the infant are evoked by gross situations. As development takes place, these situations are broken apart, analyzed, and the essential fear-provoking element isolated. This means that when the fear element is absent, concomitants will not provoke fear. Where it is present, even with new concomitants, there will be fear.

The essential fear element of the diverse total situations which provoke fear is *insecurity.* To be insecure is to be in want of safety, exposed to danger or loss, or insufficiently safeguarded against hazards and risks. When darkness is a source of fear, regardless of the total situation, the child has not distinguished the element of insecurity from its concomitants. The developmental stage corresponds to that of comprehension when the child calls all men "daddy," or all animals "dogs." When he is afraid to be alone in the dark, but not afraid to be in the dark if his mother is with him, we have a first step in the direction of differentiation. At an early stage, a child may fear strangers. Later only strangers who are too aggressive are feared. At an early stage, a child may fear all dogs; later he fears only those that are barking, growling, or threatening him. Still later he may have no fear of some dogs which growl and bark because he knows them and has learned that they will not harm him, while strange dogs growling and barking may cause fear. When children are questioned concerning their fears, they tend to specify the concrete objects or specific situations which produce their fears. On the other hand, as the threat of danger is singled out and is recognized in other situations, new fears appear. The adolescent finds in certain social situations and relationships a threat to his security, a threat which for the young child is nonexistent. Likewise, the adult finds cause for fear in many situations that do not concern a child. So with growth of understanding comes the fear of such things as contagious diseases, inflation, financial troubles, failure, disloyalty, and loss of property or employment.

Persistent fears. Unfortunately, there are numerous exceptions to the normal course of development described above. Some fears, especially those conditioned by a severe shock or painful experience, are very persistent. They carry over from childhood into adult life and constitute the unreasonable and childlike fears which we frequently see in grown-up persons. The unfortunate individuals who are afflicted by such fears do not discriminate between the insecurity element and what constituted its harmless concomitants in the situation at the time of conditioning, and they continue to be frightened by perfectly harmless situations in which these concomitants occur. So we have adults who are afraid of the dark, open bodies of water, open places, closed places, cats, fire, knives, and all sorts of objects because these things were connected with some terrifying experience of childhood.

Often the victim of such abnormal fears or phobias does not know why he is afraid, but the fear habit is so intrenched that understanding is unable to eradicate it. The original conditioning event may be forgotten while the fear lives on to torment the victim in the most harmless of situations. A teacher whom the writer once knew was afflicted by a phobia for cats. She could not bear to remain in any room if a cat was present. In her childhood she had been bitten and scratched by a cat. No reasoning concerning the harmlessness of a particular pet cat could remove that fear. She was unable to discriminate between a harmless pet and a vicious, clawing attack. She still reacted to the harmless concomitants of the original harrowing experience.

Overcoming fears. The method most frequently used by parents in attempting to relieve their children of fears is that of verbal assurance. In using it, an effort is made to convince the child that the situation is perfectly harmless and that there is no reason for being afraid. This procedure is not very effective if used alone. It may be of some help if the child has confidence in the one who is offering the explanation and if he sees that the latter is not afraid. Its use in connection with other procedures is recommended. A recognition of the unreasonableness of a fear, while a help in many cases, does not always enable one to overcome it. Also of little value are the practices of ridiculing or shaming the child, ignoring his fears, or forcing him to face or participate in the feared situation.

More effective than trying to talk a child out of his fear is an example of fearlessness. If the child sees that his parents, his teacher, or other children are not afraid, he will usually be able to face the situation more courageously. The fearless attitude of others is reassuring; it suggests that there is no real cause for alarm. Moreover, if he imitates their behavior, he may thereby acquire an adequate method of reacting to the situation.

A method which has been rather successful in overcoming fears in children is to present the feared object as a secondary part of a total situation that is pleasant. The procedure is to present the feared object first at a safe distance while the child is enjoying himself in some activity such as eating, and to bring it gradually nearer and nearer as the child becomes accustomed to facing it without emotional upset. Jones (1924) found that in this way children's fear reactions to rabbits or other small animals could be eliminated.

A study by Jersild and Holmes (1935) of methods used by parents in attempting to help their children eliminate fears indicated that the most successful procedures are: first, those which provide for the child opportunities for becoming acquainted with the fear situation by coming in contact with it frequently in his own normal activity; second, those which provide for contact with the fear stimulus first in a slight degree and then with gradually increasing intensity until it is encountered in its entirety; and third, those which help the child to develop skills which will enable him to cope successfully with the situation. A situation ceases to agitate and overwhelm an individual when he is able to make an adequate response to it. Repeated contacts with a situation without unpleasant consequences eliminates the element of strangeness, reveals the harmless character of the situation, and alters its meaning for the individual so that he no longer perceives it as threatening.

George, a boy of nine years, was afflicted with an acute fear of the water. He was an only child; his father was a physician, his mother a college graduate. His parents wanted to send him to a boys' camp, but believed he should learn to swim before going. The instructor of swimming to whom he was sent understood his fear problem and inquired into its origin. She learned that while at the beach, when he was three years old, two aunts of the boy took him into the water, where he was knocked down by a large wave and severely choked by the water. The unhappy incident had conditioned his fear.

The swimming lessons were given in a pool. The instructor spent the first half hour getting the boy to walk across the shallow end of the pool in the water. This required much patient coaxing and repeated assurances that nothing could harm him. As he timorously ventured to do it, he constantly clutched the edge of the pool. The boy did not want his instructor to go into the water with him. She surmised that he was afraid she would push or duck him, and was later convinced of this when the mother and one of the aunts came to watch the boy during one of his lessons. Impatient with the boy's hesitation, they both shouted, "Push him in!"

The lessons continued throughout the summer. He first became accustomed to the shallow water and learned to swim a few strokes. But after he learned to swim, he would not venture into the deeper water. The instructor then placed numbers at the side of the pool and urged him to work out to a farther number. This he tried, but all the time he clutched the gutter. He would not swim the length of the pool even with the aid of water wings or pole. He was afraid to jump into the water, but the instructor got him over that by having him first jump from the lowest rung of the ladder, then the second, and so on, until finally he had the courage to jump from the edge of the pool into the shallow water. But then he was still afraid to jump in where the water was deeper.

Finally on the day of the last lesson he did try jumping into the deeper water and enjoyed it. He kept on doing it past the hour for the lesson and asked the instructor if he couldn't do it some more. She told him he could if he would swim the length of the pool with the water wings. He did that, and then kept on jumping for a long time. The following summer he became a good swimmer and learned to do several kinds of diving.

In this case, we have a combined use of the various methods mentioned above. The instructor used verbal explanation and assurance, she set an example of fearlessness, she provided contact with the fear stimulus by gradually increasing degrees, she did not try to force him into the water, and she taught him a skill (swimming) for adequately coping with the deep water situation. As for the value of this treatment to the boy, if he had gone to camp with this fear, he probably would have been mercilessly teased and humiliated. What might have happened if he had fallen into the hands of a less sympathetic instructor who lacked the insight and skill of this teacher in dealing with his emotional difficulty? What if he had been pushed in as his mother and aunt advised?

ANGER

In the case of anger, as in fear, changes both in the source and in the behavior occur through experience. Most children engage in displays of anger more often than they manifest fear. This may be due to the fact that outbursts of anger are found useful for attracting attention and getting what they want, while fears are more often concealed. Boys usually display anger more often than girls, perhaps because boys are more successful in using it to gain their ends.

Changes in the causes of anger. The manifestations of anger in young children are associated with bodily restraint, interference with activities in progress, and frustrations of desires. Throughout life, the essential source of anger is some form of interference which retards the individual's advance toward his goal or frustration which blocks the way to successful achievement of his purposes. In the young child, the most frequent forms of interference are those which impede or prevent free bodily movement. Frustration appears in not being able to get some object of desire or in being prevented from continuing with some activity that has been started. To have his bottle removed unexpectedly before he has finished his feeding, to have a toy snatched away, and to be held when he wishes to retrieve the elusive ball are the kinds of situations which evoke in the youngster violent outbursts of temper.

As the child reaches the age of walking and becomes more active in manipulating things in his environment, the range of possible sources of interference and frustration rapidly increases. The mastery of language also opens new sources of irritation. At the age of six months, he will not be angered by taunting remarks or by having someone call him "names." At a later age, however, he will be quick to resent such insults. They interfere with his good thoughts of himself and conflict with his desire to command respect from others. In his play with other children, conflicts arise over playthings, and over the part to be taken in games. These developmental changes result from both maturation and learning.

As the child grows to maturity, the fundamental causes of anger are the same, though the situations differ. In general, the outbursts due to interference with physical activities decrease. During the period of adolescence, the sources of resentment and retaliation are most often encountered in social situations. For the adult, the causes of anger are often the same as those for children and adolescents; but if he is emotionally mature he does not so often become angry at inanimate objects that impede his progress, and the social situations that arouse his resentment and indignation are less often personal. He is aroused by social injustice, by brutal or criminal conduct toward defenseless persons, by exploitation of the weak, and by ruthless acts of aggression by nations. Deeds that violate his sense of decency and humanity, institutions that operate against national welfare, and practices that undermine law and order draw the fire of his anger.

In anger, as in fear, the provoking situations normally change as understanding develops. It is the meaning which the situation has for the individual that determines its effect on him, and meanings change with intellectual growth. However, emotional outbursts are subject to habit, and we often find irrational childish reactions persisting through adolescence and into adult life because they have become the habitual way of responding to certain situations. Again, under great stress, fatigue, or sometimes through the accumulative effect of many minor irritating circumstances, a person may become angry over something which under normal conditions would not arouse his ire. It also happens sometimes that a person harbors a resentment toward another who is merely associated with something which blocks the way to his goal. A jilted lover, for example, may feel resentment toward the girl's parents, who had nothing to do with her change of attitude toward him.

Changes in the overt behavior of anger. The infant's reactions to restraint are explosive and diffuse in character, poorly suited to eliminate the cause of his annoyance. Through early childhood his behavior becomes less random and more and more directed toward the thing which arouses his anger. He is likely to resort to various forms of attack, such as biting, slapping, striking, or scratching other children who interfere with his activity. If these forms of behavior are unsuccessful or are promptly squelched by elders or other children, they will soon be abandoned. If through these means the child triumphs in his purposes to get what he wants when he wants it, they may become his habitual method of dealing with interference. If they do not work, he may shift to other less aggressive forms of behavior such as screaming, throwing himself to the floor, holding his breath, pouting, or sulking. If by means of the temper tantrum or sulking he brings others to yield to his demands, these reactions are likely to become his stock methods for getting his own way.

Olson (1949) in reporting his observations reveals the wide range of vocal and motor behavior utilized by nursery school children in temper outbursts. The main vocal symptoms were crying, refusing, and screaming; but threatening, whimpering, whining plus several other kinds of vocalizing were reported. Motor behavior was primarily pushing or struggling, tensing the body, striking, refusing to move, kicking, stamping, and flight, which were only half the repertoire of responses. Whereas infant outbursts of anger are explosive reactions, by age four the anger is directed toward a frustrating object in half the instances.

Anger is displayed by children more often than fear because situations which are psychologically or physically restraining or frustrating increase tensions contributing to aggressive behavior. It should not be construed that all aggressive behavior is undesirable in either children or adults. The direct aggressive actions of young children which ensue from exploratory and energetic behavior are a source of popularity among their classmates, and it is in their direct expression that aggressive behavior becomes channelized into socially constructive activities. The distinction between aggressive and hostile feelings which are an unavoidable result of social living on one hand and aggressive behavior directed to destructive or injurious ends on the other is an important step in child development. Failure to accept anger and hostile feelings in children by shaming or censuring the feelings creates guilt feelings which find displacement in self-disparagement or in more aggressive acts. With young children, acceptance of feelings followed by redirecting or diversion of behavior produces greater success in developing positive controls of behavior than direct challenging of the aggressive behavior.

The temper tantrum is, unfortunately, so often successful that some individuals never give it up but go on using it as a means of forcing other persons to yield to their demands throughout life. It is normally a young child's way of reacting to interference and frustration. When it persists into adult life, it is considered an infantile reaction and an indication of emotional immaturity.

In the normal course of development, the child encounters difficulties in his use of the crude forms of attack and learns that these and the temper tantrums are not socially acceptable. As he grows older he usually drops these childish forms of reaction and relies more upon verbal attacks. At the age of adolescence, he may make use of epithets or sulking. The less aggressive person may withdraw from the situation and find solace in daydreams in which he pictures direful things happening to his antagonist.

The adult usually finds it expedient to restrain gross angry behavior. Resort to fist fighting between individuals is not considered respectable in most circles. Social custom dictates the legitimate manner in which insults and other annoying conduct may be redressed. The fighting of a duel was once the socially approved method of redeeming one's honor. Today, the approved methods of attack are speech-making, law suits, and, in war, bombing raids and gunfire. In one's social and business relationships, it is often necessary to conceal anger aroused by one's associates, and the emotionally mature adult is usually more skillful at doing this than a child. The individual tends to change his behavior in anger in the direction of social demands as he learns what society accepts and what it rejects.

Aggressive feelings may be released in several ways: verbally through joking, profanity, teasing, swearing, and criticizing; in fantasy by dreaming or imagining varied misfortunes happening to the thwarting person or object; through displacement by hurting or cruelty to a weaker person such as a younger brother or sister, or animal, which act may attain quite cruel and destructive proportions; in projection such as prejudice, which rids oneself of hostile feelings by attributing them to others; in delinquency and other anti-social acts; and in self-punishment. Some of the releases are more socially acceptable than others, but none are especially healthy for the individual even though they may intrude less upon the prerogatives and privileges of others.

OTHER EMOTIONS

There is a temptation to dwell on the negative aspects of children's behavior, particularly aggressive behavior because it interferes with classroom programs and disturbs other individuals. While an understanding of fear, anger, frustration, aggression, and conflict is essential, it is also important for the teacher to adopt a positive approach to children's emotions in order to foster healthy development. The satisfactory social climate of the classroom depends upon the teacher's ability to foster affectionate and pleasant interpersonal relationships. Fortunately, the positive affect of most children's groups and children far outstrips the negative. Sociometric studies reveal that choices between children usually exceed rejections by a 3 to 1 or 4 to 1 ratio, thus suggesting that teachers may be unduly concerned about "control" of children in assuming that children are innately uncontrolled, destructive, and aggressive. Fortunately, many teachers have discarded the notion that gloom and goodness go arm in arm or that a serious countenance is an essential condition of learning. Just as personality is modified through the control and channeling of negative responses to emotion, so does it develop through the nurturing of positive emotions such as happiness, love, affection, and sympathy.

The many other forms of emotional activity such as joy, love, surprise, mirth, and grief also go through developmental changes under the combined operation of maturation and learning. Joy usually comes from some signal success or the sudden fulfillment of a great desire. But with development from childhood to adulthood, the desires change and so does the character of the situations of success. The child is delighted with a new toy, the adult with a profitable business transaction or the securing of a professional honor.

The emotion designated "love" by Watson was aroused in the infant in his experiments by stimulating erogenous zones of the body. At least, it appears that in the infant, pleasure and happy states are the result of bodily stimulation. The young child's interests are primarily egocentric. His emotional attachment to his parents is probably conditioned by their association with the satisfactions of his physical wants. The gang stage just prior to adolescence shows the appearance of attachments to other persons outside the family circle. Such attachments are as a rule with members of the same sex. At this time boys like and associate with other boys but shun girls. In adolescence comes the turning to the opposite sex and the emergence of heterosexual interests and attachments. That biological factors of physiological growth, inwardly determined but stimulated from without, play a major role in this development is not to be doubted. Yet the conduct at these various stages is largely dependent upon learning in the form of becoming acquainted with the social norms and conventions and with the importance of conformity to them. In some parts of the world, the approved and generally practiced forms of courtship and love-making are quite different from those which are customary among American youth.

Regarding surprise, its change with experience can be seen in its rapid decline when the situation arousing it is repeated. The knowledge of the adult will cause him to be surprised at things which would not arouse that emotion in children, and likewise will cause him not to be surprised where a child would be. Also, with the growth of experience and understanding and with the establishment of attitudes, habits, and ideals, come changes in the situations which provoke mirth and grief and changes in the manner in which these are expressed in outward behavior.

OTHER AFFECTIVE PROCESSES

Pleasantness and unpleasantness. The emotions are characterized by strong feelings. But feelings of pleasantness and unpleasantness are experienced in many situations which do not upset one to the extent of an emotion. Some stimuli such as sweet tastes, fragrant odors, harmonious sounds, and mild warmth are conducive to pleasantness without previous conditioning. Other stimuli are naturally unpleasant; a bitter taste, a painful burn, and foul odors are most likely to be unpleasant quite apart from any previous experience.

Many stimuli are pleasant because they satisfy a need or a desire. When one is very hungry, it is pleasant to eat good food. It is pleasant to escape from danger, to be relieved from pain, to secure the new toy, and to achieve success. It is not by learning that one finds pleasure in obtaining the object of one's desire. But many desires are acquired through learning. The stamp collector's desire for a certain rare stamp to complete a series of which he is very proud, for example, can hardly be considered a natural desire. A desire for a copy of a new novel may be the outgrowth of reading a previous work by the same author. The desire to spend a week at the seashore may have been aroused by a friend's description of the good times to be had there, or by the memories of the pleasant vacation spent there last summer. Unpleasant feelings are aroused by the frustration of desire or by obstacles which impede our progress in obtaining what we want. Insofar, then, as learning contributes to the development of our needs and desires, it serves to open up new sources of pleasant and unpleasant feelings. We also acquire, through experience and conditioning, various attitudes toward objects and persons which make them capable of arousing pleasant or unpleasant feelings. Likes, dislikes, interests, and sentiments are examples of such attitudes.

Moods. Moods are affective experiences which last longer and are less intense than emotions. Many of our moods are related in quality to certain forms of emotional upsets. For example, the irritable mood is related to the emotion of anger; the timorous mood, to fear; a cheerful or jovial mood, to joy; and sadness, to grief. This relationship of the mood to the corresponding emotion makes either a likely source of the other. First, the mood may be a lingering aftereffect of the emotion. Thus, an encounter which causes an outburst of anger may leave an individual in an irritable mood and his associates may find him testy. A fright may be followed by a timorous mood, while a joyful experience leaves the individual in a happy mood. In the second place, a mood makes a person more sensitive than usual to emotional stimuli and inclines him toward a particular form of emotional reaction. The person in an irritable mood is angered at the slightest provocation; the timorous mood disposes one toward fear; and a cheerful mood easily passes to a joyful emotion.

Can the moods be trained? An unqualified affirmation that they can be would hardly be justified, because the moods are largely the reflection of one's physical condition. Buoyant health is conducive to pleasant moods. Discouragement and depressed moods are frequently connected with faulty elimination or ill health. Much can be done to avoid these depressions by safeguarding the physical health, and the correction of an ailment helps to give the world a brighter hue.

Since moods are frequently the result of emotional upsets, the development of a more stabilized emotional life helps to reduce the incidence of moods. The adolescent, at a stage in life marked by instability resulting from physical changes and psychological tensions. is particularly subject to moody spells, while the well-adjusted adult, being less often stirred up emotionally, is not so frequently the victim of moods.

While no claim is made that unpleasant moods can be wholly avoided by training, there are some things that one can do to avoid or break them up. The cultivation of a "calm frame of mind," looking for "the silver lining of the cloud" or at "the doughnut instead of the hole," and an honest effort to see the offender's point of view will help to prevent discouragement and lingering resentments. If a person finds himself in a mood of depression, he should, if he wants to throw it off, trace back through the day's experience to discover its source. He may find it in a remark of a friend which hurt or in the annoying conduct of some pupil in the classroom. An intelligent analysis of the situation will probably reveal that ordinarily such an incident would not cause this unhappy state and that fatigue, a cold, indigestion, constipation, or some other physical condition is responsible for the fact that a comparatively trivial incident left a feeling of depression or an ugly mood in its wake. An honest effort to divorce the incident from one's feelings and steps to remove the physical indisposition will do much to restore a state of equanimity.

THE EMOTIONS AND MENTAL HEALTH

Mental health is dependent upon good emotional habits. The various forms of mental ill health are characterized largely by faulty emotional reactions. Neurasthenia is one of the milder forms of mental disorder. Its outstanding symptom is fatigue brought about by emotional difficulties which the victim has been unable to resolve. Psychasthenia is identified by bad mental habits of which worry and phobias are examples. Hysteria is marked by inappropriate and excessive emotional outbursts. In schizophrenia, the emotional reactions are out of harmony with the patient's behavior and intellectual processes. Manic-depressive psychosis is primarily a disorder of emotional extremes. The foundation of mental ill health is often laid in faulty emotional habits acquired in childhood.

Today the school is recognizing and accepting its responsibility for safeguarding the mental health of the pupils. The concern of educators is with the welfare of the whole personality of the individual child. This means that not only his intellect but his social and emotional reactions must be educated. A wholesome personality is one that is well integrated. In the integrated personality the emotions, intellectual processes, and actions are coördinated so that they work together harmoniously for a happy adjustment to one's environment and for efficient intercourse with it.

In the interest of mental health, a child must learn to face reality and to make the best possible adjustment to it. Some common sources of emotional maladjustment in the school situation are: sensory defects and physical handicaps; an appearance that singles the child out from the others, such as being red-headed, fat, unusually tall, or very short; inability to do the work assigned and failure; sarcastic remarks by the teacher; and unwise handling of disciplinary problems.

The teacher should be guided by the mental hygiene point of view. She should have constantly in mind the effect of her teaching on the emotional life of her pupils. She should seek to avoid those episodes which produce emotional conflict and to help the maladjusted child solve his emotional problem.

For the sake of mental health, special opportunities should be provided for handicapped children. This will usually call for individual attention. Merely putting such children together in a special class will not be sufficient. The fact of being placed in a special class may be, and often is, the source of further emotional difficulties. Some children become resentful, others are humiliated and made to feel inferior by being segregated in a group they know has failed to keep up with the average. The handicapped child should not be placed in a competitive situation where he is certain to fail because of his handicap.

Academic work should be suited to the abilities of the children at each age level. To prevent needless failure and its devastating consequences, the work must be kept down to the child's mastery level. Realization of the importance of this matter has given rise to a tendency to postpone some subjects of instruction to later years. For example, it has been found better to present long division in the fifth grade than in the fourth.

Disciplinary measures which crush a child's spontaneity and initiative are not to be tolerated. A good disciplinarian does not seek docility and timid conformity but endeavors to train the child so that he finds satisfaction in harmonious coöperation with others rather than in creating disturbances. A child does not throw a temper tantrum because he cannot push over a brick wall or keep the milkman's horse. He may do so in the ten-cent store when his mother refuses to buy him a toy that he wants if he has learned from previous experience that he can make his mother yield by making a scene. In the former case, he has learned that he cannot do those things. In the latter, he has found that sometimes he can get his way if he makes a big enough fuss. Good discipline is consistent. It lets the child understand what he can and what he cannot do. Inconsistency and vacillation in disciplinary matters creates uncertainty, tensions, and conflicts, and encourages attempts to overcome the opposition of authority.

A well-planned activity program in which children work together in fairly small groups or committees, each contributing according to his talents and ability, each feeling that he belongs, each doing his work because of a real interest in the undertaking, and each receiving due recognition for his efforts, is a type of educational procedure which promotes mental health.

THE EMOTIONALLY WELL-EDUCATED ADULT

Throughout this chapter we have attempted to show how emotional reactions are modified and developed — in a word, learned. It has also been our purpose to point out the need for training in the emotional life and to suggest the direction which such training should take. The description of an emotionally well-educated adult sets objectives toward which we may strive in the development of emotional maturity and stability both in ourselves and in the children and students who come under our direction. Fundamentally, these objectives fall in three categories: relationships with self, with others, and with the world.

Essential in our feelings about ourself is a sense of being worthy and thinking ourselves good. We accept ourselves and our bodies and can gratify our physical needs adequately. We are consistent within ourselves and realistic in self-evaluation: we know our assets and liabilities and our strengths and weaknesses, and have knowledge of what motivates us and what mechanisms we resort to to maintain psychological comfort. In short, we are internally consistent, neither torn by conflict nor duped by self-deception. In our relationships with others we are able to give and receive affection, to share others' emotions, to express our own feelings with vigor and spontaneity, to be loyal to friends and tolerant of people without sacrificing integrity, to accept and understand social customs and restrain our behavior accordingly, to be responsible to ourself and others, remaining at the same time, sufficiently independent of group opinion and judgment to have some degree of originality and uniqueness.

In our view of the world and our place within it, we have to establish goals which are attainable, seen as socially acceptable, and toward which we can strive with some persistence. We must be able to learn from experience and to design and adapt our plans and procedures to the realities which surround us.

SUMMARY

Properly developed emotional reactions are essential to mental health, happiness, social adjustment, and a wholesome personality. Emotional activities are complex functions which involve visceral and skeletal behavior and emotional experience. An emotion starts with perception of a predicamental situation and runs its course through the affective seizure, efforts to resolve the difficulty, and a gradual recovery from the disturbance. In violent emotions, the individual is frequently unable to react in an adequate manner, but sometimes a well-fixed action trend withstands the shock and the action is carried out with unusual promptness and energy. The secret of avoiding the devastating effects of panic is to have an adequate form of response prepared before the emergency arises.

The complex emotional activity we observe in children and adults develops from a set of reactions in infants which reflect not clearly differentiated emotions but a state of excitement. Outward behavior is not a reliable indication of the character of the emotion. We judge one's emotions largely by what we know of the provoking situation.

As one grows from infancy to maturity, his fears change. The child acquires new fears through conditioning and from threats, suggestions, and imitation. The development of understanding causes the elimination of some fears and the appearance of new ones. Sometimes childhood fears persist into adult life. Some fears of children are traceable to unfortunate remarks and unwise methods of the teacher. The child tends to disguise and conceal his fears as he grows older. The teacher should avoid practices which instill fear, and assist the child in overcoming persistent fears. Effective methods for overcoming fears are verbal assurance coupled with an example of courage, the introduction of a fear object by degrees in a pleasant situation, and the development of adequate responses for coping with the situation which arouses fear.

Anger is caused by interference and frustration. The situations in which these appear change with growth in experience. Under social pressures, the behavior in anger tends to become more restrained. The other emotions are also modified through learning.

Mental health depends largely upon good emotional habits. Special opportunities should be provided for handicapped children, school-work should be suited to the child's ability, and discipline should be consistent. The child should learn to face his emotional problems realistically. Such escapes as running away, daydreaming, and rationalization should not be allowed to become habitual methods of reacting to difficulties; they do not solve the problems and sometimes lead to further troubles. A direct attack upon the source of the difficulty is usually the best way to resolve an emotional conflict, but in the case of unsurmountable obstacles, a shift in aims is desirable. Misconduct is often compensatory behavior produced by frustration.

The emotionally well-educated adult possesses stable and mature emotional habits which are in harmony with his intellect, coördinated with his behavior, and in accord with the happiness and welfare of other persons.

OVERVIEW

Goodenough, Florence, "Child Development, XIV. Emotions," *Encyclopedia of Educational Research,* W. S. Monroe, ed. New York: Macmillan Co., 1950, pp. 187-89.

SELECTED REFERENCES

Bridges, K. M. B., *Social and Emotional Development of the Preschool Child.* London: Kegan Paul, 1931.
English, O. S. and G. H. J. Pearson, *Emotional Problems of Living.* New York: Norton, 1945.
Jersild, A. R., "Emotional Development," *Manual of Child Psychology,* L. Carmichael, ed. New York: Wiley, 1954, pp. 833-917.
Prescott, D. A., *Emotion and the Educative Process.* Washington: American Council on Education, 1939.
Redl, F. and D. Wineman, *Children Who Hate.* Glencoe: Free Press, 1951.

ORIGINAL INVESTIGATIONS

Jersild, A. T. and F. B. Holmes, "Children's Fears," *Child Development Monograph,* 1935, No. 20.

Jersild, A. T. and F. B. Holmes, "Methods of Overcoming Children's Fears," *Journal of Psychology,* 1, pp. 75-104.

Keister, M. E. and R. Updegraff, "A Study of Children's Reactions to Failure, and an Experimental Attempt to Modify Them," *Child Development Monograph,* 8, pp. 241-48.

Chapter Sixteen

The Development of Attitudes and Ideals

Among the various tendencies and predispositions which are acquired and modified by learning, none is more important to individual and social welfare than attitudes and ideals. These determiners of activity are important because of the broad scope of their potent influence. They extend beyond the range of habit and they govern the use of knowledge. Their development is more difficult to manage and to appraise than is the development of skills and knowledge, but it is equally essential for the full and wholesome education of the individual.

ATTITUDES

There are many different connotations of the term *attitude* as it is used in the literature on the subject. It is used to mean almost any form of set from organic urge, bodily posture, or habit to purposes and ideals. This loose and varied use of the term simply means that a common definition or conception has not been universally adopted. G. W. Allport (1935), after sifting many definitions of *attitude,* finds certain points of resemblance from which he presents the following statement, "An attitude is a mental and neural state of readiness, organized through experience, exerting a directive or dynamic influence upon the individual's response to all objects and situations with which it is related." A state of readiness for certain forms of response is what we have called *set.* There are several different kinds of readiness or set: organic needs, social motives, habits, attitudes, and ideals.

Attitudes are like habits in being states of readiness without conscious purpose or intent. But they differ from habits in the wider scope of their control. The effective range of habit is limited to a relatively specific or particular form of response, while attitude is a directive set which may operate in widely differing situations and which promotes various forms of behavior. By attitudes we mean relatively generalized determiners of activity.

It will be readily seen that attitudes exert a directive influence on the manner in which one responds to a great variety of situations. The way one thinks, feels, and acts is determined largely by the dominant attitude at the moment. A person who has a strongly developed scientific attitude, for example, finds satisfaction in scientific research although the collection and testing of data may take many different forms. He thinks in terms of cause-and-effect relations, and is desirous of discovering the explanation of various phenomena and the influence of certain conditions. He is annoyed by violations of scientific procedures in the collecting and interpretation of data.

A boy who has a well-generalized coöperative attitude will be quick to notice situations calling for coöperation with others and will derive satisfaction from being coöperative. At camp he will cheerfully gather firewood, peel potatoes, carry water, or help pitch the tent. At home he will clean the mud off his shoes before entering the house, shovel the snow off the walk, help wash the family car, assist in taking care of the furnace, move about quietly when others are sleeping, and keep his room orderly. At school he will take part in the extracurricular activities and obey regulations. If this attitude is only partially developed, the boy may be coöperative in some of these situations and not in others.

The situational range of an attitude is frequently more restricted than it is in the cases just mentioned. One may have an attitude, for example, which operates only with respect to a particular object, or person, or even with respect to some trait of a particular person, such as a dislike for his profane language or unitdy appearance. But even here, there is a flexibility or variability of response not found in habit. If such flexibility is not characteristic of the predisposition, then it is a habit according to the distinctions we have made here.

Attitudes and personality. An individual's personality includes his attitudes, but it also includes traits. The distinction between traits and attitudes is not always clear-cut, but in general the attitude involves a fairly definite reference to things or ideas and usually is a disposition to react favorably to or against the object of reference. Traits have less definite reference and have more to do with one's manner of adjusting himself to widely differing situations. G. W. Allport makes the distinction as follows: "A trait, in short, is a man's personal and unique manner of responding to the myriad circumstances of life; it has very little reference to objects, for innumerable objects will arouse it. An individual's point of view toward war, liquor, the church, or capital punishment are clearly attitudes and not traits; but his talkative, shy, or emphatic *manner* of behaving are traits. The former are clearly less intimate and less personal than the latter."

Attitudes and social life. The object of reference in attitudes is not always social, but there are so many attitudes which refer to other persons and social issues that the character of an individual's social life is to a large extent identified with the type of attitudes which have been established in him. Therefore, the social education of the child calls for the engendering of desirable social attitudes and the elimination of undesirable ones. Friendly, coöperative, and judicial attitudes are to be fostered, as also are loyalty to school, home, church, and the government. Racial prejudices, born of ignorance and stereotyped modes of thinking, beget hatreds, unhappiness, and injustice. They should be prevented from growing, and be eliminated so far as possible. Other attitudes which are incompatible with social harmony and welfare are hostility to authority, class antagonisms, religious prejudices, and "the world owes me a living."

We are living in a world of rapidly changing social conditions. Old procedures and old solutions are inadequate to cope with the new problems which the changing order presents. The younger generation cannot be prepared to face the future demands to be made upon it by our developing in them fixed patterns of response based on past or present conditions. Our young people must be trained to make readjustments and adaptations while holding fast to the fundamental principles of democracy which we cherish. The problems of government, finance, industry, and international relations will be a challenge to their versatility and resourcefulness. Changes will inevitably come, and there must be a readiness to adjust to them. If social change is not to outrun our democratic processes, the school must instill in the young certain democratic attitudes and ideals. These, if developed, may be expected to direct creative effort along the lines of a democratic order.

Reports of studies made of the attitudes of school pupils indicate that our schools have not been particularly successful in instilling democratic attitudes. The findings indicate that a large proportion of the young people are possessed of prejudices and views which are not in keeping with democratic principles. For example, H. E. Jones (1938) found that 62 per cent of the first-year pupils of a favorably situated high school expressed a dislike for all radicals, 65 per cent agreed that foreign radicals should not be allowed to visit the United States, 71 per cent would not allow radical agitators to speak publicly in parks and streets, and 24 per cent supported the statement that armies are necessary in dealing with backward peoples.

Democracy cannot prosper in a nation whose people are heavily loaded with religious and racial prejudices and class hatreds and antagonisms. Education for democratic citizenship calls for the prevention and removal of such inimical attitudes and the establishment of such favorable ones as:

1. Belief in the "inalienable rights" of the individual
2. Acceptance of the principle of equality of privilege
3. Tolerance of the views of others and a willingness to allow these views to be expressed

4. Respect for the individuality of other persons
5. A willingness to accept social responsibilities
6. A willingness to abide by the decisions of the majority
7. A willingness to arbitrate conflicts of interests

STUDIES OF ATTITUDES OF CHILDREN AND STUDENTS

Many studies have been made to determine the nature of the attitudes of children and students. These studies have dealt with a large variety of subjects, such as racial preferences, views on various social issues, preferences for school subjects, and attitudes toward God and the church. No attempt is made here to summarize all this literature. A few studies are mentioned briefly for the purpose of illustrating the character of the work done in this field.

Racial preferences and prejudices. Beckham (1934), in a study of a large number of Negro adolescents, found that by the age of twelve most of them had experienced some form of unfavorable discrimination or humiliation because of their race. The effects most often produced were resentment, aloofness, antagonism, and in some cases a strong desire for personal achievement. A majority thought white teachers were usually fair, but a number complained that teachers showed discrimination in favor of white children in grades, positions of leadership, seating, sympathy, derogatory remarks about Negroes, and in discouraging the Negro pupils from taking part in extracurricular activities.

A study of the racial prejudices of college students by Katz and Braly (1935) showed the Americans and English to be the most favored groups. Next in order of preference came the Germans and Irish. Below these came Italians and Jews, while the Chinese, Negroes, and Turks were assigned to the least favored positions. The conclusions of this study, which are in general agreement with those of a number of other investigators, are that racial prejudice "is a generalized set of stereotypes of a high degree of consistency which includes emotional responses to race names, a belief in typical characteristics associated with race names and an evaluation of typical traits."

In a comparison of racial preferences of colored and white children in St. Louis, Meltzer (1939) found that the Negro was ranked first by the colored children and twentieth by the whites. The Japanese, Mexicans, South Americans, and Chinese were more favored by the Negro children than by the whites, while the Germans, Poles, Swedes, Jews, Scotchmen, and Greeks were less favored by the Negroes.

By means of personal interviews, a study was made of racial prejudice as it applied to 162 Italian-Americans. Fifty-seven per cent of this group stated that they had been subjected to some form of prejudicial discrimination because of their nationality. Practically all of these had experienced discrimination before the end of the period of adolescence. The children and adolescents seemed to be more distressed by the alleged discriminatory treatment than their elders. The most frequent emotional responses to such treatment were said to be anger, resentment, and hate (Kingsley and Carbone, 1938).

In general, it can be said that adolescents are inclined to have rather strong racial prejudices and that the effect of such attitudes is ill feeling, the withdrawal to itself of each racial group, the termination of social contacts, and the development of a persistent antagonism. The mingling of pupils of the various race and nationality groups in the classes and in the extracurricular activities of the public schools should do much to prevent or overcome these unwarranted antagonisms, provided, of course, that the teacher sets an example of just behavior.

Zeligs (1950, 1951) has completed several investigations of intergroup attitudes among elementary school children; these provide information regarding the prejudices and attitudes of children, and have the advantage of being comparisons of similar groups of children at a thirteen-year interval. In comparing the attitudes of sixth grade children in the same school in a midwestern community towards Irish, Finnish, several middle-European, Hindu, and Filipino groups, Zeligs found a negligible change in 13 years in the proportions of favorable and unfavorable attitudes, but a slight increase in neutral attitudes, possibly because of lack of familiarity with some of the groups mentioned. Granting the limitations inherent in attitude measurement, which aside from the technical problems assumes a close relationship between verbal response and actual behavior, the author concluded that education aimed at creating favorable intercultural attitudes left much to be desired. When asked reasons for preferences and rejections of various nationality groups listed, a series of characteristics stressing cultural similarities and differences, stereotypes with respect to intelligence, honesty, fairplay, and the like were given. In the thirteen-year period, the reasons reported reflected a shift from racial and physical characteristics to form of government and kind of leader as a basis for preference. The fact that the follow-up study occurred during the war years leads one to believe that the shift reflects wartime allegiances and attitudes. But attitudes and prejudices are in part built upon group-held norms and are not dependent upon actual experience with the discriminated group.

Prejudices against minority groups (Radke and Sutherland, 1949) are observed developing in significant proportion at about the third-grade level and showing a steady rise through the high-school years independently of any actual contact or experience with the out-group. When Zeligs (1950) asked a group of 80 twelve-year-olds to write anonymous compositions as to the nationality they would choose to be if they could not be Americans and their reasons for so choosing, nearly two-thirds selected English as either first or second choice, and two-fifths selected Russian as first or second choice, citing the similarity of English and American cultures and the bravery, loyalty, and honesty of the Russians.

Although the postwar years saw the attempt in certain quarters to attribute the prior existence of such attitudes to the subversive influence of teachers, the change in the climate of opinion really reflects a radical shift of group norms and its influence upon views expressed by members of the group. Certainly a repetition of the same question today would produce markedly different answers. This is not a reflection on the instability of attitudes as such but instead of the importance of group membership and attendant group values upon individual attitudes, particularly where the lack of direct experience prevents any other anchoring point for opinions. Chyatte, Schaefer, and Spiaggia (1951), interviewing samples of northern and southern children with respect to anti-Negro and anti-Jewish prejudices, reported that the more favorable attitudes were associated with higher educational levels rather than with economic differences.

Subject and reading preferences. The results of a questionnaire study made by Blair (1939) of the subject preferences of 1,463 students in a senior high school indicated that the subject most preferred by mentally superior boys — those with IQ above 113 — was mathematics. For inferior boys — those with IQ below 95 — shop was the most liked subject. The preference of the superior girls was English, while the favorite of the inferior girls was home economics.

From the findings of Rothney and McCaul (1938) in an investigation of the free reading choices of high-school boys, it appeared that the teaching of literature had not established a liking for the types of reading material used in the English courses. The boys in the study preferred newspapers and magazines to books. The magazines they liked best were the comic, scientific, news, and boys' publications. Others for which a preference was indicated included those devoted to popular fiction, the radio, movies, and detective stories. The most favored books were the ones which contained stories of adventure, the sea, and mysteries, and those which dealt with sports and vocations. Suggested reasons for this "poor taste" in reading matter were: the poor choice of selections studied in English courses, the disregard of the pupils' current interests, and poor teaching.

Various studies have shown that the reading interests of boys and girls differ somewhat both in childhood and in the adolescent period. Boys, for example, in the elementary school years are likely to be most interested in reading about war, athletics, and adventure, while girls like fairy tales and stories dealing with home or school life. Girls become interested in romantic novels earlier than boys. In adolescence they favor love stories and reading that deals with travel and home life. Boys of the adolescent age generally prefer such subjects as sports, outdoor life, adventure, inventions, and machinery.

As far as attitude toward school is concerned, Tenenbaum (1944) reports that 20 per cent of 639 sixth and seventh grade New York City school pupils were dissatisfied with school and 40 per cent were critical of many phases. Girls reflected more favorable attitudes than boys. Fortunately for teachers, the negative feelings were directed against the school as an institution rather than against the teacher as a person, which confirms findings of the author. Perhaps it is premature to say, "fortunately for teachers," for the possibility is real that children are reluctant and fearful of directing their criticism against an authority figure and substitute the school as a safer target. In general, however, the concept of going to school is the one that is established rather than going to a teacher, so that the attitude is more likely to be generalized.

Religious attitudes. The results of an investigation of students' attitudes toward God and church at three large universities and three denominational colleges indicated that few students were inclined to be atheistic. There appeared to be no important differences between the attitudes of the two sexes and little change in religious attitudes during the four years in college. The attitudes of the students in the denominational colleges were somewhat more favorable than those of university students.

By means of a questionnaire, Dudycha (1933) obtained an expression of religious beliefs from 852 college freshmen at the beginning of their first year in college and from 305 college seniors just before graduation. Each student was asked to indicate the nature and extent of his belief for each of 25 propositions concerning matters of religion. The freshmen showed a somewhat greater tendency toward wholehearted belief than did the seniors, but the majority of the latter indicated that they still believed most of the fundamental doctrines. Belief in the existence of God was expressed by 96 per cent of the freshmen and by 93 per cent of the seniors. There were more disbelievers than believers among the seniors only in the propositions pertaining to the existence of hell, angels, the devil, present-day miracles, and the creation of the world in six solar days.

Social and economic questions. Young adolescents are generally rather conservative with respect to sociological matters, and the tendency is for them to become more liberal with increase in knowledge and personal experience with the issues. A number of studies have thrown light on the attitudes of youths relative to social and economic problems. In regard to such issues as prohibition and communism, adolescent attitudes differ to about the same extent as those of adults and probably reflect the opinions and feelings of the older persons with whom these young people are associated.

War. During the years before World War II, a large number of studies were made of the attitudes of high-school and college students toward war. In practically all of these where definite scores were obtained by means of attitude scales, the mean scores for both men and women fell in the divisions labeled "mildly pacifistic," "strongly pacifistic," or "moderately opposed to war." The women usually were found to be slightly more pacifistic than the men. In a number of cases, the same students were retested later in their course to discover whether there were shifts in their attitudes. There were shifts in some cases by some individuals toward greater pacifism; these were offset by shifts of others in the opposite direction, leaving the mean score of the group about the same (Dudycha, 1942). But several retest studies indicated a small but definite shift toward greater pacifism (Corey, 1940; Farnsworth, 1937; Jones, 1938, 1942).

With the outbreak of war in Europe, there was some indication of a shift away from the pacifistic attitude. Then came the Pearl Harbor attack and our entry into the war in full force. Students who had been taught by the school, the church, the radio, the movies, and the press to regard war as a horrible thing and futile as a means of settling disputes between nations — students who had acquired from their teachers, parents, and pastors attitudes which set them against war — were suddenly told that they must become soldiers, fighters, and killers because arbitration and conciliation had failed. The result was confusion, doubt, and disillusionment. The emotional shock to many was great.

It was not easy to embark on a course absolutely opposed to one's deep-seated feelings and convictions. But social pressure and law made it practically impossible to do otherwise. High-pressure propaganda, fear of consequences if the war were not won, and war hysteria did much to make over the feelings and opinions of many. Others, not being able to escape from years of training, entered upon their duties with resentment against war but sustained by an urgent desire to get the "dirty mess" over as soon as possible, a faith in the possibility of an enduring peace, and confidence in their ability to manage in the future the affairs of the nation more successfully than their elders had done it.

HOW ATTITUDES ARE ACQUIRED

Attitudes spring from a number of sources. Some of these are to be found in the classroom, but many are outside of it. Since preparation for good citizenship calls for the establishment of the appropriate generalized controls of behavior as well as understanding, it is the responsibility of every teacher to contribute to some extent to the development of wholesome attitudes.

The school is certain to affect pupil attitudes. We should try to make that influence count in the right direction. This means that the development of attitudes and ideals cannot be left out of the teacher's aims and plans. Their development should be cultivated by design, not left to the hazards of growth as incidental by-products of classroom instruction. It is believed that long after the factual material of instruction is forgotten, the attitudes acquired through classroom experiences may continue as potent factors in the life and behavior of the individual. The teacher should be sensitive to the attitudes possessed by his pupils, should know the ones required for good citizenship and individual happiness, and should strive to eliminate wrong ones and to engender the desirable ones. We mention here some of the ways in which new attitudes arise.

1. Imitation. In many cases, a person simply adopts attitudes of his associates. In the case of young children, particularly, this is likely to occur without any definite awareness of the attitude and without realization that it is being assumed. This is often the case with certain religious attitudes which a child takes on in early years through home influences. It may be true also of racial or class prejudices, political attitudes, and preferences for certain types of food or music. The adolescent is inclined to conform to his group. He notices their prejudices, likes, and dislikes and copies them in order to be like the others. Adults also frequently take on uncritically the attitudes of the group to which they belong.

2. Emotional experiences. Attitudes — particularly likes and dislikes, attractions and aversions, interests and antagonisms — are often traceable to some strong emotional experience or to incidents or associations of a definitely pleasant or unpleasant nature. Humiliating or unjust treatment may set up in a child a resentful attitude toward the parents or toward the teacher from whom it was received. A timid attitude may result from a series of frights. An appreciative attitude toward good reading matter is most likely to be developed in the child who enjoys his literature class. So strong is the tendency for one to assume a favorable or unfavorable attitude toward persons or things associated with a pleasant or unpleasant experience that the process through which such attitudes are established appears to be a form of conditioning.

A teacher writes, "As a child, I spent a summer vacation with an aunt who had no children and, I suppose, didn't know what to expect of a child of my age. She believed that every girl must be a good seamstress. I had done very simple sewing before, more in the way of play than anything else, but she gave me things to do that really were too difficult for any child of my age. Naturally, I had a very hard time trying to do what she told me to do, to say nothing about sticking the needle into myself often. Invariably, what I did turned out badly and I was reprimanded severely for it each time. The effect of that has always stayed with me. Even to this day, I hate sewing and never do any unless it is absolutely necessary. That one summer's experience destroyed any desire on my part to sew, although I had previously enjoyed making dolls' clothes, even though they were not great successes. Another and far more serious effect was that I took a dislike to that aunt and never wanted to visit there again."

Falling in love with a person at first sight may be due to some trivial association wholly unworthy of the grave results it produces. If a girl is very fond of her father and the father wears a mustache, she is likely to have a predilection for young men who wear mustaches. If a few college boys behave badly on the streets, their actions turn the townspeople against the whole student body. If an actress plays the part of a despicable character, there is danger that the audience will not appreciate her superb performance in their disgust for the character she portrays. If the child has a bad time with his arithmetic, he tends to dislike the teacher, or if some disciplinary action by the teacher arouses his resentment, he may dislike not only the teacher but also the teacher's subject. It has been found that the subjects which high-school students say they like the best are the ones taught by the best-liked teachers (Corey and Beery, 1938).

3. **Informative experiences.** Attitudes are also built up by means of many different forms of experiences which add to one's fund of information or which change one's impressions. Such experiences include what we are told, what we see, and what we read. The information may be true, it may be a distortion of the truth, or it may be wholly false. It may affect our attitudes directly or by way of suggestion. It may be derived from a lecture, sermon, or conversation; from the radio, movies, newspapers, or magazines. When we learn that one whom we have regarded as a friend has been making derogatory remarks about us, our attitude becomes one of distrust. Gratitude changes to resentment when it is discovered that someone has done us a favor only to place us under obligation for his own selfish purposes. Reports of corrupt practices by politicians destroy the confidence of the public in its elected representatives. Rumors of wasteful expenditures by the government make for resentment against a mounting tax rate. Sneers at the incompetence of "brain trusters" give the general public the impression that all college

professors are visionary and incapable of thinking in practical or realistic terms. Malicious gossip destroys confidence and respect for one's neighbors. Accounts of the unprovoked invasion of a peaceful nation set us against the ruthless aggressor and arouse sympathy for the oppressed. Movies which play up the sordid aspects of war make us more pacifistic, while those which portray its glories or which picture it as a heroic crusade against aggression or a patriotic enterprise necessary for national survival incline us toward a militaristic position. Clever propaganda, true or false, is effective in turning a peaceful, war-hating nation into one eager to fight. Derogatory remarks by a teacher about other nationalities or races tend to beget racial prejudice and a false sense of superiority of one's own race. Thus, we are led to favor or to oppose, to sanction or to disapprove, to admire or to hate, according to the type of information which comes to us. For just attitudes, we must strive for the truth.

4. Deliberate cultivation. Attitudes may be deliberately cultivated. A person, for example, may cultivate in himself a friendly attitude toward his associates. The process is about the same as for the establishment of a habit. To build a new habit, one starts necessarily on the level of purposive action. To establish an attitude by design, one must practice the appropriate behavior in all the varied situations to which that attitude should apply. His purpose, being broad in scope, will be in the nature of an ideal. So, for the friendly attitude, he begins with an ideal of friendliness. By constantly being friendly with all his associates in all types of situations and through various kinds of friendly acts, he will reach the point where the general tendency to be friendly takes control and he does not each time have to think to be friendly or how to express his friendliness. If the individual is strongly prejudiced against a particular race and regards that attitude as undesirable, he can overcome it by making a practice of always treating members of that race in just as fair a manner as he treats those of his own race, making no unfair discrimination and granting to them the same privileges.

THE MODIFICATION OF ATTITUDES

Classroom instruction. There has been in recent years considerable interest in the possibility of changing and developing attitudes of children and students in the school situation and in the procedures by which this can be accomplished. In a study reported by Manske (1936) it was found that the pupils' attitude toward the Negro tended to become more liberal with ten non-indoctrination lessons about Negroes. The attitude of the teachers seemed to have little effect on the changes produced by the lessons.

That it is possible to shift attitudes of pupils in a desired direction by means of suitable instructional material has been shown by a number of studies. In one, for example, the attitudes toward certain rural social problems were modified in the desired direction through class discussion of specially prepared material dealing with the problems (McConnell, 1936). In another, the attitudes of high-school pupils toward social insurance, capital punishment, and labor unions were shifted in the direction desired and for which the instructional material was designed. As indicated by tests given before and after the instruction, the pupils became more favorably disposed toward social insurance and capital punishment, and less favorable toward labor unions (Bateman and Remmers, 1936). In a study of the superstitious beliefs of junior-high-school pupils and the effect on these beliefs of a course in general science, it was found that the regular science work had little effect in reducing them, but that special instruction designed for that purpose did decrease superstititon (Zapf, 1938). It has been shown that musical interest may be increased by suitable musical training. The measurement of the attitudes of a group of college students toward the treatment of criminals before and after taking a course in criminology showed a small shift away from punishment of criminals and respect for law and a shift in the direction of capital punishment (Smith, 1937).

Teachers can and should direct their efforts toward attitude development as well as academic growth. It is unavoidable that attitudes and opinions will develop in children; it is better that their direction be favorable. Mead (1951) suggests three learning levels which teachers should consider: the concepts and understandings, the emotional responses, and the behavioral patterns. He illustrates possible approaches with specific suggestions such as integrating textbook, classroom, and community experiences to provide experiences which develop meanings and favorable affective responses, planned voluntary personal associations with minority members, vicarious experiences through sociodrama, and others. Not to be overlooked is the fact that the satisfactions and frustrations of children in school are likely to be related to their behavior and attitude toward other groups. Children who are thwarted by having unmet needs are more likely to seek a safe target against whom they can release their hostile and aggressive feelings resulting from their frustration. Minority and religious groups represent safer targets than authority figures. Park (1951) found a decrease in prejudiced attitudes among fourth, fifth, and sixth grade pupils when their teachers made efforts to meet the children's needs for affection, belonging, achievement, and freedom from fear.

College. An extensive investigation of attitudes of college students toward war, the Negro, religion, and the church has been carried out by Jones (1938). His work included retesting to discover changes in the attitudes during the four years in college. He found that both freshmen and seniors were, generally speaking, neither strongly conservative nor strongly radical. The differences between the freshmen and the seniors were small. From a position of moderate liberalism in the freshman year, there was a tendency to become somewhat more liberal with advancement to the upper class levels. A very small correlation was found between intelligence and liberalism. Among the seniors, the majors in natural science appeared to be the most liberal while history and geography majors were the most conservative, although the differences were not large. Among the political groups represented, the Communists were the most liberal; of the religious groups, the Jews were the most liberal. The groups which were most liberal at the beginning of their college course showed less change in the direction of greater liberalism than did the ones which were more conservative at the freshman level. The tests indicated that the students were not conservative or liberal in the same degree in the various fields, and that a change in one area does not necessarily mean a corresponding change in general or with respect to the other fields studied. The author of this study points out that specificity and generality are matters of degree and that, in training for attitudes, we cannot assume that if we secure improvement in one area there will be a general spread to all areas of experience. To secure generality in attitudes, training must be directed toward generalization.

While there is ample evidence that the attitudes of students do change during their college life, it appears that attitudinal objectives have not in most cases been clearly formulated. Catalogues of colleges have been found to mention most often religious and spiritual objectives. One study revealed that only about half specified intellectual excellence, while good citizenship was mentioned by less than a third (Nelson, 1937).

Home and community influences. Many factors of home and community life serve to shape the attitudes of children and young people. Measured results have shown that motion pictures are sometimes effective in bringing about significant changes in attitude toward the subject of the pictures (Peterson and Thurstone, 1933). The prestige of the majority is a potent influence. In one study it was found that after a presidential election, more students indicated a preference for the winning party than before the election (Whisler and Remmers, 1937). An investigation by Breslaw of the factors determining political attitudes led to the conclusion that the most important influences were those of the home and of the individual's social life. These appeared to outweigh books and intellectual factors.

Failure. Failure is a fertile source of a number of unwholesome attitudes. Among these are to be found defensive attitudes; the tendency to withdraw from social life and to avoid difficult tasks; feelings of inferiority, discouragement, hopelessness; the conviction that there is no use in trying; and sometimes a smartness manifesting itself in annoying compensatory behavior. Treatment which has proven effective in overcoming detrimental attitudes brought about by failure includes encouragement, the removal of the child from overwhelming competitive situations, a convincing demonstration of the possibility of success by means of tasks suited to his ability and interests, and a liberal application of praise and recognition for efforts and achievements.

Appreciation. Education should increase the individual's sources of enjoyment. Some persons have such a full appreciation of nature that they find rich satisfaction in the beauties which it is constantly providing. They find pleasure in beautiful trees and flowers, in the color of the sunset, in the songs of birds, or in the view from a mountain top; other less fortunate souls indifferently pass these by because they have not learned to perceive nature as beautiful, pleasing, or something to be enjoyed. Likewise, people differ in their ability to enjoy art, music, and good literature. What one enjoys is determined in a large measure by training and experience. The attitude of appreciation or enjoyment is, like other attitudes, developed through learning. The school can and should enrich the lives of its pupils by the cultivation of attitudes that predispose them toward appreciative responses.

Since we learn according to our reactions, we cannot expect an attitude of appreciation to emerge from classroom lessons that are dull and uninspiring or from homework that is meaningless drudgery. If the child is to learn to like poetry, for example, he must find pleasure in hearing or reading the poetry studied in the classroom. The teacher's primary aim should be to help the child discover its beauty. Factors of knowledge or understanding which enhance the child's ability to perceive a particular poem as a thing of beauty may be expected to contribute to his appreciation; but, since appreciation is so largely a matter of the feelings, the knowledge elements should be employed only as a means to the ultimate objective, which is not understanding but enjoyment. Undue emphasis on analysis and grammatical structure will defeat the real purpose. Too often, the study of literature has missed its mark and has left the child with a dislike for rather than an appreciation of the kind of reading material used in the course. As one high-school pupil disconsolately expressed it when asked if he liked "The Rime of the Ancient Mariner" which he was studying, "Aw, all we do is to hunt for similes and metaphors."

The teacher's own attitude is important. He is not likely to succeed in training others to enjoy what he himself does not appreciate. But the teacher's appreciation does not of itself insure the adoption of his attitude by his pupils. We cannot expect, for example, the average twelve-year-old boy to find much pleasure in novels or poems that depend for their appeal on interest in romance. Not only should the teacher assign material adapted to age differences in ability and interests, but he should also be alert to the special current interests of children and tie up the assignments with them.

IDEALS

As we have endeavored to point out before, there is no sharp line of demarcation between attitudes and ideals. The distinction, we believe, lies in the degree to which the generalized control of behavior is a matter of conscious direction or the extent to which the individual has in mind the relatively broad goal of purpose. The ideal, therefore, involves an idea of an end to be achieved and a commitment of one's efforts to attain that goal. This commitment, in the form of purpose or desire, is a form of set or readiness which initiates and regulates various forms of conduct; it arises from an appreciation of the value of the conceived goal. The value of the goal is appreciated when the individual regards it as a source of satisfactions or as a means of avoiding annoyances. The generality of the determining effect of an ideal will depend upon the extent to which the individual's concept is generalized and upon the reach of his understanding of the kinds of behavior by which his purpose may be realized.

By way of illustration, consider the ideal of *honesty*. Here the individual has an understanding of what it means to be honest; he feels that honesty is worth while and purposes to be honest in all matters that come within the range of his ideal. His goal is to be an honest individual. His concept of honesty may be very imperfect, in which case, he is likely to be honest in some situations and not in others. Likewise, the ideal of *punctuality* will involve first an understanding of what it means to be punctual. But even though the individual has a well generalized concept of punctuality, his ideal will not be fully generalized and he will not be consistently punctual if he feels the need for being punctual in only some of his appointments.

Engendering ideals. The engendering of an ideal involves both the development of an adequate concept or understanding and the establishment of a motive or a goal of conduct in accord with the concept. The ideal will be complete and effective only to the extent to which we succeed in establishing both of these essential ingredients.

The conceptual aspect of the ideal may be taught directly as we would teach any concept. This is essential but not sufficient. To develop the ideal of honesty, for example, the child must be taught what honesty means. We may start with specific examples of honest conduct. We may "vary the concomitants" by means of illustrations of honesty in varied situations and in different sorts of behavior. By this procedure and by examples of dishonest conduct (contrast), we may isolate and abstract the feature of concrete acts which makes them honest. If this element is clearly grasped, it will serve as a basis for judging the honesty of various concrete forms of conduct. One of the difficulties encountered here is that adults who attempt to teach children are not always clear in their own minds about what constitutes honesty. A college student who was conscientious and who had a sincere desire to be honest once came to the writer for counsel. The day before, his help had been solicited by a fellow student during an examination. He knew that it was not right to cheat on an examination, but he wanted to know whether the faculty considered it as serious an offense to give help to another during an examination as to secure it.

To establish an ideal of neatness, children need to be taught what neatness means and all the various ways of being neat. They need to be taught what it means to be punctual, loyal, just, amiable, industrious, and so on for all the ideals which we seek to inculcate. But knowledge is not enough to insure the desired conduct, and this is probably why the direct instruction for character education has so miserably failed in most cases. An explanation of what is right, plus an admonition always to do what is right, will do little good if the motive which impels and directs behavior is not established.

Establishment of goal. The critical phase in the process of establishing an ideal is the actual adoption of the conceived standard of conduct or level of achievement as a goal. To secure this, the child must truly appreciate its value. Direct instruction alone is likely to be unsuccessful in putting the necessary motive behind the pupil's knowledge to insure its application in practice. Knowledge of right does not insure right conduct. An appeal to personal concern is usually more effective than mottoes, slogans, and admonitions; and example is more convincing than logical argument.

The effectiveness of example depends, however, upon several things. 1. It should be consistent. Occasional lapses from the ideal in the conduct of the teacher or parent will undermine the effect of many good examples. 2. The prestige of the person who sets the example is an important factor. The conduct of an admired fellow student, a highly respected teacher, a beloved parent, or public official is likely to carry more weight than that of unknown, unimportant, or disliked persons. 3. To influence a child in the desired direction, the example of good conduct should be accompanied by evidence of satisfaction derived from such conduct. If one's conformity to ideal standards appears to be annoying, it will not favorably impress the child. If the pupil sees, for example, that the teacher whom he respects derives satisfaction from carefully obeying the traffic regulations, he will be much more likely to regard that conduct as worth while than if he sees the teacher conform to the law grudgingly and under protest. 4. The effectiveness of the teacher's example is dependent to a large extent upon other influences in the child's life. If the examples and moral tone of the home and community are not in keeping with the standards of conduct which the teacher is attempting to establish, his efforts will be seriously handicapped.

Habits and ideals. Habit training as a means of securing desirable conduct is good as far as it goes. But the trouble with habit training is that it is not likely to carry over to other types of situation and behavior, and it is impossible to build specific habits to take care of the manifold situations which one is certain to encounter. Some years ago, an attempt was made to discover by experiment the extent to which habit training transferred to other situations. Children were trained for neatness in their arithmetic papers, but this produced no improvement in the neatness of papers in other classes. Bagley suggested that if neatness could be made an ideal instead of a habit, the desired generalization would be secured. Ruediger (1910) put Bagley's idea to an experimental test and found that it worked. Neatness was stressed in one subject. Neat papers were required; in addition, the teachers were directed to talk with the class about the importance of neatness in other situations, such as in dress, in the home, in business, and in hospitals. The subject of neatness was not mentioned in other classes. The greatest improvement was reported for the papers from the class in which the training was given, but there was definite improvement also in the other subjects. Ruediger concluded that by making the children aware of the need for neatness in the form of an ideal, the training in one subject was transferred to other subjects.

Where the ability to generalize is restricted, as in young children and the feeble-minded, it will be necessary to depend largely on habit training in our efforts to secure moral conduct. But, as the ability to comprehend develops, we should endeavor to go beyond the building of habits to the establishment of ideals of conduct which will direct judgments and choices along socially acceptable lines.

Character training: Jones' experiment. An excellent experimental study of the relative effectiveness of three different methods of instruction for character and citizenship was made by Jones (1936). The study was made in the public schools of Hartford, Connecticut. It included a total of 304 children in eight different classes, of which four were seventh grade, and four were eighth grade. Two of the classes, one from each grade, were used as control groups. They received no instruction in citizenship and character during the period of the experiment, which covered one whole school year.

Three different methods were used with the other three groups of each grade. Group E was given, by means of planned activity units, firsthand experience with certain problems of conduct encountered in their own lives. The units were centered around such actual events and interests as Halloween, Thanksgiving, Christmas, police, and use of the library. There were 13 such units in all. The Halloween unit, for example, planned for furthering respect for property and the rights of others, and included planning for a parade, designing of costumes, arranging parties, and other enterprises to occupy the pupil's evening in wholesome enjoyment. In this group, no attempt was made to generalize the learning. Group D was entirely a discussion group. It considered the same problems, but the instruction was wholly verbal. The third group, E-D, was taught by means of a combination of the methods used in the other two groups.

Tests of honesty and coöperation were given before and after the period of training. The results indicated that the combination of experiencing and discussion proved to be the best method for securing improvement. It resulted in measurable gains in moral behavior, though these gains were not large. The discussion method alone and the activity method alone appeared to be quite unsuccessful. From the experiencing method there appeared to be little gain other than in the specific habits practiced. Transfer effects had not been sought, and there apparently were none. The discussion method was better than the others for transfer to test situations comparatively remote from the teaching situations, but as a means for securing improvement in behavior in a specific situation it was definitely inferior to experience and training in that particular situation.

The study in general indicated that some improvement can be made in character and social behavior by means of planned instruction and that, for such improvement, we need meaningful experiences in specific situations plus discussion and instruction aimed at generalization to secure transfer of the experience to other situations.

SUMMARY

The development of attitudes and ideals is important for the welfare of the individual and of society. An attitude is a form of set or readiness for certain types of response. Its scope of control is broader than that of habit. Three fundamental attitudes are: appreciation, knowledge, and use. They and other attitudes control a wide variety of responses.

The case histories of delinquents and criminals generally reveal faulty social attitudes. The reformation of such individuals requires the correction of their attitudes. In order to maintain our democratic institutions, the school must instill in the youth of the nation democratic ideals and attitudes.

Many studies have been made of the attitudes of children and students. They have shown the prevalence of a considerable degree of racial prejudice, a difference in subject preference for pupils of high- and low-grade intelligence, reading tastes not in accord with what is studied in the English classes, and age differences in reading interests. College students do not tend to be atheistic but generally hold to the fundamental religious teachings.

Attitudes are acquired by imitation, from emotional experiences and conditioning, from various kinds of informative experiences, and by deliberate cultivation. We have experimental evidence to the effect that attitudes are modified by instruction given in the classroom. Jones found that during the four years in college, students tended to become slightly more liberal toward certain social and religious issues. Failure is the source of many unwholesome attitudes, the removal of which requires encouragement and provision for success. Physical handicaps also may give rise to troublesome attitudes. These should be remedied if possible, and if they are not remediable, the child should be taught to adjust to his misfortune. The school should seek to develop an appreciation of nature, art, music, and good literature for the purpose of providing sources of enjoyment. To this end the child should be taught to see the beauty in them.

A number of attitude tests have been devised in recent years. These are so arranged that the degree of favorableness or unfavorableness toward the topic of the test can be indicated by a score.

An ideal is a form of set or readiness in which a goal is broadly conceived. In engendering ideals it is essential to develop an understanding of what the ideal implies in the way of behavior and also to secure the adoption of the conceived standard of conduct as a goal. The conceptual aspect of the ideal can be taught by direct instruction, but the acceptance of it as a goal requires an appreciation of its value which is more likely to be secured through example.

For character education we need more than habit training. Jones' extensive study of methods of instruction in character education indicated that activity training plus discussion aimed at generalization was successful in securing measurable gains in moral behavior, while discussion alone and the activity training without discussion did not produce appreciable gains.

OVERVIEW

Harris, D.B., "How Children Learn Interest, Motives, Attitudes," *Forty-ninth Yearbook of the National Society for the Study of Education*. Chicago: University of Chicago Press, 1950, Part I, pp. 129-82.

SELECTED REFERENCES

Jones, V., "Character Development in Children," *Manual of Child Psychology*, L. Carmichael, ed. New York: Wiley, 1954, pp. 781-832.
Lewin, K., *Resolving Social Conflict*. New York: Harper, 1948.
Mowrer, O.H., *Learning Theory and Personality Dynamics*. New York: Ronald Press, 1950.
Sherif M. and M.O. Wilson, *Group Relations at the Crossroads*. New York: Harper, 1953, p. 379.

ORIGINAL INVESTIGATIONS

Adorno, T. W., E. Frenkel-Brunswik, D. J. Levinson, and R. N. Sanford, *The Authoritarian Personality*. New York: Harper, 1950.
Lewin, K., R. Lippitt, and R. White, "Patterns of Aggressive Behavior in Experimentally Created 'Social Climates'." *Journal of Social Psychology*, 1939, 10, pp. 271-99.
Mead, A. R., "What Schools Can Do to Improve Social Attitudes," *Educational Leaders*, 1951, 9, pp. 183-87.
Park, L., "Prejudice and Unmet Emotional Needs," *Journal of Educational Sociology*, 1951, 24, pp. 407-13.
Tolman, E. C., "Social Learning," *Readings in Learning*, L. Stolurow, ed. Englewood Cliffs, N. J.: Prentice-Hall, 1953, pp. 329-45.

Chapter Seventeen

Transfer of Training

When training in one situation or one form
of activity affects one's ability in other types
of activity or one's performance in different
situations we have what is commonly understood
as transfer of training. An attempt to operate
a tractor or a truck based upon one's knowledge
of operating an automobile requires transfer
of training in order to succeed in the task.
In countless ways we use the results of past learning
to meet the demands of new situations. In many
ways the results of past learning interfere with
new learning, for instance, the difficulty we
experience in correctly pronouncing a foreign
language because of our habitual manner
of pronouncing sounds.
From a social viewpoint, the real measure

494

of the effectiveness of education is the degree to which it is transferred into daily life. A fundamental premise on which the school
is based is that the training obtained in school will be useful outside
of school — in short, that it is transferable.

There is probably no question concerning learning which has
occupied the thoughts of educational philosophers and in turn affected the actual course of educational history more than that of its
transfer or applicability to lines of endeavor beyond the limits of the
sphere of actual training. Such momentous issues as what subjects
shall make up the content of the curriculum and the aims and
methods of instruction are inevitably decided according to the views,
convictions, and prejudices held by the leaders of educational thought
in regard to this problem.

Formal discipline. The modern scientific investigations of the
problem of transfer of training are set against a background of several
centuries of rationalistic inquiry concerning the mind and its training. Conspicuous in this background is the doctrine of formal discipline. This doctrine was based upon a psychology which is not
accepted by reputable psychologists of today. This psychology was
known as *faculty psychology.* It held that the mind is composed of a
set of faculties or mental powers, such as the will, memory, attention,
judgment, observation, reason, and the like.

It was believed by educational theorists that the chief concern of
education was to develop and strengthen these faculties. They reasoned, furthermore, that it was the process of learning that mattered
most, not what was acquired in the way of information or skills to be
used. The mental faculties were believed subject to improvement,
strengthening, or enlargement by exercise, much as a muscle is
strengthened by use. For this reason, subjects were included or retained in the curriculum, not because they contributed usable information, but because of their supposed value as instruments for
sharpening the intellect and toughening the fibers of the mind.

The outstanding example of the consequences of this doctrine is
seen in the dominant place held by the ancient languages in education. Latin, which had dominated the schools of the Middle Ages and
of the Renaissance, had by the end of the seventeenth century lost its
exalted position as the language of the clergy, diplomacy, the universities, and writers because of the emergence and adoption of the
vernacular languages. Having ceased to be the exclusive language

of culture and the humanities, its place in the curriculum was made secure by the argument that no other subject, except possibly formal mathematics, could equal it as an instrument of mental discipline. This view was supported by educational tradition and conservatism.

Now, according to this conception of mental training, it was supposed that the intellect or the faculties of the mind were strengthened by appropriate discipline and in that way the individual was best prepared for all of the demands of life. We therefore have the notion of a sort of blanket transfer of training from one kind of learning to any situation or activity no matter how different and remote. The study of the classics and formal mathematics was regarded as a means of generating mental power, and this reservoir of power could be drawn upon to cope with any situation. Here was a theory of transfer most sweeping in its claims, based on rationalistic speculation, not on scientific evidence.

In the elementary school, arithmetic was full of useless material selected for its supposed value in training the mind. The process of weeding this out has been occupying the attention of educators only in very recent years. Spelling included the memorizing of thousands of words the child would never use in his own writing. Much attention was given to formal grammer, not to promote good English usage, but to discipline the mind. Methods of teaching were strict and in conformity with the view that, not what the child learned, but the discipline he received in the process was the important consideration.

While the doctrine of formal discipline has been discredited by modern scientific research and is not accepted by psychologists and most educators today, it is still reflected in the public utterances of some educators and in the practices of some teachers. Recently a professor of English in an institute of technology who felt that the students tended to attach more importance to their "practical" subjects than to the academic or cultural subjects, stated in behalf of the latter in an address before a body of students that he believed in "good old mental muscle" and maintained that it could be strengthened by such studies. Unfortunately, there are still some teachers who require their pupils to memorize lists and tables of factual items which have no immediate or future value for the pupils, with a vague notion that somehow the arduous labor of memorizing will itself improve in some way the metal caliber of the victims of such practices.

Procedures in experiments on transfer. In the earlier studies on

transfer effects, the usual procedure was first to test a group of subjects to determine their ability in some one type of performance.
Then training was given these subjects in a different activity. Following training, a second test was given in the performance originally
measured but not trained. If the subjects did better in the final test
than in the initial one, the improvement was assumed to be the transferred effects of the training received on the other activity between
the tests. Such a procedure is subject to error because of the practice
effects of taking the tests. A subject may be expected to do better in a
second test in any activity because of the practice provided by the
first test. All of the improvement, therefore, indicated by the final
test cannot be attributed to the transfer effects of the intervening
training.

Later experimenters overcame this difficulty by the use of a control
group. Under this procedure, two equivalent groups are first tested
on one form of activity. Then the experimental group is given special
practice or training on a second activity. The control group is not
given this special training. Finally, both groups are again tested to discover any increase in proficiency of the first activity. In computing
the amount of transfer from the training to the performance in the
final test, the gains of the control group are subtracted from the gains
of the experimental group. The outline of this procedure is as
follows:

Experimental group	Pretest	Training	Post-test
	Activity A	Activity B	Activity A
Control group	Pretest	No training	Post-test
	Activity A		Activity A

Gains: post-test scores minus pretest scores
Transfer of training: difference in gains between experimental and control group

The practice effects from taking a test, enabling one to do better
in a second test are in themselves a form of transfer from the first
to the second test situation. This sometimes appears in experiments
not aimed at the study of transfer. In such cases, care must be taken
to prevent it from becoming a source of error. For example, in a
recent study which sought to discover the relative effectiveness of
two different forms of instruction in perceptive goal-searching,
children were asked to find a certain object in a search field consisting
of an array of 85 small objects. In one form, called visual instruction,
each child was shown a duplicate of the object he was to find. In the
other, called verbal instruction, only the class name of the search

object was given, such as "Find a button." Each child was tested once with visual instruction and once with verbal instruction. It was recognized that familiarity with the field of search gained from the first test might make the second task with the other method of instruction easier if the same field were used again. Therefore, the second method was used with a second field. Practice effects were still in evidence, however, because the average time required to find the search object was shorter under both methods of instruction when they came second than when they were first in the order of procedure.

A disadvantage of the method of studying transfer effects by giving a test in one activity before and after training in a different one lies in that fact that it is limited to one stage in the mastery of the performance tested. This will be the early stage of learning in those cases where the only practice on this performance is that offered by the first test. The rate of improvement for a given amount of practice varies at different stages of mastery, and the transfer effects might vanish after a few trails if practice on the test performance were continued until a higher degree of proficiency in it were attained. For these reasons, many researchers have employed the method of "successive practice" in their studies of transfer. In its usual form, two equated groups are used. One of these groups is given practice on activity A. Then both groups are given practice on activity B. If the former group makes better progress in Activity B under the same conditions of practice, it is presumably because of that group's previous practice on Activity A. Thus, transfer of training is seen in the influence of previous learning upon the ability to learn new materials or to acquire new skills. A number of variations of the method of successive practice have been employed.

Woodrow's experiment (1927) on memorizing provides an excellent illustration of the experimental method. Woodrow used two experimental groups, one receiving 72 hours training in memorizing nonsense syllables and poetry and the second devoting 36 hours to the same activity but spending the other 36 hours in learning how to memorize, e.g., looking for meaningful associations, using rhythmical grouping, etc. Both groups were compared with a control group on the gains made between a pre-test and a post-test measuring their memorizing ability for poetry, prose, Turkish-English vocabulary, factual items, and historical dates. The test used was a broad measure of memorizing ability. The group which spent all their time memorizing made only slightly greater gains than the control group in direct contradiction of the claims of faculty psychology, while the second experimental group made the significant gain.

Negative transfer. It sometimes happens that previous learning retards the learning of a new performance. In cases of this kind, the interference is greater than the positive carry-over and the result is called negative transfer. This has been demonstrated, for example, in card-sorting experiments in which the subject practices the sorting of cards into compartments numbered to correspond to the cards. After considerable facility has been acquired, the order of the compartments is changed and the subject is asked to place the cards according to the new arrangement. In performing the second task, the previously formed habits tend to carry the hand in the direction of the former positions of the compartments. This interferes with the making of the proper movements and retards the second learning.

If one is to master two such interfering sets of habits as those mentioned above, it has been shown experimentally that the most economical procedure is to master one thoroughly before starting practice on the second. Pyle (1928) describes an experiment in which a group of subjects sorted cards with one arrangement of boxes an hour a day for 15 days, and then switched to practice with a different arrangement of boxes for an additional 15 days. Another group practiced the two arrangements for 30 days but practiced each arrangement on alternate days throughout the whole period. Better results were obtained from the first procedure. Pyle points out by way of application of this principle that it is not advisable to attempt to learn two different systems of writing or two foreign languages at the same time.

- **Transfer in motor skills.** In the field of sensorimotor learning, practice with one bodily member or set of muscles may increase an individual's ability to achieve a similar result with other members of other neuromuscular mechanisms and with different movements.

Dogs paralyzed temporarily in the right hind leg by severing the motor nerves were given conditioning trials with buzzer and with shock on the right hind foot. The experimenters reported that when conditioning was established, some of the operated animals lifted the paralyzed member at the sound of the buzzer to avoid shock by swaying the body to the left or by standing on the toes of the left foot. During training they learned to escape shock in this way without flexing the muscles of the right hind leg. As soon, however, as the severed nerves were regenerated, they substituted without further training the flexion of these muscles to accomplish the same result in a more normal manner (Kellogg et al, 1940).

Training that transfers to corresponding members of the opposite side of the body is called *cross education*. This bilateral transfer is seen, for example, in the improvement of performance with the left hand resulting from practice with the right hand. Several experiments have explored bilateral transfer. One of them by Munn (1932) will illustrate the character of this work and the usual findings. The activity in this experiment called for eye-hand coördination. The apparatus used consisted of a wooden cup attached to a long handle from the bottom of which was suspended, by means of a string, a wooden ball. The task was to grasp the handle and flip the ball into the cup. The subjects were 100 college students, 50 men and 50 women. There were two training groups of 25 students each, and two control groups of the same number. The training groups were given 50 trials with the left hand, then 500 practice trials with the right hand, and finally 50 additional trials with the left hand. The controls received no practice with the right hand. They were given 50 trials with the left hand, rested for 45 to 60 minutes, and then practiced for 50 more trials with the left hand. The average increase in facility with the left hand from the first 50 trials to the second 50 trials was 61.14 per cent for the experimental groups and 28.5 per cent for the controls. Thus, a difference of 32.6 per cent was found in favor of the groups that practiced with the right hand, due, apparently, to the transfer effects of that practice to the use of the left hand. Comments of the subjects indicated that, during practice with the right hand, they discovered the kinds of moves which brought success, and they were able to profit by this knowledge when they came to the second set of trials with the left hand.

A number of experiments have shown transfer from the right to the left hand in mirror tracing and in other forms of sensorimotor learning. Positive transfer has also been found from the left hand to the right, from hands to feet, and from each foot to the other in the learning of an irregular maze pattern. In some experiments, the advantage of previous practice with a different member appeared mostly in the early trials and diminished as practice was continued. This advantage appears to be due to an acquaintance with the problem, familiarity with the experimental situation, greater ease and confidence, and a knowledge of procedures or movements best suited to accomplish the desired results. Having discovered during the previous practice ways and means of dealing with the situation and applying equally well to the performance with another member, the second task is partially learned when practice on it is begun.

Another experimenter studied transfer in motor learning by measuring the effect of learning one maze upon the learning of several others. He found in each case definite evidence of positive transfer effects. However, the amount of transfer varied widely, from 20 to 77 per cent, as measured by trials for the different mazes. One of the mazes used in the transfer series was similar to the maze previously learned except for a section of it which was made a blind alley. To master this maze, the subjects had to break the previously acquired habit of turning into this section. There was considerable interference from the previous practice in the mastery of this part, for the subjects who had learned the otherwise similar maze had greater difficulty in eliminating this section than did controls who had not learned that maze. For this maze as a whole, however, there was positive transfer. It appeared that the transfer effect was the net result of both facilitation and interference. Moreover, as was pointed out in the report, the wide variation in the amount of transfer for the different mazes strongly indicates that the amount of transfer from any learning depends upon the nature of the task to which the shift is made.

Transfer in verbal learning. One of the most thorough investigations in the field of memory was conducted by Sleight (1911). He used a control group and three practice groups equated on the basis of several memory tasks. There were two series of experiments, one with school children, another with college students as subjects. The materials of the test series were dates, nonsense syllables, poetry, prose, and letters. All groups were tested before and after the special memory practice. Between tests one group memorized poetry, another learned "tables," and the third practiced reproducing prose substance. The control group received no memory practice between tests. The results were varied and conflicting. In some tests there were gains for the practice group only to be offset by losses in others. In several cases, the controls gained more in the test performances than the practice groups. There was no indication that the extensive practice had produced any general improvement in memory, nor was there any evidence to support the belief in a general memory function. The results suggested that the term *memory* covers many functions both related and unrelated.

The experiments mentioned above and others reported in the older literature seemed to agree in showing that memory as a whole was not uniformly improved by practice on one kind of material or on one type of memory task. They indicated that *sometimes* there was positive transfer and that at other times the transfer effect was negative or approximately zero. They also showed rather definitely that the greatest transfer occurs in cases where the trained and tested activities were highly similar. For example, practice in memorizing nonsense syllables increased the ability to memorize other lists of such syllables, but resulted in no significant improvement with prose selections or other dissimilar materials. It therefore appeared that the amount of transfer varies with different conditions, and the aim of many of the more recent studies has been to discover more specifically the conditions favorable to the maximum amount of transfer. It has been noted that transfer frequently appeared as the result of acquiring better procedures. During the practice series, the subjects apparently learned how to learn. This was illustrated in the previously cited Woodrow experiment on memorizing.

Transfer in problem solving. A most significant series of studies has been conducted by Harlow (1949) and his students at the University of Wisconsin on the formation of learning sets of both children and monkeys. Instead of the ordinary experimental design in which the same task is presented over a series of trials and the amount of learning measured in terms of number of trials needed to reach a given level of proficiency, Harlow presented his subjects with a series of problems and plotted the improvement in performance over the series. A tray containing food-wells was presented to a monkey. Covering the wells were two objects which differed from each other in several characteristics such as color, shape, size. The monkey's task was to choose the rewarded one of the two objects by correctly discriminating the particular difference in characteristics of the objects. With children, beads and toys were substituted for the food reward.

A series of 344 problems was presented using 344 different pairs of stimuli. The first 32 problems were run for 50 trials each. The second 200 problems were run for 6 trials each. The last 112 problems were run for an average of 9 trials. The question was whether or not the subjects could *learn how to learn,* that is to improve in their ability to learn object-quality discrimination problems. Figure 17.1, adapted from Harlow's data, shows the percent of correct responses obtained during trials on early, middle, and late sets of problems.

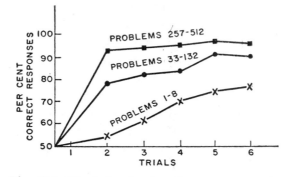

Fig. 17.1. Discrimination learning curves on early, middle, and late sets of problems (after Harlow, 1949).

The correct responses on the first trial of each series are at the chance level. In the first series of trials, improvement comes slowly, in contrast to the last series of problems in which the subject's responses indicate insight following a single trial as indicated by near perfect responses on the next attempt. The experience obtained on previous trials shows increasingly greater transfer the later the series. The animals and children *learned how to learn* on the discrimination problems, just as Woodrow's subjects had learned how to memorize in his experiment on memory. Before the formation of learning sets, improvement from trial to trial was slight, but after their formation the sudden and sharp improvement shown suggests the gradual development of insight into how to go about obtaining correct solutions. The subjects were also able to utilize the learning sets when the problems were reversed and when the task was shifted from a quality-discrimination to a position discrimination. The significance of Harlow's studies lies in providing some understanding of how human and infra-human organisms may acquire problem-solving approaches rather than trial-and-error approaches to the range of demands to be faced in any environment. Learning how to learn efficiently in a new situation, how to approach problem situations, and how to utilize previous experience to permit insight into newly encountered events permit a transformation from creatures who blindly respond either by fixed habit or by chance to creatures who can adapt "intelligently." In addition, these studies offer a possible explanation of the varying degrees of transfer which have been reported in the different studies on transfer of training.

Other studies show how experience in problem solving may transfer positively or negatively to subsequent problems. Ruger (1926), in an experiment with mechanical puzzles, found definite transfer from practice in taking a puzzle apart to putting it together. In one case, a subject took a puzzle apart 400 times without putting it together or seeing it put together. He then put it together 5 times. His average time for putting the puzzle together was just one tenth the average time for the first 5 trials in taking it apart. Since the movements involved were reversed, Ruger believed that the transfer was not due to the carry-over of motor habits but to an understanding of the construction of the puzzle acquired during practice in taking it apart.

Different positions of the puzzles required different initial manipulation. Positive transfer from one position to another was found when the subject clearly saw by analysis what adjustments were needed to use the practiced habits in the new position. But when such insight into the process required for solution was lacking, the old habits produced interference when the puzzle was changed to a new position. Practice with one puzzle transferred positively to the solution of another puzzle involving similar procedure when the subject discovered by analysis during practice the underlying principle and devised a formula for solution that was appropriate for the new puzzle. Motor habits, carried over without the benefit of analysis and generalization of procedure, led to error and negative transfer effects when they were inappropriate and to positive effects when they happened to be appropriate. Among the factors promoting transfer in puzzle solving listed by Ruger are: heightened attention to the task, shift from self-consciousness to a problem attitude, improved methods of attack, analysis and generalization of procedure, and an awareness of the similarity of the new case to the old.

A number of studies have been focused on the functions of comprehending and the solving of problems by thinking. Winch (1923) used school pupils as subjects in a study to determine whether training in solving one type of problem would improve the ability to solve other kinds of problems. Initial and end tests were given in logical reasoning. In the period between the tests, the control group worked on their usual lessons while the training group received practice in solving arithmetical problems; special attention was given to the principles involved. The end tests showed that the practice group improved significantly more in logical reasoning than the controls.

Barlow (1937) found that special training in analysis, abstraction, and generalization transferred positively to test performances consisting of giving the lesson or moral conveyed by various fables. These and other studies indicate the possibilities of positive transfer of practice in problem solving with one kind of material to reasoning in other types of problems. They indicate that transfer is achieved by acquiring an understanding of principles, by developing confident, analytical, searching attitudes, and by learning effective procedures.

Table 17.1 presents a summary of results obtained in various trans-

TABLE 17.1

AMOUNT OF TRANSFER RESULTING FROM DIFFERENT TRAINING EXPERIENCES
IN EXPERIMENTS ON TRANSFER OF TRAINING

Amount of transfer reported	*Training experience*	*Transferred to*
Maximum transfer (over 50% gains)	Marking words	Other words
	Discrimination of shades of red	Discrimination of other colors
	Mazes	Other mazes
Considerable transfer (25%-50%)	Learning sets on object—equality discrimination	Similar problems
	Estimating areas of geometric figures	Similar mazes
	Memorizing techniques	Varied memory tasks
	Mental multiplication	Adding, dividing
	Biology, geometry	Biology and geometry tests
Moderate transfer (10%-25%)	Learning nonsense syllables	Learning prose, poetry
	Poetry	Prose
	Sound intensities	Brightness intensities
	Applying principles of refraction	Hitting underwater targets
Little to negative transfer (under 10%)	Poetry, prose	Dates, syllables
	Estimating line lengths	Similar task
	Cancellation of letters	Cancellation of nouns, verbs
	Card sorting	Reaction time typing
	Computation	Reasoning
	Latin	English vocabulary
	Latin	Spelling
	Biology and geometry	Other subjects

fer of training experiments. Previous experience can affect present learning to a slight or to a great extent depending upon the presence or the absence of certain conditions. The higher the degree of similarity between the two tasks, the higher the degree of transfer. Secondly, if procedures or principles are acquired or understood during the previous training experience, the degree of transfer is likely to be greater than if not. Previous experience, however great, does not automatically insure positive transfer to new learning situations; rather, the extent to which the new is similar to the old or the degree to which the relationships between the two situations are understood determines the extent to which previous experience can be a positive factor in new learning.

CONDITIONS OF TRANSFER

Transfer by similarity. Since the time of the earliest experiments it has been recognized that the more the two performances involved have in common, the more will training in the first tend to improve the second. The important experiments by Thorndike and Woodworth (1901) led to the formulation by Thorndike of the famous and broadly accepted doctrine of *identical elements.* There might be identical elements in the content of subject matter learned, in attitudes, or in methods of procedure. Thus, training in the process of addition would transfer to learning multiplication because in multiplication the pupil uses many addition facts. The procedure in adding involved in multiplying is the same as that involved in solving problems of addition. Names and dates learned in studying American history may aid in the study of American literature where topics in the two subjects relate to the same period (identical elements of content). A searching, alert attitude developed in solving one set of puzzles may accelerate the solving of a second set, or self-confidence from success in one subject may promote achievement in another (identical elements of set).

Because the term *element,* as commonly used, refers to an unanalyzable or at least very simple constituent of a whole and because transfer may result from a common functional trend or common part-functions in themselves not simple, Woodworth (1938) suggested that it would be more appropriate to use the word "constituent" or "component" in the place of "element." The mere presence of com-

mon components does not assure positive transfer; under some conditions of training, they produce negative transfer. The amount of
transfer due to identical features of two functions varies with the
locus of identity or the phases of the functions in which identity
occurs. Identity in the response phases is conducive to far more
positive transfer than identity in the stimulus factors or initial phases.
Thus, it is easier to learn to respond to a new situation in an old
way, than to develop a new mode of responding to an old situation,
for in the latter case the interference from previously formed habits
is greater.

It has been demonstrated that subjects who have learned to respond
to a stimulus word by another word tend to give the same response
word when a word similar in *meaning* to the original stimulus word
is presented. The frequency with which a trained verbal response
will occur in this manner varies with the degree of the similarity in
meaning of the two stimulus words. Thus, if the subject is trained
to respond to the word *snake* by saying "tree," he will be more likely
to say "tree' in response to *serpent* than to the word *hen*.

Transfer by generalization. When a given response is made to
varied, though somewhat similar situations, we have a form of generalization of the conditions which initiate the function. In such cases
the effects of learning are seen to reach beyond the specific function
trained to others of a similar kind. Moreover, as we move to the level
of comprehension, we find that generalizations furnish a ready vehicle
for transfer. The child who has formed a good general concept of
dogs from numerous experiences with them readily recognizes a
strange animal of that species as a dog. If one has learned the general
nature of rivers and comes in his travels upon one he has never seen
before, he knows it is a river. Likewise, a child who learns to add with
one set of exercises, if he acquires an understanding of the principles
involved, will be able to add other sets of figures not used in his training exercises. We have seen above that subjects who grasped the principles involved in solving certain types of mechanical puzzles could
more easily solve other puzzles to which these same principles applied.

The importance for transfer of generalized experience was early
recognized and emphasized by Judd (1908). He believed experience
in one situation could be generalized and applied by the learner in
many other situations. In an experiment demonstrating his view he
had two groups of boys shoot darts at a target submerged in water.

Because of refraction of the light, the target appeared to be in a different position. Before practice the principle of refraction of light was explained to one group, while the other group received no instruction in this matter. Both groups made similar errors at first and corrected them gradually by trial-and-error. Then the depth of the target was changed. This time the instructed group saw the application of the principle to their problem and did much better than the group that had not been told about light refraction.

A similar experiment was made more recently by Hendrickson and Schroeder (1941) who had their subjects shoot BB shot at a submerged target with an air rifle. The results were substantially the same, though they found that the theoretical information also aided in learning to hit the target in the initial situation.

The importance of general principles for transfer was shown also by Woodrow in the previously mentioned memorizing experiment, in which the group that was taught the principles of good memorizing procedures showed a large degree of transfer while the group that had only routine practice showed practically no transfer.

Transfer through generalization is not merely a matter of elements trained during practice appearing as actual components of the new functions. The generalization is a form of comprehension which applies beyond the training situation to other situations of the same general class. It should be noted, however, that the mere knowledge of the principle will not insure transfer of training to new situations. Its general applicability must be realized, and the learner must be able to see the possibility of its application to the new situations.

Transfer through relationships. Somewhat akin to the third leg of a triangle is the Gestalt theorists' explanation of transfer as depending upon the transposition of relationships. The analogy of the triangle is useful because none of the three explanations are completely unrelated or detached from each other. The explanation, by way of a pattern of relationships, agrees that similarities in the two situations permit the transfer of training; but it denies that the similarity is one of content in the two situations, holding rather that the patterns of relationships are alike.

It is often claimed that competitive athletics contribute greatly to the successful performance of the American soldier in combat; this statement describes transfer of training from one situation to another. According to the similarity theory, a competitive sport such as football has component parts identical to those performed as a soldier. For instance, both situations require an aggressive attack against the opponent. Both require the ability to carry out direction or instruction. According to the relationship theory, transfer occurs because both activities involve coordinated teamwork of individuals performing related operations. The strategy involved in outthinking and outmaneuvering an opponent would count more than the specific tactics.

Transfer of attitudes and ideals. An important form of generalization through which transfer takes place is the generalization of set in the form of attitudes and ideals. Bagley many years ago called attention to the possibilities of transfer *via* this medium. His views (1922) and the experiment by Ruediger (1910) on training school children to be neat were mentioned in chapter 16. As stated there, it was found that when neatness was made a general aim (ideal) in connection with one school subject, the improvement, though greatest in that subject, did carry over to other school subjects.

The keynote of the chapter on attitudes and ideals was the importance of developing these generalized controls of conduct to insure socially acceptable forms of behavior in the many and varied situations of life for which specific habit training would be impossible. In that chapter, we considered the widespread influence of these generalized sets. One's reactions to practically any new situation is influenced by attitudes already formed. The bearing on classroom learning of such attitudes as likes, dislikes, respect, antagonism, interest, indifference, punctuality, carelessness, self-confidence, self-repudiation, courtesy, arrogance, pride in work, and fear of failure will be apparent to the most casual observer.

TRANSFER IN SCHOOL SUBECTS

Of the many studies concerning transfer in school subjects, the most crucial test of their general values was made by Thorndike in 1922 and 1923. Tests of general mental ability were given to 8,564 high-school pupils in grades 9, 10, and 11, and after one year of school-work other forms of the same tests were given to discover the intellectual advancement made. By a thoroughgoing analysis of the many different combinations of subjects studied and by a system of weighting the gains to allow for practice effects of taking the tests, for the normal intellectual growth over a year's time, for the fact that pupils with highest initial ability made greatest gains, and also for the fact that the boys gained more than the girls, it was possible to calculate the relative amount contributed by various subjects to the year's gain in the tests. The procedure was to compare the test gains in relation to programs that were alike except for a difference of one subject. If, for example, the programs of two groups equated in terms of initial test scores were alike in that they both included English, history, and geometry but different in that for the fourth subject one group took Latin while the other took chemistry, then it was possible to compare the contributions of Latin and of chemistry to the test gains in the other subjects. The results were most significant. They revealed surprisingly small differences between the various subjects in relation to the test gains and they showed the gains to depend more on initial ability or intelligence than upon any particular subject studied.

A similar study with 5,000 pupils was made later (Broyler, et al., 1927). The results agreed for the most part with those of the earlier study. The table below represents the combined results of the two studies and covers data from over 13,000 high-school pupils. It shows the subjects listed in rank order according to their computed relative contribution to the gains in the mental ability tests. The scores represent corrected weighted average differences between group VII and each of the others. They show how much the subjects of the various groups exceeded or fell short of those in group VII.

Subject	Relative effect on test gains
1. Algebra, geometry, trigonometry	2.99
2. Civics, economics, psychology, sociology	2.89
3. Chemistry, physics, general science	2.71
4. Arithmetic, bookkeeping	2.60
5. Physical training	0.83
6. Latin, French	0.79
7. English, history, business, drawing	0.00
8. Stenography, cooking, sewing	— 0.14
9. Biological sciences, argiculture	— 0.15
10. Dramatic art	— 0.48

The differences are so slight that there is no convincing evidence of the superiority of any one subject or group of subjects. It is significant that Latin, so long held up as the supreme instrument of mental discipline, should, when subjected to a fair comparison with other subjects, fall to the middle of the list.

In discussing the outcomes of his investigation Thorndike states, "After positive correlation of gain with initial ability is allowed for, the balance in favor of any study is certainly not large. Disciplinary values may be real and deserve weight in the curriculum, but the weights should be reasonable."

Studies of transfer in special subjects. *Arithmetic.* One investigator (Winch, 1911) found that practice in arithmetical computation, which improved the accuracy in the computation processes, did not improve arithmetical reasoning. This finding was based on tests given to two groups before and after one of the groups had received practice in computation exercises. We should expect, however, transfer from training in computation to *learning* to solve reasoning problems in so far as the trained computation processes entered into the actual solving of the reasoning problems.

Overman (1930) investigated transfer in arithmetic in relation to methods of teaching. His subjects were pupils of 52 second-grade classes. They were divided into 4 closely equated groups of 112 each. The training consisted of instruction and practice in addition with 3 types of examples involving two-place numbers. Tests were given to determine the extent to which this training transferred to similar addition examples involving two-place and three-place numbers and to examples in subtraction. Group A was shown simply how to do the examples with no attempt to generalize the procedure or to develop comprehension of the underlying principles. In group B, *generalizations* of the procedure were stressed and an effort was made to formulate rules applicable to similar types of examples. With group C, no attempt was made to generalize or formulate rules, but the reasons for the procedures in the specific examples were discussed. In group D the methods of B and C were combined.

The tests given before and after training showed a considerable amount of transfer for all four groups from the taught to the untaught examples. It varied from 67 per cent to 81 per cent for the different types of problems. The calculated transfer (on the basis of 100 per cent for correct solution of all untaught problems) was 59.6 per cent for group A. That generalization greatly facilitated transfer was shown by the fact that group B surpassed group A in the untaught examples by 21.5 per cent. This difference was statistically significant. Discussion of the underlying principles and reasons for the procedures in the taught examples appeared to contribute little to transfer, for group C surpassed A by only 5.4 per cent and the difference was not significant. Group D did about the same as group B, surpassing group A by 20.5 per cent. It appeared, therefore, that "rationalization" added nothing to "generalization." [1]

Geometry. The transfer values of a college freshman course in descriptive geometry were investigated by Rugg (1916) at the University of Illinois. The training group consisted of 326 freshman engineering students who took the course, while 87 students in the college of liberal arts were used as a control group. Tests were given to both groups at the beginning and at the end of the semester during which geometry was studied by the training group but not by the controls. These tests dealt with three types of material: first, "non-geometrical"; second, "quasi-geometrical"; and third, "strictly geometrical." The gains of the training group in the tests were greater in all three types of material than for the control group. This difference in gains for the two groups indicated transfer from the semester course in geometry. But the amount of transfer varied for the three types of test material, being 7 per cent for the non-geometrical, 20 per cent for the quasi-geometrical, and 31 per cent for the geometrical. When the amount of transfer was studied in relation to scholastic ability, the amount of transfer was found to correspond to ability in mathematics, but it did not correspond to differences in ability in English and modern languages. Here, again, it appears that transfer takes place according to the amount of similarity between the trained and untrained processes to the extent to which procedures of analysis and attack are generalized.

Algebra. An arithmetic test covering the fundamental operations, percentage, and problem solving was given to a group of about 200 pupils before and after taking a course in ninth-grade algebra. There appeared to be a definite improvement in the arithmetical abilities tested, but since no control group was used, it is not possible to say just how much of this improvement was directly attributable to the study of algebra (Braverman, 1939).

Chemistry. A study in the field of high-school chemistry showed that students who were given special training in the application of principles derived from the kinetic theory gained more in tests involving the application of other chemical principles than did mem-

---

[1] E. L. Thorndike, "Mental Discipline in High School Studies," *Journal of Educational Psychology,* 1924, 15, p. 98.

bers of control groups who had the usual instruction. The groups were too small to make the results statistically reliable, but the data indicate that the amount of transfer secured for applying scientific principles in new situations is related to the teaching procedures employed and that it may be increased by means of special training in the application of principles (Babitz, 1939).

Grammar. The alleged values of formal grammar for developing various types of abilities such as reasoning in other fields were examined by Briggs (1943). The subjects were seventh-grade pupils. They were divided into two equivalent groups on the basis of intelligence ratings. One group studied grammar while the other studied composition and language. The before and after tests measured the pupils' ability to see likeness and differences, to test definitions critically, to apply definitions, to make a rule or definition, and to reason in connection with various matters. With the possible exception of detecting likenesses and differences, the results indicated that there was no gain of any consequence in those aspects of the reasoning processes tested that could be attributed to the study of grammar.

Latin. The blasting of the doctrine of formal discipline by experimental evidence discredited the view that Latin is a superior means for "developing the mind." This led to a search for evidence of transfer values to be derived from the study of this language. No one who has studied this problem carefully will deny that the study of Latin has transfer values. What is objected to and what has been disproved is that this subject has a monopoly on transfer values or that it is particularly superior to other subjects in this matter. The question to be faced frankly is whether a high-school pupil will receive values commensurate with the time devoted to Latin when other subjects also afford transfer or general values plus a much larger amount of directly useful material.

In a study designed to test the value of first-year Latin for ability to read English several thousand high-school pupils were given form 2 of the Thorndike-McCall Reading Scale at the beginning of the school year, form 8 at the end of the half-year, and form 4 at the end of the year. Among those tested were pupils taking first-year Latin and those who were not studying this subject. It was assumed that if the Latin pupils gained more than the non-Latins in the tests, their superiority could be attributed to the study of Latin. After taking into account differences in initial scores, it was calculated that the

Latin pupils for the entire year gained about 1.5 times as much as the non-Latins. The system of scoring and weighting used gave the Latins a superiority of 1.7 for the whole year, and 1.8 for the first half-year. Thus, the superiority of the Latin pupils was achieved entirely during the first half-year. During the second half-year they gained no more than the non-Latin pupils (Thorndike, 1923).

Another study was undertaken to determine the influence of the study of one year of Latin on the knowledge of English words. Over 5,000 pupils in ninth-grade classes of 41 schools in several different states were given forms A, B, and C of the Carr English Vocabulary Test at the beginning, middle, and end of the school year respectively. Each test included 25 words derived from Latin, and 25 words not of Latin origin. About half of the pupils tested took first-year Latin while the other half did not. In words of Latin origin, the Latin pupils made greater gains for the year than did the non-Latin group. For words not derived from Latin, the gains of the two groups were approximately the same (Thorndike, 1923, 1924).

Other studies have indicated that the study of Latin contributes to an improvement in English vocabulary according to the amount of attention devoted in the Latin class to the matter of derivation of English words from the Latin. Not much benefit may be derived from the study of Latin on this score unless the teacher definitely gives training in English derivations (Jordan, 1942).

It has been shown that the study of Latin for one year produces some beneficial effects on the ability to spell English words of Latin origin but not for words of non-Latin origin. Here, too, the method of teaching is an important factor. If no emphasis is placed on spelling, a slight advantage may accrue from the study of Latin. Great emphasis on Latin derivations may even impair ability to spell words not derived from Latin. The most favorable results have been obtained from the development of rules and the comprehension of principles pertaining to the spelling of Latin derivatives (Coxe, 1923, 1924).

To determine the value of the study of Latin in high school as a preparation for the study of French in college, Kirby (1923) compared the grades in first-year French of students who had studied Latin with the grades of students who had not studied Latin. The Latin students made slightly better grades in the first semester of French. He found a correlation of .23 between the number of years spent in studying Latin and grades in French as compared with a correlation of .43 between French grades and intelligence. It appears from this that intelligence had more to do with the French grades than did the previous study of Latin. When the factor of intelligence was kept constant, a correlation of .22 was found for French grades and the years spent in the study of Latin, indicating a slight relationship.

A similar study by Cole (1936) likewise revealed a positive relation between the number of years spent in the study of Latin in high school and grades earned by college freshmen in first-year French. In this study, a positive relation was found also between the amount of Latin studied and grades in Spanish. Students who had studied Latin for four years made better grades in first-year French and Spanish than students who had studied Latin for two years. Since the factor of intelligence was made constant, these findings indicate some transfer effects from Latin to the study of these modern languages.

Modern foreign languages. Werner (1930) investigated the influence of the study of modern foreign languages upon the development of abilities in English. A battery of tests covering punctuation, sentence structure, language and grammar, vocabulary, reading speed, and reading comprehension was given to a large number of high-school and college students at the beginning and at the end of a school year. The gains in the tests made by the students who during the year studied French, German, or Spanish were compared with the gains of those who did not study a foreign language. The results in general indicated that the study of a foreign language did not always produce an improvement in abilities in English, that such study contributed to the development of speed and comprehension in reading, that it had a favorable effect on ability in grammar for high-school pupils but not in the case of college freshmen, that it had a negative effect on improvement in punctuation and the ability to detect faulty sentence structure, that it had no appreciable effect on the increase of English vocabulary, and that the effect of foreign language study on the development of abilities in English varied greatly with the degree of mental ability, since pupils with high-grade ability more often profited by such study and the less gifted individuals more often suffered from the interference produced by it.

An investigation of the influence of the study of French on the gains in English vocabulary was made by Woody (1930). Form I of a specially prepared test of English vocabulary, containing 25 words derived from French and 25 words of non-French origin, was given near the beginning of the school year to three groups of high-school pupils. One group was made up of pupils who were beginning the study of French and who had not taken and were not taking any other foreign language. The pupils of the second group were not taking and had not previously taken any foreign language. The members of the third group were beginning the study of Latin with no previous or concurrent study of any foreign language. Near the end of the same school year (1926-1927), Form II of the vocabulary test was administered to the same pupils. High schools in ten Michigan cities participated in the investigation.

The mean gains of the three groups for words derived from French and for words not of French origin are shown in the following table:

Language Group	French Derivatives	Non-French Origin
1. No foreign language	2.34	.68
2. Beginning French	1.29	— .08
3. Beginning Latin	2.09	.57

It will be noted that there was a gain in all but one case. The "Beginning French" group showed a slight loss on words not derived from French. The gains in words of French origin were greater for all groups than for non-French derivatives. In both types of words, the "No Language" group made greater mean gains than either of the two language groups, and the mean gains for the "Beginning Latin" group exceeded the gains of the "Beginning French" group. It is significant that the French group gained less than the other two groups in words of French derivation, for in these words we should have expected an advantage from their study of French. The factors of sex, size of initial score, and intelligence did not affect significantly the general tendency of the results.

It was suggested that the superiority of the Latin group over the French group may have been due to more attention to the matter of derivation in the Latin classes and to the fact that many words derived from French are also based on Latin roots, while the superiority of the "No Language" group may have been due to stress on business English and spelling in commercial courses taken by members of this group. The author was careful to point out that the results reflected only the conditions as they were then in the schools studied and that a different emphasis in teaching might well be expected to produce different results. They do indicate strongly that the teaching of French with no particular attention to the derivation of English words from French cannot be expected to contribute much to the development of the pupil's English vocabulary even in the case of words of French origin.

A general consideration of the evidence. These and other investigations of the transfer effects of classroom study agree in general with the laboratory experiments on the fundamental nature and conditions of transfer. They indicate that the training in one school subject transfers to the study of other subjects or to other activities not directly trained according to the degree of *similarity* between the trained and untrained activities, according to the extent to which these activities possess *common components,* and according to the extent to which the learner grasps or recognizes similarities of *relationships*. They have shown that transfer may be secured by way of *generalizations* in the form of rules and principles when the learner realizes the applicability of such rules and principles to situations or problems other than those specifically involved in his training. They have shown also that the ease and extent of transfer increases with the thoroughness of learning, with the intelligence of the learner, and with purposeful effort on the part of the teacher to secure definite transfer values.

They indicate, moreover, that any subject may, if properly taught, have some transfer value, that the differences between subjects in this respect are small, and that no one subject or group of subjects is especially superior in this respect. It appears that the most effective way to secure a desired educational outcome is to train directly for it rather than to expect it to appear as an incidental by-product of other subjects. The evidence from transfer studies supports the modern educational trend toward the teaching of that which is worth learning for its direct values, be those values social, esthetic, recreational, or utilitarian, rather than for any so-called training of the mind.

Teaching for transfer. That the method of teaching is an important factor in securing transfer from the classroom exercises to situations and activities beyond the classroom has been definitely demonstrated. If pupils are to get the fullest return from the study of a subject, it should be taught in a manner conducive to the maximum of transfer effects. Since transfer takes place through the medium of common components and generalizations, effective teaching will bear on these factors so that the outcomes will not be merely the mastery of the particular exercise for its own sake, but will spread beyond the limits of the particular conditions of the instructional situation to other situations and problems.

We may promote transfer through common functional components by devising learning exercises in keeping with the demands of real-life situations and by securing problems calling for methods of attack and analysis similar to those demanded by the problems confronted in daily living.

Some of the ways by which a resourceful teacher can accomplish this are: relating the history lesson to the novel studied in the literature class or to present political problems; relating the geography lesson to travel, to the food on the dinner table, or to the issue of world citizenship; relating the civics lesson to the current town election; relating the elementary science lesson to the family car, the radio, or aviation; relating the foreign language lesson to good English usage; and relating the geometry lesson to finding the range of an enemy target in war or to the building of a house. The essential thing is to help the learner see the many different situations and activities that contain or involve elements or features of the subject he is studying.

The teacher who desires to have the results of his instruction reach beyond the confines of the classroom and who seeks to be a true educator will, moreover, take advantage of the possibilities of transfer through generalization of experience. The principle taught by means of a classroom exercise will be developed to include far more than the specific details of that particular exercise. The learner must see the entire range of situations to which the principle applies. The use of many and varied examples will aid in accomplishing this important step. He must also be shown cases wherein the principle does not apply.

The procedures for developing generalizations were discussed in the chapter on comprehension. They include calling attention to the principle in numerous and varied concrete cases and its isolation by way of contrast through the examination of cases to which it does not apply. Only a few suggestions need to be added here. The good teacher will keep in mind that for greatest transfer, the generalization should be thoroughly mastered and completely understood. Its application in a great variety of situations and problems will need to be pointed out. The many different ways in which it may be employed in various locations, in dealing with current social problems, or in managing one's personal affairs should be indicated.

The teacher should also bear in mind the important relations of intelligence to transfer. It is easier for a child of high-grade intelligence to generalize than for one less gifted. The brighter child will be quicker to recognize elements of similarity. He will grasp the underlying principle with fewer illustrations. He will show greater facility in drawing from concrete examples the general procedures and methods appropriate for dealing with other cases. For the child of lesser intelligence, therefore, the teacher will need to intensify his effort to secure an understanding of the range of application and usefulness of rules, laws, definitions, methods of procedure, and other generalizations.

Special attention must be given to techniques of problem solving, to efficient procedures in learning, and to the best methods of dealing with controversial issues. An effort should also be made to develop ideals and attitudes which serve, as we have seen, as generalized controls of thinking, feeling, and conduct. Through these, we may expect transfer from the classroom instruction to the diverse situations and activities of life.

SUMMARY

Transfer of training occurs when the results of learning in one situation affect our performance in different situations or when training in one activity affects other forms of activity. The nature and conditions of transfer are of prime importance to education both with regard to what subjects shall be taught and to how they shall be taught.

Prior to the present century, the doctrine of formal discipline dominated educational philosophy and practice. Subjects were taught primarily for their alleged value for training the faculties of the mind, not for their intrinsic worth to the pupil. This doctrine was discredited by controlled experiments made in the early part of this century.

Many experiments on various functions — particularly action, memory, perception, and reasoning — have shown that transfer does take place and that it may be negative as well as positive. These studies have been fruitful in discovering the conditions under which transfer occurs. While the greatest improvement occurs from direct training, transfer takes place through the medium of components common to the activity trained and the activity to which the training is transferred. The greater the similarity of two functions, the more will the training of one affect the other.

Transfer also takes place through generalizations developed during training when the learner sees the applicability of a principle, rule, or method of attack to a new situation or problem. Another medium of transfer is found in ideals and attitudes.

The degree of learning is a factor in transfer. As it is increased, the tendency toward negative transference or interference is lessened and the tendency toward positive transfer is increased. There is some evidence that transfer effects are more persistent than the direct results of training.

Studies of transfer in school subjects indicate only small differences between high-school subjects in their effect on general mental ability. Studies of special school subjects indicate that the study of one subject may affect the ability to learn other subjects but that the amount and nature of transfer effects depend upon the intelligence of the pupil and the method of instruction far more than it does upon the subject.

The evidence, in general, points to the conclusion that the most effective way to realize a desired educational outcome is to train directly for it and that no subject merits a place in the curriculum solely on the grounds of its alleged values for mental training. Any subject properly taught has cultural, disciplinary, and transfer values. The direct values, therefore, are to be given the first consideration.

Every subject should be so taught as to secure the maximum spread of learning to situations and activities beyond the classroom. To this end, attention should be called to those aspects of the subject that are common to other subjects and to the various activities in which elements of the subject are employed. Generalizations should be thoroughly taught and the varied possibilities of their use and application pointed out to the learner. In teaching for transfer, we should endeavor to develop attitudes and ideals.

OVERVIEW

Andrews, T. G., L. J. Cronbach, and P. Sandiford, "Transfer of Training," *Encyclopedia of Educational Research*, W. S. Monroe, ed. New York: Macmillan Co., 1950, pp. 1483-89.

SELECTED REFERENCES

Brownell, W. A., "Theoretical Aspects of Learning and Transfer of Training," *Review of Educational Response,* 1936, 6, pp. 281-90, 337-39.

McGeoch, J. A., *The Psychology of Human Learning.* New York: Longmans, Green, 1942, pp. 394-452.

Stroud, J. B., *Psychology in Education.* New York: Longmans, Green, 1946, pp. 555-97.

Swenson, E. J., *Retroactive Inhibition: A Review of the Literature.* Minneapolis: University of Minnesota Press, 1941.

ORIGINAL INVESTIGATIONS

Hendrickson, G. and W. H. Schroeder, "Transfer of Training in Learning to Hit a Submerged Target," *Journal of Educational Psychology,* 1941, 32, pp. 205-13.

Swenson, Esther, G. L. Anderson, and C. L. Stacey, "Learning Theory in School Situations," *University of Minnesota Studies in Education.* Minneapolis: University of Minnesota Press, 1949, p. 103.

Thorndike, E. L., "Mental Discipline in High School Studies," *Journal of Educational Psychology,* 1924, 15, pp. 1-22, 83-98.

Woodrow, H., "The Effect of Type of Training upon Transference," *Journal of Educational Psychology,* 1927, 18, pp. 159-72.

Bibliography

Abom, M., "The Influence of Experimentally Induced Failure on the Retention of Materials Acquired through Set and Incidental Learning," *J. Exp. Psychol.,* 1953, 45, 225–31.

Allee, Ruth, et al., "Experimental Frustration in a Group Test Situation," *J. Abn. Soc. Psychol.,* 1951, 46, 316–22.

Allen, C. N., "Individual Differences in Delayed Reactions of Children," *Arch. Psychol.,* 1931, 19, No. 127.

Allport, G. W., "Attitudes," *A Handbook of Social Psychology,* C. Murchison, ed. Worcester, Massachusetts: Clark Univ. Press, 1935, Chapter XVII.

Alpert, Augusta, "The Solving of Problem Situations by Preschool Children," *Teachers College Contributions to Education, No. 323.* New York: Teachers College, Columbia Univ., 1928.

Ames, Louise, "Postural and Placement Orientation in Writing and Block Behavior: Developmental Trends from Infancy to Age Ten," *J. Gen. Psychol.,* 1948, 73, 45–52.

Ames, Louise and Frances Ilg, "Development Trends in Writing and Behavior," *J. Gen. Psychol.,* 1951, 79, 29–46.

Ammons, R. B., "Rotary Pursuit Performance with Continuous Practice before and after a Single Rest," *J. Exp. Psychol.,* 1947, 37, 393–411.

Anastasi, Anne and F. A. Cordova, "Some Effects of Bilingualism upon the Intelligence Test Performance of Puerto Rican Children in New York City," *J. Educ. Psychol.,* 1953, 44, 1–19.

Anderson, J. E., "Child Development: Learning and Age," *Encyclopedia of Educational Research,* W. S. Monroe, ed. New York: Macmillan, 1950, 178–80.

Andrews, T. G., ed., *Methods of Psychology.* New York: Wiley, 1948.

Ash, P., "The Relative Effectiveness of Massed versus Spaced Film Presentation," *Res. Quarterly,* 1950, 41, 19–30.

Babitz, M. and N. Keys, "An Experiment in Teaching Pupils to Apply Scientific Principles," *Science Educ.,* 1939, 23, 367–70.

Baldwin, B. T., E. A. Fillmore, and L. Hadley. *Farm Children.* New York: Appleton, 1930.

Barlow, M. C., "The Influence of Electric Shock in Mirror Tracing," *Amer. J. Psychol.,* 1933, 45, 478–87.

——, "Transfer of Training in Reasoning," *J. Educ. Psychol.,* 1937, 28, 122–28.

Barker, R. G., Tamara Dembo, and K. Lewin, "Frustration and Regression: Studies in Topological and Vector Psychology: II," *Univ. Iowa Stud. Child Welfare,* 1941, 18, No. 1.

Bartlett, F. C., *Remembering: A Study in Experimental and Social Psychology.* Cambridge, England: The University Press, 1932.

Barton, W. A., "Outlining as a Study Procedure," *Teachers College Contributions to Education, No. 411.* New York: Teachers College, Columbia Univ., 1930.

Bateman, R. M. and H. H. Remmers, "The Relationship of Pupil Attitudes toward Social Topics before and after Studying the Subjects," *Studies in Higher Educ.,* Purdue Univ., 1936, No. 31, 27–51.

Bayley, Nancy, "The Development of Motor Ability during the First Three Years," *Soc. Res. Child Devel. Monogr.,* 1935, Vol. 1, No. 1.

Baley, Nancy, and Anna Espenschade, "Motor Development from Birth to Maturity," *J. Educ. Res.,* 1941, 11, 562–72; 1944, 14, 381–89.

Beckham, A. S., "A Study of Race Attitudes in Negro Children of Adolescent Age," *J. Abn. and Soc. Psychol.,* 1934, 29, 18–29.

Beebe-Center, J., *The Psychology of Pleasantness and Unpleasantness.* New York: Van Nostrand, 1932.

Bergen, C., "Some Sources of Children's Science Information," *Teachers College Contributions to Education, No. 881.* New York: Teachers College, Columbia Univ., 1943.

Bernard, J., "The Lecture-Demonstration versus the Problem Solving Method of Teaching a College Science Course," *Sci. Educ.,* 1942, 26, 121–32.

Bernard, J. and R. Gilbert, "The Specificity of the Effect of Shock for Error in Maze Learning with Human Subjects," *J. Exp. Psychol.,* 1941, 28, 178–86.

Bingham, W., *Aptitudes and Aptitude Testing.* New York: Harper, 1937.

Birsh, H. G. and H. S. Rabinowitz, "The Negative Effect of Previous Experience on Productive Thinking," *J. Exp. Psychol.,* 1951, 41, 121–25.

Blair, G. M., "Subject Preferences of Mentally Superior and Inferior Senior High School Students," *J. Educ. Res.,* 1939, 33, 89–92.

Blankenship, A. B., "Memory Span: A Review of the Literature," *Psychol. Bull.,* 1938, 35, 1–25.

Brace, D. K., "Studies in the Rate of Learning Gross Bodily Motor Skill," *Res. Quart., Amer. Phys. Educ. Assn.,* 1941, 12, 181–85.

Braverman, B., "Does a Year's Exposure to Algebra Improve a Pupil's Ability in Arithmetic?" *Math. Teacher,* 1939, 32, 301-12.

Brener, R., "An Experimental Investigation of the Memory Span," *J. Exp. Psychol.,* 1940, 26, 467–82.

Bridges, Katherine, "A Genetic Theory of the Emotions," *J. Genet. Psychol.,* 1930, 37, 514–27.

———, "Emotional Development in Early Infancy," *Child Development,* 1932, 3, 324–41.

———, *Social and Emotional Development of the Preschool Child.* London: Kegan Paul, 1931, 187.

Briggs, L. J. and H. B. Reed, "The Curve of Retention for Substance Material," *J. Exp. Psychol.,* 1943, 32, 513–17.

Britt, S. H., "Retroactive Inhibition: A Review of the Literature," *Psychol. Bull.,* 1935, 32, 381–440.

Britt, S. H. and M. E. Bunch, "Jost's Law and Retroactive Inhibition," *Amer. J. Psychol.,* 1934, 46, 299–308.

Broadhead, R. and S. Dimond, "The Social Studies—Thinking," *Rev. of Educ. Res.,* 1950, 20, 262–63.

Brown, F., "Knowledge of Results as an Incentive in Schoolroom Practice," *J. Educ. Psychol.,* 1932, 23, 532–52.

———, "Problems Presented by the Concept of Acquired Drives," *Current Theory and Research in Motivation: A Symposium.* Lincoln, Neb.: Univ. of Nebraska Press, 1953, 1–21.

Brown, W., "To What Extent is Memory Measured by a Single Recall?" *J. Exp. Psychol.,* 1923, 6, 377–82.

Brownell, W. A. and Charlotte Chazal, "The Effects of Premature Drill in Third Grade Arithmetic," *J. Educ. Res.,* 1935, 29, 17.

Broyler, C. R., E. L. Thorndike, and Ella Woodyard, "A Second Study of Mental Discipline in High School Studies," *J. Educ. Psychol.,* 1927, 18, 377–404.

Bruce, R. W., "Conditions of Transfer of Training," *J. Exp. Psychol.,* 1933, 16, 343–61.

Bruner, J. E. and C. Goodman, "Value and Need as Organizing Factors in Perception," *J. Abn. Soc. Psychol.,* 1947, 42, 33–44.

Bruner, S., L. Postman, and E. McGinnies, "Personal Values as Selective in Perception," *J. Abn. Soc. Psychol.,* 1948, 43, 142–54.

Buckingham, B. R., and J. MacLatchy, "The Number Abilities of Children When They Enter Grade One," *Twenty-ninth Yearbook of the National Society for the Study of Education,* 1930, Part II, 473-549.

Buhler, Charlotte, *The First Year of Life.* New York: Day, 1930.

Bunch, Marion, "The Effect of Electric Shock as Punishment for Errors in Human Maze-Learning," *J. Comp. Psychol.,* 1928, 8, 343–59.

Bunch, Marion and E. P. Hagman, "The Influence of Electric Shocks for Errors in Rational Learning," *J. Exp. Psychol.,* 1937, 21, 330–41.

Bunch, Marion and Frances D. McTeer, "The Influence of Punishment during Learning upon Retroactive Inhibition," *J. Exp. Psychol.,* 1932, 15, 473–95.

Bunch, Marion and K. Wientage, "The Relative Susceptibility of Pleasant,

Unpleasant, and Indifferent Material to Retroactive Inhibition," *J. Gen. Psychol.*, 1933, 9, 157–78.

Burtt, H. E., "A Further Study of Early Childhood Memory," *J. Genet. Psychol.*, 1937, 50, 187–92.

———, An Experimental Study of Early Childhood Memory," *J. Genet. Psychol.*, 1932, 9, 157–78.

———, "An Experimental Study of Early Childhood Memory: Final Report," *J. Genet. Psychol.*, 1941, 58, 435–39.

Buxton, C. E. and C. E. Henry, "Retroaction and Gains in Motor Learning: I. Similarity of Interpolated Tasks as a Factor in Gains," *J. Exp. Psychol.*, 1939, 25, 1–17.

Cady, Helen, "On the Psychology of Testimony, "*Amer. J. Psychol.*, 1924, 35, 110–12.

Cain, L. F. and R. D. Willey, "The Effect of Spaced Learning on the Curve of Retention," *J. Exp. Psychol.*, 1939, 25, 209–14.

Caplin, D., "A Special Report on Retardation of Children with Impaired Hearing in New York City Schools," *Amer. Ann. Deaf,* 1937, 82, 234–43.

Carr, H., " The Law of Effect, I.," *Psychol. Rev.*, 1938, 45, 191–99.

Carr, H. A., "Teaching and Learning," *J. Genet. Psychol.*, 1930, 37, 189–218.

Carter, L. F. and K. Schooler, "Value, Need, and Other Factors in Perception," *Psychol. Rev.*, 1949, 56, 200–207.

Cason, H., "The Learning and Retention of Pleasant and Unpleasant Activities," *Archives of Psychol.*, 1932, 21, No. 134.

Centers, R., *The Psychology of Social Classes.* Princeton, N. J.: Princeton Univ. Press, 1949.

Children's Bureau, "Research Relating to Children," *U. S. Dept. of Health, Education, and Welfare,* 1953, Bull. 2.

Chyatte, C., et al., "Prejudice Verbalization among Children," *J. Educ. Psychol.*, 1951, 42, 421–31.

Cofer, C. N., "A Comparison of Logical and Verbatim Learning of Prose Passages of Different Lengths," *Amer. J. Psychol.*, 1941, 54, 1–20.

Collinson, L., "Chronological Acceleration and Retardation at Junior High School Level," *Contributions to Education No. 262,* Geo. Peabody College for Teachers, 1940.

Conway, C. B., "The Hearing Abilities of Children in Toronto Public Schools," *Bull. Dept. Educ. Res.,* Ontario Coll. Educ., 1937, No. 9, 132.

Cook, T. W., "Studies in Cross Education, III: Kinesthetic Learning of an Irregular Pattern," *J. Exp. Psychol.*, 1934, 17, 749–62.

Cook, W. W., "Some Effects of the Maintenance of High Standards of Promotion," *Elem. Sch. J.,* 1941, 44, 430–37.

Corey, S. M., "Changes in the Opinions of Female Students after One Year at a University," *J. Social Psychol.,* 1940, 11, 341–51.

Corey, S. M. and G. S. Beery, "The Effect of Teacher Popularity upon Attitude toward School Subjects," *J. Educ. Psychol.*, 1938, 29, 665–70.

Corner, G. W., *Ourselves Unborn.* Yale Univ. Press, 1944, 188.

Courtney, D., Margaret Bucknam, and D. Durrell, "Multiple Choice Recall versus Oral and Written Recall," *J. Educ. Res.,* 1946, 40, 456-61.

Cowen, E. L. and G. C. Thompson, "Problem Solving Rigidity and Personality Structure," *J. Abn. & Social Psychol.,* 1951, 46, 165–76.

Coxe, W. W., "A Controlled Experiment to Determine the Extent to Which Latin Can Function in the Spelling of English Words," *J. Educ. Res.,* 1923, 7, 244–50.

————, "Influence of Latin on the Spelling of English Words," *J. Educ. Res.,* 1924, 9, 223–33.

Coyne, Catherine, "British Child Evacuees Paint American Scene for America," *Boston Sunday Herald,* April 6, 1941.

Crosland, H. R., "A Qualitative Analysis of the Process of Forgetting," *Psychol. Monogr.,* 1921, 29, No. 130.

Culler, E. A., "The Law of Effect, IV," *Psychol. Rev.,* 1938, 45, 206–11.

Curti, Margaret, *Child Psychology.* New York: Longmans, Green, 2nd ed., 1938.

Dallenbach, K. M., "The Relation of Memory Error to Time Interval," Psychol. Rev., 1913, 20, 323–37.

Dalton, M. M., "A Visual Survey of 5000 School Children," *J. Educ. Res.,* 1943, 37, 81–94.

Dashiell, J. F., "The Law of Effect, V.," *Psychol. Rev.,* 1938, 45, 212–14.

Dashiell, K. M., "A Survey and Synthesis of Learning Theories," *Psychol. Bull.,* 1935, 32, 261–75.

Davis, A., "Socio-Economic Status and its Influences on Children's Learning," *Understand the Child,* 1951, 20, 10–16.

Davis, A. and R. J. Havighurst, "Social Class and Color Differences in Child Rearing," *Amer. Sociol. Rev.,* 1946, 11, 698–710.

Davis, R. A., *Psychology of Learning.* New York: McGraw-Hill, 1935.

Dearborn, W. F. and J. Rothney, *Predicting the Child's Development.* Cambridge, Mass: Sci-Art. Pub., 1941, 360.

Deese, J., R. S. Lazarus, and J. Keenan, "Anxiety, Anxiety-Production, and Stress in Learning," *J. Exp. Psychol.,* 1953, 46, 55–60.

Dewey, J., *How We Think.* Boston: D. C. Heath and Co., 1910.

Doré, L. R. and E. R. Hilgard, "Spaced Practice and the Maturation Hypothesis," *J. Psychol.,* 1937, 27, 303–12.

Douglass, H. R. and H. C. Bauer, "The Study Practices of Three Hundred Ninety-Five High School Pupils," *J. Educ. Psychol.,* 1938, 29, 36–43.

Drake, R. M., "The Effect of Teaching the Vocabulary of Algebra," *J. Educ. Res.,* 1940, 34, 601-10.

Dudycha, G. J., "Attitudes Toward War," *Psychol. Bull.,* 1942, 39, 846–58.

————, "The Religious Beliefs of College Students," *J. App. Psychol.,* 1933, 17, 585–603.

Dudycha, G. J. and Martha Dudycha, "Adolescents' Memories of Preschool Experiences,"*J. Genet. Psychol.,* 1933, 42, 468–80.

————, "Childhood Memories: A Review of the Literature," *Psychol. Bull.,* 1941, 38, 668–82.

Duncan, C. P., "The Effect of Unequal Amounts of Practice on Motor Learning before and after Rest," *J. Exp. Psychol.*, 1951, 42, 207–64.

Duncker, K., and I. Krechevsky, "On Solution-Achievement," *Psychol. Rev.*, 1939, 46, 176–85.

Dunlap, K., *Habits: Their Making and Unmaking*. New York: Liveright, 1932.

Durrell, D. D., *Improvement of Basic Reading Abilities*. Yonkers-on-Hudson, N. Y.: World Book Co., 1940.

Dynes, J. J., "Comparison of Two Methods of Studying History," *J. Exp. Educ.*, 1932, 1, 42–45.

Eames, T. H., "The Effect of Correction of Refractive Errors on the Distant and Near Vision of School Children," *J. Educ. Res.*, 1943, 37, 37–542.

———, "The Ocular Conditions of 350 Poor Readers," *J. Educ. Res.*, 1938, 32, 10–16.

———, "The Speed of Object Recognition and of Word Recognition in Groups of Passing and Failing Pupils," *J. Educ. Psychol.*, 1947, 38, 119–22.

Easley, H., "The Curve of Forgetting and the Distribution of Practice," *J. Educ. Psychol.*, 1937, 28, 474-78.

Eaton, M. T., "The Conditioned Reflex Technique Applied to a Less Specialized Type of Learning," *J. Exp. Educ.*, 1937, 6, 68–83.

Ebbinghaus, H., *Memory, a Contribution to Experimental Psychology (translated by H. A. Ruger and Clara Bussenius)*. New York: Teachers College, Columbia University, 1913, Chapter VI.

Edgerton, H. A. and S. H. Britt, "Sex Difference in the Science Talent Test," *Science*, 1944, 100, 192–93.

Edmiston, R. W., "Effects of Emphasizing 'How to Learn' upon Knowledge of Course Content and School Marks," *J. Educ. Psychol.*, 1937, 28, 371–81.

Edwards, A. L., "Political Frames of Reference as a Factor Influencing Recognition," *J. of Abn. Soc. Psychol.*, 1941, 36, 34–50.

Edwards, A. L., and H. B. English, "The Effect of the Immediate Test on Verbatim and Summary Retention," *Amer. J. Psychol.*, 1939, 52, 372–75.

Eells, K., A. Davis, et al., *Intelligence and Cultural Differences*. Chicago: Univ. of Chicago Press, 1951.

Eikenberry, D. H., "Permanence of High School Learning," *J. of Educ. Psychol.*, 1923, 14, 463–82.

English, H. B. and L. E. Allen, "Studies in Substance Learning and Retention: XI. The Effect of Maturity Level on Verbatim and Summary Retention," *J. Gen. Psychol.*, 1939, 21, 271–76.

Espenschade, Anna, "Physiological Maturity as a Factor in the Qualification of Boys for Physical Activity," *Res. Quart.*, 1942, 113–17.

Farnsworth, P. R., "Changes in Attitude Toward War during College Years," *J. Soc. Psychol.*, 1937, 8, 274–79.

Farris, L. P., "Visual Defects as Factors Influencing Achievement in Reading," *J. Exp. Educ.*, 1936, 5, 58–60.

Fay, P. J., "The Effects of the Knowledge of Marks on Subsequent Achievement of College Students," *J. Educ. Psychol.*, 1937, 28, 548–54.

Findley, W. G. and D. E. Scates, "Obtaining Evidence of Understanding," *Forty-fifth Yearbook of the National Society for the Study of Education*, 1946, Part I, 44–64.

Flügel, J. C., "A Quantitative Study of Feeling and Emotion in Everyday Life," *Brit. J. Psychol.*, 1925, 15, 318–55.

Forlano, G., "An Experiment in which the Delayed and Immediate Knowledge of Results with Monetary Reward is Compared with Delayed and Immediate Knowledge of Results," *Teachers College Contributions to Education*, No. 688. New York: Teachers College, Columbia Univ., 1936.

———, "School Learning with Various Methods of Practice and Rewards," *Teachers College Contributions to Education, No. 688*. New York: Teachers College, Columbia Univ., 1936.

Forlano, G. and M. H. Hoffman, "Guessing and Telling Methods in Learning Words of a Foreign Language," *J. Educ. Psychol.*, 1937, 28, 632–36.

Fouracre, M. H., Gladys Jann, and Anna Martorana, "Educational Abilities and Needs of Orthopedically Handicapped Children," *Elem. School J.*, 1950, Feb., 331–38.

Frank, J. D., and E. J. Ludvigh, "The Retroactive Effect of Pleasant and Unpleasant Odors on Learning," *Amer. J. Psychol.*, 1931, 43, 102–08.

Fraser, J. A., "Outcomes of a Study Excursion," *Teachers College Contributions to Education, No. 778*. New York: Teachers College, Columbia Univ., 1939.

Freeburne, C. M., "The Influence of Training in Perceptual Span and Perceptual Speed upon Reading Ability," *J. Educ. Psychol.*, 1949, 40, 321–51.

Friedman, K., "The Growth of Time Concepts," *Soc. Educ.*, 1944, 8, 29–31.

Friedman, K. and Viola Marti, "A Time Comprehension Test," *J. Educ. Res.*, 1946, 39, 62–68.

Frutchey, F. P., "Retention in High School Chemistry," *J. Higher Educ.*, 1937, 8, 217–18; also, *Educ. Res. Bull.*, 1937, 16, 34–37.

Gage, N. L. and G. Souci, "Social Perception and Teacher-Pupil Relationships," *J. Educ. Psychol.*, 1951, 42, 145–52.

Garrett, H. E., *Great Experiments in Psychology*. New York: Appleton-Century, 1941.

Garry, R. J., "Review of Research: Television," *J. Educ.*, 1953, 75, 31–33.

Gates, A. I., "The Nature and Limit of Improvement due to Training," *Twenty-Seventh Yearbook of the National Society for the Study of Education*, 1928, 27, Part I, 441–60.

———, "Recitation as a Factor in Memorizing," *Archives of Psychol.*, 1917, 6, No. 40.

Gates, A. I. and Grace A. Taylor, "The Acquisition of Motor Control in Writing by Preschool Children," *Teachers College Record*, 1923, 24, 459–68.

Gellermann, L. W., "The Double Alternation Problem: II. The Behavior of Children and Human Adults in a Double Alternation Temporal Maze," *J. Genet. Psychol.*, 1931, 39, 359–92.

Gesell, A., *Infancy and Human Growth*. New York: Macmillan Co., 1929.

———, "Maturation and the Patterning of Behavior," *Handbook of Child Psychol.*, Rev., C. Murchison, ed. Worcester: Clark Univ. Press, 1933, 217.

Gesell A. and Louise Ames, "The Development of Directionality in Drawing," *J. Gen. Psychol.*, 1946, 68, 45–61.

Gesell, A. and Helen Thompson, *Infant Behavior: Its Genesis and Growth*. New York: McGraw-Hill, 1934.

Gibson, Eleanor, "Improvement in Perceptual Judgments as a Function of Controlled Practice or Training," *Psychol. Bull.*, 1953, 50, 401–31.

Gibson, Eleanor and J. J. Gibson, "Retention and the Interpolated Task," *Amer. J. of Psychol.*, 1934, 46, 603–10.

Gilbert, G. M., The New Status of Experimental Studies on the Relationship of Feeling to Memory," *Psychol. Bull.* 1938, 35, 26–35.

Glasgrow, G., "The Relative Effects of Distinct and Indistinct Enunciation on Audience Comprehension of Prose and Poetry," *J. Educ. Res.*, 1943, 37, 263–67.

Goodenough, Florence L., "Some Special Problems of Nature-Nurture Research," *Thirty-ninth Yearbook of the National Society for the Study of Education*, 1940, Part I, 367–84.

———, "The Development of Creative Process from Early Childhood to Maturity," *J. Exper. Psychol.*, 1935, 18, 431–50.

Gould, Miriam and F. A. Perin, "A Comparison of the Factors Involved in Maze Learning of Human Adults and Children," *J. Exper. Psychol.*, 1916, 1, 122–54.

Greene, E. B., "The Retention of Information Learned in College Courses," *J. of Educ. Res.*, 1931, 24, 262–73.

Guilford, J. P., *Laboratory Studies in Psychology*. New York: Holt, 1934.

———, *Psychometric Methods*. New York: McGraw-Hill, 1936.

Guilford, J. P., ed., "Research Report No. 5," *Army Air Forces Aviation Psychology Program*. Washington: Government Printing Office, 1947.

Guilford, J. P. and K. M. Dallenbach, "The Determination of Memory Span by the Method of Constant Stimuli," *Amer. J. of Psychol.*, 1925, 36, 621–28.

Gunborg, B. G., "Difficulty of the Arithmetic Processes," *Elem. School J.*, 1939, 40, 198.

Hagman, E. R., "A Study of Fears of Children of Preschool Age," *J. Exp. Educ.*, 1932, 1, 110–30.

Hahn, H. H. and E. L. Thorndike, "Some Results of Practice in Addition under School Conditions," *J. Educ. Psychol.*, 1914, 5, 65–81.

Hamilton, H. C., "The Effect of Incentives on Accuracy of Discrimination Measured on the Galton Bar," *Arch. Psychol.*, 1929, 16, No. 103.

Harden, Luberta, "A Quantitative Study of the Similarity Factor in Retroactive Inhibition," *J. Gen. Psychol.*, 1929, 2, 421–32.

Harding, L. W. and Inez Bryant, "An Experiment on Comparison of Drill and Direct Experience in Arithmetical Learning in a Fourth Grade," *J. Educ. Res.*, 1943, 37, 321.

Harlow, H. F., "The Formation of Learning Sets," *Psychol. Rev.*, 1949, 56, 51–65.

Harter, G. L., "Overt Trial and Error in the Problem Solving of Preschool Children," *J. Genet. Psychol.*, 1930, 38, 361–72.

Havighurst, R. J. and F. H. Breese, "Relation Between Ability and Social Status in a Midwestern Community: III. Primary Mental Abilities," *J. Educ. Psychol.*, 1947, 38, 241–47.

Hayes, S. P., "Contributions to a Psychology of Blindness," *American Foundation for the Blind*, 1941, 296.

———, "What Do Blind Children Know?" *Tech Forum*, 1938, 11, 22, 32.

Haynes, H. C., "Teacher Intelligence and Pupil Thinking," *North Carolina Educ.*, 1936, 2, 306, 346–47.

Heidbreder, Edna, "Problem Solving in Children and Adults," *J. Genet. Psychol.*, 1928, 35, 522–45.

———, "Reasons Used in Solving Problems," *J. Exp. Psychol.*, 1927, 10, 397–414.

Heider, F., "Report of the Clarence W. Barron Research Dept., Psychol. Division," *A. R. Clarke School Deaf*, 1940, 73, 25–29.

Helmstadter, G. C. and D. S. Ellis, "Rate of Manipulative Learning as a Function of Goal-Setting Techniques," *J. Exp. Psychol.*, 1952, 43, 125–28.

Helson, H., "Adaptation Level as a Basis for a Quantitative Theory of Frames of Reference," *Psychol. Rev.*, 1948, 55, 297–313.

Hendrickson, G. and W. Schroeder, "Transfer of Training in Learning to Hit a Submerged Target," *J. Educ. Psychol.*, 1941, 32, 205–13.

Hertzberg, O. E., "A Comparative Study of Different Methods Used in Teaching Beginners to Write," *Teachers College Contributions to Education, No. 214.* New York: Teachers College, Columbia Univ., 1926.

Heyer, A. W., Jr. and L. E. O'Kelly, "Studies in Motivation and Retention," *J. Psychol.*, 1949, 27, 143–52.

Hildreth, Gertrude, "An Explanation of the Difficulty Reduction Tendency in Perception and Problem Solving," *J. Educ. Psychol.*, 1941, 32, 305–13.

———, "Puzzle Solving with and without Understanding," *J. Educ. Psychol.*, 1942, 33, 595–604.

Hilgard, E. R., "Methods and Procedures in the Study of Learning," *Handbook of Experimental Psychology*, S. S. Stevens, ed. New York: Wiley, 1951, Chapter 15.

————, *Theories of Learning* (rev.). New York: Appleton-Century-Crofts, 1956.

Hilgard, E. R. and D. G. Marquis, *Conditioning and Learning.* New York: Appleton-Century, 1940.

Hilgard, E. R. and D. H. Russell, "Motivation in School Learning," *Forty-ninth Yearbook of the National Society for the Study of Education,* 1950, Part I, 36–68.

Hilgard, E. R., L. V. Jones, and S. J. Kaplan, "Conditioned Discrimination as Related to Anxiety," *J. Exp. Psychol.,* 1951, 42, 94–99.

Hilgard, Josephine, "Learning and Maturation in Preschool Children," *J. Genet. Psychol.,* 1932, 41, 36–65.

Hobson, J. R., "Sex Differences in Primary Mental Abilities," *J. Educ. Res.,* 1947, 41, 126–33.

Hodd, H. B., "A Preliminary Survey of Some Mental Abilities of Deaf Children," *British J. Educ.,* 1949, 19, 210–19.

Holaday, P. W. and G. D. Stoddard. *Getting Ideas from the Movies.* New York: Macmillan, 1933.

Honzik, M. P., "A Developmental Study of the Relation of Family Variables to Children's Intelligence," *Unpublished manuscript, reported at Western Psychological Assn. meeting,* 1952.

Honzik, M. P., J. W. MacFarlane, and L. Allen, "The Stability of Mental Test Performance between Two and Eighteen Years," *J. Exp. Educ.,* 1948, 17, 309–24.

Hood, H. B., "A Preliminary Survey of Mental Abilities of Deaf Children," *Brit. J. Psychol.,* 1949, 19, 210–19.

Hovland, C. I., "Experimental Studies in Rote-Learning Theory: I. Reminiscence following Learning by Massed and by Distributed Practice," *J. Exp. Psychol.,* 1938, 22, 201–24.

————, "Experimental Studies in Rote-Learning Theory: II. Reminiscence with Varying Speeds of Syllable Presentation," *J. Exp. Psychol.,* 1938, 22, 338–53.

————, "Experimental Studies in Rote-Learning Theory: III. Distribution of Practice with Varying Speeds of Syllable Presentation," *J. Exp. Psychol.,* 1938, 23, 172–90.

————, "Experimental Studies in Rote-Learning Theory: IV. Comparison of Reminiscence in Serial and Paired-Associate Learning," *J. Exp. Psychol.,* 1939, 24, 466–84.

————, "Experimental Studies in Rote-Learning Theory: V. Comparison of Distribution of Practice in Serial and Paired-Associate Learning: *J. Exp. Psychol.,* 1939, 25, 622–33.

————, "Experimental Studies in Rote-Learning Theory: VI. Comparison of Retention following Learning to the Same Criterion by Massed and Distributed Practice," *J. Exp. Psychol.,* 1940, 26, 568–87.

————, "Experimental Studies in Rote-Learning Theory: VII. Distribution of Practice with Varying Lengths of List," *J. Exp. Psychol.,* 1940, 27, 271–84.

————, "Experimental Studies in Rote-Learning Theory: VIII. Distributed Practice of Paired Associates with Varying Rates of Presentation," *J. Exp. Psychol.,* 1949, 39, 714–18.

Hull, C. D., *Principles of Behavior.* New York: Appleton-Century, 1943.

Humphreys, L. G., "Acquisition and Extinction of Verbal Expectations in a Situation Analogous to Conditioning," *J. Exp. Psychol.,* 1939, 25, 294–301.

Humphreys, L. G. and P. L. Boynton, "Intelligence and Intelligence Test," *Encyclopedia of Educational Research,* W. S. Monroe, ed. New York: Macmillan, 1950, 600–12.

Hunter, W. S., "Experimental Studies of Learning," *Handbook of General Experimental Psychology,* C. Murchison. Worcester: Clark Univ. Press, 1934, 497–570.

Hurlock, Elizabeth, "An Evaluation of Certain Incentives Used in School Work," *J. Educ. Psychol.,* 1925, 16, 145–59.

————, "The Use of Group Rivalry as an Incentive," *J. Abn. and Social Psychol.,* 1927, 22, 278-90.

Husband, R. W. and Margaret Ludden, "Sex Differences in Motor Skills," *J. Exp. Psychol.,* 1931, 14, 414–22.

Imus, H. A., "Visual Factors in Reading," *Understanding the Child,* 1938, 7, 8–15.

Jenkins, J. G. and K. M. Dallenbach, "Obliviscence during Sleep and Waking," *Amer. J. Psychol.,* 1924, 35, 605–12.

Jenkins, Lulu, "A Comparative Study of Motor Achievements of Children at Five, Six, and Seven Years of Age," *Teachers College Contributions to Education, No. 414.* New York: Teachers College, Columbia Univ., 1930.

Jensen, M. B. and Agnes Lemaire, "Ten Experiments on Whole and Part Learning," *J. Educ. Psychol.,* 1937, 28, 37–54.

Jersild, A. T., "Training and Growth in the Development of Children," *Child Devel. Monogr. No. 10.* New York: Teachers College, Columbia Univ., 1932.

————, "Methods of Overcoming Children's Fears," *J. Psychol.,* 1935, 1, 75–104.

————, "A Study of Children's Fears," *J. Exp. Educ.,* 1933, 2, 109–18.

Jersild, A. T. and Frances Holmes, "Children's Fears," *Child Devel. Monogr.,* 1935, No. 20.

Jersild, A. T., F. V. Markey, and C. L. Jersild, "Children's Fears, Dreams, Likes, Dislikes, Pleasant and Unpleasant Memories," *Child Devel. Monogr.,* 1933, No. 2.

Johnson, D. M., "A Modern Account of Problem Solving," *Psychol. Bull.,* 1944, 41, 201–29.

Johnson, Lillian, "Similarity of Meaning as a Factor in Retroactive Inhibition," *J. Gen. Psychol.,* 1933, 9, 377–89.

Jones, E. I., "Differential Transfer of Training between Motor Tasks of Different Difficulty; USAF Human Resources Research Center," *Res. Bull.*, 1952, No. 23, 52-53.

Jones, H. E., "The Citizen Goes to School," *Nat. Parent Teacher*, 1938, 33, No. 4, 8–10.

——, "The Environment and Mental Development," *Manual of Child Psychol.*, L. Carmichael, ed. New York: Wiley, 1954, 631–96.

——, "Motor Performance and Growth: A Developmental Study of Static Dynamometric Strength," *Univ. of Calif. Publications in Child Devel.*, 1949, 1–180.

Jones, H. E., H. S. Conrad, and M. B. Blanchard, "Environmental Handicap in Mental Test Performance," *Univ. Calif. Publ. Psychol.*, 1932, 5, 63–69.

Jones, Mary, "A Laboratory Study of Fear: The Case of Peter," *J. Genet. Psychol.*, 1924, 31, 308–15.

Jones, V., "Attitudes of College Students and the Changes in Such Attitudes during Four Years in College," *J. Educ. Psychol.*, 1938, 29, 14–25, 114–34.

——, "Attitudes toward Peace and War," *J. Higher Educ.*, 1942, 13, 5–13.

——, *Character and Citizenship Training in the Public School*. Chicago: Univ. Chicago Press, 1936.

Jordan, A. M., *Educational Psychology*. New York: Holt, 1942, rev.

Judd, C. H., "The Relation of Special Training to General Intelligence," *Educ. Rev.*, 1908, 36, 28–42.

Kao, Dju-Lih, "Plateaus and the Curve of Learning in Motor Skill," *Psychol. Monogr.*, 1937, 49, No. 219, No. 3.

Katona, G., "Economic Psychology," *Scientific Amer.*, 1954, 191, 33–35.

——, *Organizing and Memorizing*. New York: Columbia Univ. Press, 1940, 319.

Katz, D. and K. W. Braly, "Racial Prejudice and Racial Stereotypes," *J. Abn. and Social Psychol.*, 1935, 30, 175–93.

Kellogg, W. N., V. B. Scott, and I. S. Wolf, "Is Movement Necessary for Learning? An Experimental Test of the Motor Theory of Conditioning," *J. Comp. Psychol.*, 1940, 29, 43–74.

Kendler, H. H. and H. C. Mencher, "The Ability of Rats to Learn the Location of Food when Motivated by Thirst—An Experimental Reply to Leeper," *J. Exp. Psychol.*, 1948, 38, 82–88.

Kimble, G. A., "An Experimental Test of a Two-Factor Theory of Inhibition," *J. Exp. Psychol.*, 1949, 39, 15–23.

Kimble, G. A. and E. A. Bilodeau, "Work and Rest as Variables in Motor Learning," *J. Exp. Psychol.*, 1949, 39, 150–57.

Kingsley, H. L., "Search; A Function Intermediate between Perception and Thinking," *Psychol. Monogr.*, 1926, 35, No. 2.

Kingsley, H. L. and Mary Carbone, "Attitudes of Italian-Americans toward Race Prejudice," *J. Abn. and Soc. Psychol.*, 1938, 33, 532–37.

Kinsey, A. C., W. B. Pomeroy, and C. E. Martin, *Sexual Behavior in the Human Male*. Philadelphia: Saunders, 1948.

Kirby, T. J., "Latin as a Preparation for French," *School and Society,* 1923, 18, 563–69.

Klineberg, O., *Negro Intelligence and Selective Migration.* New York: Columbia Univ. Press, 1935, 66.

Knotts, J. R. and W. R. Miles, "The Maze Learning Ability of Blind Compared with Sighted Children," *J. Genet. Psychol.,* 1929, 36, 21–50.

Kohler, W., *Gestalt Psychology.* New York: Liveright, 1947.

Krueger, W. C. F., "The Effect of Overlearning on Retention," *J. Exp. Psychol.,* 1929, 12, 71–78.

———, "Rate of Progress as Related to Difficulty of Assignment," *J. Educ. Psychol.,* 1946, 37, 247–49.

Kuo, Zing-Yang, "The Nature of Unsuccessful Acts and their Order of Elimination in Animal Learning," *J. Comp. Psychol.,* 1922, 2, 1–27.

———, "Ontogeny of the Embryonic Behavior in Aves: V. The Reflex Concept in the Light of Embryonic Behavior in Birds," *Psychol. Rev.,* 1932, 39, 499–515.

Lahey, M. Florence, "Retroactive Inhibition as a Function of Age, Intelligence, and the Duration of the Interpolated Activity," *J. Exp. Educ.,* 1937, 6, 61–67.

Langhorne, M. C., "Age and Sex Differences in the Acquisition of One Type of Skilled Movement," *J. Exp. Educ.,* 1933, 2, 101–8.

Larson, L. A., "A Factor Analysis of Motor Ability Variables and Tests with Tests for College Men," *Res. Quart. Amer. Ass. Health Physical Educ.,* 1941.

Lazarus, R. S. and C. W. Eriksen, "Effects of Failure Stress upon Skilled Performance," *J. Exp. Psychol.,* 1952, 44, 100–10.

Leavitt, H. J. and H. Schlosberg, "The Retention of Verbal and Motor Skills," *J. Exp. Psychol.,* 1944, 34, 404–17.

Lee, J. J., "The Crippled," *Nation's School,* 1943, 31, 22–23.

Lester, O. P., "Mental Set in Relation to Retroactive Inhibition," *J. Exp. Psychol.,* 1932, 15, 681–99.

Levine, J. and G. Murphy, "The Learning and Forgetting of Controversial Material," *J. Abn. Soc. Psychol.,* 1943, 38, 507–17.

Levine, R., I. Chein, and G. Murphy, "The Relation of the Intensity of a Need to the Amount of Perceptual Distortion," *J. Psychol.,* 1942, 13, 293-95.

Lewin, K., *Principles of Topological Psychology* (translated by F. Heider and G. M. Heider). New York: McGraw-Hill, 1935.

Lewin, K., R. Lippitt, and R. K. White, "Patterns of Aggressive Behavior in Experimentally Created Social Climates," *J. Soc. Psychol.,* 1939, 10, 271–99.

Ling, B., "Form Discrimination as a Learning Cue in Infants," *Comp. Psychol. Monogr.,* 1941, No. 2, Serial No. 86.

Longwell, Sarah, "Progressive Change in Simple Action," *Amer. J. Psychol.,* 1938, 51, 261–82.

Lorge, I., "Irrelevant Rewards in Animal Learning," *J. Comp. Psychol.,* 1936, 21, 105–28.

———, "Schooling Makes a Difference," *Teachers Coll. Rec.,* 1945, 46, 483–92.

Luh, C. W., "The Conditions of Retention," *Psychol. Monogr.,* 1922, 31, No. 142.

Lynd, R. S. and H. M. Lynd. *Middletown.* New York: Harcourt, Brace, 1929.

Lyon, D. O., "The Relation of Length of Material to the Time Taken for Learning, and the Optimum Distribution of Time," *J. Educ. Psychol.,* 1914, 5, 1–9, 85–91, 155–63.

MacCorquodale, K. and P. E. Meehl, "Cognitive Learning in the Absence of Competition of Incentives," *J. Comp. Physiol. Psychol.,* 1949, 42, 383–390.

Macmeeken, A. M., *The Intelligence of a Representative Group of Scottish Children.* London: Univ. of London Press, 1939.

Maddy, N. R., "Comparison of Children's Personality Traits, Attitudes, and Intelligence with Parental Occupation," *Genet. Psychol. Monogr.,* 1943, 27, 3–65.

Maier, N. R. F., "Reasoning in Children," *J. Comp. Psychol.,* 1936, 21, 357–66.

———, "Reasoning in Humans: III. The Mechanism of Equivalent Stimuli and of Reasoning," *J. Exp. Psychol.,* 1945, 35, 349-60.

Maier, N. R. F. and J. B. Klee, "Studies of Abnormal Behavior in the Rat: XVII. Guidance versus Trial and Error in the Alteration of Habits and Fixations," *J. Psychol.,* 1945, 19, 133–63.

Maller, J. B., "Cooperation and Competition: An Experimental Study in Motivation," *Teachers College Contributions to Educ., No. 384,* New York: Teachers College, Columbia Univ., 1929.

Mallory, J. N., "A Study of the Relation of Some Physical Defects to Achievement in the Elementary School," *George Peabody College for Teachers Contribution to Educ. No. 9.* Nashville, Tenn.: George Peabody College for Teachers, 1922.

Manske, A. J., "The Reflection of Teachers' Attitudes in the Attitudes of Their Pupils," *Teachers College Contributions to Educ., No. 702.* New York: Teachers College, Columbia Univ., 1936.

Mattson, M. L., "The Relation between the Complexity of the Habit to be Acquired and the Form of the Learning Curve in Young Children," *Genet. Psychol. Monogr.,* 1933, 13, 299–398.

Mayer, B. A., "Negativistic Reactions of Preschool Children on the New Revision of the Stanford-Binet," *J. Genet. Psychol.,* 1935, 46, 311–34.

McClelland, D. C., J. W. Atkinson, R. A. Clark, and E. L. Lowell, *The Achievement Motive.* New York: Appleton-Century-Crofts, 1953.

McCloy, C. H., "The Influence of Chronological Age on Motor Performance," *Res. Quart.,* 1935, May, 61–64.

McConnell, Robert, "Attitudes toward Certain Proposed Social Actions as Affected by Defined Educational Content," *Studies in Higher Educ.,* Purdue Univ., 1936, No. 31, 70–104.

McConnell, T. R., "Reconciliation of Learning Theories," *Forty-first Yearbook of the National Society for the Study of Education*, 1942, Part II.

McConnell, T. R., *et al.*, "The Psychology of Learning," *Forty-first Yearbook of the National Society for the Study of Education*, 1942, Part II.

McGeoch, J. A., "The Influence of Degree of Interpolated Learning upon Retroactive Inhibition," *Amer. J. Psychol.*, 1932, 44, 695–708.

———, "The Influence of Degree of Learning upon Retroactive Inhibition," *Amer. J. Psychol.*, 1929, 41, 252–62.

———, "The Influence of Four Different Interpolated Activities upon Retroactive Inhibition," *J. Exper. Psychol.*, 1931, 14, 400–13.

———, "The Influence of Sex and Age upon the Ability to Report," *Amer. J. Psychol.*, 1928, 40, 458–66.

———, *The Psychology of Human Learning*. New York: Longmans, Green, 1942.

———, "Studies in Retroactive Inhibition: II. Relationships between Temporal Points of Interpolation, Length of Interval, and Amounts of Retroactive Inhibition," *J. Gen. Psychol.*, 1933, 9, 44–57.

———, "Studies in Retroactive Inhibition: VII. Retroactive Inhibition as a Function of the Length and Frequency of Presentation of the Interpolated Lists," *J. Exper. Psychol.*, 1936, 19, 674–93.

McGeoch, J. A. and A. L. Irion, *The Psychology of Human Learning*, rev. New York: Longmans, Green, 1952, 596.

McGeoch, J. A. and W. T. McDonald, "Meaningful Relation and Retroactive Inhibition," *Amer. J. Psychol.*, 1931, 43, 579–88.

McGeoch, J. A. and Grace McGeoch, "Studies in Retroactive Inhibition: X. The Influence of Similarity of Meaning between Lists of Paired Associates," *J. Exper. Psychol.*, 1937, 21, 320–29.

McGeoch, J. A. and F. McKinney, "Retroactive Inhibition in the Learning of Poetry," *Amer. J. Psychol.*, 1934, 46, 429–36.

———, "Studies in Retroactive Inhibition: VIII. The Influence of the Relative Order of Presentation of Original and Interpolated Paired Associates," *J. Exper. Psychol.*, 1937, 20, 60–83.

McGeoch, J. A. and M. E. Nolan, "Studies in Retroactive Inhibition: IV. Temporal Point of Interpolation and Degree of Retroactive Inhibition," *J. Compar. Psychol.*, 1933, 15, 407–17.

McGeoch, J. A. and B. J. Underwood, "Tests of the Two-Factor Theory of Retroactive Inhibition," *J. Exper. Psychol.*, 1943, 32, 1–16.

McGinnis, E., "The Acquisition and Interference of Motor Habits in Young Children," *Genet. Psychol. Monogr.*, 1929, 6, 209–311.

McGraw, L. W., "A Factor Analysis of Motor Learning," *Res. Quart. Amer. Ass. Health and Physical Educ.*, 1948, 19, 22–29.

McKinney, F., "Retroactive Inhibition and Recognition Memory," *J. Exper. Psychol.* 1935, 18, 585–98.

McNemar, O. W., "An Attempt to Differentiate between Individuals with High and Low Reasoning Ability," *Amer. J. Psychol.*, 1955, 48, 20–36.

McNemar, Q., "A Critical Examination of the University of Iowa Studies of Environmental Influence upon the IQ," *Psychol. Bull.*, 1940, 37, 63–92.

————, "Opinion-Attitude Methodology," *Psychol. Bull.,* 1946, 37, 289–374.

————, *The Revision of the Stanford-Binet Scale.* Boston: Houghton Mifflin, 1942.

Mead, A. R., "What Schools Can Do to Improve Social Attitudes," *Educ. Leadership,* 1951, 9, 183–87.

Mead, Margaret, *Sex and Temperament in Three Primitive Societies.* New York: Morrow, 1935.

Melton, A. W., "Learning," *Encyclopedia of Educ. Res.,* W. S. Monroe, ed. New York: Macmillan, 1950, 668-90.

————, "The Methodology of Experimental Studies of Human Learning and Retention: I. The Functions of a Methodology and the Available Criteria for Evaluating Different Experimental Methods," *Psychol. Bull.,* 1936, 47, 119–34.

Melton, A. W. and Jean Irwin, "The Influence of Degree of Interpolated Learning on Retroactive Inhibition and the Overt Transfer of Specific Responses," *Amer. J. of Psychol.,* 1940, 53, 173–203.

Meltzer, H., "Nationality Preferences and Stereotypes of Colored Children," *J. Genet. Psychol.,* 1939, 54, 403–24.

————, "The Present Status of Experimental Studies on the Relationship of Feeling to Memory," *Psychol. Rev.,* 1930, 37, 124–39.

Miller, N. E., "Studies of Fear as an Acquirable Drive: I. Fear as Motivation and Fear Reductions as Reinforcement in Learning of New Responses," *J. Exper. Psychol.,* 1948, 38, 89–101.

Miller, N. E. and J. Dollard, *Social Learning and Imitation.* New Haven: Yale Univ. Press, 1941, 341.

Morris, W. W., "Story Remembering among Children," *J. Soc. Psychol.,* 1939, 10, 489–502.

Mowrer, O. H., "Motivation," *Annual Review of Psychol.,* Calvin Stone, ed. Stanford, Calif: Annual Reviews, 1952, 3, 419–39.

Munn, N. L., "Bilateral Transfer of Learning," *J. Exper. Psychol.,* 1932, 15, 343–53.

————, "Learning in Children," *Manual of Child Psychol.,* L. Carmichael, ed. New York: Wiley, 1954, 374–458.

Murphy, Helen, "An Evaluation of the Effect of Specific Training in Auditory and Visual Discrimination on Beginning Reading," Ed.D. thesis. Boston Univ., 1943.

————, "An Evaluation of Exercises for Developing Auditory Discrimination in Beginning Reading," Master's thesis, Boston Univ., 1940.

Murphy, Helen and Kathryn Junkins, "Increasing the Rate of Learning in First Grade Reading," *Education,* 1941, 62, 37–39.

Muscio, B., "The Influence of the Form of a Question," *Brit. J. Psychol.,* 1916, 8, 351–89.

Neff, W. S., "Perceiving and Symbolizing: An Experimental Study," *Amer. J. Psychol.,* 1937, 49, 376–418.

Nelson, E., "Attitudes Sought by Colleges," *School and Society,* 1937, 46, 444–47.

Newlun, C. O., "Teaching Children to Summarize in Fifth Grade History," *Teachers College Contributions to Education No. 404.* New York: Teachers College, Columbia Univ., 1930.

Newman, E. B., "Forgetting of Meaningful Material during Sleep and Waking," *Amer. J. Psychol.,* 1939, 52, 65–71.

Newman, H. H., F. N. Freeman, and K. J. Holzinger, *Twins: A Study of Heredity and Environment.* Chicago: Univ. of Chicago Press, 1937.

Noble, Gladys, "High School Students Report Their Fears," *J. Educ. Soc.,* 1951, 25, 97–101.

Nolte, K. F., "Simplification of Vocabulary and Comprehension in Reading," *Elem. Eng. Rev.,* 1937, 14, 119–24, 146.

Oakes, M. E., "Children's Explanations of Natural Phenomena," *Teachers College Contribution to Education No. 926.* New York: Teachers College, Columbia Univ., 1947.

O'Brien, F. J., "A Qualitative Investigation of the Effect of the Mode of Presentation upon the Process of Learning," *Amer. J. Psychol.,* 1921, 32, 249–83.

Oleron, P., "A Study of the Intelligence of the Deaf," *Amer. Ann. Deaf,* 1950, 95, 179–95.

Olson, W. C., "Symptoms in Temper Outbursts in Nursery School Children," *Child Developm.,* 1949.

Oseas, L. and B. J. Underwood, "Studies of Distributed Practice: V. Learning and Retention of Concepts," *J. Exp. Psychol.,* 1952, 43, 143–48.

Osgood, C. E., "An Investigation into the Causes of Retroactive Interference," *J. Exp. Psychol.,* 1948, 37, 133–54.

Oxendine, H., "The Grade Placement of the Physical Science Principle 'Sound is Produced by Vibrating Material' in Relation to Mental Ages," Ed.D. dissertation, Boston Univ., School of Educ., 1953.

Park, L., "Prejudice and Unmet Emotional Needs," *J. Educ. Soc.,* 1951, 24, 407–13.

Perkins, F. T., "Symmetry in Visual Recall," *Amer. J. Psychol.,* 1932, 44, 473–90.

Peterson, Ruth and L. L. Thurstone, *Motion Pictures and Social Attitudes of Children.* New York: Macmillan Co., 1933.

Piaget, Jean, *The Psychology of Intelligence.* New York: Harcourt, Brace, 1950.

Pintner, R. and J. Lev, "The Intelligence of the Hard of Hearing School Child," *J. Gen. Psychol.,* 1939, 55, 31–48.

———, "Worries of School Children," *J. Genet. Psychol.,* 1940, 56, 67–76.

Pistor, F., "How Time Concepts Are Acquired by Children," *Educ. Methods,* 1940, 20, 107–12.

Plowman, Letha and J. Stroud, "Effect of Informing Pupils of the Correctness of Their Responses to Objective Test Questions," *J. Educ. Res.,* 1942, 36, 16–20.

Postman, L. and T. G. Alper, "Retroactive Inhibition as a Function of the Time of Interpolation of the Inhibitor between Recall and Learning," *Amer. J. Psychol.,* 1946, 59, 439–49.

Postman, L. and R. Crutchfield, "The Interaction of Need, Set, and Stimulus Structure in a Cognitive Task," *Amer. J. Psychol.,* 1952, 65, 196–218.

Postman, L. and G. Murphy, "The Factor of Attitude in Associate Memory," *J. Exp. Psychol.,* 1943, 33, 228–38.

Powell, E. H., "The Full-Expression Plan." Paper presented before the National Council for Social Studies at Syracuse, New York, Nov. 23, 1940.

Prescott, D. A., *Emotion and the Educative Process.* Washington: American Council on Educ., 1938.

Pressey, Luella, "What Are the Crucial Differences between Good and Poor Students?" *Res. Adventures in Univ. Teaching.* Bloomington, Illinois: Public School Publishing Co., 1927, 4–10.

Pressey, S. L. and J. B. Thomas, "A Study of Country Children in Good and Poor Farming Districts by Means of a Group Scale of Intelligence," *J. App. Psychol.,* 1919, 3, 366–73.

Proshansky, H. and G. Murphy, "The Effects of Reward and Punishment on Perception," *J. Abn. Soc. Psychol.,* 1948, 43, 142–54.

Pyle, W. H., *The Psychology of Learning,* rev. Baltimore: Warwick and York, 1928, pp. 44–45.

———, "Transfer and Interference on Card-Distributing," *J. Educ. Psychol.,* 1919, 110, 107–10.

Radke, M. and J. Sutherland, "Children's Concepts and Attitudes about Minority and Majority American Groups," *J. Educ. Psychol.,* 1949, 40. 449–468.

Raffel, Gertrude, "Two Determinants of the Effect of Primacy," *Amer. J. Psychol.,* 1936, 48, 654–57.

Rarick, L. and R. McKee, "A Study of 20 Third Grade Children Exhibiting Extreme Levels of Achievement on Tests of Motor Proficiency," *Res. Quart.,* 1949, 142–52.

Ray, J. J., "The Generalizing Ability of Dull, Bright, and Superior Children," *George Peabody College Contributions to Education, No. 175.* Nashville, Tenn.: George Peabody College for Teachers, 1936.

Reed, H. B., "An Experiment on the Law of Effect in Learning the Maze by Humans," *J. Educ. Psychol.,* 1935, 26, 695–700.

———, "Distributed Practice in Addition," *J. Educ. Psychol.,* 1924, 15, 248–49.

———, "Factors Influencing the Learning and Retention of Concepts: I. The Influence of Set," *J. Exp. Psychol.,* 1946, 36, 71–87.

————, "The Learning and Retention of Concepts: IV. The Influence of Complexity of the Stimuli," *J. Exp. Psychol.,* 1946, 36, 252–61.

Reeder, C. W. and S. C. Newman, "The Relationship of Employment to Scholarship," *Educ. Res. Bull.,* Ohio State Univ., 1939, 18, 203–14.

Remmers, H. H., "An Experiment on the Retention of Attitudes as Changed by Instructional Materials," *Studies in Higher Educ.,* Purdue Univ., 1938, No. 34, 20–22.

————, "Measuring the Effect of a Lecture on Attitudes toward the League of Nations," *Studies in Higher Educ.,* Purdue Univ., 1936, No. 31, 105–08.

Richardson, Helen, "The Growth of Adaptive Behavior in Infants: An Experimental Study of Seven Age Levels," *Gen. Psychol. Monogr.,* 1932, 12, 195–359.

Ritchie, B. F., B. Aeschliman, and P. Pierce, "Studies in Spatial Learning, VIII. Place Performance and the Acquisition of Place Dispositions," *J. Comp. Physiol. Psychol.,* 1950, 43, 73–85.

Robinson, E. S., "The Similarity Factor in Retroaction," *Amer. J. Psychol.,* 1927, 39, 297–312.

Robinson, E. S. and C. W. Darrow, "The Effect of Length of List upon Memory for Numbers," *Amer. J. Psychol.,* 1924, 35, 235–43.

Robinson, E. S. and W. T. Heron, "Results of Variation in Length of Memorized Material," *J. Exp. Psychol.,* 1922, 5, 428–48.

Roethlisberger, F. J. and W. J. Dickson, *Management and the Worker.* Cambridge, Mass.: Harvard Univ. Press, 1939.

Rowley, Florence, "Motor Coordination in the Field of Handwriting," Master's thesis, Boston Univ., School of Educ., 1938.

Ruediger, W. C., *The Principles of Education.* Boston: Houghton Mifflin, 1910, 108–11.

Rugg, H. O., "Experimental Determination of Mental Discipline in School Studies," *Educ. Psychol. Monogr.,* 1916, No. 17.

Russell, R. D., "A Comparison of Two Methods of Learning," *J. Educ. Res.,* 1928, 18, 235–38.

Rust, M. M., "The Effect of Resistance on Intelligence Scores of Young Children," *Child Dev. Monogr.* New York: Teachers College, Columbia Univ., 1931, No. 6, 80.

Sand, Margaret C., "The Effect of Length of List upon Retroactive Inhibition when Degree of Learning is Controlled," *Archives of Psychol.,* 1939, 33, No. 238.

Sandin, A. A., "Social and Emotional Adjustments of Regularly Promoted and Non-promoted Pupils." Ed.D. dissertation, Teachers College, Columbia Univ., 1942.

Sato, T., "The Relation between Vision and School Performance," *Nihon-Gakko Eisei,* 1937, 25, 423–24.

Saugstad, P., "Incidental Memory and Problem Solving," *Psychol. Rev.,* 1952, 59, 221–26.

Schrepel, Marie and H. R. Laslett, "On the Loss of Knowledge by Junior High School Pupils over the Summer Vacation," *J. Educ. Psychol.,* 1936, 27, 299–303.

Schwartz, F. O., "Ocular Factors in Poor Readers in the St. Louis Public Schools," *Am. J. of Ophthalmology*, 1940, 23, 535–38.

Scottish Council for Research in Education, *The Intelligence of Scottish Children: A National Survey*. London: Univ. of London Press, 1933.

Seagoe, M. V., "The Influence of Degree of Wholeness on Whole-Part Learning," *J. of Exp. Psychol.*, 1936, 19, 763–68.

———, "Qualitative Wholes: A Revaluation of the Whole-Part Problem," *J. of Educ. Psychol.*, 1936, 27, 537–45.

Sears, Pauline, "Levels of Aspiration in Academically Successful and Unsuccessful School Children," *J. Abn. and Soc. Psychol.*, 1940, 35, 498–536.

Sears, R. R., "Initiation of the Repression Sequence by Experienced Failure," *J. Exp. Psychol.*, 1937, 20, 570–80.

Seashore, H. G., "Some Relationships of Fine and Gross Motor Abilities," *Res. Quart*, 1942, 13, 259–74.

Seels, L., "The Relationship between Measures of Physical Growth and Gross Motor Performance," *Res. Quart.*, 1951, May 244–50.

Sharp, W. L., "The Relationship between Speed and Efficiency of Learning on the Constant Speed Finger Maze," *J. Exp. Psychol.*, 1939, 24, 86–94.

Sherman, M., "The Differentiation of Emotional Responses in Infants," *J. Compar. Psychol.*, 1927, 7, 265–84, 335–51; 1928, 8, 385–94.

Shirley, Mary, *The First Two Years*. Minneapolis: Univ. of Minnesota Press, 1931.

Siao-Sung, Djang, "The Role of Past Experience in the Visual Apprehension of Masked Forms," *J. Exp. Psychol.*, 1937, 20, 29–59.

Silleck, S. B., Jr. and C. W. Lapha, "The Relative Effectiveness of Emphasis upon Right and Wrong Responses in Human Maze Learning," *J. Exp. Psychol.*, 1937, 20, 195–201.

Sims, Verna M., "The Relative Influence of Two Types of Motivation on Improvement," *J. Educ. Psychol.*, 1928, 19, 480–84.

Sisson, E. D., "Retroactive Inhibition: The Influence of Degree of Associative Value of Original and Interpolated Lists," *J. Educ. Psychol.*, 1936, 27, 299–303.

———, "Retroactive Inhibition: Serial Versus Random Order Presentation of Material," *J. Exp. Psychol.*, 1939, 23, 288–94.

———, "Retroactive Inhibition: The Temporal Position of Interpolated Activity," *J. Exp. Psychol.*, 1939, 25, 228–33.

Skaggs, E. B., "Further Studies in Retroactive Inhibition," *Psychol. Monogr.*, 1925, 34, No. 161.

Skaggs, E. B., S. Grossman, Louis Krueger, and W. C. F. Krueger, "Further Studies of the Reading-Recitation Process in Learning," *Archives of Psychol.*, 1930, 18, No. 114.

Skalet, M., "The Significance of Delayed Reactions in Young Children," *Comp. Psychol. Monogr.*, 1931, 7.

Skinner, B. F., *The Behavior of Organisms*. New York: Appleton-Century, 1938.

Sleight, W. G., "Memory and Formal Training," *British J. Psychol.*, 1911, 4, 386–457.

Smith, H. P. and T. R. Tate, "Improvement in Reading Rate and Comprehension of Subjects by Training with the Tachistoscope," *J. Educ. Psychol.*, 1953, 44, 176–84.

Smith, M., "Spontaneous Change of Attitude toward War," *School and Society*, 1937, 46, 30–32.

Smith, M. H., Jr., "The Influence of Isolation on Memory," *Amer. J. Psychol.*, 1949, 62, 405–11.

Snoddy, G. S., *Evidence for Two Opposed Processes in Mental Growth.* Lancaster, Pa.: Science Printing Co., 1935.

Solley, W. H., "The Effects of Verbal Instruction of Speed and Accuracy upon the Learning of a Motor Skill," *Res. Quarterly*, 1952, 23, 231–40.

Sones, A. M. and J. B. Stroud, "Review, with Special Reference to Temporal Position," *J. Educ. Psychol.*, 1940, 31, 665–76.

Sontag, L. W., S. I. Pyle, and J. Cape, "Prenatal Conditions and the Status of Infants at Birth," *Amer. J. Diseases of Children*, 1935, 50, 337–42.

Spearman, C., *Abilities of Man.* London: Macmillan Co., 1927.

Spelt, D. K., "Conditioned Responses in the Human Fetus in Utero." *Psychol. Bull.*, 1935, 35, 712–13.

Spitz, R. A., "Hospitalism: An Inquiry into the Genesis of Psychiatric Conditions of Early Childhood," *Psychoanalytic Study of the Child*, 1945, 1, 53–74.

Spitzer, H. F., "Studies in Retention," *J. Educ. Psychol.*, 1939, 30, 641–56.

Springer, N. N., "A Comparative Study of the Intelligence of a Group of Deaf and Hearing Children," *Amer. Ann. Deaf*, 1938, 83, 138–52.

Sprunt, Julie and F. W. Finger, "Auditory Deficiency and Academic Achievement," *J. Speech Hearing Disorders*, 1949, 14, 26–32.

Stacey, C. I., "The Law of Effect in the Retained Situation with Meaningful Material," *Univ. of Minn. Studies in Educ. No. 2.* Minneapolis: Univ. of Minn. Press, 1949.

Starch, D., *Educational Psychology.* New York: Macmillan Co., 1927, 168–69.

Steffens, Lottie, "Experimentelle Beiträge zur Lehre von Ökonomischen Lernen," *Zeitschrift für Psychologie*, 1900, 22, 321–82.

Stephens, J. M., *Educational Psychology.* New York: Holt, 1951.

Stolurow, L. M., *Readings in Learning.* Englewood Cliffs, N. J.: Prentice-Hall, 1953.

Strauss, A. and K. Schuessler, "Socialization, Logical Reasoning, and Concept Development of the Child," *Amer. Socio. Review*, 1951, 16, 514–23.

Stroud, J. B., *Educational Psychology.* New York: Macmillan Co., 1935.

———, "Experiments on Learning in School Situations," *Psychol. Bull.*, 1940, 37, 777–807.

———, "The Role of Practice in Learning," *Yearbook of the National Society for the Study of Education*, 1942, 41, Part 2, 353–76.

Stroud, J. B., and E. F. Lindquist, "Sex Differences in Achievement in the Elementary and Secondary Schools," *J. Educ. Psychol.*, 1932, 33, 657–67.

Stroud, J. B. and Ruth Maul, "The Influence of Age upon Learning and Retention of Poetry and Nonsense Syllables," *J. of Genetic Psychol.*, 1933, 42, 242–50.

Stroud, J. B. and C. W. Ridgeway, "The Relative Efficiency of the Whole, Part, and Progressive Part Methods When Trials Are Massed," *J. Educ. Psychol.*, 1932, 23, 632–34.

Sutherland, Jean, "The Effect of Training in Perceptual Span on Rate of Reading and Rate of Perception," *J. Educ. Psychol.*, 1946, 37, 378–80.

Swenson, Esther, "Retroactive Inhibition: A Review of the Literature," *Univ. of Minnesota Studies in Educ.* Minneapolis: Univ. of Minn. Press, 1941.

Swenson, Esther, G. L. Anderson, and C. L. Stacey, "Learning Theory in School Situations," *Univ. of Minnesota Studies in Education.* Minneapolis: Univ. of Minn. Press, 1949, 9–39.

Tenenbaum, S., "Attitudes of Elementary School Children toward School, Teachers, and Classmates," *J. Appl. Psychol.*, 1944, 134–41.

Terman, L. M. and M. A. Merrill, *Measuring Intelligence.* Boston: Houghton Mifflin, 1937.

Terman, L. M. and M. H. Oden, *Genetic Studies of Genius, Vol. IV.* Stanford, Calif.: Stanford Univ. Press, 1947.

Terman, L. M. and L. E. Tyler, "Psychological Sex Differences," *Manual of Child Psychol*, L. Carmichael, ed. New York: Wiley, 1954, 1065–1117.

Thompson, G. G. and S. L. Witryol, "A Relationship between Intelligence and Motor Learning Ability as Measured by a High Relief Finger Maze," *J. Psychol.*, 1946, 22, 237–46.

Thompson, M. E. and J. P. Thompson, "Reactive Inhibition as a Factor in Image Learning: II. The Role of Reactive Inhibition in Studies of Place Learning vs. Response Learning," *J. Exp. Psychol.*, 1949, 39, 883–891.

Thorndike, E. L., *Educational Psychology.* New York: Teachers College, Columbia Univ., 1916.

———, *The Fundamentals of Learning.* New York: Teachers College, Columbia Univ., 1932.

———, "The Gains Made in Ability in English by Pupils Who Study Latin and by Pupils Who Do Not," *School and Soc.*, 1923, 18, 690.

———, *Human Learning.* New York: Appleton, 1931.

———, "The Influence of First-Year Latin upon Ability to Read English," *School and Soc.*, 1923, 17, 165–68.

———, "The Influence of Irrelevant Rewards," *J. Educ. Psychol.*, 1933, 24, 1–15.

———, "The Law of Effect," *Psychol. Rev.*, 1938, 45, 204–5.

———, "Mental Discipline in High School Studies," *J. Educ. Psychol.*, 1924, 15, 1–22, 83–98.

Thorndike, E. L. and I. Lorge, "The Influence of Relevance and Belonging," *J. Exper. Psychol.*, 1935, 18, 574–84.

Thorndike, E. L. and G. J. Ruger, "The Effect of First-Year Latin upon Knowledge of English Words of Latin Derivation," *School and Soc.*, 1923, 18, 260–70.

Thorndike, E. L. and R. S. Woodworth, "The Influence of Improvement in One Function upon Efficiency of Other Functions," *Psychol. Rev.*, 1901, 8, 247–61, 384–95, 553–64.

Thorpe, L. P. and A. M. Schmuller, *Contemporary Theories of Learning*. New York: Ronald Press, 1954.

Thune, L. E. and B. J. Underwood, "Retroactive Inhibition as a Function of Degree of Interpolated Learning," *J. Exp. Psychol.*, 1943, 32, 185–200.

Thurstone, L. L., "Measurement of Social Attitudes," *J. Abn. Soc. Psychol.*, 1931, 26, 249–69.

Thurstone, L. L. and E. J. Chave, *The Measurement of Attitude*. Chicago: Univ. Chicago Press, 1929.

Thurstone, L. L. and Thelma Thurstone, *SRA Primary Mental Abilities, Technical Supplement*. Chicago: Science Res. Associates, April, 1954.

Tiedeman, H. R., "A Study of Retention of Classroom Learning," *J. Educ. Res.*, 1947, 41, 516–30.

Tolman, E. C., "The Law of Effect," *Psychol. Rev.*, 1938, 45, 200–03.

——, *Purposive Behavior in Animals and Men*. New York: Appleton-Century, 1932.

——, "There Is More Than One Kind of Learning," *Psychol. Rev.*, 1949, 56, 144–55.

Tolman, E. C. and C. H. Honzik, "Introduction and Removal of Reward, and Maze Performance in Rats," *Univ. Calif. Publ. Psychol.*, 1930, 4, 257–75.

Tolman, E. C., B. F. Ritchie, and D. Kalish, "Studies in Spatial Learning: II. Place Learning vs. Response Learning," *J. Exper. Psychol.*, 1946, 36, 221–29.

——, B. F. Ritchie, and D. Kalish, "Studies in Spatial Learning: IV. The Transfer of Place Learning to Other Starting Paths," *J. Exper. Psychol.*, 1947, 37, 39–47.

Tormey, T. J., "The Effect of Drill upon the Specific and General Comprehension of Historical Content," *Univ. of Iowa Studies in Educ.*, 1934, 9, No. 1, 151–81.

Trainor, Doris and Constance Rogers, "Adjustment of Non-Promoted and Regularly Promoted Children in the Same Classrooms." M.Ed. thesis, Boston Univ., 1955.

Travis, R. C., "Length of the Practice Period and Efficiency in Motor Learning," *J. Exper. Psychol.*, 1939, 24, 339–45.

Trowbridge, M. H. and H. Cason, "An Experimental Study of Thorndike's Theory of Learning," *J. Gen. Psychol.*, 1932, 7, 245–88.

Tuddenham, R. D., "Soldier Intelligence in World Wars I and II," *Amer. Psychologist*, 1948, 3, 54–56.

Turrell, A. M., "Study Methods and Scholarship Improvement," *Junior College,* 1937, 7, 295–301.

Tuttle, H. S., "Knowledge Is Powerless," *School and Society,* 1941, 54, 315–17.

Twining, P. E., "The Relative Importance of Intervening Activity and Lapse of Time in the Production of Forgetting," *J. Exper. Psychol.,* 1940, 26, 483–501.

Tyler, R. W., "Permanence of Learning," *J. Higher Educ.,* 1933, 4, 203–4.

Ulmer, G., "Teaching Geometry to Cultivate Reflective Thinking: An Experimental Study with 1239 High School Pupils," *J. of Exp. Educ.,* 1939, 8, 18–25.

Underwood, B. J., "Studies of Distributed Practice: III: The Influence of Stage of Practice in Serial Learning," *J. Exp. Psychol.,* 1951, 42, 291–95.

Underwood, B. J. and L. Oseas, (1952). See Oseas and Underwood.

Updegraft, Ruth, Louise Heiliger, and Janet Learned, "The Effect of Training upon the Singing Ability and Musical Interest of Three, Four, and Five-Year-Old Children," *Univ. of Iowa Studies in Child Welfare,* 1938, 14, 83–131.

Vandell, R. A., R. A. Davis, and H. A. Clergston, "The Function of Mental Practice in the Acquisition of Motor Skills," *J. Gen. Psychol.,* 1943, 29, 243–50.

Van Dusen, F. and H. Schlosberg, "Further Study of the Retention of Verbal and Motor Skills," *J. Exp. Psychol.,* 1948, 38, 526–34.

Van Ormer, E. B., "Retention after Intervals of Sleep and of Waking," *Archives of Psychol.,* 1932, 21. No. 137.

Van Waters, Miriam, "Social Treatment and the Attitudes of Delinquency," lecture delivered at Boston Univ. No. 27, 1939.

Wagner, Mazie and Eunice Strable, "Teaching High-School Pupils How to Study," *Sch. Rev.,* 1935, 43, 577–89.

Walker, E. L., "Drive Specificity and Learning," *J. Exp. Psychol.,* 1948, 38, 39–49.

Walker, E. L., M. C. Knotter, and R. L. De Valois, "Drive Specificity and Learning: the Acquisition of a Spatial Response to Food under Conditions of Water Deprivation and Food Satiation," *J. Exp. Psychol.,* 1950, 40, 161–168.

Warner, W. L. and L. Srole, *The Social Systems of American Ethnic Groups.* New Haven: Yale Univ. Press, 1945.

Wasserman, H. N., "The Effect of Motivation and Amount of Pre-Rest Practice upon Inhibitory Potential in Motor Learning," *J. Exp. Psychol.,* 1951, 42, 162–72.

Waters, R. H. and Z. E. Peel, "Similarity in the Form of Original and Interpolated Learning and Retroactive Inhibition," *Am. J. Psychol.,* 1935, 47, 477–81.

Watson, B., "The Similarity Factor in Transfer and Inhibition," *J. Educ. Psychol.,* 1938, 29, 145–57.

Watson, J. B., *Behaviorism.* New York: Norton, 1930.

Wellman, B. L., "Iowa Studies on the Effects of School," *Thirty-ninth Yearbook of the National Society for the Study of Education*, 1940, 39, Part II, 377–99.

Wendt, H. W., "Motivation, Effort, and Performance," *Studies in Motivation*, D. C. McClelland. New York: Appleton-Century-Crofts, 1955.

Wenger, M. A., "An Investigation of Conditioned Responses in Human Infants," *Univ. of Iowa Studies in Child Welfare*, 1936, Vol. 12, No. 1, 90.

Werner, O. H., "The Influence of the Study of Modern Foreign Languages on the Development of Desirable Abilities in English," *Studies in Modern Language Teaching*. New York: Macmillan Co., 1930, 99–145.

Wesman, A. G., "A Study of Transfer of Training from High-School Subjects to Intelligence," *J. Educ. Res.*, 1945, 254–65.

Whisler, L. and H. H. Remmers, "The Effect of the Election on High-School Pupils' Attitudes toward the Two Major Parties," *Second and Society*, 1937, 45, 558–60.

White, M. M. and Margaret McLeod Ratliff, "The Relation of Affective Tone to the Learning and Recall of Words," *Am. J. Psychol.*, 1934, 46, 92–98.

Whitely, P. L., "The Dependence of Learning and Recall upon Prior Intellectual Activities," *J. Exp. Psychol.*, 1927, 10, 489–508.

Whitely, P. L. and J. A. McGeoch, "The Curve of Retention for Poetry," *J. Educ. Psychol.*, 1928, 19, 471–79.

Wilkins, E. H., "On the Distribution of Extra-Curricular Activities," *School and Society*, 1940, 51, 651–56.

Willoughby, R. R., "Incidental Learning," *J. Educ. Psychol.*, 1929, 20, 671–82.

Wilson, G. M., *What Arithmetic Shall We Teach?* Boston: Houghton Mifflin, 1926, pp. 136–38.

Winch, W. H., "Experimental Researches on Learning to Spell," *J. Educ. Psychol.*, 1913, 4, 525–37.

———, "Further Experimental Researches on Learning to Spell," *J. Educ. Psychol.*, 1914, 5, 449–60.

———, "Further Work on Numerical Accuracy in School Children: Does Improvement in Numerical Accuracy Transfer?" *J. of Educ. Psychol.*, 1911, 2, 262–71.

———, "Transfer of Improvement in Reasoning in School Children," *British J. Psychol.*, 1923, 13, 370–81.

Woodbury, C., "The Effect of Community Status upon the Differential Adjustment of School Children." Unpublished Ed.D. dissertation, Boston Univ., 1952.

Woodrow, H., "The Effect of Type of Training upon Transference," *J. Educ. Psychol.*, 1927, 18, 159–72.

———, "Interrelations of Measures of Learning," *J. Psychol.*, 1940, 10, 49–73.

Woody, Clifford, "The Influence of the Teaching of First-Year French on the Acquisition of English Vocabulary," *Studies in Modern Language Teaching*. New York: Macmillan Co., 1930, 149–84.

Woodworth, R. S., *Experimental Psychology.* New York: Holt, 1938.

————,*Psychology*, Fourth Edition. New York: Holt, 1940, p. 441.

Wright, Susan and D. W. Taylor, "Distributed Practice in Verbal Learning and Maturation Hypothesis," *J. Exper. Psychol.*, 1949, 39, 527–31.

Wulf, F., "Beiträge zur Psychologie der Gestalt: VI. Uber die Veranderung von Vorstellungen (Gedachtnis und Gestalt)." *Psychologische Forschung,* 1922, 1, 333–73.

Young, P. T., "A Study on the Recall of Pleasant and Unpleasant Words," *Amer. J. Psychol.,* 1937, 49, 581–96.

Zangwill, O. L., "The Problem of Retroactive Inhibition in Relation to Recognition," *British J. Psychol.,* 1938, 28, 229–47.

Zapf, Rosalind, "Superstitions of Junior High-School Pupils: Part II, Effects of Instruction on Superstitious Beliefs," *J. Educ. Res.,* 1938, 31, 481–96.

Zeigarnik, B., "On Finished and Unfinished Tasks," *A Source Book of Gestalt Psychology,* W. D. Ellis. New York: Harcourt, Brace, 1938, 207.

Zeligs, Rose, "Children's Concepts and Stereotypes of Polish, Irish, Finnish, Hungarian, Bulgarian, Danish, Czechoslovakian, Hindu, and Filipino," *J. Gen. Psychol.,* 1950, 77, 73–83.

————, "Nationalities Children Would Choose If They Could Not Be Americans," *J. Gen. Psychol.,* 1951, 79, 55–68.

————, "Reasons Given by Children for Their Intergroup Attitudes," *J. Gen. Psychol.,* 1950, 78, 145–61.

Zintz, M. V., "Academic Achievement and Social and Emotional Adjustment of Handicapped Children," *Elem. School J.,* 1951, 51, 502–7.

Subject Index

549

Author Index